SACRED STORIES

INDIANA-MICHIGAN SERIES IN RUSSIAN
AND EAST EUROPEAN STUDIES

Alexander Rabinowitch
and
William G. Rosenberg,
GENERAL EDITORS

SACRED STORIES

RELIGION AND SPIRITUALITY IN MODERN RUSSIA

EDITED BY

Mark D. Steinberg

AND

Heather J. Coleman

INDIANA UNIVERSITY PRESS

Bloomington and Indianapolis

This book is a publication of

Indiana University Press
601 North Morton Street
Bloomington, IN 47404-3797 USA

http://iupress.indiana.edu

Telephone orders   800-842-6796
Fax orders   812-855-7931
Orders by e-mail   iuporder@indiana.edu

© 2007 by Indiana University Press

All rights reserved

Manufactured in the United States of America

Library of Congress Cataloging-in-Publication Data

Sacred stories : religion and spirituality in modern Russia / edited by Mark D. Steinberg and Heather J. Coleman.
    p. cm. — (Indiana-Michigan series in Russian and East European studies)
    Includes bibliographical references and index.
    ISBN-13: 978-0-253-34747-3 (cloth : alk. paper)
    ISBN-13: 978-0-253-21850-6 (pbk. : alk. paper) 1. Russia—Religion.
2. Religion and state—Russia—History. 3. Russia—History—1801–1917.
I. Steinberg, Mark D., date- II. Coleman, Heather J., date-
    BL980.R8S23 2007
    281.9′4709034—dc22

                                                                2006021427

1 2 3 4 5 12 11 10 09 08 07

Contents

⸻⟨∞⟩⸻

Acknowledgments

This book emerged out of a series of collaborations, beginning with a conference organized by the two editors and held at the University of Illinois at Urbana-Champaign (UIUC) on February 21–23, 2002. The conference opened with keynote addresses by Thomas Kselman (University of Notre Dame) and Laura Engelstein (Yale University), whose arguments and comments, along with those of the conference participants, shaped the revision of these papers, first presented at that conference, and the editors' introduction. Additional participants in the discussions included Eugene Clay, Page Herrlinger, and Scott Kenworthy, as well as Illinois faculty and students. Valuable additional comments and advice were given by Janet Rabinowitch at Indiana University Press and the anonymous readers chosen by the press. The editors thank all the participants in this project for their collegiality, their commitment to advancing the study of Russia and religion, and their patience. To the extent that this volume captures the state of a field at a vibrant moment in its history is because of the enthusiasm and cooperation of all involved.

We are also grateful to UIUC for the financial support that made the 2002 conference possible; in particular, we thank the Russian, East European, and Eurasian Center, the International Council, the College of Liberal Arts and Sciences, the Department of History, the Program for the Study of Religion, the Program in Jewish Studies, the UIUC/Ford Program "Crossing Borders: Revitalizing Area Studies," the Department of Slavic Languages and Literatures, and the Department of Anthropology. The Research Board of the University of Illinois provided a generous publication subvention. Rita Bernhard worked very hard to correct and improve the prose of diverse authors, for which we express our thanks. We are also grateful to Dawn Nichol and Dietlind Bechthold at the University of Alberta for their help in preparing the submission, the staff of the Russian, East European, and Eurasian Center, who assisted mightily with the many logistics of the conference and finances, Sharyl Corrado for her attentive proofreading, Sharon Kowalsky for preparing the index, and Jane Hedges. And, finally, the editors want to thank each other for their energetic labor, supportive criticism, and good cheer all along the journey.

SACRED STORIES

Introduction: Rethinking Religion in Modern Russian Culture

Mark D. Steinberg and Heather J. Coleman

———··◦∞◦··———

These essays reflect the dramatic growth of new research and interpretation on the long neglected history of religious life in late imperial Russia.[1] An elusive object of study, religion is understood here less as the story of institutions or fixed beliefs than as a vital terrain of social imagination and practice where everyday (and extraordinary) experience, ideas, beliefs, and emotions come together as people make sense of their lives. As in so much religious experience and expression, at the center here are stories and images, representations through which meaning gels (and disintegrates, and is reshaped). No less important, these cultural stories bridge the gap between the inner self and social existence. This work views the religious as fully and deeply entangled with the world. Belief, spirituality, and the sacred are seen not as separate, clearly bounded spheres—religion as the terrain of "things set apart and forbidden"[2]— nor as mere reflections of social and political life but, rather, as powerful and complex cultural expressions of transcendent meanings, passions, and beliefs entwined inescapably with the whole of life, in Russia and beyond. Necessarily, therefore, these sacred stories are also stories about power and resistance, community and individuality, the public sphere and private life, class and gender, and, pervading all this, modernity. Indeed, the relationships between religion and the landscape of the modern—modern forms of political power, modern social relationships and identities, modern conditions of change and crisis, and modern ideas—imbue these stories with their particular tone and urgency.

Religion and the Russian Fin de Siècle

Modern Russia, especially in the final decades of the old regime, was awash in sacred stories. As will be seen in the chapters that follow, the landscape of rapid industrialization, social transformation, and political revolution in the late nineteenth and early twentieth centuries was also a landscape of intellectual journeys of spiritual discovery, mass religious pilgrimage, nonconformist religious movements, battles over freedom of conscience, literary and artistic

1

mysticism, and the emergence of a vital new tradition of religious philosophy. In the pages of the increasingly free and widely circulating press, Russians told one another of religious healing, of lives transformed by the words of charismatic preachers like the priest Father Ioann of Kronstadt or the dissident lay preacher "Brother" Ivan Koloskov, or of conversion to new creeds. Writers, poets, artists, and philosophers increasingly described the world in mythic and mystical terms, exalted spiritual imagination and elemental feeling, spoke of the divinity of all things or of mystical "correspondences," resituated ethics on the ground of religion, turned away from both church dogma and scientific materialism and determinism toward a new spiritual faith, and often described apocalyptic visions of a coming catastrophe out of which, perhaps, great redemption would come. The imperial Russian state and its church also entered the fray, telling stories of a national religious mission and of an eternal spiritual bond between ruler and ruled. Sacred stories were to be found in unexpected places, too—in the pages of the secularist Yiddish press, in the work of avant-garde, even "Futurist," artists like Kazimir Malevich, in the verse of self-consciously proletarian poets, and even among revolutionaries articulating their own sacredly inflected story of imminent revolutionary change. Modernization and the modern were entwined through all these stories. Modern life unsettled social, political, and intellectual hierarchies and knowledges. Quite tangibly urbanization, modern rail transport, and the rapid expansion of popular literacy and the press worked together with other new social and economic realities to cause many people to experience their faith in novel ways and to send others in search of new, more appropriate forms of spirituality and transcendent meaning for a modern age. Just as the encounter with modernity made people more self-conscious as individuals, it also heightened self-awareness about religious belief, the presumed boundaries of the sacred and the secular, and the place of religion in their country and the world.

Orthodoxy, the established religion of the empire, found itself in a paradoxical position. Russia's last two tsars, Alexander III (reigned 1881–1894) and Nicholas II (reigned 1894–1917) championed an "Orthodox" conception of the monarchy and the empire. Both personally devout, father and son sought to "resacralize" the monarchy by revitalizing the role of Orthodoxy in imperial ceremony and by sponsoring festive commemorations of great religious events in the nation's past and the canonization of new Russian saints. Religion also played an enhanced role in state social and educational policy, as Konstantin Pobedonostsev, influential adviser to the tsars and lay director of the Holy Synod, aimed to "convert the Russian people and Russian society to a native, religious form of social thought and action" through the wide dissemination of religious reading matter, by sponsoring a network of parish primary schools, and by encouraging the opening of new monasteries, convents, and charitable institutions.[3] Religion was politicized also in the form of anti-Semitic policies, restrictions on the non-Orthodox faiths of the many national minorities of the empire, and a renewed attempt to combat the public expression of religious dissent by Old Believers and sectarians. Indeed, it remained illegal to leave the Orthodox Church until 1905. Yet, despite this government sponsorship, the Orthodox Church faced a pastoral and identity crisis at the turn of the twentieth century, as churchmen wrung their hands at the godless condition of educated society and the ignorance of the masses, and chafed under the harness of state obligations.[4] When the state tacitly acknowledged the increasing pluralism of Russian society by decreeing religious tolerance during the Revolution of 1905, the state church was forced to confront its own relativization.[5]

In these years large numbers among the educated urban elites, typically the most imbued with modern secular ways of knowing and seeing, sought spiritual meaning. Many returned to the church and sought to revitalize their faith. But even more evident were nonconformist paths of spiritual searching, sometimes termed "God-seeking" (*bogoiskatel'stvo*). Writers, artists, and intellectuals in large numbers were drawn to private prayer, mysticism, spiritualism, theosophy, Nietzschean philosophy, Eastern religions, and other idealizations of imagination, feeling, and mystical connections between all things. A fascination with elemental feeling, with the unconscious and the mythic, proliferated along with visions of coming catastrophe and redemption. Aptly "Golgotha" represented, in the works of many writers and artists, the essential spirit of the time: a metaphor of suffering and death containing the transcendent promise of salvation. The visible forms of God-seeking were extensive, from relatively formal organizations such as the Religious-Philosophical Society of St. Petersburg or the Russian Theosophical Society to informal circles and salons, séances, and gatherings in private apartments for prayer and even liturgies. In 1909, in a sensation-creating volume of essays under the title *Vekhi* (Landmarks or Signposts), a group of leading left-wing intellectuals, mostly former Marxists, repudiated the materialism and atheism that had dominated the thought of the intelligentsia for generations as leading inevitably to failure and moral disaster. The only path to Russia's regeneration, they argued, was through the sacred principle of the absolute autonomy and value of the individual, including in his or her inward life, through spiritual and moral awakening to sacred truths. No less, they joined many intellectuals in rejecting universalizing historical narratives (specifically, Marxist Messianism) in favor of what Petr Struve, one of the contributors to the volume, called a faith that was ultimately "diffident, intimate, undemonstratable."[6] At the same time some Marxists elaborated a re-enchanted Marxism. Feeling the cold rationalism, materialism, and determinism of traditional Marxism inadequate to inspire a revolutionary mass movement, they insisted on the need to appeal to the subconscious and the emotional to create a new faith that placed humanity where God had been but retained a religious spirit of passion, moral certainty, and the promise of salvation.[7] In a similar spirit, some individual clergy worked to revitalize Orthodox faith, most famously Father Ioann of Kronstadt, who, until his death in 1908, emphasized Christian living and sought to restore fervency and the presence of the miraculous in liturgical celebration.[8]

Among the lower classes a similarly renewed vigor and variety in religious life and spirituality flourished in the early years of the twentieth century, and intensified still further after the upheavals of 1905. In the countryside we see widespread popular interest in spiritual-ethical literature; nonconformist moral-spiritual movements; an upsurge in pilgrimage and other devotions to sacred spaces and objects (especially icons); persistent belief in the presence and power of the supernatural (apparitions, possession, walking-dead, demons, spirits, miracles, and magic); renewed vitality of local "ecclesial communities" actively shaping their own ritual and spiritual lives, sometimes without clergy, and defining their own sacred places and forms of piety; and the proliferation of what the Orthodox establishment branded as "sectarianism," including both non-Orthodox Christian denominations, notably Baptists, and various forms of deviant popular Orthodoxy and mysticism.[9] Among the urban poor, the often-described decline in Orthodox belief and practice may be partly questioned by evidence of high rates of communion and confession.[10] Even more noticeable, traditional religious patterns were challenged in the city not only by secular values but also by competing forms of religious faith and enthusiasm. We see much the same dissatisfaction as among the more educated with an established church that often did not seem to satisfy spiritual, psychological, or moral needs. This popular urban religious revival, often nonconformist and functioning outside the established church, included gatherings in taverns to talk about religion; followers of individual mystics and healers; adulation of Lev Tolstoy along with a growing Tolstoyan movement; the charismatic movement known as the "Brethren" (*brattsy*), which attracted thousands of workers to an ideal of moral living, the promise of salvation in this life, and impassioned preaching; and growing congregations of religious dissenters, frequently branded by the Orthodox Church hierarchy as "sectarian."[11]

Russia at the fin de siècle, as elsewhere in the modernizing world, experienced a remarkable upheaval of religious invention, creativity, and conflict, of intense competition about the sacred and its place in private lives and public culture. Religious ideas and experiences and conceptions of the sacred were intimately intertwined with emerging definitions of the self, the negotiation of the public sphere, the elaboration of national identity, and the articulation of new ideologies. The Symbolist poet Alexander Blok spoke of this age as witnessing a volcanic upheaval of the "elemental" through the "crusted lava" of modern civilization.[12] Yet, until recently, religion and spirituality have not been treated as central to our understanding of this age of crisis and change, but have been pushed to the margins of analysis, dismissed as the whimpers of a dying tradition against secularizing progress, sidelined in favor of what were perceived as more "real" social, economic, and political forces in Russian society. This volume exemplifies the scholarly work that has been bringing this neglect to an end. This new work, however, has sought not only to fill gaps in our knowledge and understanding of the Russian past. The goal has also been to explore, along with scholars of other places and times, critical theoretical questions about the nature of religion and the sacred and their role in modern times.

Religion and Culture

What does it mean to study religion and the sacred? In this collection the discourses, practices, and boundaries of religion vary considerably, ranging from narratives of pilgrimage, confession, and miraculous healing to religious writing about secular concerns, the language of sacred community, ethical philosophy, and, finally, visual and symbolic expressions of the sacred. If there is something essential amid this diversity, clearly it is not simply the church, which once stood at the center of religious studies but here is only one of many important locations of religious practice and discourse. The effort to name and fix the category of "religion" is characteristically modern. The common definition of "religion" as a clearly bordered set of beliefs, practices, and communal institutions, as a "system" of symbols and emotions that formulate some coherent conception of the "order of existence," has been usefully criticized in recent work as too limiting and, specifically, as a modern, and Western, definition imposed on other times and places, on other meanings and practices.[13] And like so much of the modern project to make the human world "legible," to order it by means of controlling knowledge, this effort to fix and bound the definition of religion tends to falter in the face of ubiquitous unpredictability and ambiguity.[14] A historical approach, however, partly addresses these uncertainties. "Religion" and the related but not synonymous categories of "belief," "spirituality," and "sacred" are not self-evident in meanings or boundaries. The same can be said of "secular" and "profane," which might appear to be antonyms of the sacred but are not, as several of the authors in this volume argue. In late imperial Russia, as elsewhere, these words carried the weight of well-established meanings, but they were also built and continually remade in the practices of people living in the variety and flux of place and time—in social and political relationships and in efforts to make the world comprehensible, meaningful, at least bearable, and possibly even filled with joy and hope. The varied stories in this collection meet in a common recognition of the persistent power of the religious in modern times to construct and voice meaning, but also of the persistent multiplicity and multivocality (*raznorechivost'*) of the religious. These categories remain elusive, but, as living practices they are of compelling value as evidence of historical experience and agency.

The question of how to define religion is not new. The field of religious studies itself was born a century ago amid new questions about the definition of "religion," about the relationship between religion, the sacred, and spirituality, and between subjectivities and material experience. As the founders of modern theories of religion confronted the variety of human religious experience around the globe, as well as a decline in the institutional power of traditional churches in the lives of many Europeans, some proposed a broad notion of the "sacred" as a means of defining that which is essentially religious. Émile Durkheim famously asserted that religions share not a belief in the supernatural but a division of the world into sacred and profane spheres. The sacred becomes religion only when systematized by beliefs and practices that unite believers into a community. This distinction between a theologically and institutionally defined religion and the more general mysterious, transcendent, awe-inducing, symbolic, and powerful qualities of the sacred was an important early insight pointing to the necessity of studying both organized religion and a wider sphere of spiritual experience and sacred meaning.[15]

Until the mid-1950s, however, religious history remained primarily the history of institutional churches and formal theology. When the history of the Church was the main subject, of course, problems of definition were necessarily less acute. But newer scholarship, influenced by social and cultural history, has had to face these questions directly as it turned to view religion as something experienced and shaped in social practice, as a product of a complex dialogue between institutions, inherited ideas, and individual human agency.[16] Indeed, one of the core insights in the scholarly literature over the last couple of decades on the history of religion in modern Europe is that the phrase "to be religious" has had quite different meanings attached to it according to place, local culture, education, class, and gender. Thus, it is argued, the history of religious beliefs and practices is one of appropriation, adaptation, variety, and even the unexpected. Religious feeling and devotion in modern Europe has been seen to be remarkably persistent—whether linked to organized communities of believers or more loosely associated with a spirit of the mysterious, transcendent, and awe-inspiring—but also complexly varied, shaped around historical memory, identity, and sentiment, as well as around the flux of social and political relations and conflicts.[17]

Thomas Kselman has proposed "belief" as a more flexible category with which to conceptualize the subject of religious history. Unlike traditional church history and, ironically, the studies of "popular religion" that challenged it—for both tend to accept the misleading dichotomy between official religion and the beliefs of the laity—"belief can be used to cover the relatively unsystematic formulations of laymen without rigidly distinguishing these from the commitments of the clergy." As many of the essays in this volume demonstrate, the laity were neither blind (nor true) followers of the established faith, nor autonomous (nor false) practitioners of a distinctive popular faith covered by a veneer of formal religion; rather, they were active participants in the making of "belief." As Kselman argues, "belief restores the element of agency to the historical subject, who combines, amends, and rejects elements drawn from the religious environment."[18] But even "belief" may be too limiting, for it suggests confidence and faith—what Clifford Geertz called the "aura of factuality."[19] Mikhail Bakhtin contrasted "faith," the codification and fixing of a belief system, with a more elusive "feeling for faith" (*chuvstvo very*). Such a feeling might be, as it was for Bakhtin, imbued with metaphors like the Incarnation and the Passion, yet remain, as Caryl Emerson has described it, "restless, engaged, at risk, conscious of being on the boundary with another and different substance."[20] More recently Jacques Derrida has distinguished the "experience of belief," marked by confidence and trust, from "the religious," which he describes as "vaguely associated with the experience of the sacredness of the divine, of the holy, of the saved or the unscathed [*heilig*]," but also of "hesitation" before the vain "temptation of knowing."[21]

The emphasis on "experience" and "feeling" in these efforts at definition is essential, whether it is an experience of "faith" and "belief" or a more "vaguely associated" experience of the sacred, the holy, and the transcendent. Religion functions, it has often been argued, to give order and comprehensibility to the experience of life in the world—especially to the chaos, evil, and suffering of everyday life—and, perhaps, of the beyond. Belief in the miraculous can express a sense of more profound reality, one that can give meaning to even the uncanny and the ambiguous, and, of course, to evil and suffering. At the very least, religion has been a ground for ethics, for the knowledge of right action in relation to essential and transcendental truth.[22] But religion, spirituality, and the sacred also serve to express feelings about the world as a place of mystery and awesome power, to give form to imagination, to voice nostalgia for lost perfection, and to articulate potent feelings of awe and the sublime.[23] This is the more difficult terrain in the interpretation of religion. The literature on the history of religion and spirituality has elaborated its social functions better than it has described and theorized its subjective power. Indeed, scholars have even spoken of the "principled difficulty in contemporary cultural studies" of seriously addressing belief and faith.[24] Yet clearly religion provides both emotional and interpretive knowledge, evoking transcendent moods and offering social and ethical meaning.

The cultural stories people tell one another are at the center of how these varieties of religious form and function are understood. In viewing religious life in late imperial Russia through the prism of culture (as complexes of symbols, ideas, and practices that people use to make sense of, and shape, their world), scholars have treated religious cultures "as not merely inherited or imposed" but "also made and remade by the people who live them." Religion, in other words, is processual and performative, and is constructed of diverse and contested meanings.[25] Language and narrative are often at the heart of these cultural practices. In this volume we see sacred words believed to heal the body and the self, and words assumed to have the power to transform the world. We see sacred stories intertwined with stories of community and nation. And, of course, we see that narratives of the sacred, even when as scripted and formulaic as prayer or confession, or as inherited as the story of the Passion, remain subject to elaborations, appropriations, even counter-narratives. People continually construct, as Nadieszda Kizenko comments in her essay, "their own versions of the sacred." But they also believe deeply, as almost all these authors demonstrate, in the sacred "power of the word."

These words and stories reflect social realities but also transform them by changing the way people perceive and act. This is not a simple matter of how social experience shapes or is shaped by religious language, or how religious belief shapes or is shaped by the meanings of words. Rather, this is a subtle story of inseparability, in the construction of meaning, of the social and the sacred, of the word and its practices. What is required here is to uncover the "social imaginary" of religious expression and practice: the complex linkages between material experience, the language of representation, emotional experience, and belief.[26] Implicit is the reminder not to lose sight of the agency of historical actors, even amid the many social and cultural constraints in which people live and think about life.[27]

These differences of religious definition, function, and practice, and their interrelations, are explored in the stories presented here. These chapters concern institutionalized practices and unquestioning belief in the miraculous and the presence of God, but also more elusive forms of spiritual experience and expression. They explore the existential and moral ordering of the world but also expressions of spiritual feeling and uses of religious language and argument that were distinctly restless and hesitant. Above all, they examine powerful words and stories—as expressions of tangible and elusive experience, of the social and the subjective, of meaning and feeling, and of belief, uncertainty, and desire.

Entangled with the World

Religion, spirituality, and the sacred are understood here as fully inhabiting social and political life. This should not be confused with functionalist approaches to religion, which seek to expose the "underlying social structures or unnoticed psychological distresses" that are said to "form the real root of religious behavior."[28] Even Émile Durkheim, who was instrumental in developing an interpretive model for religion as the social product of people acting as communities to constitute themselves in the world, understood that the religious was no mere "reflection" of the social but remained a social phenomenon in its own right, engaged in continual interaction with worldly life. This dialogue with the world is a central theme in these chapters.

Modernity stands at the center of these dialogues. The essays in the volume speak often of the modern and describe modernity as being "embraced," "accommodated," and "adapted," but also "confronted" and "opposed," through religion and spirituality. Most concretely, we see Russians using modern means of communication to tell their stories, even to experience the sacred: newspapers, journals, magazines, pamphlets, advertising, printed and mass circulated religious images, the railroad, even a "modern consumer industry of holy objects." We also see the sacred as a constituting factor of the emerging modern public sphere, that critical space of civic involvement between the private life of the individual and the institutional power of the state. As Russians sought to find a place for individuals and individual expression, and for alternative forms of community, in Russia's increasingly vibrant if still fragile civic life, religion and the sacred were rarely distant. Finally, modern ideas pervade these sacred stories: these chapters speak of complex interrelations between religious vocabularies and "secular rationalism," worldly notions of justice and morality, modern ideas of the self, and still more radical forms of philosophical humanism and individualism.

Conventionally the discourse of modernity tells a tale of inexorable secularization. The rationalization and disenchantment of the world through rational knowledge and organization, the displacement of religion from the center to the margins of public life, the privatization of religion—all these processes are considered to be the hallmarks of modern life. There can be no denying that in Russia, as in western Europe and North America, the processes of economic, social, and political modernization in the nineteenth and twentieth centuries destabilized traditional institutional and theological hierarchies and paved the way for the emergence of competing new individual identities. Yet, for all that this story of secularizing modernity explains, it also masks a great deal. As Derrida recently warned, if we continue to imagine a world where reason and religion, science and religion, and modernity and religion are inevitably opposed to each other, we risk being unable to see, let alone explain, the "return of the religious" in our own age.[29] In recent years historians, sociologists, and anthropologists of religion have reexamined and challenged these venerable binary oppositions in response to widespread evidence of the continued vitality of religion and the sacred in modern life. Without entirely rejecting the notion of secularization, they have suggested that it is only one element of a more complex story of religious change in the modern age. They have emphasized, in particular, that the late nineteenth and early twentieth centuries, the period traditionally seen as marking the victory of rationalist modernity, was, in fact, one of terrific religious mobilization, resulting in part from intense religious conflict and invention.[30] Modernization itself created an unprecedented self-consciousness about religious faith and practice. It shook up assumptions about the relationship between religion and nation, about the individual conscience, and about the very nature of religion itself.[31] Some philosophers and cultural critics have suggestively pointed to an even more imbricated and paradoxical relationship: "secularization" as the "hostile foundation of religion but also its driving force"; "religious belief" as "modernity's estranged self."[32] It is useful, in this regard, to keep in mind that "modernity" itself is not simply a story of rationalistic and scientific modernization: the cult of reason, the doctrine of progress, confidence in science and technology, the secular concern with time. It is also, as much recent historical scholarship has shown, a story of dynamic displacement, rupture, and flux. But perhaps the most essential sense of modernity may be found in the volatile dialogue between its two mutually dependent selves: inherently critical, restless, and insatiable but also endlessly seeking to overcome, even deny, this self through the disenchanting artifice of reason, legibility, and homogeneity.[33]

On this ambiguous and conflicted terrain, religion often found itself, in modern Russia as in other modernizing nations and empires, less and less central to the social organization of public life and even to everyday social practice, but persistently, even increasingly, important to experiencing, interpreting, and constructing the modern. As these chapters reveal, people still sought to experience the transcendent and the divine, although their reasons and definitions were changing. No less, they brought religious beliefs, narratives, images, and emotions into a critical dialogue with the modern everyday: with urban and industrial life, with illness and death, with the greater mobility of individuals in search of work and opportunity, with the disruption of family life and new roles for women, with the growth of a vibrant and often disorienting public sphere, with increasing social and cultural difference, with new ideas about the world and the self, and with revolution. The national cults of various saints, Christine Worobec shows, were modern phenomena, made possible by modern transport, mass media, and orchestration by the state church, and healing visions and experiences were shaped by expectations and narrative patterns made available by the widespread circulation of miracle tales to an increasingly literate public; at the same time miraculous cures were made subject to the verifications of modern medicine and rational investigations. The transformation of the Solovetskii Monastery during the nineteenth century from cloister to mass pilgrimage destination, examined here by Roy Robson, was aided by modern transport and media, although some participants were troubled by the commercialization and mass character of modern pilgrimage. Authors of letters of confession to Father Ioann of Kronstadt, as Nadieszda Kizenko demonstrates in her essay, shaped the ages-old narrative script of confession to fit their own purposes, and to reflect the conditions and values of the world in which they lived. For many educated female penitents, for instance, it was quite natural to seamlessly combine traditional religious language with the modern language of psychological self-analysis. Facing the intensifying modern life around them, Russians spoke often, as we see in these chapters, of "new times" and "new desires," and the worldly and the sacred were inseparably intermingled in how they experienced and constructed both time and desire.

A critical terrain on which these dialogues were played out in imperial Russia was the public sphere, which was dramatically emerging as an arena where individuals and groups could articulate the values that form the basis of a modern civil society, such as the inviolability of the individual conscience and freedom of speech and assembly; construct new identities; and mold public opinion.[34] Scholars have generally expected the values of this public sphere to be secular; indeed, for many, a public sphere infused with religious values would not be modern. Yet many essays in this volume suggest that contests over religious values and their public expression brought new voices into the Russian public sphere and played a central role in promoting individualistic and pluralistic values and secular legal principles. Paul Werth demonstrates that religious affiliation was an important arena where the state and its subjects communicated over the question of individual rights, where different stories about the meaning of freedom of conscience competed, and where notions of citizenship and of the relationship of the individual to the group and of the group to the state were rethought. Similarly Heather Coleman reveals how, by telling stories about religious violence in the countryside, villagers and various elites debated pressing questions of freedom of conscience, constitutional order, representative politics, and national identity, and convinced many government bureaucrats that, if only in the interest of preserving order, some sort of legal acceptance of religious pluralism was necessary. And Nicholas Breyfogle shows how members of the Molokan sect, in seeking to establish prayer houses, created the kinds of associations commonly considered to be the building blocks of a public sphere and implicitly promoted notions of religious pluralism. Thus conflict over religious values and the desire to freely express religious beliefs, as well as the formation of organizations based on shared religious objectives, all played a fundamental role in pushing open the boundaries of public debate in late imperial Russia and offering new models of citizenship that would not favor one religious affiliation over another. In this respect, Russia resembled other countries, such as Great Britain, where the pressure of religious dissidents for more *religious* rights played a crucial role in the early evolution of the public sphere and the legal acceptance of civic pluralism.[35] Religious pluralism is the distinguishing feature of a secularizing society and a modern public sphere, not the absence of religious organizations and spiritual values.[36]

The construction and defense of community was often central to these stories of religion in the public sphere. The creation of a "moral community," Durkheim argued in his 1912 study of "religious life," was crucial to the functions of religious belief and practice;[37] of course, the notion of moral community was also partly what the nineteenth-century Slavophiles had in mind in speaking of *sobornost'* (conciliarity, a community of values and faith) as the basis for a regenerated and reintegrated social and spiritual order in Russia. We continually see religion entwined with stories of defining, building, and defending but also with negotiating the created boundaries of communities. We see this most vigorously in Coleman's stories of religious violence and Werth's account of state policing of confessional boundaries. Very often, difficult questions of identity were central to these stories—matters of experience and self-identification no less complex and multiple than religion itself. In the minds of many, Orthodoxy and *tserkovnost'* ("churchness," i.e., belonging to the ecclesial community of the Russian Orthodox Church) were essential to the definition of Russian nationality. Rituals and discourses around a revered icon, Vera Shevzov shows, helped bind together both local communities and a national community as sharing in a defining sacred history and its remembrance. Likewise, many religious minority groups defined themselves as communities of difference (or by the difference others saw in them). For the Molokans, for example, the new desire to pray together in their own buildings, despite a long history of Molokan critique of the physical church, reflected a growing inclination to make themselves into a tangible civic as well as spiritual community.

As these discussions of community, difference, and tolerance suggest, fundamental questions of power, and resistance, are often crucial to these stories of religion and the world. William Wagner describes the efforts of Orthodox writers to extol in sacred terms the virtues of women's obedience and submissiveness but also their arguments about the essential spiritual equality of men and women, both equally capable of living a life of faith and piety. Gregory Freeze finds in debates about divorce a struggle—and a losing one for those defending traditional authority—not only over the power of the church to regulate civic life but also over the moral authority of patriarchy as a cultural and social system. The declaration of freedom of conscience, Werth shows, provoked a wave of requests to change confessional affiliations that threatened to destabilize the special and privileged relationship of the Orthodox Church to the Russian state, and raised difficult questions about the religious construction of national identity and the boundaries of "Russian" and "alien" within the empire. Related questions about the role of the state in enforcing adherence to Orthodoxy as a definition of community and nation, and fear that the growth of non-Orthodox Christian confessions was a cause of social disorder, are basic to Coleman's chapter, as is a more localized and bloody contest over power and order, both partly rooted in a deep fear of difference as the source of disorder. Clearly religion functioned here as "an eminently political thing," to paraphrase Durkheim, as communities (empire, nation, church, confessions, village) constituted themselves in the world.

Class and gender—critical categories of public experience, identity, community, difference, and power—were entwined with how the sacred was understood and used. The essays in this volume join the ongoing reassessment of the relationships between class, "popular culture," and religion. Works on popular religion have tended to focus on the distinctive ways that ordinary people fashioned religious practices to suit local circumstances, customs, and mentalities. This approach emphasized the agency of the laity in accepting, rejecting, or reformulating the teachings of religious institutions. But just as historians of popular culture have, in recent years, criticized models that too strictly separated popular from "high" culture and overemphasized elements of resistance over those that were shared across class lines, historians of religion have increasingly questioned the overly simple contrasts between high and low, clerical and lay, rational and emotional, and spontaneous and conscious religiosity that were usually implied in the concept of "popular religion."[38] Thus Kizenko and Worobec, for example, highlight how religiosity was at once experienced differently and shared across class lines. Both argue that laypeople from across the social spectrum took seriously the teachings of the clergy and engaged with them in introspective, active ways. Religious piety was not just the characteristic of presumably ignorant, premodern peasant mentalities and practices but was also meaningful to educated, urban Russians. Still, the awareness and enactment of class difference—of different experience and its understanding—is inescapable. Gregory Freeze sees a growing chasm between official and popular Orthodoxy in attitudes toward marriage and the family. When Russians went on pilgrimage, Worobec and Robson show, the "better public" (literally the *chistaia publika*, or "clean public") kept themselves away from the diseased, dirty, and pustulous bodies of the poor. Indeed, practices of class discrimination at religious sites and during religious ceremonies repeatedly reminded lower-class Russians that in the community of Orthodox believers, where all should have faced God as equals in both sin and dignity, as in the idealized worldly community of the nation, some were more equal than others. At the same time, the poor themselves, drawing on religious notions of pollution and sin, could feel their own debasement as a class, as Kizenko and Mark Steinberg find in lower-class confessions and poetry, although these could variously be expressions of self-deprecating guilt, a desire to escape, or defiant anger. Clearly "popular religion"is best understood neither as passive accommodation or internalization of prescribed beliefs nor as a defiantly separate and autonomous plebeian culture but as a dialogic cultural practice that can simultaneously embrace, resist, appropriate, and rearrange forms and meanings.

Gender, too, was part of these dialogues between the sacred and worldly experience and identity. Scholars have long debated the "feminization of religion" in modern Europe, visible, for example, in the greater relative persistence and even rise of female observance and piety, and of a supposedly "feminine" tendency toward spiritual sentimentalism and irrationality.[39] In this volume Worobec and Kizenko explore more subtle workings of gender in narratives of the sacred.[40] In stories of healing miracles, Worobec finds men and women (and different classes) equally attracted to saints' cults but sees subtle gendered differences in individuals' troubles and desires, and in definitions of disease (including possession) and miraculous healing. Similarly Kizenko questions simplistic claims that confession was a "religious genre more congenial to women" but also observes important differences in men's and women's confessional voices. Wagner and Freeze explore discourses of gender in which male and female become matters of both sacred values and secular relationships—including the contemporary belief that women were more pious and thus represented a moral force beneficial to the family and, by extension, to the whole social and political order. Religious attitudes about women (including among women themselves) were shaped by the interplay of church teachings, secular ideas, changing economic and social conditions for women, and lay and religious activism by women themselves. Arguments were constructed, in ways not easy to disentangle, of both profane and sacred materials.

The religious was entwined with the construction not only of communities and collective identities but also of the self—with individual experience, personal self-knowledge, and self-assertion. The self and its social and moral meanings preoccupied many Russians in the final decades of the old order.[41] The characteristically modern, Western idea of interior and autonomous personhood, reflexively aware, actively self-fashioning, and endowed by nature with a universal humanity and dignity, became a powerful presence in modern Russia. This modern "effort to map inner space," and to draw political and social lessons from these discoveries, was closely linked with religion and the sacred. At the very least, the widespread notion of the intrinsic value of personhood (*lichnost'*) was viewed as immanent in the making of humanity in the "image and likeness" of God. The sacred narrative of the self was also connected to notions of the mystery of being, the transcending "unknowability" of God and hence of the individual human person, creating a pervasive "otherness" within all creation that results in an encompassing sacredness. The self-consciousness so central to modernity helped to constitute a heightened self-awareness about belief and faith that was one of the defining features of modern religiosity.[42]

Notions of self-knowledge, personal dignity and will, and self-realization pervade the stories of the religious and the sacred explored here. Equally we see the central importance of inward feeling and faith, the critical but interpretively difficult terrain of feelings, emotions, and subjectivities.[43] Liberal Orthodox theologians, for example, as Wagner describes, increasingly spoke of the personal autonomy of women and even emerging "notions of self," constructions that in turn emphasized, as Christian values, personal moral and spiritual development, individual self-realization, and the inherent "human dignity" of women. Women themselves, Freeze shows, sometimes challenged official notions of the marital sacrament to defend their own personal dignity and rights as grounded in values of personal self-esteem and of love and affect in marriage. As Werth demonstrates, the 1905 decree promising freedom of religious "conscience" was viewed by many, including in the government, as recognition that faith was a "personal affair," a matter of "individual" belief not of external structures of law or even birth (although this view was vehemently rejected by many others in power). Religious dissenters, of course, like the Baptists discussed by Coleman, often assumed faith to be a matter of personal choice and inward conversion (although this is precisely what so offended many Orthodox communities that they were provoked to violence). But the Orthodox, too, practiced an often personal and inward faith. Miraculous healing, Worobec shows, often involved individual promises made to saints and personal tokens of affection, as well as individual cure. Pilgrimage, both Robson and Worobec describe, involved individual decisions to leave a community, even to act against the will of relatives, in the pursuit of healing (or as a mark of individual gratitude for healing) or of other uplifting experiences, including the personal pleasures of travel and unusual encounters. Confession, as Kizenko discusses, was a characteristic practice of intimacy and revelation—of the self but always in relation to God and others—that often involved "eclectic and personal" interpretations of religious formulas to express personal concerns and needs. And Shevzov's chapter shows how, even when dealing with such a strongly communal narrative as that of the Kazan icon, Orthodox pastors often chose to preach to the individual about the internal processes of human spiritual development. At the center of the impassioned language of worker-poets, and of the meanings with which they infused images like martyrdom and crucifixion, Steinberg describes, was the self: feelings of "dignity" continually "wounded," and feelings of an "interior distance" from others and even from the present time and place, led to individual "wandering" in search of "truth," healing, and salvation. Like these worker-poets, the new Jewish "heroes" in the stories of the Russian-Jewish ethnographer and writer S. An-sky, as Gabriella Safran describes, believe in the ideal—indeed are made by it—of an elevated self and community empowered by the sacred force of feeling, speech, and word. Similarly, religious thinkers of the Silver Age like Dmitry Merezhkovsky, Viacheslav Ivanov, and Pavel Florensky (discussed by Bernice Rosenthal and Paul Valliere) and mystical-oriented artists like Kazimir Malevich (examined by Alexei Kurbanovsky) explored the deification of the human person, above all through the power of feeling, of inward passion, even ecstasy. At the heart of so many of these sacred narratives we see the "inner space" of the self, although inescapably entwined with other spaces and other selves.

The essays in this volume repeatedly draw our attention to the ambiguity of the boundaries between the sacred and the profane, the religious and the secular, the spiritual and the physical. The perceived boundary between sacred and secular was especially unstable in these years. Sarah Stein observes, through close attention to narrative, the fuzziness of the divide between what have traditionally been treated as the very separate worlds of "observant" and "secular" Jews in late imperial Russia. Stein shows that the secularizing agenda of the editors of the first Yiddish daily newspaper published in Russia, *Der fraynd*, was constantly undermined by the sacred stories that were the experience of their readers. This tension, she argues, reflected a pervasive uncertainty: for Russian Jews in this period, the boundaries between "religious" and "secular" Jews were profoundly unclear—indeed, they were being invented by advocates of a secular Yiddish culture such as the editors of *Der fraynd*. Likewise, Rosenthal meditates on the irony that, owing to the affinities between Nietzschean ideas and Orthodox thought, Friedrich Nietzsche, that herald of the death of God, played a central role in inspiring and reshaping the thought of writers and thinkers dedicated to a revitalization of Orthodoxy in the modern age.

The boundaries of sacred and secular were continually violated in the quest, widespread in early-twentieth-century Russia, for a modern mysticism. Safran identifies a search for such a mysticism, for a spiritual energy divested of formal religious content, in An-sky's retelling of the Hasidic legend of a *rebbe* who puts God on trial. We see much the same search in the work of the artist Malevich, in the poetry of workers, and in the thinking of many leading philosophers. Valliere, for example, shows us the fashioning of a highly original new Russian tradition of religious philosophy animated by the desire to overcome the gap between religion and modern secular civilization through a theology of "culture." These philosophers viewed modern Russian cultural history itself as constituting a sacred story and sought to ground modern civilization in the sacred without necessarily tying either to religious institutions.

At every turn we see sacred narratives and practices questioning dichotomies and transgressing boundaries. We also encounter constant efforts, sometimes quite desperate and even violent, to sustain and police these boundaries. At issue, for example, were definitions of male and female natures and roles, of national and confessional "moral communities," of religious and secular words, stories, spaces, images, and people, and of the secular and sacred in the work of philosophy and art. The questioning, contesting, and guarding of these boundaries were not only a matter of words and stories. In the search for answers or solutions (including healing), individuals looked to the law or revolution, turned violently against one another, "converted" from one faith to another (although it often seemed to them that they were simply turning to the truth), or crossed the boundaries of both place and perception by taking to the road as pilgrims and wanderers.

We see in many of these essays striking evidence of the ambiguity of even the most solid boundary: that between the physical and the spiritual. Material objects and places—icons, relics, burial sites, churches, crypts, scraps of cloth, stones, water, words, visual symbols—reach across the presumed divide to make present and tangible the healing power of saints and the divine. These boundary crossings were only made more frequent and complex as holy objects became entangled with modern forms of production and commerce. For some fin-de-siècle religious intellectuals, notions such as "holy flesh" alluded not only to the historical incarnation but also to a sanctification of the body and sexuality. In any case, they argued, all dichotomies, including the physical and the spiritual, would be reconciled finally by the apocalyptic Second Coming of Christ.

It is, of course, characteristic of the modern age, with its pervasive ruptures, displacements, and flux, that interpretive boundaries became fraught and uncertain. However, one should not overstate the modernity of all this. Religion has long been a form of experience and interpretation that reaches across the lines supposedly separating, for example, the living from the dead or the present world from transcendent spaces. There is nothing inherently modern, for example, about the powerful and often unsettling liminal experiences of pilgrimage or ecstatic prayer or the miraculous. Orthodox Christianity, especially, often takes place precisely on this boundary of the physical and the spiritual. Sacraments and icons are manifestations of the presence of the transcendent, eternal, and sacred in the physical and temporal present. And, of course, the essential ambiguity of the boundaries between spirit and matter, sacred and secular, human and divine is exemplified by the foundational image of the incarnate, suffering, and dying Christ. When the experiential transgressions and displacements of the religious occur in modern conditions of flux and rupture they can become especially intense.

The full history of the upheaval of religion and spirituality in Russia and its place within the whole of Russia's history in those critical years of change and crisis has yet to be written. But the essential research and interpretation is being done, enriched by new sources (some of them inaccessible before the post-communist opening of archives and other collections), new questions, and new approaches. This work offers stories that fill gaps in our knowledge of the Russian past but that also force us to rethink Russia's modern experience. In the process critical interpretive questions are raised regarding the definition of the religious, especially in relationship to the modern; the place of narrative in the construction of vision and understanding; the connections between sacred stories and everyday life in the world; and the relationships between religion and politics, class, gender, and the individual self.

Notes

1. For a list of published works in this still relatively new field of sustained scholarly study, see the bibliography, "Further Reading."

2. Émile Durkheim, *Elementary Forms of Religious Life,* trans. and ed. Karen E. Fields (New York, 1995), 44 (French original published in 1912).

3. Richard S. Wortman, *Scenarios of Power: Myth and Ceremony in Russian Monarchy,* Vol. 2, *From Alexander II to the Abdication of Nicholas II* (Princeton, 2000), 239–242. See also Gregory L. Freeze, "Subversive Piety: Religion and the Political Crisis in Late Imperial Russia," *Journal of Modern History* 68 (June 1996): 310; and A. Iu. Polunov, *Pod vlast'iu ober-prokurora. Gosudarstvo i tserkov' v epokhu Aleksandra III* (Moscow, 1996).

4. See, for example, G. L. Freeze, "Handmaiden of the State? The Church in Imperial Russia Reconsidered," *Journal of Ecclesiastical History* 36, no. 1 (January 1985): 100–101; Gregory Freeze, "'Going to the Intelligentsia': The Church and Its Urban Mission in Post-Reform Russia," in *Between Tsar and People: Educated Society and the Quest for Public Identity in Late Imperial Russia,* ed. Edith Clowes, Samuel Kassow, and James West (Princeton, N.J., 1991), 215–221.

5. Paul R. Valliere, "The Idea of a Council in Russian Orthodoxy in 1905," in *Russian Orthodoxy under the Old Regime,* ed. Robert L. Nichols and Theofanis George Stavrou (Minneapolis, Minn., 1978), 186.

6. Quoted in Aileen Kelly, *Toward Another Shore: Russian Thinkers between Necessity and Chance* (New Haven, Conn., 1998), 174.

7. A. V. Lunacharskii, "Ateizm," *Ocherki po filosofii marksizma: filosofskii sbornik* (St. Petersburg, 1908), esp. 115–116, 148–157; idem, *Religiia i sotsializm,* 2 vols. (St. Petersburg, 1908 and 1911). See also George L. Kline, *Religious and Anti-Religious Thought in Russia* (Chicago, 1968), chap. 4; and Jutta Scherrer, "'Ein gelber und ein blauer Teufel': zur Entstehung der Begriffe 'bogostroitel'stvo' und 'bogoiskatel'stvo,'" *Forschungen zur osteuropaeischen Geschichte* 25 (1978): 319–329; idem, "L'intelligentsia russe: sa quete de la 'vérité religieuse du socialisme,'" *Le temps de la réflexion* 2 (1981): 134–151.

8. A. S. Pankratov, *Ishchushchie boga* (Moscow, 1911); Nicolas Zernov, *The Russian Religious Renaissance of the Twentieth Century* (New York, 1963); Kline, *Religious and Anti-Religious Thought in Russia;* Temira Pachmuss, *Zinaida Gippius: An Intellectual Profile* (Carbondale, Ill., 1971), chap. 4; Christopher Read, *Religion, Revolution and the Russian Intelligentsia, 1900–1912* (London, 1979); Maria Carlson, *"No Religion Higher Than Truth": A History of the Theosophical Movement in Russia, 1875–1922* (Princeton, N.J., 1993); Catherine Evtukhov, *The Cross and the Sickle: Sergei Bulgakov and the Fate of Russian Religious Philosophy, 1890–1920* (Ithaca, N.Y., 1997); Bernice Glatzer Rosenthal, ed., *The Occult in Russian and Soviet Culture* (Ithaca, N.Y., 1997); Nadieszda Kizenko, *A Prodigal Saint: Father John of Kronstadt and the Russian People* (University Park, Pa., 2000); Laura Engelstein, "Holy Russia in Modern Times: An Essay on Orthodoxy and Cultural Change," *Past and Present* 173, no. 1 (November 2001): 129–156.

9. Freeze, "Subversive Piety," 308–350; Gregory Freeze, "Counter-Reformation in Russian Orthodoxy: Popular Response to Religious Innovation, 1922–1925," *Slavic Review* 54, no. 2 (summer 1995): 305–339; Jeffrey Burds, *Peasant Dreams and Market Politics* (Pittsburgh, Pa., 1998), chap. 7; W. Arthur McKee, "Sobering Up the Soul of the People: The Politics of Popular Temperance in Late Imperial Russia," *Russian Review* 58, no. 2 (April 1999): 212–233; A. Etkind, *Khlyst: Sekty, Literatura, Revoliutsiia* (Moscow, 1998); Laura Engelstein, *Castration and the Heavenly Kingdom* (Ithaca, N.Y., 1999); Christine Worobec, *Possessed: Women, Witches, and Demons in Imperial Russia* (DeKalb, Ill., 2001); Steinberg, *Proletarian Imagination,* chap. 6; Heather J. Coleman, *Russian Baptists and Spiritual Revolution, 1905–1929* (Bloomington, Ind., 2005), chap. 3; Vera Shevzov, *Russian Orthodoxy on the Eve of Revolution* (New York, 2004).

10. Simon Dixon, "The Orthodox Church and the Workers of St. Petersburg, 1880–1914," in *European Religion in the Age of Great Cities, 1830–1930,* ed. Hugh McLeod (London and New York, 1995), 121; idem, "How Holy Was Holy Russia? Rediscovering Russian Religion," in *Reinterpreting Russia,* ed. Geoffrey Hosking and Robert Service (London, 1999), 29–30.

11. Pankratov, *Ishchushchie boga;* A. S. Prugavin, *"Brattsy" i trezvenniki* (Moscow, 1912); A. I. Klibanov, *Istoriia religioznogo sektantstva v Rossii* (Moscow, 1965), N. Tal'nikov, "Sektanty v Peterburge (iz nabliudenii i vpechatlenii)"—a series of articles in *Peterburgskii listok* during 1907–1908; Engelstein, *Castration and the Heavenly Kingdom.*

12. Aleksandr Blok, "Stikhiia i kul'tura" (December 1908), in *Aleksandr Blok, Andrei Belyi: Dialog poetov o Rossii i revoliutsii,* ed. M. F. Pianykh (Moscow, 1990), 396–405.

13. Clifford Geertz, "Religion as a Cultural System," in idem, *The Interpretation of Cultures* (New York, 1973), esp. 89–103, quote at 90; Talal Asad, "Religion, Nation-State, Secularism," in *Nation and Religion: Perspectives on Europe and Asia,* ed. Peter van der Veer and Hartmut Lehmann (Princeton, N.J., 1999), 4.

14. On this impossible modernist drive for legibility, see James C. Scott, *Seeing Like a State* (New Haven, Conn., 1998). Of course, much of Michel Foucault's work similarly explores the modern drive to know and control, although with less certainty about its limitations and failures.

15. Daniel L. Pals, *Seven Theories of Religion* (New York, 1996), 99, 165; Phillip E. Hammond, ed., *The Sacred in a Secular Age: Toward Revision in the Scientific Study of Religion* (Berkeley, Calif., 1985), 4, 167. Durkheim, *The Elementary Forms of Religious Life,* esp. 21–44.

16. Thomas Kselman, ed., *Belief in History: Innovative Approaches to European and American Religion* (Notre Dame, Ind., 1991), 1–7.

17. Caroline Ford, "Religion and Popular Culture in Modern Europe," *Journal of Modern History* 65, no. 1 (March 1993): 152–175. See also, for example, David Blackbourn, *Marpingen: Apparitions of the Virgin Mary in Nineteenth-Century Germany* (Oxford, 1993); and Suzanne Desan, *Reclaiming the Sacred: Lay Religion and Popular Politics in Revolutionary France* (Ithaca, N.Y., 1990). This work on modern Europe, as well as recent work on Russia, has been especially influenced by innovative historical studies of early modern popular religion. See especially Natalie Zemon Davis, *Society and Culture in Early Modern France* (Stanford, Calif., 1975); Carlo Ginzburg, *The Cheese and the Worms* (Baltimore, Md., 1980); David Warren Sabean, *Power in the Blood: Popular Culture and Village Discourse in Early Modern Germany* (Cambridge, 1984).

18. Kselman, *Belief in History,* 7.

19. Geertz, "Religion as a Cultural System," 109.

20. Susan M. Felch and Paul J. Contino, eds., *Bakhtin and Religion; A Feeling for Faith* (Evanston, Ill., 2001), 1, 16–20, quote at 188 (from the afterword by Caryl Emerson). This discussion especially concerns Bakhtin's book, *Problems of Dostoevsky's Poetics,* trans. Caryl Emerson (Minneapolis, Minn., 1963).

21. Jacques Derrida, "Faith and Knowledge: The Two Sources of 'Religion' at the Limits of Reason Alone," in *Acts of Religion,* ed. and intro. by Gil Anidjar (New York, 2002), 68, 70. "Faith and Knowledge" was originally published in Jacques Derrida and Gianni Vattimo, eds., *La Religion: Seminaire de Capri* (Paris, 1996).

22. For some classic statements on the function of religion, see Mircea Eliade, *The Sacred and the Profane: The Nature of Religion* (New York, 1959); idem, *Myths, Dreams, and Mysteries* (New York, 1960); Peter Berger, *The Sacred Canopy: Elements of a Sociological Theory of Religion* (New York, 1967).

23. See, for example, the work of Mircea Eliade and Clifford Geertz, "Ethos, World View, and the Analysis of Sacred Symbols," in Geertz, *Interpretation of Cultures,* 126–141.

24. Gauri Viswanathan, *Outside the Fold: Conversion, Modernity, and Belief* (Princeton, N.J., 1998), xv.

25. Natalie Zemon Davis, "From 'Popular Religion' to Religious Cultures," in *Reformation Europe: A Guide to Research,* ed. Steven Ozment (St. Louis, Mo., 1982), 323, 331; Caroline Ford, "Religion and Popular Culture in Modern Europe," *Journal of Modern History* 65 (March 1993): 154, 175. See also William H. Sewell Jr., "The Concept(s) of Culture," in *Beyond the Cultural Turn: New Directions in the Study of Society and Culture,* ed. Victoria E. Bonnell and Lynn Hunt (Berkeley, Calif., 1999), 35–61.

26. Sarah Maza, "Stories in History: Cultural Narratives in Recent Works in European History," *American Historical Review* 101, no. 5 (December 1996): 1515.

27. Kselman, *Belief in History,* 7.

28. Pals, *Seven Theories,* 13.

29. Derrida, "Faith and Knowledge," in Anidjar, *Acts of Religion,* 65.

30. See, for example, van der Veer and Lehmann's introduction to, and Asad's "Religion, Nation-State, Secularism" in, van der Veer and Lehmann, *Nation and Religion,* 3–12, 178–196; McLeod, *European Religion in the Age of Great Cities,* 9–24; Hugh McLeod, *Secularization in Western Europe, 1848–1914* (New York, 2000).

31. Lucian Hölscher, "Secularization and Urbanization in the Nineteenth Century: An Interpretative Model," in McLeod, *European Religion in the Age of Great Cities*, 263, 266–267.

32. Maurizio Ferraris, "The Meaning of Being as a Determinate Ontic Trace," in Derrida and Gianni Vattimo, *La Religion*, 172; Viswanathan, *Outside the Fold*, xiii–xiv.

33. Marshall Berman, *All That Is Solid Melts into Air: The Experience of Modernity* (New York, 1982); Zygmunt Bauman, *Modernity and Ambivalence* (Ithaca, N.Y., 1991); idem, *Intimations of Postmodernity* (London, 1992), esp. intro. and chap. 9; Arjun Appadurai, *Modernity at Large* (Minneapolis, Minn., 1996); Rita Felski, *The Gender of Modernity* (Cambridge, Mass., 1995).

34. Clowes, Kassow, and West, *Between Tsar and People*; Joseph Bradley, "Subjects into Citizens: Societies, Civil Society, and Autocracy in Tsarist Russia," *American Historical Review* 107, no. 4 (October 2002): 1094–1123.

35. See, for example: Peter van der Veer, *Imperial Encounters: Religion and Modernity in India and Britain* (Princeton, N.J., 2001), 27–28; Viswanathan, *Outside the Fold*, chap. 1; David Zaret, "Religion, Science, and Printing in the Public Spheres in Seventeenth-Century England," in *Habermas and the Public Sphere*, ed. Craig Calhoun (Cambridge, Mass., 1992), 212–235.

36. Berger, *The Sacred Canopy*, chap. 6.

37. Durkheim, *The Elementary Forms of Religious Life*.

38. David D. Hall, "Introduction," Robert Orsi, "Everyday Miracles: The Study of Lived Religion," and Danièle Hervieu-Léger, " 'What Scripture Tells Me': Spontaneity and Regulation within the Catholic Charismatic Renewal," in *Lived Religion in America: Toward a History of Practice*, ed. David D. Hall (Princeton, N.J., 1997), esp. viii–ix, 25. See also Kselman's introduction to his *Belief in History*.

39. Caroline Ford briefly reviews recent scholarship on the feminization of religion. See Ford, "Religion and Popular Culture," 167–169.

40. See also Worobec, *Possessed*; and Kizenko, *A Prodigal Saint*.

41. See Oleg Kharkhordin, *The Collective and the Individual in Russia: A Study of Practices* (Berkeley, Calif., 1999); Laura Engelstein and Stephanie Sandler, eds., *Self and Story in Russian History* (Ithaca, N.Y., 2000); and Steinberg, *Proletarian Imagination*.

42. See suggestive comments in Randall Poole, "The Apophatic Bakhtin," in Felch and Contino, *Bakhtin and Religion*, esp. 151–156; Foucault, *Religion and Culture*, 5, 32; See also Simon Critchley and Robert Bernasconi, *The Cambridge Companion to Levinas* (Cambridge, 2002), esp. 33–35, 63–66, 91, 188, 241–244, 255–258.

43. For a recent critical discussion in what is a growing theoretical and historical literature on the study of emotions, see Barbara H. Rosenwein, "Worrying about Emotions in History," *American Historical Review* 107, no. 3 (June 2002): 821–845.

1

Miraculous Healings

Christine D. Worobec

An examination of religious literature published in the last decades of imperial Russia reveals the tangible hope of a cure that Russian Orthodoxy
offered to the disabled and diseased, as well as to their relatives and, indeed,
all believers who feared they might fall ill. Through their prayers for the intercession of the Mother of God, Christ, the saints, and other holy persons, and
with vows to visit saints' graves, the sick and disabled often believed they
could receive God's mercy and grace. Miraculous cures at the graves of saints
or through visions of holy persons in dreams were regular occurrences in
late imperial Russia. The narratives describing these cures reveal a Russian
Orthodoxy not stuck in medievalism and obscurantism but relevant to people's
lives, regardless of gender and class. The sacred stories demonstrate individual
or collective experiences with the divine. Miraculous cures, to be certified as
such, had to be witnessed by others, and some posthumous miracles ascribed
to holy persons had to be verified through an investigation by the Holy Synod.
Print culture not only disseminated the stories of the miraculous throughout
European Russia but also beckoned the infirm to visit local and national shrines
that enjoyed the imprimatur of the Russian Orthodox Church and the support
of pilgrims who believed that prayers at a shrine were "more efficacious."[1]

In addition to recording healings ascribed to divine forces, the miracle tales
demonstrate the ways that the Orthodox Church in later imperial Russia confronted and embraced elements of modernity. The Holy Synod tried to shape
popular piety in the face of formidable challenges posed by competing faiths
and ideologies, including Old Belief, sectarianism, Shtundism (or Evangelical
Christianity), secularism and scientific rationalism, and atheism. Its use of mass
communications, verification of miracles, the demotion of demon possession
from acceptable to fraudulent behavior, and representation of a shrinking percentage of peasants among recipients of the miraculous pinpointed a religious
establishment that had adopted modern notions and means, even though its

22

belief in the possibility of miracles was decidedly antimodern.[2] By simultaneously promoting pilgrimages, trying to control the definition of what constituted a miracle, and catering to the aesthetic needs of the upper classes, the Church may have helped to exacerbate the tensions between upper and lower classes in imperial Russia.

The turn of the twentieth century in Russia is a rich period for examining miracle narratives, for the Russian Orthodox Church canonized six holy men in the reign of Nicholas II, beginning with the glorification of Archbishop Feodosii of Chernigov in September 1896 and ending with that of Metropolitan Ioann of Tobolsk in 1916. The Holy Synod also confirmed Anna Kashinskaia's sainthood in 1909. This flurry of canonizations represented a departure from the Synod's reticence in recognizing posthumous miracles of holy persons, as attested by its recognition of only four new saints over the course of the entire nineteenth century. Unwittingly influenced by secular rationalism, in spite of their railing against it, late-eighteenth-century ecclesiastics had become skeptical of the possibility of miracles in the modern age, particularly those reportedly experienced by commoners. They were also wary of acknowledging miracles because of the growing numbers of schismatics, sectarians, and converts to other Christian denominations who questioned the legitimacy of Orthodox saints and were prone to attack the Russian Orthodox Church for exploiting holy relics for financial gain. At the same time, the scrutiny of popular practices with regard to miracles had the unintended and undesirable consequence by the early nineteenth century of turning the faithful away from the Orthodox Church and into the hands of Old Believers and sectarians. In response, the Holy Synod relaxed its skepticism toward miracles. By the mid-nineteenth century the Synod began to publish regular accounts of miracles in the religious press, even though it remained cautious about recognizing new saints and continued to assert its control over miracle-working icons.[3] As Gregory Freeze has demonstrated, many of the early-twentieth-century canonizations came about because the state sought to re-sacralize the failing autocracy and bring it closer to the masses of Orthodox believers. Tensions between the Holy Synod and the autocracy, the dubious character of some of the candidates for sainthood, and the scandal surrounding the corrupted remains of Serafim of Sarov resulted in a disastrous public relations campaign for both government and Church.[4] A counter-narrative, however, may be found at the level of the miracles stories that attested, in the believers' minds, to the holiness of individual saints.

This essay examines 247 miracles ascribed to the intercessory powers of Serafim of Sarov (canonized in 1903), Bishop Ioasaf of Belgorod and Oboiansk (canonized in 1911), and Bishop Pitirim of Tambov (canonized in 1914). In the case of Saints Serafim and Ioasaf, the miracle narratives were printed in diocesan newspapers, religious journals, and individual publications that had passed the Holy Synod's censors.[5] The 110 miracles performed by Serafim posthumously and the 102 attributed to Ioasaf outnumber the officially verified miracles for each.[6] They include miracles recorded prior to the canonization ceremonies as well as accounts of miracles that occurred during and after the ceremonies of glorification. Not all of them, therefore, had their information authenticated by an official church commission. In the case of Pitirim of Tambov, the record includes thirty-four official miracles (involving thirty-five individuals)[7] verified and sanctioned by a committee, with additional information coming from nineteen cases in which lay and ecclesiastical commissioners could not validate the miracle.[8] The mixture of official and nonofficial miracles provides evidence about the Church's agenda in the late imperial period as well as its own and its followers' understandings of communities of believers. At the same time, conclusions reached in this essay can only suggest trends that will have to be tested against miracle narratives connected to other saints, both those officially recognized by the Church and those not sanctioned.

Methodologically this essay employs quantitative and content analysis. The breakdown of recipients of miracles by geographical origin, estate, age, and gender reveals both differences and similarities between these saints' cults; and comparison of the miracles with those from the mid-eighteenth century elucidates both continuities and discontinuities over time. Given the wide range of illnesses represented in the miracle tales, statistical analysis is less illuminating in this regard than content analysis. Information gleaned from eyewitness descriptions of the canonization celebrations themselves and medical records demonstrate the degree to which medicalization of illness had taken place. Finally, content analysis also illuminates the rituals of the saints' cults as well as the importance of the press in disseminating information about holy persons, encouraging pilgrimages, and stimulating miracles.

Geographically the recipients of cures before, during, and after the canonizations of Serafim of Sarov, Ioasaf of Belgorod, and Pitirim of Tambov reveal saints' cults of varying national impact. Whereas the glorification of Serafim of Sarov had been carried out at the express orders of the royal family, the canonizations of Bishops Ioasaf of Belgorod and Pitirim of Tambov were instigated by the Church. Of the three, Serafim of Sarov (1754–1833),[9] a simple monk who served as spiritual elder or adviser to all supplicants regardless of class origins, enjoyed the greatest popularity among the faithful. Throughout the nineteenth century the Sarovskaia Uspenskaia Hermitage, where Serafim's remains rested, drew pilgrims from far and wide.[10] In order to establish a record that could later be used to argue in favor of Serafim's sanctity, monks at the hermitage had regularly noted the miracles attributed to him. Dismissing the validity of those miracle accounts because they could not be verified, the Holy Synod set up a separate commission in 1892 to investigate newer miracles. After repeatedly delaying Serafim's canonization, the Synod finally bowed to the appeal of Nicholas II on the anniversary of Serafim's birth in July 1902 that Serafim be glorified the following year.[11] The miracles attributed to him before, during, and after the 1903 canonization ceremonies involved individuals from an impressive range of provinces. Twenty-nine percent of the recipients came from unidentified locations, and only 15.5 percent were from the immediate provinces of Tambov and Nizhnii Novgorod. A slightly higher percentage (17.3) stemmed from Penza, Saratov, Voronezh, Riazan, and Vladimir provinces, all located around Tambov. A significant 38 percent of miracle beneficiaries, on the other hand, were residents of regions outside the circumference of the latter area. They came from as far away as Siberia in the Northeast and Astrakhan in the East to St. Petersburg in the North and Riga in the West. The report of the peasant Ivan Kharitonov Shazhkov of the village of Zaplavnoe, Tsarevskii uezd (district), Astrakhan Province, that he had walked one thousand versts to Sarov in fulfillment of his vow to make the pilgrimage there and seek the saint's help surely must have impressed the readers of his miracle narrative.[12] The cult of Ioasaf of Belgorod (located in Kursk Province) had less of a national reach than that of Serafim, with 33 percent of the individuals reporting miracles because of his intercession identifying themselves as residents of Kursk Province. Just over one-third did not specify their place of residence; 13.7 percent came from provinces bordering Kursk (Orel, Voronezh, Chernigov, Poltava, and Khar'kov); and 17.3 percent came from provinces outside those areas, ranging from Minsk in the West to Tashkent in the East; Ekaterinoslav in the South and Kostroma in the Northeast. Unlike the Serafim and Ioasaf cults, the cult surrounding Pitirim had, in keeping with most miracle cults, strictly a local cast: all beneficiaries of his miracles resided in Tambov Province.

At both the national and local levels, print culture played a significant role not only in disseminating information about holy persons and their posthumous miraculous cures but also in promoting the possibility of the miraculous in the modern age and begetting new miracles.[13] Owing to popular demand, portraits and vitae of holy men were circulated well before their glorifications. Thus we read about a noblewoman's gradual healing from what appeared to have been a stroke (paralysis was accompanied by a sagging of the lower jaw, a crooked mouth, and loss of speech) in 1815, as a result of her husband's placing a portrait of Ioasaf of Belgorod at the head of her bed and then traveling to the saint's grave where he ordered a thanksgiving service (*moleben*) for the holy man. Numerous other references are made in other miracle narratives to the beneficial effect of Ioasaf's portrait, including one instance when a mother, through prayer, beseeched the saint's help in saving her two-year-old daughter from pneumonia and used his icon to provide her daughter with spiritual and medicinal treatment: she poured water over the icon in a vessel, wet the child's head with the "holy" runoff, and had the child drink some of the water.[14] Posthumous miracles ascribed to Serafim of Sarov are replete with references to individuals and their relatives reading Serafim's vita before they received a miraculous cure through the holy man's intercession. By means of the hagiography, believers learned about his reputation as a holy man and a healer of disease, followed his advice about how to seek a cure and lead a full Christian life, and, influenced by the iconography on the printed page, pictured in their minds an image of the saint.

Dreams of Saints Serafim, Ioasaf, and Pitirim, generally prompted by the print media, are another common feature of the miracle narratives. Some of the nocturnal visions occurred without the benefit of saints' portraits as had been the case in the medieval period, but the vast majority of miracle recipients who had divinely inspired dreams of holy men evidently were influenced by the print iconography. A vision generally followed the reading of a blessed person's vita. The beneficiaries of nocturnal visitations invariably described the clothing of the holy men as either generic monk's garb or the brilliant vestments they wore in their graves. Sixteen-year-old Elizaveta Feodorova Letunova, for example, who had been suffering from epilepsy for about six years, described Pitirim as a monk wearing "a *klobuk* [monk's hood], ... with a long greying beard," and "holding a small wooden black box [of herbs] in his left hand." In describing Pitirim to her mother, she insisted that he was not a figment of her imagination, because the man who came before her looked very much like the depictions of St. Pitirim in two pamphlets a neighbor had left them.[15]

In the dream visitations a holy man did various things: he ordered an ill person well, commanded the infirm or the parents of small children to travel to his shrine to seek healings, or insisted that those who were ill vow to visit his grave in gratitude for the healing they were about to receive. Playing a didactic role, he might admonish a father for postponing his child's baptism, order an ill person to pray to a particular icon, or command the sick to "serve God and the Tsar" in order to receive a cure.[16] Saints appearing in dreams also chastised persons for not carrying out their pilgrimage vows. Nocturnal visions prompted by mass-produced literature could thus result in a healing but served a larger didactic purpose of sharing with believers the proper actions of a Christian seeking a saint's help to attain God's mercy.

In preparation for the glorification of saints, religious publications increased their reportage of miracles, and this in turn begat other miracles. Already in 1909, two years before the glorification of Ioasaf of Belgorod, the wife of

A. P. Ivanov of Stavropol, who had been diagnosed with incurable stomach cancer that caused days of severe vomiting, sought Ioasaf's help after a friend showed her newspapers that listed his miracles. The friend had also advised her to send a telegram to Belgorod, presumably to the bishop.[17] Other telegrams to the Bishop of Belgorod beseeched him to pray before the saint's grave on a sick relation's behalf and, in some cases, to hold a service of intercession (*moleben*) at the same site. The bishop's office responded to all such requests by disseminating information about Ioasaf and mailing to each supplicant an icon of the holy man as well as a pamphlet detailing his vita and miracles.[18] Reading a newspaper account of a miracle could convince the sick to abandon scientific medicine in favor of spiritual means. Thus when, at the beginning of 1910, the Mel'nikovs read aloud a story in a Kursk newspaper about Ioasaf healing a boy of cancer, their precocious young daughter, who had been wasting away from a five-year bout with cholic, refused to take her medicine and accept yet another doctor's examination; instead she announced that she would seek the holy man's help through prayer.[19] Whether it was the child or the parents who decided to turn to Ioasaf was irrelevant; the article gave patient and relatives hope for alternative means for a cure that was credible within their belief system. A priest, learning from a Church bulletin about the impending transfer of Ioasaf's holy remains from his tomb to a glass-cased reliquary, and then reading the story to his congregation, immediately vowed to travel with his son to the saint's grave if his dying son were cured of pleurisy. The cleric was pleased to report that he had been able to carry out his vow.[20] Such bargaining with a deceased holy person was not unusual in the miracle narratives. Mass-circulated literature clearly influenced the way readers handled illness, providing them with tangible proof of God's mercy.

Religious newspaper and journal reports also encouraged villagers to time pilgrimages to coincide with canonization and translation of relics, times when a saint's power was thought to be heightened. The elder Anatolii at the famous Optina Hermitage counseled Klavdiia Pavlova Malinina, the wife of the Ranenburgsk urban school inspector, to seek Ioasaf's help for her debilitating rheumatism by traveling to Belgorod in time for the translation of his relics. This advice came only after the woman's ailment had been eased but not cured by carrying through Anatolii's directive that she bathe in the holy waters connected to the cult of St. Tikhon.[21] In 1903 a young woman who believed that she was possessed by demons after her cure at St. Serafim's grave explained that her travels to the Sarovskaia Uspenskaia Hermitage had been precipitated by hearing that Serafim was to be glorified. "When news reached our village of Novo-Kurchak (Bobrov District, Voronezh Province) that our Father the Tsar had ordered . . . that the holy remains of the elder Serafim be opened ," she reported, "our peasants, both young and old, decided to go to Sarov on pilgrimage. They seized me, I was ill at the time, and my godchild Kostia, who had been blind since birth."[22] The lists of miracle stories published by the Church in popular religious magazines and pamphlets to coincide with canonizations convinced individuals suffering from various afflictions that they needed to take advantage of the opening of saints' relics to seek out new cures.[23] Others postponed their pilgrimages until after the glorification ceremonies, when news of new miracles at the grave were reported in newspapers or by word of mouth.

The magnitude of literature circulated for a saint's glorification can only be suggested by the impressive local activities of Kursk's Znamensko-Bogorodichnoe Missionary and Educational Brotherhood. Beginning in 1909 the brotherhood undertook to acquaint believers within Kursk Province with the life of Ioasaf of Belgorod. Its members organized processions in his honor, sub-sidized publications of the saint's vita, and provided the clergy with devotional literature having to do not only with the saint's life, his posthumous miracles, and his teachings but also with anti-sectarian advice. The brotherhood boasted that over the course of two years it had published one million copies of leaflets, brochures, and books largely at its own expense.[24] Rising literacy rates and the mass circulation of literature were drawing Russians of all classes to various pilgrimage sites, although, as in the case of Pitirim, those sites could still retain a fairly local flavor and constituency. That Pitirim's cult had a limited following should not be surprising, given that the popularity of most saints' cults was regional. The greater national resonance of both Serafim of Sarov and Ioasaf of Belgorod was more unusual and part of the modernization of the Russian Orthodox Church.

The democratizing effect of the mass circulation of pictorial representations, vitae, miracles, and other information about the three saints was reflected only to a degree in the estate representation in the miracle narratives of beneficiaries of miracles. On the one hand, the saints' cults of Serafim, Ioasaf, and Pitirim exemplify communities of believers that stemmed from all groups in society. On the other hand, the portrayal of peasants in the miracle stories attributed to Ioasaf and Pitirim was not as robust as in the cases of Serafim or Dmitrii of Rostov, an eighteenth-century saint.

The distribution of beneficiaries of miracles by estate and occupation is shown in table 1.1 and includes a profile of 243 individuals who were recipients of 232 miracles accredited to the intercession of Dmitrii of Rostov. Dmitrii had been the metropolitan of Rostov from 1702 to 1709, and the miracles attributed to him occurred between 1753 and 1762, that is, both before and after his 1757 canonization.[25] Compared to the eighteenth-century miracles, it is not surpris-ing that more townspeople were represented in the early-twentieth-century

Table 1.1. Breakdown of Beneficiaries of Miracles by Estate

Estate	Attributed to Serafim (%)	Attributed to Ioasaf (%)	Attributed to Pitirim(%)	Attributed to Dmitrii (%)
Civil Service	0.9	0.0	11.4	13.2
Ecclesiastics*	9.1	12.7**	8.6	13.2
Merchantry	7.3	2.0	11.4	5.3
Townspeople	14.5	22.5	28.6	9.5†
Military***	6.4	6.9	8.6	14.4
Nobility	7.3	16.7	11.4	7.4
Peasantry	33.6	21.6	14.3	31.7
Others	5.5	3.9	5.7	2.9
Unknown	15.5	13.7	0.0	2.5
Total	100.1	100.0	100.0	100.1

Note: The glorification of Serafim, Ioasaf, Pitirim, and Dmitrii occurred, respectively, in 1903, 1911, 1914, and 1757.
* Includes women religious
** One of the miracles includes an indeterminable number of clergy, which means that this figure is artificially low
*** Includes Cossacks
† These are *posadskie* and *slobodskie liudi* (tax-paying and non–tax-paying lower urban classes)

miracles, given the growth in urbanization in the second half of the nineteenth century. Nor is the decline in the military unexpected in the modern period, because the military reforms in 1874 made conscription universal and shortened the length of military service considerably.

The increased relative weight of the nobility and the decline in peasant representation in the miracle tales attributed to Ioasaf and Pitirim, however, bear comment. It appears that both Ioasaf's and Pitirim's cults were more urban-centered, and in the case of Pitirim they attracted more members of the social elite. The Church's demotion of demon possession, which had become almost exclusively a peasant affliction and is discussed below, also accounts for the lower numbers of peasants. The rudimentary nature of medical care in the countryside also guaranteed that fewer peasants would be involved in official miracle tales, as doctors' testimonies about individuals' medical histories became critical in the decision making of commissioners charged with verifying miracles. Even non-verified miracle tales referred to the inability of medicine to cure the ailments in question. Peasants who had not sought medical care because of the expense and their distrust of doctors were clearly disadvantaged when they reported miraculous cures. Serafim's more popular resonance with villagers is understandable, given his role as a spiritual elder who practiced humility and led a life of poverty.

When gender is considered, women's representation in the eighteenth-century miracle tales is similar to their representation in the nineteenth- and early-twentieth-century cults. Women, adolescent girls, and female children (ranging in age from a few months to ten years) accounted for just over 50 percent of the recipients of miracles attributed to Dmitrii of Rostov (53.5 percent), Serafim of Sarov (53.6 percent), Ioasaf of Belgorod (57 percent), and Pitirim of Tambov (57 percent). These figures change only slightly if adults are considered separately from children. The miracle narratives give no indication that parents favored male over female children in seeking cures. Nor do they support a conclusion that religion was being feminized in the modern period.[26] All the saints' cults examined here attracted both women and men. Their grave sites were equally accessible to men and women, a far cry from the medieval period when monasteries were reluctant to allow entry to women for fear that their bodily pollution would defile sacred spaces.[27] Miracles, then, essentially "cut across lines of class, sex, age, and status" and therefore were critical social bonds between recipients and witnesses "as participants in a sacred community."[28]

The saints' accessibility to all believers was also made possible by the availability of material objects linked to the saints that facilitated miraculous healings. We have already seen the ways in which believers used the saints' icons to try to effect healings. The miracle narratives also repeatedly refer to the miraculous properties of holy water, holy oil from the votives illuminating icons in the saints' crypts, wadding from the saints' coffins, and pieces of the saints' clothing. Some of the cures involving these substances and articles occurred at the individual saint's grave site, and others took place at the sickbed because relatives or acquaintances had brought the material objects back from the holy sites. A cure sometimes resulted from applying the cotton wadding of a saint's coffin to the diseased part of the body, placing a saint's miter on the ill person's head, or covering a sick person's face with a saint's paten bearing an embroidered illustration of the saint.[29] Other miracles were facilitated when a sick person applied holy oil from the votives in front of the holy person's icons to an infected area of the body or donned the saint's cross or his stockings.[30] Although the use of such objects did not guarantee a cure, it appeared to believers that using them increased the possibility of a healing. A cleric, who always had some oil and wadding from Ioasaf of Belgorod's grave on hand, explained that intercession of a saint was crucial in imbuing the holy substances with curative power. In relating a miracle story, he noted that he had administered the oil to four children with eye ailments, but only one of them regained her sight as a result of St. Ioasaf's intervention.[31]

Orthodox teachings did not frown upon such faith in holy objects and the merging of "the boundaries between the material and the spiritual."[32] These teachings stemmed from the New Testament examples of miraculous cures tied to the touching of Christ's clothing (Luke 9:43–48) and the application of hand-kerchiefs or aprons that had been handled by Paul himself (Acts 19:11–12).[33] According to the cleric Sergei Goloshchapov, the elements of a saint's crypt and his clothing were considered holy objects.[34] Metropolitan Antonii went further, explaining that "even the earth upon which a saint walked acquires healing strength," as did "earth from Serafim's grave, the stone on which he prayed, the spring which he dug."[35] So important were such materials that a substantial, if controlled, modern consumer industry of holy objects developed at pilgrimage sites both within and outside monasteries' walls.

The ecclesiastical hierarchy forbade monasteries and churches from selling the objects from the saints' crypts, thereby trying to raise standards among the clergy and also reacting to the criticism of sectarians, other religious groups, and skeptics that the Church was only interested in financial gain in promot-ing saints' cults. The Church hierarchy was also concerned with the potential defilement of relics. In the case of Ioasaf of Belgorod, for example, a legend circulated that priests who had once served in the Troitskii Cathedral and sold bits of the saint's hair and beard to worshipers were driven insane and suffered other misfortunes as a result of the saint's ire.[36] Included in the list of miracles attributed to St. Ioasaf, the vengeance legend was meant to be a deterrent to greedy members of the clergy.

While prohibiting crass commercialization of the saints' relics and cloth-ing, the Holy Synod did permit monasteries to sell candles, *prosphora* (small communion loaves), holy water, holy oil, portraits of saints, postcards, rosaries, and crosses. It also allowed monasteries to receive donations and use some of the profits on food, housing, and medical services for poor pilgrims. Dmitrii Ivanovich Rostislavov, a prolific nineteenth-century author who wrote about the Russian Orthodox Church and clergy, and was disturbed by the intrusion of profane money into sacred spaces, explained the pilgrims' understanding of their responsibilities, which involved various offerings, once they arrived at their destinations. The faithful felt obliged to buy candles at the shrine, which they then placed before icons and a saint's crypt, and to make small contribu-tions to the collection plate circulated during the liturgy and to collection boxes located near holy relics and miracle-working icons. Their pilgrimage rituals also involved ordering and paying for services of intercession or thanksgiving at a saint's shrine and purchasing several *prosphora* for themselves as well as rela-tives and neighbors who were unable to go on a pilgrimage. Pilgrims who could not afford to make cash donations for every service instead made offerings of ribbons, towels, and cloth. So considerable were these material donations of cloth that the monasteries had to sell the items to peddlers and traders.[37] Pilgrims could also buy holy objects and other paraphernalia from peddlers who set up their stalls outside the gates of the monasteries.

Although the profane certainly mixed with the sacred in these transactions for spiritual relief, the donations pilgrims made must be understood within the context of the rituals that were integral to pilgrimages and to the fulfillment of individual pilgrims' vows. Exchanges of all types occurred at the pilgrimage sites, as pilgrims attempted to execute the provisions of the contract they had made with their patron saints, in return for which they expected "material and spiritual favors."[38] The physical burden of making the pilgrimage on foot, especially for the sick and crippled; the fasting, confession, and communion that often took place at a holy site; and visitation of pilgrimage stations— locations where a saint had experienced visions and other manifestations of God's grace, prayed incessantly, and received visitors—all prepared the penitent for the climax of communion with the saint at the grave site.[39] However, only the tactile sensation of kissing and kneeling at the grave itself, followed by the ordering of a special service in the saint's honor, ultimately released pilgrims from their vows. Donations in money and kind at various points were tangible representations of the pilgrims' sincerity. In return for the curative powers they anticipated from a saint's clothing and personal belongings, they gave mementoes and offerings to the saint and his patrons as tokens of their affection and as representations of their individuality. The souvenirs they purchased were an indispensable part of the rituals of thanksgiving and remembrance.

While rich and poor alike served as recipients of miracles and the dreams of saints, and indulged in the same practices involving holy objects, they did not enjoy the same access to holiness during canonization celebrations, which emphasized class differences. The luxurious nature of the first-class passenger cars to the Arzamas train station and the availability of expensive carriages to transport the wealthy the sixty versts to the Sarovskaia Uspenskaia Hermitage contrasted sharply with the primitive third-class rail cars that poor peasants occupied as well as their travel by cart or on foot. Once at the pilgrimage destination, however, all pilgrims would have expected to participate equally in the glorification ceremonies and have the same access to the relics of honored saints. This was not to be the case, however. The presence of the royal family at the glorification of Serafim of Sarov, and the corresponding security requirements, necessitated tickets of admission which were distributed only to members of the upper classes and to church officials. Thus thousands of pilgrims and parish priests huddled in the courtyard around the main cathedral, desperately hoping to hear sounds of the liturgical services that might drift into the courtyard. Tens of thousands more found themselves completely removed from the sacred events.

Even though Nicholas II and his family were not present at the 1911 glorification ceremonies for Ioasaf of Belgorod, the attending police issued tickets for the purpose of controlling the crowd.[40] The Kursk Znamenskoe Bogoridchnoe Missionary and Educational Brotherhood was able to obtain a mere one hundred tickets for its own members, visiting clergy, and the "poor and crippled." Indeed, pilgrims were not allowed to wander about the city or enter the monastery freely at that time. The Church organized services for the pilgrims in village squares and in front of the tents and barracks where they were housed.[41] On the first anniversary of Ioasaf's canonization, the priest Porfirii Amfiteatrov made a point of commenting on the sharp contrast in the nature of the crowd of pilgrims who attended the all-night vigil compared to the gathering of worshipers in the cathedral for the glorification ceremonies. "If on that night the previous year one could see only glittering full-dress uniforms and elegant dress, then on this night, to the contrary, one could find mainly the meager clothes of poor people who had access to the cathedral and [the area enclosed by] the cathedral fence."[42] Amfiteatrov obviously felt that the poorer pilgrims were more loyal devotees of the saint than their wealthier counterparts.

The segregation of the poor from the rich occurred not only during the glorification ceremonies themselves but also at the springs or wells that were believed to have miraculous properties. At Sarov, bathing in Serafim's spring did not involve full immersion. Rather, bathhouses were segregated by gender for modesty's sake, and then each of those bathhouses was divided into two areas: one for the elite, the other for the masses.[43] Water flowed continuously out of a sluice for commoners, who might be naked or partially clothed, whereas the water for the rich came from a faucet.[44] The protection of the rich from the pustulous and vermin-ridden bodies of the poor suggested a Church that was sensitive to notions of upper- and middle-class decorum. That sensitivity in turn implied that not all individuals were equal in the eyes of God.

Social divisions are also evident in educated society's descriptions of the sick at holy sites, which painted an oppressive picture of poverty-stricken and crippled peasants. Commenting on the ill pilgrims who sought the help of Serafim of Sarov, an anonymous correspondent for *Pravitel'stvennyi vestnik* found disturbing the numerous "bodies of the sick, emaciated, corrupted by illness or deformity":

Along the road to the spring . . . one can see a multitude of ill [persons]. Here on a stretcher—made of two sticks with a cloth stretched over them—they are carrying an ill girl; in a cart they are leading a sick man whose legs are paralyzed; a pale, weak, sick woman, having put her arms around the shoulders of two women, hardly moves her legs, every minute using up her breath from exhaustion; a hunchbacked old woman goes on two crutches; holding the stick of a boy leading him, a blind man walks with his head held high; behind him a boy hops on a crutch with a bent leg; a woman moves on her legs and arms, like a four-legged [animal], contorted at the waist.[45]

This and other similar descriptions pinpoint the centrality of the ill at saints' shrines. "Usually relegated to the unseen margins of society," they now "took centre stage."[46] Momentarily claiming the spotlight and seeking preternatural intervention, the pilgrims not only disturbed witnesses around them but also humbled them. The same author who was made uncomfortable by the multi-tudes of the sick also remarked on the "joyous exclamations of those healed," noting that "the Lord's mercy does not abandon them."[47] Medical science and the larger community might have failed the indigent, but God did not.

While the above description focuses on physical infirmities, the types of illnesses described in the miracle tales of the early-twentieth-century saints' cults defy easy classification. Worshipers did not identify Saints Serafim, Ioasaf, and Pitirim with specific diseases. Ailments ranged from endemic diseases such as typhus, measles, diphtheria, consumption, and dysentery to abscesses, paralysis, tuberculosis of the bones, peritonitis, rheumatism, and other life-threatening problems to congenital defects. The presence of medical doctors on commissions set up to investigate the validity of miracles, as well as testimonies from doctors about their patients' treatments, reveal a growing influence of medical science on the identification and treatment of illnesses in late imperial Russia. Surprisingly illnesses that today might be identified as psychosomatic do not prevail in the miracle tales. The stories highlight, instead, the limitations of medical science in spite of its growing authority and the possibility of the miraculous in a modernizing world.

The medical and religious story of the Tambov townswoman Elizaveta Kononova Troshina poignantly demonstrates the limitations and in this case cruelty of late-nineteenth-century medicine vis-à-vis women, and the solace that spiritual faith provided them. Troshina's claim that she had been cured of her nervous affliction because of God's grace, which she received as a result of Pitirim's prayers and the holy water she drank from his well, turned out to be insufficient evidence to deem her cure miraculous. The commissioners charged with verifying miracles attributed to Pitirim could not determine whether the medicines administered by doctors to the poor woman or the holy water had been instrumental in the healing of an incurable "serious nervous disorder."

One can only imagine the woman's disappointment in not having her cure recognized as miraculous after what she had suffered. The record tells us that in 1893, when Troshina was twenty-four years old, she developed a nervous disorder that almost drove her mad. Hospitalized for three months, from 27 August until 30 November, in the Tambov Provincial Zemstvo Psychiatric Hospital for the Insane, she was treated not only with medicines and hypnosis but also intrusive and unnecessary surgery.[48]

The hospital log, which was produced for the benefit of the commission investigating Pitirim's miracles, provides a biography of Troshina written by a medical expert who consciously set her up as a candidate for hysteria. It describes her as having been a child "distinguished by a changeable mood," a characteristic psychiatrists associated with hysteria, and repeatedly frightened by an alcoholic father. Her four-and-a-half-year marriage bore no children, but the economic and emotional bases for the marriage, according to the record, were good. Although she exhibited "sufficiently abrupt mood changes," she felt well. Then the record makes the following value judgment, "She did not like to work, and more often sat with some kind of handiwork or read a novel." The medical staff at the zemstvo (rural administration) hospital was obviously concerned that Troshina was rising above her station. Handiwork was not for the hardworking lower classes but a sign of refinement, and novels were the stuff that rotted women's minds. Since her confinement in the hospital, she turned to religious books and "was indifferent to music." These descriptions lead to the fact that three years earlier the woman had been subjected to a gynecological treatment requiring her to syringe her vagina with mercuric chloride. Rather than reflecting on the possible harmful effects of the mercuric chloride, the medical record paints an unflattering picture of a woman who began to obsess about being poisoned. A year later, the report continues, Troshina's obsession turned into an idée fixe that she was being punished for her sins. Troshina's fifty prostrations before God each morning and evening to fulfill the penance she had imposed upon herself left her weakened and "in a hysterical state." Suspecting a serious gynecological problem as the root cause of her mental condition, the doctors performed an examination on 1 September which revealed that the woman had signs of gonorrhea as well as endometriosis. The log, then, essentially concealed the woman's history of venereal disease, for which she was administered the mercuric chloride in the first place, until it established that the woman was mentally unstable. It subsequently went on to note that after the uterine examination, the woman immediately began to obsess about the possibility of the doctors operating on her, as if the idea of an operation were ludicrous. As time passed and no operation was performed, the woman's "obsessions weaken somewhat. She becomes happy, sleeps better, and wants to work." Instead of recognizing the woman's valid fears, the log comments that "the ill woman is completely impressionable. Thus, for example, the doctor's advice to carry out an easy operation on her uterus caused a serious hysterical condition." As it turned out, the so-called easy operation, which was performed on 13 October, involved the removal of Troshina's cervix. In other words, Troshina's obsessions were a direct result of her having been traumatized by the doctors themselves. After a period of calm, Troshina's obsessions, for which hypnosis had no effect, returned. In the end, a defiant Troshina signed herself out of the hospital on 30 November 1893, after her mother had given her holy water from Pitirim's grave. Her tortures came to an end within two months, during which time she had the opportunity to visit Pitirim's grave several times, have services said for him, and drink water from his well. Troshina testified under oath in 1897 that she was completely healthy because of the holy Pitirim's intercession on her behalf. Medical drugs and hypnosis, she pointed out, had absolutely no effect until after she drank holy water from Pitirim's well. Even her doctors, she stressed, had deemed her incurable.[49] Troshina's earlier fears of doctors had been well founded, and her recovered health served as testimony to the elevation of the individual or the self over the objections of medical doctors who had mutilated her body.

The impact of medical science on classifications of illness by the early-twentieth-century may also be seen in relation to *klikushestvo* or demon possession. A comparison of the illnesses cured in the eighteenth-century miracle tales of Dmitrii of Rostov with the early-twentieth-century narratives reveals a shrinking number of individuals believed to have been possessed by demons. As I chronicle elsewhere, demon possession became feminized in the late eighteenth-century because state and Church demoted the phenomenon in the Petrine period from acceptable to fraudulent behavior. Casting doubt on the possibility of possession in an increasingly rational world, authorities were now identifying the loss of control over the body as a feminine rather than masculine trait. The feminization of possession victims in officially verified miracles continued apace in the course of the nineteenth-century so that, by the mid-nineteenth century, demoniacs were exclusively women; at the same time the medical diagnosis of hysteria as an alternative descriptor of women's loss of control appeared in the miracles stories. Doctors' greater access to and influence over upper- and middle-class women resulted in confining to the peasant class those demoniacs who still figured prominently in the miracles ascribed to Feodosii of Chernigov, a late-seventeenth-century archbishop of Chernigov canonized in 1896. Demoniacs, nonetheless, appeared far less frequently in the miracles attributed to Serafim, Ioasaf, and Pitirim. Demotion of demon possession had to do with the Church's embrace of scientific rationalism and the medical profession's refusal to recognize possession as a legitimate affliction, preferring instead to see some of these women as suffering from hysteria. As the appearance of demoniacs lessened in the miracle tales, so, too, did the number of peasants, as attested in the miracle cycles of Ioasaf and Pitirim. At the same time religious commentators did not dismiss demoniacs altogether from their writings, noting their presence among the crowds of pilgrims, as well as the cacophony of their shrieks in the midst of religious ceremonies. Once again, these women demonstrated the limitations of medicine in a world God continued to govern.[50]

Although the overwhelming majority of miracle tales focused on the cure of illness, a minority involved conversion and punishment narratives. In the late imperial period, the Russian Orthodox Church felt besieged by competing religions as well as by atheism. In a report about the glorification of Feodosii of Chernigov in 1896, a cleric framed his remarks with specific reference to "the attacks of the Tolstoyans, Shtundists, and other sectarians on the validity of miracles."[51] A parish priest reported that many of his peasant parishioners in Petrovskii khutor in Novooskol'sk uezd, Kursk Province, were constantly being exposed to sectarian ideas and pressure to convert to Shtundism on their travels in various Ukrainian provinces collecting rags. He was pleased to announce, however, that none of them was tempted away from "pure and strong Orthodoxy," especially since one of their co-villagers had miraculously been cured of a life-threatening ailment after visiting Ioasaf's grave.[52] Given the need for the Church's vigilance and publication of anti-sectarian literature in tandem with glorification ceremonies, it is not surprising that the miracle stories contain conversion and punishment narratives.

While the early-twentieth-century saints could not claim to have converted two thousand Old Believers, as had the uncorrupted remains of Feodosii of Chernigov in 1896, conversions still took place. Thus, for example, we read about the sixty-year-old Old Believer peasant woman, Dar'ia Ermilova, from Nikol'sk uezd, Samara Province, who came to Sarov in July 1903 for the canonization ceremonies. Unfortunately the sacred story does not explain Ermilova's motivation for traveling to Sarov but notes that, once she was there, she witnessed numerous cures at Serafim's holy spring, "understood all the deceit of the teachings of the Old Believers," and decided to convert to Orthodoxy. One Old Believer peasant, Sitnov of the village of Stepurino in Bogorodskii uezd, Moscow Province, who mocked Serafim and declared that he would disregard the decision of the village assembly forbidding work in the fields on the day of the glorification, was not so lucky: he was struck dead. As word of Sitnov's punishment at the hands of St. Serafim spread, according to the miracle narrative, other Old Believers in the vicinity refrained from working in the fields on

19 July, the day of the canonization.[53] In another miracle tale a Baptist railway worker suddenly suffered paralysis right in front of his fellow workers immediately after he challenged Serafim's sanctity, the holiness of saints in general, and the possibility of miraculous cures.[54] Even a philosopher-unbeliever, despite his denial of the existence of miracles, God, and personal salvation, could not stay away from the Sarov Hermitage during the canonization festivities. Placing his hand on the cross at the saint's grave, the atheist found himself thrown several versts by a mini-earthquake. The event so frightened him that he sobbed that "his life's work was destroyed."[55] Such tales of vengeance "encouraged believers to call on supernatural intercession" and touted the superiority of true Orthodoxy.[56]

Orthodox individuals also risked bringing the wrath of the saint down upon their heads if they insulted a saint or did not fulfill their vows by traveling to the saint's resting place to give proper thanks and to order a thanksgiving service for the saint. In an obviously didactic miracle story, Kondratii Il'in Mordasov, a peasant of the village of Borshchevo in Kozlovskii uezd, Tambov Province, had suddenly become mute when he had too much to drink at a christening in the town of Kozlov and refused to take his mother-in-law home so that she could prepare for her trip to the Sarov Hermitage. Mordasov recovered his speech only after he asked for Serafim's forgiveness and ordered a prayer service to be said before Serafim's icon in Kozlov's Arkhangel'sk church, and then another prayer service in his own parish the following Sunday. The recovery was not immediate but was delayed a day after the Sunday memorial service, when Mordasov arose in the morning and made the sign of the cross.[57] According to another miracle narrative, the husband of a peasant woman who had suffered from a "woman's ailment" soon contracted a liver disorder as a just reward for callously objecting to his wife's going on a pilgrimage to Belgorod for the translation of Ioasaf's relics. His wife, who had defied her husband by going on the pilgrimage and had become the beneficiary of a miraculous cure through Ioasaf's intercession, refused to get her husband the medical treatment he needed, and he subsequently died![58] The tale suggested that the man's earlier actions, not those of his wife, were responsible for his death.

Punishment tales of this sort were didactic, stressing the importance of an individual's respect for the veneration of saints and of restraint from alcoholic excess. In highlighting the superiority of a male saint's authority over that of a husband, the third example involved the empowering of a woman to assert her independence from her spouse in seeking help for herself. Indeed, many ill persons had to resist the pleas of relatives to remain at home rather than embark on a risky trip to a faraway shrine. Obedience to a saint took precedence over obedience to a family member. Since women were rarely victims of punishment tales, the Orthodox Church in the early-twentieth-century may have been more concerned with losing men than women from their flocks as a result of growing urbanization and secularization.

The miracle tales connected to the cults of Saints Serafim, Ioasaf, and Pitirim in early-twentieth-century Russia reveal a vibrant Orthodoxy that enveloped local and national communities of believers from all social classes. The thaumaturgical arsenal of saints' cults was still powerful in an age when medical science had limited if increasing impact. By disseminating information about saints and their miraculous cures, mass-circulated literature drew believers' attention away from their individual parishes to much larger congregations of believers at the regional and sometimes national levels. The Serafim and Ioasaf cults attracted the sick from a wide geographical base. Mass communications not only helped to keep the possibility of the miraculous alive in a modernizing world but also served to teach the faithful about Orthodox practices. The individuals who came forward to tell their stories about miraculous cures did so to celebrate their encounters with God's grace and mercy through the compassion of saints. They sometimes had to assert the self over family members' objections to their traveling to saints' shrines. At all times they asserted the self against a variety of afflictions, but all the while as participants in a larger story of redemption. Mass-produced literature also reminded believers about the constant need for vigilance against competing faiths and the continuing relevance of Orthodoxy in their lives.

Although early-twentieth-century miracles cut across gender and socioeconomic lines, the declining representation of peasants in the miracle cults of Ioasaf and Pitirim suggests a disturbing trend in Orthodoxy. Suspicion was increasing regarding miracles among commoners, whose dependence on spiritual healing was greatest, and also regarding some of their ailments such as demon possession. The social divide experienced by the lower classes at the glorification ceremonies and at the saints' springs was a constant reminder that, in a community of believers, some were more equal before God than others. The egalitarian nature of visions of saints was somewhat belied by practices on the ground.

Notes

1. "Palomnichestvo," in *Khristianstvo: Entsiklopedicheskii slovar'*, vol. 2, ed. S. S. Averintsev, A. N. Meshkov, and Iu. N. Popov (Moscow, 1995), 278.

2. Here I am borrowing from Victor Turner and Edith L. B. Turner's definition of "modern pilgrimage." See their *Image and Pilgrimage in Christian Culture: Anthropological Perspectives* (New York, 1978), 18–19.

3. Christine D. Worobec, *Possessed: Women, Witches, and Demons in Imperial Russia* (DeKalb, Ill., 2001), 25; and Vera Shevzov, "Miracle-Working Icons, Laity, and Authority in the Russian Orthodox Church, 1861–1917," *Russian Review* 58, no. 1 (January 1999): 26–48.

4. Gregory L. Freeze, "Subversive Piety: Religion and the Political Crisis in Late Imperial Russia," *Journal of Modern History* 68, no. 2 (June 1996): 308–50; and idem, "Tserkov', religiia i politicheskaia kul'tura na zakate staroi Rossii," *Istoriia SSR,* no. 2 (1991): 107–19.

5. The 110 miracle stories relating to the cult of Serafim of Sarov were taken from "Blagodatnia istseleniia po molitvam Prepodobnago ottsa Serafima Sarovskago," *Tambovskiia eparkhial'nyia vedomosti* 44, no. 30, 26 July 1903, 903–6; "Blagodatnyia znameniia prepodobnago Serafima, Sarovskago Chudotvortsa," *Tambovskiia eparkhial'nyia vedomosti* 44, nos. 23–24, 26–28, 7–14, 28 June, 5–12 July 1903, 639–45, 675–81, 745–52, 797–803, 829–34; *Chudesa pri otkrytii moshchei prepodobnago Serafima Sarovskago* (Moscow: Otd. tip. Tovarestva I. D. Sytina, 1903); "Chudesa v Sarove," *Russkii palomnik* 18, no. 32 (9 August 1903): 557–58; "Chudesnoe istselenie po molitvam ottsa Serafima Sarovskago ot neplodstva zheny Kineshemnskago kuptsa Kharlampiia Bobkova," *Tambovskiia eparkhial'nyia vedomosti* 44, no. 20, 17 May 1903, 542–47; "Chudo po molitvam Prepodobnago Serafima Sarovskago," *Tambovskiia eparkhial'nyia vedomosti* 44, no. 35, 30 August 1903, 689–90; Nikolai Remizov, "Dva sluchaia blagodatnoi pomoshchi ottsa Serafima," *Tambovskiia eparkhial'nyia vedomosti* 44, no. 34, 7 June 1903, 645–47; S.N.R., "V pamiat' svetlago torzhestva otkrytiia sv. moshchei Prepodobnago Serafima, Sarovskago Chudotvortsa, 19 iiulia 1903 goda," *Tambovskiia eparkhial'nyia vedomosti* 44, no. 27, 5 July 1903, 779–96; *Zhitie, chudesa i istseleniia Prepodobnago Serafima, Sarovskago Chudotvortsa* (Odessa, 1907); "Zhizn' i chudesnyia istseleniia v Sarove vo dni otkrytiia moshchei prepod. Serafima," *Vera i razum,* no. 14 (July 1903): 440–47. The 102 miracle stories attributed to Ioasaf of Belgorod were culled from "Chudesnoe istselenie nemoi-razslablennoi po molitvam sv. Ioasafa," *Kurskiia eparkhial'nyia vedomosti,* nos. 51–52, 23–30 December 1911, 515–19; "K proslavleniiu Sviatitelia Iosafa," *Kurskiia eparkhial'nyia vedomosti,* nos. 12, 16, 19 March, 22 April 1911, 112–13; 151–52; "Noviia chudesa Sviatitelia Iosafa," *Kurskiia eparkhial'nyia vedomosti,* nos. 51–52, 23–30 December 1911, 524; "Novye sluchai blagodatnoi pomoshchi po molitvam Sviatitelia Iosafa, Belgorodskago Chudotvortsa," *Kurskiia eparkhial'nyia vedomosti,* nos. 14–15, 2–15 April 1911, 135–36; no. 24, 1 July 1912, 539–41; no. 28, 1 September 1912, 698–703; no. 7, 22 February 1912, 155–59; nos. 12–13, 1–8 April 1912, 294–99; no. 17, 8 May 1912, 394–98; no. 31, 15 October 1912, 850–56; no. 34, 1 December 1912, 998–1000; "Novye sluchai chudesnago istseleniia po molitvennomu predstatel'stvu Sviatitelia Ioasafa. (Iz doneseniia na imia Ego Vysokopreosviashchenstva)," *Kurskiia eparkhial'nyia vedomosti,* no. 32, 12 August 1911, 320; Ioann Shchegolev, "Chudesnoe istselenie po molitvam Sviatitelia Ioasafa, Belgorodskago Chudotvortsa," *Kurskiia eparkhial'nyia vedomosti,* nos. 18–19, 13 May 1911, 172–73; *Skazanie o zhizni, podvigakh i chudesakh sviatitelia i chudotvortsa Ioasafa, Episkopa Belogradskago i Oboianskago, predlagaemoe blagochestvomu vnimaniiu Kurskoi pastvy Soborom kurskikh episkopov* in *Kurskiia eparkhial'nyia vedomosti, no.* 31, 5 August 1911, 64–92; P. Skubachevskii, "Belgorodskiia torzhestva: V pechatleniia ochevidtsa," *Vera i razum,* no. 19 (October 1911): 118–28; "Sluchai chudesnago istseleniia devochki ot slepoty po molitvam Sviatitelia Ioasafa," *Kurskiia eparkhial'nyia vedomosti,* nos. 14–15, 2–15 April 1911, 137; "Sluchai nebesnoi pomoshchi bol'nomu po molitvam i predstatel'stvu Ugodnika Bozhiia Sviatitelia Ioasafa. (Iz doneseniia Igumenii Kurskago Sviato-Troitskago zhenskago monastyria Emilii na imia Ego Vysokopreosviashchenstva)," *Kurskiia eparkhial'nyia vedomosti,* no. 36, 9 September 1911, 343; "Sviatitel' Ioasaf i uroki iz ego zhitiia," *Kurskiia eparkhial'nyia vedomosti,* no. 26, 1, 8, 15 July 1911, 239–43, 255–58, 274–76; I. Vasil'ev, "K proslavleniiu sv. Ioasafa Gorlenko," *Kurskiia eparkhial'nyia vedomosti* no. 5, 29 January 1911, 32–33; "Zaiavlenie krest'ianina sela Starago-Gorodishcha, P. F. Uvarova," *Kurskiia eparkhial'nyia vedomosti,* nos. 14–15, 2–15 April 1911, 136.

6. In 1892 a commission set up by the Holy Synod recognized twenty-eight miracles ascribed to Serafim of Sarov as legitimate; three years later the Synod requested local officials

to continue collecting eyewitness accounts of miracles. The Synod credited St. Ioasaf with having performed fifty-four miracles. See Freeze, "Subversive Piety," 317 n. 334.

7. Because one of the miracles involved two individuals, I count the one miracle as two in the database.

8. Rossiiskii gosudarstvennyi istoricheskii arkhiv (RGIA), f. 796, op. 195, d. 1449 [Kanonizatsiia Pitirima].

9. Natal'ia N. Chugreeva, ed., *Prepodobnyi Serafim Sarovskii: Agiografiia. Pochitanie. Ikonografiia* (Moscow, 2004), 9. Almost all biographies of Serafim of Sarov give his birth date as 1759; Chugreeva's recent study, based on archival records, however, moves that date back to 1754.

10. Precise figures of pilgrims are hard find. An 1848 publication claimed that as many as four thousand pilgrims at any one time visited Serafim's shrine, presumably on major feast days connected to Serafim's life and the miracle-working icons of the Mother of God that had cured Serafim's illnesses and thus were an integral part of his cult. Cited in D. I. Rostislavov, *Opyt issledovaniia ob imushchestvakh i dokhodakh nashikh monastyrei* (St. Petersburg, 1876), 108.

11. Worobec, *Possessed*, 55–56.

12. *Zhitie, chudesa i istseleniia Prepodobnago Serafima*, 120–21.

13. Archimandrite Nikodim credited the press with spreading information about the holiness of ascetics to commoners, although he was also disturbed that the reporters sometimes mistakenly confused persons who had not been canonized but were thought by the laity to be holy with canonized individuals. See his "Nekanonizovannye sviatye i vopros o tserkovno-narodnom ikh pochitanii," *Strannik* (January 1903): 45–46.

14. *Skazanie o zhizni*, 73. The practice whereby "believers 'consumed' or 'absorbed' the power of divine grace by means of drinking the water in which an icon [or a copy of an icon] had been washed" was common among Russian Orthodox believers. See Vera Shevzov, "Poeticizing Piety: The Icon of Mary in Russian Akathistoi Hymns," *St. Vladimir's Theological Quarterly* 44, nos. 3–4 (2000): 367.

15. RGIA, f. 796, op. 195, d. 1449, ll. 68–680b., 410b.

16. *Skazanie o zhizni*, 65–66.

17. Ibid., 82.

18. "Novye sluchai blagodatnoi pomoshchi," no. 17, 8 May 1912, 394–95; no. 31, 15 October 1912, 850–51.

19. Vasil'ev, "K proslavleniiu sv. Ioasafa Gorlenko," 32–33.

20. Shchegolev, "Chudesnoe istselenie," 172–73.

21. "Novye sluchai blagodatnoi pomoshchi," no. 28, 1 September 1912, 698–99.

22. *Zhitie, chudesa i istseleniia Prepodobnago Serafima*, 132.

23. Worobec, *Possessed*, 83.

24. "Otchet o sostoianii i deiatel'nosti Kurskago Znamensko-Bogorodichnago Missionersko-prosvetitel'nago Bratstva za 1911 god (Prodolzhenie)," *Kurskiia eparkhial'nyia vedomosti*, no. 16, 1 May 1912, 263–73.

25. "Prilozhenie XXIV: Kopiia s zapiski o chudesakh Preosviashchennago Dmitriia Mitropolita Rostovskago," in *Opisanie dokumentov i del, khraniashchikhsia v arkhive Sviateishego Sinoda* (1752; rpt., Petrograd, 1915), 32:983–1150.

26. Arguments for the feminization of congregations have been made with regard to modern Western European countries. The issue has not yet been investigated systematically in the Russian case. For an argument in favor of feminization of religion in late imperial Russia on the basis of the saints' cults of Ioann of Kronstadt and Kseniia of Petersburg, see Nadieszda Kizenko, "Protectors of Women and the Lower Orders: Constructing Sainthood in Modern Russia," in *Orthodox Russia: Belief and Practice under the Tsars*, ed. Valerie A. Kivelson and Robert H. Greene (University Park, Pa., 2003), 211–38.

27. Both Serafim's and Pitirim's crypts were located within monasteries. In the nineteenth century, monasteries concerned with the inundation of pilgrims and the presence of women established skete at some distance from the main pilgrimage sites. Closed off

to women, the sketes promoted a contemplative life that rejected worldly concerns for the resident monks. See Scott M. Kenworthy, "The Revival of Monasticism in Modern Russia: The Trinity-Sergius Lavra, 1825–1921" (Ph.D. dissertation, Brandeis University, 2002), chap. 2. For a discussion of the lower representation of women in miracles reported at monasteries in the medieval period, see Isolde Thyrêt, "Muscovite Miracle Stories as Sources for Gender-Specific Religious Experience," in *Religion and Culture in Early Modern Russia and Ukraine*, ed. Samuel H. Baron and Nancy Shields Kollmann (DeKalb, Ill., 1997), 115–31.

28.	Michael E. Goodich, *Violence and Miracle in the Fourteenth Century: Private Grief and Public Salvation* (Chicago, 1995), 151.

29.	*Skazanie o zhizni*, 73, 75–76.

30.	Ibid., 76, 78.

31.	"Sluchai chudesnago istseleniia devochki," 137.

32.	Ruth Harris, *Lourdes: Body and Spirit in the Secular Age* (New York, 1999), 293.

33.	Richard Kieckhefer, *Magic in the Middle Ages* (Cambridge, 1989); and Kh. V. Poplavskaia, *Palomnichestvo, strannopriimstvo i pochitanie sviatyn' v Riazanskom krae, XIX–XX vv.* (Riazan, 1998), 86 n. 171.

34.	Sergei Goloshchapov, "Vera v chudesa s tochki zreniia sovremennoi bogoslovskoi nauki," *Vera i razum*, nos. 5–6 (February–March 1912): 676.

35.	Antonii, "Neobkhodimoe raz'iasnenie," *Vera i razum*, no. 12 (June 1903): 378.

36.	*Skazanie o zhizni*, 72.

37.	According to Rostislavov, the Nilova Monastery, in 1873, "received 26,858 arshins of cloth from pilgrims." See his *Opyt issledovaniia*, 132, 114, 110. For biographical information about Rostislavov, see Alexander M. Martin's excellent introduction to Dmitrii Ivanovich Rostislavov, *Provincial Russia in the Age of Enlightenment: The Memoir of a Priest's Son*, ed. and trans. Alexander M. Martin (DeKalb, Ill., 2002).

38.	For the notion of shrines as sites of exchange rituals, see John Eade and Michael J. Sallnow's introduction to their edited volume, *Contesting the Sacred: The Anthropology of Christian Pilgrimage* (Urbana, Ill., 2000), 24, 26.

39.	One of the several pilgrimage stations at the Sarovskaia Uspenskaia Hermitage included the prayer stone on which Serafim had reputedly kneeled for one thousand days (Stephen Graham, *The Way of Martha and the Way of Mary* [New York, 1915], 129).

40.	Freeze, "Subversive Piety," 327.

41.	"Otchet o sostoianii," 272, 270.

42.	Porfirii Amfiteatrov, "Pervaia godovshchina otkrytiia sv. moshchei Sviatitelia i Chudotvortsa Ioasafa, Episkopa Belgorodskago," *Kurskiia eparkhial'nyia vedomosti*, no. 31, 15 October 1912, 858.

43.	"Izvestiia i zametki," *Vera i razum*, no. 14 (July 1903): 442 n.

44.	See the photograph of the bathhouse for male commoners at Sarov in Y. Barchatova et al., *A Portrait of Tsarist Russia: Unknown Photographs from the Soviet Archives*, trans. Michael Robinson (New York, 1989), 220. By 1915 several taps and pipes had been installed in the bathhouse to conduct water from the holy spring (Graham, *The Way of Martha*, 129). In the early Soviet period, separate sections for men and women in the bathhouse remained, but unsurprisingly the separate facilities for the rich and poor had been dismantled. The pilgrim Elena Apushkina, in visiting the bathhouse in 1925, described having to descend "a damp and cold stone ladder" to access the icy holy water. See her "Tri palomnichestva," in *V gosti k batiushke Serafimu*, comp. and ed. Sergei Fomin (Moscow, 1997), 149–50.

45.	Reprinted in "Izvestiia i zametki," 441. For a similar description, see the quotation from a 1903 article in *Novoe vremia*; translated in Freeze, "Subversive Piety," 325.

46.	Harris, *Lourdes*, 285.

47.	"Izvestiia i zametki," 441.

48.	RGIA, f. 796, op. 195, d. 1449, ll. 980b.–990b., 131–370b.

49.	RGIA, f. 796, op. 195, d. 1449, ll. 132–1330b., 99.

50. Worobec, *Possessed*, 52–60.

51. "Po povodu tserkovnykh torzhestv v Chernigove," *Vera i razum*, no. 18 (September 1896): 478.

52. Bulgakov, "Novye sluchai chudesnago istseleniia," 320.

53. *Chudesa pri otkrytii moshchei prepodobnago Serafima Sarovskago*, 30, 31.

54. A truncated version of the story may be found in ibid., 32; a fuller account appears in "Groznyi sud Bozhii nad khulitelem prep. Serafima Sarovskago," *Vera i razum*, no. 16 (August 1903): 498–99.

55. "Chudo v Sarovskoi pustyni," *Vera i razum*, no. 16 (August 1903): 503–504.

56. Goodich, *Violence and Miracle*, 23.

57. "Chudo po molitvam Prepodobnago Serafima Sarovskago," 689–90.

58. "Novyia chudesa Sviatitelia Ioasafa," 524.

2

Transforming Solovki: Pilgrim Narratives, Modernization, and Late Imperial Monastic Life

Roy R. Robson

························

Nestled in the White Sea, near the Arctic Circle and buffeted by storms or ice for nine months every year, Solovki (also known as Solovetskii) was an unlikely pilgrimage destination.[1] The storied monastery had weathered political, military, and religious tempests since its founding in the 1420s. From the famed piety of its founders, Saints Zosima and Savvati, to its holding out against a seven-year siege by the tsar's own army during a monastic uprising, Solovki was among the most famous holy places in all of Russia. Its renown tempted pilgrims to make a long, difficult journey to see its celebrated walls, huge cathedrals, and legendary riches.

By the early twentieth century expanded opportunities and interest in pilgrimage helped to produce a minor genre—the Solovki pilgrim narrative.[2] These narratives were based on the model provided by two well-known works from the mid-nineteenth century, S. V. Maksimov's *A Year in the North* (*God na severe*), which went through many editions starting in the mid-century) and V. I. Nemirovich-Danchenko's *Solovki: Recollections and Tales from Travels with Pilgrims* (*Solovki: vospominaniia i razskazy iz poiezdki s bogomol'tsami*, published in 1884). The pilgrim books published at the turn of the century were both less professional and less extensive in their approach than the two more famous volumes. The narratives are useful, however, because they describe the pilgrim experience at Solovki and offer entrée to issues raised by the dramatic expansion of pilgrimage to the islands during the period. This essay considers six pilgrim narratives printed during the late imperial period and one published recently from a manuscript of that time.[3] The narratives introduce us to themes important to pilgrimage in the period and provide a framework for discussing both the pilgrims' notion of the meaning of travel and the impact of pilgrimage on the monastery itself. Most important, the stories show the impact that modernization had on the monastery.

The authors of these narratives—which were often published from diaries—represented a cross-section of the pilgrim population itself.[4] Two of the works were published by members of the clerical estate—the eminent Bishop Evdokim (Meshcherskii) and a group of seminarians from the Tobol'sk Theological Academy. The background of three other authors—K. Kokovtsov, S. D. Protopopov, and N. Trush—can be inferred only from their texts. They were apparently of the "better society" that traveled by first-class, but little else is known of their background. Of the three, Protopopov styled himself as the most worldly, fretting over provincial life:

> Farewell, Arkhangel'sk! I abandon you without regret. This city is flat like a pancake and poorly built like a village. In dry weather, clouds of dust float along the streets; after rain—mud. There is no local newspaper, and there is nowhere to buy the capital's news. In two hundred years Arkhangel'sk hasn't climbed the first step of culture.[5]

The last Russian pilgrim used in this study was the Tot'ma peasant A. A. Zamaraev, who kept a journal from 1906 to 1922. Although the trip to Solovki occupied but a small part of his diaries, Zamarev's work offered a firsthand look at travel by the middle and poor peasants who comprised the vast majority of pilgrims.

The English priest included here—Father Alexander Alfred Boddy—published detailed descriptions of his extensive travels, including his volume *With Russian Pilgrims: An Account of a Sojourn in the White Sea Monastery and a Journey by the Old Trade Route from the Arctic Sea to Moscow*. Although Fr. Boddy was not a Russian pilgrim, his descriptions often provided detail to the picture outlined by the Russian books.[6]

Background

"Short-term pilgrims"—known as the "three-day pilgrims" because of the time spent on the islands—had come to Solovki in the eighteenth and early nineteenth centuries in relatively small numbers. Rarely did more than one thousand faithful arrive each year.[7] Several events helped to raise that number, however. In 1826 Archimandrite Dosifei (Nemchinov) ordered two three-mast ships to be built for the monastery—the *Nikolai* and the *Savvati*—named for the White Sea's two patron saints. Although these were not specifically bought to carry pilgrims, they may have been in response to an earlier Arkhangel'sk provincial law forbidding the monastery from carrying pilgrims in its own boats.[8] Then, in 1836, the monastery built its first large-scale hostelry—named the Arkhangel'sk Guesthouse—to house pilgrims. With expanded ship connections and accommodations, pilgrimage grew to the islands. By mid-century some eight thousand pilgrims arrived at Solovki each year.

Living conditions for pilgrims on the islands also improved in the latter half of the century, following an investigation into the scandalously poor treatment of pilgrims during the 1830s. As a result of the investigation, the monastery constructed "two extensive two-story wooden structures built for accommodating pilgrims; a three-story, stone, sixty-foot-long building, for the various established workers and masters; a two-story stone building for the lodging of monastic servants; an extensive wooden building with a stone foundation on Muksalma Island" (near the main monastery) and a new bakery and cookhouse that increased production dramatically.[9]

The Allure of Solovki

Why did so many faithful want to travel to Solovki, the northernmost pilgrimage destination in Europe?[10] Our diarists offered little reason for their trip—Zamaraev wrote simply, "Tomorrow I want to begin my travel to the Solovetskii Monastery."[11] Protopopov assumed his readers would know why that was the place to go; he opened his work advising that "June and July are the best times for a trip to Solovetskii."[12] Kokovtsov, however, was more reflective:

> In June 1900 it was suggested that I carry out a trip to the Solovetskii Monastery which I had intended to do earlier. Both then and now, this ancient abbey has had its historians and its annalists. The beauty of northern nature, with its overgrown forests and its terribly beautiful ocean, were conveyed by S. V. Maksimov, V. I. Nemirovich-Danchenko, and others; it is comparatively rarer to read about the educational meaning of the Solovetskii society and the spiritual-educational aspect of its activities.[13]

Indeed, the many printed reports, travelogues, pilgrim stories, and guides to the monastery served to entice pilgrims to Solovki's remote shores. Although Maksimov's and Nemirovich-Danchenko's books were undoubtedly the most important memoirs, scores of other books and pamphlets were published on the subject. A number of travel guides for pilgrims appeared, with detailed information about routes to Solovki, places to stay, travel costs, and appropriate times for travel. Newspapers in the North, especially in Arkhangel'sk, published the sailing times for steamships embarking for the islands.[14] The monastery added its own guides, histories, and pamphlets commemorating important events.

The monastery had also gained considerable cache for its role in defending Russia during the Crimean War, a rare bright spot in a disastrous period of Russian history.[15] On 6 July 1854 (o.s.), the HMS *Brisk* and the HMS *Miranda* lobbed shells at the monastery walls, scarring buildings and landing inside churches. No one was seriously hurt, and holy objects remained largely undamaged. In fact, unexploded shells were found *behind* icons, which remained unharmed. Based on descriptions of miraculous occurrence and heroic defense, one observer sent by the Holy Synod reported that all who were on the islands deserved medals of commendation.[16]

This conflation of Russian nationalism and religion had a particularly modern ring to it. The monastery actively promoted the linkage, memorializing spots where British bombs had hit its buildings and opening its armory (filled mostly with outdated pikes, muskets, and cannon balls) as a testament to its role in defending the motherland. Fifty years after the event, institutional memory of the British attack was fresh and each of the diarists recounted the skirmish. Even Zamaraev—not usually a stickler for detail—noted the following:

I saw and hefted shot in the fortress, English. All the shot and splinters are gathered in one heap, where there is a chapel. In the walls and on the fortress were many holes, all closed up and marked with black paint. The captain of the English squadron was Erasmus Ommanei, the frigates *Brisk* and *Miranda* bombed on 6 and 7 July.[17]

Protopopov, who rarely showed any excitement in his description of the monastery, wrote that "in the history of the Solovetskii Monastery, this bombardment of 1854 makes up one of the most interesting pages."[18] The most obvious connection between nationalism and faith came on 4 August 1912, when the British returned a bell to the monastery that had been taken as a prize during the fighting. The bell was transferred from a British steamer to the monastery's own *Vera* and brought ashore with the pomp usually accorded only visiting heads of state—red carpet, pealing bells, singing choirs, and fresh flowers. The archimandrite compared the bell's return to the Jews receiving back the Ark of the Covenant. The monastery immediately published a long pamphlet marking the occasion, tempting more pilgrims to see the bell in its original home.[19]

Because of its heritage as both a religious shrine and a site of patriotic defense of the motherland, travelers to Solovki were sometimes grouped as "pilgrims" versus "tourists." Bishop Evdokim, remembering his first views of the White Sea, wrote, "The thought of a tourist, of course, was concentrated exclusively on the picture unfolding before his eyes. But the thought of the pilgrim is unconsciously carried away on this watery plane to the place of great works and *podvigi* [heroic deeds], to Solovki."[20] This seems rather too fine a distinction: without exception, the pilgrims themselves wrote about the astounding natural beauty of the White Sea area, noting interesting flowers, trees, and animals—even whales. Tourists, on the other hand, also took part in the life of the monastery during their stay.

Modernization Begets Pilgrimage

The romantic picture of Russian pilgrims portrayed them as wanderers, trudging "on foot, in bands of fifty or sixty persons—men, women, children, each with a staff in his hand, a water bottle hanging from his belt; edifying the country as they march along, kneeling at the wayside chapel, and singing their canticles by day and night."[21] By the late nineteenth century, however, pilgrim transport had taken on modern characteristics, including huge barges, trains, and steamships. Moreover, the pilgrim trade became a major source of income for Solovki.

Although itinerant preachers and wandering pilgrims had been known for centuries in Russia, pilgrimage became a mass phenomenon only in the latter half of the nineteenth century. Emancipation of the serfs, coupled with rapid advances in technology, gave pilgrims both the opportunity and the means to travel. Thus the faithful needed only a desire to see the holy sites and a small amount of money. Emancipation had an immediate impact on Solovki—receipts for the transportation of pilgrims jumped from 3,351 rubles in 1860 to 12,937 rubles in 1861.[22]

In 1870 an English travel writer described the "mastering passion" and "untamable craving" for religious travel among Russians: "One of these lowly Russ surprised me on the Jordan at Betharbara; and only yesterday I helped his brother to cross the Dvina on his march from Solovetsk [sic]. The first pilgrim had visited the tombs of Palestine, from Nazareth to Marsaba; the second, after toiling through a thousand miles of road and river to Solovetsk [sic], is now on his way to the shrines at Kief [sic]."[23] A generation later, Bishop Evdokim wrote: "Here are priests, candidates of the academy, priests [sic], pupils of seminaries, hieromonks, monks, nuns. There is a merchant, here is a soldier, there a bureaucrat, here a group of peasant men and women."[24] The vast majority of pilgrims to Solovki were "peasants of the provinces of Arkhangel'sk, Olonets, Vologda, and Viatka; but, among them, it was common to encounter pilgrims who had traveled many thousands of versts."[25] The seminarians agreed, noting that "from this mass of gray *chuyki* [overcoats] worn by the people of the northern borders who comprise the majority of the public" could be seen peasant clothing from the central provinces, Riazan, and "the elegant figures of the servants of Mars."[26]

As might be expected, pilgrim narratives emphasized the journey itself, especially the period before arriving at the monastery. The short-term pilgrims invariably traveled during the brief navigable season on the White Sea, roughly from the end of May through the end of August. In fact, about 80 percent of the faithful traveled to Solovki in the first half of the navigable season, almost all from Pentecost to mid-July.

Shortly after emancipation, the monastery bought a used steamship to ferry the faithful and other goods from the mainland to the islands. On 15 August 1862 the *Vera* made its maiden voyage from Solovki. It cost the monastery 24,479 rubles, paid over five years.[27] Soon Solovki added three more steamships—the *Nadezhda* in 1863, the *Solovetskii* in 1881, and the *Mikhail Arkhangel* in 1887. Finally, the *Vera* was completely overhauled in 1902 and refit for more pilgrims. Instead of buying used ships, the monastery soon had enough money to look abroad for new, high-quality steamers. The *Solovetskii*, for example, was built by a Norwegian company to carry both cargo and pilgrims in its holds and on deck.[28]

Within a single generation, the monastery became one of the most important steamship companies in the Russian North. With four ships in its line, Solovki flew its own maritime flag—the Russian tricolor with the letters "S. M." emblazoned on it. Plying the waters from Kem' and Arkhangel'sk to Solovki, and carrying both passengers and cargo, the monastery used the newest technology to link itself to mainland Russia for three months a year. The monastery took great pride in running its own affairs, captaining its boats with monks, and undertaking major repairs at the dry dock on Solovki, the only such dock on the White Sea. Describing the captain of the *Vera*, one observer wrote in 1870 of "this dwarf, in a monk's gown and cap, with a woman's auburn curls, the captain of a sea-going ship!"[29] Even more colorful was the story of the *Vera*'s first year on the White Sea, illustrating the importance Solovki placed on developing its own maritime affairs:

> At first these holy men felt strange on deck; they crossed themselves; they sang a hymn; and, as the pistons would not move, they begged the Scottish engineer to return; since the machine—having been made by heretics—had not grace enough to obey the voice of a holy man. They made two or three midsummer trips across the gulf, getting helpful hints from the native skippers and gradually warming to their work. A priest was appointed captain, and monks were sent into the kitchen and the engine-room.[30]

The importance of the ferries was immense. Holding 400 to 450 passengers and steaming from mid-May to mid-September, the monastery's ships carried thousands of pilgrims to the monastery each week. Thus the number of pilgrims visiting Solovki grew tremendously, from about 6,000 in 1863 (just after the *Vera* was put into service) to around 24,000 in 1900, when all four ships were in service. In 1863 the monastery had realized a profit of 2,914 rubles from the *Vera*.

After losing money in 1864, the steamships were again profitable until 1913. Moreover, their profit rose continually, except during the 1905 Revolution. By the eve of World War I Solovki was realizing a profit of more than 50,000 rubles per year on steamship tickets alone. An average of 11 percent of Solovki's yearly income was derived from the four ships.[31]

Most pilgrims came to Arkhangel'sk, where they had to arrange for passage to the monastery. The huge increase in pilgrimage during the late imperial period manifested itself in the city, which could barely contain the seasonal increase in visitors. Most problematic was the monastery's city house (*podvor'e*) at Solombal'skoe, outside Arkhangel'sk, where thousands of pilgrims sometimes waited days for the next sailing of the islands' steamers. By monastic tradition, visiting the *podvor'e* was free—once a pilgrim made it to Arkhangel'sk, the monastery paid for a bed and tea. The monastery, however, simply could not keep pace with the flood of pilgrims desiring its hospitality. Up to 900 people sometimes found shelter at the Solombal'skoe *podvor'e*, a building designed to house fewer than 150. The situation grew progressively worse in the early twentieth century, and the monastery experienced "extreme need" for a guest house. (During the war the Sololmbal'skoe *podvor'e* even housed "citizens of hostile powers who were arrested from the ships and boats of Arkhangel'sk.")[32] In 1917 the monastery finally petitioned the Holy Synod to build its own hotel in the city of Arkhangel'sk to house the hundreds of pilgrims who could not be cared for at the *podvor'e*.[33] The revolution intervened, however.

Descriptions of the monastery regularly included comments on the huge income derived from pilgrims, which came not only from the steamships but also from the shops, the poor boxes, and the offertories during the liturgy. The seminarians marveled at the shops' wealth; Protopopov grumbled about illiterate (but wealthy) pilgrim women who thought nothing of paying thirty to forty rubles for icons, oleographs, and neck crosses but loudly complained when paying three to five kopeks for baggage transfer. He guessed that even the "simplest" pilgrims spent one or two rubles at the shops and kiosks. In fact, from 1863 to 1913 the monastery consistently made more than 40 percent of its annual income from serving pilgrims, not including income derived from selling food, fur coats, or other goods produced on the island. The monastery's total income rose by 71 percent from 1863 to 1913, with the increase directly related to the number of pilgrims arriving each year. (The only significant downturn in income occurred during the Russo-Japanese War and the 1905 Revolution, when pilgrimage plummeted.)[34] Through its aggressive development of pilgrimage, Solovki became second only to the St. Sergius—Holy Trinity Lavra in the yearly income monasteries made. This was particularly impressive, given the former's remote location. St. Sergius—Holy Trinity, on the other hand, was able to draw pilgrims from the Moscow region, with a far higher population density than in the Far North.

Class Distinctions in Pilgrimage

Although the monastery prided itself on welcoming all manner of Russian folk, and although most Solovki monks were peasants, the pilgrims' experiences varied by wealth and class. Undoubtedly the vast majority of pilgrims came from among the peasantry, and most of Solovki's resources went to providing them with food and shelter. Still there were clear differentiations between the rich and the poor, that is, between the "better public" (*chistaia publika*) *and* the "dull public" (*seraia publika*). Protopopov noted that "the majority of pilgrims are common people. Many of them make the journey by foot, suffering all the discomforts of traveling in third and fourth class and by 'common tickets.'"[35] Poor pilgrims could also find work on the river boats carrying wood to fuel the steamers or helping to push boats off sandbars and shoals. The most generous aid, however, came directly from the monastery. The cost for passage on the monastery's steamships was kept artificially low, and the monastery regularly provided free passage to the poorest pilgrims.[36] Finally, three-day peasants did not have to pay for room or board while at the monastery.

Travel was highly segregated onboard both commercial fleets and those of the monastery. The least expensive method of travel was on the deck of wooden river barges that made their way to Arkhangel'sk. Hundreds of pilgrims and other travelers crowded there, able to cruise very cheaply. Both the barges and monastery steamers provided four classes of travel, the latter offering 12 places in first class, about 100 in second class, and another 350 in third and steerage classes. Group differentiation was bolstered when the pilgrims arrived on Solovetskii's dock. As the pilgrims exited the steamers, monks shepherded them into rooms at the monastic guest houses. The "better" pilgrims were led to the Preobrazhenskaia hostelry. An imposing, three-story stone building that had taken six years to build (1859–1865), the Preobrazhenskaia opened its main doors right onto the dock. Even at that hostelry, however, some pilgrims were pushed together into rooms with strangers, sleeping on the floor when there were too many people for the four couches furnishing the room.[37] The authors related their experiences in the Preobrazhenskaia: rooms number 1 and 6 on the middle floor—there were seventy rooms in all—were the very best: clean, with beautiful views and upholstered furniture. (This is where Fr. Boddy stayed.) The third floor was worse than the second, and the first floor worst of all.[38]

The "lesser" pilgrims were herded to the two older guest houses. Although the Arkhangel'sk Guest House proudly showed off its scars from British bombs,

Figure 2.1.   View toward the Solovetskii Monastery from a guest house.
Library of Congress, Prints & Photographs Division, Prokudin-Gorskii Collection.

by the early twentieth century it had fallen into disrepair. Some forty-five people packed into a single room. Fr. Boddy remembered that "the place, whenever
I visited it, was crammed with pilgrims reclining on the sloping counters which
did duty as beds. It was somewhat like the steerage on our great Atlantic steamers, where all sorts and conditions of men, women, and children come together."
An earlier observer claimed that, in the guest houses, he saw "everything: fighting, profligacy, and theft."[39]

Finally, distinctions at the monastery were reinforced during mealtimes.
Three times a day, "simple folk" went to the "needy refectory" or the "women's
refectory," whereas monks, long-term workers, and the "better" guests ate at the
brothers' refectory. Trush reported: "Experience and practicality is evident in the
monastic-refectory in this regard, as [it is able] faultlessly to assign the mass
of people [for meals], as was done in the guest houses, dividing men into two
parties and directing one to the lower refectory and the other to the brothers'
and then women to their particular one."[40] Apparently, however, this system did
not always work. For some meals, the peasant Zamaraev ate among the *seraia*

publika; but on the last day of his pilgrimage, he noted: "We ate lunch together with the brothers. Here the food was better, in four courses, in the Uspenskii Church."[41]

Although pilgrimage was overwhelmingly a peasant activity throughout the early twentieth century, the *chistaia publika* also developed an interest in Solovki. Protopopov wrote, almost conspiratorially, that "people who know Solovetskii well recounted to me in confidence that the former severity of monks in this monastery is gradually beginning to change. The growing contingent is not only literate but also cultivates a [higher] cultural-clerical level of the monastery. Year in and year out, the number of pilgrims from the 'better' class grows."[42] Protopopov undoubtedly saw this as progress, and long overdue—Valaam Monastery had already begun providing more comfortable hostels for its pilgrims. If Solovki would only orient itself to the "better class" and get rid of its bedbugs, Protopopov wrote, it, too, would develop a pilgrim trade based on Russia's higher classes.[43]

Thoroughly Modern Traditions

Without doubt, the vast growth in pilgrimage at the end of the imperial period changed the religious experience of pilgrims to Solovki. On the one hand, the daily activities undertaken over three days remained rather constant, but, on the other, the practice of those activities differed significantly over time, taxing both the pilgrims and the brotherhood.

Pilgrim narratives described similar experiences at the monastery. Upon arriving early in the morning after the night crossing, time was taken up finding a room at one of the various hostelries and getting acquainted with the monastic kremlin. Always the most succinct of the narrators, Zamaraev wrote that "the monastery is large, beautiful. Many temples and bureaucratic buildings are visible, rich ones. The fence around the monastery for thirteen hundred paces is made of large stones, as are the towers."[44] Others, as one might expect, were more colorful in their initial descriptions of the monastery. Bishop Evdokim wrote: "I quickly climbed to the deck. Before my eyes unfolded a staggeringly wonderful picture. . . . And just in front of us, in all its glory, pouring out in evening color sunlight, lay the holy cloister of Solovetskii with its great sacred places."[45]

Pilgrims generally took part in a number of traditional activities during their stay on Solovki. Although none was significantly different from religious devotions available at any parish church, these activities took on heightened meaning at the monastery. The most important was the taking of communion and the receiving of *prosphora*, the bread blessed during Eucharist commemorations.

Every few days, the archimandrite of Solovetskii—Fr. Ioanniki for most of the early twentieth century—served the liturgy himself. From the time of Peter I, who bestowed this honor, Solovetskii's archimandrite was allowed to serve an "archimandrite's service" exactly like that of a bishop. This caused some excitement among the pilgrims, many of whom rarely witnessed a hierarchal liturgy. Zamaraev noted, "The archimandrite served. Communion lasted until one in the afternoon."[46] The seminarians agreed, writing that "on another day—a Sunday—the solemn liturgy was served by the archimandrite himself with many of the brothers. There were a lot of people in the church. They served with grandeur. It is true that they sang, as always, loudly and not particularly harmoniously; still the "archbishop's service" of the archimandrite produced a strong impression on those present. The liturgy ended around one."[47]

At the end of the liturgy, prosphora was handed out to all the faithful in pieces, and whole small loaves (with a small triangle taken out for use in the communion chalice) were returned to pilgrims who brought them from the special prosphora chapel outside the monastery walls. From the earliest days of the monastery, Solovki's prosphora was considered to be particularly holy, carried home to loved ones and consumed during sickness to hasten a believer back to health. To fill the demand, Solovki had to import ever-increasing amounts of flour and expand the bakery. In return, prosphora sales accounted for significant income for the cloister.

After liturgy, pilgrims regularly stood in line for hours to venerate the relics of Saints Zosima and Savvati. Although many churches and local monasteries might have had reliquaries, few could compete with the sacred power invested in these two saints, the founders of Solovki. Bishop Evdokim asked, "Is it necessary to speak of the feeling of fullness in our souls when we bowed down before those shrines? No, it is not necessary. I wanted to lay on the floor forever in front of those saints in fear and trembling, wanted to be the dust and perpetually be trampled upon before them."[48] It was an impressive sight; Fr. Boddy wrote that "countless offerings of candles were blazing around the tombs of the saints of Solovétsk [sic], and the floor of the chapel, with its black and white pavements, was covered with a dense mass of kneeling humanity all worshiping toward the rich shrines glittering with gold—a contrast to the two simple old men who lie there."[49]

In addition to the founders' bodies, the monastery's exceptional collection of other saints' relics and wonder-working icons also attracted the pilgrims. Miracle-working icons included a "Slavianskaia" Theotokos; an image of the Savior painted by St. Eleazar himself; and the wonder-working "Sosnovskaia" Theotokos that saved the monastery from bombardment by the British. (This last icon was Kokovtsov's first stop in the monastery.)[50] Objects from the saints' own lives provided a tangible link to their holiness—chief among these was a stone cross brought to the islands by St. Zosima.

In late afternoon, the monks began to serve intercessory services (*moleben*) and services for the dead (*panikhida*). Although these services were regularly available at home, to have the monks of the holy island pray for one's family was a high point of the pilgrimage. Trush noted that the monastery had therefore developed a system to serve the spiritual needs of thousands: pilgrims queued at the cashier near the back of the church and paid for their service. Priest-monks stood there, too, ready to take the faithful into a corner of the church to celebrate the service. Once finished, the priest came back to the cashier to pick up another believer.[51] In this way, the monks could serve five hundred to six hundred of these short services per day. This placed extreme demands on the monks who served the pilgrims and upset the daily routines established for the rest of the year. As early as 1863 the monastery leadership had to implore monks to serve in this capacity, saying that all consecrated monks of any rank needed to serve in rotating shifts at the churches. In fact, anyone who "could sing even a little" was called to the Troitskii-Zosima Cathedral to help serve at the saints' tombs. Notably the document also exhorted the monks to treat the pilgrims "cordially, affectionately, and with decent respect, and to bear all their imperfections tolerantly."[52] This intimated the stress undoubtedly felt by the monastic community when confronted by thousands of pilgrims. The most stern monks were castigated for sending pilgrims away in tears.[53]

The great number of intercessory and memorial services celebrated at the monastery highlighted how sheer magnitude changed the quality of the pilgrims' religious experience. Some writers grumbled that there were far more peaceful and accessible monasteries in Russia that could provide a deeper spiritual experience for pilgrims than could be offered by the mass character of all the religious activities on Solovki. This view, however, missed a central point about the sanctity of Solovki: herds of pilgrims arriving by the boatload only heightened the monastery's appeal as a sacred place, as thousands of candles were a better sacrifice to the saints than one single candle burning in front of their crypts. The mass nature of Solovki's pilgrim experience—made possible largely by changes in technology—rather than undermining its sanctity actually increased it.

Enormous financial growth, fueled by pilgrimage, significantly affected the internal life of the monastery. The upheaval experienced during the pilgrimage season was overwhelming but relatively short. The pilgrims began to arrive in late May or early June, and by August almost all of them had left the islands. The task of cleaning up, fixing up, and preparing for the next summer's onslaught, however, became a major task for the brothers of Solovki. This was accomplished through a series of large public-works projects that brought new technology to the monastery, sometimes introducing innovations to the Russian North. Between 1895 and 1917, for example, the monastery built its own electric station, telegraph service, horse farm, fisheries, and other major projects, largely based on income provided by the pilgrims.

The large building and development projects favored by Solovki's long-serving archimandrite, Ioanniki, had little support among the brothers of the monastery who regarded him with suspicion—especially after 1907 when he decided to build a turbine mill. One brother told Protopopov that "the father abbot fancies himself an engineer-shipbuilder . . . hmm . . . I don't know if this should be [said]." Other pilgrims, however, praised the archimandrite. In the words of the seminarians:

> The archimandrite approached. This is a stocky person with energy and small expressive eyes, the typical Russian peasant. His manner and method of treatment show his origin, but in his eyes one sees intelligence, and in his step and in his characteristic features—between his brows—uncon-querable energy. This is a man of action—a child of the gloomy North. He makes no allowances for the monks and maintains strict discipline. The monks are afraid of him but respect him; they elected him their leader for his outstanding intellect, boundless energy, and excellent understanding of the monastery and all its procedures, from the time when the archi-mandrite began his career from among the *trudniki* [working pilgrims] and then became a novice.[54]

Although he fought back vigorously and continued to modernize the mon-astery, the archimandrite received increasingly harsh condemnations: in 1911 a former teacher of theology at Solovki went so far as to call Ioanniki a "nihil-ist," a "practical atheist" who ran the monastery with the unbridled power of a Pope.[55] Formal charges were brought against Ioanniki, related in part to his misuse of funds, but he was not removed from his post until 1917. By that time the Russian press had begun reporting on problems at the monastery and so the Holy Synod was forced to act.

These problems may have had little effect on the pilgrims. In fact, Ioanniki's policies probably helped the monastery to attract more pilgrims—the great wealth and modern miracles to be seen there provided ever-more exotic reasons to visit Solovki. And despite the many monasteries one could visit throughout the North, Solovki continued to captivate the imagination of Russian pilgrims. It may be that pilgrims simply preferred rich monasteries to poor ones, but the faithful also saw in Solovki a monastery where they could encounter the sanctity of Russia's medieval saints while experiencing the great wealth developed by modern methods.

Concluding Observations

The peasant A. A. Zamaraev wrote down the particulars of his trip home from Solovki: "At last, on 13 June somehow we left aboard the ship *Vera*, which departed at 2:00 in the afternoon. The weather is calm."[56] With him on the trip back to Tot'ma, via Arkhangel'sk, Kotlas, and Velikii Ustiug, were hundreds of like-minded souls, looking forward to arriving home. What was the meaning of their experiences? The more descriptive of our authors offered a few thoughts on their journeys. Kokovtsov remarked that the importance of Solovetskii had changed over the centuries—"In our day it cannot have the complete *propagation* of the Word of God as in the fifteenth century, but it expresses itself in the *maintenance* of the Orthodox way."[57] Here Kokovtsov intimated that the faith needed maintenance, that Solovki was a defender of tradition against a sea of change. Protopopov was not so sure: "It is said that the faith of the people is falling and weakening, that rationalism is spreading. How might this be reflected in a monastery, the income of which acts as a good thermometer of religious temperature? Alas!—in the absence of good writings about monastic life, and being unable to establish the necessary facts without the assistance of monastic powers, this question, for me, must remain unanswered."[58]

Protopopov may have been more satisfied with his spiritual temperature taking had he analyzed his fellow pilgrims' experiences rather than monastic ones. The throngs of believers that came to Solovki in the waning years of the empire represented a high level of popular religious commitment among a certain segment of the population. There seems to be little evidence—given the narratives offered here—that pilgrims had become more rational in their approach to religion. Indeed, just the opposite was true: the traditional forms of worship and piety at the monastery during these years, rather than suffering a decline, were in fact reinforced.

Yet a transformation had been occurring, and the outlines of that change could be seen in the pilgrim narratives. Solovki, long proud of "working only for itself," was now linked to the laity in ways it had never experienced. When the monastery's first steamship arrived, the pilgrim experience at Solovki likewise changed forever. Remarkably this remote monastic outpost became among the most-often visited holy places in Russia. With its mammoth influx of visitors, the monastery sometimes seemed to be more income-driven than spirit-filled, and some guests came away disgusted with the amount of money the monastery made.

Most pilgrims, however, continued to experience the monastery in deeply religious ways, as attested by the huge number of requiem and intercession services celebrated each day on the islands. Likewise, the vast amount of communion bread sold for personal commemorations also illustrated the central place of prayer in the pilgrims' activities. The English priest—Fr. Boddy—summed up this aspect of Solovki's pilgrim culture: "I had been to a great number of services in Russia ... but never was more impressed than at Solovetsk [sic]. There was such earnestness and simple devoutness in these pilgrim faces. They had come across the Ural from Siberia, from the steppes of the Cossacks of the Don, from the forest of northern Russia, had traveled for weeks and weeks, and at last here they were in the Holy Place itself, and almost overwhelmed with devout emotion."[59]

Although Fr. Boddy was emphasizing the continuation of piety in Russian culture, he also introduced another puzzle, as yet unexplored. These narratives hinted that thousands of pilgrims crisscrossed the empire and far beyond, but we still do not know the extent of their travels. (Protopopov suggested that some had been in Kiev before making their way north.)[60] Was it possible to attach a size, shape, and meaning to the movement of believers across Russia? Was Solovki's transformation—from cloister to pilgrim Mecca, capable of housing and feeding thousands of pilgrims at once—a singular occurrence or part of a larger change in popular religion in the late imperial period? These areas are ripe for examination.

Notes

1. Solovki was the popular name for the Solovetskii Monastery and the island archipelago on which it stood. The complete formal title was the Savior-Transfiguration Solovetskii Stavropigial'nyi Men's Monastery.

2. These narratives were not produced in a vacuum, of course. Pilgrimage to many religious shrines had become popular among Russians, and the Holy Land often seemed awash in Russian pilgrims. See, for example, Boris Romanov, Puteshestviia v sviatuiu Zemliu: zapiski russkikh palomnikov i puteshestvennikov, XII–XX vv. (Moscow, 1995). I have not yet compared the Solovki narratives to those written about other Russian holy sites or Palestine.

3. V. V. Morozov and N. I. Reshetnikov, eds., Dnevnik totemskogo krest'ianina A. A. Zamaraeva 1906–1922 gody (Moscow, 1995).

4. Alexander A. Boddy, With Russian Pilgrims: Being an Account of a Soujourn in the White Sea Monastery and a Journey by the Old Trade Route from the Arctic Sea to Moscow (London, 1893); Episkop Evdokim (Meshcherskii), Solovki: stranichka iz dnevnika palomnika (St. Petersburg, 1904); K. Kokovtsov, Poezdka v solovetskii monastyr' (St. Petersburg, 1901); S. D. Protopopov, Iz poezdki v solovetskii monastyr' (Moscow, 1903); Solovki i Valaam: dnevnik studentov-palomnikov (Moscow, 1901); and N. Trush, Solovki v avguste 1905 g. (Moscow, 1905). In addition, a recent dissertation from Moscow State University has offered a huge amount of raw data on the economic life of the monastery in this period, culling from many archival sources. I will quote regularly from the material found in T. Iu. Samsonova, "Solovetskii monastyr': khoziastvennaia

deiatel'nost', sotsial'nyi sostav i upravlenie vtoraia polovina 19–nachalo 20 veka" (Moscow, 1997). Finally, I am indebted to A. A. Soshina, a historian at Solovki, for her paper "Palomniki i palomnichestvo v solovetskii monastyr' v xvi–nach. xx vv." (Solovki: Ob'edinennaia direktsiia Solovetskogo gosudarstvennogo istoriko-arkhitekturnogo i prirodnogo muzeia-zapovednika [SGIA PMZ], 1991).

5. Protopopov, *Iz poezdki v solovetskii monastyr'*, 9.
6. Fr. Boddy was a particularly interesting character in his own right. See Gavin Wakefield, *The First Pentecostal Anglican: The Life and Legacy of Alexander Boddy* (Cambridge, 2001).
7. Soshina, "Palomniki i palomnichestvo v solovetskii monastyr'," 8.
8. *Vidy Solovetskogo monastyria, otpechatanye s drevnykh dosok, kraniashchikhsia v Tamoshnei Riznitse* (St. Petersburg, 1884), 3. See also Gosudarstvennyi arkhiv Arkhangel'skoi oblasti (GAAO), f. 4, op. 3, d. 664, 1822 g., quoted in Soshina, "Palomniki i palomnichestvo v solovetskii monastyr'," 11.
9. Rossiiskii gosudarstvennyi istoricheskii arkhiv (hereafter, RGIA), f. 797, op. 4, d. 15909, ll. 740b.–75 and Archimandrite Dosifei, *Letopisets Solovetskii na chetyre stoletiia ot osnovaniia Solovetskago monastyria do nastoiashchago vremeni*, (Moscow, 1847), 160–162.
10. Solovki was the northernmost pilgrimage shrine in all of Europe. See Mary Lee Nolan and Sidney Nolan, *Christian Pilgrimage in Modern Western Europe* (Chapel Hill, 1989), 31–32.
11. V.V. Morozov and N. I. Reshetnikov, *Dnevnik totemskogo krest'ianina A. A. Zamaraeva*, 43.
12. Protopopov, *Iz poezdki v solovetskii monastyr'*, 1.
13. Kokovtsov, *Poezdka v solovetskii monastyr'*, 1–2.
14. See, for examples, *Pravoslavnyia russkiia obiteli*, (St. Petersburg, 1910; repr. St. Petersburg, 1994); and *Putevoditel' po solovetskim ostrovam* (St. Petersburg, 1900). Often the pilgrim narratives also gave detailed instructions for travel to the monastery. For information on Arkhangel'sk newspapers, see Samsonova, "Solovetskii monastyr'," 105.
15. See, for example, *Solovetskii monastyr' i opisanie bombardirovaniia ego anglichanami 7-go iulia 1854 goda* (Moscow, 1855). Boddy gives one of the best analyses of the conflict in his *With Russian Pilgrims*, 98–126.
16. RGIA, f. 797, op. 1858–61, d. 28, l. 50b.
17. V. V. Morozov and N. I. Reshetnikov, *Dnevnik totemskogo krest'ianina A. A. Zamaraeva*, 47.
18. Protopopov, *Iz poezdki v solovetskii monastyr'*, 22.
19. *Vozvrashchenie iz Anglii plennogo monastyrskogo kolokola v Solovetskuiu obitel'* 4 avgusta 1912 g. (Moscow, 1913).
20. Evdokim, *Solovki*, 5.
21. William Hepworth Dixon, *Free Russia*, 2 vols. (Leipzig, 1872), 1:50.
22. Samsonova, "Solovetskii monastyr'," 139.
23. Dixon, *Free Russia*, 1:48.
24. Evdokim, *Solovki*, 10.
25. Kokovtsov, *Poezdka v solovetskii monastyr'*, 35.
26. *Solovki i Valaam*, 84.
27. For a lengthy description of the economic impact of the steamships, see Samsonova, "Solovetskii monastyr'," 103–108.
28. The monastery explicitly wanted to develop pilgrimage by acquiring new, faster, and larger steamships. See, for example, RGIA, f. 799, op. 1879, d. 898, ll. 1–10b.
29. Dixon, *Free Russia*, 1:58.
30. Ibid., 1:64.
31. For raw data and some analysis, see Samsonova, "Solovetskii monastyr'," 107–109.
32. Ibid., 173.
33. Ibid., quoting RGIA, f. 799, op. 31, d. 252, l. 13.

34. Ibid., 175–76.

35. Protopopov, *Iz poezdki v solovetskii monastyr'*, 26.

36. Free passage accounted for about 5–10 percent of all tickets, which did not significantly diminish the steamships' profits. See Samsonova, "Solovetskii monastyr'," 106, 201.

37. See Protopopov, *Iz poezdki v solovetskii monastyr'*, 18, for a more complete description.

38. Even the higher-class pilgrims were not necessarily sophisticated. Protopopov reported that the walls of his room were dirty and covered with graffiti: "'In 1887 here was the merchant son Nikolai Gubanov'" (*Iz poezdki v solovetskii monastyr*, 18). A later inhabitant added, after Gubanov's name, "fool and pig." Kokovtsov provided a more positive description of the Preobrazhenskaia (*Poezdka v solovetskii monastyr'*, 29–30).

39. P. F. Fedorov, *Solovki. Zapiski imperatorskago russkogo geograficheskogo obshchestva po otdeleniiu etnografii* tom xix, vyp. i. (Kronstadt, 1889) 70.

40. Trush, *Solovki v avguste 1905 g.*, 12. It is interesting that the travel guides to Solovki noted the various dining rooms but did not explain the class differentiation each one connoted. See *Putevoditel' po solovetskim ostrovam*, 9.

41. V. V. Morozov and N. I. Reshetnikov, *Dnevnik totemskogo krest'ianina A. A. Zamaraeva*, 47. See also Trush, *Solovki v avguste 1905 g.*, 12.

42. Protopopov, *Iz poezdki v solovetskii monastyr'*, 40.

43. To this end, the monastery trumpeted pilgrimage by the royal family. In the late nineteenth century more royals than ever had made their pilgrimage to Solovki. Grand Prince Aleksei Aleksandrovich came to Solovki via Arkhangel'sk in 1870. Grand Prince Vladimir Aleksandrovich arrived on the clipper *Zabiaka* for a three-day pilgrimage on 16–18 June 1885. The monastery publicly celebrated the pilgrimage by Her Royal Highness Elizaveta Feodorovna in *Poseshchenie solovetskogo monastyria e.i.v. velikoi kniaiznei Elisaveti Feodorovnoi v iulee 1913 goda*, (Moscow, 1915).

44. V. V. Morozov and N. I. Reshetnikov, *Dnevnik totemskogo krest'ianina A. A. Zamaraeva*, 46.

45. Evdokim, *Solovki*, 8.

46. V. V. Morozov and N. I. Reshetnikov, *Dnevnik totemskogo krest'ianina A. A. Zamaraeva*, 47. Considering that many priests would have been present to offer the gifts to the faithful, the number of pilgrims communing on that day must have been overwhelming to have the service continue that late into the afternoon.

47. *Solovki i Valaam*, 100–101.

48. Evdokim, *Solovki*, 14.

49. Boddy, *With Russian Pilgrims*, 88.

50. Kokovtsov, *Poezdka v solovetskii monastyr'*, 31.

51. Trush, *Solovki v avguste 1905 g.*, 12.

52. Rossiiskii gosudarstvennyi arkhiv drevnykh aktov (RGADA), f. 1201, op. 4, d. 788, l. 19. Quoted in Samsonova, "Solovetskii monastyr'," 171.

53. Samsonova, "Solovetskii monastyr'," 53.

54. *Solovki i Valaam*, 102.

55. Samsonova, "Solovetskii monastyr'," 62.

56. V. V. Morozov and N. I. Reshetnikov, *Dnevnik totemskogo krest'ianina A. A. Zamaraeva*, 48.

57. Kokovtsov, *Poezdka v solovetskii monastyr'*, 74.

58. Protopopov, *Iz poezdki v solovetskii monastyr'*, 40.

59. Boddy, *With Russian Pilgrims*, 84–85.

60. Protopopov, *Iz poezdki v solovetskii monastyr'*, 26.

3

Scripting the Gaze: Liturgy, Homilies, and the Kazan Icon of the Mother of God in Late Imperial Russia

Vera Shevzov

————··◄◦►··————

At the beginning of the twentieth century, during a sermon on the feast of Russia's well-known miracle-working Kazan icon of the Mother of God, a Russian Orthodox priest beckoned his listeners to "gaze upon the image of the Queen, gaze with ardent and fervent prayer."[1] Recent studies in religion and visual culture have shown that such seemingly simple exhortations are anything but straightforward.[2] Included among the numerous questions raised by such exhortations are those that concern the very act of religious seeing and the cultural dynamics that contribute to it. "Looking upon" an icon in Russian Orthodoxy was indeed a complex act. On the one hand, a believer's apprehension of an icon was deeply personal: how one perceived a sacred image largely depended on who one was, the state of one's mind, and where and when one came upon it. On the other hand, the act of the devotional gaze involved more than a single individual and a detached image. Icons and believers were also part of a broader faith community that provided a living environment in which icons were both produced and received.

One of the most prominent aspects of that environment was the sacred community's liturgical worship. As the historian Margaret Miles has argued for Western Christian medieval visual experience, "the individual viewer confronted the image as a member of an interpreting community, and the image itself was also part of the ... liturgical presentation of an ordered cosmos of being, reality, and value."[3] In this sense, in modern Russia, too, the production and reception of an icon were not simply attributable to the iconographer and the individual believer, respectively, but involved broader religious, cultural, and even political processes. Nowhere was this more evident in late imperial Russian Orthodoxy than in the veneration of its nationally recognized miracle-working icons, most of which were of Mary, the Mother of God. These icons not only enjoyed specially designated feasts on the Church's liturgical calendar but also had special liturgical services composed in their honor. Orthodox liturgical worship consisted largely of chanted established rehearsals of foundational narratives and sacred stories that formed the basis of the community's "life-world."[4] It also included, with increasing frequency from the eighteenth century on, homilies or paraliturgical talks in which a presiding bishop or priest would expound on a topic related to the sacred celebration. On the feast of a particular icon of Mary, ecclesial narratives and the Church's visual culture were thereby integrated in a mutually transformative way. On the one hand, Old and New Testament narratives and apocryphal stories gained new meaning as they were woven together in honor of a particular image of Mary. On the other hand, liturgical texts and the homilies spoken on the feast framed the icon of Mary with stories that themselves became part of the phenomenon of that particular icon. This essay examines the "sacred rhetoric" of the liturgical and homiletic

Чуд. икона Божіей Матери, именуемой Казанской.

СКАЗАНІЕ

О ЧУДОТВОРНОЙ ИКОНѢ БОЖІЕЙ МАТЕРИ, ИМЕНУЕМОЙ

КАЗАНСКОЙ.

I.

Икона Казанской Божіей Матери, находящей-ся въ Казанскомъ соборѣ, написана на кипа-рисной доскѣ съ предвѣчнымъ Младенцемъ на лѣвой рукѣ, благословляющемъ десницею всѣхъ прибѣгающихъ съ вѣрою къ Ея покрову и по-мощи. Икона эта какъ святыня и украшеніе гра-да святаго Петра празднуется 8 іюля съ котора-го начинается ея исторія, передаваемая такъ:

Figure 3.1. The Kazan icon of the Mother of God as depicted in a pamphlet that recounted the icon's life. *Skazanie o chudotvornoi ikone Bozhiei Materi, imenuemoi Kazanskoi,* 3rd ed. (Moscow, 1888).

culture associated with a particular icon of Mary, namely, the Kazan icon of the Mother of God, in order to understand better the broader narrative context in which the Orthodox believer viewed it and, in turn, the multidimensionality of religious viewing itself.[5] While it might be impossible to determine the way and extent to which this rhetoric may have stirred the imagination of any given believer, that it was spoken and that it influenced the believer's perception of the icon would be difficult to deny.

I have chosen to focus on the Kazan icon for several reasons. First, it was the most widely publicly revered of Russia's twenty-eight nationally recognized miracle-working icons of the Mother of God.[6] The Church celebrated the icon on two days, 8 July and 22 October. The latter date was also a state holiday. Many businesses and government offices were closed, and liturgical services were conducted throughout the empire.[7] That the Kazan icon was an extremely popular image among the laity, with a copy found in most homes and certainly in most churches, added to the salience of its national celebration. Moreover, the icon's liturgical and homiletic framing was not merely an annual or bian-nual event that was intermittently forgotten; the stories and themes intoned on the icon's feasts would have continued to resonate through their association with the icon's countless copies and with other Marian icons and feasts, and thereby would have helped to sustain the Kazan icon's vitality as a sacred sym-bol in modern Russia. With what sacred stories, we might ask, was the Kazan icon liturgically associated? How did they present the figure of Mary and what significance did they ascribe to her icon? How did liturgical texts and sermons represent believers, both individually and collectively, and what did these texts demand of them?

The Kazan Icon of the Mother of God: The Story

The feasts in honor of the Kazan icon reflected two key phases in the icon's life, a life which began to form in the sixteenth century.[8] The first phase took place in 1579 in Kazan, not long after the Russians established rule over that territory. In that year a fire had destroyed that city's Kremlin fortress, an event which, according to the story, the indigenous Muslim population interpreted as a sign of God's wrath on the Russian people. That same year a ten-year-old girl, Matrona Onuchina, had several dreams of an icon of Mary, in which Mary directed her to inform the local bishop and city authorities about an icon buried beneath the ashes. Hearing about these dreams, Matrona's mother dismissed them as products of a child's vivid imagination. In the final dream, however, the icon appeared to Matrona emitting fiery rays. The account maintains that Matrona heard Mary's voice come from the icon and say: "If you do not follow my words . . . I will appear on another street and in a different city, and you will become ill until your sinful life ends." This time, frightened, Matrona begged her mother to follow Mary's directives. The mother reported these events to the local bishop and to city officials but to no avail, as they, too, doubted the validity of Matrona's experiences.[9]

At this point in the story, Matrona's mother took matters into her own hands. She went to the site and, joined by bystanders and Matrona, began digging. Matrona found the icon, which was undamaged. With news of the discovery quickly spreading, the local bishop recognized his mistaken judgment and, together with local clergy, carried the icon in a procession to the local parish church. Along the way the first healing took place—a blind person regained sight after praying before the image. Soon after, 8 July became a local feast day in Kazan. The first recorder of the icon's story was Ermogen, the patriarch of Russia from 1606 to 1612, who, while a parish priest in Kazan, had reportedly witnessed events associated with the discovery of the icon.

The second phase in the life of this icon is connected with Russia's Time of Troubles in the early seventeenth century. At that time Russia was afflicted by domestic political turmoil, as well as foreign intervention from Poland and Sweden. As the icon's story maintains, Poles had decided to place the son of their own King on the Russian throne and thereby gain rule over Russia. The patriarch at the time—the same Ermogen who penned the story of the finding of the Kazan icon—called the Russian people to rally against the foreign interventionists. In response, several militia forces were formed, one of which carried a copy of the Kazan icon. Led by Prince Dimitrii Pozharskii from Kazan and Kuzma Minin, a butcher by trade, from Nizhnii Novgorod, the militia moved on Moscow against great odds. They spent three days in preparation for battle, fasting and praying before the Kazan icon. On the eve of the battle, St. Sergius of Radonezh reportedly appeared in a dream to the Greek archbishop of Elasson, Arsenius, whom the Poles had imprisoned, and in the dream stated: "God has hearkened unto the supplications of his servants and, for the sake of the entreaties of his Mother, his divine judgment has been turned to mercy. In the morning the Lord God will give this city into the hands of the Orthodox Christians and will cast down your enemies." According to the story, Russian troops learned about this dream and, empowered by it, liberated Moscow from the occupying Polish forces on 22 October 1612.

After the defeat of the Poles, the newly established tsar, Mikhail Romanov, instituted 22 October as a day of annual commemoration of the Kazan icon in the city of Moscow. The later, empire-wide celebration of the Kazan icon was prompted by a personal event in the life of the ruling family. In 1649 Tsar Alexei Mikhailovich declared 22 October a nationwide feast, as his son, Dmitrii

Figure 3.2. Matrona finding the Kazan icon of the Mother of God.
Skazanie o iavlennoi Kazanskoi ikone Bozhiei Materi (Moscow, 1907).

Alekseevich, was born on its eve in 1648.[10] At the end of the eighteenth century, during the reign of Emperor Paul, the Holy Synod added the celebration of the icon to the list of annual tsar's feasts that commemorated the name days of members of the imperial family and events central to the life of Russia.[11]

The story behind the Kazan icon, then, involves various themes that make it more than simply a visual depiction of Mary, the mother of Jesus. Accordingly, the unadorned message to "Gaze upon the image of the Queen; gaze with ardent and fervent prayer" was only seemingly plain-speaking.[12] The acts of gazing upon and praying before an image of the Kazan icon, especially on the occasion of its feast, situated the believer at the interface of the visual, literary, historical, and oral dimensions of Russia's Orthodox culture. The notion of gazing upon an icon must therefore take into account not merely the personal religious sentiments of each individual believer toward the depicted figures of Mary and the Christ child but also the icon's story, or life, in all its complex social and political dimensions, along with its interpretations in the worshiping community. How, we might ask, was the story of this icon incorporated into the ritual life of the Church, and what message did clergy emphasize in their sermons on the feast of the icon? In other words, when believers came to church to celebrate one of the feasts of this icon, what would they have heard and with what might they have resonated?

The Kazan Icon in Liturgical Word and Song

Composed in large part in the sixteenth century, the liturgical hymns for the feast of the Kazan icon did not speak directly about the Kazan icon.[13] Instead, they spoke about Mary and her image in general and situated both in the broader Christian meta-narrative of human redemption. Mary was contemplated mainly for her role in the central event of Christian salvation history, the Incarnation. As the Mother of God, she was "the restoration to life" who granted life to the world. Liturgical hymns spoke about Mary's icon, too, in terms of a universal Christian story; they did not refer to a specific icon associated with Kazan or even with Russia. The vespers and matins services for the feast connected Mary's icon with the "old" part of the Christian story in that it was compared to the Ark of the Covenant, the symbol of divine presence in the midst of Israel. These services also tied the icon to the "new" part of sacred history by their references to the well-known story of the first icon of Mary reportedly painted by the Evangelist Luke. According to that story, Mary blessed her own image. The liturgical hymns for the Kazan icon indicated that this was not a one-time event; they envisioned Mary's relationship with her images as ongoing, resulting in the perception of these icons as "inexhaustible wellsprings" of her grace. While not specifically mentioning the Kazan icon, therefore, liturgical hymns and readings recited narratives that provided a broader context for the story of the Kazan icon.

Hymns and readings also suggested that the intimate relationship between Mary and her image was not insular and involved believers as well. Gazing meant not only viewing but actively revering the icon through established gestures and words of praise. Liturgical texts also directed believers' emotions. The texts indicated that the act of veneration involved a proper emotive disposition that included tears of compunction, a contrite heart, unfailing hope, and love. These were not a matter of mere etiquette; they were a matter of salvation, because, according to the liturgical texts, Mary aided only those who honored her in a proper manner.

Accordingly, the liturgical texts for the 8 July and 22 October feasts stated that Mary's help and mediation had their limits. "If one does not revere the all-holy Mother of God, and does not venerate her icon," one liturgical text bluntly stated, "let him be anathema." "For she puts to shame and destroys them that honor her not." This was the other side of Mary; she who joyfully granted healing to all the ailing who came in faith before her also "wounded the heretical like a shaft from a bow." Texts praised Mary as an "insuperable dominion of might who crushed the audacity of the enemy that was directed against us" (referring to the Orthodox faithful). She was "a sword against our enemies." In this context, the radiance of Mary's icon did not balm and heal as much as it blinded and "darkened the countenance of the ungodly and put them to shame."

Allusions to Mary's might and rhetoric concerning enemies and victory, however, occupied a relatively minor place in the liturgical texts. The notion of "enemy" was also often left undefined: the term might have alluded to general "dark circumstances" or to personal iniquities as much as to political opponents or foreign aggressors. Moreover, the services did not associate the notions of victory or might with any particular historical event or time, including those in the Kazan icon's story. Most of the hymns and texts, in theory, could have been used for the feasts of Mary's numerous other miracle-working icons, especially the nationally known ones.

Regarding any references to the individual believer, the liturgical services offered relatively little. The hymns mostly spoke in the collective "we," with general appeals addressed to "assemblies of pious Christians" and the "multitude of faithful." Occasionally the undifferentiated collective took on more contours with references to emperors and princes, hierarchs, monks, and laypeople, rich and poor, orphans and widows, old and young. The lack of attention to the individual, however, is not particularly surprising since, in the Orthodox liturgical tradition, it was mainly the penitential and Lenten services and hymns that contained the soul-searching language aimed at the individual.

Liturgical scholars such as Catherine Pickstock have argued that modernity was characterized by "the refusal of liturgy," insofar as modernity attempted to deny the ontological "givenness" of the transcendent and its natural enchantment of the world; to turn exclusively to the temporal and the immanent as the standard for the "real"; and to attribute an essential self-sufficiency to humans and to the world.[14] From this perspective, a genuinely liturgical act—one that recognized the world as a means of God's "revelation, presence and power"—became an act of resistance vis-à-vis "the modern."[15] Insofar as the celebration of the Kazan icon of the Mother of God was liturgical, it not only reiterated some of the most vital principles of the Orthodox faith. Through its assumptions about divinity, history, time, and modes of being, it also signaled dissent from certain "modern ways" of thinking. Insofar as the believer's gaze upon the icon was a liturgical act, it set itself against modern ways of seeing.

In 1867 the story of the Kazan icon found a new hearing in the liturgical life of the Church. In that year a state official (*stats-sovetnik*), Nikolai Elagin, petitioned the Holy Synod to review for publication a new hymn he had composed, an *akathistos* in honor of the Kazan icon.[16] In his petition Elagin claimed that he had been encouraged in his efforts by many people who had expressed their desire to have an *akathistos* hymn specifically in honor of this icon.[17] In contrast to the annual liturgical services in honor of the Kazan icon and to the general *akathistos* in honor of the Mother of God, an *akathistos* dedicated specifically to this icon, he maintained, would recall many more details of its story. "Pious feelings generated by prayer before the icon," he wrote, "desire to remember miracles in recent times performed by the Mother of God by means of this icon." The recollection of more contemporary experiences associated with the icon, he argued, would reaffirm peoples' faith in the Virgin Mary's protection of the Russian land.

Elagin's proposal to publish an *akathistos* hymn in honor exclusively of the Kazan icon of the Mother of God was itself part of a trend in nineteenth- and early-twentieth-century Russian Orthodox liturgical life. As a genre, *akathistoi* hymns had developed from an original Byzantine hymn in honor of the Mother of God composed perhaps as early as the fifth century. Although widely known in Russia's western borderland and southern regions in the seventeenth century, only at the end of the eighteenth and the beginning of the nineteenth century did central Russia begin seeing the composition and publication of numerous *akathistoi* hymns. From the mid-nineteenth through the first decade of the twentieth century, the genre enjoyed its own "golden age," with the Holy Synod approving some 130 new *akathistoi* for publication. But even this figure did not reflect the full range of activity related to the composition of these hymns. Not only had ecclesiastical censors during this period denied publication of at least 300 more *akathistoi* hymns, but others were composed and used locally, and never found their way to the offices of ecclesiastical censors in St. Petersburg or Moscow.[18]

The widespread appeal of these hymns stemmed in part from the fact that individual believers could chant them privately or in small groups without the presence of clergy.[19] Also, except for the ancient *akathistos* to the Mother of God, *akathistoi* to saints or icons of the Mother of God were never liturgically pre-scribed although clergy were free to supplement prescribed liturgical services with the chanting of *akathistoi* hymns. Clergy also turned to the *akathistoi* hymns for inspiration for their sermons.

In 1867 the Holy Synod approved Elagin's proposed *akathistos* in honor of the Kazan icon not only for publication but for church use as well. The text saw more than ten editions between 1868 and 1900.[20] In contrast to vespers and mat-ins on the feast of the Kazan icon, this new *akathistos* more fully incorporated the icon's story and consequently was more historically specific. Although it also rehearsed the story of Mary's role as intercessor and healer in salvation history, it paid substantially more attention to her involvement in Russia's history in particular. It recounted not only the reported appearance of the icon in Kazan and its role in the Russian victory over the Poles during the Time of Troubles but also told of later events with which it became associated such as Peter the Great's eighteenth-century victory over the Swedes, the icon's placement in St. Petersburg as that city's guardian and Russia's victory over Napoleon.[21] Whereas the liturgical services in the icon's honor presented Mary in terms of universal enlightenment, the *akathistos* hailed her as the "Protection of the Land of Russia, defense and confirmation of Orthodoxy therein, and indestructible shield of the faithful." The *akathistos* hymn thus remembered Mary and her icon in terms of military imagery. It praised them as "shields" and "standards of victory to the Orthodox forces" against foreign adversaries; Mary was the "deliverance from foreign invasions," "the strength of warriors," the "tower and rampart in the day of battle."[22] The texts for prescribed liturgical services emphasized Mary as defender of the Orthodox faithful, but these allusions were more prominent in the *akathistos*. Moreover, against the backdrop of references to specific historical events, such rhetoric acquired more politically charged overtones.

Such military language itself was not new; Eastern Orthodox Christians had applied it to the figure of the Mother of God since the sixth century, if not earlier, and therefore it would not have been jarring to the liturgically trained ear of an Orthodox believer in nineteenth-century Russia. Modern historical-critical approaches, however, cast a shadow over such imagery. At a time when many West European Christians, mainly Protestant intellectuals, were rethink-ing the Christian story and attempting to "demythologize" it in order to fit modern, "enlightened" sensibilities, the continued introduction of such imagery in Orthodox worship could only highlight the diverse worldviews between Christian intellectuals who became preoccupied with the positivity of history and those whose primary concern lay in discerning history's sacred meaning.[23]

As with the liturgical services in honor of the Kazan icon, the *akathistos* hymn offered relatively little for personal spiritual reflection. As a hymn primarily of thanksgiving and praise, it contained only brief allusions to Mary's "mindful attention" to the condition of human souls. The *akathistos* hymn remained focused on the collective "we" and the celebration of those events that helped protect that "we" from destruction.

Drawing on the work of Susanne Langer, the anthropologist Stanley Tambiah has argued that ritual can be viewed not so much as a "free expression of emotions" than as a "disciplined rehearsal of right attitudes."[24] Seen from this perspective, the liturgical celebrations in honor of the Kazan icon provided an annual occasion for Russia's Orthodox urban and rural worshiping communities to recollect and reaffirm the roles of Mary and her icon in salvation history. In this sense, liturgy helped to impart meaning to and sustain the life of an icon. The introduction of an *akathistos* hymn to honor the Kazan icon, in particular, modernized, to some extent, the centuries-old liturgical celebration of that icon. Although repeating, in refrain, Mary's role as "helper of the Christian race," the hymn refocused attention away from the broader scheme of sacred history—from creation to the end of time—to Russia's role in that history. Focusing on Mary as a "defense for the Russian Church, the bulwark and glory of its hierarchy and the strengthening of the Orthodox faithful against every foe," the *akathistos* hymn infused a national sensibility into its liturgical rehearsal of "right attitude" toward Mary and her icon.

The Homily and the Kazan Icon: Retelling the Story

Although an ancient Christian practice, preaching became a subject of renewed interest and debate among Russia's Orthodox clergy during the second half of the nineteenth century. Many churchmen became aware of the need to modernize their preaching and to balance contemporary social and political interests of their flock with their main concern as pastors—namely, salvation of souls.[25] Many churchmen also became more aware of the potential power that the homily offered as a form of mass communication. With more than forty thousand churches within the Russian Empire at the beginning of the twentieth century, the collective voice of pastors held the potential, at least, to be heard.[26] Sermons were a means by which clergy could help sustain memories, values, and beliefs that they considered central to the Orthodox faith in a modern age.

The second half of the nineteenth century also saw a proliferation of published homilies. While sermons of well-known bishops and priests found their way into publication in the eighteenth and early nineteenth century, published sermons were part of a general publications boom of Orthodox religious and devotional literature that began in the 1860s. Homilies, "words" (*slova*), and more informal "discussions" (*besedy*), often penned by less prominent churchmen, filled newly founded religious journals and diocesan newspapers. They also began appearing in record numbers in published collections of sermons. The trend in publication helped to bring the sermon from a geographically and confessionally limited "listening" and believing audience into the broader sphere of a reading public. An unbeliever with an eye for polemics might have read printed homilies just as easily as a fellow priest might have read them while searching for inspiration for his own sermons. Historians may wonder about the relationship between the published and spoken sermon and about the differences in the experience of both;[27] yet, as words in honor of the Kazan icon of the Mother of God, they both became part of that icon's culture.

While recognizing the potential that preaching in Russia held, some churchmen also criticized the general lack of creativity and modern appeal of many late nineteenth- and early twentieth-century sermons. In 1879 Nikolai Barsov, professor of pastoral theology and homiletics at the St. Petersburg Theological Academy, for instance, maintained that sermons in Russia were remarkably impersonal and uniform—"as soldiers lined up in file"—and suffered from a general lack of character.[28] We might conclude that, as a storytelling medium, the sermon in modern Russia was ineffectual. Such a conclusion, however, would be shortsighted not only because such a sweeping generalization cannot be substantiated but, more important, because it misunderstands the place and role of the sermon in Russia's Orthodox liturgical culture. Many clergy understood divine services as a timeless journey in which the presiding priest led the faithful to a meeting between humans and the divine, much like Moses led his people to Sinai. Sermons, on the other hand, as one priest reminded his readers in 1904, were neither sacramental in nature nor an essential part of liturgy. Moreover, he maintained that the priest as preacher was not a vessel of God comparable to the prophets.[29] The priest's purpose, according to this view, was to cultivate believers' ability to make the liturgical journey and to enlighten them regarding their faith.

Seen in this light, sermons in late-nineteenth-century Russia shared with liturgy the feature of having formal, traditional, and anticipated patterns, suggesting that sermons, too, were often ritual-like. It would not have been uncommon, for instance, for a sermon delivered in one diocese on the occasion of the feast of the Kazan icon to be similar to those delivered by priests in other dioceses, not only that same year but in years past. With respect to the framing of the Kazan icon, such shared narratives within churches throughout the Russian Empire helped to focus and offer coherence to otherwise potentially disparate personal attitudes, imaginings, and sensibilities associated with the icon.

Finally, we might also remember that, as a genre, sermons were not necessarily exclusively "official" in their tenor. Although intended as prescriptive texts that edified and directed believers' thoughts and sensibilities, sermons likely also drew upon and resonated with emotions, associations, and stories known and held by believers. Priests and bishops, after all, were also a part of the believing community and shared many of the same sentiments and sensibilities as their parishioners.[30] Some Orthodox clergy thought about the sacred words of liturgy in this manner as well. They understood liturgical texts as having given form to sensibilities that were already present among the laity, although only in the form of "vague intuitions." The view of liturgy and sermons as expressing feelings and views shared by laity and clergy alike precludes approaching them in terms of unilaterally clerical or exclusively institutional narratives.

From among the more than three hundred sermons in honor of the Kazan icon that I have read, more sermons and talks, not surprisingly, were published for the 22 October feast than for the 8 July feast, given that the former was a national holiday. That does not mean that more clergy delivered sermons on that day. It simply means that we have more opportunity to learn about how clergy presented that icon in relation to the Time of Troubles than with respect to the annexation of Kazan, although clergy frequently discussed both episodes on each of the icon's feast days.

Homilies offered clergy the occasion to expand upon those stories recalled during the feast's liturgical services (including its *akathistos* hymn) or to introduce other ones associated more directly with the scriptural readings for the day. It is not surprising, therefore, that some churchmen spoke not at all about the Kazan icon but about the Gospel readings for this feast: Mary's visitation to Elizabeth as told in the Gospel According to Luke (1: 39–49, 56) and Christ's visit to the home of the two sisters, Martha and Mary (Lk: 10: 38–42; 11: 27–28). When commenting on these texts, churchmen tended to focus on Mary as a model of human salvation and on the spiritual types of Martha and Mary.

In the majority of cases for both the 8 July feast and the 22 October feast, however, clergy retold the two major episodes in the Kazan icon's life. In this sense, they followed the spirit of the *akathistos* hymn. "I think that first I should tell you the history of the appearance of the miracle-working icon of the Mother of God in the city of Kazan, although this event is remembered not today but on 8 July." With this, the priest Grigorii D'iachenko in 1898 began a model discussion for the feast of 22 October.[31] The recounting of these events offered churchmen an occasion to associate Mary and her icon with history and thereby stir their listeners' historical imaginations.

Sermons consistently cultivated an association between history, memory, and Marian icons. Icons of the Mother of God were carriers of collective memories that, as one priest said, were central to history and therefore necessary to remember.[32] Thus the feast of the Kazan icon was a "sacred celebration of memory,"[33] a day that offered a "live stimulus to remember reverentially."[34] The need to remember applied not only to the past but also to the present. Clergymen urged their audience to contemplate the past as preserved through stories associated with the Kazan icon in order to secure a proper discernment and reading of present events.[35] The icon in this sense offered "useful memories."[36] In order to tap these memories, the priest Mikhail Klichanskii urged his listeners to "carry themselves in their thoughts" back to the Time of Troubles.[37]

Proper veneration of the icon in churchmen's minds therefore carried a historical dimension: it involved not only an awareness of the "presence" of the prototype depicted on the icon and meditation on the broader Christian narrative but also reflection on the various ways the image had been involved in the corporate life of a people. Accordingly, the icon of the Mother of God carried a believer's "imaginative gaze" upward, beyond this world, and also focused that gaze in time.[38] The feast offered an occasion when thoughts could be carried back in time in order to investigate "thoroughly with the mind and heart" the lessons history offered. As a priest from the Astrakhan diocese noted in 1904, the feast of the Kazan icon called for the faithful to exercise their "mind's eye" with regard to the past.[39] Another referred to the exercise of memory associated with this feast as "awakening us from our forgetfulness."[40]

By closely associating Mary's image with the movement and meaning of history, churchmen enunciated a view of history that differed somewhat from the more classical versions of Christian philosophies of history. Traditional Christian readings of history sought meaning in divine providence, usually thought of as ordered by God the Father and Christ the Incarnate Son. In modern Russia, in contrast, Orthodox believers often also added the image of Mary to the forefront of events.[41] Marian icon stories, for instance, conceived of history not simply in terms of a covenantal relationship between God and humans but also as a working relationship with Mary. Preachers traced this relationship back to Mary's adoption of the disciple John at the foot of the Cross and interpreted John as symbolizing the entire human race.[42] In her role as overseer of history, clergy spoke of Mary as a woman and mother with "holy audacity" and "maternal boldness"—as one who ceaselessly pursued her spiritual intuitions regarding humanity and its fate.[43]

Preaching the Kazan Icon: Russia, Russians, and the Religious Other

Preachers regarded Mary as the spiritual mother of all humanity and, as a result, recognized her role in the lives of all Christian peoples.[44] Nevertheless, they attributed Russia's "chosenness" to a special relationship with Mary: "We Russians find ourselves under her special protection and defense," stated Bishop Makarii of Viatka in 1885.[45] In 1911 the priest A. Antoninov confirmed this sentiment when he stated, "Russia is a place chosen by her preferentially from all lands of the earth for her . . . sojourn in the world."[46] Some clergy maintained that this special relationship developed at the time of the baptism of Rus' in the late tenth century. "The Mother of God chose Rus' from its very cradle as her inheritance, and preserves, protects, and raises it among all nations and kingdoms and peoples," explained the priest Ioann Sabinin from the Tver diocese in 1893.[47] Some twenty years earlier, in 1870, Bishop Antonii of Perm went so far as to state that Russia, with its acceptance of Christianity, received a "special right" to Mary's protection.[48] Churchmen indicated as proof of this "chosenness" the multitude of specially revered icons of Mary and countless stories of her "workings" that could be found in most Russian villages, towns, or cities.[49] Clergy directly linked the course of Russia's history with Mary, referring to the history of Russia as a "chronicle of miracles manifested by the Mother of God."[50] Such beliefs about Mary's close connection to Russia's history led one priest to maintain in 1899 that, were it not for Mary, Russia's history might have followed a completely different course.[51]

The theme of the collective destiny of Orthodox Christians in Russia and of Russia itself was a favored theme in sermons. In addressing this topic, churchmen attempted to turn believers away from seeing themselves as isolated individuals standing before an icon of the Mother of God to viewing themselves as part of a sacred body. Homilies worked to open the private and highly personal devotional gaze to an additional communal dimension of veneration. In doing so, they attempted to connect personal fates to the fates of others standing before her image.[52]

The underlying assumption in the sermons of many clergy (although few articulated it explicitly) was that God related to peoples and to nations in much the same way that He connected to individuals. One sermon explained that "a people, like an individual, was a type of moral person (*lichnost'*) and every people was destined to realize its moral tasks."[53] On a related note, the well-known conservative priest Ioann Vostorgov wrote, in 1894, that for each people, God appointed a certain place to live, a time to act, and a task to fulfill for the good of the world.[54] Accordingly, in contrast to liturgical hymns that spoke of Mary and her icon in terms of salvation history broadly understood, sermons in honor of the Kazan icon were similar to its *akathistos* hymn in that they typically situated both the icon and Mary more specifically in the context of Russia's history. This feast, as another priest noted in 1908, "calls forth thoughts of the fate of our fatherland and the relationship of divine providence to it."[55]

The themes of divine providence and the workings of peoples and nations echoed ideas found in Orthodox dogmatic textbooks. Such textbooks occasionally had sections devoted to the relationship between divine providence and "kingdoms and peoples." Fr. N. Malinovskii, dean of the Podolsk and later the Vologda diocesan seminary and author of a dogmatic theological textbook, found inspiration for his thought on the role of various peoples in God's divine plan in the Book of Acts, 17: 26–27:

> From one ancestor God made all nations to inhabit the whole earth, and He allotted the times of their existence and the boundaries of the places where they would live, so that they would search for God and perhaps grope for Him and find Him.

Fr. Malinovskii explained that God guided not only individuals but also entire societies, since the perfection and well-being of each person depended in part on his or her social surroundings. He referred to an ongoing divine census, of sorts, by which every newborn person is registered within the nation or people (*narod*) in which he is born. To each people, Malinovskii maintained, God had appointed its time and its own place on earth, the limits of its existence and multiplication, and the degree of its prosperity. Every people had its own will that guided it to a particular goal, which was distinct from the goals of other peoples. Despite these differing goals, however, within the general flow of world events one could perceive a single, unified will guiding matters to a single end.[56]

The idea of Russia's special role in the plan of divine providence and the "sacred feelings for the homeland" that such a notion cultivated found increasing criticism among Russia's educated circles at the end of the nineteenth century, partly because of the influence of Leo Tolstoy's writings on the subject of patriotism.[57] In 1909 the priest N. P. from the Perm diocese apparently met enough resistance to the notion of patriotism that he felt compelled to justify the notion of "love for the homeland" as a Christian sensibility, and one that did not in and of itself sow discord among peoples and nations. Patriotism, he claimed, was a "great spiritual force" in the life of every people that enabled them to attain goals for the general welfare of all. N. P. emphatically denied that love for one's native land contradicted the teachings of Christ. If a person loved his or her parents more than mere acquaintances, he asked rhetorically, did this mean that this love contradicted the teachings of Christ? The love of one's parents, he maintained, did not preclude the love of others. Moreover, Christ's teaching on love toward all humans did not prescribe an undifferentiated, equal love of all. Thus love for one's homeland and for one's own people did not preclude the possibility of love or respect for other nations and peoples.

N. P. based his reasoning on the example Christ himself set. He argued that Christ displayed special feelings toward his inner circle of disciples and, among these, toward his beloved disciple, John. Furthermore, Christ loved his own Jewish people and bemoaned the fate of their land, Jerusalem. Nevertheless, such displays of special devotion toward close ones and toward one's native land did not undermine or lessen Christ's teaching about love for one's neighbor. Accordingly, N. P. maintained, the apostle Paul could insist on both the following principles: "there is no longer Jew or Greek . . . for all are one in Christ Jesus" (Gal 3:28) *and* "Whosoever does not provide for relatives, and especially for family members, has denied the faith and is worse than an unbeliever" (1 Tim 5:8).[58]

Sermons for the feasts of the Kazan icon inspired thoughts not only about Mary and Russia, but also about the religious Other. The subject of Russia and the religious Other arose in the consideration of Mary's involvement with Russia on two fronts—the East, where Russia and Orthodoxy met Islam, and the West, where Russia and Orthodoxy met Catholicism and Protestantism. The story of the Kazan icon, especially in relation to the Kazan region, inspired priests to speak about Orthodox missionary efforts and the religious conversion of non-Russian peoples at the eastern frontiers. According to the story of the finding of the icon, Orthodox Christians who lived in this region were a minority and their faith gradually weakened in the face of the Islamic majority.[59] The annexation of Kazan, therefore, according to late imperial preachers, pertained not only to the struggle between two long-time neighboring enemies but to a "war of faiths" as well.[60]

Nineteenth- and early-twentieth-century priests presented the finding of the icon as an appearance of Mary to a fledging group of Christians in an alien land. As the priest Vasilii Mikhailovskii stated in 1893, the icon was a divine means of enlivening the faith among the newly converted Muslims in the Kazan lands.[61] Moreover, its discovery confirmed that the annexation of this territory by Tsar Ivan IV had been an act pleasing to God. As one priest from the Smolensk diocese stated in 1876, "the Mother of God wrestled Kazan from the hands of the impious and handed it the Orthodox kingdom of Russians."[62] In 1891 the bishop of Kazan, Pavel, maintained that the Mother of God gave this icon as a reminder of the destiny of Christianity in Russia: it was ordained that it should enlighten the "dark region of Islam and paganism" with the light of Christian truth.[63]

The character of the sermons for the national celebration of the Kazan icon on 22 October was somewhat different from that for the 8 July feast. Whereas discourse about the Kazan icon concerning Russia's eastern regions had an expansionist tone, the discourse had a more protective emphasis when speaking about the icon's role vis-à-vis the West. The feast of 22 October commemorated the Russian victory over the Poles and Swedes during the Time of Troubles and the establishment of the Romanov dynasty. It was a period when everything was "falling, collapsing, and perishing."[64] Churchmen depicted the struggle not merely as a political one in which Russia almost lost its independence to "uninvited guests" [the Poles]. They presented it as an inter-confessional contest as well, between the Orthodox on one side and the Protestant Swedes and Catholic Poles on the other.[65] It was a time when both the Russian state and the Orthodox Church faced the question "to be or not to be."[66]

Sermons maintained that Poles had sought Russia's spiritual subjugation along with its political destruction. The priest P. Vinogradov described the Time of Troubles as a period of "evil plundering by Western heretics" who desired to lead the Orthodox into the "delusion" of "Latinism."[67] The main aggressors were the "Papists" and "Jesuits," whom Orthodox clergy depicted as the "inveterate enemies of Orthodoxy" who had never abandoned their hopes to Catholicize the Orthodox East and who thereby guided the Poles in their actions.[68] Clergy maintained that the Time of Troubles was a darker period in Russia's history than the Tatar yoke, since, in their view, during the Tatar yoke no one "touched the most valuable of our holy things, the Orthodox faith."[69] From the clergy's point of view, the feast of the Kazan icon was, above all, a spiritual independence day that celebrated the self-determination of Orthodoxy and its preservation from foreign influence. It marked the Church's securing of "the purity of its faith and its ancient traditions" from the "evil trickery of Western heretics, who desired to subject Orthodoxy to another faith."[70]

Rhetoric that combined the memory of Mary, her icon, and notions of sacred history with direct references to the Islamic East and the Christian West might suggest at first glance that Russian Orthodox churchmen promoted an association between the Kazan icon of the Mother of God and a sense of Russian national superiority. That generally was not the case, however. Many clergymen saw the icon's story speaking as much to Russian Orthodox peoples as to the "newly converted." Sermons generally did not associate the icon's appearance with any supposed intrinsic superiority or virtue of the Russian people. Taking his cue from the Gospel reading of the day, the priest I. Leporinskii from the Kazan diocese compared the Virgin Mary's visitation to her kinswoman Elizabeth with Mary's visitation (through her icon) to the Kazan lands. By her visitation, Mary "opened the eyes of their hearts to a vision of truth, and poured forth the joyful light of faith from the newly enlightened city onto our entire land." Yet, unlike Elizabeth who had been worthy of Mary's visit, Leporinskii explained, Russians had not been. Russians, no less than their Islamic counterparts, were living in darkness; the light shown by the icon was meant to enlighten them as much as anyone else.[71] Thus, although *Russia* as such might have been seen as destined to "guard Orthodoxy in the world and to attract all peoples to it," clergymen warned that not all *Russians* were living up to their collective task or were worthy of such divine blessings.[72]

From this perspective, Russians enjoyed no "ethnic election." Their "chosenness" depended not on their "Russianness" but on the extent to which they were faithful Orthodox Christians. Thus, although some clergy spoke of the feast as a "twofold sacred day for every truly Russian person"—both a "spiritual celebration" and a "great national holiday"—the two aspects of the feast, according to their own logic, were inseparable.[73] To be genuinely Russian and to reap the benefits of Mary's protection as a Russian meant to be a committed Orthodox Christian. According to Fr. Michael Zelenev from the Tambov diocese in 1890, Orthodoxy was the basis on which Russian ethnic identity was determined. He maintained that Orthodoxy "transformed the Tatar and any other foreigner (*inorodets*) into a Russian in soul and heart," while the abandonment of the faith transformed "a Russian into a non-Russian, if not into an enemy of the homeland."[74] The Kazan icon was supposed to remind believers of that association.

Clergy spoke at even greater length about the faults with Russia and Russians in their sermons for the feast of 22 October. Although Poles and Swedes, in their view, may have caused turmoil and taken advantage of Russia's situation, they were not the ones directly responsible for Russia's fate. Clergymen placed this blame on Russians themselves. As the priest Porfirii Alekseevskii from the Moscow diocese noted in 1916, "it was as if 'our own' united with foreigners on purpose in order to torture and torment Rus' until the end."[75] Thus Russia's clergymen interpreted the Time of Troubles as a period when God had manifested His righteous indignation with the Russian people, namely, with those at the political helm.[76] "Traitors of the fatherland," stated a priest in 1891, "forgot their Orthodox faith and their honor and valor as Russians, and greeted the enemy with bread and salt."[77]

Prompted by the Kazan image to recall their ancestors' demeanor in difficult times, nineteenth- and early-twentieth-century preachers frequently brought the icon's story to bear on contemporary domestic and foreign events such as the Polish Uprising of 1863, the war with the Ottoman Empire in 1877–1878, and the assassination of Tsar Alexander II in 1881. From their perspective, the icon's story offered lessons for overcoming seemingly hopeless situations. They told the story not only to galvanize a sense of corporate strength and responsibility but also to inspire collective self-improvement. Churchmen repeatedly emphasized several lessons. First, they accentuated the power of unity: Russians defeated the foreign aggressor because they stood as "one person."[78] In 1896 the bishop of Kharkov, Amvrosii, pointed to the story's two heroes—the leaders of the militia, Kuzma Minin and Dimitrii Pozharskii, the common person and the prince, respectively—as symbols of solidarity among diverse peoples.[79] The unity their ancestors had shown was a "sacred unity" facilitated by a common Orthodox faith: "the Orthodox faith inspired the hearts of the Russian people and raised all of Rus' as one person."[80] In the beginning of the twentieth century certain priests saw unity threatened not only by the decree of religious tolera-tion, and the open religious pluralism that was developing, but also by what appeared to them as indifference to these changes on the part of the faithful.[81]

Second, clergy combined their discussions of patriotism with that of prayer. They looked to the story of the Kazan icon, in particular, in order to offer thoughts on the proper posture and frame of mind demanded from a people who hoped for divine protection. In this context, homiletic "sacred rhetoric" sometimes sounded like a form of Russian Orthodox civil religion. Clergy, for instance, often recounted the words attributed to Kuzma Minin when he heeded the call to rally for Moscow: "Our native land is perishing; the time has come to stand for the faith and for Russia! Let us gather, old and young . . . Let us sell our homes, pawn [*zalozhit'*] our wives and our children, and redeem the father-land!"[82] Clergymen portrayed Minin as the embodiment of heroism. They found his call for self-sacrifice for the homeland especially appealing in times of acute domestic hardship such as the famine that distressed central Russia in 1891.[83]

Dedication to and self-sacrifice for the homeland, however, were not enough to guarantee its well-being. Clergy routinely underscored, for instance, the sto-ry's detail of a three-day period of prayer and fasting by the militia and believers in and around Moscow.[84] Churchmen reminded their listeners that it was only after this collective act of purification that a change occurred in the way events unfolded.[85] Ultimately, in their view, neither military might nor political power was responsible for Russia's victory. The deciding factor, they insisted, was the simple faith of their ancestors.[86] In focusing on this particular detail, clergy urged their listeners to fall in line with their ancestors and to look to them for a standard of what amounted to an Orthodox-based civic piety.[87] Gazing at the Kazan icon, in this context, meant being strengthened and inspired by a per-ceived collective heroism of a generation past whose own plights were imagined as equally if not more difficult than those of contemporary viewers.

The telling of the Kazan icon story entered a new phase in June 1904, when the icon was stolen from Kazan. From then on, few sermons failed to mention this event or to offer some interpretation or lesson learned. Although rumors spread about the identity of those involved in the crime, with some

Russians apparently even considering Japanese involvement as a way of bringing about domestic unrest during wartime, clergy as a rule looked to Russia and to Russians and spoke in terms of collective responsibility.[88] They depicted the incident in a dismal light, as an omen that God and Mary had rescinded their protection of Russia, had turned their faces from it, especially regarding its eastern fronts.[89] In Kazan itself, newspapers reported a pervasive sense of abandonment amid the population.[90] The priest Aleksandr Zelenetskii claimed that the theft signified Russia's current "time of troubles," and testified to God's righteous indignation with his people for their deviation from the true way of life.[91] Fr. Ioann Vostorgov saw the event as a sign that Russia was failing in its messianic mission, primarily because of the people's (*narod*) inability to live up to it. In his view, the light of Christianity was fading among the Russian people themselves, as demonstrated by the fact that the theft of the Kazan icon had not led to a "nationwide outcry."[92] Reflecting back on other incidents in sacred history—especially to the story of the Ark of the Covenant and its capture from the midst of Israel (1 Samuel 4: 21–5: 3; 2 Kings 24)—clergy maintained that God did not spare holy items in his indignation; he allowed the icon to be stolen because of the collective sins of the Russian people.[93]

While delivered within the broader, liturgical context of the Christian meta-narrative of human redemption, sermons in honor of the Kazan icon tended to shift believers attention from the universal to the particular regarding human history. Sermons recalled the stories associated with this particular icon, in contrast to the power of Mary's image in general, and in so doing informed the personal, religious act of seeing with national, collective sensibilities. The Kazan icon, in this sense, was not only an Orthodox icon in the traditional sense—one that testified to the Incarnation and its implications for understandings of body and matter—but also an evolving national icon that gave believers a way to make sense of their collective task and fate as Orthodox Christians and Russian citizens. While meant to elicit feelings of thanksgiving and hope, sermons also sounded a note of caution. The story of the Kazan icon was not a story of divine control or manifest destiny in which the individual believer had little role to play. Clergy tied notions of divine protection of the nation to human cooperation. To address this aspect of the Kazan story, preachers turned to the topic of the individual.

The Kazan Icon: Appeals to the Individual

Although sermons spoke about Mary's involvement in the destiny of Russia, they also noted that her activity was even more notable regarding individuals.[94] Unlike the liturgical services and the *akathistos* hymn, sermons often more directly addressed matters of the heart and soul. Such interest in the individual was partly driven by the idea that the collective fate of Russia depended on the development of virtues in each of its inhabitants. Clergy reminded believers that they could not count collectively on her unconditional aid; Mary saved only the good and the God-fearing from calamity.[95] On other occasions Mary's role concerning Russia went unmentioned, as clergymen focused their thoughts entirely on the relationship between Mary and the individual.

Just as there was a storyline for the relationship between Mary, Russia, and Orthodox Christians, so, too, was there a narrative that directed the individual's relationship with Mary. In explaining the Mother of God's perceived aid to individuals, clergy drew on principles traditionally related to the veneration of icons and reiterated themes found in the liturgical hymns for this feast. In 1891 the bishop of Kazan, Pavel, explained that the Mother of God offered her icon as a pledge of her love to humans and as a sign of her vow to intercede for Christians. Clergy described her icons as acting like a "second conscience" since they reminded each believer of his or her duty to imitate the qualities of Mary.[96] Churchmen maintained that, for those who exercised their "eyes of faith" before an icon of Mary, the icon would be a sign of Mary's "palpable presence" and would enable believers to relate directly to her.[97] Such a relationship, clergymen maintained, could help order a believer's thoughts and sensibilities, and raise a person's awareness to a new level.[98]

In presenting the virtues and ideals for which believers should strive, preachers pointed to two models. Above all, they turned to Mary, the Theotokos: "Gazing reverentially at the icon of the Mother of God, let us remember the virtues with which she was adorned."[99] Such virtues included the expected steadfast faith, humility, chastity, and an "unquenchable love of God."[100] Preachers seemed aware that some of their listeners might regard such virtues as passive or weak in an age of modernization. Yet they defended them as active and powerful forces in their own right. Evil, one priest noted, could be defeated only by humility, as the "evil one," too, was an intelligent activist who could match ascetics in their capacity to fast and not sleep. Only humility and meekness remained beyond his grasp.[101] Clergy also turned to another Mary, the sister of Lazarus, who was mentioned along with her sister, Martha, in the Gospel reading for the feast of the Kazan icon (Lk: 10: 38–42; 11: 27–28). In these sermons churchmen emphasized the importance of priorities and prayer in the ordering of human life. Fr. Dimitrii Kastal'skii maintained that, without careful and sober scrutiny of commitments and goals, individuals, in their daily strivings, might overwhelm themselves and those around them with anxieties that ultimately destroy the spirit.[102]

The subject of prayer found its place in sermons inspired by both the Mother of God and Mary, the sister of Lazarus. A priest from Tambov Province,

Andrei Flegmatov, identified prayer, along with the change of heart and mind accompanying it, as the main lesson of the Kazan icon's feast.[103] Only prayer could transform the individual. It brought the individual before the face of God, whom clergy identified with light and life. It ordered human thought and changed the quality of its content.[104] Only through prayer could the human soul achieve genuine greatness and glory, despite human destitution.[105] Thus, without prayer, believers could not expect aid from Mary.[106] In 1897 Bishop Vladimir of Orenburg maintained that prayer before Marian icons actually drew Mary to the icon. Mary saw, as it were, the "zealous and diligent prayers" of believers and, in turn, drew closer to them. Her perceived presence, in his estimation, largely depended on the disposition of those who gazed upon her icon.[107]

A figure sermons often glaringly neglected as a model was Matrona, the young child who reportedly found the Kazan icon initially. Although she was a central figure in the early life of the icon, many clergymen failed to mention her by name in their retelling of the story. When they did mention her, they sometimes omitted the significant detail that both ecclesiastical and civil officials at first dismissed her experiences and that only through her own perseverance was the icon discovered. It is difficult to imagine that such oversight was not deliberate; Matrona, after all, confounded the institutional authority of the Church. When clergymen did choose to single her out as a figure to emulate, they focused on her purity: God chose to reveal his help through her, because in her purity she was transparent to the workings of the Spirit.[108] Strikingly absent was the recognition of Matrona's boldness and perseverance in the face of "the establishment." Although the icon story preserved these character traits in the historical memory of the Church, their valuation would largely be left to lay members of the community.

***

The art historian David Morgan has recently reminded us of the reciprocity between language and perception in human consciousness. "Language and vision, word and image," he writes, "are deeply enmeshed and collaborate powerfully in assembling our sense of the real."[109] This synthetic view applies aptly to liturgy and the icon in Russia's religious culture. Twice annually the Kazan icon in late imperial Russia enjoyed public liturgical services and special homilies in its honor throughout the empire. Through chant, hymn, and speech, liturgy and homily contributed to scripting believers' gazes by associating Mary's image with particular ideas about the nature of history and Russia's role in that history; with distinct attitudes toward one's "own" and the "other"; with insights into the workings of the individual's soul (at least in the case of sermons); and with emotions and patterns of behavior deemed proper with respect to God, homeland, self, and other. Liturgical texts and homiletic words, however, did not form a static or monochromatic fixture around the Kazan icon. Their effects were dynamic and combined with numerous other factors in conditioning what believers might have sensed and apprehended in gazing at the Kazan icon.

The Kazan icon remained a highly revered, living image throughout the late imperial period. Evgenii Poselianin, one of Russia's most well-known catalogers of miracle-working icons, lists more than sixty-five copies of the Kazan icon that were specially revered throughout the Russian Empire at the end of the nineteenth and beginning of the twentieth century. By all accounts, many others never found their way into an ecclesiastical or ethnographic record. Believers' associations, with their local or personal image of the Kazan icon, may have had little to do with discourse about the Islamic East or Christian West; as public and private images, these icons were involved in their own local stories, most of which spoke to values and issues not directly connected with the fate of the nation. Yet the more general themes alluded to by the national services in honor of the Kazan icon and sermons on the 8 July and 22 October—Mary's role in history, Mary's presence through her icon, and the power she had to influence individual lives—were ones confirmed by the stories of people's own local and personal icons. Thus the experiences with their own copies of the Kazan icon, or even with another icon of the Mother of God, may well have enhanced believers' identification with the stories of Russia's collective past when gazing upon a Kazan icon.

In many ways the story of the Kazan icon and the sermons it inspired cultivated what Anthony D. Smith has called the "deeper cultural resources" and "sacred foundations" from which future generations might draw their own interpretations of Russia's past and present.[110] The belief in being sacredly chosen, the sense of belonging to a homeland regarded as somehow sacred, the value of communal and individual self-sacrifice for the welfare of the homeland, and a desire to recover the spirit of an age past that displayed particular communal heroism—each of these themes that Smith emphasizes in the development and sustenance of a sense of national identity were found in these sermons.

One final point is worth considering. In her book on the precious decorations of ancient Russian icons, between the eleventh and the fourteen centuries, I. A. Sterligova has shown that, in medieval Russia, an icon and the precious decorations frequently adorning it (such as gemstones, strands of beads, or coverings of precious metals) were considered an organic whole and were viewed as such by believers. Beginning in the eighteenth century, that understanding started to shift and churchmen frequently considered the two separately, seeing the embellishments as mere additions superfluous to the icon's genuine meaning.

By the nineteenth century, some educated believers such as Prince Eugene Trubetskoi, author of the well-known *Theology in Color,* viewed the encasings *(rizas)* that covered many icons as "imprisoning" them and hiding their spiritual meaning.[111] Others, however, such as the philosopher V. V. Rozanov, the theologian Fr. Pavel Florenskii, and the writer Ivan Bunin, appreciated the precious items with which believers decorated the icons and viewed them positively as an aspect of a holistic sacred visual experience.[112] If the sacred stories communicated by liturgical services, prayers, and homilies provided their own type of frame for the Kazan icon of the Mother of God, did believers, both clergy and laity, recognize them as an essential complement of the Kazan image, or did some view them as distracting accretions to a more authentic iconic message? In either case, these stories contributed to defining the Kazan icon as a sacred national symbol not only in prerevolutionary Russia but, as evidence suggests, in communist times as well. The extent to which these same narratives might influence the believers' gaze in postcommunist Russia or the ways that they might be transformed or renewed, especially in the context of civil society, remains to be seen. Russia's most recently instituted civil holiday—the Day of National Unity—falls on the feast of the Kazan icon (22 October/4 November) and thereby introduces yet another chapter in the icon's life.

Notes

This essay is part of a larger forthcoming study on Mary in modern Russia. I thank the National Council on Eurasian and East European Research, under the authority of a Title VIII grant from the U.S. Department of State, as well as the Mellon Foundation, for supporting the research that made this essay possible. It goes without saying that the views expressed here are my own and not those of any of these organizations and agencies.

Abbreviations

ArEV	*Arkhangel'skiia eparkhial'nyia vedomosti*
AsEV	*Astrakhanskiia eparkhial'nyia vedomosti*
BEV	*Blagoveshchenskiia eparkhial'nyia vedomosti*
DEV	*Donskiia eparkhial'nyia vedomosti*
DCh	*Dushepoleznoe chtenie*
EkEV	*Ekaterinburgskiia eparkhial'nyia vedomosti*
EnEV	*Eniseiskiia eparkhial'nyia vedomosti*
IaEV	*Iaroslavskiia eparkhial'nyia vedomosti*
IKE	*Izvestiia Kazanskoi eparkhii*

KavEV	*Kavkazskiia eparkhial'nyia vedomosti*
KazEV	*Kazanskiia eparkhial'nyia vedomosti*
KhEV	*Khersonskiia eparkhial'nyia vedomosti*
KEV	*Kievskiia eparkhial'nyia vedomosti*
MEV	*Moskovskiia eparkhial'nyia vedomosti*
MTsV	*Moskovskiia tserkovnyia vedomosti*
NEV	*Nizhegorodskiia eparkhial'nyia vedomosti*
NovEV	*Novgorodskiia eparkhial'nyia vedomosti*
OEV	*Orenburgskiia eparkhial'nyia vedomosti*
PEV	*Permskiia eparkhial'nyia vedomosti*
PodEV	*Podol'skiia eparkhial'nyia vedomosti*
PTEV	*Pribavleniia k Tulskim eparkhial'nym vedomostiam*
PTsV	*Pribavleniia k tserkovnym vedomostiam*
REV	*Riazanskiia eparkhial'nyia vedomosti*
SEV	*Saratovskiia eparkhial'nyia vedomosti*
SmEV	*Smolenskiia eparkhial'nyia vedomosti*
StEV	*Stavropolskiia eparkhial'nyia vedomosti*
TEV	*Tambovskiia eparkhial'nyia vedomosti*
TavEV	*Tavricheskiia eparkhial'nyia vedomosti*
TTsOV	*Tavricheskii tserkovno-obshchestvennyi vestnik*
TobEV	*Tobol'skiia eparkhial'nyia vedomosti*
TvEV	*Tverskiia eparkhial'nyia vedomosti*
UEV	*Ufimskiia eparkhial'nyia vedomosti*
VEV	*Viatskiia eparkhial'nyia vedomosti*
VCh	*Voskresnoe chtenie*
VD	*Voskresnyi den'*
VolEV	*Volynskiia eparkhial'nyia vedomosti*
VorEV	*Voronezhskiia eparkhial'nyia vedomosti*

1. "Prazdnik Kazanskoi ikony Bozhiei Materi," *Bozhiia Niva: Sbornik pouchenii na ves' god,* comp. Sv. M. Menstrov (St. Petersburg, 1910), 482–88. For an exposition of the "imaginative gaze" of the Orthodox believer with respect to icons, see Nicholas Constas, "Icons and Imagination," *Logos* 1, no. 1 (1997).

2. Examples of recent studies of religion and visual culture include David Morgan, *The Sacred Gaze: Religious Visual Culture in Theory and Practice* (Berkeley, Calif., 2005); S. Brent Plate, ed., *Religion, Art, and Visual Culture: A Cross-Cultural Reader* (New York, 2002); David Morgan, *Visual Piety: A History and Theory of Popular Religious Images* (Berkeley, Calif., 1998); David Freedberg, *The Power of Images: Studies in the History and Theory of Response* (Chicago, 1989); Margaret Miles, *Image as Insight: Visual Understanding in Western Christianity and Secular Culture* (Boston, 1985).

3. Miles, *Image as Insight,* 8–9.

4. For the notion of "life-world" related to liturgy, see Catherine Pickstock, "Liturgy, Art, and Politics," *Modern Theology* 16, no. 2 (April 2000): 160.

5. For the notion of "sacred rhetoric," see John Corrigan, ed., *Religion and Emotion: Approaches and Interpretations* (New York, 2004), 17.

6. For a discussion of icons of the Mother of God in Russia's Orthodox culture, see Vera Shevzov, *Russian Orthodoxy on the Eve of Revolution* (New York, 2004), 171–257.

7. For descriptions of some of these festivities, especially in Kazan, see "O prazdnovanii v gorode Kazani trekhsotletiia ot obreteniia chudotvornoi ikony Bozhiei Materi, imenuemoi Kazanskoiu," *IKE* 14 (1879): 396–405; "Prazdnovaniia 8-ogo iiulia 1885 goda v Kazanskom zhenskom pervoklassnom Bogoroditskom monastyre," *KavEV,* chast' neoffitsial'naia 18

(1885): 726–29; Ochevidets, "Prazdnik Kazanskoi Bozhiei Materi 8 iiulia v m. Kakhovke," *TTsOV* 22–23 (1915): 900–902.

8. "Povest' o chestnom i slavnom iavlenii obraza prechistoi Bogoroditsy v Kazani," *Patriarkh Ermogen: Zhizneopisanie, tvoreniia, istoricheskie predaniia, chudesa i proslavlenie* (Moscow, 1997), 41–58.

9. Nineteenth-century retellings of the story of the Kazan icon occasionally varied with respect to Matrona's age and the exact words Matrona heard from the Mother of God. For examples, see *Skazanie o iavlennoi Kazanskoi ikone Bozhiei Materi, byvshikh ot neia chudesakh, ustanovlenii povsemestnago prazdnovaniia ei v Rossii v 1649 g.* (Moscow, 1907); *Zhitiia sviatykh, na russkom iazyke izlozhennyia po rukovodstvu chet'ikh-minei sv. Dimitriia Rostovskago*, vol. 11 (Moscow, 1910), 184–87; S. V. Bulgakov, *Nastol'naia kniga dlia sviashchenno-tserkovno-sluzhitelei* (1913; reprint, Moscow, 1993), 253–54.

10. *Skazanie o iavlennoi Kazanskoi ikone Bozhiei Materi*, 25–27; Bulgakov, *Nastol'naia kniga*, 421.

11. Rossiiskii gosudarstvennyi istoricheskii arkhiv (hereafter, RGIA), f. 796, op. 79, d. 861.

12. Sv. M. Menstrov, "Prazdnik Kazanskoi ikony Bozhiei Materi," *VD* 42 (1908): 486.

13. I. V. Pozdeeva, "Sluzhba Kazanskoi ikone Bogoroditsy po Kazanskomu ekzempliaru izdaniia XVI veka," *Drevniaia Rus': Voprosy medievistiki* 1 (2002): 116–24. Citations are from the services for 8 July, *Miniia mesiats iiulii* (1893; reprint, Moscow, 1996), 151–72; and 22 October, *Miniia mesiats oktobrii* (1893), 161–69. The services are virtually identical. A translation of these texts by Isaac E. Lambertsen can be found in *The Kazan Icon of the Mother of God: History, Service, and Akathist Hymn* (Liberty, Tenn., 1988).

14. Catherine Pickstock, "Liturgy, Art, and Politics," 167; Russell A. Berman, "Creation and Culture: Introduction to 'Toward a Liturgical Critique of Modernity,'" *Telos* 113 (fall 1998): 3–11; Alexander Schmemann, "Worship in a Secular Age," *St. Vladimir's Theological Quarterly* 16, no. 1 (1972): 3–16.

15. Pickstock, "Liturgy, Art, and Politics," 163–64.

16. *Akathistoi* hymns belonged to the genre of liturgical music and services that developed from the original Byzantine *akathistos* in honor of the Mother of God. The precise dating and authorship of this hymn have been a matter of debate. See Vasiliki Limberis, *Divine Heiress: The Virgin Mary and the Creation of Christian Constantinople* (New York, 1994), 89–90.

17. Aleksei Popov, *Pravoslavnye russkie akafisty, izdannye s blagosloveniia Sviateishago Sinoda* (Kazan, 1903), 251–53.

18. Ibid., 425–44.

19. During the late nineteenth century the Holy Synod approved publication of *akathistoi* in honor of various icons of the Mother of God. For the most comprehensive study of *akathistoi* hymns in Russia, see ibid. For the depiction of the icon of the Mother of God in these hymns and for the criticism of the *akathistos* genre in the late nineteenth century, see Vera Shevzov, "Poeticizing Piety: The Icon of Mary in Russian Akathistoi Hymns," *St. Vladimir's Theological Quarterly* 44, nos. 3–4 (2000): 343–73.

20. Popov, *Pravoslavnye russkie akafisty*, 253.

21. *Akafist presviatyei Bogoroditse iavleniia radi chudotvornyia eia ikony Kazanskiia* (St. Petersburg, 1890).

22. *Akafist*, Kondak IV, Ikos V.

23. It was not uncommon for clergy to recall the Byzantine legacy of the Mother of God's aid to Orthodox Christians. See Diakon I. Bukharev, "Krestnyi khod v Moskve 22 oktiabria," *MEV* 43 (1969): 4–5; Sv. A. Zhukov, "Slovo v den' prazdnika Kazanskoi Bozhiei Materi (22 oktiabria)," in *Sbornik pouchenii na voskresnye i tabel'nye dni* (Pochaev, 1912), 41–42.

24. Stanley J. Tambiah, "A Performative Approach to Ritual," *Proceedings of the British Academy* 65 (1979): 125–26; Susanne K. Langer, *Philosophy in a New Key* (New York, 1951).

25.   Prot. Grigorii D'iachenko, *Propovednicheskaia entsiklopediia* (Moscow, 1903), viii. For a general review of the history of preaching in Russia, see I. K. Smolich, *Istoriia russkoi tserkvi, 1700–1917*, trans. B. B. Vika, F. K. Kon'kova, et al., in *Istoriia russkoi tserkvi*, vol. 8, pt. 2 (Moscow, 1997), 18–53. The Russian word *propoved'* can be translated either as "homily" or "sermon." I use the two interchangeably in this essay.

26.   "Vedomost' o tserkvakh za 1900," *Vsepoddanneishii otchet ober-prokurora Sv. Sinoda po vedomstvu pravoslavnago ispovedaniia za 1900 god* (St. Petersburg, 1903), vedomost' 3; Amvrosii, arkhiepiskop Kharkovskii, *Zhivoe slovo* (Kharkov, 1892), 27–28, 82.

27.   Larissa Taylor, ed., *Preachers and People in the Reformations and Early Modern Europe* (Boston, 2001), x.

28.   N. I. Barsov, *Istoricheskie, kriticheskie i polemicheskie opyty* (St. Petersburg, 1879), 410. Also quoted in Smolich, *Istoriia russkoi tserkvi*, 35.

29.   S. Kokhomskii, "Otnoshenie propovedi k bogosluzheniiu," *RSP* 18 (1898): 1–7.

30.   Katherine Ludwig Jansen, *The Making of the Magdalen: Preaching and Popular Devotion in the Later Middle Ages* (Princeton, N.J., 2000), 6–7.

31.   Prot. Grigorii D'iachenko, comp., "Beseda o prazdnike v chest' Kazanskoi Bozhiei Materi," *Obshchedostupnyia besedy o bogosluzhenii Pravoslavnoi tserkvi* (Moscow, 1898), 819.

32.   R. I. G., "Pouchenie v den' prazdnovaniia chudotvornoi Kazanskoi ikone Bozhiei Materi," *SEV* 45 (1877): 580–85.

33.   Arkhimandrit Antonin, "Slovo v den' prazdnovaniia v chest' Kazanskoi ikony Presviatoi Bogoroditsy, 22 oktiabria," *PTEV* 21 (1879): 231–34. Also see A. Voskresenskii, "Ob'iasnenie prazdnikov Pravoslavnoi tserkvi uchenikam sel'skikh shkol," *VCh* 27 (1864–1865): 651–52.

34.   Sv. Nikolai Tripol'skii, "Slovo v den' ikony Kazanskoi Bozhiei Materi," *VolEV* 20 (1875): 786.

35.   Arkhiepiskop Antonii (Shokotov), "Slovo v den' Kazanskiia ikony Bozhiei Materi, govorennoe v 1854 g.," *Slova i rechi vysokopreosviashchennago Antoniia, arkhiepiskopa Kishinevskago i Khotinskago* (St. Petersburg, 1862), 114–19; "Pouchenie v den' prazdnovaniia v chest' Kazanskiia ikony Bozhiia Materi," *REV* 4 (1865): 89–90; Sv. Feodor Tolerov, "Slovo v den' prazdnestva chudotvornomu obrazu Presviatyia Bogoroditsy Kazanskiia," *REV* 6 (1866): 207–9; Tripol'skii, "Slovo v den' ikony Kazanskoi Bozhiei Materi," *VolEV* (1875); Sv. Evfimii Setsinskii, "Slovo v den' Kazanskoi ikony Bozhiei Materi," *PodEV*, chast' neoffitsial'naia 44 (1900): 1–4; Prot. A. Antoninov, "Slovo v den' prazdnovaniia v chest' Kazanskoi ikony Presviatyia Bogoroditsy," *EkEV* 45 (1911): 1001–1002; "Prazdnik Kazanskoi ikony Bozhiei Materi, *DEV* 31 (1913): 917–20; A.V., "Pouchenie na 22-e oktiabria," *IaEV* 41 (1915): 897–98.

36.   Prot. Svetovidov, "Slovo v den' Kazanskiia ikony Bozhiei Materi," *NEV* 23 (1864): 7–14; Episkop Aleksandr, "Slovo v den' Kazanskiia ikony Bozhiei Materi," *EnEV* 18 (1892): 336–43.

37.   Sv. Mikhail Kliuchanskii, "Pouchenie v den' prazdnika v chest' Kazanskoi ikony Bozhiei Materi," *VorEV*, chast' neoffitsial'naia 19 (1902): 469–75; Sv. Stefan Tronin, "Slovo v den' Kazanskoi ikony Bozhiei Materi, 22 oktiabria," *BEV*, otdel neoffitsial'nyi 15 (1905): 341–46.

38.   For a discussion of the "imaginative gaze" with respect to the iconographic image in Eastern Orthodoxy, see Constas, "Icons and the Imagination."

39.   A.V., "Slovo v den' Kazanskoi ikony Bogomateri," *AsEV* 22 (1904): 982. Three decades earlier, the priest Nikolai Tripol'skii from the Volhynia diocese urged his audience to "penetrate the annals of history with the eyes of faith" ("Slovo v den' ikony Kazanskoi Bozhiei Materi," *VolEV* [1875]: 786). For other examples, see "Pouchenie v prazdnik Kazanskoi ikony Bozhiei Materi 22 oktiabria," *SmEV*, otdel neoffitsial'nyi 19 (1888): 819–23; Sv. Ioann Sabinin, "Slovo v den' Kazanskoi ikony Bozhiei Materi," *TvEV* 23 (1893): 624.

40.   Arkhiepiskop Antonii (Shokotov), "Slovo v den' Kazanskiia ikony," *Slova i rechi* (1862), 114–19.

41.   C. T. McIntire, *God, History, and Historians: An Anthology of Modern Christian Views of History* (New York, 1977).

42. Sv. A. Tupatilov, *Slovo v den' prazdnovaniia Kazanskoi Bozhiei Materi* (Chernigov, 1901); Sv. Victor Zlatomrezhev, "Pouchenie v den' Kazanskoi ikony Bozhiei Materi (22 oktiabria)," *SEV*, otdel neoffitsial'nyi 23 (1902): 1088–92; Sv. Lev Murogin, "Slovo v den' prazdnika Kazanskoi ikony Bozhiei Materi," *IaEV*, chast' neoffitsial'naia 45 (1915): 973–78; Prot. V. I. Soloviev, "Pouchenie v den' prazdnovaniia ikony Bozhiei Materi Kazanskiia," *Poucheniia protoiereia Ivanovo-Voznesenskago Pokrovskago sobora V. I. Solovieva* (Vladimir, 1915), 78–80.

43. For example, see "Slovo proiznesennoe Sofronieiu, episkopom Turkestanskim v prazdnik iavleniia ikony Presviatyia Bogoroditsy, imenuemyia Kazanskoiu," *KhEV* 19 (1872): 363–70; Sv. Nikolai Troitskii, "Slovo v prazdnik Presviatyia Bogoroditsy Kazanskiia," *PTEV* 21 (1885): 261–62; Sv. Petr Belyi, "Slovo v den' Kazanskiia ikony Bozhiei Materi," *Sbornik slov i pouchenii sviashchenno-sluzhitelei Ekaterinoslavskoi eparkhii*, vol. 2 (Ekaterinoslav, 1891), 214–19; Sv. Egenii Popov, "Slovo v den' Kazanskoi ikony Bozhiei Materi," *StEV* 19 (1902): 1138–42.

44. See, for example, Varlaam (Denisov), *Slovo preosviashchennago Varlaama, episkopa Orenburgskago v den' vynosa iz goroda Orenburga chudotvornoi Kazanskoi ikony Bozhiei Materi* (St. Petersburg, 1867); Sv. V. Rozaliev, "Slovo v den' prazdnovaniia Kazanskoi Bogomaternei ikone (8-go iiulia)," *Slova, besedy i rechi* (Stavropol, 1884), 259–69.

45. "Slovo v den' prazdnovaniia Kazanskoi ikone Bozhiia Materi, proiznesennoe Preosviashchenneishim Makariem, Ep. Viatskim i Slobodskim, v Viatskom Spasskom sobore," *VEV* 5 (1885): 579–85; Tripol'skii, "Slovo v den' ikony Kazanskoi Bozhiei Materi," *VolEV* (1875): 786–88; Prot. Andrei Flegmatov, "Pouchenie v den' Kazanskoi ikony Bogoroditsy," *SEV*, otdel neoffitsial'nyi 42 (1881): 330; Sv. Patrikii Petrovskii, *Sbornik vydaiushchikhsia besed iz zhurnala "Vestnik Voennogo Dukhovenstva" za 1890–1897*, vol. 3 (St. Petersburg, 1901): 46–50; Prot. Petr Il'inskii, "Slovo v den' Kazanskiia ikony Bogomateri," *AsEV* 22 (1906); Antoninov, "Slovo v den' prazdnovaniia v chest' Kazanskoi ikony," *EkEV* (1911): 997–1003.

46. Antoninov, "Slovo v den' prazdnovaniia v chest' Kazanskoi ikony," *EkEV* (1911): 997.

47. Sabinin, "Slovo v den' Kazanskoi ikony Bozhiei Materi," *TvEV* (1893): 624.

48. Antonii, ep. Permskii, "Pouchenie v den' Kazanskoi Bozhiei Materi," *PEV*, otdel neoffitsial'nyi (1870): 347; Murogin, "Slovo v den' prazdnika Kazanskoi ikony," *IaEV* (1915): 973–78.

49. Troitskii, "Slovo v prazdnik Presviatyia Bogoroditsy Kazanskiia," *PTEV* (1885): 263; S.P.S., "Slovo v den' Kazanskoi Bozhiei Materi," *Pouchitel'nyi glas pastyria v khrame Bozhiem* (St. Petersburg, 1861): 57; Vladimir, Episkop Orenburgskii i Ural'skii, "Slovo v den' Kazanskoi ikony Bozhiei Materi," *OEV* 21 (1897): 767–71; Prot. I. Soloviev, "Slovo v den' prazdnovaniia Kazanskoi ikony Bozhiei Materi," *TvEV*, chast' neoffitsial'naia 22 (1907): 703–706.

50. Antoninov, "Slovo v den' prazdnovaiia v chest' Kazanskoi ikony," *EkEV* (1911): 1000; Sv. M. Grigorevskii, "Slovo v den' Kazanskoi ikony Bozhiei Materi," *ArEV*, chast' neoffitsial'naia 21 (1896): 589–91.

51. Prot. Petr Il'inskii, "Slovo v den' Kazanskiia ikony Bogomateri," *AsEV*, chast' neoffitsial'naia 23 (1899): 1192–96; Grigorevskii, "Slovo v den' Kazanskoi ikony Bozhiei Materi," *ArEV* (1896): 593.

52. For a discussion of the notion of divine election in light of national identities, see Anthony D. Smith, *Chosen Peoples* (New York, 2003), 44–94.

53. I. Poliakov, "Slovo v den' prazdnovaniia Presviatoi Bogoroditse, chudotvornyia Eia ikony Kazanskiia (22 oktiabria), *SEV*, otdel neoffitsial'nyi 39 (1883): 401–403.

54. Prot. Ioann Vostorgov, "Velikoe prizvanie russkago naroda" in *Polnoe sobranie sochinenii*, 5 vols. (St. Petersburg, 1995), 1:69–73; Tripol'skii, "Slovo v den' ikony Kazanskoi Bozhiei Materi," *VolEV* (1875): 787.

55. Menstrov, "Prazdnik Kazanskoi ikony Bozhiei Materi," *VD* (1908): 483.

56. N. Malinovskii, *Ocherki Pravoslavnago dogmaticheskago bogosloviia* (Kamenets-Podolsk, 1904), 403–405; for similar views, see *Besedy i slova arkhiepiskopa Khersonskago i Odesskago Nikanora* (Odessa, 1903), 204–207.

57. For a collection of Leo Tolstoy's writings related to the subject of patriotism, see *War, Patriotism, Peace,* ed. Scott Nearing (New York, 1973).

58. Protoierei N. P., "Slovo v den' prazdnovaniia v chest' Kazanskoi ikony Bozhiei Materi," *PEV* 31 (1909): 641–45. Fr. N. P.'s views resonated with those of other churchmen who responded to Tolstoy's writings. For example, see Prof. A. A. Bronzov, "Predosuditelen li patriotizm?" *Khristianskoe chtenie* 5 (1900): 710–45; *Besedy i slova arkhiepiskopa Khersonskago i Odesskago Nikanora,* 207–10.

59. "Kazanskaia ikona Bozhiei Materi," *VD* 40 (1898): 470–72.

60. "Proiskhozhdenie prazdnika v chest' Kazanskoi ikony Presviatyia Bogoroditsy, 22 oktiabria," *VEV* 21 (1896): 1030–31.

61. Vasilii Mikhailovskii, *Slovo v den' Kazanskoi ikony Bozhiei Materi* (St. Petersburg, 1893), 5; "O prazdnovanii v gorode Kazani trekhsotletiia" *IKE* (1879): 396–405; Ep. Pavel (Lebedev), *Slovo proiznesennoe ego Vysokopreosviashchenstvom Vysokopreosviashchenneishim Pavlom, Arkhiepiskopom Kazanskim i Sviazhskim v den' Kazanskiia ikony Bozhiei Materi 22 oktiabria 1888 goda* (Kazan, 1891); Episkop Aleksandr, "Slovo v den' Kazanskiia ikony Bozhiei Materi," *EnEV* (1892): 336–43; Sv. Evgraf Evarestov, "Pouchenie v den' prazdnovaniia Kazanskoi ikone Bogoroditsy," *UEV,* otdel neoffitsial'nyi 19 (1894): 64; "Kazanskaia ikona Bozhiei Materi," *VD* 40 (1898): 470–72; Sv. A. Barkhatov, "Iavlenie Kazanskoi ikony Bogoroditsy. Pouchenie na 8-oe iiulia," *Tserkovnye besedy* (St. Petersburg, 1904), 43; Sv. G. Kliucharev, "Razmyshlenie po povodu pokhishcheniia Kazanskoi ikony Bozhiei Materi," *StEV* 7 (1905): 407–16; Prot. I. Dolinskii, "V den' iavleniia Kazanskoi Bozhiei Materi 8 iiulia," *Polnyi godichnyi krug slov i pouchenii* (Rybinsk, 1907), 301–303.

62. Sv. Pavel Losevskii, "Slovo na osviashchenie khrama v chest' ikony Presviatyia Bogoroditsy Kazanskiia v sele Budine, Bel'skago uezda," *SmEV,* otdel neoffitsial'nyi 16 (1876): 415–21.

63. Ep. Pavel (Lebedev), *Slovo proiznesennoe ego Vysokopreosviashchenstvom,* 3–5; "Kazanskaia ikona Bozhiei Materi," *VD* 40 (1898): 470–72; "Proiskhozhdenie prazdnika v chest' Kazanskoi ikony Presviatyia Bogoroditsy, 22 oktiabria," *VEV* (1896): 1030–31; Sv. Vasilii Boshchanovskii, "V den' Kazanskoi ikony Bozhiei Materi (22 oktiabria)," *Sbornik pouchenii na Paskhu i vse voskresnye dni, dvunadesiatye prazdniki, Novyi god, dni Bogorodichnye, sviatykh, vysokotorzhestvennye i na raznye sluchai* (Sergiev Posad, 1912): 327–33. In some dioceses where the Muslim population was substantial, local missionary brotherhoods—whose main concern was to facilitate the conversion of Muslims in their region to the Orthodox faith—took their name from the Kazan icon. See *TEV* 6 (1876): 152.

64. Sv. Roman Nadezhdin, "Slovo v den' Kazanskiia ikony Bogomateri," in *Propovedi na vse voskresnye i prazdnichnye dni* (St. Petersburg, 1865): 670–75.

65. Sv. N. Liubimov, "Pouchenie v den' chudotvornoi ikony Kazanskoi Bozhiei Materi," *KEV* (1891): 549–54; "Skazanie o proiskhozhdenii oktiabr'skago prazdnika Kazanskiia ikony Bogomateri," *TEV,* chast' neoffitsial'naia 15 (1861): 348–49; N. I. Florinskii, *O tom, po kakomu sluchaiu otechestvennaia tserkov' nasha prazdnuet presviatoi Bogoroditse 22 oktiabria* (Vladimir, 1864); Sv. Porfirii Vinogradov, *Slovo v den' Kazanskoi ikony Bozhiei Materi, 22 oktiabria* (St. Petersburg, 1872); "Slovo na den' Kazanskiia ikony Bozhiei Materi," *MEV* 46 (1889): 613–14.

66. "Prazdnestvo Kazanskoi ikony Bozhiei Materi," *TobEV,* otdel neoffitsial'nyi 19/20 (1890): 419–21; Efremov, *Slovo v den' prazdnovaniia Kazanskoi ikone Botomateri;* Prot. F. Vasiutinskii, *Slovo v prazdnik Kazanskoi ikony Presviatyia Bogoroditsy* (Chernigov, 1910).

67. Vinogradov, *Slovo v den' Kazanskoi Bozhiei Materi,* 3.

68. Grigorevskii, "Slovo v den' Kazanskoi ikony Bozhiei Materi," *ArEV* (1896): 589–91; Voskresenskii, "Ob'iasnenie prazdnikov Pravoslavnoi tserkvi uchenikam sel'skikh shkol," *VCh* (1864–1865): 646–52; Vinogradov, *Slovo v den' Kazanskoi ikony Bozhiei Materi;* Sv. Mikhail Zelenev, "Pouchenie v den' Kazanskoi ikony Bozhiei Materi, 22 oktiabria," *TEV,* chast' neoffitsial'naia 22 (1890): 1109–15; Vladimir, episkop Orenburgskii i Ural'skii, "Slovo v den' Kazanskoi ikony Bozhiei Materi," *OEV* (1897): 767–71; D'iachenko, *Obshchedostupnyia besedy,* 819; Il'inskii, "Slovo

v den' Kazanskiia ikony Bogomateri," *AsEV* (1899): 1192–96. Arkhimandrit Sergii, "Slovo v den' Kazanskiia ikony Bozhiei Materi," *NovEV* (1904): 1426.

69.   Voskresenskii, "Ob'iasnenie prazdnikov Pravoslavnoi tserkvi uchennikam sel'skikh shkol," *VCh* (1864–1865): 646–52; *Rech', skazannaia protoiereem D. Borisoglebskim po sluchaiu moleb-stviia na Aleksandrovskom rynke v Sankt-Peterburge v den' iavleniia Kazanskiia ikony Presviatyia Bogoroditsy 8 iiulia,* 5–6.

70.   Vinogradov, *Slovo v den' Kazansoi Bozhiei Materi.* This sermon was delivered in 1865; Nadezhdin, "Slovo v den' Kazanskiia ikony," 670–75.

71.   Prot. I. Leporinskii, "Pouchenie v den' iavleniia ikony Bozhiei Materi Kazanskiia," *IKE* 15 (1871): 475.

72.   Ep. Pavel (Lebedev), *Slovo proiznesennoe ego Vysokopreosviashchenstvom,* 12.

73.   Florinskii, *O tom, po kakomu sluchaiu;* R. I. G., "Pouchenie v den' prazdnovaniia," *SEV* (1877): 580–85; Il'inskii, "Slovo v den' Kazanskiia ikony Bogomateri," *AsEV* (1899): 1193; Sv. I Artinskii, "Slovo v den' Kazanskoi ikony Bozhiei Materi, 22 oktiabria, 1901," *DEV,* otdel neoffitsial'nyi 31 (1901): 760–62.

74.   Zelenev, "Pouchenie v den' Kazanskoi ikony Bozhiei Materi," *TEV* (1890): 1109–15.

75.   Prot. Porfirii Alekseevskii, "Pouchenie v den' Kazanskoi ikony Bozhiei Materi, 22 oktiabria," *MTsV* 43–44 (1916): 632–34.

76.   Alekseevskii, "Pouchenie v den' Kazanskoi ikony Bozhiei Materi, 22 oktiabria," *MTsV* (1916): 632; Nadezhdin, "Slovo v den' Kazanskiia ikony," 670; "Slovo na den' Kazanskiia ikony Bozhiei Materi," *MTsV* (1889): 613.

77.   Liubimov, "Pouchenie v den' chudotvornoi ikony Kazanskoi Bozhiei Materi," *KazEV* (1891): 551.

78.   "Proiskhozhdenie prazdnika v chest' Kazanskoi ikony Presviatyia Bogoroditsy, 22 oktiabria," *VEV* (1896): 1030–31; Il'inskii, "Slovo na den' prazdnovaniia v chest' Kazanskoi ikony Bogomateri," *AsEV* 22 (1892); Il'inskii, "Slovo v den' Kazanskiia ikony Bogomateri," *AsEV* (1899).

79.   "Slovo preosviashchennago Amvrosiia, arkhiepiskopa Kharkovskago v den' iavleniia ikony Bohziei Materi, imenuemoi Kazanskoi," *PTsV* 28 (1897): 951–57.

80.   Grigorevskii, "Slovo v den' Kazanskoi ikony Bozhiei Materi," *ArEV* (1896): 589–91; Nikolai, Episkop Tavricheskii, "Pouchenie skazannoe v tserkvi s. Veselianki v den' Kazanskoi ikony Bozhiei Materi," *TavEV,* chast' neoffitsial'naia 22 (1901): 1511–19; Zhukov, "Slovo v den' prazdnika," *Sbornik pouchenii,* 41–44.

81.   Soloviev, "Slovo v den' prazdnovaniia Kazanskoi ikone Bozhiei Materi," *TvEV* (1907): 703–706; A.V., "Slovo v den' Kazanskoi ikony Bogomateri," *AsEV* 22 (1904): 982–87; Zelenev, "Pouchenie v den' Kazanskoi ikony Bozhiei Materi," *TamEV* (1890): 1109–15.

82.   Florinskii, *O tom, po kakomu sluchaiu;* Grigorevskii, "Slovo v den' Kazanskoi ikony Bozhiei Materi," *ArEV* (1896): 589–91; Kliuchanskii, "Pouchenie v den' prazdnika," *VorEV,* chast' neoffitsial'naia (1902): 469–75; V. L., "Pouchenie v den' Kazanskoi ikony Presviatoi Bogoroditsy," *IaEV* 41 (1909): 833–36.

83.   Il'inskii, "Slovo na den' prazdnovaniia," *AsEV* 22 (1892).

84.   Voskresenskii, "Ob"iasnenie prazdnikov Pravoslavnoi tserkvi uchenikam sel'skikh shkol," *VCh* (1864–1865): 646–49; Sv. Nikolai Iunitskii, "Slovo v den' Kazanskoi ikony Presviatyia Bogoroditsy," *Propovedi na vse voskresnye i prazdnichnye dni* (St. Petersburg, 1865), 678; Prot. Evgraf Megorskii, "Slovo v den' prazdnika Kazanskoi ikony Bozhiei Materi (22 oktiabria)," *Slova, poucheniia i rechi* (St. Petersburg, 1894), 284–89; Prot. D. T—tskii, "Slovo na den' prazd-novaniia v chest' Kazanskoi ikony Bozhiei Materi, 22 oktiabria," *EkEV,* otdel neoffitsial'nyi 45 (1907): 747.

85.   Prot. Georgii Popuzhenko, "Slovo v den' prazdnovaniia v chest' Kazanskoi ikony Bozhiei Materi," 22 oktiabria, *KhEV* 13 (1873): 377–81.

86.   Megorskii, "Slovo v den' prazdnika Kazanskoi ikony Bozhiei Materi (22 oktiabria)," *Slova,* 284–89; Tupatilov, *Slovo v den' prazdnovaniia Kazanskoi Bozhiei Materi* (1901); Prot. N.

Liubimov, "Pouchenie v den' chudotvornoi ikony Kazanskoi Bozhiei Materi," *Slova i rechi* (Moscow, 1914), 130–31.

87. Arkhiepiskop Antonii (Shokotov), "Slovo v den' Kazanskiia ikony," *Slova i rechi* (1862): 114–19; "Pouchenie v prazdnik Kazanskoi ikny Bozhiei Materi, 22 oktiabria," *SmEV*, otdel neoffitsial'nyi 19 (1888): 819–23; Sergii, Arkhiepiskop Khersonskii i Odesskii, "Slovo v den' Kazanskiia ikony Presviatyia Bogoroditsy," *KhEV* (1892); Tupatilov, *Slovo v den' prazdnovaniia Kazanskoi Bozhiei Materi* (1901); "Slovo na den' Kazanskiia ikony Bozhiei Materi," *MTsV* (1889): 614.

88. For commentary in a secular newspaper on this event and how it was interpreted by believers, see "Malen'kii fel'eton: sviatotatstvo," *Novoe vremia*, 7 July 1904, no. 10182.

89. Prot. Petr Uspenskii, "Pouchenie na den' Kazanskoi ikony Bozhiei Materi," *TEV* 45 (1904): 1340–45; *O pokhishchenii Kazanskoi ikony Bozhiei Materi* (Kazan, 1905); I. M. Pokrovskii, *Pechal'naia godovshchina so dnia pokhishcheniia iavlennoi chudotvornoi Kazanskoi ikony Bozhiei Materi* (Kazan, 1905); "Slovo proiznensennoe Permskim eparkhial'nym propovednikom v kafedral'nom sobore v den' Kazanskoi ikony Bozhiei Materi, 22 oktiabria," *PEV* 32 (1909): 669–70.

90. *Kazanskii telegraf*, 11 July 1904, no. 3458.

91. Prot. Aleksandr Zelenetskii, "Slovo v den' Kazanskiia ikony Bozhiei Materi, 22 oktiabria 1905," *IKE* 42 (1905): 1254.

92. The local Kazan press, the national religious press, and diocesan newspapers generally reported the crime and followed the case in some depth. The general Russian secular press, however, was more sporadic in its reporting of the crime. Often the theft of the icon was reported in a one- or two-sentence notification. This was perhaps not surprising given that secular attention was focused on the Russo-Japanese War, the death of Anton Chekhov in June 1904, and the assassination, in July, of the Minister of the Interior Viacheslav Plehve.

93. "Slovo Vysokopreosviashchennago Arseniia, Arkhiepiskopa Khar'kovskago i Akhtyrskago," *Vera i razum* (1904): 449; Episkop Vissarion, "Gnev Bozhii na russkuiu zemliu," *Dushepoleznoe chtenie* 12 (1904): 483–88; Kliucharev, "Razmyshlenie po povodu pokhishcheniia Kazanskoi ikony," *StEV* (1905): 407–16; Sv. Bazarianinov, "Po povodu sviatotatstvennoi pokrazhi iavlennoi chudotvornoi Kazanskoi ikony Bozhiei Materi," *TEV* 6 (1905): 269–79; A. Vysotskii, "Po povodu pokhishcheniia chudotvornoi Kazanskoi ikony Bozhiei Materi," *Izvestiia po Kazanskoi eparkhii za 1905* (Kazan, 1905): 348–53.

94. Antoninov, "Slovo v den' prazdnovaiia v chest' Kazanskoi ikony," *EkEV* (1911): 1000; Grigorevskii, "Slovo v den' Kazanskoi ikony Bozhiei Materi," *ArEV* (1896): 589–91; for other examples where both individual and collective are stressed, see Megorskii, "Slovo v den' prazdnika Kazanskoi ikony," *Slova, poucheniia i rechi* (1894): 284–89.

95. Sergii, Arkhiepiskop Khersonskii i Odesskii, "Slovo v den' Kazanskiia ikony Presviatyia Bogoroditsy," *KhEV* (1892); Sabinin, "Slovo v den' Kazanskoi ikony Bozhiei Materi," *TvEV* (1893): 627–28; A.V., "Slovo v den' Kazanskoi ikony Bogomateri," 670–75.

96. Ep. Pavel (Lebedev), *Slovo proiznesennoe ego Vysokopreosviashchenstvom, 2.*

97. Efremov, *Slovo v den' prazdnovaniia Kazanskoi ikone Bogomateri, 22 oktiabria* (Chernigov, 1898).

98. Antonii, ep. Permskii, "Pouchenie v den' Kazanskoi Bozhiei Materi," *PEV* (1870): 348–49; "Slovo v den' iavleniia Kazanskoi ikony Bozhiei Materi," *IKE* 16 (1879): 444–49.

99. P. Ia., "Slovo v den' iavleniia chudotvornoi ikony Bogomateri v Kazani," *VolEV*, chast' neoffitsial'naia 22 (1882): 697–701.

100. P. Ia., "Slovo v den' iavleniia chudotvornoi ikony Bogomateri v Kazani," *VolEV* (1882); Varlaam (Denisov), *Slovo preosviashchennago Varlaama, episkopa Orenburgskago* (St. Petersburg, 1867); Rozaliev, "Slovo v den' prazdnovaniia Kazanskoi Bogomaternei ikone (8-go iiulia)," *Slova, besedy i rechi* (1884), 263–64; Sv. S. Kamenetskii, "Pouchenie v Bogorodichnye prazdniki," *IaEV*, chast' neoffitsial'naia 31 (1913): 609–11.

101.   I. Butik, *Slova i poucheniia* (Kishinev, 1877), 176; Prot. Sergii Bel'skii, "Slovo v prazdnik v chest' Kazanskoi ikony Bozhiei Materi," *TEV*, chast' neoffitsial'naia 46 (1900): 1159–63; Prot. Dimitrii Kastal'skii, "Zaboty ob izlishnem: slovo v den' prazdnovaniia Kazanskoi ikone Bozhiei Materi 8 iiulia 1890," *DCh* (August 1890): 415–20; Prot. V. I. Solov'ev, "Pouchenie v den' prazdnovaniia ikony Bozhiei Materi Kazanskiia," in *Poucheniia protoiereia Ivanovo-Voznesenskago Pokrovskago sobora* (Vladimir, 1915), 32–34; 78–80.

102.   Kastal'skii, "Zaboty ob izlishnem," *DCh* (August 1890): 415–20.

103.   Flegmatov, "Pouchenie v den' Kazanskiia ikony," *SEV* (1881): 79; Afonskii, "Slovo v den' prazdnika Kazanskoi ikony Bogomateri," *SmEV* (1876): 614.

104.   Sv. A. Zhukov, "Slovo v den' iavleniia ikony Bozhiei Materi, imenuemoi Kazanskoi (8 iiulia)," *Sbornik pouchenii* (1912): 22; Antonii, ep. Permskii, "Pouchenie v den' Kazanskoi Bozhiei Materi," *PEV* (1870): 348–49.

105.   Sv. G. Melanovskii, "Slovo v den' iavleniia Kazanskoi chudotvornoi ikony Presviatyia Bogoroditsy," in *Pouchitel'nye slova* (Kazan, 1879), 175–78.

106.   Arkhimandrit Antonin, "Slovo v den' prazdnovaniia," *PTEV* (1879): 233.

107.   Vladimir, episkop Orensburgskii i Ural'skii, "Slovo v den' Kazanskoi ikony Bozhiei Materi," *OEV* (1897): 767–71. For the notion of Mary gazing at believers through her icon, also see Episkop Vissarion, "Zhivoi i obil'nyi istochnik," *DCh* 10 (1898): 249–52.

108.   Sv. P. Skorodumov, *Sbornik vydaiushchikhsia besed iz zhurnala 'Vestnik Voennogo Dukhovenstva'* (St. Petersburg, 1901): 207–209.

109.   Morgan, *Visual Piety*, 9.

110.   Smith, *Chosen Peoples*.

111.   Eugene N. Trubetskoi, *Icons: Theology in Color* (Crestwood, N.Y., 1973), 41.

112.   I. A. Sterligova, *Dragotsennyi ubor drevnerusskikh ikon XI–XIV vekov: proiskhozhdenie, simvolika, khudozhestvennyi obraz* (Moscow, 2000), 5–14.

4

Written Confessions and the Construction of Sacred Narrative

Nadieszda Kizenko

————·•◈•·————

Confession has probably captured the imagination of more people, and been interpreted more broadly, than any sacrament in Christianity. Whether it is Jean-Jacques Rousseau writing his "letter to the world" or Protestant polemicists publishing scandalized penny tracts about what goes on between a priest and a woman at the sickbed or in the darkened booth, confession has become a symbol of both intimacy and revelation. Whether one interprets the term broadly, as a metaphor, or narrowly, in the sense of a religious sacrament, confession weighs heavy with connotations of dark secrets clutched closely to one's breast and only finally revealed to another human being who is standing in for God. Confession has been a staple of autobiography, a literary genre, and transformed nearly beyond recognition in the television talk show at the turn of the twenty-first century.

Despite these latest versions of "open" confessions, confession had become something secret after several centuries of Christianity.[1] And although ample numbers of penitentials—the lists of questions used by priests to those coming to them for confession—survive from different periods, and have served many historians as indicators of religious belief and practice, this source suffers from several obvious drawbacks.[2] First, penitentials are prescriptive, not descriptive. Just because a priest had a list of possible questions available does not mean that he stuck to the list or that the people he asked admitted to committing those sins. We have only one side of what was always a dialogue, and we cannot be sure even of that. Second, with the exceptions of confessions involving the mute or the deaf, confessions were oral, not drawn or written. They survived only in the memories of their participants. Finally, the confession was, by definition, secret. For all these reasons, whatever surviving traces of confession we have are necessarily one-sided and inconclusive at best.

Among the only exceptions to the silence of the penitents are the confessions sent to Father Ioann of Kronstadt (1829–1908), a charismatic Russian priest with a reputation for holiness.[3] In a particularly immediate way, they demonstrate the simultaneous internalization and appropriation of religious formulas. Even as people took part in a ritual that most expresses one's submission to the traditional authority of the Church—namely, the confession—they displayed a range of behavior and expression that argues against their biddability. These confessions show that while religion was a dominant force in the worldview of many Russians, its interpretation was more eclectic and personal than has been allowed previously. They illustrate the remarkable theological and liturgical literacy of some Russian Orthodox believers—and also the extent to which this literacy did or did not affect their behavior. The contrast between the confessions of women and men illuminates the extent to which gender could inform religious experience.

Above all, these confessions illustrate one of the central themes of this volume: the nature of narrative in relation to the construction of the sacred. The confession was supposed to follow a familiar script. And, indeed, the similarities in the confessions examined here show just how well people who confessed knew this "master narrative." On the other hand, the confessions also reveal an astonishing ability of their authors to make the template fit their own purposes. These confessions genuinely demonstrate that storytelling and narrative, however ritualized, allowed people to construct their own versions of the sacred, and impose their own vision on the master script.

The confessions sent to Father Ioann pose several methodological problems. Almost all are undated, making it difficult to hazard any assumptions about trends or changes over time. Geographic generalization is even more problematic, as only a few people included their address in the letter. Class identification is also complicated: with the obvious exceptions of women who write about the temptations they encounter as schoolteachers, house maids, or nuns, or such clues as writing paper of good quality, the most precise categories possible in most cases are "highly educated," "passable grammar," or "barely literate."

Quantitative analysis of the confessional letters is difficult as well because of the high degree of individual variation and the relatively small sample size—a total of 163 letters. This makes it hard to determine something as basic as whether the correspondents are typical Orthodox Christians or religious virtuosi, exceptional in every respect. Through a judicious comparison with confessional manuals, popular devotional literature, clerical accounts, and liturgical texts, however, it becomes easier to place these documents in their modern Russian context. Most important, however, is their uniqueness. Except for the recent scandalous taping of confessionals in Italy, until now most of our information on confessions—whether Orthodox Christian or Roman Catholic—has been secondhand.[4] Simply put, the confessions discussed here are the only examples of contemporary religious confessions that exist, and provide the first concrete material about what was legally required of millions of Russian Orthodox Christians every year.[5] Approached imaginatively and carefully, these confessions can tell us more about religious experience in late imperial Russia.

Preliminary Observations

Any discussion of confession requires us to bear in mind several peculiarities of the Orthodox confession as a genre—the penitentials, the literature, the prayers, the language, and the ritual. The most obvious point is that the Orthodox Church does not have the anonymity of the Roman Catholic confessional. Rather than being separated from the priest by a barrier or from other parishioners by a booth, the confessor was visible and audible not only to the priest but often to others standing in line. Although the Orthodox were accustomed to the relative openness characterizing confession, their choosing to write Father Ioann rather than approach their parish priest suggests a desire for privacy quite apart from having the counsel or absolution of a holy man. "I am too ashamed to tell this to my parish priest" is a common motif in the confessional letters.[6]

There is, then, the matter of confessional formulas. The similarities in these confessions and the repetition of certain formulas clearly indicate that those raised as Orthodox Christians were trained in how to confess. How, then, can one determine how much of the expressed is conventional and how much is personal (albeit using conventional language)? The issue of standardization would have become increasingly prevalent during the nineteenth century, when the Orthodox Church hierarchy, as part of a campaign to educate the laypeople as to their responsibilities (particularly in cities, where it was feared they might lose the moorings of tradition provided by the village), began to circulate the "standard" confession of St. Dimitrii of Rostov so people would have a model against which to measure their lives.[7] The literate pious also had at their disposal a daily confession, which followed the daily evening prayers in the prayer book, reminding them of the general categories of sin.[8] And, in fact, many sins are not specific to class or gender: 90 percent of the writers confess to pride, envy, hatred, anger, despair, miserliness, and bearing a grudge (*zlopamiatstvo*).[9] In a sense, the opposition between conventional and personal is moot. The extent to which conventions influenced the confession itself reveals their interpenetration.

Figure 4.1. "The Devil Flees as the Angel Crowns Penitence."
Nineteenth-century engraving. *Spiritual Instructions to the Penitent*
(Moscow, 1901).

With these caveats, quantification is useful in noting a basic gender difference. Of the163 letters, 121 came from women and 34 from men (8 letters were
either from couples writing as a unit or gender could not be determined). That
more women than men wrote their confessions can be attributed to various factors: women were generally more religiously observant; they saw confession

as a more congenial religious genre; they were more likely to seek out a cel-ebrated charismatic healer; and they were more apt to put their confessions in writing.

Let us approach each issue in turn. The feminization of piety has been dis-cussed in various historical contexts, but still lacking are the exhaustive local studies necessary to propose such a paradigm for Russia.[10] We can say, how-ever, that, based on both the confessions and other letters sent to Father Ioann, women were indeed more likely to seek out a charismatic priestly figure who emphasized an emotional conversion and a less perfunctory, formal sacra-mental life—and also provided emotional and practical help. Whether men's religious needs and desires in late imperial Russia were better served in other ways than confession, or whether men were less observant, is not possible to determine based on this sample.

As to whether the confession was a religious genre more congenial to women, there is no evidence to suggest that, before the possibility of visiting Father Ioann or writing him, women confessed their sins with any more enthu-siasm or frequency than their male relatives. On the basis of guides for priests concerning confession, such as S. V. Bulgakov's *Nastol'naia Kniga,* it was appar-ently difficult just to persuade anyone to come more than the requisite once a year.[11] Some priests noted a slightly greater tendency toward compunction on the part of women but no greater frequency.[12] The higher proportion of women writing their confessions to Father Ioann thus appears to have more to do with Father Ioann himself than with confession as a form of religiosity.

But that the confessions were *written* must not pass unnoticed. It is possible, for example, that an equal or perhaps even higher percentage of men than women personally sought out Father Ioann.[13] Crucial here is the question of physical access to Father Ioann, which has two aspects. First, more areas of an Orthodox Church are open to men than to women: virtually any male may pass behind the doors of the iconostasis and enter the altar; almost no laywoman, how-ever holy, may do so. For this reason, the eyewitness accounts of men, ranging from visiting students to lawyers to fellow clergy, describing their encounters with Father Ioann in the altar, safe from the press of the crowds and in rela-tive privacy and comfort, obviously have no female counterparts.[14] Moreover, the physical pressure of people wishing to see and touch Father Ioann often meant that only the strongest and most physically importunate triumphed; some women, particularly desperate to see Father Ioann, were reportedly run over by the wheels of his carriage.[15] On May 17, 1900, during an extraordinarily crowded service in St. Andrew's Cathedral, one woman was crushed to death.[16] Women may therefore have written their confessions to Father Ioann because it was physically difficult to speak to him in person. Finally, almost all available evidence suggests that men were more likely to be literate than women, so it was not their literacy that drove more women than men to write to Father Ioann.[17] The marked differences in the confessions of women and men are examined in a later section of this essay, but the differences lie less in the kinds of sins mentioned (with obvious exceptions such as going to church while menstruating or having had an abortion) than in the language used to describe those sins. Here I concentrate on elements common to most confessions, on class differences, and, finally, on variations according to gender.

Common Elements

A particularly Orthodox theme is the relation to images, particularly icons. Although this is more characteristic of the less educated, it occurs among the upper classes as well. What the writers perceive as blasphemy actually suggests the important role the images had in their lives. Such actions as cursing, fearing, or defacing images reveal their very potency. Any tension or resentment people felt in their relationship with the divine often expressed itself in direct, physical action. Even an educated and repentant ex-Tolstoyan man was prone to attach an importance to external symbols and their overt defilement. He confesses that,

> I laughed at and abused God's temple, the service, and all religious actions such as prayer and performance of the sacraments, regarding this as delusion on the part of the people.
> I mocked holy books.
> I violated icons.
> I hammered a metal cross into my axe instead of a wedge.
> I spat Holy Communion out of my mouth.
> I shot my revolver at a photo-postcard of you.[18]

Because this man and others like him ascribe their actions to the influence of Lev Tolstoy, such explicit evidence of the connection between Tolstoy's teachings and the violation of revered Orthodox symbols may well have contributed to Father Ioann's animosity toward the novelist. More typical incidents of "blasphemy," however, are those from this peasant woman:

> I was careless toward icons, I venerated the icons while menstruating, I looked closely into icons, I stand disrespectfully in church and laugh, curse, and am adulterously attracted to every man I see.[19]

If the sins were grave enough, and had never been confessed (even if committed during childhood), they were added:

> I found an image of the Savior in a prayer book, and I began to prick it with a needle although I did not know for sure that this was the Lord but my soul ached when I did this and some invisible force made me do this, I could not restrain myself, I was eight years old.[20]

Nor was blasphemy the exclusive preserve of the uneducated. One educated young woman describes her extreme blasphemy as an affliction as well as a sin:

> I am in dismay about my sin, which I could not bring myself to tell to our spiritual father. I have tried to fight it, but nothing helps. When I am in church I constantly have bad thoughts about communion; or when I venerate an image I want to spit at it. Others pray to God; I have ideas about praying to Satan or to a joker. I envision the Chalice or icons fouled in a bad place.[21] I wish God would at least show me why I am afflicted with such a harsh sin.[22]

Sexual Mores

The Russian Orthodox Church strictly limited the periods during which married people could engage in sexual relations. A couple was prohibited from relations on Saturdays and Sundays, Wednesdays and Fridays, holidays and the eves of holidays, all the fasts (seven weeks before Easter, six weeks before Christmas, two weeks before the Dormition, and a variable amount of time—from whenever Trinity Sunday fell to June 29—for the apostles Peter and Paul).[23] Thus roughly two-thirds of the year was off-limits to *married* people; *unmarried* people, who were supposed to abstain year-round, felt the burden of their disobedience even more strongly if it fell during a proscribed period.

The difficulty people had in complying with these strictures emerges clearly in their confessions, in which "breaking the fast" in this sense was nearly as common as slander and drunkenness. Educated people were slightly less likely than those who were less educated to confess breaching these restrictions (although it is not clear whether this is because the former regarded such lapses as less sinful, did not know of the prohibitions, or were more conscientious). Most of the people who sent their confessions to Father Ioann, however, took holidays seriously. One woman wrote:

> My mind was occupied only with fornication, *I did not respect holidays,* everyone went off to church while I pretended to be sick so that I could stay home for the sake of fornication. . . . Then I got married. My husband

was originally like a human being, but I made an animal out of him, even
worse than an animal. He imitated me in everything, and I knew no fear,
not on holidays and not of communion, we would fornicate immediately
*after receiving the Holy Mysteries and on the eve of receiving communion and on
Easter and on Annunciation.* In a word, there was no fear of God.[24]

A similar note occurs in the confession of a woman named Vasilisa:

I sinned against God and before you, Father Sergiev, I committed a fleshly
sin with my *kum*[25] and I did not keep the feasts, neither with my *kum* nor
with my husband.[26]

The identification of sexual relations with one's spouse on holidays with
fornication is evident in the confession of a woman who, after describing how
she and her husband "defiled themselves with fornication" on Trinity Sunday,
adds that "besides my husband, I fornicated with a pilgrim."[27] And others
confessed:

When I lived with my husband I did not honor God's holy days, defiling
them with fornication, even great feasts such as Trinity Sunday and the
Protection of the Mother of God [*Pokrov*], I did not honor the Mother of
God, and the Bright Resurrection of our Lord I did not keep in purity . . .[28]
. . . On the holiday of the Protection of the Mother of God I engaged in
fornication with a man in church, and then went up like to a dog to be
anointed with holy oil; I wonder at God's Mercy, how did the Lord not
strike me down at that moment . . .[29]
. . . I tempted an administrator on Great and Holy Saturday [the eve
of Easter] before the late liturgy, then I went to the neighbors' to get
some milk and became completely deaf and then remembered that I had
sinned, that people do not even eat bread on a day like this; then, at that
very minute, the bells began to ring for the liturgy, and then I guessed
how grievously I had sinned. Then once when three holidays fell on one
day—Sunday and St. Nicholas and Isaiah[30]—I fornicated during early
liturgy and crawled through a window to [meet] an officer.[31]

Thus holidays were not merely occasions when religious events were
abstractly commemorated but were palpable presences in the lives of those who
confessed to Father Ioann, requiring physical as well as spiritual observance.

The notion of lust (*blud*) as desire (*pokhot', vozhdelenie*) is strikingly rare
in the confessions. Instead, there are many variations of the multifarious *blud*.
Dictionaries render this as "lechery" or "fornication" but, as the confessions
show, its meaning was more fluid and encompassed a greater range of activity
than either definition might suggest. The people's use of this term rather than

pokhot' or *vozhdelenie* confirms Eve Levin's suggestion regarding an earlier historical period that the Russian Orthodox Church cared relatively little about what its members *thought* sexually; it was concerned, instead, with what they actually *did*. Still, the easy use of the term *blud* suggests that sometimes individuals themselves identified thought with action.

Their confusion, perhaps deliberate, is not surprising. Many Orthodox prayers, including those recited before having Communion, routinely have the penitent refer to him- or herself as "a fornicator," or to ask God to "cleanse me as thou didst cleanse the adulteress," whether or not he or she has engaged in sexual thought or activity. Fornication is a metaphor for the general, chronic spiritual impurity of physical beings. (Note that angels, to underscore their distinction from humans, are referred to as *bodiless* hosts). The Russian term for the prodigal son is *bludnyi syn*. Nor could the linguistic connection of the verb *bludit'sia* to such words as *zabluzhdat'sia* (to err, to be mistaken) or *zabludit'sia* (to lose one's way, to get lost) have encouraged a rigorously limited use of the verb. Can one really believe a maid from Yaroslavl, for example, when she writes that she "fornicates every minute of every day"[32]—particularly given that she also finds time to steal food from her employers, sing and dance with soldiers in the tavern, and gossip with the other servants?

Another confession from a woman named Minodora suggests the confusion that might emerge:

> Once I sinned against Sunday, spending the whole night in drunkenness, and then drank also with the husbands of others. Then I sensed during the reading of the Gospels[33] that *this means adultery*, and now my heart aches over my sins and with tears I beg you, sweet Father, please pray to my [guardian] angel.[34]

Thus it is exceedingly difficult to generalize about sexual mores based on these confessions. Perhaps the only element one can identify with certainty is the overwhelmingly negative perception of sexual activity, in whatever form. Nowhere in the confessions is there any notion of sex as a benign or even favorable force to channel and even enjoy; men and women alike consider it a fundamental impurity that should be uprooted, or at least struggled against. The perception of sexual activity as unclean emerges from the requirement of washing oneself after sexual relations and before entering a church; hence one woman appears to refer to the physical, rather than spiritual, aspects of impurity, when she mentions that she "dared to approach the Holy Chalice dirty after a man, and, when, in a woman's condition [e.g., during menstruation], often also approached dirty and venerated the holy icons and the cross."[35]

While there is a high degree of specificity, as when one woman writes that she "fornicated with children of the female sex," there is little evidence in the confessions to suggest that—in contrast with Church teaching—the people who wrote regarded sexual activity with children or adults of the same sex as more or less sinful than with those of the opposite sex.[36] The less educated virtually never use such terms as "unnatural," as if they view sexual activity itself as unnatural or at least always sinful. Although the sinfulness of homosexual activity is acknowledged, these confessors apparently do not view it as substantially or inherently worse than illicit heterosexual activity. Consider the language this woman uses regarding her attraction to a girl:

> Please save me from the fornicating enemy and from the sin of Sodom. Batiushka [Father] dear, I love one girl and, if I touch her, the flames of Hades and impurity burn me . . . I wish to be rid of this sin and I want to love with pure, divine love.[37]

While this woman recognizes that her attraction to the girl is sinful, her language is no different than that used by women attracted to men, or men attracted to women. The fact of sexual attraction and activity is the sin, not its object. Another woman, however, expresses an explicit distaste towards attraction between women when she writes of her own attraction for "another maiden":

> I have fallen in love passionately with her; I have fallen into the sin of adultery.[38] I sinned with her through passionate kisses and sinful glances, we satisfied our desires in this way during the time of the Divine Liturgy and at night [and] during your mass confession.[39] Even during Great Lent I spent time with her during your service and during communion when everyone was repenting, I was sinning . . . I had condemned others, saying how could a maiden love another maiden and for my condemnation I fell into the same sin.[40]

Most interesting is that this woman believes that harshly judging or condemning others is worse than any sin for which one might judge them: she believes she was punished with a lesbian attraction specifically because she had condemned it.

There is one area, however, where the object of one's desire matters a great deal. The taboo on sexual relations with either blood or spiritual kinfolk has already been noted. The villagers were clearly aware of it, regularly specifying degrees of relation. This would appear to be part of a general tendency by the less educated to be as specific as possible in detailing their sins (and a countervailing tendency by the more educated to generalize).

Communion

A similar concern with the concrete emerges in the attitude toward communion. Father Ioann's wish to transform the relation of his flock to the Eucharist assumes a new urgency in the context of these letters. While they show profound reverence toward the sacrament, this reverence tends all too easily to slide into literality and great fear.[41] The references to communion in the letters of both the educated and the less educated are striking in their physicality and in the importance attached to the prescriptions surrounding the sacrament. The letters to Father Ioann show that communion, despite being a legal requirement, was far from a formal, empty, or abstract action but was charged with literal, potent significance for many people from all social groups.[42]

One man confessed, for example, that occasionally he had eaten before communion.[43] One educated woman bewailed her distraction and lack of reverence at communion:

> How carelessly, how idly, with what thoughts and with a heart in what a state did I partake of the Holy Mysteries![44]

Such sentiments suggest that communion was seen as a state requiring all one's concentration and dedication. But the exalted emphasis placed on communion could lead to rebelliousness and questioning. Some who wrote Father Ioann, for example, shared his occasional Eucharistic doubts. An educated woman described such an occurrence:

> Having partaken of the Holy Body of Christ, I bit it apart to taste it specifically; I wanted to determine whether this was really Body and not bread, and I also had the effrontery to think, well, if this is not what it is, then go ahead, God, punish me right here where I stand, and if you do not punish me, then it means that You do not even exist, and with these thoughts I left the church and did not go to communion or pray at all for thirteen years.[45]

Whereas the educated tended to confess such "intellectual" sins of doubt or distraction toward the Eucharist, people of the lower class who wrote Father Ioann reported communion-related sins that were almost exclusively physical and external, for example, whether one had previously fasted and abstained from sexual relations or, at most, whether one had approached in a state of due piety. Eating non-Lenten food was also seen as an "unlawful" transgression and a defamation of the sacrament, which was only supposed to enter a body that had been purified through fasting. Even more serious were acts of explicit physical defamation, even accidental ones. Both laity and clergy had a keen sense of the holiness of the Eucharistic elements and feared "defiling" them in any way. This fear was fostered by elaborate restrictions such as specifying that any garments on which infants might have coughed up communion be burned; if any of it fell on the floor, the carpet or floorboards were to be either scrubbed clean or burned as well.[46] In such a climate, it is not surprising that one person confessed, "I dropped part of the Holy Gifts out of my mouth."[47] Another man described the process of guilt in greater detail:

> I saw how after communion my brother spat it out and I could see the holy blood and body of the Lord, and I shrank from picking it up. I do not remember how old I was but for some reason I also crumbled the Holy Mysteries on the floor.[48]

Partaking of communion in an unworthy state was particularly sinful if that state involved alcohol. One villager confessed:

> Once I had communion while I had a hangover, I partook of the Holy Mysteries without knowing what I was doing: I thought it was *prosphora* and wine, nothing more.[49]

Partaking of communion had effects that extended beyond the short term. The prayers that were read after communion enjoined one to spend the remainder of the day "in sobriety and continence and speaking as little as possible, so that on that day one would honorably contain within oneself the received Christ."[50] Based on the confessions sent to Father Ioann, some people did feel a sense of the divine dwelling within them, if only temporarily. Thus succumbing to temptation soon after having had communion was seen as substantially worse than if one's communion had taken place some time ago. One woman rebuked herself—and Father Ioann—on just such an occasion:

> You gave me communion, Batiushka, and said that the Lord would extinguish all my passions, and when I went to bed the night of the day I had communion the enemy attacked me so fiercely that by morning I fornicated with myself.[51]

Class Differences

Class differences occasionally emerge in predictable vices. Highly educated people mention idleness and overeating much more frequently than the barely literate, for example.[52] But class differences emerge most palpably in the tone of the confession. Educated women are more inclined to treat their confessions as psychological self-analyses, although they continue to use religious language to describe their states, whereas the less educated tend to accept unambiguously the definitions of the Orthodox Church, calling a sin (in the definition of the Church) a sin and to describe actions committed in as much detail as possible. Better-educated women express their sins in milder terms than their less-educated counterparts. Although the following woman mentions envy, deceit, judging, breaking the fasts, and taking offense in the same language peasant women do, for example, she then changes her tone. The use of the qualifiers "not always" or "sometimes" is also more characteristic of the better educated:

> In prayer I have *tended* to veer toward quantity rather than quality; I *rarely* examine myself spiritually; *sometimes* I have spiritual pride and *do not always* struggle against it . . . I *do not always* sympathize with the poor or with my neighbors . . . I laughed, I was *occasionally* unrestrained in food and drink . . .[53] I was enthusiastic about music and worldly pleasures, I carried out my whims; I was *not always* fair with the servants.[54]

Other concerns and expressions, such as being proud of one's learning or lacking simplicity of heart, are also characteristic of the educated. The educated women who wrote Father Ioann consistently refer to their coldness, or stoniness, which is nearly absent in the confessions of the less educated. The less educated, by contrast, concentrate less on their inner lives and more on their actions. Less-educated men and women alike regarded their sources of amusement as sinful activities, which hardly occurs in the confessions of the educated. They consistently and duly confessed going dancing, singing songs, telling tales, clapping hands while playing games, and going to the theater or masquerades.[55]

On first glance it would appear that any pleasure people took in popular culture was mixed: they appear to have felt guilty about *all* non-Church culture, however universal it was among their contemporaries. One must remember, however, that the clergy had inveighed against popular customs, particularly those accompanying such feasts as Christmas and Theophany, practically since the introduction of Christianity to Russia. While their audience clearly understood their message, as is evident from the dutiful reporting of all forms of revelry in confessions, the clergy's lack of success in changing the behavior of their parishioners is also evident: their sermons inveigh against the same customs in the same terms in the sixteenth and the early twentieth centuries.[56] On the basis of the confessions to Father Ioann, it seems as if the clergy and the people had reached a tacit understanding in which the clergy would accept the behavior of the people as long as the people accepted the judgment of that behavior by the clergy. Different women wrote:

> I am a universal adulteress, in my youth I went to fairs, drank wine and all kinds of drinks with all the men, I sang all kinds of bad songs . . . and in the theaters and at fairs I watched all kinds of comedies with delight . . .[57]

... When I was a nanny in Petrov there was a tavern beneath us and I would go there to amuse myself, to listen to dances and songs, this was a great consolation to me ... [58]

... I allowed myself to carouse and have a good time ... now however the Lord in his mercy has visited me with sorrows, sicknesses ... I thank the Lord that he has visited me with these sicknesses because of my cursed sins. [59]

Other sins specific to the less educated include cursing the animals and the weather (especially the wind). Attempting to predict the weather is also regarded as sinful. [60] They are more prone to stealing, itemizing all the items: "knives, forks, threads, needles, scissors, linen, featherbeds, a pillow, and one hen which I sold to buy vodka." [61] The less educated also mention more frequently such physical sins as not keeping the fasts or eating holy bread after having eaten ordinary food (holy water and bread that had been blessed in church was supposed to be the first food one ate in the morning, when one was still pure from the night's fast and had not sullied oneself with unsanctified food). The opinion that one should wear one's best clothes to church, or at least "decent" ones, was shared by all classes, but only the poorer people confessed going to church dirty or not going to communion for lack of "decent clothing."

Class differences emerge most palpably, however, in relation to food. The educated writers hardly mention it, while detailed references to stealing food, eating more than one's share, and even the monastic sin of "eating in secret," which acquires a practical meaning in large, poor families unanticipated by the desert fathers, are a staple of the letters from the less educated. [62] One woman writes:

I have no love at all, when Mother would leave me my little brother to watch I would take his food and eat it or give him the worst bits which he could not eat and this boy died, maybe because of me ... I will eat something secretly and Mother will ask me about it and I lie and so irritated my mother that she begged God to die rather than to continue to suffer at the hands of her children, but she could not break my stubbornness, and all this through eating in secret [*tainoiadenie*] ... When our house burned down and one poor little widow took us in for a while, when she went out begging I took the best bits of food from her too. [63]

Houseservants had additional temptations:

I constantly stole food from my masters and ate secretly to satiety, and also at another employment I stole and ate secretly, I ate to fill ... I cooked up pastry and licked up half of it in secret . . . When I lived at the Mazaevs', I would steal sweetmeats from the shops and secretly bake them for myself . . . During the fasts I would steal meat and milk and eat them, I engaged in *chrevobesie*.[64]

Nevertheless, some confessions suggest convincingly the caution one must exercise in attempting to attribute class levels. The following account, from a woman who was apparently a merchant or a shopkeeper, illustrates the mixture of worldliness, piety, superstition, and bad grammar that hardly lends itself to easy categorization:

I went to my marriage wreath while menstruating, defiled myself with my husband . . . I cast spells . . . I do not have children.[65] We defile Sundays and holidays, do not keep the fasts, I took a false oath, I acted evilly in court, I bought myself off . . . I made the help work on Sundays,[66] I accepted stolen goods and made out false promissory notes . . . I went to wizards and to doctors,[67] I believed in the devil and not in God . . . The world has never seen such an adulteress until me, I should not even look up at heaven . . . I took interest from the poor . . . I cannot struggle against sleep the moment I pick up a holy book or stand to prayer.[68] . . . Dear spiritual father, tell me how to struggle against the devil; every night he arouses my desires in my sleep, I cannot save myself.[69]

Barely literate women in particular show an astounding familiarity with religious language. They freely cite phrases from the Psalms, the Gospels, the lives of the saints, and the rituals of the Orthodox Church. In the middle of describing how she gossiped with the maid and the cook, a nanny will sigh, "O Lord, my sins are greater than the sands of the sea and the earth."[70] Another woman quotes Psalm 50 (it is read frequently during Orthodox services and is one people would have been likely to know by heart) so casually one might think she meant it literally: "I was conceived in iniquity and in sins did my mother bear me."[71] Another woman writes, "Like the fruitless fig tree, like the foolish virgins, I do not have the oil of good deeds, I will be left outside the doors of the heavenly bridal chamber."[72] They compare themselves to the saints using the analogies standard for contemporary sermons, saying, "I sinned for many years but offer little repentance, while the saints cried their whole lives over one single sin."[73] The extent to which the psalms in particular were part of many people's ordinary language is evident from the ease with which they interpolate them into the rest of their text:

In my heart I have the root of all evil, it is like an overgrown swamp, wherein are innumerable things creeping, both small and great beasts.[74]

Curses, Spells, and Incantations

Curses invoking the name of God, the larger category in which blasphemy falls, appear to have been a standard feature of lower-class, especially peasant, life. (It seems to vanish when peasants move to cities.) Why is it omnipresent there and virtually absent among the more educated?[75] The most likely reason may have been the powerlessness of the lower classes to alter their circumstances. The strict limits placed on the peasants' lives, the lack of opportunity to significantly alter their circumstances (particularly in the case of women), created a state of nearly constant anger and frustration. If there was little one could do to address the direct causes of one's rage, one had to vent it nonetheless. Curses and imprecations were among the only ways available to challenge authority (parents, husbands, priests) or to rail at oppressive circumstances (families generally, domestic animals, the elements, children). Just as blasphemy was viewed as rebellion against a God that could not be thrown off,[76] so, too, was cursing seen as rebellion against various elements of a life that could not be thrown off. It would be mistaken, however, to regard cursing someone as a harmless way of venting one's spleen. As the confessions to Father Ioann show, cursing was regarded as a potent action with potentially dire consequences:

> Once in anger I said to my husband, "I could just stab you—" this was not said from the heart, but still I killed him with these words,[77] for he was consumptive . . . After these words of mine he fell sick and died without Christian consolations, without communion or extreme unction.[78]

Invoking the Devil was as dangerous as cursing God: "I said 'Devil's place,' I called the demon to sleep . . . I reviled God."[79]

The relation between parent and child, and especially between mother and child, was the most susceptible to cursing and the most fraught with evil consequences. The high degree of formalized respect and filial piety that was supposed to characterize parent-child relations was evidently a source of great strain for both sides. One tended to curse those who were the closest at hand. Mothers with large extended families and visiting relatives particularly felt the tension. One hapless woman wrote:

> Father Ioann, mentor of all sinners, please pray for my sins. I had six children, the youngest was eight weeks old and then, during Big Lent, when my husband's parents were here, I sinned against Clean Thursday like this: I said, "Oh, I wish at least half of you would just die!"—That night we went to sleep, my husband first, me next, then the little child, and then the rest of the family. When we woke during the night, the child, who had

been completely healthy, was not alive. Then I felt such sorrow and grief in my heart.[80]

A similar sense of being trapped by one's family and circumstances emerges in another woman's confession to Father Ioann:

> I cursed my children, saying, "I wish you did not exist," and the Lord heard my prayer, my children Vasili and Anna climbed up onto the stove and never got off, they died at twelve o'clock ... I was also injured during a fire as a result of which my arms and legs go into spasms ... Please forgive me, help me, and absolve me.[81]

This confession is striking for its terseness. There is no emotion or any reference to guilt, often considered superfluous. Repentance appears to be implied in the very act of confessing. The writer is interested in release and absolution. She states the facts of the case plainly, without embellishment. Notice, however, the implied link between the injury from the fire and the sins described before it: the injury from the fire is punishment for her sins—hence the need for absolution from a holy man before she can ask for healing.

The casting of spells, as an explicitly magical activity, was regarded as essentially different from cursing. Cursing was done in the heat of the moment and was usually a response to a chronic, rather than particular, affliction; using the tools and methods of male and female witches was premeditated and aimed at a specific result, whether injuring someone's livestock or winning someone's love. Priests, moreover, were particularly concerned with whether people had consulted wizards (*volkhvy*), fortune-tellers or "women repugnant to God" (*baby bogomerzkiia*) and routinely inquired into such activity during confession.[82] People sending in their confessions to Father Ioann would thus have anticipated such queries and addressed them in advance:

> People practiced sorcery for me and I gave them money for this, eleven rubles, and when he was conjuring, the wizard placed seals on my back and on my chest. Then I went to a sorceress who read cards ...[83]
> ... I spat in what people were to drink so that men would love me, I washed my sick sister with water from a corpse ...[84]
> ... I foretold the future using cards, I went to soothsayers.[85]

The line between magic and the holy may have been strictly drawn—the writers always sought to distinguish between the two and called them by their respective names—but they coexisted all the same. After describing the sorcery above, for example, the same woman writes that "after all these sins I went to see one *starets* [elder] and he clapped his hands over [my] naked body and said that after this I would not sin any more."[86]

Religious acts could be "inverted," thus summoning the reverse effect. A conventional act of piety was to write down the names of the living or the dead whom one wished the priest to commemorate during the liturgy and pass the list to the altar. In an attempt to do harm to someone still alive, people would include that person on the list of those reposed; one woman did so to make the man she sought love her and pine for her.[87]

Gender Variations

As suggested above, both sexes have most sins in common, but the thirty-four men were more likely than women to repent for drinking, working on holidays, laziness, showing disrespect for or cursing parents and priests, playing cards, and, of course, beating their wives. A higher proportion of men confessed to having venereal disease. One wrote, "I sinned and have been sick with an impure disease from that sin for three years. Doctors cannot help me, only God can; I promise to live by the commandments; please pray for me."[88] Men were also more likely to fear that their souls would perish because they would be driven to suicide.[89]

By contrast, the women who sent their confessions to Father Ioann appear to have internalized the ideas and self-excoriations contained in the standard prayers before communion—particularly the assumption that one is guilty of every sin in existence and more sinful than any other creature—more than the men. One of these, the prayer by Simeon Metaphrastes with its exhaustive litany of wrongs committed and extravagant bemoaning of one's wretched state, reinforced the sense of all-pervading culpability. Such expressions as "What evil have I not committed?" were more than rhetorical; they were internalized and accepted as literal truth by those who read them. The prayer stated, among other things:

> See, Oh Lord, my humility, and forgive all my sins! See how my trans-gressions have increased more than the hairs of my head. For what evil have I not committed? What sin have I not wrought? What evil have I not imagined within my soul? *I have done the deeds as well:* fornication, adultery, pride, blasphemy, idle talk, unseemly laughter ... [list of sins continues for a page]. I have defiled my *every* sense and member and was the devil's worker in *all* ways.[90]

Notably one did not have to be literate to be acquainted with such prayers. Priests in many churches regularly assigned a person to read the prayers before communion aloud to fill in the time when the priests took communion at the altar or while parishioners were waiting in large numbers for confession.[91]

Thus people who could not read the prayers in private could still absorb them. Although the prayers themselves are not gender-specific, it was mostly women who echoed them in their letters to Father Ioann, constantly exclaiming, as one woman did, "Is there another such damned, lawless, adulteress on earth as I?"[92] Another woman wrote:

I crave to be the slave of God, I implore [Him, you] to allow me to be among the number of His children, to accept me as a sheep of his flock . . . I have not had men in my life, but I have sinned against the Lord more than all the rest of the world.[93]

Another educated woman used even more extreme language:

I am a woman hyena, as I have no love. I am a human animal, attempting to take my own life—my life, which others have so carefully sought to preserve. . . . I am the worst sinner from the creation of the world: I have had no thoughts of God, of sin, of eternity, etc. I am a universal criminal: mother killer, wife killer, the killer of a completely normal, healthy woman, a despairing suicide, the breaker of every word of the Gospels.[94]

Women regularly mention attempting to abort their children or kill them after they are born. Shame is cited as a reason more often than economic problems. Sometimes their attempts to rationalize their actions before Father Ioann and God were quite elaborate:

It seemed to me that I had forfeited my innocence and I was afraid of rebuke and I asked the Lord if it would be better if I had a dead child, only not to be rebuked, but I did not know what the lot of these dead children was[95] and so I vowed to go to Pochaev or to send ten rubles to the Mother of God anything only to be free of rebuke and there was a miracle of God over me: the Sovereign Mistress saved me from disgrace, and the child was stillborn.[96] Perhaps it might have been possible to revive him,[97] but his nose was flattened; in a word, it was an ugly nose and so I did not attempt to revive him, thinking that they would all laugh at him anyway.[98]

Most striking is that none of the women expresses concern at her lack of knowledge of the Orthodox faith, whereas it is a recurrent concern of the few men who sent their confessions to Father Ioann. One man who repents for cursing his children, eating before communion, not praying or going to church on Sundays and holidays, and earning his mother's curses closes with the words, "Also, dear Batiushka, please pray to God and bless me a sinner so that God would grant me to understand Divine reading and Divine reading in God's temple."[99]

The following letter from Semën, Prince Shcherbatov's cook, is particularly eloquent in expressing the desire for understanding:

> March 15, 1908
>
> *Confession.*
>
> Today I visited you, Batiushka, and received your blessing to send you a written confession.[100] I do not sense any particular or grievous sins in me besides the usual human ones.[101] But I do have a grievous sin, which is that I do not know how to pray consciously and with profound faith.
>
> If my parents taught me from childhood to go to church frequently and to recite my prayers, they were still not able to do so in such a way that I would continue to go now.[102] They never even explained to me what our Orthodox faith actually is, and I still do not know now. They go to church and pray fervently; whereas I—if I go at all—then I mostly listen to the singing, look at the ceremony, but I am utterly far from the prayer I see in others, my thoughts literally wander, I become offended at myself, but I cannot do anything with myself to chase away these thoughts and to pray like everyone else.
>
> And so to go to church is to sin all the more. Not to go is to earn the imprecations of my parents and to be some kind of an unbelieving idol. Which is also bad and sinful. I decided to come to you, Batiushka, to confession, to acknowledge this sin, and to ask you to teach me how to pray the way every religious Orthodox person ought to pray . . .
>
> I want to believe and to pray, but not according to tradition or out of decency, but consciously, with profound understanding, and with an open soul.[103] When my comrades and acquaintances teach me to believe in some new teachings of Tolstoy or others, I would like to be able not only to object to their arguments but bring them to reason as well.
>
> The sinner Semën, the cook of Kn. Shcherbatov.
>
> I fast and have Communion each year.[104]

These confessions show that, although most sinners shared many qualities that illuminated common attitudes, nevertheless differences regarding class and gender persisted. People who wrote their confessions, moreover, varied greatly when it came to the "master narrative" of the oral confession which they clearly knew very well. The individuality of the themes they chose to emphasize, the sins they felt they needed to mention, the way they wrote their stories—all this suggests that the confession, far from being an externally imposed form of control hostile critics felt it to be, could also be a way for people to rethink both their lives and their life stories.

But this happy discovery is less surprising than the very existence of these confessions. In fact, the presence of the confessions in Father Ioann's archive poses a delicate pastoral question. Written confessions were discouraged in Orthodox practice unless they served as a supplement to a conventional spoken confession. Did written confessions such as these serve as an occasional supplement to the mass confessions Father Ioann instituted? Did they remove the unease people may have felt that perhaps the depth of their sins prevented them from receiving absolution along with everyone else at St. Andrew's in Kronstadt? Were the written confessions simply a function of geographical distance that made it impossible for confessors to travel? And if the confessors were not absolved, and if their aim was not absolution but counsel, then can these confessions even be classified as such?

The only case where late-nineteenth-century Russian pastoral practice had fully approved the use of a written confession was when the confessor was a literate deaf mute who would arrive in church and present the priest with his list of sins.[105] In this case, however, the priest was supposed to burn the written confession in front of the confessor, both to soothe the person's conscience and to avoid the possibility that the confession would fall into someone else's hands. The latter precaution reinforced the emphasis on the secrecy of the confessional, which was constantly reiterated in pastoral practice.[106]

Why did Father Ioann not destroy the confessions he received once he answered them? (The few that could be dated to 1898 remained in his possession for as long as ten years). Whether he used them as a reference or kept them as a reminder of the extent and poignancy of human frailty or simply filed away everything automatically without ever having the chance to go through the files to destroy them remains unknown. He never referred to the confessions in his diaries nor, apparently, in his conversations with those who set down their reminiscences, so one may only guess at his motives. Whatever the motives were, they have made it possible for us to know something of the contents of the hearts and minds of the people in late imperial Russia who would approach a parish priest—albeit a most unusual one—and to know something of what they wished to unburden.

Notes

1. For analyses contemporary with the confessions discussed in this paper, see S. I. Smirnov, *Dukhovnyi otets v drevnei vostochnoi tserkvi. Istoriia dukhovnichestva na vostokie* (Sergiev Posad, 1906); and A. I. Almazov, *Tainaia ispoved' v pravoslavnoi vostochnoi tserkvi: opyt vneshnei istorii,* 3 vols. (Odessa, 1894–1895).

114 Nadieszda Kizenko

2. The most subtle and imaginative treatment of Orthodox penitentials remains N. Suvorov, "Veroiatnyi sostav drevneishago ispovednago i pokaiannago ustava v vostochnoi tserkvi," *Vizantiiskii vremennik* 8 (1901): 357–434; 9 (1901): 378–417. Eve Levin has attempted to extrapolate conclusions for behavior on the basis of confessional manuals used by priests in *Sex and Society in the World of the Orthodox Slavs, 900–1700* (Ithaca, N.Y., 1991). Gregory L. Freeze has analyzed the potential of the confession as a means of enforcing discipline; see his "Wages of Sin: the Decline of Public Penance in Imperial Russia," in *Seeking God: The Recovery of Religious Identity in Orthodox Russia, Ukraine, and Georgia* (De Kalb, Ill., 1993), 53–82. For a valuable comparison, see Thomas N. Tentler, *Sin and Confession on the Eve of the Reformation* (Princeton, N.J., 1977).

3. The confessions are in the Central State Historical Archive of Saint Petersburg, TsGIA SPb, f. 2219, op. 1, d. 31.

4. See the discussion of privacy and secrecy in Giordano Bruno Guerri, *Io ti assolvo. Etica, politica, sesso: i confessori di fronte a vecchi e nuovi peccati* (Milan, 1993), 9–13.

5. Although Soviet historians emphasized occasional examples of people not confessing in a given year, statistics for those observing the obligation remained high through the end of the Russian Empire. Cf. B. G. Litvak, "Russkoe pravoslavie v XIX veke," in *Russkoe pravoslavie: vekhi istorii* (Leningrad, 1975), 122–25; and Gregory L. Freeze, *The Parish Clergy in Nineteenth-Century Russia* (Princeton, N.J., 1983), xxix. I am not discussing confession as a literary or autobiographical genre here, although I do so in the monograph I am currently preparing on confession in modern Russia.

6. The phenomenon of people preferring to confess sins which they were most loath to admit to any priest other than the one they knew best was not restricted to Russia. Jean Delumeau notes the popularity enjoyed by traveling missionaries in Roman Catholic Europe precisely because they provided a confessional alternative, and even argues that one cause of the Reformation was a reluctance to confess (*Sin and Fear: the Emergence of a Western Guilt Culture, 13th–18th centuries* (New York, 1977), 471–75). Several nineteenth-century manuals for priests addressed this problem, stating that if a priest encountered confessants from another parish who were seeking to confess only mild sins to their own parish priest and more serious ones to a priest they did not know, they were to be sent back as attempting to fool God Himself. See Georgii Diachenko, *Voprosy na ispovedanii detei* (Kiev, 1890), 87.

7. Cf. the argument of Gregory L. Freeze, "'Going to the Intelligentsia': The Church in Its Urban Mission in Post-Reform Russia," in Edith W. Clowes, Samuel D. Kassow, and James L. West, eds., *Between Tsar and People* (Princeton, 1991).

8. This standard formula appears in every prayer book published in the nineteenth century. Quoted here from editions contemporary with these confessions: *Molitvoslov* (Kiev, 1881), 44–45; and *Molitvoslov* (Moscow, 1904), 254–55.

9. This sin, which might seem relatively insignificant, was regarded by Russian and Ukrainian laity and clergy alike to be particularly offensive to God. One publication describes it as the most offensive sin: See Evstratii Golovanskii, *Tysiacha dvesti voprosov sel'skikh prikhozhan o raznykh dushepoleznykh predmetakh s otvetami na onye byvshago prikhodskago ikh sviashchennika,* 2nd ed. (Kiev, 1869), 52.

10. For contemporary North America, see Ann Douglas, *The Feminization of American Culture* (New York, 1977). For contemporary Europe, see Philippe Boutry and Michel Cinquin, *Deux Pèlerinages aux XIXe Siècle, Ars et Paray-le-Monial* (Paris, 1980), 150ff.

11. See the introductory comments to confession in S. V. Bulgakov, *Nastol'naia Kniga,* 1000ff.

12. Ibid., 1002.

13. Eyewitness accounts suggest that the proportion of women to men in St. Andrew's Cathedral was equivalent. For example, see V. M., *Dva dnia v Kronshtadte, iz dnevnika studenta* (Sergiev Posad, 1902), 60–74; I. K. Surskii, *Otets Ioann Kronshtadtskii,* 2 vols. (Belgrade, 1938–1941, reprint, Forestville, Calif., 1979–1980, 1:66–68; Mikhail (Semenov), *Otets Ioann Kronshtadtskii. Polnaia biografiia s illiustratsiiami* (St. Petersburg, 1903), 1:310–18.

14. See the accounts of Konstantin Fofanov, Rossiiskii gosudarstvennyi arkhiv literatury i isskustva (RGALI), f. 525, op. 1, d. 41, l. 60b.; Surskii, *Otets Ioann Kronshtadtskii,* 1:10–12; Al. Serebrov, *Vremia i Liudi, Vospominaniia* (Moscow, 1960), 30–35; and V. M., *Dva dnia v Kronshtadte,* 61–64.

15. The incident was reported in *Tovarishch* to condemn the "fanaticism" that Father Ioann inspired (*Tovarishch,* no. 16 [April 21/May 4, 1906]: 2).

16. Reported in *Svet,* no. 132 (May 18, 1900); quoted in V. M., *Dva dnia,* 73–74.

17. For a discussion of literacy patterns, see Jeffrey Brooks, *When Russia Learned to Read: Literacy and Popular Literature, 1861–1917* (Princeton, N.J., 1985), 3–34.

18. TsGIA SPb, f. 2219, op. 1, d. 31, l. 32.

19. Ibid., l. 63.

20. Ibid., l. 67. The writers' ability to remember their sins is remarkable.

21. "A bad place" was the expression used in parts of Russia for an outhouse.

22. TsGIA SPb, f. 2219, op. 1, d. 31, l. 234.

23. Bulgakov, *Nastol'naia Kniga,* 1005. Marriages were forbidden to take place on Saturdays, Tuesdays, and Thursdays, and on the chief holiday and fasting periods also because of the prohibition on sexual relations.

24. TsGIA SPb, f. 2219, op. 1, d. 31, ll. 67–68.

25. The term *kum* denotes spiritual, as opposed to blood, kin: a *kum* could be the father of one's godchild, the child of one's godparent, and so on. Incest in these cases was more harshly judged than incest among blood relatives.

26. TsGIA SPb, f. 2219, op. 1, d. 31, ll. 67–68.

27. TsGIA SPb, f. 2219, op. 1, d. 31, l. 1920b.

28. Ibid., l. 192.

29. Ibid., l. 212. The use of the simile "like a dog" in this confession is apt as well as colorful. The Russian Orthodox regarded dogs as so unclean that they were generally not even allowed in the house, let alone in church. If a dog did manage to get into a church, the church had to be specially purified by the priest before being used again. The singling out of dogs, as opposed to other animals, comes from the belief that the devil was most likely to assume their guise, or that of black cats. See Linda J. Ivanits, *Russian Folk Belief* (Armonk, N.Y., 1989), 39.

30. All three are mentioned because the sin becomes a "triple" sin: one is insulting Isaiah *and* St. Nicholas *and* the Lord.

31. TsGIA SPb, f. 2219, op. 1, d. 31, ll. 690b. –70.

32. Ibid., l. 69.

33. The woman is apparently referring to the phrase rendered in the King James Bible as "Be not drunk with wine, wherein is excess; but be filled with the Spirit" (Ephesians 6:18). In the Church Slavonic translation, however, the phrase is, "Do not get drunk on wine, wherein is fornication [*v nemzhe est' blud*]." Along with the rendering of the prodigal son as *bludnyi syn,* this is an example of the variations of the term *blud* in Church Slavonic and its consequent tendency to be all-encompassing.

34. TsGIA SPb, f. 2219, op. 1, d. 31, l. 1170b.

35. Ibid., l. 2500b.

36. Ibid., l. 192. For a discussion of the Orthodox position on homosexuality and bestiality, see the canons of St. Gregory, Bishop of Nyssa, 500–503, and the canons of St. Basil the Great, 383–84, both in *Pravila svv. Otsev s tolkovaniami* (Moscow, 1912).

37. TsGIA SPb, f. 2219, op. 1, d. 31, l. 2170b.

38. The following description of what in her mind constitutes "adultery"—some form of sexual activity between two unmarried women—shows again how much care one must exercise in interpreting the expressions in the confessions.

39. The perceived contrast between the holiness of the external occasion and the sinfulness of one's inner activity (lustful thoughts or glances) exacerbates the sense of sin this woman feels.

40. TsGIA SPb, f. 2219, op. 1, d. 31, ll. 237–2370b.

41. This is not surprising, given that the prayers before communion repeatedly stressed the "dread and terror" one *ought* to feel, and considering that the priest summoned the faithful to the chalice with the words "with *fear of God* and faith draw near" (*Service Book: The Divine Liturgy of St. John Chrysostom* [Jordanville, N.Y., 1999], 118).

42. The evidence of the confessions is corroborated by other sources. In her memoirs, the aristocratic Galina von Meck, for example, vividly describes the fear of being irresistibly impelled to spit communion out of her mouth (Galina von Meck, *As I Remember Them* [London, 1973], 124).

43. TsGIA SPb, f. 2219, op. 1, d. 31, l. 141.

44. Ibid., l. 163.

45. Ibid., ll. 258–59.

46. Bulgakov, *Nastol'naia Kniga*, 987.

47. TsGIA SPb, f. 2219, op. 1, d. 31, l. 62.

48. Ibid., l. 680b.

49. Ibid., l. 103.

50. *Pravilo Molitvennoe Gotoviashchimsia ko Sviatomu Prichashcheniiu i ezhednevnoe vechernee i utrennee* (Vladimirova, 1948), 282.

51. TsGIA SPb, f. 2219, op. 1, d. 31, l. 2110b.

52. This is not surprising, given the scale of meals indicated for masters relative to servants in the cookbook Bible of the time, that of Elena Molokhovets (translated into English as *Classic Russian Cooking: Elena Molokhovets' "A Gift to Young Housewives,"* trans. Joyce Toomre (Bloomington, Ind., 1993).

53. As opposed to the laconic term "gluttony" (*ob"iadenie*) used by the less educated.

54. TsGIA SPb, f. 2219, op. 1, d. 31, l. 96.

55. This may also have been a function of Father Ioann's unusually strong and well-publicized antipathy toward the theater. See, for example, *O svetskoi zhizni: urok blagodatnoi zhizni po rukovodstvu o. Ioanna Kronshtadtskago* (Moscow, 1894), esp. 15ff.

56. See N. V. Rozhdestvenskii, ed., "K istorii bor'by s tserkovnymi bezporiadkami, otgoloskami iazychestva i porokami v russkom bytu XVII v.," Ch OIDR, 1902, no. 2, pt. 4, 1–31.

57. TsGIA SPb, f. 2219, op. 1, d. 31, l. 71.

58. Ibid., l. 69.

59. Ibid., l. 113–1130b.

60. Ibid., l. 252a.

61. Ibid., l. 245.

62. Caroline Bynum has argued that food, rather than sex or money, was and remains the central concern in economically strained cultures ("Medieval people often saw gluttony as the major form of lust, fasting as the most painful renunciation, and eating as the most basic and literal way of encountering God.") See Caroline Walker Bynum, *Holy Feast and Holy Fast: The Religious Significance of Food to Medieval Women* (Berkeley, 1987), 2 and chap. 2.

63. TsGIA SPb f. 2219, op. 1, d. 31, l. 65.

64. Like its counterpart, *gortanobesie*, this now obscure sin denoted rolling food around in one's mouth to savor it before swallowing (like wine tasters) (ibid., ll. 69–690b.).

65. This sign of God's disfavor, evoking the Old Testament, is perceived and described as a sin.

66. Obviously only an employer or landowner could confess this sin.

67. Equating these two examples of nonclerical aid (i.e., wizards and doctors), or perceiving that it is sinful to seek aid from a nonclerical source rather than relying on God's mercy, is noteworthy. This attitude should be viewed in the context of the contemporary debate on whether insuring one's property is acceptable from a religious point of view.

68. The reference to being overcome by sleep the instant one begins to pray is common in theological and edifying texts.

69. TsGIA SPb f. 2219, op. 1, d. 31, l. 203.

70. Ibid., l. 69. The reference is to the prayer of Manasses, King of Judah, read at Great Compline.

71. Ibid., l. 92a0b.

72. Ibid., l. 224. This reference to the New Testament parables has several possible sources: the three "Bridegroom" services during Holy Week, the Great Canon of Andrew of Crete, or the iconographic treatment of the subject, often used to decorate women's refectories in monasteries.

73. Ibid., l. 2480b.

74. The reference is to Psalm 103, read or sung at the beginning of every Vespers or All-night Vigil service.

75. Educated rural landowners and their families also appear to have been immune: on the basis of the confessions to Father Ioann, elaborate cursing was not a generally rural occurrence but largely a peasant phenomenon.

76. Not easily, at least, and not before 1905. Some priests writing their diocesan reports in 1905–1907 speak with dismay of the evident wonder their parishioners expressed at hearing anti-and nonreligious sentiments for the first time in their lives. See *Otchet Olonetskoi eparkhii za 1905 g.*, no. 2101, 1. 24ob, and *Otchet Orlovskoi eparkhii za 1907 g.*, no. 2227, 1. 12, quoted in Liubov Emeliakh, *Antiklerikal'noe dvizhenie krestian v period pervoi russkoi revoliutsii* (Leningrad, 1975), 122–25.

77. The notion that one could kill someone symbolically as well as literally was part of confessional language; priests were instructed to pose the question in the section of the confession that pertained to the sixth commandment.

78. TsGIA SPb f. 2219, op. 1, d. 31, ll. 68–68ob.

79. Ibid., l. 630b.

80. Ibid., l. 117.

81. Ibid., l. 121.

82. See S. Smirnov, "Baby bogomerzkiia," in *Sbornik statei, posviashchennykh Vasiliiu Osipovichu Kliuchevskomu . . .* (Moscow, 1909), 221.

83. TsGIA SPb, f. 2219, op. 1, d. 31, l. 98.

84. Ibid., l. 1120b.

85. Ibid., l. 193.

86. Ibid., l. 98.

87. Ibid., l. 2040b.

88. Ibid., l. 101.

89. See, for example, ibid., l. 198.

90. *Velikii Chasoslov,* repr. in Ep. Dimitrii, *Domashnii molitvoslov dlia userdstvuiushikh* (Kharbin, 1943), 154–55; emphasis added.

91. Bulgakov, *Nastol'naia Kniga,* 979 n. 3.

92. See, for example, TsGIA SPb, f. 2219, op. 1, d. 31, l. 2120b. (Men also compare themselves to the prodigal [*bludnyi*] son, but this is comparatively rare. See ibid., l. 213.)

93. Ibid., ll. 111–120b.

94. Ibid., l. 1090b.

95. Un-christened and stillborn children fell into the category of *zalozhnye pokoiniki.* The problem thus was not only a taxonomic one of how these children ought to be classified but a lurking concern that they might be in the grasp of the evil one. This concern may be one effect of the absence of the Roman Catholic notion of purgatory.

96. Even a sinful act can be miraculous. This underscores the objective sense of miracles or divine intercession.

97. This was not a fanciful notion. There were so many cases of "apparently dead" (*mnimoumershie*) people that both clergy and laity had evolved standard procedures before proceeding with a funeral to determine whether a person was actually dead—burning a part of

the body, inserting a steel needle, tying a finger to test the circulation, and so on. See Bulgakov, *Nastol'naia Kniga*, 1207ff.

98. TsGIA SPb, f. 2219, op. 1, d. 31, l. 92. For the canonical position on abortion and those who facilitate it, see canons 2 and 8 of St. Basil the Great, canon 21 of the Council of Ancyra (314), and canon 91 of the Council of Trullo (692).

99. Ibid., l. 130.

100. This is valuable evidence: perhaps others also obtained Father Ioann's blessing before sending their confessions to him, suggesting that it was a form both sides found efficacious.

101. No villager writes anything like this; it may the influence of an aristocratic milieu.

102. This ascription of responsibility to one's parents rather than to oneself is also a departure from the usual confession in which one assumes all blame for one's actions. It is impossible to speculate about how recent such a "psychological" approach to confessions was.

103. Those qualities stressed by the Protestant Reformation, by the Protestant-type Russian sects such as the Pashkovites and the Shtundisty—and by Ioann Kronshtadtskii.

104. Note the identification by *soslovie* (estate)—typical for the lower classes—and the mention of previous fasting and communion, as if in tacit response to the first question a priest would usually ask at confession (TsGIA SPb, f. 2219, op. 1, d. 31, ll. 47–48).

105. Bulgakov, *Nastol'naia Kniga*, 1014.

106. See, for example, the Ecclesiastical Regulation (Supplement, point 9), *Napominaniie sviashchennikam*, Zabelin, 208ff. If a priest told the family of a confessant what he had heard at confession, for example, he was supposed to be defrocked (quoted in Bulgakov, *Nastol'naia Kniga*, 1036).

5

"Orthodox Domesticity": Creating a Social Role for Women

William G. Wagner

⚊⚊⚊⚊⚊◆⚊⚊⚊⚊⚊

Petitioning the Council of the Russian Orthodox Church that met between August 1917 and September 1918 for the restoration of the office of deaconess, Liudmila Gerasimova, a journalist and self-professed specialist in agriculture, argued that "the Church, *the state*, and *humanity*" would benefit in important ways from this action. As deaconesses, she asserted, "women will engage in culturally enlightening activity in a religious spirit . . ., especially in such areas as agriculture, medicine, crafts, and useful trades for the countryside, . . . proclaim the Christian truths of the knowledge of God and undertake the moral and spiritual enlightenment of the people, . . . engage in economic-managerial activity in *the Church*, the organization of the parish, charitable activity [and] the declaration of the joyful news of the Gospels to adults, youth, and children and its proclamation to female Christian lay students . . . [and] participate in the liturgy and the management of the church economy." To achieve these objectives, Gerasimova envisaged the formation of "settlements of female intelligentsia" that would "find their best use in the cultural-educational religious mission of the village deaconess."[1] Gerasimova's conception of the office of deaconess therefore corresponded with the proposals advanced in the early twentieth century by such women as Abbess Ekaterina of the Holy Mother of God Convent in Lesna, Sedlets Province, and the Grand Duchess Elizaveta Feodorovna, founder and Mother Superior of the Martha and Mary Cloister in Moscow, who advocated an active social role for women through the creation of autonomous communities of deaconesses dedicated to missionary work and service to the poor and needy.[2]

A majority of the delegates at the Council, an exclusively male body, agreed that the Church and society had much to gain from such a widening of the social activity of women. Proposing to broaden the role of women in the Church, for example, the Committee on Church Discipline declared that "at the present time the position of women in general has changed, and education and all forms of labor and social activity have become accessible to them. Women, moreover, much more than men, have preserved a true religiosity and an ardent devotion to the Church." Hence "the expansion of the activity of Christian women in all educational, charitable, and even missionary organizations, sanctified moreover by the experience of the ages, will only benefit the affairs of the Church and enrich its complement of actors by the influx of new creative forces, so necessary for the Church at the present time."[3] Responding to the pleas of advocates such as Gerasimova, Abbess Ekaterina, and Grand Duchess Elizaveta Feodorovna, the committee also supported restoration of the office of deaconess, asserting that "the position of the Church in the period through which we are living, a period that in many ways recalls the first centuries of Christianity, awakens memories of the useful service of deaconesses to the early Church and summons Russian women believers to the special service of their Church through the office of deaconess."[4] Yet, in redefining the role of women in the Church, the committee was careful to ensure that its proposals did not challenge male clerical authority and remained consistent with what its members believed were the particular moral and psychological qualities and the natural and divine calling of women. Hence, while generally granted equality in parish and diocesan governance, women were considered too delicate to be included in certain diocesan bodies; although women were to be permitted to serve as sextons (*psalomshchiki*), those doing so would not be considered members of the clergy; and deaconesses would not enjoy the autonomy envisaged by Abbess Ekaterina and Grand Duchess Elizaveta Feodorovna but would perform a more modest role under the guidance and authority of parish clergy.[5] Through its actions the Council therefore attempted to accommodate, but also to contain and direct, the aspirations and religious energy of women.

The actions of the Church Council regarding women represented the culmination of a debate over the nature and role of women that had been taking place within the Orthodox Church, and between representatives of the Church and lay society, since the 1860s. As occurred in other areas of Church life and thought during these decades, the ideal of womanhood conveyed in Orthodox writings and the roles considered appropriate for women were contested and in flux, destabilizing structures of authority and providing women with alternative images that could be used to interpret, fashion, and give meaning to their lives. Tracing the development of the images of womanhood articulated by Orthodox writers in the late imperial period, this essay advances three broad arguments. First, revealing a capacity to accommodate as well as to oppose important aspects of modernity, the image of womanhood defined by Orthodox writers included not only conservative variants but also variants that emphasized the personal autonomy of women and encouraged them to engage in a wide range of social activities. In the latter case, paralleling trends in contemporary Europe, Russian Orthodox writers attempted essentially to widen the social roles open to women by projecting outward, into the public sphere, what they perceived as the particular domestic, maternal, and moral qualities of women.[6] Second, these images of womanhood reflected the diverse responses of Orthodox writers to lay criticisms of the teachings and policies of the Church with respect to women, to changing socioeconomic and cultural conditions, and to the growth both of education and employment outside the home for women and of religious activism by women themselves. Third, the contested ideals of womanhood contained in Orthodox writings during the late imperial period also reflected different strategies for reestablishing order and sexual balance within society and for preserving the social and moral authority of the Church in conditions perceived as both socially destabilizing and threatening to the Church. Again, even though some of these strategies were efforts to resist social and cultural modernity, others attempted to meet its challenges from an Orthodox Christian perspective. Paradoxically, however, the efforts of Orthodox writers to create an open dialogue within the Church, and between the Church and lay society, over competing images of womanhood and Church policies, as well as practices regarding women, thereby widening the opportunity for women to shape their own identities, only added to the problems of internal disunity and governance confronting the Church in the early twentieth century.[7]

Since the term "Orthodox writings" can encompass a broad range of genres, it should be noted at the outset that in this essay the term refers to official sources through which representatives of the Church attempted to shape the identity and behavior of women, and to the scholarly studies and polemical writings in which clerical and lay members of the Church debated the nature and proper role of women both among themselves and with secular critics. The volume of such writing, which includes catechisms, religious textbooks, instructional literature, sermons and other forms of public address, articles in scholarly and popular religious journals, scholarly treatises, polemical tracts, and so on, increased enormously in the late imperial period, as academic and publishing infrastructures developed, education expanded, and literacy rates rose. It was through such works, as filtered through personal experience, that the attitudes which informed the actions of delegates to the Church Council with respect to women were largely shaped. The authors of these works, it should be added, were almost exclusively male, reflecting not only cultural prejudices but also male dominance of the positions that provided an authoritative voice within the Church and access to the media of public discourse. As will become apparent, these authors can be grouped according to distinct tendencies. Given the values,

conceptions, and proposals distinguishing different tendencies, it seems ana-
lytically both useful and legitimate to characterize them as "conservative," "liberal," "reformist," and so on, especially since the positions these authors adopt
on a range of issues, from women and divorce to parish reform, were generally
consistent with one another and paralleled broader ideological trends in late
imperial Russia.

By the 1830s to 1850s, with respect to women, marriage, and the family, these
forms of Orthodox writing had come to project a domestic and maternalist ideal
of womanhood that was similar to the one found in secular literature at this
time. Hence, although little research has been done on the evolution of ideals of
womanhood in general in imperial Russia prior to the mid-nineteenth century,
and almost none on developments in Orthodox teachings and writing on this
theme, it would appear that a number of the trends noted by Catriona Kelly
and Diana Greene in advice literature for women, journals directed at parents
and children, and other literary sources between the mid-eighteenth and mid-
nineteenth centuries also affected Orthodox ideals of womanhood.[8] In particular, Orthodox writers appear to have assimilated the notion of "natural
motherhood" and the "ideology of separate spheres" that began to appear in
secular literature in the early nineteenth century, as well as to have been influenced by conceptions of mothers as educators of their children and moral arbi-
ters within the family, as had been propagated somewhat earlier.[9] These ideas
were combined with earlier Orthodox ideals that stressed both the subordinate
position of women in the family and their central role in managing the domestic
affairs of the household.[10] This mixture produced an ideal that included elements of patriarchy, equality, and complementarity.

With respect to patriarchy, Orthodox writers believed that the authority of
husbands and fathers was essential for the maintenance of stability and moral
order within the family, and for securing the interests and welfare of the family
as a whole. As expressed in an instructional essay on the family published in
Addenda to the Works of the Holy Fathers in 1844: "Although a wife is not a servant
but a true helpmeet of her husband, in the management of the household she
nonetheless must submit completely to her husband as the head of the family.
Otherwise there will not be unity, order, and peace in the domestic community."[11] This essentially functionalist justification for female subordination to
superior, and unitary, male authority was reinforced by appeals to both nature
and divine ordination. Hence naturalist conceptions of women as weak and
prone to emotionalism were combined with scriptural passages to demonstrate
that wives should submit to a husband's authority and that women in general
were in need of male guidance and control.[12] Continuing a long tradition in
Russian Orthodox writings on this theme, some authors also asserted that Eve's

primary responsibility for humanity's fall into sinfulness demonstrated the need for male suspiciousness of and authority over women, although this argument appears to have become less common—at least in print—by the 1840s.[13]

If the ideal of patriarchy led Orthodox writers to extol the virtues of obedience, submissiveness, and patience in women, even to the point of enduring an abusive relationship "as a trial from God,"[14] in other ways women and men were considered equal. Perhaps most critical, from a Christian perspective, Orthodox writings portrayed women and men as sharing an equal capacity for faith, piety, and salvation, and an equal ability to make moral choices and live a Christian life. Similarly, Orthodox moral teaching did not distinguish between women and men regarding their responsibilities to themselves, their families, and society, and their contribution to their families and to society were considered equally worthy.[15] Seeking to restrain the exercise of patriarchal power by husbands, moreover, Orthodox writers frequently reminded them that "marriage is the truest and most holy union of friendship," and "friendship most commonly exists between equals."[16] The husband, therefore, was enjoined "always to see his wife as a helpmeet, to seek her advice and agreement on family matters, and to accept [her advice] with respect and attention," even though his will prevailed in the event of disagreement.[17]

Although equal in important respects, however, women and men remained different both by nature and divine design, with diverse if complementary callings. Expressing a common view, for example, the influential Metropolitan Filaret (Drozdov) of Moscow declared in 1854 that "the appointed place of a man is in the life both of the family and society beyond the family circle," whereas "the appointed place of a woman is in the life of the family."[18] Similarly, in an essay on the vocation of women published in 1862, the priest D. Sokolov asserted that women "are neither equal nor unequal [with men]; their character is different and wisely suited to a different goal. . . . Hence nature itself has made women capable of fulfilling the calling assigned them by the word of God."[19] According to Sokolov, echoing other Orthodox authors, the particular calling of a woman was "to make her home a sanctuary of order, peace, and happiness, where, after his occupations outside the home, her husband can find peace and diversion (*razvlechenie*)."[20] Equally important, as Arkhimandrit Vladimir (later Bishop of Sarapul') stated in a sermon in the 1860s, "The primary care of children lies in particular with the mother: children are closest of all to [their] mother, and she is their first mentor and guide."[21] Thus, although Orthodox writers generally charged both parents with the upbringing of their children, they commonly assigned to mothers the task of educating children, especially in their early years. The particular qualities with which Orthodox writers presumed women had been endowed for the fulfillment of their domestic and maternal calling were essentially the same as those stressed in the domestic ideal propagated in Europe and the United States at the time. These included modesty, humility, selflessness, self-denial, patience, tolerance, tactfulness, tenderness, compassion, industriousness, practicality, physical dexterity, intuitiveness, and piety. While highly valorized and perceived as essential for the stability, welfare, and survival of the family, and thereby also of society and the state, however, the role of women remained "secondary and dependent" relative to that of men.[22] For Orthodox writers, then, the complementarity of the natures and roles of women and men served to reinforce the subordinate status of women and to confine them to the domestic sphere.

Indeed, prior to the 1860s, the only social activity outside the home for laywomen regularly recognized by Orthodox writers was charitable work. Even this activity, however, was identified with the domestic and maternal role of women, with the empresses and other prominent aristocratic women serving as models. In his address in 1834 at the graduation ceremony at the school for girls established by the Women's Patriotic Society, attended by the school's patron, Empress Aleksandra Feodorovna, for example, the archpriest Petr Myslavskii declared, "Sovereign! Among the many titles by which You are distinguished, the most complimentary for [the graduates] and for You is that of their tender and unforgettable Mother!"[23] Extending this sentiment to women in general, Sokolov asserted that through charitable work even single women could fulfill their high calling and become "a mother for all." In this way, their lives "would not pass without purpose or usefulness."[24] Often implicit in such writings, but never mentioned, was a further social role for single women, that of governess in a wealthy family or teacher at the girls' schools patronized by royal and aristocratic women. But, as Myslavskii's remarks indicate, the latter schools were compared to the family, and their patronesses represented in maternal terms. The principal objective of such schools, moreover, was to train women for their domestic roles.[25] The underlying assumption, then, was that, for most women, their domestic role encompassed the whole of their social role.

This domestic ideal remained the most commonly represented image of women in Orthodox writings until the end of the imperial period. From a conservative perspective, it was defended not only by references to women's natural and divine calling and to social and state utility but also by a "fundamentalist" mode of reasoning that emphasized the literal, timeless, and prescriptive meaning of the Scriptures and other authoritative texts.[26] From the 1860s on, moreover, the domestic ideal constituted an important component of the strategy articulated by conservative Orthodox writers for restoring social and sexual order and balance in what they perceived as conditions of increasing social disintegration and moral decay. In this sense, women were to play a vital role in the conservative strategy for managing the effects of social, economic, and cultural change. Through their role in the family, women were to inculcate and reinforce the moral values, social and sexual relations, and attitudes toward authority that undergirded the tsarist social, political, and ideological order. Expressing concern over the sexual mores and practices especially of urban youth in a speech in 1901, for example, A. A. Bronzov, a professor at the St. Petersburg Ecclesiastical Academy, asserted: "It is necessary that in the family, and precisely in the family, truly Christian seeds be implanted. . . . [O]nly in such conditions, introduced firmly and intelligently, will evil disappear, and disappear by itself."[27] Through its defense of the patriarchal family, and its reinforcement of the position and role of women within it, the Church in turn would likewise contribute to the restoration of social and sexual order, and, in the process, maintain its own social and cultural authority and influence.

A reformist or liberal variant of this Orthodox ideal of domesticity, however, also developed gradually from the 1860s on, although it was articulated most fully only in the early years of the twentieth century. It differed from its conservative counterpart in two key respects: first, by placing greater emphasis on the equality of women and men and on the development of women as autonomous beings; and, second, by promoting an expansion of the public role of women. Regarding the former, the greater stress on the personal autonomy of women by reformist or liberal Orthodox writers reflected both a general trend concerning notions of the self in nineteenth-century Russian culture and an attempt by Orthodox theologians and reformers in the late nineteenth and early twentieth centuries to redefine the relationship between the personal and the social in a way that gave greater importance to the moral development of individuals and recognition to individuals as having value in themselves.[28] Applying these notions to the relationship between spouses within marriage, for example, Archpriest Petr Smirnov declared to Countess Maria Sheremeteva and Count Aleksandr Gudovich at their wedding in January 1900 that "two people are two separate worlds. Each of us is endowed by the Creator with the gifts of distinctiveness [*samobytnost'*] and freedom, and on each of us lies the imprint of diverse influences. For a complete concord of thoughts and desires to be established between these two different human natures, much work and effort is necessary."[29] Addressing the question of the social role of women in a sermon dedicated to the Holy Martyr St. Alexandra in April 1916, Archpriest Aleksandr Glagolev asserted that Christianity "summoned women equally with men to active participation in the creation and renewal of a life in Christ and in His Church."[30]

Of course, even liberal Orthodox writers generally retained a belief in the different and complementary natures of women and men, and hence did not challenge the belief that the family represented the natural and primary sphere of activity for most women. At the same time, however, they described personal moral and spiritual development and individual self-realization as essential Christian goals that women and men should be able to pursue equally. From this perspective, marriage was portrayed as a voluntary and companionate partnership in which each spouse assisted the other to develop morally and spiritually, and to achieve self-realization and salvation. This idea of mutual development was expressed ultimately by the concept of "completion," which held marriage to be necessary for the self-realization of individual women and men, because it enabled them to combine their complementary natures and thereby compose a human whole. Asserting that the idea of original human androgyny articulated by thinkers from Plato to Jacob Böhme was explained by the Christian ideal of marriage, for example, Aleksei Govorov, in his treatise on the "woman question" published in 1907, contended that,

> each of these two halves [i.e., women and men] is only a one-sided manifestation of [the human essence.] Only both of them together constitute a single and complete human being. Only a married couple results in a microcosm of complete humanity, not only in the physical, but also in the spiritual and moral sense.[31]

Such ideas led reformist or liberal Orthodox writers to reject patriarchal conceptions of spousal relations and authority as incompatible with the basic equality of women and men, and consequently both a source of marital instability and an impediment to the process of completion as well as the personal moral and spiritual development of each spouse. To diminish the impact of the scriptural passages and other texts cited by conservatives in defense of patriarchy and women's inferior status, reformist or liberal Orthodox writers either contextualized them historically, relativized them, or found other interpretations that weakened their prescriptive force. Govorov, for example, described New Testament admonitions to wives to obey their husbands in silence as "provisional and historically conditioned," and intended not to demean women by subordinating them to the arbitrary will of their husbands but to "protect women in a defenseless time, out of respect for their personality and their dignity."[32] Thus, to ensure order and sexual balance within marriages, reformist or liberal Orthodox writers called for a more equal distribution of authority between spouses within marriage and advocated the liberalization of the rules governing divorce, albeit with the latter still firmly under the jurisdiction of the Church.[33]

At the same time Orthodox writers acknowledged and legitimized an active role for women outside the family. This social role was characterized as deriving from, and therefore consistent with, both the natural qualities and the domestic role and divine calling of women. Liberal and reformist Orthodox writers thus followed a strategy similar to that employed at this time by women and feminists in other parts of Europe and the United States, that is, using prevailing ideals of domesticity and femininity to expand the boundaries of acceptable social and civic activity for women.[34] This strategy offered opportunities for both expanding the social role of women and limiting this role within narrowly drawn boundaries, as argued by one N. M. Parunov in a book, published in 1873, directed at women: "A woman by her very nature," Parunov asserted,

> and a Christian woman by her direct calling, is presented in our time with no other activity than matters of lofty service to others [*svoim blizhnim*], since she can perform this activity incomparably better than a man owing to an abundance of sympathy, tender-heartedness, diligence, and patience. Only such activity, including service to the injured, care of the ill, and the education and upbringing of children, is possible for women beyond their lofty and principal obligations in the family. But, of course, this work is not for all women, but only for those who have been deprived of the possibility of performing their obligations in the family.[35]

Speaking at the ceremony to commemorate the twenty-fifth anniversary of the Isidorov Women's Diocesan School in St. Petersburg in 1896, A. I. Ponomarev, the instructor of rhetoric at the school, similarly told those in attendance that the occupation of teacher in a village school "opened the way for women from clerical families to fruitful social activity and, in the event of need, to an economically independent, honorably noble, and enlightened existence."[36] Over time, the list of occupations deemed appropriate for women expanded, to include teacher, nurse, paramedic, midwife, doctor, missionary, social worker, and even writer.[37] To a significant extent, of course, this list reflects the social backgrounds of both the authors and their intended audience, although Orthodox writers also recognized that, for women from the poorer strata of society, more menial work outside the home often was necessary. Nonetheless, at least for some authors, occupations such as teacher and writer "revealed the supreme calling that is possible only for women" and provided a woman not only with "a lofty meaning for her personal life but also indicated her important role in the general life of humanity."[38]

By arguing that the occupations and social activities that women engaged in should be consistent with their feminine nature and domestic calling, reformist and liberal Orthodox writers were attempting simultaneously to widen and contain the field of social activity open to women in ways that directly or indirectly preserved superior male authority and the authority of the Church. Indeed, some authors believed that women's expanded social activity would make an important contribution to the revitalization of the social authority and influence of the Church, as well as to the restoration of social stability and order. For such authors, the expansion of women's social role thus constituted part of a general strategy for adapting the Church to social, economic, and cultural change through a program of reform that accepted such change but sought to guide it, in part through the reinterpretation of Church doctrine and teachings and the revision of Church policies.

A series of articles written in 1903 by the archpriest and academic Iakov Galakhov, who played a key role in persuading the Church Council of 1917–1918 to take up the issue of the role of women in the Church, provides an example of this line of argument. Stressing the essential spiritual and moral equality of women and men, Galakhov contended that the Christian view of marriage and of the relations between the sexes generally helped to preserve social stability by reinforcing the natural division of labor between women and men. In particular, by providing both sexes with an equally worthy and respected role in the family and society, Christian teaching prevented disruptive and destabilizing competition between women and men. By elevating the position of women in the family and society, Galakhov argued, Christianity historically had restored the equality between women and men lost by humanity's fall from Grace. This restored balance, however, and therefore social stability in general, had been upset both by industrialization and the economic development of the nineteenth century, which had deprived women of much of their productive role in the home and forced them to look elsewhere for employment, and by scientific rationalism, which had undermined the ideological foundations of Christian marriage. The result, Galakhov claimed, was renewed competition and conflict between the sexes and an altered view of marriage that, together, led to moral degeneration and social decay. But in contrast to conservative authors, Galakhov maintained that the solution to these problems did not lie in a return to the past or an attempt to enforce a literalist interpretation of Church dogma. Rather, balance between the sexes, within the family, and within society generally could be restored only by accepting the expansion of women's employment outside the home but ensuring that such employment assumed forms corresponding to women's natural roles as mother, helpmeet of her husband, and nurturer of her children.[39]

Govorov made a similar argument in response, in particular, to feminist and socialist criticisms of the impact of Christianity on women and proposals for women's emancipation. According to Govorov, the negative/positive dualism in the Christian image of women—that is, women as agents of both temptation and redemption—also existed in the definition of women found in all ancient and modern societies. After the Fall, in pre-Christian societies, the negative side of this dualistic image predominated, and "a woman no longer was considered a person, but only a thing, which in itself had neither independence nor rights but was valued only by the degree of its utility to a man."[40] Christianity, Govorov argued, had reemphasized the positive side of the duality and thereby elevated the position of women, making them, in theory, equal with men. "Here for the first time," he contended, "we encounter equality of rights for men and women; here is revealed the possibility, in principle, of progress in the sense of the free development of the moral personality of a woman together with a man."[41] Although Christianity recognized "the moral dignity of the individual personality,"[42] however, this ideal had not been realized in practice for women because of historical circumstances and the persistence of pre-Christian traditions and prejudices. Nonetheless, Govorov claimed, the "woman question" in contemporary Russia and Europe essentially represented an attempt to realize the ideal of equality originally inspired by Christian teaching. He therefore concluded that, contrary to the criticisms of feminist and socialist critics of the Church, the Christian ideal of womanhood constituted a principal cause of the improvement of the status and rights of women over time. In fact, Govorov asserted, the socialist ideal, both in general and regarding women in particular, "derives its nourishment from the ideological content of Christianity."[43]

Govorov then traced, from the earliest times to the present, what he characterized as the gradual improvement in the status of women in Russia, defined as the growth of individual freedom, opportunity for self-realization, and autonomy, attributing (but not effectively demonstrating) significant causal influence on this path of progress to Christian ideals. Since the 1860s, he asserted, the contours and content of the "woman question" also had been shaped by the abolition of serfdom (in 1861), economic change, and industrialization, the result of which had linked the goal of women's emancipation with the ideal of socialism. In Govorov's view, however, by reducing life to its external aspects and seeking to regiment everyone into a "factory-style existence," socialism was spiritually impoverishing. "Here," he declared, "there is not a trace of personal interests or the higher inner satisfaction of the spirit."[44] Moreover, he claimed, socialists and feminists, to achieve their objectives, sought especially to undermine the institution of the family, "since the type of state depends on the type of family hearth, and the type of family hearth [depends] on the type of woman who manages it." Hence "a fundamental transformation of the forms of life must begin with a change in family structure."[45] But, he contended, especially given the critical socializing role of the family, socialist and feminist efforts to undermine it threatened the stability of society and the survival of state order. He concluded that the family, therefore, urgently needed to be reinforced through a reassertion of the Christian ideal of love. Yet at the same time Govorov advocated expanding formal education for women, with the curriculum the same as for men. By providing women with equal education while preserving their role in the family, he believed that both the universally human and specifically feminine aspects of women's personalities would be developed; the pernicious effects of the feminist and socialist denial of what he claimed was an essential aspect of women's humanity, their maternal and feminine natures, would be avoided; and women would be able to fulfill their calling of the Christianization of society through both their social and maternal activities.[46]

Galakhov's and Govorov's arguments clearly indicate that, by the early twentieth century, reformist and liberal no less than conservative Orthodox writers perceived that the Orthodox Church and society in general were confronting serious social and moral problems as a result of economic, social, and cultural change. In this context many authors in their writings, and clergymen in their sermons, began to stress the salutary influence women could exert on society through their domestic and social activities because of their allegedly superior moral virtues and more intense and steadfast religiosity. In such writings and sermons, women now were portrayed as providing a critical antidote to the dangers of modernity and as important agents of Christianization as well as defenders of the Church and the faith; in the latter instance, women were modeled on such predecessors as Mary and the other women who had witnessed Christ's crucifixion, Martha and Mary, and early Christian martyrs such as Alexandra, Catherine, and Barbara.[47] Sentiments and concerns such as these, in fact, led even conservative writers to accept a limited expansion of women's social role, again chiefly as teachers and nurses.[48]

By the early twentieth century, then, Orthodox writers—primarily liberal and reformist but also, to a lesser degree, even conservative and neo-Slavophile—had articulated an ideal of womanhood that combined domestic and social roles for women. In this ideal, although women remained primarily mothers and wives, they could also be social actors within boundaries defined by what was deemed their particular nature and divine calling as women. Through both their domestic and social activities, women were perceived as making a valuable contribution to the moral, spiritual, and material well-being of their families and of society as a whole. For many Orthodox writers, this contribution played a vital role in the different strategies they proposed for preserving social stability and reinforcing the authority of the Church in the turbulent conditions of early-twentieth-century imperial Russia. Certainly, within this ideal of womanhood, women's social activity continued to be circumscribed, and women remained subordinate to the authority of the Church and to male authority more broadly. These limitations support the arguments of contemporary theologians such as Elizabeth Johnson and George Tavard that any anthropology or ideology of complementarity is unlikely to result in full equality for women, as it will lead inescapably to the delineation of separate spheres of activity for men and women which then tend to become differentially valued.[49] Acceptance of an ideology of complementarity thus had a limiting effect on the practical proposals advanced even by liberal and reformist Orthodox writers in comparison with their secular counterparts.[50] Nonetheless, both the particular ideal of womanhood promoted by such Orthodox writers and the uncertainties produced by the debate they were engaged in provided openings for a further expansion of the autonomy and social role of women that at least some women were able to exploit.

Although the developments that provoked and shaped this debate over womanhood among Orthodox writers are still unclear, such writers were responding in part both to secular challenges to the teachings and authority of the Church and to changes in the socioeconomic condition, educational opportunities, and religious activism of women after the early 1860s. A common feature in both conservative and reformist Orthodox writings on women and marriage during this period, for example, was the attempt to disprove the claims made by radicals and feminists, and later by socialists as well, that the Orthodox Church and religion in general were among the chief causes of the oppression of women. As the arguments of Galakhov and Govorov indicate, Orthodox writers attempted to refute such claims by demonstrating that historically, and in comparison with non-Christian religions, Christianity, in fact, had elevated the familial and social status of women by proclaiming their essential equality with men and by valorizing their particular social roles. Such writers depicted women in pre-Christian, pagan, and other non-Christian societies as being, in contrast, little more than instruments to further the interests of kin groups or the chattel and sexual objects of their husbands, a rhetorical strategy suggesting the moral inferiority of non-Christian cultures and societies in general.[51] After criticizing the allegedly demeaning and slavish position occupied by women in earlier pagan societies and under Islam, for example, Archbishop Pavel (Lebedev) of Kazan, in a sermon given at the Kazan Mother of God Convent in 1888, declared:

> Under Christianity, a woman is as free and independent as a man in her choice of [a way of] life and activities. By nature as human as a man, she can independently choose to perform those services open to women, compose independent communities together with other women similar to herself, and pursue a moral life in the same way as a man, even surpassing him in the heights of her moral achievements. In any event, under Christianity a woman is not an object of her parents or her husband, and she is raised not only for marriage but also for an independent and autonomous life.[52]

Although in this sermon Pavel clearly had in mind the ability of Christian women to make moral choices and to choose a religious life, his words and his call to the sisters of the Kazan Mother of God Convent to serve as a model for the liberation, via Christianization, of Muslim women demonstrate how Orthodox authors often assimilated into their ideal of Christian womanhood many of the terms and concepts used by their opponents. Indeed, as we have seen, Govorov contended that feminist and socialist ideals of women's emancipation represented merely flawed and debased manifestations of a precedent and underlying Christian conception of equality between the sexes that promised a more complete and fulfilling resolution of the "woman question" for women.

Similarly the general involvement of Orthodox clerics, scholars, and writers in several prominent public debates regarding women after the 1860s, most notably those over marriage and divorce, also helped to modify and diversify the image of women in Orthodox writings. As I indicated elsewhere, in the course of these debates Orthodox scholars and writers developed an array of arguments both supporting and opposing various reforms of family, marriage, and divorce law that entailed sharply divergent conceptions of marriage, the ideal relationship between spouses, and the relative natures and roles of women and men. The competing arguments were grounded in different conceptions of the past and varying interpretations of Church doctrine as well as in diverse understandings of the relevance of historical and social context for the definition and practical application of Church doctrine. Very broadly, those favoring reform emphasized a companionate ideal of marriage, the development of marital and family relations in a progressive direction over time, and the need to adapt Church doctrine to existing social and historical conditions; their opponents, on the other hand, stressed the need for and naturalness of strong patriarchal authority within marriage and the family, the congruence of this family structure with Russian cultural traditions, and the ahistorical prescriptiveness of Church doctrine. Similar ideals, divisions, and modes of argumentation characterized the other groups that played a prominent role in these debates, including jurists, medical professionals, state officials, journalists, and political activists.[53] Hence it would appear that the images of women articulated by Orthodox writers after the early 1860s were shaped in part by general cultural trends and modes of public and professional discourse during this period.

The expansion and transformation of education for women, the growth of female employment outside the home, and the penetration of women into occupations previously closed to them—all of which occurred after the late 1850s—seem also to have influenced Orthodox ideals of womanhood. Prior to the late 1850s formal education for women had been limited, both in extent and content. The relatively small number of schools that existed generally drew their students from a single social estate (*soslovie*), and their curriculum was oriented toward preparing women for their roles in the family and, in the case of the nobility, in polite society. With the expansion of education for women after the late 1850s, however, schools grew socially more mixed and the curriculum in women's secondary schools and higher educational institutions became academically more rigorous, more closely resembled the curriculum for men at parallel levels, and grew more oriented toward preparing women for occupations outside the home. The growth of education for women at the secondary and tertiary levels was particularly rapid in comparative terms, with women constituting approximately half the number of secondary students in the entire empire by 1913 and nearly a third of all students in higher educational institutions by 1915.[54] The graduates of these schools found an expanding range of employment opportunities in fields such as education, health care, journalism, publishing, writing, charity and social work, ethnography, and administration, as well as in the arts.

Although some Orthodox writers condemned these trends and sought ways to resist them, and others grudgingly acknowledged them but attempted to limit their extent and impact, writers such as Galakhov and Govorov actively promoted the expansion of education and employment for women while simultaneously trying to channel the latter in directions that preserved the domestic ideal of womanhood and its underlying conception of feminine nature. Likewise, in seeking to mobilize Orthodox women in defense of the Church, Orthodox writers often advocated and legitimized the participation of women in various occupations and roles in the Church—for example, teaching, missionary work, writing, even preaching—from which they previously had been excluded or to which their access had been severely limited.[55] In doing so, they reflected the evolution of Church policy itself regarding education and employment for women after the mid-1860s. If prior to then formal education for the daughters of clergymen had been limited in extent and motivated chiefly by concerns over the eligibility to marry, beginning in the 1860s Orthodox dioceses were encouraged to establish Diocesan Women's Schools to provide a broader and more rigorous secondary education for women, chiefly but not exclusively those from the clerical estate. The number of such schools grew rapidly during the latter half of the nineteenth and early twentieth centuries, with seventy-four established by 1913. Although the graduates of these schools entered a range of occupations, the majority were employed as teachers, especially in the rapidly growing network of parish schools maintained by the Church.[56] Hence the Church itself, in part to provide for the daughters of its clergy and in part to protect the faithful from the temptations of non-Orthodox religions as well as from harmful secular influences, became a significant source of education and employment for women in the late imperial period.

Finally, the image of women and their appropriate social role reflected in Orthodox writings appears also to have been influenced by women's own social and religious activities in the late imperial period. Although scholars have not explored this topic systematically or comprehensively, women clearly played an increasingly prominent role in the charitable and social welfare organizations and the reform movements that emerged in late imperial Russia.[57] While most of these organizations and activities were not explicitly religious in nature, many had a religious—and specifically Orthodox—foundation, and functioned with the support and sanction of the Church. Beginning in 1844, for example, with the foundation of the Holy Trinity Community of Sisters of Mercy in St. Petersburg, communities of women were formed to provide care for the sick and infirm as well as other social services. Although most Orthodox "Brotherhoods"— voluntary organizations composed of lay and clerical members who engaged in various missionary, charitable, and educational activities—appear to have been comprised predominantly or exclusively of men, some included or consisted chiefly of female members and directed their attention to women.[58] Women also appear to have played a significant role in the charitable activities organized by parish councils.[59]

The rapid expansion and transformation of female Orthodox monasticism during the nineteenth and early twentieth centuries, particularly after the 1850s, provide a similar example of increased social engagement by women under the umbrella of the Church. Between 1764 and 1850, the number of Orthodox convents increased from 68 to 123; by 1914, the number had risen to 475. Similarly the number of female monastics grew rapidly, from 1,671 in 1796 to 8,533 by 1850, and to 73,299 in 1914.[60] During the second half of the nineteenth century, in fact, Orthodox monasticism became overwhelmingly female. The growth in the number of convents and female monastics, and the parallel increase in the number of less formal women's religious communities over the same period, was accompanied by a dramatic expansion of the social welfare and educational activities undertaken by these communities. Such activities included providing shelter for orphans and the elderly and medical care for the poor, offering famine relief, and operating parish and vocational schools for girls.[61] Commending such social engagement by female monastics in a sermon given sometime in the 1860s, Bishop Ioann (Sokolov) of Smolensk called it a persuasive reply to the growing skepticism of secular society toward the legitimacy of monastic life.[62] Indeed, beginning in the 1860s, all monastic communities were officially encouraged to provide some form of social welfare or educational service, and the social engagement of particular convents and women's communities frequently were cited by Orthodox writers as both a model for monastic reform and a defense of monasticism against clerical as well as lay criticism.[63]

An example of how the social activity of women during the late imperial period could serve as a catalyst for the refashioning of images of womanhood in Orthodox writings is provided by V. V. Ostroumov, the priest and religious instructor at the Second Moscow Women's Gymnasium during the 1870s and 1880s. In his address to the graduating class in 1875, Ostroumov presented a fairly conservative and conventional set of images of womanhood, idealizing the domestic and maternal roles of women, and attempting to dissuade the students from aspiring to any role in society beyond the family and domestic affairs. "Always with tender love and true maternal concern," Ostroumov told those gathered, "the gymnasium has prepared you for the useful life to which you have been committed since childhood.... Human affairs are generally divided into two large classes: domestic affairs, which appertain primarily to women, and affairs of social service, which appertain primarily to men." Yet "currently in several of the most educated countries, women, as if in defiance of their nature and of higher [i.e., divine] authority, seek to take the place of men in the spheres not only of social and civil life but even of the Church," an example, Ostroumov made clear, not to be emulated by the students.[64] Three years later, however, specifically citing the performance of Russian female nurses in the Russo-Turkish War, Ostroumov now told the graduating class that their natural qualities as women suited them for other vocations as well, especially nursing and teaching. Although "the majority of you will enter social life in the capacity of either members of your families or the educators and guides for members of families other than your own," Ostroumov declared to his soon-to-be former students, "a few of you [will step into] the social positions now opening for women.... [But] if a Christian woman has occasion to be called to social activity broader than the family, nonetheless even here she will be all the more capable, energetic, and influential the more her work demands the operation of a Christian-developed heart."[65] Similarly the engagement of convents and women's religious communities in social welfare and educational activities preceded and provided the basis for their adoption as a model for monastic social engagement in general.

Conversely, like women in the United States and Western Europe during the nineteenth century, Orthodox women in imperial Russia also invoked the evolving images of women in Orthodox writings after the early 1860s to expand their activities and opportunities. Perhaps least controversial in this regard was the use of the ideals of a religious life, socially engaged monasticism, and the compassionate, nurturing, and self-sacrificing character of women to legitimize the foundation of women's religious and service communities that were either partly or wholly dedicated to providing education and various forms of welfare services to the local population. In a letter to Metropolitan Sergei of Moscow in 1894 regarding the foundation of a new women's religious community on one of her estates, for example, Countess Orlova-Davydova specified that "the essential goal of [the community], in addition to the performance of regular prayers, would be to serve the needs of the local population, to tend the ill, to instruct and educate young girls, and so on."[66] In an arrangement that was not uncommon, the countess then served as head of the community during her lifetime.[67] Similarly, after 1905, Abbess Nina of the Moscow All Sorrows Convent and Abbess Ekaterina of the Holy Mother of God Convent in Lesna drew on the images of women as educators and propagators of the faith, as well as on the movement of women into teaching positions at the secondary level, to lobby—ultimately successfully—for the establishment of a Women's Theological Academy that could train women to teach at the secondary level and engage in missionary work. Opened initially in 1916, the Academy had to close briefly because of a lack of funds but was reopened the following year, after Nina procured financial support from a wealthy widow. Enthusiastically describing the ceremony to mark the reopening of the Academy, a writer in the *Moscow Church Voice* declared, "One need not even speak of how necessary educated Christian women are. In the person of these enlightened Christian women, the Church will receive an energetic and vital force for the enlightenment of the people." Moreover, "in addition to the normal role of teachers in secondary and primary schools, the future graduates of the Academy, having a higher theological education, must occupy even the position of religious instructor [*kafedry zakonouchitel'skie*]."[68] Seeking a wider and more formalized role in the Church, women also figured prominently among advocates of the restoration of the office of deaconess in the Church, a movement that grew stronger in the early twentieth century and whose goal appeared about to be realized in 1918 when the Church Council was dissolved under the impact of intensifying revolution.[69]

How far such efforts might be taken, particularly in the wake of the 1905 Revolution, is demonstrated by a pamphlet published in 1906 by one E. Liuleva.[70] Counterposing the New to the Old Testament and what she described as the actual teachings of Christ to their alleged distortion by the Church in certain historical circumstances, Liuleva advanced a Christian argument for the emancipation of women and their full equality with men. In doing so, like Gerasimova did later in her petition to the Church Council, Liuleva built on but radically extended many of the ideas and arguments that male Orthodox writers had been advancing since the early 1860s. Liuleva's pamphlet thus reveals the potential for the reworking and multiple interpretations of these latter ideas and the images of womanhood contained in them, even though it is not clear how widely her views were shared.

Liuleva portrayed Christ as a radical liberationist who "destroyed all differences of existence between people that divided them into men and women, rich and poor, and strong and weak. . . . Above all, of course, He put an end to the enslavement of the physically weak, i.e., women, recognizing that the body is generally powerless and only the spirit can be powerful and hearty." Hence "the law of slavery and submission was replaced by the commandment of universal brotherly love, freedom, and equality."[71] Applying this idea to marriage, Liuleva argued that within a genuinely Christian marriage spouses were completely equal and their relations were based on mutual love, respect, and friendship. The legal and canonical norms governing marriage, divorce, and the family should thus be reformed accordingly. Furthermore, Liuleva continued, "Christ posited the principle of the liberation of women and gave them access to the only work necessary for humanity, the seeking of the Kingdom of God and service to His truth and to Him Himself."[72] Consequently, she contended, all who believe in God can serve Him equally and without distinction. For women, this meant that their activities were not confined to the domestic sphere but included active participation in society and in the Church. Noting the activity of deaconesses and other women in the early Christian Church, Liuleva argued that women therefore should be allowed to play an equally active role in contemporary society and the Church, including participation in Church governance. In explaining the failure of Christ's liberating message to have been realized up to then, Liuleva cited the Church's alleged absorption and perpetuation of discriminatory attitudes and practices toward women which, she claimed, had existed in biblical Jewish and early pagan societies, a process that had led women to gradually be excluded from the active role in Church life which they initially had enjoyed. After their position had reached its nadir in medieval society, however, "women slowly have conquered for themselves the rights given them by Christ and have struggled ceaselessly for their human dignity, independence, and freedom. But always along their way they have collided with the inertness of the Church, with its deadening ritual, and with its insistent miscomprehension of the spirit of the Christian religion."[73] Nonetheless, despite the regressive influence of the Church on the position of women, Liuleva asserted that its doctrines and teachings had prepared the way for a new reception of Christ's liberationist teachings. Hence she concluded that "women not only can but must insist on their independence and freedom, and their obligation before God and humanity, to throw off the chains placed on them."[74]

Although unusual in its radicalism, Liuleva's pamphlet nonetheless reflects the key issues affecting women that were being debated within the Russian Orthodox Church in the last decade of the old regime. The intensity of these debates, of course, should not be exaggerated. The Church confronted a number of divisive issues during these years, and of those perceived as directly related to women, only the reform of divorce law could be counted among the most contentious.[75] In conjunction with the other issues under debate, however, and in a manner strikingly similar to broader patterns in late imperial Russia, the emergence within Orthodox writings of competing images of women and their proper social role contributed to the development of what might be called "public politics" within the Church during the latter part of the nineteenth century. Such politics both created pressure for the reform of Church policies and practices, with respect not merely to women and divorce but also to Church governance, parish life, monasticism, and a host of other issues, and posed problems for Church governance and unity. In effect, during the latter half of the nineteenth century, an institutional structure and publishing infrastructure had emerged that made discord within the Church both unavoidable and a matter of public discourse. Prior to the February Revolution of 1917, the relationship between the Orthodox Church and the tsarist state paradoxically had helped to contain this discord by limiting the mechanisms available for the resolution of major disputes within the Church over policy, governance, and similar matters. Once the February Revolution eliminated this obstacle, however, the Church Council that met in 1917–1918 revealed the potential for both the mediation and containment of discord and a schism in the Church.

As noted above, the Church Council convened in August 1917 and continued to meet through three sessions, spanning nearly a year. Viewed from the perspective of its ability to formulate policy and mediate disputes, its outcome was ambiguous, reflecting in part the tension between its organizational structure and procedural rules, on the one hand, and both the deep divisions among the delegates and their commitment to an ideal of "conciliarism" (*sobornost'*), on the other.[76] Hence the structure and the procedures the Council followed enabled it to adopt a wide range of measures that apparently resolved many issues that had provoked public disagreement over the past two decades, and thereby, at least in the view of their advocates, enabled the Council to adapt Church policies and practices to changed conditions. Regarding women, these measures included an extensive liberalization of divorce law and a substantial expansion of women's role in the Church in ways that generally reflected the ideals of womanhood promoted by liberal and reformist Orthodox writers since the 1860s.[77] In the future, for example, women would take part in parish and diocesan governance on a basis generally equal with that of men, would be permitted to hold the lower clerical position of sexton (but would not be included in the clergy), and would play a wider liturgical role. The formation of "sisterhoods," which were to perform a variety of educational, missionary, and charitable functions, was encouraged.[78] It seems likely, too, that the Council would have reestablished the office of deaconess had it been able to continue its work.[79] Through such measures, the Council intended to expand the social role of women under the auspices of the Church, and, in the process, reinforce the Church's moral and social authority.

However, the debates within the Church Council on all these issues were extraordinarily heated, especially on the subject of divorce, and it was unclear that the minority would accept the decisions of the majority which they often characterized as unorthodox, contrary to fundamental Christian doctrine, socially harmful, and driven by "party-mindedness."[80] Most of the bishops, moreover, frequently found themselves in the minority along with those that either opposed reform or thought that the measures the Council majority adopted were too radical.[81] Thus, even though the Church Council adopted reforms that revealed the Church's capacity to adapt to changing conditions and attitudes, and even though the process of adopting these reforms also revealed a resolve to end internal conflicts, the schism in the Church in the 1920s was presaged by cleavages within the Council and a reluctance by many delegates to accept majority decisions that was reinforced by a notion of conciliarity questioning the legitimacy of the form of politics dominating the Council.[82]

In the course of the nineteenth and early twentieth centuries, then, the image of womanhood in Orthodox writings grew more diverse and complex. Earlier images of woman as redemptrix and temptress remained, but the domestic and maternal ideal of womanhood predominated. This ideal, too, was complicated, however, with conservative and liberal variants. Both views, of course, perpetuated a conception of the fundamental differences in the nature of women and men, and thus also a belief in the necessity, and appropriateness of their different if complementary roles in society and the Church. Both sides also sought to restrict women's activities within boundaries acceptable to the Church and, in so doing, preserve the authority of the Church. Both also held that women's domestic roles were essential to the stability and survival of society, the polity, the state, and the Church. But the liberal variants of the image of womanhood in prerevolutionary Orthodox writings also placed greater emphasis than their conservative counterparts on the essential equality of women, on their autonomy as individuals, and on the importance of their self-realization as moral and spiritual human beings. This self-realization included active participation within society and the Church, provided this activity remained consistent with what was considered women's essential nature and with their domestic and maternal roles. Much of the internal debate over womanhood, and the interaction between the images of women contained in Orthodox writings and women's actual activities, revolved around determining where the boundaries of women's appropriate social activity lay. But at the same time that the debate

over womanhood within the Church helped to stimulate public discourse over
the intersection of religion and gender that individual women could draw on
to shape their own identities, the dynamic and substantive contents of the
debate revealed the complex and ambiguous relationship of Orthodoxy to the
emergence of social and cultural modernity in late imperial Russia, and also
demonstrated that religion at this time continued to provide meaning in the
lives of many women.[83]

Notes

I acknowledge with gratitude that research for this paper was supported in part by grants
from Williams College and from the International Research and Exchanges Board (IREX),
with funds provided by the National Endowment for the Humanities, the U.S. Department
of State, and the U.S. Information Agency. None of these organizations is responsible for the
views expressed.

1.   Italics in original. GARF, f. R-3431, op. 1, d. 327, ll. 8–90b.
2.   *Zhurnaly i protokoly zasedanii Vysochaishe uchrezdennago Predsobornago Prisutstviia*, 4
vols. (St. Petersburg, 1906–1907), 4: 83; on this issue in general, see 2: 28–31, 79, 102–104; and
4: 83–86); Igumeniia Ekaterina, "O diakonissakh. (Po povodu stat'i sviashch. V. Uspenskago),"
Tserkovnyia vedomosti, no. 15/16 (1908): suppl., 728–29; *Materialy k zhitiiu prepodobnomuchenitsy
velikoi kniagini Elizavety. Pis'ma, dnevniki, vospominaniia, dokumenty*, 2nd ed. (Moscow, 1996),
20–25, 30–34, 50–55, 225–33; GARF, f. R-3431, op. 1, d. 327 (especially ll. 8–90b.); d. 326, ll. 11–66;
and d. 514, envelope 28[a], l. 157; and E. V. Beliakova and N. A. Beliakova, "Obsuzhdenie voprosa
o diakonissakh na Pomestnom Sobore 1917–1918 gg.," *Tserkovno-istoricheskii vestnik*, 8 (2001):
139–61.
3.   GARF, f. R-3431, op. 1, d. 136, ll. 2, 90.
4.   GARF, f. R-3431, op. 1, d. 327, l. 21.
5.   GARF, f. R-3431, op. 1, d. 136 (all); d. 172, ll. 8–32; d. 325 (all); d. 328 (all) (relating to
the role of women in the Church); d. 50, ll. 24–48; d. 89, ll. 20–20[zh]; d. 472, ll. 1–1[b] (relating to
women in parish, diocesan, and central Church governance); d. 129 (all); d. 130, ll. 5–7, 40–48,
60–64, 92; d. 387 (all); and d. 580 (all) (relating to women's schools and women as teachers); and
*Sobranie opredelenii i postanovlenii Sviashchennogo Sobora pravoslavnoi rossiiskoi tserkvi 1917–1918
gg.* (Moscow, 1994), 47–48. See also E. B. Beliakova, *Tserkovnyi sud i problemy tserkovnoi zhizni*
(Moscow, 2004), 422–65.
6.   Hazel Mills, "Negotiating the Divide: Women, Philanthropy and the 'Public Sphere' in
Nineteenth-Century France," in *Religion, Society and Politics in France since 1789*, ed. Frank Tallett
and Nicholas Atkin, 29–54 (London, 1991); and Karen Offen, *European Feminisms, 1700–1950:
A Political History* (Stanford, Calif., 2000), 100–102; but, on Russia, cf. Diana Greene, "Mid-
Nineteenth-Century Domestic Ideology in Russia," in *Women and Russian Culture: Projections
and Self-Perceptions*, ed. Rosalind Marsh, 78–97 (New York and Oxford, 1998).
7.   On these problems, see James Cunningham, *A Vanquished Hope: The Movement for
Church Renewal in Russia, 1905–1906* (Crestwood, N.Y., 1981); Sergei Firsov, *Russkaia tserkov'
nakanune peremen (konets 1890-kh–1918 gg.)* (Moscow, 2002); and Vera Shevzov, *Russian Orthodoxy
on the Eve of Revolution* (Oxford, 2004).

8. Catriona Kelly, *Refining Russia: Advice Literature, Polite Culture, and Gender from Catherine to Yeltsin* (Oxford, 2001), 15–16, 22–32, 35, 43–45, 55–58, 62–63, 65–68, 111–36; and Greene, "Mid-Nineteenth-Century Domestic Ideology in Russia."

9. Kelly, *Refining Russia*, 22–32, 62–63.

10. T. B. Riabova, "Ideal zhenshchiny—pravitel'nitsy doma v pozdnee srednevekov'e (Po russkim i ital'ianskim istochnikam)," in *Zhenshchiny i rossiiskoe obshchestvo: nauchno-istoricheskii aspekt. Mezhvuzovskii sbornik nauchnykh trudov* (Ivanovo, 1995), 31–46; Carolyn Johnston Pouncey, ed. and trans., introduction to *The Domostroi. Rules for Russian Households in the Time of Ivan the Terrible* (Ithaca, N.Y., 1994), 27–28; and Natalia Pushkareva, *Women in Russian History, from the Tenth to the Twentieth Century*, trans. Eve Levin (Armonk, N.Y., 1997), 36–43, and passim.

11. "O semeinykh obiazannostiakh," *Pribavleniia k Tvoreniiam Sviatykh Ottsov, v Russkom Perevode* (1844), chap. 2, 429.

12. For examples, see Gedeon (Arkhiepiskop poltavskii i pereiaslavskii), *Slovo v den' vypuska vospitannits poltavskago instituta blagorodnykh devits, proiznesenoe v institutskoi tserkvi* (Poltava, 1845); S. Mikhailovskii, "Obiazannosti suprugi-khristianki," *Dukhovnaia beseda* 41 (1858): 55–74; and Arkhimandrit Fotii, "Vzaimnyia khristianskiia otnosheniia suprugov," *Strannik* 8, pt. 2 (1861): 63–69.

13. "Nastavlenie khristianskoe," in *Tvoreniia izhe vo sviatkkh ottsa nashego Tikhona Zadonskago* (reprint, Pskov, 1994), 5: 159–64; and D. Abriutskin (sviashchennik), *Uroki iz sviashchennoi istorii Vetkhago zaveta, chitannye vospitannikam instituta korpusa gornykh inzhenerov* (St. Petersburg, 1841), 7–9.

14. Mitropolit Filaret (Drozdov), *Sobranie mnenii i otzyvov Filareta, mitropolita moskovskago i kolomenskago, po uchebnym i tserkovno-gosudarstvennym voprosam* (Moscow, 1885–1888), 5: 71 (no. 588).

15. "O semeinykh obiazannostiakh," 417.

16. V. Bazhanov, *Ob obiazannostiakh khristianina*, 4th ed. (St. Petersburg, 1858), 120, 124.

17. *Pravoslavnoe nravstvennoe bogoslovie*, 3rd ed. (Kostroma, 1859), 325.

18. Filaret, *Sobranie mnenii*, 3: 572 (no. 399).

19. D. N. Sokolov (sviashchennik), *Naznachenie zhenshchiny po ucheniiu slova Bozhiia* (St. Petersburg, 1862), 15, 22.

20. Ibid., 37.

21. Arkhimandrit Vladimir, nyne Episkop Sarapul'skii, *Pastyrskie trudy za tridtsat' piat' let sluzheniia sv. tserkvi (1866–1901 gg.). Izbrannyia propovedi i stat'i religiozno-nravstvennago soderzhaniia* (St. Petersburg, 1901), 124.

22. Sokolov, *Naznachenie zhenshchiny*, 9. See also I. Petrov (sviashchennik), *Rech', govorennaia, 20-go ianvaria 1865 goda, vo 2-i Admiralteiskoi shkole S.-Peterburgskago zhenskago patriotiches-kago obshchestva, pred panikhidoiu ob ustopei Predsedatel'nitse Soveta etogo Obshchestva, Stats-Dame Eia Imperatorskago Velishestva Grafine Kleopatre Petrovne Kleinmikhel* (St. Petersburg, 1865).

23. P. N. Myslavskii (Protoierei), *Rech', proiznesennaia Eia Imperatorskomu Velichestvu, i slovo, propovedannoe v tserkvi patrioticheskago instituta, pri vypuske blagorodnykh vospitanits, okonchivshikh kurs ucheniia* (St. Petersburg, 1834), 3.

24. Sokolov, *Naznachenie zhenshchiny*, 66.

25. On formal education for women at this time, see E. Likhacheva, *Materialy dlia istoriia zhenskago obrazovaniia v Rossii* (St. Petersburg, 1890–1895), vol. 3; and Robin Bisha, Jehanne M Gheith, Christine Holden, and William G. Wagner, comps. and eds., *Russian Women, 1698–1917. Experience and Expression. An Anthology of Sources* (Bloomington, Ind., 2002), chap. 4.

26. For examples, see William G. Wagner, *Marriage, Property and Law in Late Imperial Russia* (Oxford, 1994), 146–49, 182–84, 195–200; and the references to the debates over the reform of divorce law, the role of women in the Church, and the restoration of the position of deaconess at the Church Council of 1917–1918 cited in notes 1 and 5 above and 77–81 below.

27. A. A. Bronzov, *O khristianskoi sem'i i sviazannykh s neiu voprosakh* (St. Petersburg, 1901), 10. See also Arkhimandrit Sergei, *Znachenie zakona proiskhozhdeniia liudei chrez rozhdeniia. Slovo*

v den' rozhdeniia blagochestiveishei gosudaryni imperatritsy Marii Feodorovny (14 noiabria) (Moscow, 1881); E. Mertsalov, *Pouchenie v den' tezoimenitstva Blagochestiveishei Gosudaryni Imperatritsy Aleksandry Feodorovny, proiznesennoe v Petrozavodskom kafedral'nom sobore, 23 aprelia 1896 g. (O prizvanii zheny khristianki)* (Petrozavodsk, 1896); K. V. Efremov (protoierei), *Rech', skazannaia pri zakrytii kratkosrochnykh pedagogicheskikh kursov dlia uchitelei i uchitel'nits tserkovnykh shkol chernigovskoi eparkhii* (Chernigov, 1900); and A. A. Astapov, "Zhenshchina khristianka," *Dushepoleznoe chtenie*, (1901), chap. 2, 245–49.

　　28.　Laura Engelsten and Stephanie Sandler, eds., *Self and Story in Russian History* (Ithaca, N.Y., 2000); L. A. Filipovich, *Filosofskii analiz pravoslavno-bogoslovskoi kontseptsii nravstvennykh kachestv cheloveka* (Kiev, 1989); Wagner, *Marriage, Property and Law*; and idem, "Family Law, the Rule of Law, and Liberalism in Late Imperial Russia," *Jahrbücher für Geschichte Osteuropas* 43, no. 4 (1995): 519–35.

　　29.　P. A. Smirnov (protoierei), *Rech' k novobrachnym protoieria P. A. Smirnova* (St. Petersburg, 1900), 5.

　　30.　A. A. Glagolev (protoierei), *Slovo v den' pamiati Sv. Muchenitsy Aleksandry i tezoimenitstva Gosudaryni Imperatritsy Aleksandry Feodorovny (23 aprelia 1916 goda) (Zhenshchina na sluzhenii rodine v godinu tiazhkago ispytaniia)* (Kiev, 1916), 4.

　　31.　A. V. Govorov, *Zhenskii vopros v sviazi s istoricheskimi sud'bami zhenshchiny* (Kazan, 1907/ 1908 [both years are given]), 6–7. See also Arkhimandrit Mikhail, "*Zakonnyi"brak (Problemy braka, materinstva, shkoly). Sbornik statei* (St. Petersburg, 1908), 17–18; I. M. Gromoglasov, "O vtorykh i tret'ikh brakakh v pravoslvanoi tserkvi," *Bogoslovskii vestnik* 9 (1902): 36–39; P. Levitov,"O brachnom soiuze i ego znachenii v oblasti polovykh otnoshenii," *Khristianskoe chtenie* 7 (1905): 66, and, in general, 65–84; and G. G. Popovich, "Polozhenie zhenshchiny v bibleiskoi sem'e i obshchestve," *Trudy Kievskoi Dukhovnoi Akademii* 1 (1916): 62, 77.

　　32.　Govorov, *Zhenskii vopros*, 30.

　　33.　Wagner, *Marriage, Property and Law*, 145–46, 169–205, and passim.

　　34.　In addition to the works cited in note 4 above, see Karen Kennelly, "Ideals of American Catholic Womanhood," in idem, ed., *American Catholic Women: A Historical Exploration* (New York and London, 1989), 1–16.

　　35.　M. N. Parunov, "*U baby volos dolog, da um korotok.*"*Narodnyia chteniia* (St. Petersburg, 1873), 20.

　　36.　A. I. Ponomarev, *Zhenshchina v dukhovnoi sem'e v sviazi s istoriei prikhodskago dukhovenstva na Rusi* (St. Petersburg, 1896), 10.

　　37.　For examples, see A. M. Matiushenskii (protoierei), *Proshchal'noe slovo vospitannitsam saratovskoi mariinskoi zhenskoi gimnazii* (Saratov, 1914), 3; A. Voznesenskii (sviashchennik), *Rukovodstvo k domashnemu religiozno-nravstvennomu khristianskomu vospitaniiu detei. Kurs VIII-go klassa zhenskoi gimnazii* (Orel, 1888), especially 8–20; Palladii, episkop ladozhskago, *Rech' preosviashchennago Palladiia, eipiskop ladozhskago, vikariia s. peterburgskago, po privedenii k prisiage serdobol'nykh sester, v Ekaterinskoi tserkvi, pri vdov'em dome (12 marta 1867 g.)* (St. Petersburg, 1867); F. P. Preobrazhenskii (sviashchennik), *Naputstvennoe slovo pervomu vypusku sester miloserdiia iverskoi obshchiny, sostoiashchii pri Moskovskom mestnom komitete Rossiiskago obshchestva "Krasnago Kresta"* (Moscow, 1896); Arkhimandrit Anastasii, *Privetstvie Kazanskoi obshchine sester miloserdiia krasnago kresta, v den' 25-letiia eia sushchestvovaniia* (Kazan, 1911); and P. Smirnov, "Zhenshchina v dele oslableniia staroobriadcheskago raskola," *Khristianskoe chtenie* (1905), 1: 50–51, 5:609–33, 6:799–810.

　　38.　S. V. Strakhov (sviashchennik), *Rech' k okonchivshim kurs vospitannitsam mariinskago uchilishcha damskago popechitel'stva* (Moscow, 1893), 6–7.

　　39.　I. Galakhov (sviashchennik), "Zhenskii vopros, ego prichiny i otsenka s khristianskoi tochki zreniia," *Khristianskie chteniia* (1903), 6:924–35, 7:94–107, and 8: 217–34.

　　40.　Govorov, *Zhenskii vopros*, 5.

　　41.　Ibid., 7.

　　42.　Ibid., 12.

43. Ibid., 23.
44. Ibid., 52.
45. Ibid., 52–53.
46. Ibid., especially 63–64, 91–94.
47. For examples, see Feofan (Govorov) (Episkop), *Na raznye sluchai. Slova episkopa Feofana*, 2nd ed. (Moscow, 1897), 9–10; I. V. Preobrazhenskii, *V podarok materi i docheri. Sobrnik nravstvenno-nazidatel'nykh statei*, 4th ed. (St. Petersburg, 1900), 19–31, 85–128, 151–53; Glagolev, *Slovo v den' pamiati Sv. Muchenitsy Aleksandry*, 1–4; and Feodor (Episkop), "Rech' pri otkrytii zhenskikh bogoslovsko-pedagogicheskikh kursov v Moskve," *Bogoslovskii vestnik* 10/12 (1916): chap. 3, 177–81.
48. For example, see Bronzov, *O khristianskoi sem'i*, 36–37; N.Vladimirskii, *Poslednyi urok. Proshchal'naia rech' k okanchivshim kurs v 1914 g. vospitannitsam Eparkhial'nago zhenskago uchilishcha* (Kazan, 1914), 8–16; N. N., *Osnovy zhizni* (Moscow, 1899), esp. 8; Amvrosii, Arkhiepiskop Khar'kovskii, *Rech' Preosviashchennago Amvrosiia, Arkhiepiskopa Khar'kovskago, po sluchae tridtsatiletnei godovshchiny so vremeni preobrazheniia Khar'kovskago zhenskago Eparkhial'nago uchilishcha po novomu ustavu. "O znachenii iskusstva v dele vospitaniia i obrazovaniia"* (Khar'kov, 1898); and P. Levitskii (sviashchennik), *Da ne smushaetsia serdtse vashe! Slovo pred blagodarstvennom molebnom po sluchaiu sto pervago vypuska iz Instituta Imperatritsy Marii v Peterburge okonshivshikh kurs vospitannits* (St. Petersburg, 1912), esp. 4, 9, 11.
49. Elizabeth A. Johnson, *Truly Our Sister: A Theology of Mary in the Communion of Saints* (New York and London, 2003), 47–70; and George H. Tavard, *The Thousand Faces of the Virgin Mary* (Collegeville, Minn., 1996), 229.
50. I am indebted to Randall Poole for this insight.
51. For other examples, see K. L. Kustodiev (protoierei), *Opyt istorii bibleiskoi zhenshchiny. Istoriia vetkhozavetnoi zhenshchiny* (St. Petersburg, 1870), Parunov, "U baby volos dolog," 5–9; A. Nadezhdin, "Zhenshchiny v istorii khristianskoi tserkvi," *Strannik* 11 (1872): 141–86; and idem, *Prava i znachenie zhenshchiny v khristianstve* (St. Petersburg, 1873). On the way such arguments inherently promote a negative image of the comparative group, see Johnson, *Truly Our Sister*, 185–88.
52. "Slovo, proiznesennoe Ego Vysokopreosviashchenstvom, Chlenom Sviateishago Synoda, Vysokopreosviashchenneishim Pavlom, Arkhiepiskopom Kazanskim i Sviiazhsikm, v den' Kazanskiia ikony Bozhiei Materi, 22 oktiabria 1888 goda v Kazanskom Bogoroditskom zhenskom monastyre," *Pravoslavnyi sobesednik* 10 (1890): 7 (1st pagination).
53. Wagner, *Marriage, Property and Law*, chaps. 3, 4.
54. *Rossiia 1913 god. Statistiko-dokumental'nyi spravochnik* (St. Petersburg, 1995), 328–29, 331, 341, 347.
55. In addition to the works cited in note 37 above, see S. V. Troitskii, *Diakonissy v pravoslavnoi tserkvi* (St. Petersburg, 1912).
56. I. V. Preobrazhenskii, *Vserossiiskaia pravoslavnaia tserkov' po statisticheskym dannym s 1840–41 po 1890–91 gg.* (St. Petersburg, 1897), 202–18; O. D. Popova, "Eparkhial'nye zhenskie uchilishcha v kul'ture provintsial'nogo goroda," in *Regional'naia istoriia v rossiiskoi i zarubezhnoi istoriografii. Tezisy dokladov mezhdunarodnoi nauchnoi konferentsii 1–4 iiunia 1999 goda* (Riazan', 1999), chap. 1, 75–80; "Eparkhial'nye zhenskie uchilishcha v Rossii," *Pedagogika*, 3 (1999): 85–91; and I. K. Smolich, *Istoriia russkoi tserkvi 1700–1917* (Moscow, 1996), 2: 100–115.
57. But see also, on the development of organized charitable and social work after the late 1850s, S.V. Pashentseva, *Zhenskie blagotvoritel'nye obshchestva Rossiiskoi imperii* (Moscow, 2003); G. N. Ul'ianova, *Blagotvoritel'nost' moskovskikh predprinimatelei, 1860–1914* (Moscow, 1999); and Adele Lindenmeyr, *Poverty Is Not a Vice: Charity, Society, and the State in Imperial Russia* (Princeton, N.J., 1996); and on social work by women, see Laurie Bernstein, *Sonia's Daughters: Prostitutes and Their Regulation in Imperial Russia* (Berkeley, Calif., 1995).
58. *Kalendar' i spravochnaia kniga dlia materei i uchitel'nits na 1876* (St. Petersburg, 1876), 86–89, 238–47; "Vdova serdobol'naia," in *Entsiklopedicheskii slovar'*, izd. F. A. Brokgauza i I. A.

Efrona (St. Petersburg, 1892), vol. 10 (V^a), 679; "Sestry i brat'ia miloserdiia," in ibid., vol. 58 (XXXIX^a), 713–15; John Shelton Curtiss, "Russian Sisters of Mercy in the Crimea, 1854–1855," *Slavic Review* 25 (1966): 84–100; P. A. Ilinskii, *Russkaia zhenshchina v voinu 1877–1878 g.* (St. Petersburg, 1879); F. L. German, *Zaslugi zhenshchin v dele ukhoda za bolnymi i ranenymi* (Khar'kov, 1898); *Zhurnaly i protokoly zasedanii Vysochaishe uchrezhdennogo Predsobornago Prisutstviia*, 2: 15; and A. A. Papkov, *Tserkovnyia bratstva. Kratkii statisticheskii ocherk o polozhenii tserkovnykh bratstv k nachalu 1893 godu* (St. Petersburg, 1893).

59. For example, see *Otchet za 1907 [1910, 1911] g. po Prikhodskomu Sovetu pri Sergievskoi tserkvi, goroda N. Novgoroda* (Nizhnii Novgorod, 1908, [1911, 1912]); and, in general, Glennys Young, *Power and the Sacred in Revolutionary Russia: Religious Activists in the Village* (University Park, Pa., 1997), 23–26; but cf. Gregory L. Freeze, *The Parish Clergy in Nineteenth-Century Russia: Crisis, Reform, Counter-Reform* (Princeton, N.J., 1983), 289–95.

60. Smolich, *Istoriia russkoi tserkvi*, 1: 669.

61. E. B. Emchenko, "Zhenskie monastyri v Rossii," in N. V. Sinitsyna, *Monashestvo i monastyri v Rossii XI–XX veka* (Moscow, 2002), 245–84; Brenda Meehan-Waters, "Popular Piety, Local Initiative and the Founding of Women's Religious Communities in Russia, 1764–1907," in *Seeking God: The Recovery of Religious Identity in Orthodox Russia, Ukraine, and Georgia*, ed. Stephen Batalden (Dekalb, Ill., 1993), 83–105; idem, "From Contemplative Practice to Charitable Activity: Russian Women's Religious Communities and the Development of Charitable Work, 1861–1917," in *Lady Bountiful Revisited: Women, Philanthropy, and Power*, ed. K. D. McCarthy, 142–56 (New Brunswick, N.J., 1990); O. Bukova, *Zhenskie obiteli prepodobnogo Serafima Sarovskogo* (Nizhnii Novgorod, 2003); and William G. Wagner, "The Transformation of Female Orthodox Monasticism in Nizhnii Novgorod Diocese, 1764–1929, in Comparative Perspective," *Journal of Modern History*, forthcoming.

62. P. Lakhotskii (protoierei), *Propovednicheskaia khristomatiia. Posob'e pri izuchenii nauka o tserkovnom propovednichestve v dukhovnykh seminariiakh* (St. Petersburg, 1912), 310–13.

63. See, for example, Arkhimandrit Evdokim, "Inoki na sluzhbe blizhnim," *Bogoslovskii vestnik* 11(1902): 305–58.

64. "Rech' okonchivshim kurs ucheniia vospitannitsam Moskovskoi 2-i zhenskoi gim-nazii, v 1874/ 75 g.," in *Rechi, proiznesennyia zakonouchiteliami moskovskikh zhenskikh gimnazii, okonchivshim kurs vospitannitsam onykh* (Moscow, 1892), 32, 33, 34, and, in general, 31–38.

65. "Rech' okonchivshim kurs ucheniia vospitannitsam Moskovskoi 2-i zhenskoi gim-nazii, v 1877/ 78 g.," in ibid., 50, 55, and, in general, 50–59.

66. RGIAgM, f. 203, op. 400, d. 1, ll. 1–10b. See also ll. 7–70b.

67. Ibid.

68. Odin iz uchastnikov, "V zhenskom Bogoslovsko-pedagogicheskom institute," *Moskovskii tserkovnyi golos* 36 (19 October 1917): 5–6. See also Feofan, "Rech' pri otkrytii zhen-skikh bogoslovsko-pedagogicheskikh kursov"; and *Zhurnaly i protokoly zasedanii Vysochaishe uchrezdennago Predsobornago Prisutstviia*, 4:83.

69. See the sources cited in note 2 above.

70. E. Liuleva, *Svobodnaia zhenshchina i khristianstvo* (Moscow, 1906). I have not been able to identify Liuleva.

71. Ibid., 4.

72. Ibid., 7.

73. Ibid., 13.

74. Ibid., 25.

75. A sense of the issues confronting the Church is provided by *Zhurnaly i protokoly zasedanii Vysochaishe uchrezhdennago Predsobornago Prisutstviia*, 4 vols.; and *Otzyvy eparkhial'nykh arkhiereev po voprosu o tserkovnykh reforme*, 2 vols. (Moscow, 2004); see also the sources cited in note 7 above.

76. For different assessments of the Church Council, see Catherine Evtuhov, *The Cross and the Sickle: Sergei Bulgakov and the Fate of Russian Religious Philosophy, 1890–1920* (Ithaca,

N.Y., 1997), 189–206; Roman Rössler, *Kirche und Revolution in Russland: Patriarch Tichon und der Sowjetstaat* (Köln, 1969); I. Smolitsch, "Die Russische Kirche in der Revolutionszeit vom März bis Oktober 1917 und das Landeskonzil 1917 bis 1918," *Ostkirchliche Studien*, 14 (1965): 3–34; idem, *Istoriia russkoi tserkvi. 1917–1997* (Moscow, 1997), 9–47; and A.V. Kartashev, "Revoliutssia i sobor 1917–18 g.," in *Bogoslovskaia mysl'. Trudy pravoslavnago bogoslovskago instituta v Parizhe* (Paris, 1942), 75–101.

77.   GARF, f. R-3431, op. 1, d. 105, ll. 26, 45–89; d. 106, ll. 6–8, 43–102; d. 107 (all); d. 108, ll. 2–12; d. 109, ll. 2–17, 25–30; d. 110, ll. 13–29; d. 111, ll. 3–48; d. 113, ll. 2–12, 19–83; d. 114 (all); d. 115 (all); d. 122, ll. 10, 13–17; d. 130, ll. 24–35, 48–49, 85–93; d. 154, ll. 2–25; d. 157, ll. 5, 8–80b, 11–12; dd. 264–65 (all); d. 552 (all); d. 588 (all) [all relating to divorce]; and the sources cited in note 5 above.

78.   See the sources cited in note 5 above.

79.   GARF, f. R-3431, op. 1, dd. 326–27; Beliakova and Beliakova, "Obsuzhdenie voprosa o diakonissakh," 149–61; and Beliakova, *Tserkovnyi sud*.

80.   GARF, f. R-3431, op. 1, d. 105, ll. 45–71 (25–28); d. 110, ll. 13–14; and d. 192, ll. 116, 121–23.

81.   GARF, f. R-3431, op. 1, d. 154, ll. 2–25; d. 192, ll. 116–23, 159, 188; and d. 588, ll. 3–5.

82.   On the Church schism of the 1920s, see, especially, Edward E. Roslof, *Red Preists: Renovationism, Russian Orthodoxy, and Revolution, 1905–1946* (Bloomington, Ind., 2002), M. V. Shkarovskii, *Obnovlencheskoe dvizhenie v russkoi pravoslavnoi tserkvi XX veka* (St. Petersburg, 1999); A. Levitin-Krasnov and V. Shavrov, *Ocherki po istorii russkoi tserkovnoi smuty* (Moscow, 1996); and *"Obnovlencheskii" raskol* (Moscow, 2002).

83.   On these points, see, especially, Laura Engelstein, "The Dream of Civil Society in Tsarist Russia: Law, State, and Religion," in *Civil Society before Democracy: Lessons from Nineteenth-Century Europe*, ed. Nancy Bermeo and Philip Nord (Lanham, Md., 2000), 23–41; and idem, "Holy Russia in Modern Times: An Essay on Orthodoxy and Cultural Change," *Past and Present* 173 (2001): 129–56.

6

Profane Narratives about a Holy Sacrament: Marriage and Divorce in Late Imperial Russia

Gregory L. Freeze

·•◦⊷∞⊶◦•··

Nineteenth-century Russia had exalted the family as the bedrock of stability, but that very institution underwent profound change in the final decades of the ancien régime. Apart from reports about "family division"(*semeinyi razdel*) and the "hooliganism" of rebellious youth, the most dramatic sign of family breakdown was the explosive increase in the number of divorces, which sky-rocketed from a few *dozen* in the 1850s to a few *thousand* by 1914. This family crisis affected not only elites but even peasants—the putative bastion of traditional patriarchy and piety. Little wonder that the "marital question" now pervaded public discourse,[1] impelling one prelate to complain that "people now speak of illegal cohabitation without inhibition, as something ubiquitous and commonplace."[2] A liberal church journal concurred: "The breakdown of the family, despite the extreme difficulty of the divorce process, is one of the most serious social ills at the present time. Some obtain a divorce by paying out thousands of rubles to hire false witnesses and to bribe officials; others, who lack such means, simply desert their wives and children and take up relations outside the law."[3]

To explore this neglected sphere, this essay relies mainly on diocesan, not central, Church archives. Although the latter are still useful (especially in reflecting policy changes), those files omit the original narratives—the plethora of petitions, depositions, court hearings, verdicts, and appeals. The "extract" sent to St. Petersburg constitutes but a pale reflection of the original file. More important, Church authorities in St. Petersburg reviewed only cases already approved by the diocesan authorities, *not* the vast majority that had been denied or terminated. To see the full panoply of divorce (those rejected, not only those approved), this essay examines all the pertinent files in the Lithuanian diocese from 1905 to 1914, allowing for a close examination of an important borderland area (the Lithuanian diocese), characterized by a strong Orthodox base but also fraught with confessional, not just class and gender, issues.[4]

Several broad conclusions are suggested in this essay:

First, the archival files, if "failed divorces" are included, reflect a level of family breakdown far greater than that suggested in official divorce statistics.

Second, the divorce files indicate a "democratization" of divorce, affecting the underclass, and not just the elite, with marked geographic differences and a strong impact not on the old but on the relatively young.

Third, the legal process created a profound gap between the privileged and non-privileged: whereas the former could script a quick divorce, the latter routinely became mired in the maze of ecclesiastical justice.

Fourth, men and women used opposing narrative strategies to obtain divorce: the former sought to reassert patriarchy, the latter to contest it.

Fifth, the divorce files reveal a gap between official and popular Orthodoxy: in contrast to the Church's sacramentalist conception of marriage, the laity's view in divorce litigation was secular (as traditional patriarchy or modern partnership).

Sixth, borderland context—with confessional differences—left a clear imprint on rhetoric and legal strategy.

Finally, the divorce question had a profound impact on the Church: overwhelmed by a tidal wave of complicated legal cases, driven to deny divorce and alienate litigants, the Church simultaneously found its administration paralyzed and its authority among the faithful steadily eroding.

The "Traditional" Family Order and Post-Reform Challenge

In Russia, as in the West, institutional control over marriage was a relatively modern phenomenon; the difference was that in Russia it came only in the first half of the nineteenth century.[5] The medieval Church had formal authority but, for several reasons, lacked the means to regulate marriage: the geographic dispersion of the population, the primitive communications, its miniscule administration, the uncodified and contradictory law, and the lack of rudimentary documentation of metrical books. By the early nineteenth century, however, the Church had developed the administration and documentation needed to regulate marriage and divorce, an institutionalization process that culminated in the *Charter for Diocesan Consistories* (1841).

Legal divorce consisted of several distinct stages. The first was a formal request (*proshenie*) citing specific grounds for divorce (along with filing fees, copy of the marriage certificate, and pertinent documents). The second stage was the formal exhortation for reconciliation (*primirenie*), where the local priest implored both parties to reconcile and terminate the proceeding.[6] If the plaintiff refused, the diocesan consistory (the bishop's advisory council) scheduled a hearing (*sudogovorenie*) and conducted its investigation, obtaining depositions from witnesses and neighbors, making a nationwide search (if one spouse had disappeared), and obtaining medical opinions (in the case of sexual incapacity and insanity). With this evidence in hand, the consistory compiled a summary (shown to the litigants for confirmation) and prepared a draft verdict for the bishop to confirm or reject. If he approved, an "extract" was sent to the Holy Synod (the ruling council of the Church in St. Petersburg) for review and confirmation. Significantly the Church did not address the material aspect of divorce (division of property, child custody and support, and alimony); although such issues sometimes intruded into the diocesan files,[7] they were outside the jurisdiction of the Church and left either to arbitration (*treteiskii sud*) or to state courts (*okruzhnoi sud*).

This cumbersome procedure made divorce virtually impossible, which was precisely what the Church intended. In the spirit of post-Napoleonic restoration, which spurned the liberalization of divorce and exalted the family as the bedrock of political stability, the Russian Church did everything possible to avert marital dissolution. It buttressed policy with a new theology: in contrast to the traditional "reproductionist" conception of marriage as necessary for "the propagation of mankind," the new sacramentalist doctrine underscored the "indelibility" of the marital sacrament and hence the unacceptability of frivolous human attempts to dissolve "holy unions,"[8] whether through separation or formal divorce. While retaining earlier grounds for marital dissolution (permanent disappearance, adultery, Siberian exile with loss of all rights, premarital impotence, premarital insanity, bigamy, and various lesser grounds), the nineteenth-century Church made divorce so difficult that it was effectively limited to easily documented cases of bigamy and Siberian exile. The chances of success were slim: even of those cases already approved by bishops, 70 percent were rejected in the Synodal review.[9] Compared to continental Europe, where divorce generally became easier (or, in Catholic countries, at least annulment and separation), the Russian Church was uniquely restrictive. Some clergy even warned of a destructive impact, as it drove increasing numbers into dissent—especially against the Old Belief, which now represented not only the old *rites* (liturgical practices) but also the old *rights* (to marry and divorce without ecclesiastical control).

After the 1860s, however, the divorce rate steadily increased and, by 1914, far exceeded the twofold increase in population.[10] In absolute numbers, the approved divorces jumped from 71 in 1860 to 1,171 in 1900 and then to nearly

4,000 by 1913. That was a twenty-eight-fold increase in the divorce rate per 100,000 Orthodox faithful (from 0.14 in 1860 to 3.9 in 1914), with an even higher (thirty-three-fold) increase when compared to 1,000 new marriages (from 0.13 to 4.34). That significantly narrowed the gap between Russia and most European countries, the number being only three times higher in France and eight times higher in Germany. The grounds for divorce also underwent a significant change: whereas the main cause before the 1880s had been disappearance, the grounds subsequently shifted to adultery, which rose to 41 percent in 1900 and catapulted to 90 percent by 1913. The divorce rate, moreover, varied considerably across the realm, with high rates in urbanized provinces like St. Petersburg and Moscow and far lower rates in the agricultural heartland.[11]

Notably these official statistics include only divorces that were approved, not those denied—not to mention the "informal divorces" of those who never bothered to formalize the dissolution of a marriage. The Synod did assemble interesting data on divorces filed at the diocesan level but, for various reasons (chiefly denial and termination), these were never brought before the Synod for approval. The total number of divorce cases grew exponentially, from about 200 in the mid-nineteenth century to 15,502 in 1913—an increase of 7,000 percent. In addition to new applications each year, the Church accumulated an ever-growing backlog of unresolved, contested divorces; by 1913 it was processing nearly 40,000 cases. As before, the Church continued to reject the vast majority of divorce applications—reflecting, as we shall see, the profound gulf between ecclesiastical views of marriage and those of the laity.

The overburdened Church bureaucracy did not assemble, much less analyze, data about the profile of litigants in divorce. As contemporaries noted, however, divorce ceased to be a prerogative of the privileged and had become increasingly common among the lower classes, especially workers,[12] where migrant labor and separate residence inevitably took its toll on marital stability. The data on Lithuanian diocese confirm such impressions: nobles comprised just 9 percent of the litigants, with the rest consisting of petty officials and military personnel (46 percent), townspeople (10 percent), and peasants (35 percent). As for gender distribution, the female proportion of plaintiffs (60 percent) was only moderately higher, showing that men were also seeking to dissolve marriages. And these litigants were usually young, rarely over forty years of age. Hence the surge in the divorce rate was owing not to greater longevity but to a higher incidence of marital breakdown, often in the early years of a union.

A multiplicity of factors, of course, contributed to this exponential increase in marital breakdown and divorce. One was law, especially a Synodal decree of 1904 permitting those found guilty of adultery, after a suitable penance,[13] to remarry; freed from a permanent ban on remarriage, spouses more readily agreed to register (even fabricate) extramarital sex to obtain a divorce. The emergence of the legal profession, which gained the right to represent litigants (and actively solicited clients),[14] served both to ensure a higher rate of success and to shield litigants from the indignities of a court appearance.[15] Some clergy even blamed the lawyers for the growing demand, and expectations, for a prompt divorce.[16] More fundamental were the profound social changes associated with urbanization and industrialization; migrant labor (*otkhodnichestvo*), in particular, which divided a family's residence and nullified community control, was an oft-cited factor.[17] Equally important were the cultural changes, the erosion of traditional norms that impacted not only the city but also the countryside. Apart from a general rise in feminine self-consciousness, women could increasingly expect favorable treatment even from a patriarchal institution like the Church, which tended to privilege women and posit female piety as a weapon against irreligion.

Despite the escalating caseload, the Church sought to treat each case with consummate vigilance. Even if sympathetic toward one party, the consistory—given the bishop's and Synod's review—strictly enforced the rules on procedure, grounds, evidence, fees, and documents. Although some cases were straightforward (e.g., the easily documented bigamy and Siberian exile),[18] others were complex: claims of premarital insanity and premarital sexual incapacity required medical confirmation, and adultery—the main grounds for divorce—needed two "eyewitnesses." In the latter case, a contrite confession or material evidence (such as love letters and photographs)[19] were useless if the plaintiff could not provide the two eyewitnesses. For example, when Captain Ivan Nemilov admitted to his transgression but only one person witnessed the act of intercourse, the consistory denied the divorce.[20] A lax consistory risked censure by the prelate; Archbishop Tikhon (Belavin)—the future patriarch of Russia—repeatedly overturned the recommendation of his consistory, declaring that the witnesses in adultery cases had not actually *seen* the alleged fornication.[21] When both the consistory and bishop proved inattentive, the Synod routinely intervened to quash a favorable decision. Thus, in one case, "upon examination of the circumstances" the Synod found that the testimony of several witnessed failed to meet the legal requirements and resolved "to annul the decision of the Lithuanian Diocesan Authority," leaving the marriage in force.[22] Such oversight, and reprimands, naturally made diocesan authorities more meticulous in enforcing the law.[23]

This vigilance sometimes led to surprising reversals, with divorce being granted in favor of the defendant, not the plaintiff, after the consistory conducted its investigation into the facts. Thus, after one man sued for divorce (on the grounds of his wife's "permanent disappearance"), the consistory quickly located the missing wife; when she proved that the plaintiff had been in an insane asylum and was currently living with another woman, the consistory promptly ruled in her favor.[24] In another case, a peasant claimed that his wife "leads a profligate life" and demanded a divorce. As the consistory soon discovered, however, the plaintiff was deranged, a condition apparent from the outset of the union[25] but sharply aggravated by the 1905 Revolution: overcome by delusions that he had been elected chairman of the State Duma, the plaintiff sold his farm inventory and prepared to go to St. Petersburg, with the expectation of marrying a tsarevna—and hence his urgent need for divorce. The consistory not only denied his suit but sympathetically counseled his wife that she could file for divorce on grounds of his premarital insanity.[26] Some plaintiffs simply misjudged their witnesses[27] or, when confronted with negative testimony, preferred a divorce in the spouse's favor to no divorce at all.[28]

Divorce Narratives

However impressive the divorce statistics, more revealing still are the texts—the petitions, sworn statements, court hearings, and depositions. As one might expect, these files are packed with half-truths and outright lies;[29] the documents—often contested by the other party and witnesses—must be treated critically. Nevertheless, even the pathologically mendacious sought to convince by invoking the presumed norms in ecclesiastical courts. At the same time, litigants inevitably reflected their own station in life, specifically with respect to three key variables: class, gender, and confession.

Class: Privileged and Popular Narratives

Although a binary elite-popular model is simplistic—for example, some peasant plaintiffs showed legal acumen, while some educated ones revealed surprising ignorance[30]—files do reflect the social status of the litigants. Means, not simply education, made the difference: the privileged could employ a lawyer to craft an airtight petition, represent them at hearings, and, if necessary, fabricate evidence, in particular, two eyewitnesses in adultery cases. Even without a lawyer, the educated could rely on published guides to script a credible legal suit. By contrast, the ill-informed, legally unrepresented, often rural litigant stumbled through the divorce process: such litigants often failed to send the requisite documents or fees, applied for divorce on nonexistent grounds, failed to produce credible witnesses, and, most important, lacked the tacit consent of the other spouse. Although the divorces differed greatly in detail, most divorce cases fit roughly into the paradigms shown in table 6.1, with the remainder falling somewhere in between.

Table 6.1. Two Paradigms of Divorce

Stage	Privileged	Popular
Petition for divorce, accompanied by fees and documents	Brief statement, sometimes prepared with the assistance of a lawyer	Sometimes correctly compiled but often incomplete—lacking a specific grounds for divorce or the requisite fees and documents
Exhortation to the two parties to reconcile	Promptly performed, with both sides refusing to reconcile	Often delayed; frequently the defendant challenges the petition or seeks to reconcile
Court hearing	Held within a few weeks, the defendant repeats confession; one or both parties are represented by an attorney	Delayed for months, even years, as the defendant ignores or rejects summonses to appear at the court hearing
Sworn depositions of witnesses	The witnesses confirm the substance of the original accusation	Witnesses prove difficult to locate, fail to confirm the plaintiff's claims, or even testify on behalf of the defendant
Compilation of case summary (*zapiska*), countersigned by the two parties as to accuracy	The case abstract is promptly compiled by the consistory and then signed by the two parties or their lawyers	The case abstract is eventually composed, but confirmation by the parties is sometimes delayed by the inability to locate one of the parties
The bishop confirms or rejects the consistory's recommended verdict;	Within a few months of the original petition, the consistory approves the divorce; both parties sign	After one, two, or more years, the consistory sometimes approves the original petition but, more often,

(*Continued*)

Table 6.1.   (Continued)

Stage	Privileged	Popular
if approved, the parties either accept or register "dissatis-faction"	that they are "satisfied" with the verdict	either denies divorce or rules in favor of the initial defendant; the losing side sometimes declares his or her "dissatisfaction" with the outcome
If approved by the bishop, there is a final review by the Holy Synod	The Synod approves the divorce, usually within a couple of months	In the few cases where the divorce proved success-ful, the Synod upholds the diocesan recommendation
Delivery of the divorce certificate, with the guilty party swearing agreement to perform penance	Delivery of the final divorce certificate, with confirmation of receipt by the two parties	Delivery is sometimes impeded by the inability to locate the plaintiff or defendant

The Privileged Narrative

The slick narrative of the educated (or at least the well-heeled), especially if constructed with the assistance of a lawyer, ensured prompt divorce. The initial petition, typically laconic, contained the obligatory information, documents, and fees.[31] Its purpose was not to convince but to conform—that is, to satisfy the technical requirements of ecclesiastical justice. That meant observing the bureaucratic niceties (documents, fees, and forms), citing valid legal grounds, arranging a mutual refusal to reconcile, attending the hearing (in person or through a lawyer), and providing the requisite evidence. To succeed, the plain-tiff needed documentation that was complete and legal, and did not have to provide prolix descriptions of marital breakdown but only had to satisfy the legal requirements.

This strategy worked best, of course, when the divorce was tacitly consen-sual. Indeed, given the Church's antipathy to marital dissolution, only collusion could avert interminable proceedings and a potential denial. And spouses who opposed divorce, for whatever reason, had multiple weapons at their disposal.

Apart from overt non-cooperation (to delay, if not sabotage, the process),[32] spouses could challenge the credibility of witnesses or lodge accusations of perjury.[33] These tactics were remarkably effective. Thus, in the case of a colonel who sued for divorce in 1909, immediately trouble was afoot: the plaintiff refused to reconcile, but his wife, who had already hired a lawyer, agreed to resume conjugal life. At the hearing, moreover, her lawyer produced a letter from her husband proposing "that they divorce and that she assume the guilt." Her lawyer also questioned the credibility of his two witnesses: one was a convicted perjurer, the other a "divorcee." The consistory eventually rejected the witnesses' depositions and denied the divorce.[34] Moreover, the defendant had the option of filing a countersuit (*vstrechnyi isk*), a right that could be used to intimidate or, if pursued and successful, could even shift the guilt to the plaintiff. Indeed, the contested divorce ran the risk that the consistory would find *both* parties guilty and, given the "guilt principle" (whereby only an innocent spouse could dissolve the union), deny the divorce altogether.[35] Little wonder that such contested divorces involved enormous passion, sometimes to the point of homicide.[36]

A consensual divorce, by contrast, glided smoothly through the system and almost invariably invoked adultery as the grounds for dissolution.[37] The barriers to divorce on these grounds were considerable—not only public opprobrium but, after 1904, the mandatory penance and waiting period to remarry. Although some, especially women, refused to bear the stigma and others resented the penance and waiting period for remarriage, spouses now found a consensual divorce far more palatable. Of course, they also had to resolve thorny issues of child custody and financial settlement—matters outside the purview of the Church but of vital importance to litigants. While the non-privileged could neither buy off a spouse nor afford a lawyer, those with means had a much easier time. Clearly consent to divorce could be expensive; as one wife warned: "I received your letter today and agree to everything—that is, I agree to the divorce, but I warn you that I have no money for the divorce and you will have to conduct it at your own expense. This means, you assume the guilt, pay the costs of divorce, and give me one-third of your income each month." She warned that the divorce can "cost four hundred to five hundred rubles," and if the husband sent the money, "I will immediately file for divorce." If he demurred, she warned that "in vain do you think that you can secure a divorce without my consent."[38]

If the parties came to an agreement (for material gain or simply for manumission from a detested spouse), divorce was certain and speedy. Such suits increasingly adduced adultery as grounds and offered the two eyewitnesses, who usually saw the spouse having intercourse with prostitutes[39] or with anonymous women in hotels where the doors never seem to be locked.[40] While most testimony was pro forma, some was graphic—whether from vivid memory or a determination to ensure a favorable ruling.[41] Rarely did adultery cases cite specific paramours who, apart from the ignominy, became liable to penance.[42] Hence these suits ran like clockwork; sometimes requiring only a few months,[43] they routinely were approved by the bishop and Synod. Some were transparently consensual: both spouses categorically rejected reconciliation,[44] the guilty party cheerfully confessed to infidelity,[45] and both parties signed that they were "satisfied" with the consistory's decision to grant a divorce.[46] Some files even alluded to negotiations,[47] cited specific financial arrangements,[48] or candidly declared their mutual agreement to terminate the union.[49] Thus one husband not only confessed to adultery but noted the couple's mutual agreement to divorce: "We separated about five years ago and no longer live together; after considerable reflection, we decided to give each other our freedom, to unfetter our hands, to divorce, and hence there cannot be any talk about our further living together."[50] The paperwork in most cases was brief, devoid of extraneous detail, although some volunteered self-serving excuses, invoked modern language about "incompatibility of character,"[51] or cited "irreconcilable differences" because of social origin, upbringing, character, and education.[52] Litigants occasionally offered ancillary documents, such as written agreements for material support—a further indication of consensual divorce.[53] The Church overlooked such collusion: as long as the couple provided eyewitness testimony, their suits sailed through the consistory—notwithstanding suspicion and occasional complaints about collusion, lawyering, and witness perjury.

The Non-Privileged

Divorce was infinitely more complicated for the disadvantaged. Their divorce applications, often transcripts of oral statements by illiterates, were far less legal and far less successful. It was not for taciturnity; indeed, they tended to be prolix and personal, to foreground transgressions and perfidy, but they often failed to specify valid (sometimes, *any*) grounds for divorce or to evince a minimal awareness of divorce law and procedure.[54] Such suits were often incomplete (lacking basic documents and information), interrupted (with vanishing litigants—even plaintiffs, not just defendants), and unpredictable (with plaintiffs becoming defendants). These litigants obviously lacked the wherewithal for a consensual divorce; they could neither hire lawyers nor buy a spouse's collusion. Instead, plaintiffs tended to rely on a homespun sense of morality and justice, not the *Charter of Ecclesiastical Consistories*. Cultural deprivation also took a toll, as the disadvantaged tried to decipher the bureaucratese of consistory rulings. One litigant was so "undeveloped" (in the consistory's phrase) that he misunderstood its verdict: mistakenly believing that the consistory had ruled against him, he filed an appeal to protest a ruling in his favor![55]

Moreover, the non-privileged underestimated the consistory's capacity to verify facts and enforce the law. For example, when plaintiffs filed for divorce on grounds of congenital sexual incapacity, some did not realize that the mandatory medical examination by the state medical board would immediately expose any falsehoods.[56] More common were false claims about a spouse's "disappearance," which required not only absence for at least five years but proof that the spouse could not be found. Plaintiffs, especially peasants, assumed that the consistory either could not locate missing spouses or would not bother to do so.[57] To their astonishment, however, the consistory conducted a full-scale national search, interrogating fellow villagers as to the whereabouts and date of disappearance, sending inquiries to state offices for residential registry, and publishing a "wanted" announcement in the Church's central newspaper.[58]

The non-privileged often lacked even a rudimentary knowledge of the procedures and legal grounds for divorce. Some petitions, for example, failed to provide the requisite information or even to cite the grounds for divorce. Ignatii Kharitonchik, in a handwritten letter to the consistory, complained that his wife led a "depraved life" and had abandoned him; without further ado, he naïvely asked the consistory "to divorce her from me."[59] A peasant woman correctly noted that "the permanent disappearance of one spouse gives grounds for the other spouse to enter into a new marriage" but wondered what must be done to prove the disappearance.[60] Another plaintiff made excellent headway (the advertisement in the *Tserkovnye vedomosti* failed to locate the spouse), but—evidently from sheer ignorance—candidly admitted seeing his wife three years earlier, causing the consistory to dismiss the suit (as less than the minimum disappearance of five years).[61] A peasant woman made a similar blunder: when she acknowledged at the court hearing that she had received a letter three years earlier from her "missing" spouse, the consistory automatically dismissed her suit.[62] In the case of premarital sexual incapacity, the Church required a minimum of three years of cohabitation before it would consider such applications, rejected premature applications, and allowed only the "innocent" party to file suit. Hence, when one peasant sued for divorce two years after his marriage (explaining that his wife abandoned him because "I was incapable of having conjugal relations"), he received a summary rejection from the consistory.[63]

The most striking feature of popular divorce suits, however, was not their legal ignorance but their patent "illegality": the vast majority of popular divorce petitions appealed to nonexistent legal grounds or invented new ones. As in the case of marital impedimenta (such as fourth marriage and kinship), the popular classes took issue with canon law in the name of equity and common sense. Thus some naïve plaintiffs simply invoked unrecognized grounds: venereal diseases like gonorrhea and syphilis, afflictions like epilepsy and leprosy, post-marital insanity,[64] propensity for "unnatural sex,"[65] and even physical defects such as "deafness."[66] The cunning also reinterpreted legal grounds in radically new ways. Thus some expanded "incapacity" from physical deficiencies or deformities (as required by law) to denote the failure to perform conjugal duties because of desertion, illness, and insanity. For example, one peasant explained that his wife's conjugal incapacity was the result of "a bladder ailment that causes her to wet the bed."[67] And some sought divorce on patently nonexistent grounds. When another male complained that his wife "is capable of conjugal relations but cannot bear children," the consistory explained that infertility was not grounds for divorce.[68] In rejecting a divorce application based on the wife's "wretched character" and "grave illness," the consistory explained that "the law does not recognize illness and intolerable character of a spouse as legitimate grounds for seeking to dissolve a marriage."[69]

The greatest chasm between canon and custom concerned desertion and disappearance. Whereas Church law required a "permanent disappearance" for a minimum of five years, the popular classes tended to regard mere desertion, for whatever reason, as sufficient grounds. Thus, after the consistory located a missing spouse and denied divorce, the rebuffed plaintiff appealed its verdict, insisting that desertion was sufficient reason to dissolve the marital union, but met with a summary rejection by the Synod.[70] Some plaintiffs insisted that separate residence alone was sufficient grounds for divorce. Thus one husband voiced confidence that twelve years of separate residence was "legal grounds" for divorce.[71] Other petitioners assumed that malicious desertion, not physical disappearance, was legitimate grounds for divorce. One peasant angrily complained to the Synod that the consistory had "mocked" him by locating his wife and ignoring his need for a spouse to run his household: "As if failing to understand his request, for some reason the consistory took upon itself a police function and, instead of liberating him from his wife (who is such in name only), admonished him that his wife had been successfully located, lives in such-and-such a place, so go and get her, but it said not a single word about my request to dissolve the marriage." He furiously protested that "he had not asked the consistory to find his wife (whom he morally does not regard as such and who has not lived with him since the day of their marriage)."[72]

Gender: Male and Female Narratives

Divorce cases are dialogic, with opposing gendered perspectives on marital relations. The discourse is particularly transparent for the non-privileged; whereas the elite had less reason to argue (the aim was to comply, not convince), the crude and often verbose statements of lower-status groups relied less on law than on popular, gendered logic. These male and female narratives thus present opposing views on the central concepts of "family person" (*semianin* and *semianinka*) and patriarchy.

Male Narratives

Although some privileged males invoked a modern "affect" theme,[73] most male narratives (especially from the non-privileged) based their argument on patriarchal power and prerogatives. One common theme was the claim that the wife was a poor "family person" (*semianinka*), that is, insufficiently devoted to the interests and needs of her family. Although a few men invoked this shortcoming to rationalize their own infidelity,[74] most emphasized the wife's failure to perform her economic function in the household. For example, one peasant recounted that, although he "respected and did not beat his wife," she proved a poor partner once she realized that "in my house one has to work" and to care for his children from a prior marriage.[75] Another peasant complained that his wife "not only began to fornicate with anyone who came along" but was also a "poor housekeeper."[76] Another male villager declared that "he does not wish to live with his wife," not just because she was unfaithful but also because "she did not look after order in the household and wasted money earned with such difficulty."[77] In one case the wife's shortcoming as housekeeper proved to be the last straw: "Rusin left his wife because a cat in the apartment grabbed and ate a pound of salted pork, (*salo*) and, as he left, he shouted that he does not need a housekeeper like that."[78] Another peasant complained that his wife, in his absence, had "sold the horse and cow, squandered the money, sold off the grain and linen, and carried away the remaining grain and hid it with a neighbor." When he returned, his wife surreptitiously prepared food at a neighbor's and attempted "to starve me to death and did not give me a clean change of clothes." Such a life, he complained, was "intolerable and bitter." Realizing that, "without a horse, I am not a householder, I decided to leave my wife, Elizaveta Osipova, and her home," and indeed he concluded that he "would be better off to become a hired laborer [*batrak*] than to suffer the misfortunes of a life with her."[79]

Some men candidly cited the need for a good housekeeper as the principal motive for seeking divorce.[80] Stressing the material basis of marriage, they declared that a peasant household cannot function without a wife as field worker, homemaker, cook, child care provider, and the like.[81] One thirty-year-old peasant, abandoned by his wife, wailed that "I do not have a housekeeper" and simply "cannot remain thus, since my entire economy is being ruined."[82] Another expressed similar ideas: "Being forty years old, as a household head with a full allotment of land, I need a wife, for otherwise I shall lose my property."[83] In the words of one villager, the lack of a housekeeper had caused his small children and his "entire household economy" to fall on hard times.[84] Some peasants were willing to take *any* woman: one man whose wife had deserted him asked the consistory either to have her returned or to give him a new one, given the economic urgency: "The absence of a wife-worker has a harmful impact on my household economy, where I alone am the only work force."[85] Another peasant needed a divorce so that he could remarry—and thereby provide care for his aged parents, younger sisters, and the family household.[86]

Males also invoked patriarchy when stressing that they had performed *their* duty as head of the household. That included not only their role as "provider" (and the wives' failure to show respect)[87] but also the patriarchal duty to "correct" errant wives and save them from their sinful ways. More revealing was the tendency of males to invoke the "correction" theme, either reflecting internalized patriarchal values or perhaps representing a shrewd manipulation of the Church's own teachings about the husband's responsibility. Thus one man, who accused his wife of desertion and becoming a "streetwalker," stressed that he had made every effort to bring her to her senses: "I, as her husband, wishing to persuade her of her terrible error, went to her and tearfully asked and implored her to abandon this way of life and to return to me and the children and to live as the law requires."[88] Another man accused his wife of "liberties" (*vol'nosti*) in the presence of other men, despite his best efforts to set her on the right path: "All this upset me terribly, and I repeatedly sought to instruct her to take the path of truth, but in response to my exhortations she only laughed and continued to behave as before."[89] Similar themes pervade another man's divorce petition, which castigated his wife's "bad conduct and disregard for family responsibilities" and rued that "my exhortations proved in vain."[90]

Female Narratives

Notably some women also invoked the patriarchal narrative—not, of course, to affirm the male's right to dominate but instead to demonstrate that he had failed to fulfill his duty as a "family man" (*semianin*). Thus some female plaintiffs claimed that their spouses had not provided material support for the family and hence failed to satisfy the requirements of the patriarch as provider. As one petitioner complained, her husband had "abandoned the family and does not give the means of support to her and the children."[91] Another female defendant, responding to her husband's divorce suit, swore that he had "abandoned her without any cause" and had "even deprived her of the essential means of support."[92] Some narratives redefined the trope of "family man" to link the "provider" theme with infidelity, for the womanizing had a deleterious impact on the family's financial situation. One woman, stressing that her husband was a poor "family man," complained that he had failed to "show a love for family life" and instead chased other women.[93] The reference point of such argumentation was profane: it castigated the philanderer not for sinning against the Lord but for neglecting his patriarchal responsibility to the family.

More common was not the inversion but the repudiation of patriarchy. At one level, some women challenged the domesticity that underlay dependence and instead asserted their own economic self-sufficiency. Some justified economic independence by emphasizing how the husband's failure to provide had forced them to work outside the home.[94] Indeed, they cited this need to justify a formal divorce, which provided the documents for separate residence—a precondition for employment and economic independence.[95] Thus, in demanding divorce from a husband who had vanished seven years earlier, one woman stressed not only that she could no longer make ends meet but that she had to be the main provider and to educate her children.[96] Although most women stressed that dire necessity had forced them to seek outside employment (perhaps to avoid flaunting liberationist rhetoric before a conservative prelate), an audacious few asserted their right to economic independence. One such woman wrote her husband to demand a divorce and warned that "no one can use coercion and force me to live in any way that I do not wish."[97] An engineer's wife declared that she "does not wish to reconcile (for many reasons)," but also because she wished "to live completely free in all respects."[98] Another woman testified that she had left her husband, "regards herself as having the right to live just as she wishes," and had begun a course of study to become a midwife.[99] Although most female litigants inscribed the status of their husband, Evgeniia Prigorinskaia identified herself not by her husband's rank but by her position as a "female official in the Central Telegraph Bureau of Vil'na."[100]

Female petitions frequently invoked affect as the cause of marital breakdown—either because of early, coerced marriage[101] or because the husband's behavior (infidelity, abuse, and alcoholism) denied affect and invalidated the marriage. One woman declared that her husband had married solely for material gain, and, once his expectation of receiving "a significant dowry of three thousand to five thousand rubles" did not materialize, conjugal life became impossible.[102] Another explained that she had married her husband because of her "thoughtlessness, youth, [and] inexperience," because she had been "a poor (and illegitimate) waif," and because her "own mother and other people persuaded her to marry because of his wealth."[103] Spurning the priest's appeal to reconcile, another woman declared that she "does not love her husband and under no condition will she go back together with him."[104] A female peasant declared: "I would rather be dead than live with him—they forced me to marry him, but I shall never live with him."[105] Another woman explained that she had never loved her prospective husband and had married "solely because of coercion on the part of her parents."[106] One female plaintiff implored the consistory to dissolve her nominal marriage and to give her the opportunity "to marry a person who will love me and help me in my life."[107] More radical still, some women invoked love to justify their own infidelity. One woman who confessed her love for another man offered this justification: "Whether I behaved well or badly is another question, but the die is cast, and I am bound by ties most sacred for me—love."[108] Another woman admitted that she had never felt affection for her husband and, "unable to endure the alienation," had found someone "for whom she feels serious attraction," and therefore categorically refused to reconcile and return to her husband.[109]

But the main thrust of the attack on patriarchy was the domestic abuse that figured so prominently in contemporary discourse and provided female litigants with a powerful and credible rhetorical weapon. Such arguments were predictable in the case of a noblewoman who had married a peasant and left when he "began to starve me, torment me, beat me," adding that "he never treated me like a wife, but like an animal."[110] Non-privileged women voiced the same sentiments. One peasant woman, for instance, described how her "husband beat me and mocked me, as few people would indeed treat an animal"—a statement attesting as much to her own self-assertion as his brutality.[111] Another female peasant declared that "our marriage was not some holy union but a means for an evil person to torment and torture an innocent woman."[112] Female litigants used such rhetoric in an effort to persuade the all-male consistory to intercede on behalf of a "poor, defenseless woman." Another female petitioner offered written evidence of her husband's infidelity but openly begged for protection: "I gave my husband everything—my youth, virginity, and health; but in every possible way he mocked a weak, defenseless woman, and even wishes to blacken my name forever." She implored the consistory to "intercede for my innocence and helplessness"—and it did.[113] The rhetoric worked. Moreover, as a reflection of women's growing sense of self-esteem, some litigants expanded abuse to denote mental, not just physical, maltreatment—as in the case of a peasant woman, who complained not only about constant physical abuse but also about the denigration and scorn.[114]

Although peasant women had always negotiated and resisted patriarchy, they now had a new weapon: divorce court. Even when the woman agreed to reconcile, she used this venue to negotiate new terms for marital relations, consenting to cohabitation only if the husband agreed to certain conditions and vowed to treat her properly. One condition was an end to physical abuse; for instance, one female peasant agreed to reconcile in 1908 "but only if he does not beat me, as he has done until now."[115] Others demanded more—both respect and proper treatment. To quote one deposition: "If [my husband] will give his word not to permit himself to insult me and will treat me as a husband should, then I will forgive him for all the past and resume our conjugal life."[116] Likewise, a wife who castigated her husband for "coarse and brutal treatment" agreed to return only if he asks her "forgiveness for the insults" and promises "that this will not recur."[117]

In sum, the conception of marriage was sharply gendered: the male narrative invoked a material, economic conception of the conjugal union, whereas the female narrative posited something closer to a "companionate" marriage—one based on partnership (not patriarchy), mutuality (not subordination), love (not material need).

Religion: Profane and Confessional Narratives

Despite the Church's attempt to inculcate a sacramentalist view of marriage (as an indelible, permanent sacrament), the rhetoric of divorce litigation offers little evidence that this teaching had much effect. Rarely did litigants invoke sacred or ecclesiastical language; the main exception was an occasional reference to the "violation of the holy sacrament" in adultery cases.[118] One male peasant waxed eloquent about the sanctity of marriage but declined to give it priority: "However horrifying the consequences of the sacrament of marriage and the punishment of adultery, and however great may be the service before God of those people who forgive adulterous wives, I reaffirm my suit and refuse to reconcile with my wife."[119] Despite the catechization, sermons, and religious instruction in schools, sacramentalism had little impact on discourse among the laity.

Instead, the divorce files convey a secular, not sacred, conception of marriage. When the rhetoric of the privileged invoked the modern notion of "incompatibility of character," that implicitly took precedence over the matrimonial rite.[120] Thus Mikhail Naletov refused to reconcile with his wife: "the incompatibility of our characters, the frequent family disputes, and many other reasons make it impossible for us to continue our family life together."[121] Another revealing locution was "civil marriage," denoting a "this-worldly" union and casually invoked by some narratives as normal and legitimate. One woman, who had her own career and openly admitted to leaving her husband, demanded that her illegitimate children bear their real father's name, declaring outright that "I am living in a civil marriage."[122] Another woman who had abandoned her husband seven years earlier declared that she was "living in a civil marriage" with someone she loved.[123] Some litigants treated a Church marriage as a formality, protesting that the nominal spouse was not "really" a husband or wife and demanding immediate dissolution of the union. One official, for instance, stressed that his wife left ten years ago and hence in no meaningful way was his spouse—a tacit rejection of the sacramental view of marriage.[124]

Although essentially profane, narratives were sometimes "confessional"—that is, reflecting or manipulating the confessional tensions of late imperial Russia. This factor was particularly salient in a borderland diocese like Lithuania. Although the Church itself did not discriminate against non-Orthodox litigants (for example, granting divorces to innocent Catholic spouses from misbehaving Orthodox partners),[125] litigants sometimes played the confessional card in seeking special treatment. Thus, in addition to accusations of infidelity, Mariia Dudko stressed that, "from the first days of our marriage, there were disputes and quarrels over religion: I am Russian and Orthodox, Kazimir Polish and a zealous Catholic." In another deposition she explained: "I am Orthodox, sincerely believe, while he is a zealous Catholic, with whom I have nothing in common."[126] She added that he "insistently demanded that I convert to Catholicism and insulted my nationality," thus making our marital life "intolerable."[127] A male plaintiff made similar accusations against his Catholic wife, who, "since the time of 17 April 1905 [i.e., since the freedom of conscience in religious relations]," became openly aggressive and "ridiculed our Orthodox Church and the fact that I belong to the party of true Russian patriots."[128]

Although claims of confessional abuse did not outweigh legitimate grounds and evidence, they could win a sympathetic hearing in the consistory.[129] One husband recounted how his wife had mistreated him and, *en passant,* noted that she began "to abuse my Orthodox faith"—a remark that a consistory reader underlined in his review of the case.[130] Such appeals were particularly effective in a borderland diocese like Lithuania, where confessional rivalry was strong and left the Orthodox vulnerable, particularly after the 1905 manifesto on freedom of conscience. That was apparent in a kinship case in 1906, when the Synod approved a request to marry within the fourth degree because of the "special circumstances" in Lithuania diocese.[131]

Religious conversion, moreover, was a powerful tool in divorce strategies. On the one hand, some Catholic spouses converted to Orthodoxy and, within weeks or even days, filed for divorce.[132] Significantly the Church tolerated these suspicious conversions; given the massive defection to other confessions after 1905,[133] it was obviously desperate for converts, whatever the motive. On the other hand, some Orthodox believers threatened "apostasy" if the Church spurned their demands—a credible threat after the manifesto of 17 April 1905 decriminalized conversion from Orthodoxy. One peasant couple, forced to live out of wedlock because of canon laws on kinship, declared that they preferred not to convert to Catholicism, "since they do not wish to betray the faith of their fathers," but threatened to do so if that was the only way to legitimize their eight children.[134] One male peasant petitioned the emperor demanding permission to remarry (explaining that, as a middle-aged man, he needed a woman); otherwise, he warned, he could "have a fit of rage and switch religion."[135]

The Church was well aware that its restrictive canons made apostasy attractive, especially to faiths with more liberal rules and procedures,[136] and after the manifesto on freedom of conscience in 1905 agreed to reinstate apostates who had abjured Orthodoxy for mundane reasons. Thus a peasant couple petitioned in February 1912 to reconvert from Lutheranism to Orthodoxy, explaining that they had abandoned their fathers' faith two years earlier, but only because the local bishop had denied their application to marry (because of consanguinity in the fourth degree). The local priest supported their petition: "They converted from Orthodoxy to Lutheranism not because of religious motives but in order to conceal their illicit cohabitation." Citing a Synod decree of 12 September 1911 permitting re-conversion if the apostasy was based solely on marital considerations, the consistory approved their petition.[137]

The Politics of Divorce

Although most bishops opposed a liberalization of divorce, they could hardly ignore the devastating impact the issue had on the Church and its relationship to the laity. One problem was the sheer volume of divorce cases that gradually paralyzed ecclesiastical administration: in 1913 consistories recorded 15,502 new petitions, but they already had a backlog of 23,017 cases, making a total workload of 38,519 cases. And to contend with this avalanche of litigation was the same, minuscule Church administration configured and funded by a 1869 statute, well before the explosion in divorce cases. Inevitably consistories were only able to process a decreasing proportion of new files, impelling the chief procurator to warn, in 1916, that diocesan administration stood on the verge of collapse. The St. Petersburg consistory, for example, reported in 1905 that only 15 percent of the divorce cases were unresolved; over the next eight years it received 6,632 new files, with the proportion of unresolved cases skyrocketing to 86 percent. As an official inspection of the consistory observed: "Obviously, despite all the experience and zeal, the staff of the divorce branch alone cannot perform the work (which has increased twofold); at the same time, as the total number of cases has increased, the number of unfinished cases has grown as well."[138] Similar conditions prevailed everywhere; the local press in Vladimir, for example, duly reported that "the consistory is buried in divorce suits."[139] In Ekaterinoslav, similarly, the number of cases had jumped from 180 to 320 in 1905–1906 to nearly 1,200 four years later.[140] The avalanche of divorce cases in turn buried the Synod: whereas the Synod had processed a mere 200 files in 1850, by the inter-revolutionary years it received some 8,000 files annually, triggering proposals to establish a mini-Synod to concentrate solely on divorce cases. As the St. Petersburg diocesan gazette warned: "Marriage and divorce cases are tying up the administrative work of the Synod; these files comprise about half the total volume of files passing through the general meetings of the Synod."[141]

Not only were there more cases, there was also more to the cases: "democratization" of divorce generated a surfeit of lawsuits that were often incomplete, incoherent, and invalid. The consistory therefore spent a lot of time and energy seeking to obtain the documents or fees, to locate and depose defendants and witnesses (sometimes even plaintiffs), and to secure information and medical assessments from state authorities. It was particularly difficult to deal with rural litigants, especially those who were illiterate or semi-literate; they could not afford legal counsel and conducted their cases according to their own lights. Although the consistories attempted to instruct litigants (by distributing printed forms), a large proportion of lawsuits foundered on formalities and added to the administrative overload.

Diocesan authorities also had to contend with willful resistance, as defendants, in an effort to delay or sabotage divorce proceedings, deliberately refused to cooperate.[142] Given the Church's lack of police powers,[143] bishops could not force litigants to cooperate, even when warned by a plaintiff that his wife "plans to go off somewhere to hide and thereby delay my case."[144] Indeed, often the best defense was not to contest but to procrastinate, relocate, or disappear.[145] Some non-cooperation was involuntary: spouses who had relocated since the marital breakdown found it prohibitively expensive to return for the hearing.[146] The process could be further delayed by requests to transfer the case to another diocese, where one or the other spouse currently resided.[147] And many dioceses, especially the more culturally and economically backward, had a particularly high proportion of improper, incomplete applications that tied up work in the consistory.[148]

The result was a glacial pace in contested divorces, which dragged on for years and often ended without resolution. The privileged found such delays particularly vexing and, aware of the prompt results obtained by well-connected peers, expected the same for themselves.[149] For litigants from the lower classes these delays were onerous; that was especially true for men in urgent need of a wife to run a household, or for women in need of documents to secure legal residence and independent employment. The diocesan archives are replete with irate letters and suits by impatient, frustrated litigants. One peasant, who had sued for divorce from his adulterous wife in October 1907, badgered the consistory for information about the progress on his case, stressing (in a note from early 1908) that "my family has encountered great ruination." Three years later, after numerous petitions, the exasperated plaintiff filed yet another complaint: "Until now there has still not been any kind of result. . . . I have already suffered considerable expenditures for this case, since all petitions have to be covered with stamps, the metrical copies and petitions are not prepared gratis, but I have not received any resolution."[150] Women plaintiffs complained that these unconscionable delays exposed them to abuse and deprived them of the documents needed to support themselves.[151] One female plaintiff complained that "the case is now dragging on for a second year, and the consistory has not told me the status of my case—whether a divorce has been granted or not. I am extremely upset as to why I have not heard anything for so long."[152] Infuriated by these delays, litigants appealed to the Synod,[153] to local civil authorities,[154] and even to influential functionaries in the State Duma[155] to intercede and help resolve their cases. Some litigants were relentless; one filed nineteen petitions and two appeals to the Synod, impelling the Lithuanian consistory to issue orders that he "not disturb diocesan authorities with his baseless requests."[156]

As the chief procurator of the Synod noted in 1907, such delays, although often not the fault of the Church, provoked numerous complaints and became a staple of "attacks in the newspapers and journals," undermining the authority of the Church. Contemporary studies showing that this restrictive system was a modern invention, hallowed by neither custom nor canon, reinforced the perception of its illegitimacy in the eyes of believers.[157] The procurator therefore urged the consistories to act sympathetically, especially toward those who litigated without benefit of legal counsel.[158] Subsequently consistories did in fact try to aid litigants by supplying printed instructions and occasionally volunteering advice on how best to proceed.[159]

Compounding the slowness was a transparent disparity based on class. Most obvious was the inability of the lower classes to avail themselves of the legal services that guaranteed a quick divorce. Nor could they count on special treatment, in contrast to the privileged and well-connected. That special treatment, for example, was apparent in cases involving insanity, such as the Spiridonovich case in 1914: a high-ranking courtier, who candidly admitted that his wife's mental illness was post-marital, nonetheless induced the Church to grant a divorce. Ordinary litigants, on the other hand, could expect summary rejections. Perhaps even more painful was the confrontational dialogue in "illegal" divorce applications. Female plaintiffs, for example, who sued for divorce on grounds of physical abuse, received terse rejections from the consistory. Thus, when one peasant woman petitioned Archbishop Tikhon to intercede (describing how her drunken husband subjected her and the children to beatings "with his fist and a club"), the consistory sent her a list of the legal grounds for divorce, with a note that "the causes cited in the petition, i.e., the brutal treatment of the husband, are not grounds for a marital dissolution."[160] Such responses made petitioners increasingly truculent, indeed to the point of committing apostasy. Cognizant of such popular discontent, even the infamous arch-reactionary and chief procurator K. P. Pobedonostsev had earlier advised a more lenient approach to divorce: "If one is too adamant in enforcing all the Church laws, this could result in provoking a whole revolution against the Church."[161]

That indeed proved to be the case. Perhaps the most revealing declaration of popular resentment came in the summer of 1917 in a declaration by a peasant believer in central Russia, sent to the All-Russian Assembly of Clergy and Laity. The author, a semi-literate peasant, appealed to "Comrade Citizens" at the assembly to enact far-reaching reform in marital and divorce law. Apart from celebrating the fact that the nation now had the "victory of freedom awaited for centuries," the author complained that this freedom, thus far, had failed to include divorce reform: "Comrade Citizens, we have every freedom, but we just do not see the freedom of divorce, so that this question remains very sensitive." He warned darkly that, "without bloodletting, they will not give us the freedom of divorce, so we peasants suffered from this for several centuries but could do nothing about it," unlike the nobles and merchants, who had "freedom in marriage and divorce." That this freedom now be extended to the peasantry was essential:

> However, as for us peasants, freedom in marriage and divorce was very difficult, but we also desire to be free in this important matter. In this case, we ask you, Comrade Citizens, to settle this question at your church council. Do this as quickly as possible and do not make us resort to bloodletting over this important issue. We peasants will take this matter very badly [if nothing is done], and you yourselves will see what happens: it will be unpleasant for you to answer to the people.

The author therefore demanded that the Church act immediately "so that we may be free spouses, free from each other, and may blood not flow over this matter."[162] By the end of the year, as the Bolsheviks secularized marriage and radically liberalized divorce, they essentially responded to these popular demands for expeditious divorce. As the bishop of Kaluga candidly observed, many believers responded favorably to this decree and deemed it the single most useful action that the Bolsheviks had taken since the October seizure of power.[163]

Conclusion

As these protests suggest, the divorce question figured prominently not only in shaping public discourse but also in fueling popular discontent with the Church. To be sure, such criticism—and abortive attempts at reform—were long-standing, with the first broad plan of reform dating back to the Great Reforms.[164] But the issue became truly explosive as divorce democratized and brought the Church face to face with the popular classes and their conception of legitimate grounds and fair procedures. Although the Church, if reluctantly, addressed the issue of reform, such talk served only to whet appetites and raise expectations, not to redress grievances or justify existing policy. In short, marital breakdown and divorce paralyzed the Church's capacity to function (given the flood of divorce cases), exacerbated discontent among the laity with its rules and procedures, and undermined the moral authority of the Church even among the faithful.

More important, the family crisis, aggravated by the failure to reform divorce procedure, was an integral component of the broader revolutionary process, fusing the quotidian and domestic with the larger meta-narrative of revolution. That link was particularly evident in the rhetoric of female litigants. Apart from the audacious tone ("I will not live with him—I'd rather look at a dog than at him"),[165] the petitions, with striking frequency, invoked revealing political categories like "tyrant" to describe the patriarchal power of the husband. Thus one female peasant described how her husband had "tyrannized" (*tiranil*) her in filing for divorce.[166] Another female litigant asked the consistory to dissolve her marriage with "a husband, a person generally of depraved life, who was in prison for crimes, and in the course of their twelve-year joint life tyrannized her."[167] In rebutting accusations of adultery, another peasant woman declared that, after a few years of marriage, her husband "began to drink, be jealous without cause, and tyrannize [her]."[168] Another woman, after describing how her husband had subjected her to beatings, taken her property, and left her without support, asked "to be free from such a husband-tyrant."[169] Similar ideas permeated another divorce petition cataloguing physical abuse and the "tyrannizing" perpetrated by the husband.[170] Another plaintiff complained of "all the insults, torments, tortures, and other hard-hearted relations of my husband toward me," recounting how he had even attempted to take her life but she had "been saved from the barbaric hands of the hard-hearted tyrant" and returned to her home village.[171] Another wife testified that, "in terms of his character, my husband in everyday life is extremely insufferable, a despot, nit-picking, and coarse."[172]

Thus the divorce question united the family crisis with the broader social crisis. For the privileged and educated, at least, the century-old teaching about the family as the bedrock of political stability boomeranged; the seemingly ubiquitous breakdown of the family reinforced and personalized the sense of impending cataclysm. Most significant, especially for the popular classes, the family crisis made the revolutionary process deeply personal; the broader crisis unleashed by social change and political turmoil had alighted at the family hearth, profoundly affecting attitudes toward the dominant institutions. The breakdown of the family was thus an integral part of the revolutionary process, turning even the pious into malcontents seeking either to refurbish traditional patriarchy or to construct a modern partnership, but under no circumstances willing to tolerate the status quo.

Notes

1. For post-reform sermons about family breakdown, see M. Kheraskov *Slova, poucheniia i rechi* (Vladimir, 1886), 624.

2. P. E. Immekus, *Die Russische-Orthodoxe Landpfarrei zu Beginn des XX. Jahrhunderts nach den Gutachten der Diözesanbischöfe* (Würzburg, 1978), 214–15.

3. F. B., "O prichinakh raspada sem'i," *Tserkovnyi vestnik*, no. 37 (12 September 1913): 1150–52.

4. Lietuvos Valstybes Istorijos Archyvas (hereafter, LVIA), f. 605 (Litovskaia dukhovnaia konsistoriia).

5. See G. L. Freeze, "Bringing Order to the Russian Family: Marriage and Divorce in Imperial Russia, 1760–1860," *Journal of Modern History* 62 (December 1990): 709–48.

6. In most cases, of course, the plaintiff and often the defendant refused to reconcile. Ol'ga Kalashnikova, accused of adultery after four years of marriage, declared, "I do not wish to reconcile with my husband and have no intention of returning to him" (LVIA, f. 605, op. 9, d. 1230, l. 15). Exhortations, of course, sometimes did bring about reconciliation (see, for example, d. 851, l. 10–100b.), but that was relatively rare.

7. Failing a private settlement, litigants resolved such matters in state courts. See, for example, a petition demanding that the husband provide three hundred rubles per annum as alimony and child support, in LVIA, f. 448 (Vilenskii okruzhnoi sud), op. 1, d. 82.

8. Rossiiskii gosudarstvennyi istoricheskii arkhiv (hereafter, RGIA), f. 797, op. 81 (otd. 2, st. 3), d. 414, l. 10b. (1911 resolution).

9. *Izlecheniia iz vsepoddanneishego otchet ober-prokurora po vedomstvu dukhovnogo ispovedaniia za* 1850 (St. Petersburg, 1851), 50.

10. It bears noting, moreover, that divorce statistics capture only part of the marital dissolution; tens of thousands (mostly women) obtained separate residence permits tantamount to legal separation, and untold numbers resorted to self-divorce through desertion and illegal cohabitation.

11. Thus, whereas the national prewar average was 3.5 divorces per 1,000 marriages, the rate was 19.0 in Petersburg, 11.4 in Moscow, and 8.0 in Kiev dioceses. Although the rate was significantly lower in rural dioceses (for example, 2.0 in Kursk diocese), here, too, the absolute number and frequency had risen dramatically since the mid-nineteenth century.

12. See, for example, the report from Vladimir in *Staryi vladimirets*, no. 15 (20 August 1908): 2.

13. In May 1904 the Synod justified the concession as necessary to combat the proliferation of common-law marriages: "Having been deprived of the opportunity to enter into another legal marriage," those forbidden to remarry entered into illicit relationships, "with the number

of cohabitations and illegal marriages recently increasing" (RGIA, f. 797, op. 74 [otd. 2, st. 3], d. 225, ll. 8–10). The penance for the guilty party was normally seven years but was routinely reduced, by petition, to the two-year minimum; see, for example, LVIA, f. 605, op. 9, d. 1724, l. 117–170b., d. 1376, l. 314.

14. Advertisements such as the following cluttered the pages of the conservative newspaper *Novoe Vremia*: "Divorce cases are conducted with incredible speed, extremely cheaply, and with a guarantee. They are conducted by a lawyer with a higher education and many years' experience" (no. 12370 [19 February 1913]).

15. For typical cases where lawyers represented *both* spouses, see LVIA, f. 605, op. 9, d. 1920, ll. 214–17; and d. 1919, ll. 2167–690b.

16. In particular, after an inspection of the St. Petersburg consistory showed a huge increase in divorce applications (from 247 in 1900 to 557 in 1906), with a corresponding increase in paperwork for the understaffed office workers), the official report attributed the increase to "the establishment of offices and bureaus in St. Petersburg with people actively engaged in the marital-divorce trials (who assume not only the management of the case in the consistories but also in creating the artificial circumstances of a grounds for divorce)" (RGIA, f. 797, op. 797, op. 2, st. 3, d. 145, ll. 280b.–29.

17. The impact of migrant labor and the factory was a staple in ecclesiastical discourse; see, for example, RGIA, f. 796, op. 442, d. 2622, l. 19.

18. Siberian exile cases (based on the verdict in a state court) received automatic approval; see, for example, the 1913 case in LVIA, f. 605, op. 9, d. 1376, ll. 201–202.

19. To be sure, material evidence could expedite a case. For example, one plaintiff, who produced not only credible witnesses but also love letters from her adulterous spouse, secured a divorce in just four months (LVIA, f. 605, op. 9, d. 1265, ll. 50–52). Nevertheless, such evidence did not obviate the need for two eyewitnesses. Thus, although one husband produced a love letter, the consistory denied divorce when the witnesses failed to corroborate his accusations (d. 875, ll. 237–43).

20. LVIA, f. 605, op. 9, d. 1360, l. 100.

21. Thus, in a case where eyewitnesses reported seeing the husband on a couch with a partially undressed female, Tikhon overruled the consistory's recommendation of divorce because the witnesses "do not know, but only think" that he committed adultery (LVIA, f. 605, op. 9, d. 1919, ll. 2–3; d. 1920, ll. 218–200b).

22. Thus one witness testified that "in the second year of marriage, after abandoning his wife, Anna, Zhitnovich began to live separately, taking in other women as kept women and apparently engaged in fornication with them. But I was not an eyewitness to the adultery." Another witness declared outright that he did not know "in detail" of any fornication. A third witness gave a sworn statement that Zhitnovich had abandoned his wife, described him as a "terribly violent" person who "beat his wife," and denied any knowledge of Zhitnovich's mistresses (LVIA, f. 605, op. 9, d. 1228, ll. 39–41, 49–500b., 540b).

23. Typical negative judgments, citing the lack of credible eyewitness testimony, can be found in LVIA, f. 605, op. 9, d. 1724, ll. 1–4; d. 984, ll. 113–140b.; and d. 1376, ll. 232–330b.

24. LVIA, f. 605, op. 8, d. 937, ll. 1–95.

25. Although, prior to the wedding, people warned that her fiancé was "not in his right mind," she had been forced by her "landless position" to marry. Soon after the wedding, however, her husband began to exhibit "abnormality, expressed in all aspects of peasant family life: he beat, cursed, and raped me during Lent and pregnancy (and on the day after I gave birth), stripped naked and walked around the hut, and beat his late mother for interceding on my behalf" (LVIA, f. 605, op. 9, d. 9242, l. 26).

26. LVIA, f. 605, op. 9, d. 9242, ll. 110–1100b.

27. Thus, when one peasant sued for divorce, the witnesses testified on behalf of his wife (LVIA, f. 605, op. 9, d. 1724, ll. 305–307).

28. After a husband sued for divorce because of his wife's adultery, the wife filed a countersuit, forced him to admit a sexual tryst in a hotel, and won a favorable ruling from the consistory (LVIA, f. 605, op. 9, d. 1500, ll. 209–110b).

29. Because of the guilt principle and adversarial procedure, a plaintiff had to demonstrate not only the spouse's guilt but also his or her own innocence, often embroidered with claims that infidelity arose "from the very outset." The following declaration was typical: "After my marriage to A.V. Moro in 1904, I did not long enjoy a tranquil family life and the happiness of a spouse. For reasons not dependent on me, my husband began to abuse spirits and to spend his time in taverns and in places of dubious morality" (LVIA, f. 605, op. 9, d. 1877, l. 1).

30. For example, one nobleman sued for divorce "on the grounds of her incapacity for conjugal relations, which is expressed in her ill health." Since divorce could be granted only on grounds of *premarital* sexual incapacity (and indeed the couple had two children), the consistory summarily rejected his petition (LVIA, f. 605, op. 9, d. 984, ll. 91–92).

31. When a provincial secretary filed for divorce in 1913, he submitted a brief and notarized request: "On the basis of article 45, point 1 in volume 10, part 1, of the Civil Code, I request the Ecclesiastical Consistory to dissolve my marriage with Ekaterina Aleksandrovna Zakharova and to permit me, as the innocent party, to enter into a new marriage if I wish to do so" (LVIA, f. 605, op. 9, d. 1682, l. 3).

32. For an instructive example, see Gregory L. Freeze, "Krylov v. Krylova: 'Sexual Incapacity' and Divorce in Tsarist Russia," in *The Human Tradition in Modern Russia*, ed. William Husband (Wilmington, Del., 2000), 5–17.

33. It was widely believed that litigants often suborned witnesses, encouraging defendants to exploit such suspicions and to challenge the veracity of hostile eyewitnesses. For example, one male defendant claimed to have heard "personally" from the eyewitnesses that "they had been bought off by his wife and would receive from her one hundred rubles each for their testimony" (LVIA, f. 605, op. 9, d. 1376, l. 305).

34. LVIA, f. 605, op. 9, d. 1376, ll. 48–500b.

35. Similarly, after one husband declined to pay a third of his salary (and, later, his pension) as alimony, the woman filed a countersuit that ultimately led the consistory to deny divorce on grounds of mutual adultery (LVIA, f. 605, op. 9, d. 1920, l. 690b).

36. By far the most sensational case involved Mariia and Aleksandr Dem'ianovich, with each accusing the other of adultery (in her case an affair with the son of a wealthy Jewish banker). In the midst of the case, after newspaper reports of a public encounter (where her husband slapped her paramour in public), the consistory received the report of a police investigation recounting how Aleksandr had tracked the lovers to Warsaw, caught them in a hotel, and shot his adversary to death. In an extraordinary act of imperial intervention, Nicholas II—taking into account the circumstances, perhaps inspired by the anti-Semitic subtext—reduced the murderer's punishment to three months' incarceration in a military guardhouse. Ultimately the consistory found both spouses guilty of adultery and denied divorce (LVIA, f. 605, op. 9, d. 875, ll. 180–89).

37. Adultery, despite the stigma, was preferable to other grounds, such as insanity and sexual incapacity (which required certification by the state medical office that the condition was premarital) and claims of disappearance (which ran the risk that the spouse would be located). By contrast, adultery enabled collusion, with real or well-fabricated extramarital sex guaranteeing automatic divorce. Thus the exponential increase in divorce on grounds of adultery was owing as much to the judicial procedure of the consistory as to any revolution in sexual mores.

38. LVIA, f. 605, op. 9, d., ll. 89–890b.

39. The anonymous prostitute scenario (usually with the husband's confirmation of witness testimony) was routine for the well-scripted divorce (LVIA, f. 605, op.9, d. 788, ll. 48–500b.; d. 1376, ll. 144–47; and d. 741, ll. 290–93).

40. As a variant of the bordello, the hotel, where the adulterer had a tryst with an anonymous woman, provided an alternative, with witnesses barging into an unlocked room and finding the couple engaged in intercourse. For example, one witness offered this testimony: "On 24 September 1911, at 1:00 A.M. (together with a colleague Benediktovich), after returning from the theater, I dropped in to see an acquaintance, Aleksandr Sergeevich Pravdin, in the hotel 'England.'" Without knocking on the door, they "entered the hotel room and found Pravdin undressed and in bed with some woman, also naked, their position leaving "no doubt that they had performed coitus"(LVIA, f. 605, op. 9, d. 1500, ll. 1770b.–78).

41. In a 1914 case, a witness affirmed that the husband had a weakness for "pretty women of promiscuous behavior" and described how he had been invited to a tryst with two "interesting young girls." When the second female failed to appear, the bored witness described how he peeped through a wall divider and saw "Grigorii Grigor'evich lying with his girl and performing the act of coitus" (LVIA, f. 605, op. 9, d. 2096, ll. 243–45). The testimony was not without mirth. One witness testified how a young officer, looking "red-faced and confused," dashed into his room, "holding up his trousers (which had dropped to his knees) in one hand, and his cap and coat in the other," and explained that he had just finished having "unnatural sex" with another officer's wife when the husband unexpectedly approached the apartment (d. 2003, ll. 1e–1f).

42. For a rare case in which a lover confessed and testified against a defendant, see LVIA, f. 605, op. 9, d. 1702, ll. 66–67.

43. Whereas the botched or contested divorce could last for years and often failed to reach a final terminus, a well-orchestrated consensual divorce required only a few months. Although mere mortals could never compare with the imperial family (the emperor's sister, Grand Duchess Ol'ga Aleksandrovna, for example, obtained a divorce from the Synod in just two days on the unproven, uninvestigated grounds of her husband's sexual incapacity [RGIA, f. 796, op. 205, d. 267, ll. 1–20b]), the well-connected did not have to wait long. Lt.-General Pavel Karlovich Rennenkampf (the same figure whose disastrous military leadership in 1914 earned him the sobriquet of "Rennen von Kampf") obtained a divorce from his youthful but bigamous wife in a mere four weeks (LVIA, f. 605, op. 9, d. 741, ll. 323–38). Although such speed was unusual, colluding couples routinely secured a divorce in a few months. For example, the fon Dreiers filed for divorce on 21 April 1909 and obtained a favorable decision from the consistory and bishop on 9 June 1909 (LVIA, f. 605, op. 9, d. 1226, ll. 1–290b.).

44. For example, both Leonid and Liudmila Rusinov refused to reconcile (LVIA, f. 605, op. 9, d. 788, ll. 231–340b).

45. Some defendants confessed at the exhortation and court hearing. One obliging husband declared that he "recognizes himself as guilty of violating conjugal fidelity through adultery," volunteered that he has "cohabited with one woman for years" (but refused to divulge her name), and raised no objections to the two witnesses who would testify against him (LVIA, f. 605, op. 9, d. 958, ll. 19–190b).

46. For typical examples, see LVIA, f. 605, op. 9, d. 984, l. 126; and d. 855, ll. 1–52.

47. In 1910 Nikolai Bogdanovich explained the delay in replying to the consistory order with the words: "I and my wife's lawyer are conducting written negotiations" (LVIA, f. 605, op. 9, d. 1223, l. 17).

48. In one case from 1912, the male defendant allegedly agreed to assume the guilt if his wife would pay him five hundred rubles, sign over her dowry of nine hundred rubles and their savings, and put various other assets in his name (LVIA, f. 605, op. 9, d. 1500, ll. 78–89).

49. Thus one man refused to reconcile "because I agree to the divorce with her and have no obstacles or claims" (LVIA, f. 605, op. 9, d. 1350, l. 12).

50. The divorce was well arranged, with the witnesses providing the requisite evidence, leading the consistory to grant the divorce eight months later (LVIA, f. 605, op. 9, d. 1363, ll. 17, 61, 64).

51. Incompatibility of character figured in some governmental records, such as the reform proposal of the Ministry of Justice in 1902 (RGIA, f. 1412, op. 241, d. 15, ll. 1–14). Such

notions occasionally appeared in divorce cases, with one priest relaying a spouse's explanation for the marital breakdown: "The main cause of their unhappy marital life allegedly lies in the fact that their characters, views on life, habits, and needs are totally and diametrically opposed to one another" (LVIA, f. 605, op. 9, d. 1877, l. 10).

52.   In a case involving a male peasant and noblewoman, the local priest gave this explanation of the marital breakdown: "It seemed to me that the clear, obvious reason for their mutual disagreements is the unequal position of the husband and wife: he is a peasant with an elementary [school] education, whereas she is the daughter of a general [and] received a secondary education (albeit incomplete because of her parents' death)" (LVIA, f. 605, op. 9, d. 939, ll. 7–70b).

53.   One divorce case refers explicitly to the financial settlement—a payment of five hundred rubles, a promissory note for another five hundred rubles, and a monthly alimony of fifteen rubles per month for a period of three years—given on the condition that the wife not block the divorce (LVIA, f. 605, op. 9, d. 847, ll. 38–380b.).

54.   For example, one peasant woman whose husband vanished four months after the wedding was aware of an 1895 imperial decree authorizing expedited divorce, but she wrongly assumed that divorce was automatic and had no inkling of the mandatory search-and-discovery procedure (LVIA, f. 605, op. 9, d. 1688, ll. 1–3).

55.   LVIA, f. 605, op. 9, d. 788, ll. 59–630b.

56.   For example, one peasant claimed that his new wife, "a few days after the wedding, proved incapable of conjugal relations," which in turn led them to separate. He claimed that her infirmity was premarital and that he had, out of pity, hitherto remained silent about her deformity. To his dismay, the consistory ordered a medical examination, which showed her to be perfectly healthy, causing his request for a divorce to be denied (LVIA, f. 605, op. 9, d. 741, ll. 101–105).

57.   In most cases the investigation confirmed the permanent disappearance (e.g., LVIA, f. 605, op. 9, d. 1833, ll. 1–44; d. 984, ll. 130–36). Although peasants and townspeople were involved in the majority of cases, the privileged occasionally filed for divorce on these grounds (e.g., d. 1920, ll. 7–80b.; and d. 741, ll. 128–37).

58.   For example, a peasant woman filed for divorce in 1913, claiming that her husband had disappeared a few months after their marriage in 1907; the consistory, however, promptly located the missing spouse and denied the divorce (LVIA, f. 605, op. 9, d. 1690, ll. 1–61). Such searches could go far afield; in 1908, for instance, the consistory, with the help of the St. Petersburg Address Office, located the missing husband in the capital (d. 957, l. 22). The Church weekly, *Tserkovnye vedomosti,* with an obligatory subscription by every parish church in the country, also helped to locate missing spouses. In one case, for example, the missing wife reported that she learned about a divorce suit against her in *Tserkovnye vedomosti,* adding that her husband knew perfectly well where she was living since she worked with his own brother (d. 1265, ll. 1–29).

59.   LVIA, f. 605, op. 2, d. 2423, ll. 130–310b.

60.   LVIA, f. 605, op. 9, d. 957, ll. 1–10b.

61.   LVIA, f. 605, op. 9, d. 741, ll. 12–210b.

62.   LVIA, f. 605, op. 9, d. 875, ll. 224–270b.

63.   Despite this clever logic, the consistory noted that the marriage had taken place just two years earlier and hence failed to satisfy the five-year minimum (LVIA, f. 605, op. 9, d. 2423, l. 93).

64.   The articulate challenge to the strict requirement of post-marital insanity came from an influential courtier, Major-General Aleksandr Spiridonovich. He recognized that "insanity of one spouse, according to the laws of the Russian Empire, currently does not provide grounds for the dissolution of a marriage," but argued that "it is insistently suggested by life as grounds and was even included in a draft law on divorce." His courtly connections, if not his logic, served him well, for the consistory ultimately concluded that his wife's dementia originated before

the marriage (LVIA, f. 605, op. 9, d. 2032, ll. 1–37). Other plaintiffs were less fortunate. One peasant, for example, petitioned to divorce his wife of nineteen years, claiming that her relatives had deceived him about her mental state at the time of the marriage. The consistory rejected the petition (observing that the couple had eight children and that he had waited too long to claim insanity) and merely advised him to sue the relatives for fraud in a civil court. After the plaintiff appealed to the Synod, the latter directed the consistory to seek an official medical opinion as to whether the mental illness was premarital. When the local Medical Board filed a negative view, the consistory reiterated its earlier decision (d. 1358, ll. 1–94).

65. One female peasant sued for divorce on grounds of adultery, with the added claim that her husband was a homosexual prostitute. A witness confirmed her claim, testifying that the husband had deserted his wife, and asked, "Why should he live with his wife, when he can earn money himself like a woman," and boasted that "men invite him to their train compartment and use him like a woman" (LVIA, f. 605, op. 9, d. 788, ll. 43–47).

66. One woman refused categorically to "live with [her husband] because he is completely deaf" (LVIA, f. 605, op. 9, d. 984, ll. 197–990b).

67. LVIA, f. 605, op. 9, d. 741, ll. 411–120b.

68. LVIA, f. 605, op. 9, d. 1376, l. 90.

69. LVIA, f. 605, op. 9, d. 788, ll. 98–105.

70. As the Synod explained in a resolution (10 April 1910) on an appeal by a disgruntled plaintiff: The abandonment of one spouse by the other, and their separate residence, no matter how long this might last, does not belong to the number of legally recognized grounds for the dissolution of marriages" (LVIA, f. 605, op. 9, d. 1265, ll. 1–2; d. 1239, ll. 1–29).

71. LVIA, f. 796, op. 9, d. 1897, ll. 6, 120b.

72. The plaintiff went on to explain why he was so adamant: since his wife left twenty-four years earlier, he had lived with another woman and already had children he wished to legitimize (LVIA, f. 605, op. 9, d. 741, ll. 364–72 [petition to the Synod]).

73. For example, a telegraphist stressed that he had "married out of love"—he had even contemplated suicide when the object of his affections initially spurned his advances. Although his ardor prevailed, the wife proved unfaithful, leading him to think that he "would suddenly die from a broken heart" (LVIA, f. 605, op. 9, d. 1905, l. 590b).

74. Thus an assistant accountant complained that "from the first years of the marriage my wife did not exhibit love for family life, being drawn to other men" (LVIA, f. 605, op. 9, d. 1693, l. 2).

75. LVIA, f. 605, op. 9, d. 1684, ll. 11–110b.

76. LVIA, f. 605, op. 9, d. 1706, l. 1.

77. LVIA, f. 605, op. 9, d. 282, l. 4.

78. LVIA, f. 605, op. 9, d. 1265, ll. 269–71.

79. LVIA, f. 605, op. 9, d. 1431, l. 16.

80. Such argumentation took a somewhat different form among the privileged, who saw the wife's economic independence, not her failure as a housekeeper, as the main cause of the marital breakdown. Thus one nobleman complained that his wife left him to go to St. Petersburg, with "the goal of completing the gymnasium course of studies in order to achieve a separate economic life, independent of the means of her husband" (LVIA, f. 605, op. 9, d. 1919, ll. 131–36).

81. For typical references to the need for a housewife, see the petitions from a peasant, in LVIA, f. 605, op. 9, d. 1500, ll. 424–26.

82. LVIA, f. 605, op. 9, d. 2027, l. 1.

83. LVIA, f. 605, op. 9, d. 875, l. 2670b.

84. LVIA, f. 605, op. 9, d. 2423, l. 93.

85. LVIA, f. 605, op. 9, d. 945, l. 1.

86. LVIA, f. 605, op. 9, d. 945, l. 37.

87. In an elaborate response to the priest's exhortation to reconcile, an irate husband categorically refused, citing not only his wife's infidelity but also her disrespect, demonstrated not only in her disparaging comments, "from the first days of our conjugal life, that she had married a Yid" but, worse still, in her "lack of desire to have sexual relations with me and, especially, in her sarcasm with respect to this matter" (see LVIA, f. 605, op. 9, d. 1695, ll. 24–240b).
88. LVIA, f. 605, op. 9, d. 1724, l. 1.
89. LVIA, f. 605, op. 9, d. 1235, ll. 1–2; see also d. 1230, ll. 1–10b.
90. LVIA, f. 605, op. 9,d. 1233, ll. 2–20b; see also d. 1265, ll. 287–89; and d. 1684, l. 1.
91. LVIA, f. 605, op. 9, d. 875, 490b.
92. LVIA, f. 605, op. 9, d. 1265, l. 2600b.
93. LVIA, f. 605, op. 9, d. 1724, ll. 84–86.
94. See, for example, the statement by a peasant wife, in LVIA, f. 605, op. 9, d. 846, l. 32.
95. Anna Gerasimonik, for example, complained that, without a passport, "I cannot go anywhere to earn a living" (LVIA, f. 605, op. 9, d. 2423, l. 1590b).
96. LVIA, f. 605, op. 9, d. 1426, ll. 3–4.
97. LVIA, f. 605, op. 9, d. 1416, ll. 9–100b.
98. LVIA, f. 605, op. 9, d. 1265, ll. 121–24.
99. LVIA, f. 605, op. 9, d. 1724, ll. 294–970b.
100. LVIA, f. 605, op. 9, d. 1376, ll. 144–47.
101. Thus, a peasant woman refused to reconcile, adding, "I was coerced into marrying him" (LVIA, f. 605, op. 9, d. 846, l. 32).
102. LVIA, f. 605, op. 9, d. 875, l. 481.
103. LVIA, f. 605, op. 9, d. 984, ll. 197–990b. Another woman complained that "they married me off before I had completed my sixteenth year," and indeed to a man she had specifically rejected (LVIA, f. 605, op. 9, d. 1879, l. 10b).
104. LVIA, f. 605, op. 9, d. 788, l. 390b.
105. LVIA, f. 605, op. 9, d. 984, l. 1460b.
106. LVIA, f. 605, op. 9, d. 875, ll. 384–93.
107. LVIA, f. 605, op. 9, d. 1879, l. 2.
108. LVIA, f. 605, op. 9, d. 1724, l. 62.
109. LVIA, f. 605, op. 9, d. 948, ll. 1–58.
110. LVIA, f. 605, op. 9, d. 939, ll. 27–28.
111. LVIA, f. 605, op. 9, d. 1228, l. 10. In reporting this plaintiff's refusal to reconcile, the local priest wrote that her neighbors confirmed her husband's "brutal treatment" (l. 8).
112. LVIA, f. 605, op. 9, d. 788, l. 2350b.
113. LVIA, f. 605, op. 9, d. 1500, ll. 198–202.
114. LVIA, f. 605, op. 9, d. 1879, ll. 1–2.
115. LVIA, f. 605, op. 9, d. 956, l. 13.
116. LVIA, f. 605, op. 9, d. 1873, ll. 22–220b. (28.6.1915).
117. LVIA, f. 605, op. 9, d. 1500, l. 2090b.
118. Thus one woman accused her husband of "violating the sanctity of marriage through adultery and illicit cohabitation" with another woman (LVIA, f. 605, op. 9, d. 1368, l. 1).
119. As it turned out, the husband was not only demented, having been repeatedly incarcerated in psychiatric asylums, but was also hypocritical. Confronted with evidence that he had a mistress, he confessed that a woman had been living with him for two years and refused to sunder the relationship: "Under no circumstances will this woman leave me, since she also takes care of the household, that is, washes my clothing, bakes bread," and so forth (LVIA, f. 605, op. 8, d. 937, ll. 1–95).
120. At a consistory hearing on 16 October 1906, both spouses emphasized the incompatible character argument: the wife testified that "the entire cause of her application for divorce is the incompatibility of their characters, and the husband concurred that "they had

permanently separated ways because of the incompatibility of characters" (LVIA, f. 605, op. 9, d. 741, ll. 453–54).

121. LVIA, f. 605, op. 9, d. 1691, ll. 1–65.

122. LVIA, f. 605, op. 9, d. 1724, l. 62.

123. LVIA, f. 605, op. 9, d. 948, ll. 1–58.

124. He met a predictable rebuff: the consistory denied the divorce with the explanation that desertion and separate residence did not constitute grounds for divorce (LVIA, f. 605, op. 9, d. 875, ll. 178–79).

125. Thus, in cases where Catholics sought divorce from errant Orthodox spouses, the consistory treated these fairly and, if the evidence warranted, granted the divorce; see, for example, LVIA, f. 605, op. 9, d. 1724, ll. 98–101.

126. LVIA, f. 605, op. 9, d. 1897, ll. 20–200b.

127. LVIA, f. 605, op. 9, d. 1857, l. 1. Amazingly the file includes evidence that the entire narrative was the product of her husband's advice. In an undated letter in the file, the husband gave this advice: "If you wish to petition for a divorce, consult a clever person as to where one first files the request. I agree to give you the divorce and indicate legal grounds that your husband does not live [with you] for twelve years, that he is a Pole and you are a Russian, and that your husband wants you to adopt the Polish [Catholic] faith. This is a legal ground, and you can obtain a divorce" (d. 1897, l. 7).

128. LVIA, f. 605, op. 9, d. 851, ll. 1, 8.

129. Thus one peasant woman described how, from the outset of her marriage, her husband "began to beat me and to ridicule me every way possible," and, for good measure, added that, "as a Catholic"—these words underlined in blue by the consistory—he "sought to force me to convert to Catholicism, but, as a true Orthodox believer, I did not wish to do this." Seeing that she would not convert, he "abandoned me and, for three years now, we live separately, receiving no support for myself or our daughter" (LVIA, f. 605, op. 9, d. 944, ll. 1–2).

130. LVIA, f. 605, op. 9, d. 1431, l. 16.

131. LVIA, f. 605, op. 9, d. 1376, ll. 255–560b.

132. For example, Tat'iana Balkovskaia converted on 20 May 1910 and filed for divorce five days later (LVIA, f. 605, op.9, d. 1350, ll. 1–96).

133. See the data summarized in G. L. Freeze, "Lutheranism in Imperial Russia: Critical Reassessment," in Luther zwischen den Kulturen, ed. Hans Medick and P. Schmidt (Göttingen, 2003).

134. LVIA, f. 605, op. 9, d. 1724, l. 290–900b.

135. LVIA, f. 605, op. 9, d. 875, ll. 258–62.

136. Thus, according to the governing statute adopted in 1832, the Lutheran Church in the Russian granted divorce for "mean-spirited desertion," "lack of affection," infectious diseases, insanity, "dissolute life," "and "severe criminality, including unnatural sex." See Heidi Whelan, Adapting to Modernity: Family, Caste, and Capitalism among the Baltic Germans (Cologne, 1999), 122–23.

137. LVIA, f. 605, op. 9, d. 1724, ll. 122–24.

138. RGIA, f. 797, op. 96, d. 271, ll. 216–19.

139. Staryi vladimirets, no. 15 (20 August 1908), 2.

140. RGIA, f. 797, op. 82 (otd. 1, st. 1), d. 74, l. 93–930b.

141. "Tserkovno-obshchestvennaia zhizn'," Izvestiia po S.-Peterburgskoi eparkhii, nos. 17–18 (15 September 1912): 28.

142. Specifically, whether from a sense of shame or sheer contempt for ecclesiastical courts, some defendants categorically refused to participate. Ol'ga Kalashnikova informed the consistory that she "will not come to such a hearing," since she does not "wish to endure the shame and to meet" with her husband (LVIA, op. 605, op. 9, d. 1230, ll. 27–28).

143. In one case, in which a widower cohabited with the wife of his deceased brother and had had one illegitimate child, the local priest explained that he attempted repeatedly to

combat this incest but to no avail. When he denied the couple communion, "all this had no effect, but apparently only hardened the hearts"of the couple, who "ceased coming to church and making confession with me" (LVIA, f. 605, op. 9, d. 2009, ll. 1–10b.) The consistory could only suggest that the priest threaten to initiate a police investigation and prosecution in a civil court (d. 1919, ll. 101–10b).

144.   LVIA, f. 605, op. 9, d. 951, l. 89.

145.   For a search announcement in *Senatskie vedomosti,* see LVIA, f. 605, op. 9, d. 955, l. 42.

146.   Thus, in response to accusations of adultery, Sofiia Uspenskaia admitted her guilt but refused to journey from Kharbin to Vil'na for the consistory hearing (LVIA, f. 605, op. 9, d. 788, ll. 263–66).

147.   For a typical case, where the litigants request transferring the divorce to Perm diocese, see LVIA, f. 605, op. 9, d. 959.

148.   This differential partly explains the geographic patterns in rejection rates. Thus a diocese like St. Petersburg, with higher cultural and literacy levels and with a larger corps of attorneys to shepherd suits, had a 66 percent approval rate; Kursk, by contrast, had only a 15 percent approval rate (RGIA, f. 796, op. 181, g. 1900, d. 3456, ll. 1–30).

149.   One defendant, who plainly consented to divorce, complained to the Lithuanian diocesan authorities about undue delays and claimed to know others who had obtained the divorce within two months. Archbishop Tikhon, aware of the realities of consistorial business, placed a large question mark along that assertion (LVIA, f. 605, op. 9, d. 1877, ll. 67–670b).

150.   LVIA, f. 605, op. 9, d. 848, ll. 17, 89–90, 91.

151.   Sof'ia Kovshik, for example, appealed to the consistory to "speed up the dissolution of the marriage," explaining that "I have no means to live without documents" and later emphasizing that she had to support her mother and daughter (LVIA, f. 605, op. 9, d. 1685, ll. 1–46).

152.   LVIA, f. 605, op. 9, d. 1420, l. 42.

153.   LVIA, f. 605, op. 9, d. 1866, ll. 16–160b.

154.   For a petition to the head of city administration for assistance, see LVIA, f. 605, op. 9, d. 1866, ll. 26–260b.

155.   Thus, in 1914, the right-wing Duma deputy, V. M. Purishkevich, asked the chief procurator's office to ensure the prompt disposition of a case from his home province (RGIA, f. 797, op. 84 [otd. 2, st. 3], d. 20, ll. 1–8).

156.   LVIA, f. 605, op. 2, d. 2423, ll. 1–20b.

157.   See "O kanonicheskikh osnovaniiakh k razvodu," *Tserkovnyi vestnik,* no. 26 (30 June 1905): 801–803.

158.   As the chief procurator noted, these cases showed that "delays in the processing of marital and divorce cases are a rather common phenomenon in many consistories." While not all the fault lay with the Church (given the problems posed by distance, obstreperous and ignorant litigants, and the like), these delays nonetheless constituted a hardship, especially for the lower classes: "In particular, this slowness proves very onerous for peasant petitioners, who, having been deprived of the possibility of entering into a new marriage, suffer great material harm from the lack of a housewife in the home" (RGIA, f. 797, op. 77 (otd. 2, st. 3), d. 495, ll. 3–6 ob. [circular of 22 October 1907]).

159.   For example, to facilitate matters, the Lithuanian consistory sent printed forms (with a checklist of requisite documents or fees) to litigants who ignored statutory requirements. See, for example, LVIA, f. 605, op. 9, d. 1431, l. 3, d. 1694, ll. 1–2; d. 1689, ll. 1–37; d. 939, l. 100; and d. 1706, ll. 7–70b. In the case of a peasant whose wife had emigrated to the United States, the consistory denied divorce on grounds of permanent disappearance (since she was alive and her whereabouts known) but advised the plaintiff to seek a divorce on grounds of adultery because she had written about remarrying, "since this is permitted in America." See d. 2423, ll. 111–14.

160.   LVIA, f. 605, op. 2, d. 2423, ll. 41–410b., 45–450b.

178 *Gregory L. Freeze*

161. Otdel rukopisei Rossiiskoi gosudarstvennoi biblioteki (OR RGB), f. 126, k. 3, d. 9, l. 305 (diary entry of A. A. Kireev for February 1884).

162. RGIA, f. 796, op. 177, g. 1896, d. 3771, ll. 8–80b.

163. As Bishop Feofan of Kaluga wrote in February 1918, virtually everyone condemned the sluggish and inept procedures used in ecclesiastical courts "as too complex and full of red tape, and as excessively formalistic and narrow, failing to correspond to diverse aspects of modern life." See Gosudarstvennyi arkhiv Rossiiskoi Federatsii (GARF), f. r-3431, op. 1, d. 264, ll. 8–14 (Bishop Feofan to the Synod, 1 February 1918).

164. See G. L. Freeze, *The Parish Clergy in Nineteenth-Century Russia: Crisis, Reform, Counter-Reform* (Princeton, N.J., 1983), 340–45.

165. LVIA, f. 605, op. 9, d. 1500, l. 195.

166. LVIA, f. 605, op. 9, d. 850, ll. 1–2.

167. LVIA, f. 605, op. 9, d. 265, l. 2070b.

168. LVIA, f. 605, op. 9, d. 1500, l. 1940b.

169. LVIA, f. 605, op. 9, d. 1431, ll. 1–10b.

170. LVIA, f. 605, op. 9, d. 1879, l. 10b.

171. LVIA, f. 605, op. 9, d. 1909, ll. 24–240b.

172. LVIA, f. 605, op. 9, d. 2015, ll. 1–10b.

7

Arbiters of the Free Conscience: State, Religion, and the Problem of Confessional Transfer after 1905

Paul W. Werth

————••◦∞◦••————

Among the many prerogatives the Russian autocracy arrogated for itself was the right to ascribe confessional affiliation to its subjects. For the most part, of course, the government accepted its subjects' own declarations concerning their religious allegiances and, although establishing incentives for conversion to Orthodoxy, generally considered that believers would naturally remain in the faith of their parents and ancestors. Nonetheless, for the purposes of upholding the predominance of Orthodoxy over other faiths—and also of Christianity over heterodoxy—in certain instances the government felt justified in rejecting believers' declared religious allegiances. And because the state sternly prohibited the interference of the representatives of one foreign faith in the affairs of another, even conversion among non-Orthodox faiths usually required the state's permission.[1] In short, in order both to maintain the existing hierarchy of religious confessions and to regulate their interaction, the state implicitly proclaimed itself the ultimate arbiter of religious identity in the Russian Empire.

By the late nineteenth century the state was finding it more and more difficult to exercise this prerogative. While growing numbers of formally Orthodox subjects sought to return to the religions from which they or their ancestors had been converted earlier, new religions began to draw ever more adherents from the ranks of the Orthodox. Compelled by the state's civil and criminal law to remain in Orthodoxy against their convictions, such believers became, simultaneously, ever more frustrated with their position and ever more hopeful that full legal recognition of their religious beliefs would soon be granted. Many state officials themselves became increasingly uncomfortable with the idea of deploying secular law and police power for the purpose of

179

maintaining religious discipline, arguing that this was both incompatible with modern values and, ultimately, ineffective. In response to these difficulties, and in line with these growing doubts, in April 1905 the autocracy substantially liberalized religious legislation and, in October, explicitly granted "freedom of conscience" to the empire's population.

This article examines the repercussions of this dramatic reform for the definition of religious affiliation in Russia. Focusing principally on the legal and administrative adjudication of believers' requests for "confessional transfer" in the years after 1905,[2] I argue that if the state made important concessions to the religious aspirations of the empire's subjects, it nonetheless refused to relinquish its prerogatives as the ultimate arbiter of their confessional status and thus remained deeply implicated in their religious affairs. Even as some officials such as Sergei Witte and Petr Stolypin promoted religious reform as part of a larger project of eroding particularism in favor of Russia's civic trans-formation and the establishment of a "national politics," the state's fundamen-tally confessional foundations placed profound limits on both the ability and inclination of most officials to construe religious identity purely as a matter of individual choice.[3] Thus even as believers became more self-aware of their beliefs and conscious of their dignity as individuals, their religious experience remained conditioned to a significant degree by state imperatives.

From "Religious Toleration" to "Freedom of Conscience"

The religious reform of 1905 was clearly a product of the revolutionary crisis of that same year, but there were crucial antecedents to the idea of freedom of conscience in the years and even decades leading up to 1905. Already by the 1880s the refusal of many putative "converts" to Orthodoxy from earlier eras to make peace with their formal Orthodox status provided compelling proof that religious convictions were not reducible to bureaucratic ascription and that the law's blanket prohibition on "apostasy" from Orthodoxy required modification.[4] By the early twentieth century issues of religious freedom became prominent in intellectual and scholarly circles. Legal scholars more openly condemned existing statutes as being outdated, motivated primarily by political expediency, and confused in their equation of nationality and confession.[5] Religion, ecu-menism, and individual freedom became central issues for a vibrant segment of the Russian intelligentsia in the Silver Age, while the Orthodox Church's condemnation of Lev Tolstoy in 1901 raised the question of religious freedom to a broader public.[6] By the early twentieth century issues of religious liberty and freedom of conscience, albeit in various forms, occupied a prominent place in public discourse.

Even the autocracy itself, which engaged in modest reform efforts on the eve of 1905, began to make gestures toward modifications in confessional policy. Although retreating from an early draft that referred directly to freedom of conscience, the emperor, in a manifesto of February 1903, promised "to strengthen the steadfast observance by the authorities concerned with religious affairs of the guarantees of religious toleration contained in the fundamental laws of the Russian Empire."[7] By late 1904 another decree went considerably further and instructed the government not only to eliminate immediately "all constraints on religious life not directly established by law" but also to review existing provisions on the rights of non-Orthodox groups.[8] The resulting review led to a decree of 17 April 1905, which substantially liberalized the empire's religious order. Transfer from one Christian faith to another was now fully legalized, some sects received at least implicit recognition, and Old Belief even gained something close to the status of a recognized non-Orthodox Christian faith.[9]

Still, the confessional order that emerged subsequently was neither complete nor entirely coherent, since the April decree provided for the definitive resolution of many issues only through further legislative deliberation. The October Manifesto, granted later in 1905 by an autocracy even deeper in crisis, made matters still more complex, by both explicitly granting Russia's citizens "freedom of conscience" and establishing a deliberative assembly (the Duma) that would considerably complicate the legislative process. Because new draft laws designed to effectuate "freedom of conscience" became the object of intense legislative contestation and were ultimately never approved, it remained unclear throughout the period from 1905 to 1917 whether, and how, the October Manifesto's proclamation of a broad but poorly defined "freedom of conscience" actually superseded the more modest, but also more concrete, provisions of the April decree.[10] Non-Orthodox believers were eager, of course, to invoke the Manifesto, arguing that it eliminated all the ifs, ands, and buts contained in the April decree.[11] The government was less certain. The Department of the Religious Affairs of Foreign Confessions noted in 1906 that the "freedom of conscience" identified in the Manifesto "should undoubtedly be understood as a broadening of the confessional relief granted by the decree of 17 April and as the granting to each person of complete self-definition in matters of religion."[12] But subsequent practice showed that this "self-definition" would, in fact, not be "complete" and instead would be conditioned primarily by the stipulations of the April decree. The state essentially came to regard the Manifesto as a *promise* of "freedom of conscience" to be realized in forthcoming legislation, whereas the April decree and a series of supplementary administrative rulings would regulate affairs until that new legislation could be produced.

Even in theoretical terms, attempts to define "freedom of conscience" produced no real consensus. At one end were those contending that this concept
implied the elimination of all limitations on religious life, the right to hold no
religious beliefs at all, and—with a view toward concurrent developments in
France—the full separation of church and state. The concern of such commentators was the establishment of a "rule-of-law state" (*pravovoe gosudarstvo*), as
well as the recognition of faith as an affair of individual concern. They tended to
regard the April decree as a positive step in the expansion of religious freedom
but emphasized its partial character, its many qualifications and limitations, and
its failure to establish full freedom of conscience.[13] Other observers believed
that freedom of conscience could be secured only by maintaining certain limitations on religious activity. These writers, many of them Orthodox clerics on the
front lines of the post-1905 interconfessional struggle, rejected the proposition
that the freedom of personal, individual confession required unrestricted liberty in terms of public confession, the formation of religious associations, and
so on. For such commentators, freedom of conscience did not imply freedom of
"propaganda" (i.e., proselytism) or the freedom to "seduce" (i.e., to convert others by assaulting the truth claims and sacred objects of their religions). In this
view, the conscience of each person deserved *protection* from the encroachments
of others, especially when those encroachments took extreme or "fanatical"
forms.[14] In an important memorandum of 1906, the department itself offered a
quite broad definition of "freedom of conscience" but immediately added that
this freedom was subject "to limitations based on the requirements of state
order."[15] In short, the meaning of "freedom of conscience" remained unclear
and contested throughout the last decade of the old regime.

Regulating Confessional Transfer

If in some respects the 1905 reform simplified the administration of Russia's
confessional heterogeneity (for example, by permitting the transfer of numerous
"recalcitrants" to non-Orthodox faiths), then in other respects it created new
problems in its wake or left old questions unresolved. In terms of the transfer
of confessional status after 1905, four issues proved particularly complex: (1) the
transfer of some former Uniates to Catholicism; (2) the problem of conversion
from Christianity to non-Christian faiths; (3) the problem of Jewish conversion
to other faiths; and (4) the matter of recognizing new faiths and sects. It is in
considering contests over these particular cases of transfer that the remaining
tensions between personal dignity and will, on the one hand, and the imperatives of the state, on the other, become most readily manifest.

Returning to Catholicism

The largest number of transfers after 1905 was from Orthodoxy to Catholicism and included many former Uniates, who had been bureaucratically "reunited" with Orthodoxy in 1839 and 1875. The April decree had legalized conversions among Christian confessions, and such transfers should therefore have been fairly straightforward. But complications arose almost immediately, because that decree failed to stipulate, even provisionally, how subjects were to go about changing their confessional status. Denied affiliation with Catholicism for decades, former Uniates scarcely felt compelled to wait for a well-defined procedure to appear. Instead they began transferring immediately, and Catholic authorities, lacking any guidance beyond the April decree itself, improvised a system for accepting these people into their Church. By the time the Department of the Religious Affairs of Foreign Confessions established basic rules for transfer as a supplement to the April decree in August (circular 4628), tens if not hundreds of thousands of "recalcitrants" had been accepted into Catholicism. Nor were Catholic authorities informed of this circular in a timely fashion, so that in some cases they continued to employ their own system until 1908.[16] As a result, many people now effectively belonged to two confessions at once, since they had been accepted into Catholicism but had not yet been officially excluded from the ranks of the Orthodox.

Believing that they were Catholic, such transferees faced numerous complications when they discovered that the state did not share their assessment. Converts were prosecuted and even punished for having their children baptized by Catholic rite or for burying their dead in Catholic graveyards. Students in schools and gymnasiums were suddenly barred from Catholic religious instruction and informed that they would be examined in Orthodoxy. Spouses were informed that their seemingly straightforward marriages were, in fact, "mixed" (i.e., interconfessional), that they had violated the law by having a Catholic ceremony, and that their children would have to be raised in Orthodoxy. Meanwhile, many Catholic priests found themselves under criminal prosecution for "knowingly administering Catholic rites to people of the Orthodox faith."[17]

The government had, of course, foreseen a mass exodus of formally Orthodox people to Catholicism after the April decree, and therefore had not intended for the registration process to inhibit such transfers. But to the extent that confessional affiliation remained one of the central aspects of a person's socio-legal status, the government could not permit transfers to occur in a haphazard fashion, without proper registration. For the most part senior officials sought to accommodate the transferees while ensuring such registration. Interior minister Petr Stolypin and department director A. Kharuzin noted in 1909 that most of the transferees had acted in good faith and that the government's mode of action "should exhibit particular care and deliberation." Warsaw Governor-General Georgii Skalon argued that the converts should, without question, be considered Catholic, and that nowhere had the April decree indicated that confessional transfer depended on prior exclusion from Orthodox metrical books. The governor of Vilnius added in 1909 that requiring the converts to go through the formalities of transfer "could undoubtedly be interpreted as an attempt once again to force them to return to Orthodoxy and as an arbitrary measure."[18]

Despite these good intentions, however, nothing concrete was done, and with time—especially after Stolypin's assassination in 1911—the state became less accommodating. Most remarkable, in an appeals case in 1910, the Senate decided that any person who remained Orthodox according to official records should be considered "knowingly Orthodox" (*zavedomo pravoslavnym*) until those records had been changed. On this basis, in 1913, the department instructed the governor of Minsk Province that such people, until the transfer was official, "should be considered Orthodox even if they factually confessed the Roman Catholic faith." There were also reports that the governor had begun to assert that "permission" of the authorities was required for transfer, even though circulars referred only to the *registration* of transfer.[19]

Apparently only when three Catholic members of the State Council lodged a protest against the prevailing situation in January 1915 did a final resolution appear. Appealing primarily to a basic sense of justice, the councilors also referred to the Great War, noting that many people in question were now "defending the honor and dignity of their homeland with weapons in their hands and are risking their lives each and every hour." It was critical that they "may calmly regard the future of their families, confident that nothing threatens either their conscience or their religious views."[20] The government finally decided that all those who left Orthodoxy before 1 November 1905, when circular 4628 *should* have been known to everyone, were recognized as Catholic from the day of their acceptance by Catholic authorities. All others would be regarded as Orthodox until they went through the procedure outlined in circular 4628. Thus ten years after the initial reform of April 1905, the government finally created an order covering all eventualities. Yet, notably, this resolution appeared only in July 1915, when many of the transferees already found themselves under German occupation and thus beyond its purview.[21]

Transfers to Heterodoxy

If technical considerations occupied a prominent place in the experience of would-be Catholics, the issue of permitting the conversion of Christians to non-Christianity was, by its very nature, more controversial. The Committee of Ministers, in its deliberations leading to the April decree, had addressed this question with considerable circumspection, arguing that, in general, the state should neither recognize nor criminalize such conversion. Yet the committee had also recognized that a certain category of people existed who, "in reality," confessed a heterodox faith, despite their formal ascription to Orthodoxy, and who should therefore be permitted to return to the faith of their ancestors. Adopting a rather convoluted formulation that reflected this ambivalence, the April decree thus granted the right of exclusion from Orthodoxy to "those people who are registered as Orthodox but who in fact confess that non-Christian faith to which they themselves or their ancestors belonged before their adherence to Orthodoxy."[22]

It bears emphasizing that the April decree did not actually recognize *conversion* to heterodoxy but rather the need to rectify the *inaccurate ascription* of certain subjects to Orthodoxy. The interested parties accordingly had to demonstrate, first of all, that they had actually practiced the non-Christian faith in question *before* April 1905—despite this representing a violation of the law at the time. How, precisely, were they to do this? Ruling on the basis of an earlier 1907 decision, the Senate declared in 1911 that "the very desire of a given person to be excluded from Orthodoxy" should serve as "proof of confession of a non-Christian religion" for the purposes of invoking the April decree.[23] Yet, despite this ruling, which seemed to reduce the whole matter to the declarations of each individual, numerous requests from Finnic-speaking Maris in Viatka Province, where a modestly sized movement for recognition as pagans developed, were rejected, with the justification that the petitioners had fulfilled their "Christian obligations" before 1905 and therefore could not be regarded as having confessed paganism "in reality" before then.[24] The standard for pre-1905 "confession" of heterodoxy thus remained high.

Petitioners also had to demonstrate a connection to "ancestors" who had confessed the religion they now sought to embrace officially. On the one hand, this stipulation made it possible only to *return* to one's historic religion; accordingly, attempts of those baptized from paganism or shamanism to convert to Islam or Buddhism were rejected.[25] On the other hand, the question arose: How far back in time could one claim to have had heterodox "ancestors" in order to receive satisfaction? In its 1907 bill to the Duma and in its own administrative dealings, the interior ministry ruled that "ancestors" should be construed to include only parents and grandparents—that is, those whom the petitioner "could have encountered while he was still alive and with whom it was possible to have had a more or less close moral connection and whose direct influence he could have felt."[26] Thus, in one of the very few cases in which Maris were permitted to return to paganism, the interior ministry acknowledged that the two petitioners' ancestors and relatives "were and remain pagans, and their father transferred to Orthodoxy only in 1865" with the goal of receiving material benefit. The context in which the petitioners lived and their recent family history suggested that their connection with paganism had never been broken.[27] In contrast, a few of the baptized Tatars who requested permission as Muslims had their petitions rejected when they claimed that their ancestors had been baptized shortly after the conquest of Kazan in 1552.[28] Here the connection with Islam was simply too distant for the state to fulfill their request.

These complications generally derived from the fact that the larger question of whether to recognize conversion to *any* faith—Christian or heterodox—remained open, especially after the appearance of the October Manifesto. While the Ministry of Justice contended in 1906 that conversion to a non-Christian faith was still "unconditionally prohibited" for all citizens regardless of their initial confessional status, the interior ministry wrote that the refusal to recognize conversions to non-Christian faiths "would currently contradict the spirit of the Manifesto of 17 October."[29] By the time it produced its draft law for the Duma on confessional transfer in March 1907, however, the interior ministry had retreated somewhat from that permissive position. The draft, although stopping short of criminalizing conversion to heterodoxy, still refused to recognize it, and when, in 1909, the Duma moved to reinstate such recognition, Stolypin personally defended the original draft.[30] This question of whether to recognize conversion from Christianity to heterodoxy was a central factor in the failure of the draft ever to make it past the State Council for legislative approval.[31]

Unsuccessful petitioners could not comprehend how these restrictions were compatible with "freedom of conscience." Indeed, they contended that officials who were unwilling to register them in new faiths openly violated the will of the sovereign. As one group wrote to the interior ministry in 1910, regarding its members' exclusion from Orthodoxy, "we will [then] be satisfied in our conscience and convinced that the will of the Sovereign Emperor is being fulfilled unquestioningly for the benefit of the people who adore him." Another group wrote that its members had been petitioning to be recognized as pagans for three years, "but artificial impediments have been erected." Having been referred back and forth between different government agencies, "we are unable to gain any explanation [for the rejection] and we cannot comprehend why we encounter such obstacles and red tape.... Thus, instead of the desired peace, tranquility, and happiness heralded from the heights of the throne, smoldering irritation is growing and the gracious law is being blatantly violated." Still another group of thirty-seven petitioners, complaining about the efforts of the local clergy to block their recognition as members of the pagan sect "Kugu

Sorta," asked, rhetorically, "Should the clergy abolish the manifesto and the decrees of the Sovereign Emperor and prevent us from praying to God as our conscience dictates, as the Sovereign Emperor has allowed?"[32] A similar petitioner concluded that, because of the rejection of his petition, "I am left without conscience, and such a situation is, I believe, desirable to neither the Sovereign Emperor nor the government."[33]

Yet even as state authorities refused to recognize conversion to heterodoxy, they did not actively persecute such petitioners. True, some pagans who had rejected Orthodoxy were fined for having buried their dead outside Orthodox cemeteries and without Orthodox rites.[34] But the official position was that unauthorized transfer to non-Christianity should not result in criminal prosecution or "consequences that hamper [the apostate's] religious convictions." Thus, when one Mari with Kugu-Sorta sympathies complained that he had been selected against his will as watchman for the local Orthodox church, the department upheld his complaint. The Mari in question could not be officially excluded from Orthodoxy and given Kugu-Sorta status, but at the same time he "cannot be persecuted for his belonging to it [Kugu Sorta], nor can he be compelled to fulfill any obligations with respect to the Orthodox Church."[35] Stolypin and his associates generally faced the unenviable task of reconciling two scarcely compatible imperatives: to be as deferential as possible to people's religious beliefs and aspirations (so long as they did not represent a political threat to the state) while not antagonizing the political right wing, which was crucial to the success of Stolypin's other reform projects and to his very political survival. Given the precariousness of Stolypin's position by 1909, it simply made little sense to violate the sensibilities of the believing Orthodox majority for the sake of a relatively small number of would-be pagans.[36] Still, Stolypin tried to ensure that even these pagans could at least practice their faith, even if that practice would not be given official sanction.

But merely eluding active persecution clearly was not enough for many who sought recognition as non-Christians. Aside from their marriages lacking legal force without Orthodox sanction, these petitioners believed that state recognition conferred a certain legitimacy on their choice of religion. Thus one group admitted that its members were able to practice their faith without interference, "but at the same time it should be noted that our religious teaching, since it does not have governmental approval, is effectively private and illegal [*iavliaetsia kak by chastnym, nezakonnym*], and on that basis we cannot freely make use of all the religious rights granted to us."[37] In short, freedom of conscience for many meant not only that the state would not inhibit its citizens' religious practice but that it would also respect their convictions enough to recognize their spiritual choices.

The Problem of Jewish Transfer

The transfer of Jews to other faiths raised a series of particular problems, as Jews were not understood to be a confessional group like most others. Indeed, the department was reluctant even to address the so-called Jewish problem in the context of religious reform because "at the base of particularistic legislation about Jews is not merely a confessional marker; the law distinguishes Jews as a particular alien group [*inorodcheskaia gruppa*], which is placed in particular conditions in light of its national particularities."[38] Nonetheless, cases involving the desire of Jews to convert to other religions, or of converted Jews to return to Judaism, were bound to arise, and this required the government to contemplate how the legitimate religious needs of Jews could be balanced against the supposed need to protect Russian society from Jewish exploitation and intrigue.

Most significant in this regard was determining when, and under what circumstances, religious conversion could liberate Jews from the general restrictions imposed on that population. Before 1905 Jewish converts to Christianity had been emancipated from legal restrictions, although an epidemic of seemingly insincere conversions by the late nineteenth century had raised doubts about this practice.[39] Some baptized Jews hoped to remain free from such restrictions after their return to Judaism on the basis of the April decree. However, in 1907 the Senate concluded that the April decree merely abolished criminal prosecution for the return to a non-Christian faith but did not terminate restrictions against those confessing non-Christian faiths. Thus Jews who had received the right to settle beyond the Pale based solely on their conversion to Orthodoxy "are subject [upon reconversion to Judaism] to exclusion from those communities to which they are ascribed and expulsion to the Pale of Settlement."[40] Those wishing to confess Judaism would be Jews in all senses of the term, legal restrictions included. This principle, moreover, was extended to Jews who converted to any other non-Christian faith (e.g., Islam).[41] Only Christianity could begin to erase a Jew's Jewishness.

Even here, the state refused to treat all forms of Christianity equally. If Jewish conversion to Catholicism, Lutheranism, and Orthodoxy terminated legal restrictions on the convert, then conversion to Christian sects, which became more frequent after 1905, ultimately did not. The department reported in 1909 that the Christian sectarian movement in the Russian South, and especially in Odessa, enjoyed "particular sympathy" among Jews.[42] Already regarding the Baptist faith as "a most dangerous [sect]," the government now fretted that "the interference of Jews in the sectarian movement, in light of their tendency to intrigue, may give sectarianism a completely undesirable political tint."[43] Moreover, the government feared that these various Christian sects would merely be used as a front behind which Jews could continue their practice of Judaism after their liberation from legal restrictions. The interior ministry, accordingly, began to argue for a more restrictive conception of Christianity in order to prevent Jews from making use of the "extremely primitive organization of sectarian communities" to become Christians only nominally. Assistant Minister S. E. Kryzhanovskii wrote to the Senate that the law permitting emancipation of converted Jews had been written when the term "Christian confessions" had referred to "entirely defined religions," whose dogmas and teachings were stable, generally known, and fully recognized by the state. In contrast, the sects in question lacked even recognized clergies, and "contemporary rationalistic sectarianism in all its innumerable branches does not represent anything definite and stable in either dogmatic or canonical respects." Conversion of a Jew to one of the given sects should therefore not be considered conversion to Christianity in the sense the law implied, and, accordingly, Jewish converts to Christian sects should not be liberated from legal restrictions applied to Jews.[44] Although the Senate explicitly endorsed this opinion only in 1912, from at least 1910 the interior ministry was instructing its subordinates to remind Jews wishing to convert that their acceptance into Baptist, Evangelical, and even Russian-sectarian (e.g., Molokan) communities would *not* exempt them from legal restrictions imposed on Jews.[45] Still, the government did not prohibit such conversions outright and was even willing to recognize them, as long as the baptisms were conducted in accordance with the law. Thus Leon Rosenberg, the head of the "Evangelical-Christian Protestant community of the Baptist rite" in Odessa received the interior ministry's approval to baptize a number of Jews once he had submitted certificates attesting to their successful examination in Christianity.

If Jews could at least convert to other heterodox faiths and to Christian sectarianism, albeit without being liberated from legal restrictions, they were not at all eligible for acceptance into the Karaite community, a small "sect" within Judaism whose members in Russia constituted a distinct confessional group subject to its own statutes. Decidedly privileged compared to rabbinical Jews, Karaites incurred few of the prejudices held against Jews generally.[46] They had obtained privileges in 1795 from Catherine II on the condition that they not accept any rabbinical Jews into their ranks. Petitions on the part of Jews wishing to join the Karaite community had thus been rejected in the past, for as the Karaite Spiritual Board itself declared in 1911, "the guiding motive [of such petitions] is the selfish and base goal to make use of the civil rights granted to Karaites or other privileges, or in order to satisfy a feeling of love" between a Jew and a Karaite. The Karaite faith, the board concluded, "is not in the least interested in filling its ranks with unbelieving adherents who regard religion as a means of attaining their material aspirations and who, of course, will be bad Karaites."[47] In this case the government's suspicions dovetailed with the Karaites' desire to maintain the insularity of their community. In any event, by 1907 the government established, as a condition for any confessional transfer, that the religious leadership of the target community actually agree to accept the potential convert.[48]

New Religions and Sects

The very existence of sects, whether Christian or Jewish, brings us finally to the issue of new religions. Although Russia's existing system of confessional administration made no concrete provision for the appearance of new religious teachings, nonetheless the eventual recognition of Baptists as a religious community in the 1870s, and the government's attempt to manage schism among Mennonites in the 1860s, and among Lutherans in the Baltic region in the 1890s suggest that the state was open to legalizing new confessions under certain conditions.[49] Thus state authorities had attempted—slowly and with considerable confusion—to establish some kind of system for dealing with this problem before 1905. The interior ministry noted in 1906 that, even without the proclamation of new freedoms, this was a lacuna that needed to be filled; the proclamation of "freedom of conscience" placed this question "at the top of the list."[50]

The existing system recognized several major confessions, and the law also referred to a series of tolerated sects (e.g., Hernhutters, Baptists, and Scottish colonists). Most of these confessions or sects had some kind of statute or at least basic rules governing their religious affairs, and these statutes and rules were combined into a single volume of the Law Code in 1857 (reissued in 1896).[51] Finally, in practice, a few other confessions functioned by special arrangement, such as the Anglican Church, which was administered directly by the British Embassy.[52] All other religious groupings essentially existed outside the law.

The dynamic religious situation in Russia by the end of the nineteenth century was scarcely compatible with this system. Primarily (but not only) among the Protestant faiths, various new religious teachings had begun to appear from around the mid-century: Baptists, Evangelical Christians, the "Jerusalem Friends," the "Gyupfers," Seventh-Day Adventists, the "Catholic and Apostolic community," the New Brothers and Sisters, Malevantsy, the "Free Confession," the Busch Brothers, the Separatists, the Free Church of Christ, the Mariavites, and even a "Syrio-Nestorian Evangelical Church."[53] New teachings had also formed among non-Christian religions, such as Burkhanism in the Altai region, Kugu Sorta (a reformed animism) in Viatka Province, and the so-called Vaisovtsy among Volga Muslims.[54] If anything, the proliferation of new movements was accelerating at the turn of the century, thus confirming the proposition that alienation from established churches and even crises of faith produced new forms of religiosity as often as secularism and atheism.[55] Many of these groups were very small, of course, but others—most notably Baptists, Evangelical Christians, and Mariavites—could claim tens of thousands of adherents.[56] The significance of these groups, moreover, did not depend so much on size. Rather, their very existence raised basic theoretical questions concerning the relationship of state power to different confessions in the new order. The religious aspirations of these sectarians presumably warranted satisfaction if the principle of "freedom of conscience" was to be upheld, yet the inconstancy and indeterminacy of their dogmas and "clergy"—as we saw in the context of Jewish transfer—cast grave doubts on the advisability of allowing them to maintain their own metrical records. It was also far from self-evident that the state, in the name of "freedom of conscience," should actively facilitate schism among confessions that had long been recognized and effectively integrated into the existing system of confessional administration.

In fact, a clear definition of what constituted a "sect" did not even exist, and although some groups accepted this designation, others decisively shunned it. Writing in 1910, Mennonites argued that, in contrast to the interior ministry's draft laws, imperial legislation had historically regarded them "not as a Protestant sect" but "as one of 'several communities of the Protestant confession.'" Identifying them with new sects, they argued, "would impose upon us completely new forms of church life" and would imply that their dogmas represented "heresy" and "false teaching" regarding some mother church.[57] Other groups, however, believed that as "sects" they would be entitled to recognition under the law of 17 October 1906, which provided for the registration of Old Believer and sectarian communities. Maris in Viatka Province who sought recognition as pagans were quick to define themselves as "sectarians" of one stripe or another. Thus one adherent to Kugu Sorta declared, "I became a sectarian" (*ia sdelalsia sektantom*), while another group wrote that its members belonged "to the sect 'Old-Adam faith,' that is, to the sect to which our grandparents and great grandparents belonged." Others stated that they belonged to "the religion 'Adam-Ilan,' or the 'Adam-Ilan' sect." And some stated explicitly that they were entitled to recognition and registration under the 1906 law, and even referred to the resolutions of the Duma when it discussed legislation on Old Believers in May 1909.[58] The department finally decided in 1911 that the attempts of Maris to characterize themselves as "sectarians" were specious, since that law "makes provision only for those sects that appear among Orthodox Christians and, moreover, retain Christian teaching, whereas the sect 'Kugu Sorta' represents paganism."[59]

By far the largest case of a potentially new religion after 1905 concerned the Mariavites—a movement inspired by the visions of one Feliksa Kozlowska. Arising in the 1890s, this movement eventually became a rebellion of dissident Catholic priests against the Church hierarchy. Although Mariavites had not actually sought to break from the Church and had even appealed directly to the Pope in 1903, the Vatican dismissed Kozlowska's visions as hallucinations, and the Polish episcopate condemned the dissident priests in early 1906. In an encyclical that same year, the Pope ordered the Mariavites to disband and to submit to the Polish hierarchy, and, when they refused, he excommunicated the group's leaders. Thus was born "the first schism in Polish Catholicism since the Reformation."[60]

The interior ministry had difficulty making sense of this crisis and was therefore initially reluctant to interfere. By the spring of 1906, however, conflicts between Mariavites and loyalist Catholics over Church property had become so violent—eight persons were killed in one such a confrontation—that the imperial government could no longer stand aside. Notably the Catholic hierarchy itself turned to the government for protection from the Mariavites, arguing that renegade priests could join other faiths if they wished but were not entitled to consider themselves Catholics while inciting the population against the episcopate. Because Catholic priests performed important functions of state service, the hierarchy argued, the government should aid in removing the Mariavites from their positions and ensuring the Church's control of its property, that is, the parish churches and other buildings that were the objects of intense conflict.[61] In fact, the Catholic Church in Russia had been granted full control over the appointment and removal of its own parish clergy in December 1905, as part of the implementation of religious reform earlier that year. Some in the government were therefore reluctant to interfere in these matters at this time and perhaps even took pleasure in watching the Polish Church struggle with the consequences of its newly won freedoms.

Nonetheless, while seeking to secure the needs and protect the interests of *both* the Mariavites and the members of the official Church, the interior ministry made fairly clear in 1906 that its preference lay with the latter. "Not considering itself called upon to protect either the purity of the dogmas of the Roman Catholic Church or its integrity, the ministry, on the other hand, considered it incompatible with the dignity of the government to grant any kind of particular protection to a new religious movement with the goal of inflicting harm on Catholicism." The Pope, siding unequivocally with what imperial authorities called "orthodox Catholics" (*pravovernye katoliki*), indicated that the Mariavites would have to be regarded as a sect, entirely separate from the Catholic Church. But the state could not be neutral in effectuating this divorce. If the proclamation of freedom of conscience entitled sects to "legal and independent existence," nonetheless such sects "may not, in the opinion of the ministry, enjoy identical rights with religions existing in the state that have already been recognized by law, and whose protection is the duty of the government, on an equal basis with the defense of the legal rights of the Orthodox Church." "The church in question is a state institution," the ministry continued, and therefore Catholic authorities "may obviously rely fully on the government's defense of their legal rights."[62] The ministry thus proposed a set of temporary rules for the Mariavites that declared them a recognized sect with the right of free confession and entrusted their metrical records to civil officials (based on the Baptist model). The rights of the loyalist Catholic clergy and the property of the Church were to be protected.[63] In short, even in the case of Catholicism—surely the foreign confession that had shown itself to be the least reliable and the most politicized in the eyes of the government—the satisfaction of the religious rights of new sectarians could not be realized at the expense of a recognized and properly constituted confession.

This preference for the established Catholic Church turned out to be temporary, however. Having separated from the Catholic Church in 1906, the Mariavite movement developed quickly thereafter, drawing adherents primarily from the peasantry and the working class. The Mariavites eventually established 74 communities with some 160,000 adherents and 32 priests. By approving a statute for this group in 1909; by recognizing them as an "independent religious teaching" in 1912 with the right to keep metrical records; and by establishing a system for the appointment of Mariavite bishops with imperial confirmation, the state created a full-fledged new confession in Russian Poland, entirely independent of its mother church in institutional terms. By 1913, recognizing that the 1906 rules left virtually all Church property (including parish churches) in the hands of the Catholic Church, the government was even subsidizing the Mariavites and granting their clergy free transport on imperial railways.[64]

Several reasons accounted for this reorientation. First, in 1909, the Mariavites joined forces with the "Old Catholic" movement in Europe, which had broken with the Pope over the declaration of papal infallibility in 1870 and established the so-called Utrecht Union of Churches centered in the Netherlands.[65] Presumably the Mariavites' affiliation with an established church institution facilitated their recognition as a distinct confession in Russia. Second, the Mariavite clergy strictly refrained from engaging in politics and condemned nationalism as being incompatible with universal Christian love. A cause for hostility on the part of many politicized Poles, socialist as well as nationalist, this circumstance obviously made the group attractive to a government facing far more politics than it wished.[66] Finally, by 1914 if not earlier, the government had recognized that the movement represented a useful weapon against the troublesome Catholic clergy, who "expend on this embittered battle with the 'internal enemy' the energy that previously was enlisted for the purposes of opposing Russian interests and the government in one form or another." Accordingly, the government should cease protecting a hostile Catholicism from the Mariavites "for the sake of abstract juridical principles."[67]

Conclusion

By almost any measure, believers in Russia enjoyed greater religious freedom after 1905 than before that time. Even when the state denied its citizens the confessional affiliation of their choice, Stolypin aspired to eliminate obstacles to these peoples' free exercise of that faith. Thus the state effectively allowed the exercise of conscience while refusing to recognize its consequences. Ultimately this was a political necessity in Russia, especially given the mobilization of the Right and Stolypin's greater commitment to other reform projects, such as his land reform. But within the parameters established by such imperatives, Stolypin and his associates sought to establish a substantial degree of religious freedom for the citizens of the empire.

Still, the confessional foundations of the Russian Empire's political, social, and administrative system placed significant limitations on prospects for change. For all but the most radical reformers, religion continued to represent a fundamental source of morality and stability, and therefore signified something that the state could never afford to regard with the kind of indifference implied by the separation of church and state.[68] Nor did state officials at any point contemplate placing all confessions on an equal footing, insisting instead that the Orthodox Church was and would remain "predominant and ruling." For those empowered to regulate the relationship between Russia's many faiths, the question after 1905 was never *whether* the Orthodox Church would be privileged over other confessions but to what extent and in what specific ways.

If the state remained ideologically committed to religion (generally) and Orthodoxy (specifically), it also remained dependent on religious institutions and personnel for basic elements of its administration. Because, in almost all cases, clergies rather than civil officials maintained metrical books, transfers of Russia's subjects from one confession to another would have had to be carefully regulated to guarantee the integrity of these important records. Accordingly, the department admitted in 1906 that freedom of conscience could be fully realized only with the introduction of fully secularized civil records, which in turn implied non-confessional graveyards, civil oaths, and even civil marriage.[69] And precisely because of the confessional character of the metrical books, the

Ministry of Justice stated unequivocally in 1906 that, "under no circumstances can change of faith be regarded as the exclusive affair of the conscience of individual persons."[70] It was probably these concerns—at once almost purely technical and yet absolutely fundamental—that represented the single greatest obstacle to the recognition of new religions and sects even if, as in the case of the Mariavites, the government was able to reach an accommodation with some of them. And even as local officials clearly articulated strong reservations about "freedom of conscience" in the western provinces, the archival evidence suggests that it was, first and foremost, the complications arising from registering transfers and maintaining metrical books that hindered the recognition of some former Uniates as Catholics. To the extent that the state in old-regime Russia had been constructed on confessional foundations, extensive religious reform required an overhaul of the state apparatus that few officials found either ideologically acceptable or practically feasible.

The religious reform of 1905 is perhaps best understood as representing the state's partial accommodation with a new, more dynamic religious reality in Russia in the early twentieth century. As implemented in practice, the reform tenaciously upheld certain prerogatives for the state in regulating confessional transfer but at the same time acknowledged the increasingly pluralistic character of Russian society. Perhaps as long as official religious status retained legal significance—as a category that conferred rights, imposed restrictions, and served as an expedient tool for the governance of the empire's population—the state could never afford to surrender entirely the control over its regulation, and, as a result, citizens' expressions of religiosity would always remain at least partially circumscribed.

Notes

Support for the research of this essay was provided by the National Council for Eurasian and East European Research (NCEEER) and by the International Research and Exchanges Board (IREX), with funds provided by the National Endowment for the Humanities, the U.S. Information Agency, and the U.S. Department of State, which administers the Russian, Eurasian, and East European Research Program (Title VIII).

1. *Svod Zakonov Rossiiskoi Imperii* (St. Petersburg, 1857), vol. 11, pt. 1, arts. 4, 6, and 8.

2. Proposed legislation and administrative practice in these years tended to refer to "transfer" (*perekhod*) rather than "conversion" (*obrashchenie*), thereby acknowledging that the operation in question often involved a change in formal confessional status rather than a transformation in religious consciousness as such.

3. On the establishment of "national politics" (i.e., a politics extending across the entire country), see Charles Robert Steinwedel, "Invisible Threads of Empire: State, Religion, and Ethnicity in Tsarist Bashkiria, 1773–1917" (Ph.D. dissertation, Columbia University, 1999), 267–313; and Francis William Wcislo, *Reforming Rural Russia: State, Local Society, and National Politics, 1855–1914* (Princeton, N.J., 1990). On Russia's confessional foundations, see Robert D. Crews, "Empire and the Confessional State: Islam and Religious Politics in Nineteenth-Century Russia," *American Historical Review* 108, no. 1 (February 2003): 50–83.

4. A. Iu. Polunov, *Pod vlast'iu Ober-Prokurora: Gosudarstvo i tserkov' v epohku Aleksandra III* (Moscow, 1996); and Paul W. Werth "The Limits of Religious Ascription: Baptized Tatars and the Revision of 'Apostasy,' 1840s–1905," *Russian Review* 59, no. 4 (2000): 493–511. On the origins of these groups, see Theodore R. Weeks, "Between Rome and Tsargrad: The Uniate Church in Imperial Russia," in *Of Religion and Identity: Missions, Conversion, and Tolerance in the Russian Empire*, ed. Robert Geraci and Michael Khodarkovsky (Ithaca, N.Y., 2001); A.V. Gavrilin, *Ocherki istorii Rizhskoi eparkhii XIX veka* (Riga, 1999), 73–182; and Paul W. Werth, "Coercion and Conversion: Violence and the Mass Baptism of the Volga Peoples, 1700–1764," *Kritika: Explorations in Russian and Eurasian History* 4, no. 3 (2003): 543–70.

5. For such a critique, see M. A. Reisner, *Gosudarstvo i veruiushchaia lichnost': sbornik statei* (St. Petersburg, 1905). For a positive assessment, see M. Krasnozhen, *Inovertsy na Rusi: K voprosu o svobode very i o veroterpimosti*, Vol. 1, *Polozhenie nepravoslavnykh khristian v Rossii*, 3rd ed. (Iur'ev, 1903).

6. Christopher Read, *Religion, Revolution, and the Russian Intelligentsia, 1900–1912: The Vekhi Debate and Its Intellectual Background* (New York, 1980), 13–39; Catherine Evtuhov, *The Cross and the Sickle: Sergei Bulgakov and the Fate of Russian Religious Philosophy* (Ithaca, N.Y., 1997); Georgii Florovsky, *Puti russkago bogosloviia* (Paris, 1983), 452–99; Pål Kolstø, "A Mass for a Heretic? The Controversy Over Lev Tolstoi's Burial," *Slavic Review* 60, no. 1 (2001): 81–85; Sergei Firsov, *Russkaia tserkov' nakanune peremen: konets 1890-kh–1918 gg.* (St. Petersburg, 2002), 99–125.

7. *Polnoe Sobranie Zakonov Rossiiskoi Imperii* (hereafter, *PSZ*), 3rd series, vol. 23, no. 22581 (26 February 1903). On the earlier draft of the manifesto, see B.V. Anan'ich, ed., *Vlast' i reformy: Ot samoderzhavnoi k sovetskoi Rossii* (St. Petersburg, 1996), 445.

8. *PSZ*, 3rd series, vol. 24, no. 25495 (12 December 1904).

9. *PSZ*, 3rd series, vol. 25, no. 26126 (17 April 1905).

10. Informed treatments of the legislative process include Peter Waldron, "Religious Reform after 1905: Old Believers and the Orthodox Church," *Oxford Slavonic Papers* 20 (1987): 110–39; A. A. Dorskaia, *Svoboda sovesti v Rossii: Sud'ba zakonoproektov nachala XX veka* (St. Petersburg, 2001); and Diliara Usmanova, *Musul'manskaia fraktsiia i problemy "svobody sovesti" v Gosudarstvennoi Dume Rossii, 1906–1917* (Kazan, 1999), 81–122.

11. See, for example, Rossiiskii Gosudarstvennyi Istoricheskii Arkhiv (hereafter, RGIA), f. 796, op. 442, d. 2110, ll. 260b–27; RGIA, f. 821, op. 133, d. 515, ll. 600b.–61.

12. RGIA, f. 821, op. 10, d. 260, l. 121. The Department of the Religious Affairs of Foreign Confessions, in the Ministry of the Interior, had jurisdiction over all non-Orthodox religions and confessions in the empire.

13. See, especially, Reisner, *Gosudarstvo*, 390–423, as well as Usmanova, *Musul'manskaia fraktsiia*, 81–86; Dorskaia, *Svoboda sovesti*, 32–39; K. K. Arsen'ev, *Svoboda sovesti i veroterpimost': Sbornik statei* (St. Petersburg, 1905); V. K. Sokolov, "Svoboda sovesti i veroterpimost' (istoriko-kriticheskii ocherk)," *Vestnik prava* 5 (1905): 1–31; and Laura Engelstein, "The Dream of Civil Society in Tsarist Russia: Law, State, and Religion," in *Civil Society before Democracy: Lessons from Nineteenth-Century Europe*, ed. Nancy Bermeo and Philip Nord (Lanham, Md., 2000), 34–36.

14. M. Krasnozhen, *K voprosu o svobode sovesti i o veroterpimosti* (Iur'ev, 1905); idem, "Granitsy veroterpimosti," *Pribavleniia k Tserkovnym vedomostiiam* 34 (20 August 1905): 1429–32; "O bezuslovnoi svobode veroispovedaniia v Rossii," *Kholmsko-Varshavskii eparkhial'nyi vestnik* 18 (1905): 214–16; Nikon (Episkop Vologodskii i Totemskii), *Svoboda sovesti imeet svoi granitsy* (St. Petersburg, n.d. [probably 1910]); Koren, "Svoboda sovesti, ili inkvizitsiia," *Kholmsko-Varshavskii eparkhial'nyi listok* 39 (25 September 1905): 469–71.

15. The department defined freedom of conscience as "the right of each person with a sufficiently mature self-consciousness to recognize or declare his faith, or even the absence of such, with no limitations or any adverse legal consequences." See *Spravka o svobode sovesti*, (St. Petersburg, 1906), 3.

16. Department circular no. 4628 (18 August 1905), in RGIA, f. 821, op. 133, d. 540, ll. 3–4. On the improvisation by Catholic authorities, see RGIA, f. 821, op. 10, d. 260 ll. 227–34; and LVIA, f. 378 (BS, 1905), b. 403.

17. RGIA, f. 821, op. 10, d. 260, ll. 218, 2330b, 2310b; "Zapiksa chlenov Gosudarstvennago Soveta Meishtovicha, Skirmunta, i Lopatinskago" (15 January 1915), in RGIA, pechatnye zapiski, folder 743, 1–10, and appendixes.

18. RGIA, f. 821, op. 10, d. 260, ll. 2180b.–219, 222, 2250b.

19. "Zapiska chlenov Gosudarstvennogo Soveta," 5, 7, 73.

20. Ibid., 10.

21. RGIA, f. 821, op. 10, d. 260, ll. 219, 238–40. I have addressed the issue of transfer to Catholicism after 1905 in greater detail in "Trudnyi put' k katolitsizmu: Sovest', veroispovednaia prinadlezhnost' i grazhdanskoe sostoianie posle 1905 g.," in *Lietuviu Katalikų Mokslo Akademijos Metraštis*, vol. 26 (Vilnius, 2005), 447–75.

22. *PSZ*, 3rd series, vol. 24, no. 26126 (17 April 1905), section 1, article 3. For the committee's deliberations, see N. P. Solov'ev, ed., *Polnyi krug dukhovnykh zakonov* (Moscow, 1907), 8–14.

23. RGIA, f. 821, op. 10, d. 275, ll. 20–240b.

24. See, for example, Gosudarstvennyi Arkhiv Kirovskoi Oblasti (hereafter, GAKO), f. 582, op. 150, d. 118, l. 3.

25. RGIA, f. 821, op. 8, d. 796; RGIA, f. 821, op. 133, d. 284, ll. 10b, 6; RGIA, f. 821, op. 133, d. 572; and RGIA, f. 821, op. 8, d. 798. The Senate ruled in 1906 that the guidelines for transfer from Orthodoxy to a non-Christian faith pertained also to transfer from another Christian faith to non-Christianity. See RGIA, f. 821, op. 133, d. 540, ll. 5–500b. (Department circular no. 3192 of 5 June 1906).

26. "Zakonoproekt Ministerstva vnutrennikh del: Ob izmenenii zakonopolozhenii, kasaiushchikhsia perekhoda iz odnogo ispovedaniia v drugoe" (no. 1473, 20 February 1907), in *Missionerskoe Obozrenie* (1908), 202.

27. GAKO, f. 582, op. 148, d. 91, ll. 16–160b.

28. RGIA, f. 821, op. 8, d. 796, l. 880b.

29. RGIA, f. 821, op. 10, d. 260, ll. 64, 121. In a 1906 memorandum the interior ministry explicitly included "paganism" under the heading of non-Christian faiths.

30. RGIA, f. 821, op. 10, d. 39, ll. 283–88.

31. Modified by the Duma, the draft was blocked by the State Council and languished in a committee formed to reconcile the differences. See RGIA, f. 821, op. 10, d. 265, ll. 88–1040b.

32. RGIA, f. 821, op. 133, d. 430, ll. 50b., 10–100b., 18.

33. RGIA, f. 821, op. 133, d. 515, l. 600b.

34. RGIA, f. 821, op. 133, d. 515, ll. 2–20b. In this case a twenty-five-ruble fine was assessed on villagers. See also RGIA, f. 821, op. 133, d. 515, l. 143.

35. RGIA, f. 821, op. 133, d. 430, ll. 39–390b.

36. Far-right protesters against the pending bill on confessional transfer identified the recognition of conversion from Christianity to heterodoxy in the Duma's version of the bill as among its most objectionable elements (RGIA, f. 821, op. 10, d. 39, ll. 216–60).

37. RGIA, f. 821, op. 133, d. 515, ll. 670b.–68.

38. *Spravka o svobode sovesti*, p. 36. The interior ministry expressed similar concerns about limitations on "persons of Polish origin" (*litsa polv'skago proiskhozhdeniia*), because they "have not a confessional but a political foundation" (39–40). On the problem of defining Poles, see L. E. Gorizontov, *Paradoksy imperskoi politiki: Poliaki v Rossii i russkie v Pol'she* (Moscow, 1999), 100–118. On the largely unsuccessful attempts to address the Jewish problem separately after 1905, see Abraham Ascher, *P. A. Stolypin: The Search for Stability in Late-Imperial Russia*

(Stanford, 2001), 164–17; and Hans Rogger, *Jewish Policies and Right-Wing Politics in Imperial Russia* (Berkeley, 1986), 83–106.

39. John D. Klier, "State Policies and the Conversion of Jews in Imperial Russia," in Geraci and Khodarovsky, *Of Religion and Empire*, 93, 108.

40. RGIA, f. 1284, op. 224, d. 125, l. 12.

41. RGIA, f. 821, op. 133, d. 540, ll. 11–110b. (Department circular no. 1213 of 15 April 1909).

42. RGIA, f. 821, op. 133, d. 283, ll. 11, 14–15.

43. RGIA, f. 821, op. 133, d. 283, l. 110b. Although Baptists had been among those benefiting from the more liberal religious order after 1905, the state remained convinced of their "harm." For details, see Heather Coleman, *Russian Baptists and Spiritual Revolution, 1905–1929* (Bloomington, Ind., 2005).

44. RGIA, f. 821, op. 10, d. 273, ll. 10–12.

45. RGIA, f. 821, op. 133, d. 283, ll. 7, 630b., 83, 85

46. See "Evrei-Karaimy," *Zhurnal Ministerstva vnutrennikh del,* pt. 1 (1843): 263–84. According to the 1897 census, there were merely 12,894 Karaites in the empire, most of them in Crimea. See P. Luppov, "Statisticheskiia dannyia o naselenii Rossiiskoi Imperii (po perepisi 1897 goda)," *Pribavleniia k Tserkovnym vedomostiam* 12 (19 March 1905): 512.

47. RGIA, f. 821, op. 133, d. 802, ll. 3–6; RGIA, f. 821, op. 10, d. 492.

48. RGIA, f. 821, op. 133, d. 515, l. 248; RGIA, f. 821, op. 10, d. 492, l. 430b. (Ministry of the Interior circular no. 6428, 5 November 1907).

49. RGIA, f. 381, op. 8, d. 3707; RGIA, f. 821, op. 5, dd. 975, 980, 998, 1020. I addressed the problem of sects within the foreign faiths, in "Schism Once Removed: State, Sects, and the Meanings of Religious Toleration in Imperial Russia," in *Imperial Rule*, ed. Alexei Miller and Alfred J. Rieber (Budapest, 2004), 85–108.

50. *Spravka o svobode sovesti,* 19.

51. *Svod zakonov Rossiiskoi Imperii,* vol. 11, pt. 1, *Ustavy dukhovnykh del inostrannykh ispovedanii* (St. Petersburg, 1857; new edition, 1896).

52. RGIA, f. 821, op. 5, d. 935.

53. On these groups, see "Liuteranskiia sekty v Estliandskoi gubernii" (Revel, 1893) (in RGIA, f. 821, op. 5, d. 1020, ll. 1–330b.); I. Lindenberg, "Protestanskiia sekty v Pribaltiiskom krae." *Rizhskiia eparkhial'nyia vedomosti* 10–15 (1891): 340–56, 376–82, 416–28, 455–57, 487–92, 507–12; and Iulii Osterblom, *Noveishiia religioznyia dvizheniia v Estliandii* (St. Petersburg, 1885); S. Smirnov, "Nemetskie sektanty za Kavkazom," *Russkii vestnik* 57 (1865): 230–57; S. D. Bondar', *Adventizm 7-go dnia* (St. Petersburg, 1911); idem, *Sovremennoe sostoianie russkogo baptizma* (St. Petersburg, 1911); and idem, *Sekta mennonitov v Rossii (v sviazi s istoriei nemetskoi kolonizatsii na iuge Rossii)* (Petrograd, 1916).

54. RGIA, f. 821, op. 133, d. 430, ll. 8–120b.; Andrei Znamenski, *Shamanism and Christianity: Native Encounters with Russian Orthodox Missions in Siberia and Alaska, 1820–1917* (Westport, Conn., 1999), 228–38; Paul W. Werth, "Big Candles and 'Internal Conversion': The Mari Pagan Reformation and Its Russian Appropriations," in Geraci and Khodarkovsky, *Of Religion and Identity,* 144–72; the draft of the book, which was never published, by S. G. Rybakov, "Novyia techeniia v russkom iazychestve: Sekty v iazychestve cheremis, votiakov i chuvash: vera 'Kugu-Sorta' i drugiia" (1915) (in RGIA, f. 821, op. 133, d. 643); E. V. Molostvova, "Vaisov Bozhii Polk," *Mir Islama* 1, no. 2 (1912): 143–52; M. Sagidullin, *K istorii Vaisovskogo dvizheniia* (Kazan, 1930); Michael Kemper and Diliara Usmanova, "Vaisovskoe dvizhenie v zerkale sobstvennykh prosh-enii i poem," *Ekho vekov/Gasyrlar avazy* 3–4 (2001): 86–122.

55. New forms of veneration and religiosity were also characteristic of Orthodox Russians in this period, of course, and the teachings of the Baptists made their way from German to Russian communities as well. See Coleman, *Russian Baptists;* Nadieszda Kizenko, *A Prodigal Saint: Father John of Kronstadt and the Russian People* (University Park, Pa., 2000); and J. Eugene Clay, "Orthodox Missionaries and 'Orthodox Heretics' in Russia, 1886–1917," in Geraci and Khodarkovsky, *Of Religion and Empire,* 38–69.

56. *Statisticheskiia svedeniia o sektantakh (k 1 ianvaria 1912 g.)* (St. Petersburg, 1914), which counted just under four-hundred-thousand sectarians of both Orthodox and other Christian origins. Mariavites are not included in this list, which apparently did not encompass the Kingdom of Poland.

57. *Dokumenty, otnosiashchiesia k veroispovednym voprosam mennonitov* (Gal'bshtat, 1910), pp. 6–10, 22–34.

58. RGIA, f. 821, op. 133, d. 430, ll. 1, 4, 220b.; RGIA, f. 821, op. 133, d. 515, ll. 64–640b. The Maris' claim that their beliefs constituted "the faith of Adam" or the "faith of Abraham" (*Adam-Ilanskaia vera, vera Avraamova*) was based on the proposition that their ritual sacrifices were essentially those described in the Old Testament and therefore had biblical sanction (RGIA, f. 821, op. 133, d. 515, ll. 99–1010b.). For an Orthodox refutation of this proposition, see Daniil Fedorov, *Pravda li, chto vera iazychnikov i iazychestvuiushchikh cheremis est' vera Avraama?* (Sergiev Posad, 1914).

59. RGIA, f. 821, op. 133, d. 515, l. 66.

60. Robert E. Blobaum, *Rewolucja: Russian Poland, 1904–1907* (Ithaca, N.Y., 1995), 248. The short history provided here is based on ibid., 247–49; Nikolai Reinke, *Mariavity* (St. Petersburg: Senatskaia tipografiia, 1910); Jerzy Peterkiewicz, *The Third Adam* (London, 1975), 7–34; and RGIA, f. 1276, op. 2, d. 601, ll. 1–2.

61. RGIA, f. 1276, op. 2, d. 601, ll. 20b.–40b. On confrontations, see also Gosudarstvennyi Arkhiv Rossiiskoi Federatsii (hereafter, GARF), f. 102 (O.O.), 1906, II otd., d. 12, ch. 2; Reinke, *Mariavity*, 15–16; and Peterkiewicz, *The Third Adam*, 35.

62. The interior ministry cited an imperial charter to the Kingdom of 14 February 1832 (article 5), which stated that "the Roman Catholic faith, as the faith confessed by the larger part of OUR subjects in the Kingdom of Poland, will always be an object of the government's particular care" (RGIA, f. 1276, op. 2, d. 601, l. 20).

63. RGIA, f. 1276, op. 2, d. 601, ll. 9–18. The Council of Ministers approved the ministry's position with only a few minor revisions. Temporary rules for the Mariavites—intended to govern the new community until more comprehensive legislation on the formation of new religions and sects could be passed–went into effect in November 1906.

64. RGIA, f. 1276, op. 2, d. 601, ll. 91–97; Ralph Tuchtenhagen, *Religion als minderer Status: Die Reform der Gesetzgebung gegenuber religiösen Minderheiten in der verfassten Gesellschaft des Russishcen Reiches, 1905–1917* (Frankfurt, 1995), 219–24.

65. Reinke, *Mariavity*, 24; Peterkiewicz, *The Third Adam*, 39–43; "Starokatoliki i mariavity," *Kolokol*, no. 1051 (11 September 1909): 1. For the declaration on this issue by the Mariavite bishop Jan Kowalski, see "Mariavity," *Golos Moskvy*, no. 10 (14 January 1910).

66. On the apolitical orientation of Mariavites, see "Pol'skaia natsional'naia tserkov'," *Vilenskii vestnik*, no. 2049 (16 April 1910): 2; and "Mariavitizm v Tsarstve Pol'skom," *Vilenskii vestnik*, no. 2073 (15 May 1910): 1–2.

67. RGIA, f. 1276, op. 2, d. 601, ll. 540b.–56.

68. See, for example, the draft law of 1907 "Ob izmenenii zakonopolozhenii, kasaiushchikhsia perekhoda iz odnogo ispovedaniia v drugoe," in Marian Radwan, ed., *Katolicheskaia tserkov' nakunune revoliutsii 1917 goda: Sbornik dokumentov* (Lublin, 2003), 145–46; and RGIA, f. 821, op. 10, d. 265, ll. 90–1040b.

69. *Spravka o svobode sovesti*, 11–17. Such civil records existed only for two groups—Old Believers and Baptists—precisely because the state either refused to recognize their religious leaders as legitimate "clergies" or was unwilling to trust them with such an important administrative function. For a broader consideration of the significance of metrical books, see Charles Steinwedel, "Making Social Groups, One Person at a Time: The Identification of Individuals by Estate, Religious Confession, and Ethnicity in Late Imperial Russia," in *Documenting Individual Identity: The Development of State Practices since the French Revolution*, ed. Jane Caplan and John Torpey (Princeton, N.J., 2001), 67–82.

70. RGIA, f. 821, op. 10, d. 260, ll. 640b.–68.

8

Tales of Violence against Religious Dissidents in the Orthodox Village

Heather J. Coleman

·────◦∞◦────·

In early January 1911 the Cossack village of Batalpashinskaia came to blows over the burial of a Baptist. In a telegram to the Kuban district authorities, a local Baptist preacher wrote that the trouble began when the Baptists started to dig a grave for their deceased leader, Afanasii K. Iurchenko. A crowd gathered and refused to allow the burial. For two days the body was moved from place to place as the population spat on the corpse, threw cigarette butts into the coffin, and ridiculed the Baptists. Several of the believers were beaten. Finally, the Baptists were forced to bury Iurchenko on the estate of a wealthy Baptist family twenty versts away.[1]

Later that same month the Batalpashinskaia village assembly resolved to ask its leader, the Ataman, to appeal for the expulsion of twelve Baptists from the village in order "not to allow the sectarians completely to corrupt our younger generation and to relieve the village of great danger." According to the resolution, "after the sectarians' sermons, [the youth] absolutely refuse to respect their parents, the Ruler, [and] their religion, which is undesirable and injurious both for us Cossacks, as well as for the whole state. Furthermore, the sectarians desecrate the Orthodox religion and Orthodox sacred objects, which offends and troubles the religious feelings of truly Orthodox Christians."[2]

This episode was covered in newspapers, investigated by the central government in St. Petersburg, and touted by supporters of sectarians as an example of the plight of religious dissidents in the Orthodox village. Although the basic chain of events is relatively clear, the details vary with the telling. According to one report from the Department of Police in the Ministry of Internal Affairs, for example, as the Baptists dug Iurchenko's grave, a religious discussion began among the curious who had gathered to watch. The Orthodox reported that, when the Baptists were asked why they had not prepared a cross for the grave, they allegedly responded that "dogs just run to piss under your crosses." By the time the Baptists left to collect the body, the Orthodox crowd, which had swelled to several hundred people, decided they would not allow the burial of "one of the blasphemers and insulters of the cross" and began to shovel dirt back into the grave. When the Baptist funeral procession arrived at the cemetery, the Orthodox crowd began shouting: "We don't need apostates; we will not allow them to be buried on our land, get out of here." The local Ataman, in an effort to calm the crowd, ordered that a section of the cemetery be set aside for Baptists. However, the crowd gathered round and threw the earth back into the grave as the Baptists attempted to dig, all the while yelling, "We won't allow him to be buried on our land at any cost." According to the police, when the Baptists finally gave up and carried the body away for burial on private land, Orthodox villagers accompanied them all the way, whistling and beating on empty buckets.[3]

But who were the true instigators? Did the Baptists indeed make such derogatory comments about Orthodox graves? Or did the Orthodox remark, as reported in a local newspaper, that they would rather have a dog buried in their cemetery than a Baptist? And what about the people interviewed by the local police who remembered the crowd shouting, "Beat the non-Christians [*nekhristei*]" and "Go beat the Baptists"?[4] Were fists involved or only jeers? Did Iurchenko die from a heart attack he suffered during a violent attack on his congregation in their prayer house on New Year's Day, as some sources claim, or did he die of natural causes, as asserted by the local police?[5] All we can be certain of is that the Cossacks of Batalpashinskaia considered the Baptists a sufficient threat that they took measures to expel them from their midst. Yet even the intentions behind this resolution are murky. Its wording was clearly designed to demonstrate the significance of the villagers' local problem to the Orthodox Church and the Russian state . But did they have other, more practical reasons for wanting to rid themselves of the Baptists? After all, as Jeffrey Burds has shown, Orthodox families had all kinds of material motives for denouncing their relatives as religious dissidents to the religious and civil authorities.[6] Certainly, similar appeals by Orthodox villagers for the expulsion of their religious dissidents were turned down precisely because the authorities believed that the complainants simply wanted more land.[7]

Accounts of these cases are so common that undoubtedly persecution did occur, even if the details are often clouded. This essay explores several stories of religious violence between Orthodox and Baptist villagers in late imperial Russia, and examines how these stories were communicated to, and used by, observers in educated society. These tales meant one thing in the village and another as they were transmitted beyond. Orthodox peasants regarded conversion to the Baptist faith as a disruption to a community imbued with traditional cultural and religious norms. Leaving the Church and performing non-Orthodox rites in an Orthodox milieu aroused enmity within the family, interfered with the administration of the village, and ruptured the ritual unity of village life. Faced with this unwanted dissidence, peasants defended the Orthodoxy of their villages with their fists, but also with complaints to local and central authorities. In fact, both Baptist converts and their Orthodox opponents constructed narratives of violence that would further their respective goals by appealing to the sensibilities of various elites in church, government, and educated society. But they could not always control the reception of these stories, for in late imperial Russia religious issues were a crucial element in the intense debates about civil rights, the relationship between the state and society, and the organization of public life.[8] Baptists' supporters appropriated these tales for their own purposes, namely, to promote their particular visions of the nature of the Russian community as a whole, and of the place of the Orthodox Church and the suitability of freedom of conscience in Russian society.

Problems between Baptists and their Orthodox neighbors offer a fruitful object of study both because of the Baptists' position in the Russian Empire and because of their particular ability to publicize their legal problems. First, the Baptist faith was the fastest growing non-Orthodox religious denomination among the Slavic population of the Russian Empire. It was also highly controversial within both educated society and the families and village communities that confronted the challenge of conversions in their midst. In 1894 the Council of Ministers forbade "shtundists," an umbrella term for Russian evangelicals of various types, to meet for prayer. As a result, during the 1890s, hundreds of converts suffered arrest, imprisonment, or exile. Nicholas II's decree on religious toleration of 17 April 1905 removed the legal prohibition on Orthodox people converting to other Christian faiths and cancelled the anti-shtundist legislation. Thereafter the Baptists began to organize openly and rapidly to increase their ranks. But although their legal position markedly improved, their dealings with the police did not end, for it remained forbidden to convert the Orthodox.[9] Moreover, what had been decreed in distant St. Petersburg was not necessarily played out in day-to-day relationships.

The Baptists were good at making this fact known. From the 1890s right up to the 1917 Revolution and beyond, one Ivan P. Kushnerov, a member of the Kiev Baptist community, made it his mission to defend evangelicals brought to trial for holding shtundist meetings, for publicly preaching non-Orthodox teachings, or for other religious crimes. He systematically collected materials dealing with the legal position of Russian evangelicals and used these to pester government officials, also publicizing them relentlessly in the evangelical press that blossomed after 1905. Newspaper writers and commentators interested in religious affairs frequently relied on these reports as their source of information.[10] As a result, Baptist examples dominated press reports on violence against religious dissidents. Finally, certain characteristics of the Baptist faith may have contributed to the disproportionate number of reports of violence against Baptists. These include the practice of public baptism by full immersion, a strong evangelistic drive, and the rejection of traditional hierarchies embodied in the Baptists' congregational church structure. All these features ensured that conversion could not remain a secret for long. Indeed, several observers commented on the particular frequency and severity of attacks on evangelicals compared to other religious dissidents.[11]

Defining and Defending the Orthodox Community

Orthodox families were understandably troubled when one of their number abandoned the ancestral religion. Many such families would appeal to the local priest or Orthodox missionary for help in bringing an apostate back into the Orthodox fold.[12] Numerous reports, in both government archives and the Baptist and secular press, describe the friction arising from new Baptists' refusal to perform the everyday rituals of Orthodox life, such as contemplating icons and crossing themselves. Sometimes this conflict led to violence within the family. For example, at the *khutor* (village) of Balka Vasil'eva in the Don district, where virtually all the inhabitants were Baptists, a man appeared at a meeting brandishing a whip and proceeded violently to attack his wife and drag her away.[13] Such tension and violence arose not only over pressure on dissidents to return to Orthodoxy but also because Orthodox families complained that Baptist converts placed undue pressure, sometimes even of a physical nature, on their wives and other relatives to become Baptists, too.[14]

The sectarians' refusal to reverence icons particularly offended the religious sensibilities of their families and neighbors. In every Orthodox home, a display of icons, illuminated by a burning lamp, presides from the corner of the room and sacralizes the home. Moreover, each person would have had a personal icon, received at baptism, which accompanied him or her through life's rites of passage and finally to the grave.[15] By contrast, the Baptists rejected the use of icons, affirming an unmediated relationship between the believer and his or her God and a simple style of worship to complement this belief.

As a result, new believers faced the problem of deciding what to do with their now superfluous icons. Some converts removed the icons from their houses and laid them at the church door.[16] Others were less reverent, as attested by the many complaints about converts selling, burning, or even using their icons as shutters.[17] If all family members were not ready to part with their sacred images, trouble might ensue: in 1909 in the city of Konotop, for example, a Cossack, Taras Khomenko, was tried by the district court and sentenced to three months' arrest at the police station (*pri politsii*) for taking down the family's icons, smashing them, and burning them in the stove while his Orthodox mother and wife were at church.[18] Of course, Orthodox family members could also get the upper hand in the battle over icons: in the village of Grishino, Ekaterinoslav Province, one woman's husband threw her out of the home for her refusal to revere the icon.[19]

Not only was the actual disposal of icons troublesome to family and friends but so, too, were the Baptists' explanations of their actions. Baptists' condemnation of the contemplation of icons as "idol worshiping" did not endear them to their fellow villagers. Numerous complaints country-wide suggest that whatever words the Baptists actually used, Orthodox listeners heard blasphemous disrespect for their most sacred objects. Villagers throughout Russia told police and priests that Baptists had described their icons as "planks." In one case in Kiev Province in 1909, a young peasant, Filipp Grigor'evich Litvin, was sentenced to two weeks in jail for blasphemy after refusing to kiss the cross proffered by the local priest during a pastoral visit to Litvin's Orthodox wife, Martena. Litvin allegedly pointed to the cross, and said: "to kiss it would be the same as kissing a plank." Litvin's defender, Kushnerov, did not deny that Litvin had compared the cross to a board but told the court that the statement should be seen as the blunt expression of a simple person trying to engage in discussion with a priest. Later, in a statement appealing his conviction (probably written by Kushnerov), Litvin claimed that the incident had never taken place, although he acknowledged having said in a public debate with the local psalmist that he did not kiss icons because he regarded them as "ordinary items made by the hands and will of a human."[20]

The practice of adult baptism also presented a direct challenge to Orthodox teachings and to notions of family and community. Scholars of the radical Protestant tradition have pointed out that social separation and conflict is implied in the very practice of baptizing (and especially re-baptizing) only adults. As John Bossy argues regarding the Anabaptists in the Reformation, "believers' baptism was a doctrine of division, and not just in the eyes of princely bureaucrats and unity-haunted municipalities; it provoked a growl from the average soul in defence of his conviction that through their baptism he and his children were living in Christianity."[21] Likewise, in his study of Baptist history, William Henry Brackney contends that the congregational form of the Baptist community—the congregation as a covenant of converted adults—"represented an absolute break" with the established church because it "bypass[ed] tradition altogether and ma[de] a compact with God Himself."[22] For Orthodox peasants, baptism did not merely mark an earlier spiritual transformation, as the Baptists taught.

Rather, the ritual itself conferred both salvation and membership in the community. Thus, when a fight erupted over the burial of an un-baptized Baptist baby in the cemetery of a village in Kiev Province, the Orthodox objected on the principle that they themselves did not inter un-baptized children in the graveyard. [23] And, similarly, the secret police report into the funeral incident in Batalpashinskaia, described above, found that Orthodox families resented Baptist members who "insisted that their children not be baptized and that previously baptized children who had not yet switched to the sect and were accustomed to the Orthodox faith be forced not to cross themselves and to forget completely about the cross and the Church."[24]

Sometimes these offended families took matters into their own hands. In 1910, for example, a young Baptist named Petr Kofanov from the Cossack village of Vladimirskaia, Kuban district, complained to the Department of Spiritual Affairs that, while he and his wife were away from home working on the steppe, his parents had persuaded the village priest to baptize their year-old daughter according to the Orthodox rite. He appealed for the baptism to be declared illegal and for his family's religious rights to be protected, correctly pointing out that, according to the law of 17 April 1905, when both parents transferred to another faith, children under the age of fourteen automatically followed them. An investigation ensued, and the local police took statements from all those involved. The results emphasize the importance of baptism for the Orthodox as a sign of membership in the community on earth and in heaven. The grandparents, left to care for the child while her parents were away, were distressed at the child's un-christened state. In the words of the grandfather, "looking at the child, who hadn't been baptized according to our Orthodox ritual, I felt sad in spirit." And so they asked the local priest to perform the ritual on the little girl, and he agreed. In his summation for the Ministry of Internal Affairs, the local police chief reported that, when he told the villagers about Kofanov's claim that his rights were violated, they all took umbrage on the grounds that all Kofanov's ancestors had been Orthodox and that he alone had suddenly decided a couple of years earlier to become a Baptist. [25] This case illustrates how Orthodoxy was an integral part of family and community identity, an identity that was sealed by infant baptism. In the neighbors' eyes, the heritage of the Kofanov infant superseded the parents' individual rights.

Conflict over ritual life and faith could spread beyond the walls of the family hut to become the basis for village action. Villagers frequently sought to prevent new converts from being baptized. The Baptist practice of baptism by full immersion meant that their baptisms were mostly public events that attracted considerable attention. Sometimes this interest was relatively benign, [26] but government files and the press were replete with examples of confrontation, often violent, incited by the public spectacle of evangelicals' baptisms. For example, F. T. Kolmyk, from the village of Gostochaevskaia, Kuban region, reported to the journal *Baptist* that, in early 1910, his congregation had attempted to baptize three converts, but family and village sanctions had foiled them. On their way down to the riverbank, the mother of one of the new converts ran up to her son and, with the words, "Where are you going, Maksim?" hit him on the head so hard with a stick that his face was covered with blood. As they waited for Maksim to wash his head, the Baptists knelt in prayer. A large crowd gathered and grew increasingly agitated, until finally Kolmyk announced that the baptism would not take place. Later, he reported, the Baptists learned that the river had been filled to overflowing with thorns and other prickly things.[27] Similarly, during Easter 1911, the village of Romanovka in the distant Amur district was thrown into turmoil over local Baptists' plans for an open-air baptism. As the pastor began to baptize the candidates in the lake, a crowd of Orthodox onlookers started to whistle, laugh, and make banging noises. Some women in the crowd even began to sing obscene songs. Then, as the Baptists headed back to their prayer house following the baptism, they were mocked by some of the Orthodox, apparently "in a state of drunkenness owing to the Easter holiday." A fight broke out: some attacked the Baptists, while others broke the windows of the prayer house. According to the liberal newspaper *Riech'* (Speech), the result was "a full-fledged pogrom.[28]

Some villages, like Batalpashinskaia, attempted finally to resolve their dissidence problem by exercising their traditional right to turn over to the state undesirable elements for banishment.[29] These cases show the extent to which peasant perceptions of morality, community, and legality were intertwined.[30] For example, the Baptist missionary Vasilii Skaldin reported an incident in a settlement where a branch of his congregation had rented a prayer house. The village assembly had gathered and decided to expel the Baptists. When the Baptists arrived at their prayer house that Sunday, they found it surrounded by a mob of armed peasants who shouted, "[We do not want you] to meet here or corrupt our families." To the Baptists' pleas that they were practicing their faith by the will of the tsar and the permission of the governor, the uncompromising voice of popular justice responded: "We recognize nothing; we have our law and we passed a verdict to expel you and we want to know nothing more.[31] Just as religious rioters during the Reformation regarded their violence as a legitimate defense of the doctrine the government had failed to uphold, so the villagers sought to restore the traditional boundaries of their community by rooting out heresy.[32] Thus Orthodox villagers made explicit the connection between family disruption and village politics that religious dissidence had aroused.

The communities that took action against their Baptist members had two broad complaints: that Baptist evangelizing was intolerable and that the Baptist presence interfered with village administration. As expressed in the minutes of one village assembly that tried to expel its Baptists in 1907:

> [The Baptists] boldly appear everywhere with their propaganda, in the streets and in homes, and, in trying to make converts to their teaching, do not stop at any public sacrilege, any effrontery and even blasphemy against the Orthodox Church, holy icons, rituals, sacraments; their impertinence and the importunity with which at every instance, upon every meeting with Orthodox people, they try to spread their teaching has lately become intolerable.[33]

Local converts were bad enough, but many villages regarded Baptist missionaries as a particular nuisance. As one government official who interviewed both sectarians and Orthodox in settlements across the Steppe region reported, "The population especially does not tolerate wandering sectarian preachers, brands them with the nickname of 'corruptors [*soblaznitelei*] of the people,' and vigilantly ensures that this element does not penetrate its milieu."[34] The Baptists regretfully confirmed this. In the annual report of their missionary work for 1907, for example, they described one missionary who was threatened with an axe and many cases where the village authorities had taken action to get rid of the religious intruders.[35]

The other common complaint of communities about their Baptists was that, as one village put it in its appeal to the governor to exile a group of new converts, they "undermine the social structure of the life of our settlement.[36] Not only did conversion shake up family relationships but religious dissidence wrecked havoc on a village system in which management of the religious aspects of life was closely woven into secular village administration. Although the village and parish communities were administratively and juridically distinct, the village assembly was "responsible for deciding on various collections to be taken within the community," including the compulsory "donation" from all villagers toward the construction and maintenance of the local church. [37] Now the Baptists were refusing to participate in what their neighbors regarded as an inseparable part of village life, the Church. In February 1907 the Baptist legal defender, Kushnerov, reported in the evangelical magazine, *Bratskii listok* (Brotherly leaflet), that, in various areas of Kiev Province, village assemblies were drawing up resolutions (*obshchestvennye prigovory*) "according to which our brother-Baptists are assessed taxes for the construction and repair of Orthodox churches at rates of 38 rubles, 68 kopecks, and lower. Despite their poverty and the harvest failure, this requisition is exacted from them by force, and their appeals to be released from torture and penalties are also left 'without satisfaction' by the governor." "Such a requisition," commented Kushnerov, "is not a 'voluntary donation.'"[38]

The Baptists' refusal to participate financially in the religious life of the village was not the only factor that brought public enmity. Because Orthodoxy marked one's belonging in the village, indeed was integral to its shared institutions, the public performance of non-Orthodox rituals such as baptisms and funerals violated the very nature of the community. The police superintendent (*ispravnik*) of Konotop uezd, Chernigov Province, underscored this situation in a 1910 report. He stated that the Baptists' public prayer and performance of rituals generated interest in their teachings but were also the main source of friction between them and their Orthodox neighbors. These practices, he reported, provoked "indignation and hatred among the simple people, who are firm in the Orthodox faith, [and] often entail clashes, particularly in instances . . . where, according to their understanding, the interests of the Orthodox Church are violated, for example—the burial of shtundists in Orthodox cemeteries."[39]

That reports of community conflict over the burial of a local Baptist were common is not surprising, since the funeral brought together issues of religious legitimacy and questions relating to the allocation of space and resources in the village. For example, in the spring of 1910, in the village of Gurovtsy, Kiev Province, when the Baptists were heading to the local cemetery with the coffin of one of their number, they were met on the road by a crowd of peasants led by the priest bearing a cross. The priest declared that he would not allow the burial of a Baptist in the Orthodox cemetery.[40] The Baptists complained to the local police officer, who informed the priest that there was a new law allowing sectarians to be buried in Orthodox graveyards. The priest responded that he cared only about canon law. An investigation into this incident, initiated by the metropolitan of Kiev, suggested that the peasants had sought the assistance of their priest because they objected to the burial of a Baptist in their cemetery on two counts: the Baptists had not shared in the expenses of fencing off the cemetery; and they regarded the graveyard as a holy place, which would be desecrated by the burial of people who had rejected Orthodoxy.[41] Tales of angry crowds comparing Baptists' corpses to those of dogs, such as we saw in Batalpashinskaia, reinforce this idea that villagers believed that apostates had separated themselves from the human community.[42]

Confrontations in Russian and Ukrainian villages over the presence and activities of religious dissenters certainly could have a basis in nonreligious motives. Just as often, however, such goals seemed to be secondary or nonexistent. Students of popular summary justice emphasize the way that both mockery and ritualized violence offer a means of shaming fellow villagers for stepping outside the accepted moral boundaries of the local community.[43] As Stephen P. Frank argues, rather than being meaningless, popular summary justice, or *samosud,* was a "response to some threat against the community or a challenge to village norms and authority.[44] Similarly Natalie Zemon Davis suggests that religious violence is particularly intense, "because it connects intimately with the fundamental values and self-definition of a community."[45] Reactions to the apostasy of fellow villagers clearly show the centrality of religious norms in the definition of community and family.

Villagers feared the appearance of religious dissent in their midst. As one convert remembered, when sectarians walked through the village, "women tried to make the sign of the cross over all the places where they had walked. Some villagers said that they needed to find a daredevil who could unexpectedly put a cross around their necks, and then the Satanic specter would go away and they would again become like everyone else.[46] Rumors also circulated that the shtundists practiced blood rituals whereby the new convert had to sign his name in blood, or that the arrival of religious dissidence in the village showed that the Antichrist had come.[47] Compounding this fear was a sense of shame. One man told his newly converted son-in-law to leave his house, saying, "because of you, I am ashamed to walk the streets.[48] These rumors and accusations expressed common people's perceptions of the limits of legitimate religious activity and the requirements for respectable membership in the community.

Conversing about Religious Strife in the Village

Orthodox Church authorities, government officials, the sectarian press, and secular observers of various political persuasions all took an interest in the problem of violence against religious dissidents in the villages. [49] Agreeing on what that violence signified was another story. For some, it was evidence that the Orthodoxy of the peasantry needed protection; for others, it pointed to the pernicious influence of Orthodox priests on the people. Some argued that improved civil rights for religious dissenters would solve the problem of violence, whereas others viewed that violence as a troubling sign—or even convincing proof—that the village was too backward for modern notions such as freedom of conscience. The practices of exiling and isolating religious dissidents had a long pedigree, but now state and society considered the new option of granting rights to these dissidents.[50] As Russian society faced challenging new questions about freedom of conscience, constitutional order, representative politics, and national identity in the late imperial period, analysis of the religiosity and the values of the people become crucial. Urban elites of various persuasions took up the stories they had heard from Orthodox or Baptist villagers and used them to advance their own views on these issues.

The Baptists worked hard to publicize these episodes both for reasons of internal community development and in order to draw the attention of Russian lawmakers to their plight. Publishing frequent—and no doubt embellished—accounts of violent encounters in the evangelical press that emerged after 1905 seems to have created a common identity as an unfairly persecuted people, one that drew strength from the example of the first Christians. [51] At the same time Kushnerov and the editors of evangelical journals and newspapers also used these accounts to educate local believers about their rights. Descriptions often ended with statements to the effect that "the promised freedom of confession of faith still remains on paper, but in life, especially in the village, everything remains as it has always been," and readers were entreated to send in complaints, so they could be publicized and passed on to government officials.[52] Indeed, local communities did borrow such storylines in their appeals to the central authorities for assistance. For example, in a 1910 petition to the Department of Spiritual Affairs of the Ministry of Internal Affairs, a group of Baptist peasants from Voskresenskaia volost', Ekaterinoslav Province, complained that the township elder (*starshina*) had ejected them from his office with the words, "We'll beat you up so long as there are only a few of you!" And these petitioners asked: "Where on earth is the freedom of confession and conscience bestowed by our ruler if even the authorities pay no attention to it?"[53]

Baptist leaders also ensured that writers interested in the cause of religious freedom heard about their troubles by personally informing them of incidents and by constantly reporting them in their own magazines, which often served as the source for later articles and investigations in the secular press. [54] In early 1909 the Duma speaker and Octobrist deputy Nikolai Khomiakov reported that "news reaches us about the most savage reprisals in the villages. . . . When I was told about them, I could not believe my ears. After the priest gave a sermon that inflamed the passions, two peasants who had fallen away to the Baptist faith were taken to the village administration and, there, their father was forced, on threat of death, to flog his own sons with the prickly branches of a plum tree." For Khomiakov, such incidents raised concerns about the possibilities for real legal change: "I don't know," he continued, "to what extent the law on freedom of religion, which we are now working out in the State Duma, can be implemented, if such barbarity takes place."[55]

Khomiakov clearly had his doubts about the ability of law to change popular behavior, but most of those who reacted with sympathy to accounts of religious violence did not share these anxieties. Long before such stories could be told in the Duma, participants in the burning debate of the late nineteenth century over freedom of conscience and religious questions in general were using them to show the necessity of legal, indeed constitutional, change in the Russian Empire.[56] In the liberal journal *Viestnik Evropy* (Herald of Europe) in 1901, K. K. Arsen'ev recounted at length two violent attacks on Baptists in order to argue that "the beating of sectarians is one of the outward signs of the evil that will only be eliminated through enlightenment and religious tolerance.[57] Similarly the jurist A. M. Bobrishchev-Pushkin, a former assistant procurator of the Senate, arrived at similar conclusions in his years of reviewing appeals of religious cases, and pointed out in his well-known book on the legal status of sectarians that violence between shtundists and their communities showed the need to highlight the different interests of church and state in Russian legislation.[58] Most clearly influential was a detailed review of legislation regarding sectarians that Varvara I. Iasevich-Borodaevskaia first read to the Juridical Society at St. Petersburg University in 1903. In it she used various brutal cases of rural conflict between Orthodox and Baptists to demonstrate that the Russian state needed to withdraw from enforcing adherence to Orthodoxy.[59] In early 1905 the chairman of the Committee of Ministers, Sergei Witte, had this document printed and distributed to his fellow ministers in the period leading up to Tsar Nicholas II's decree on religious toleration.

The recounting of these incidents became even more prevalent after 1905 as a way to discuss the disappointment liberals and populists felt with the outcomes of the 1905–1907 revolutionary settlement, but also for struggling with the problem of whether the Russian peasantry was ready for democracy. Writing in 1908 and 1909, the well-known commentators S. Mel'gunov and A. Prugavin both made a direct connection between an alleged resurgence of popular attacks on Baptists and the change in the political fortunes of the liberation movement after 1907. As Mel'gunov argued in 1908, "Reaction is growing, and, along with it, reports about the persecution of sectarians are becoming more frequent."[60] Prugavin connected this phenomenon to the revival of the old demons of village life:

> Beatings of sectarians are starting up again in various parts of Russia. Attacks on Baptists and shtundists and incidents of fierce beatings are becoming increasingly common. In most cases these attacks take place, as in the past, with the favorable assistance, sometimes even the participation, of representatives of village authority, the police, and even the clergy; the initiative frequently belongs to the latter.[61]

This is one of many examples of how the Baptists' allegations that their popular mistreatment originated with the clergy struck a chord with many elements of the liberal and leftist intelligentsia. Such incidents reinforced the tendency of these observers to regard the clergy as intellectually and politically backward representatives of state power in the village. The Baptists were aware of these inclinations and exploited them to their advantage. Many of the beatings reported in petitions and in the press were alleged to have followed a sermon criticizing the Baptists. For example, the Baptists in the village of Gurovtsy, described above, complained bitterly that the village priest was responsible for stirring up enmity toward them and claimed that he had sparked a beating of Baptists by hitting a man named Iatsyk in the chest and shouting, "Get out of here, Shtundist!" A diocesan investigation of the case rejected this account of events and, instead, praised the priest as an energetic young pastor who had brought new life to a previously demoralized Orthodox parish. Like many other parish priests, especially after 1905, this priest had devoted great energy to countering Baptist inroads in his congregation by organizing public debates with the sectarians in the parish school building and special missionary evenings. According to his bishop, it was the priest's fear that his Orthodox flock might resort to violence against the Baptists that led him to support their appeal to have leading sectarians evicted.[62]

It is difficult to ascertain fully the role that priests and missionaries played in fomenting anxiety about the presence of religious dissidents, for the priests generally denied any involvement in—and often the very existence of—acts of brutality. [63] There are certainly many allegations of priests standing by as villagers pummeled their religious dissidents.[64] However, just as it is unclear what Baptists actually said that offended their Orthodox interlocutors, it is not always certain that a priest truly suggested attacks on sectarians or whether this was the message villagers took from a sermon regarding Baptist theological errors. From a religious viewpoint, Orthodox parish priests had a pastoral responsibility to warn their flocks and protect them against what they no doubt genuinely perceived to be heresy. And clearly many families trusted the priests to perform this role when faced with the apostasy of a son or daughter.

Believing and emphasizing these accusations was necessary, in part, to retain the liberal and populist faith in the potential of the people. For example, when the liberal newspaper *Riech'* reported the incident of the crowd mocking the Baptists of the village of Romanovka when they attempted to perform a baptism, as described earlier, the reporter concluded that someone must have incited the "picture of a full pogrom" that ensued, as

> our simple people usually relate very tolerantly to all non-Christian and non-Orthodox people. The sight of people praying, regardless of how strange the form of prayer, never arouses even simple mockery in the Russian person, not to mention enmity and violence. How indeed the celebrated "placidity" of the Russian peasant had to be turned upside down in order to lead him to such a pogrom! And they are leading them.[65]

"They" were the reactionary forces of the Orthodox clergy and their supporters in the radical right wing. Mel'gunov made a similar argument about the inherent tolerance of the Russian people, in a 1908 article titled "'Religious fanaticism' and the Mission." Commenting on the many recent press reports of crowds beating up sectarians, he protested the conservative press's view of these incidents as proof of the population's rejection of the idea of freedom of religious speech. Rather, he said, "thousands of facts bear witness to the full religious tolerance characteristic of the popular masses [*narodnaia massa*]." To him, the cases showed that popular violence was the result purely of the "unculturedness" of the rural population and the malevolent actions of outsiders, in the form of the local police, the clergy, and Orthodox missionaries.[66]

For Iasevich-Borodaevskaia, these incidents revealed not only the inadequacy of the laws of 1905 and 1906 that had allowed sectarians publicly to organize congregations and gather to worship, while banning their proselytizing, but also the fact that even these inadequate laws had yet to be fully implemented. Writing after the failure of the Duma to pass freedom of conscience legislation in 1909–1910, she complained that the problem of violence would not be resolved until the legal rights of religious dissidents were guaranteed. She decried that their lives were governed by administrative decrees and circulars that could be withdrawn or changed, that official permission was required to hold their meetings, and that they remained subject to administrative exile at the whim of bureaucratic authorities.[67] She concluded that so long as policy on sectarians remained a matter of administrative procedure rather than legal rights, confusion would reign and the dissidents would be unable to defend themselves. She did not despair, however. Equating the sectarians with the people (*narod*), she argued that they could still look to their elected representatives for help:

> The people have a mother-caregiver—the State Duma—which keenly listens to the moaning of the people, but not everything reaches her. At present, the delegates of the Duma have the great task of supporting the people, guarding the people's rights, and directing all their creative energies to developing immovable laws for the people based on the principles of fairness.[68]

Gradually, inevitably, she asserted, freedom of conscience was becoming "an indestructible fact of reality and enter[ing] into life not as a privilege for some estate but as an inalienable, legal right, to be enjoyed equally by all citizens of Russia."[69]

Russian evangelicals actively assisted authors such as Iasevich-Borodaevskaia in their publicizing of persecution, but they could not always control how these ideas were used. For example, in 1913 a group of fifty Duma deputies, representing leftist and center-left parties, presented a complaint to the Duma regarding persecution of religious dissidents. Speaking on behalf of the group were two Social Democrats, Petrovskii and M. I. Skobelev. Although they were careful to assert their atheist credentials, the speakers went on to take up the cause of religious sectarianism as a peasant movement unfairly persecuted by Orthodox missionaries. Skobelev compared the "vile attacks on sectarianism" described in the "objective research into the history of the sectarian movement of Bonch-Bruevich and Mrs. Iasevich" to the sufferings of the early Christians.[70] Soon after, an editorial in the evangelical weekly newspaper, *Utrenniaia zviezda* (Morning star), applauded the Social Democrats' initiative but also hastened to point out that religious sectarianism was not a political movement. "Sectarianism is not an estate [or] class movement; it is first of all a Christian, not a peasant [*khristianskoe, a ne krest'ianskoe*] movement, although most of its members are peasants," the author declared. And he warned: "The involvement of sectarianism (as a whole) in the political struggle is a completely impossible matter—this must be understood."[71]

Members of the Orthodox clergy, especially its missionary wing, also evinced considerable concern about the violent encounters between evangelicals and Orthodox parishioners. In contrast to the liberals and leftists, they generally did so in order to bemoan the government bureaucracy's alleged lack of concern for promoting Orthodoxy and protecting popular faith. For example, at a conference on anti-sectarian missionary activity in the Khar'kov diocese in 1896, participants warned that when administrative authorities refused to endorse village resolutions expelling religious dissidents tension intensified. "This situation," the report declared, "excites the energy of the shtundists even more, and dispirits the Orthodox or even gives them an excuse for summary justice [*samosud*] and reprisals [*samorasprava*]."[72] This theme that the Orthodox layperson felt abandoned by the Russian state also dominated the widely read study of Baptists written by Bishop Aleksii (Dorodnitsyn), who had served as anti-sectarian missionary in Kherson and Ekaterinoslav dioceses in the last fifteen years of the nineteenth century. Describing the decision of a village in Kherson Province to expel its Baptists, he wrote: "It takes a lot to make our Little Russian intolerant and even more for an entire commune of Little Russian peasants to pull together for any sort of collective endeavor, and therefore it is very likely that the Baptists' insults directed at the holy things of the Orthodox Church and their laughter at the Orthodox, so modestly referred to in the resolution, exceeded all measures of tolerance."[73] Although he bewailed the peasantry's tendency to resort to brutality, he excused it as a frustrated response to the civil administration's failure to protect the peasantry from Baptist disturbances. The result, he wrote, was that "the Orthodox people, having lost faith that they will be defended from the sectarians' violent actions, either peacefully switch to shtundism or else unpeacefully switch from fists and rods to pitchfork and axe."[74] Dorodnitsyn's goal in retelling the stories of Baptist blasphemy and Orthodox reprisals was to demonstrate the wisdom of the repressive measures of the pre-1905 era. Although he was writing several years after the 1905 revolution, the conclusion of his section on village conflict—and, indeed, of the entire book—was that only when Tsar Alexander III had taken a personal interest was the bureaucracy shaken out of its complacency and the law of 1894 instituted, which forbade the provocative public activities of the Baptists. Dorodnitsyn's failure to address changes since then, let alone the current situation, reinforced the argument that banishing the Baptists was the true solution to the problems they created. [75] It was the tsar who solved problems, not the state bureaucracy and certainly not the Duma.

For the reactionary press and some right-wing Duma deputies, religious conflict and violence generally served as evidence that the state had abdicated its responsibilities to the Orthodox masses by proclaiming religious toleration in 1905. For example, a 1909 article in the Moscow newspaper *Vieche* (named after the medieval Russian popular assembly), titled "Fruits of 'Freedom of Conscience,'" described how the Baptists so "tried the tolerance" of the population of a particular village that the villagers felt forced to break the windows in the dissidents' prayer house, bringing on a violent fight. [76] Thus violence was the result of a state policy that did not defend the Orthodoxy of Russian society. The newspaper *Kolokol* (The bell), published by the reactionary Vasilii M. Skvortsov, who also happened to be the editor of the anti-sectarian journal *Missionerskoe obozrienie* (Missionary review), reinforced this point by printing reports from villagers complaining that the Baptists used freedom of conscience to destroy village life. In one example, a "villager" from Spasskoe, Stavropol' Province, wrote in that, as a result of Baptists' abuse of freedom of conscience, his village had recently been forced to witness a "blasphemous parody of a baptism." He then asked, "[Who will] protect us from mass conversions?"[77] Father Ganchzhulevich, a Duma deputy from Volynia, similarly declared, during the May 1909 Duma debates on freedom of conscience, that, until 17 April 1905, the shtundists, Roman Catholics, and Orthodox of his rural parish had lived peacefully, but after the toleration edict, the non-Orthodox had become belligerent and fomented discord.[78]

Amid all these arguments about the meaning of violence in the village stood the Russian state, specifically the Ministry of Internal Affairs. [79] These frequent reports of violence arising from religious dissidence produced a dilemma for policy makers in St. Petersburg who fielded appeals for help, actively followed press reports about sectarians, and regularly investigated acts of violence. On the one hand, as a result of all the rhetoric and violent incidents, officials began to associate Baptist activity with social disorder. For example, bureaucrats in the

Interior Ministry supported the decision of the Kherson governor not to allow Baptists in the village of Dobrovelichkovka to hold a public baptism, as it "could arouse the natural feeling of irritation among the Orthodox who see the public performance of the ritual as an abasement and insult to the Orthodox religion."[80] On the other hand, because the government was primarily concerned with preserving order, the authorities in St. Petersburg sometimes found themselves acting as the defenders of religious dissidents against the actions of their Orthodox neighbors.[81] Officials charged with investigating complaints about persecution made by local communities and low-level government administrators often returned to the point that, since 1905, the laws on freedom of conscience were incomplete and contradictory, allowing Baptists to interpret them one way and local communities another. Writing on this theme in a 1911 report to Prime Minister Petr A. Stolypin, one bureaucrat recounted, on a recent fact-finding trip to the Steppe region, that "in almost all the settlements where Orthodox are the majority, numerous complaints were lodged by Baptists about oppression and persecution by their fellow villagers. In tears they told [me] about their cheerless existence, constantly in fear of being beaten, not daring to leave the house, to light a fire in the hut, without risking attack or outrage." This situation, the official believed, in which laws were unclear, merely encouraged the Baptists to see themselves as martyrs.[82]

Within the village, these discourses of religious violence were about defining the nature of the community and its limits. They also concerned change. In their reactions to outsiders or to those who set themselves apart from the traditional community and its mores, Orthodox peasants revealed their own values and the place of religious identity and ritual in their definition of community. But Russian villagers, whether Baptist or Orthodox, knew they had an audience. These incidents demonstrate the agency of both peasant communities and the evangelicals these communities rejected to use the perceptions of various elites to further their own collective goals. Just as the evangelicals made sure that their liberal and left-wing supporters heard of their plight and blamed the priests whom their supporters would assume had acted in an intolerant and brutal manner, so, too, were village assemblies eager to play on the beliefs of government and right-wing observers about the Russian peasant devotion to defending Orthodoxy or the relationship between Orthodoxy and political reliability. Once these stories were appropriated by their urban listeners, they became grist for the mill of intellectuals' debates about the nature of the Russian soul, the suitability of Western European models of religious tolerance to the Russian milieu, and the political implications of religious change. Both their currency in these debates and the government's struggle to address the disorder caused by religious dissidence reveals how pragmatic exigencies were intertwined with ideological ones in the process of pushing open the public sphere and expanding the possibilities for individual expression in late imperial Russia.[83]

Notes

Some portions of this chapter are drawn from Heather J. Coleman, *Russian Baptists and Spiritual Revolution, 1905–1929* (Bloomington, Ind., 2005).

1. Rossiiskii gosudarstvennyi istoricheskii arkhiv (hereafter, RGIA), f. 821, op. 133, d. 301, l. 53. The director of the Department of Spiritual Affairs of the Ministry of Internal Affairs launched his investigation based on this telegram (l. 52). It was reprinted in "Telegramma," *Utrenniaia zviezda*, no. 3 (21 January 1911): 3.

2. RGIA f. 821, op. 133, d. 301, ll. 49–50.

3. RGIA f. 821, op. 133, d. 301, ll. 38–39. This is a particularly well documented case; although it is impossible to know all the details of such incidents, there seems to be general agreement at least about the basic chain of events. See: ll. 38–9, 49–50, 52, 53, 55, 77, 78–81.

4. RGIA f. 821, op. 133, d. 301, ll. 57, 61.

5. Report from the newspaper *Terek*, no. 3924, 1911, reprinted in V. I. Iasevich-Borodaevskaia, *Bor'ba za vieru* (St. Petersburg, 1912), 386–87; RGIA f. 821, op. 133, d. 301, l. 750b.

6. Jeffrey Burds, "A Culture of Denunciation: Peasant Labor Migration and Religious Anathematization in Rural Russia, 1860–1905," in *Accusatory Practices: Denunciation in Modern European History, 1789–1989*, ed. Sheila Fitzpatrick and Robert Gellately (Chicago, 1997), 54.

7. See, for example, RGIA, f. 1284, op. 222 (1891), d. 89, ll. 6–60b., 9–90b.

8. Laura Engelstein, "The Dream of Civil Society in Tsarist Russia: Law, State, and Religion," in *Civil Society before Democracy: Lessons from Nineteenth-Century Europe*, ed. Nancy Bermeo and Philip Nord (Lanham, Md., 2000), 32; A. Iu. Polunov, *Pod vlast'iu ober-prokurora: Gosudarstvo i tserkov' v epokhu Aleksandra III* (Moscow, 1996), 97–98.

9. See Coleman, *Russian Baptists and Spiritual Revolution*.

10. Examples of newspaper articles that list the Baptist press as their source include RGIA f. 1284, op. 185 (1907), d. 39, ll. 250, 301, 3460b. (I. M. Tregubov, "V zashchitu gonimykh sektantov," *Rus'*, 21 July 1907; idem, "Presliedovaniia sektantov," *Rus'*, 5 April 1907; idem, "Vtoroi moi otviet 'Osvied. Biuro,'" *Rus'*, 26 October 1907); Christianus, "Pod znakom svobody soviesty," *Riech'*, 2 July 1911. See also Iasevich-Borodaevskaia, *Bor'ba za vieru*, 385.

11. See, for example: A. Prugavin, "Raskol i biurokratiia," *Viestnik Evropy* 44, no. 11 (November 1909): 174–75; and S. Mel'gunov, *Tserkov' i gosudarstvo v Rossii. V perekhodnoe vremia. Vypusk vtoroi. Sbornik statei (1907–1908)* (Moscow, 1909), 107. There were, of course, reports of violence and conflict related to other dissident groups. See, for example, Vladimir Bonch-Bruevich, *Novyi Izrail. Materialy k istorii i izucheniiu russkago sektantstva i staroobriadchestva*, vol. 4 (St. Petersburg, 1911), 385–95.

A disproportionate number of these accounts deal with Cossack and Ukrainian communities apparently because of the geographic concentration of Baptists in the Ukrainian and southeastern parts of European Russia, Kushnerov's location in Kiev, and perhaps the elite's perceptions of the periphery as particularly wild. Still, patterns of behavior did not differ significantly whether the protagonists were Cossacks or Russian or Ukrainian peasants.

12. Gosudarstvennyi muzei istorii religii (hereafter, GMIR), f. 2, op. 16, d. 155, l. 18; *Baptist* no. 18 (23 March 1911): 102.

13. *Baptist* (July 1908): 30.
14. Examples include RGIA f. 821, op. 133, d. 194, ll. 450b., 3420b.; and d. 195, l. 750b.
15. Pierre Pascal, *The Religion of the Russian People,* trans. Rowan Williams (London, 1976), 16–18.
16. "Iz obshchestvennoi khroniki," *Viestnik Evropy* 18, no. 1 (January 1883): 456; Nikandr Larin, "Sektantstvo v Tambovskoi gubernii (s. Lipiagi, Borisogliebskago uiezda)," *Missionerskoe obozrienie,* no. 4 (April 1908): 606.
17. For example, RGIA, f. 821, op. 133, d. 310, l. 1750b.; RGIA, f. 821, op. 133, d. 301, l. 38; and Episkop Aleksii (Dorodnitsyn), *Religiozno-ratsionalisticheskoe dvizhenie na iugie Rossii vo vtoroi polovinie XIX-go stolietiia* (Kazan', 1909), 410.
18. RGIA, f. 821, op. 133, d. 194, ll. 12, 15.
19. *Otchet Baptistskago Missionerskago Obshchestva za 1907–1908 god. God pervyi* (Odessa, 1909), 24.
20. GMIR, Koll. 1, op. 8, d. 13, ll. 1, 40b., 29.
21. John Bossy, *Christianity in the West, 1400–1700* (Oxford, 1985), 110.
22. William Henry Brackney, *The Baptists* (New York, 1988), 3.
23. RGIA, f. 1284, op. 185 (1907), d. 39, l. 318.
24. RGIA, f. 821, op. 133, d. 301, ll. 38–380b.
25. RGIA, f. 821, op. 133, d. 301, ll. 20–270b.
26. See accounts in *Baptist,* no. 10 (1911): 79; no. 4 (October 1907): 15; no. 5 (November 1907): 15.
27. *Baptist,* no. 10 (1910): 79. Note that these incidents were not restricted to isolated villages. In the factory town of Bezhitse, on the outskirts of Briansk, a congregation of Baptist workers drew the enmity of their Orthodox neighbors by walking through the streets of the town to the river Desna, singing psalms. According to the governor of Orel Province, this upset the Orthodox population and "frequently the boys of the workmen [*mal'chiki masterovykh*] threw rocks at the Baptists when they started to sing in the street" (RGIA, f. 1284, op. 185 [1908], d. 83, l. 520b.).
28. RGIA, f. 821, op. 133, d. 254, ll. 74–75. The elder also alleged that a struggle had taken place between the Baptists and a man who did not want to allow his wife to take baptism.
29. Stephen P. Frank, *Crime, Cultural Conflict, and Justice in Rural Russia, 1856–1914* (Berkeley, Calif., 1999), 236–37.
30. Cathy Frierson, "Crime and Punishment in the Russian Village: Rural Concepts of Criminality at the End of the Nineteenth Century," *Slavic Review* 46, no. 1 (spring 1987): 57.
31. In this case, after the beating, Skaldin informed the police and the police had since protected them, posting a policeman at the door during meetings (*Baptist,* no. 10 [2 March 1911]: 77). Cases of villages attempting to expel their religious dissidents were very common. For other examples, see RGIA, f. 821, op. 133, d. 93, l. 45; *Baptist,* no. 5 (November 1907): 21; RGIA, f. 1284, op. 221, d. 75, l. 790b.
32. Natalie Zemon Davis, *Society and Culture in Early Modern France* (Stanford, Calif., 1975), 160–65.
33. GMIR, f. 2, op. 16, d. 155, ll. 12–14. In both this and the Batalpashinskaia case, the governor refused to endorse the decision of the village assembly. But even after 1905, some cases were approved. See, for example, in the same file, ll. 17–18.
34. RGIA, f. 821, op. 133, d. 289, l. 490b.
35. *Otchet Baptistkago,* 16, 17–19, 29–32, 36.
36. GMIR, f. 2, op. 16, d. 155, l. 3. In this case, again, the complainants drew attention to the resulting dangers to the state.
37. Vera Shevzov, "Popular Orthodoxy in Late Imperial Rural Russia" (Ph.D. dissertation, Yale University, 1994), 274–75.
38. *Bratskii listok* (February 1907): 36.
39. RGIA, f. 821, op. 133, d. 194, ll. 150b.–16.

40. RGIA, f. 797, op. 80 (2 otd., 3 st.), d. 390, l. 90b.

41. RGIA, f. 797, op. 80 (2 otd., 3 st.), d. 390, l. 5. In the end, the Baptists were able to bury their dead in the ground alongside the cemetery fence. The Church authorities said that in this way the village was complying with the law requiring that a section of the cemetery be set aside for sectarians: the village had declared three *morgy* (1 *morg* = 1.25 acres) as cemetery land but for financial reasons had only enclosed one *morg,* but the land where the Baptist was buried was technically cemetery land. For similar problems with the interment of Old Believers, see Iasevich-Borodaevskaia, *Bor'ba za vieru,* 98–99.

42. RGIA, f. 821, op. 133, d. 301, l. 590b; and *Bratskii listok,* no. 7 (July 1910): 8. Other evidence suggests that peasants regarded the bodies of suicides, sectarians, and un-baptized babies as dangerous after death (Frank, *Crime, Cultural Conflict, and Justice,* 201). Notably, in the same period, some French peasants, too, apparently objected to secular burials in their churchyards by making loud pig-like noises during the ceremony (Hugh McLeod, *Secularization in Western Europe 1848–1914* [New York, 2000], 250).

43. Stephen P. Frank, "Popular Justice, Community and Culture among the Russian Peasantry, 1870–1900," *Russian Review* 46 (1987): 244.

44. Ibid., 263.

45. Davis, *Society and Culture in Early Modern France,* 186.

46. I. Semenov, "S rodnykh polei," *Khristianin,* no. 4 (1924): 54. For a report of similar behavior, see Vasilii Skaldin, "Ot neviezhestva k istinie," *Slovo istiny,* no. 36 (May 1914): 421.

47. Skaldin, "Ot neviezhestva k istinie," 421; N. I. Makarevskii, *Sbornik obrashchenii na evangel'skii put' zhizni* (St. Petersburg, 1914), 30; GMIR, f. 2, op. 16, d. 190, l. 4.

48. Skaldin, "Ot neviezhestva k istinie," 421. For another example, see Minaeva, "Razskaz o svoem obrashchenii," *Drug molodezhi,* nos. 9–10 (September 1913): 104.

49. On the urban press's general fascination with incidents of village violence as examples of a retrograde and alien culture, see Frank, "Popular Justice," 257, 264. Innumerable accounts in the press describe popular beatings of Baptists; see, for example, Vladimir Bonch-Bruevich, "Presliedovanie baptistov v Rossii," *Viestnik Evropy* 45, no. 6 (June 1910): 160–83; "Izbienie evangelistov," *Riech',* 23 April 1908; "Presliedovanie Odesskikh sektantov," *Novaia Rus',* 21 May 1909; "Napadenie na sektantov," *Riech',* 18 January 1911; "Nasilie v molel'nie baptistov," *Riech',* 17 April 1913, 4; "Gonenie na sektantov," *Birzhevyia viedomosti,* 2 June 1913; "Ubiistvo sektantskago propoviednika," *Riech',* 16 June 1913, 5; see also the clipping found in RGIA, f. 821, op. 133, d. 301, l. 5 ("Plody 'svobody soviesty' [Iz Tuapsa]," *Vieche,* 20 August 1909).

50. On the exile of religious dissidents in the early nineteenth century, see Nicholas B. Breyfogle, "Heretics and Colonizers: Religious Dissent and Russian Colonization of Transcaucasia, 1830–1890" (Ph.D. dissertation, University of Pennsylvania, 1998), chaps. 1 and 2, esp. 96–97, on communities "liberating" themselves from sectarians.

51. The inspiration of the early Christians infused a special report on persecution in 1909 and other evangelical writings; see, for example, "Goneniia nashego vremeni," *Bratskii listok* (May 1909): 2–18; D. I. M., "S nashego polia," *Baptist,* no. 11 (November 1908): 23; and S. Bielousov, "Vpechatlieniia ot s"iezda," *Baptist,* no. 44 (27 October 1910): 347–48. At the 1910 Baptist Congress, sixteen delegates rose and were recognized as people who had suffered persecution for their faith (RGIA, f. 821, op. 133, d. 263, l. 13). Naturally other minority religious groups also had a well-developed sense of martyrdom linked to their rejection by the broader community (Breyfogle, "Heretics and Colonizers," 95).

52. *Otchet Baptistskogo,* 19.

53. RGIA, f. 821, op. 133, d. 194, l. 42. In a similar example from Voronezh Province, a group of Baptist peasants claimed that after they were violently dragged to the village assembly (*skhod*) where, in the presence of the village priest and the elder (*starosta*), they were "beaten half to death with sticks and kicks," they appealed to the village constable (*uriadnik*) for protection and he told them: "You needed to be beaten up like that" (RGIA, f. 1284, op. 185 [1908], d. 72, l. 40).

220 *Heather J. Coleman*

54. In addition to Kushnerov, for example, the Baptist leader V. G. Pavlov was a major source of information and primary documents on Baptist life and persecution for the most prolific researcher of Russian religious sectarianism, the Bolshevik V. D. Bonch-Bruevich, in the late nineteenth century, when both were in exile abroad, and in the 1910s, when Pavlov was editor of *Baptist* in Odessa (GMIR, f. 2, op. 16, d. 62, l. 27).

55. I. Teneromo, "Religioznyia iskaniia nashikh dnei," *Mir,* nos. 11–12 (April 1909): 48. This case appears to have been investigated (RGIA, f. 821, op. 133, d. 301, ll. 221, 275).

56. On this atmosphere, see Polunov, *Pod vlast'iu,* 97.

57. "Iz obshchestvennoi khroniki," *Viestnik Evropy,* no. 9 (September 1901): 428–30; reprinted in slightly different form in K. K. Arsen'ev, *Svoboda soviesti i vieroterpimost'. Sbornik statei* (St. Petersburg, 1905), 199–201.

58. A. M. Bobrishchev-Pushkin, *Sud i raskol'niki-sektanty* (St. Petersburg, 1902), 43–46, 50–53.

59. Iasevich-Borodaevskaia, *Bor'ba za vieru,* xiii, 1–108, esp. 63–74, 95–105.

60. Mel'gunov, *Tserkov' i gosudarstvo v Rossii,* 107.

61. Prugavin, "Raskol i biurokratiia," 174–75.

62. RGIA, f. 797, op. 80 (2 otd., 3 st.), d. 390, ll. 30b., 6, 110b. For the activities of other parish priests, see I. S-skii, "K voprosu o tom, kak podniat' religiozno-nravstvennoe nastroe-nie pravoslavnykh, uderzhat' ikh ot ukloneniia v sektantstvo i uluchshit' ikh otnoshenie k sluzhiteliam Tserkvi," *Missionerskoe obozrienie,* no. 1 (January 1906): 178–86; Vasilii Luzanov, "Kakimi sredstvami mozhet raspolagat' prikhodskii pastyr' v bor'be s shtundo-baptizmom? (Iz zapisok pastyria-missionera)," *Missionerskoe obozrienie,* no. 10 (October 1906): 438–42. On how a priest's words against "idolaters," whatever his intentions, could spark religious riots during the Reformation, see Davis, *Society and Culture,* 153.

63. See, for example, RGIA, f. 1284, op. 185 (1907), d. 39, ll. 151–520b.

64. RGIA, f. 1284, op. 185 (1907), d. 39, ll. 151–520b; and f. 1284, op. 185 (1908), d. 72, l. 40.

65. Christianus, "Pod znakom svobody soviesty," *Riech',* 2 July 1911. quote at 5.

66. S. Mel'gunov, "'Religioznyi fanatizm' i missiia," *Russkiia viedomosti,* 25 July 1908, reprinted in Mel'gunov, *Tserkov' i gosudarstvo v Rossii,* 150–56. Another article making exactly the same point is I. Larskii, "Na rodinie. Missionerskii s"iezd," *Sovremennyi mir* 9, no. 167 (September 1908): 47–48. On the politicized representation of rural people, see Cathy A. Frierson, *Peasant Icons: Representations of Rural People in Late Nineteenth-Century Russia* (New York, 1993).

67. Iasevich-Borodaevskaia, *Bor'ba za vieru,* 376–77, 389. On the freedom of conscience legislation, see Peter Waldron, "Religious Reform after 1905: Old Believers and the Orthodox Church," *Oxford Slavonic Papers,* New Series no. 20 (1987): 110–39.

68. Iasevich-Borodaevskaia, *Bor'ba za vieru,* 391.

69. Ibid., 392.

70. *Utrenniaia zviezda,* no. 19 (10 May 1913): 2.

71. Ibid., 1–2.

72. *Zhurnal zasiedanii missionerskago sovieta po sektantskim dielam Khar'kovskoi eparkhii, byvshikh 2–5 sentiabria 1896 goda* (Khar'kov, 1896), 33, found in RGIA, f. 1574, op. 2, d. 126, l. 62.

73. Aleksii (Dorodnitsyn), *Religioznoe-ratsionalisticheskoe dvizhenie,* 409.

74. Ibid., 424. See page 510 where he explains that "the people organically felt the threatening trouble and struggled with the sect, but it was the battle of a dark, unenlight-ened, and impotent [*bezpravnoi*] mass, which did not know how to defend its convictions through word and action and therefore [the battle] was carried out in a disorderly, spontaneous way."

75. Ibid., 509–10. For an example of similar arguments, made in 1914, about the violence Baptists did to the Orthodox family and village, and the responsibility of the state to protect the Orthodox, see Al. Vvedenskii, "Gosudarstvo i tserkov' v otnoshenii k sektantam," *Golos Tserkvi* 3, no. 3 (March 1914): 204–11; no. 5 (May 1914): 162–67.

76. "Plody 'svobody soviesty' (Iz Tuapse)," *Vieche,* 20 August 1909, found in RGIA, f. 821, op. 133, d. 301, l. 5. Other examples include RGIA, f. 821, op. 133, d. 194, ll. 12, 15. See also Burds, "A Culture of Denunciation," 53.

77. "Selianin," "Baptistskaia propaganda," *Kolokol,* no. 1266 (11 June 1910). Clipping found in RGIA, f. 821, op. 133, d. 194, l. 7.

78. *Gosudarstvennaia Duma, Stenograficheskiia otchety,* Third Duma, session 2, 24 May 1909, 1939–1941.

79. See Paul W. Werth's essay in this volume.

80. RGIA, f. 821, op. 194, d. 254, l. 33.

81. See, for example, RGIA, f. 821, op. 133, d. 194; f. 1284, op. 185, d. 49, l. 60; f. 1284, op. 185 (1908), d. 83, l. 78; *Baptist,* no. 10 (1911): 77; no. 11 (1908): 39; no. 15 (1910): 116; *Bratskii listok,* no. 9 (1909): 10; and Iasevich-Borodaevskaia, *Bor'ba za vieru,* 75.

82. RGIA, f. 821, op. 133, d. 289, l. 490b.

83. A similar pragmatism can be seen in the evolution of religious toleration in the United States. See William G. McLoughlin, *Soul Liberty: The Baptists' Struggle in New England, 1630–1833* (Hanover, N.H., 1991), ix–xi.

9

Prayer and the Politics of Place: Molokan Church Building, Tsarist Law, and the Quest for a Public Sphere in Late Imperial Russia

Nicholas B. Breyfogle

⸺⸺·◦⦚◦·⸺⸺

On January 30, 1892, the Baku police entered a building belonging to I. F. Kolesnikov with orders forcibly to seal it and evict those on the premises. The authorities believed that Kolesnikov had built and was operating a Molokan prayer house without the necessary state authorization, and they wanted to put a stop to this "crime." It was neither the first nor last time in the late imperial period that tsarist authorities compulsorily shut down—or even razed—churches, temples, or other spiritual buildings erected by any one of Russia's numerous sectarian denominations (*sektanty*). In this case, however, the police intervention was only one episode in a longer confrontation between Kolesnikov and the tsarist state over civil and religious rights for Molokans. The affair ultimately involved two trials. The first stemmed from an ultimately unsuccessful lawsuit Kolesnikov filed against the Baku provincial governor, Rogge, claiming that the seizure of his property had been an arbitrary and unlawful violation of his rights as a Russian subject. The second was a widely publicized criminal trial held in the chambers of the Baku Justice of the Peace at which Kolesnikov was found guilty of illegally constructing a Molokan church.

Although Kolesnikov's story is one of twofold legal defeat, it was nonetheless a watershed moment for Russia's Molokans, both symbolically and in their lived experience. In response, they lauded Kolesnikov for championing their demands for religious rights despite state opposition. Most important, however, Kolesnikov's case represented the first significant indication—and

222

simultaneously also a future catalyst—of a series of fundamental changes in Molokan communities that would appear with ever accelerating speed from the 1880s on. These changes involved Molokan religiosity, their communal and institutional development, and their aspirations to take part in tsarist Russia's evolving public sphere.

On one level, construction of a prayer house, whether permitted or not, represented a significant transformation in the religious practice of these non-conformist Christians. For most of their existence, they theologically eschewed specially designated sacred spaces of any sort, believing instead that true Christians could meet to worship God anywhere. During the nineteenth century, Molokans had few if any church buildings and most often met in rooms of private houses for prayer services.[1] This practice blurred, for Molokans, the distinction between sacred and secular space (as well as private and public space), a distinction that both the tsarist state and the Orthodox Church upheld in their religious policies. By the end of the century, however, Molokan notions of sacred space were changing, although the community continued to debate the spiritual necessity of church buildings long after they began to build them. The shift to church building offers a small window onto the mechanisms of religious change among Molokans. Notably doctrinal or theological considerations, while certainly significant, seem not to have played the defining role in bringing on this shift (or at least do not appear in the documentary record). Instead, personal conflicts and what we might call practical considerations (such as changing tsarist laws, space issues, and efforts to unite discrete, small congregations) were decisive.

On another level, the Kolesnikov prayer house is indicative of a broader process of religious and social institutionalization within the Molokan community. This institutionalization, in turn, illuminates both the Molokans' increasing presence in Baku's public sphere and also their growing restiveness for expanded public roles and civil rights. Despite Antonio Gramsci's famous claim that Russian "civil society is primordial and gelatinous," recent scholarship has unveiled the existence of tsarist Russia's own configuration of civil society with an active public sphere—one defined in part by extensive interconnections and symbioses between state and society.[2] Yet these recent studies have tended to focus on secular individuals and institutions as the building blocks of the public sphere at the expense of the contributions of religious communities.[3] In another context, Peter van der Veer has recently argued that "religion [was] crucial for the creation of the public sphere" in both Great Britain and India, pointing, in the case of the former, to the "organizational activities" and "new communications networks" of evangelical Christianity in Western Europe as "instrumental in creating a modern public sphere on which the nation-state could be built."[4] Similarly the Kolesnikov case underscores that, for Molokans, like religious minorities throughout Europe, the development of sacred architectural space through church building was intricately linked with their aspirations and engagement in Russia's public life. Churches offered a physical presence where individuals could meet freely not only for worship but also to advance their religious, social, and political agendas through a burgeoning print culture, educational programs, philanthropic activities, business endeavors, and critical efforts to expand their religious and civil rights.[5]

Throughout, the Kolesnikov incident sheds light on the nature of tsarist religious policy and the parameters of religious toleration in the transitional period between 1864 and 1905. During these years tsarist officials extended, in uneven stages, partial toleration to religious nonconformists such as sectarians and Old Believers. With each post-emancipation legislative act (such as in 1864, 1874, and 1883), the government endeavored to extend certain privileges and civil liberties to religious minorities, while simultaneously striving to maintain the preeminence of the Orthodox Church and to prevent the spread of other Christian communities. As the Kolesnikov trials underscore, it was a delicate balancing act that required tsarist officials to police ever more permeable boundaries of acceptability. Ideas of religious toleration were open to diverse interpretations by different administrative units, and tsarist officials (at various levels) did what they could to construe the laws in ways they found most beneficial. Simultaneously these changing laws energized many religious communities, the Molokans among them, to take advantage of the new rights and to use the Great Reform judicial structures to push for even greater freedoms. The tension between religious toleration and support for the Orthodox Church took on new characteristics after the watershed religious laws of 1903–1905, which brought an end to official religious discrimination (although unofficial maltreatment persisted) and extended religious civil rights including not only toleration (*veroterpimost'*) but eventually certain forms of freedom of conscience (*svoboda sovesti*). Offering the possibility of a relatively unrestrained public spiritual and communal life, the post-1905 era was a golden age of sorts for Molokans, who rapidly expanded their activities in Russian society and their demands for civil rights.[6]

Molokan History and Religion

Molokans first appear in the Russian written record in the mid-eighteenth century, particularly in the southern Russian provinces of Tambov and Voronezh, and developed during the nineteenth century into one of the numerically largest Christian nonconformist communities, with congregations across the empire, from the Caucasus to Siberia, Ukraine, and Central Asia.[7] They can be classified as one of Russia's "indigenous" Christian sects (along with Dukhobors, for example) that broke away from the Orthodox Church to embrace different forms of theology and practice. They are distinguished by their Russian origin from "imported" Western Protestant sects, such as Baptists and Mennonites, and also from Old Believers (*staroobriadtsy*), who considered themselves the true practitioners of Orthodoxy.

As part of a state effort to segregate these nonconformists from Orthodox Russians, beginning in 1830 tens of thousands of Molokans migrated to the South Caucasian regions of the Russian Empire, either through forcible exile or voluntary resettlement. Although the settlers suffered greatly in their early years in hostile surroundings, in time they proved to be not only model Russian colonists but also among the most prosperous of the empire's peasants. Approximately one thousand of these Molokans came to live in Baku, where some, like Kolesnikov, became relatively wealthy.

Religiously, Molokans denied the legitimacy of the Orthodox Church and its sacraments, saints, churches, signs of the cross, icons, and relics. They refuted the need for priests and hierarchies (or any other mediators in a relationship with God).[8]

Molokans also believed that the Scriptures constituted the only true source of religious authority, but they interpreted these texts in allegorical or spiritual terms. For example, they did not practice water baptism because they understood the word "water" in the non-literal sense of "living water" (John 7:38) and believed that baptism was concluded by hearing the word of God and living in a godly way. The Molokans' teachings also had important social and political components, which led them to question the power of the tsarist state, refuse military service, and preach social equality and an end to serfdom.

Molokans and Churches: Theology and Law

Kolesnikov's construction of a separate prayer house went against long-standing Molokan beliefs regarding the need for special buildings designated as sacred spaces. For most of their existence, Molokans met to pray in the private residences of particular members of their congregations or outdoors in the woods or fields. As such, Molokan religious services required few material objects: usually a table for the Bible and perhaps other religious texts, and occasionally benches to seat the congregation, with men and women seated separately. As one Russian musicologist noted on a visit to the Tiflis Molokans in the early twentieth century: "The temple, without the least adornment, with no gold, silver, precious stones or rich stuffs, with no burning of expensive incense, made a deep impression. Its magnificence did not consist in the showy richness of the place, but in sincere religious disposition." A Molokan added, "We do not believe that our places of worship need to be ornamented in any way with pictures, images, stained windowpanes. The sincerity of man is the best ornamentation of His place of worship."[9]

As such, Molokans attached little importance to special buildings believing instead that the true "church" of Christ was not in a place but in the meeting of true believers, wherever they may be.[10] A Molokan author, N. F. Kudinov, noted: "About Churches and splendorous temples, they said it is not the place that paints the people but the people the place. The Church of Christ or the temple of God is the gathering together of the faithful in God, in accordance with the teachings of the apostles." He pointed to several texts in the New Testament to provide scriptural support, such as 1 Corinthians 3:16, "Do you not know that you are God's temple and that God's Spirit dwells in you?" and 1 Peter 2:5, "and like living stones be yourselves built into a spiritual house."[11]

While Molokans themselves eschewed formal churches for doctrinal reasons, the laws of the tsarist state, which closely guarded the prerogatives of the Orthodox Church, also imposed a prohibition against church building. Molokans, to a certain degree, made a virtue out of necessity, since, even if they wanted to build separate prayer houses, they were legally barred from doing so. The state's concern with Molokan churches developed out of their trepidation over Old Believer churches, chapels, and monasteries. As was often the case in tsarist religious policy, Molokans were initially subsumed in this prohibition directed at Old Believers.[12] By the late 1830s, however, tsarist laws and administrative practice increasingly came to target Molokan religious life specifically in an effort to stamp out the sect. A decree of February 13, 1837, for example, banned Molokan services for worship, whether they took place in private homes or in huts specially constructed for such purposes. Any Molokan church that was discovered was to be torn down immediately, the parts sold off and the owners punished.[13]

These statutes directly impeded Molokan religious life. Kolesnikov pointed out in his petitions that tsarist restrictions were part of the reason they had "gather[ed] together in private residential houses" in order to worship God.[14] In fact, whatever the foundations of their faith said about churches, there were certain Molokan communities that would have built some form of designated prayer house had it not been for tsarist prohibitions. Molokans from the village of Topchi in Shirvan Province, for instance, petitioned the emperor in 1838 complaining that the local administration was preventing them from opening a communal chapel in which to conduct their religious services.[15] In addition, unlike most of their co-religionists, Molokans of the Don branch (*Molokane Donskogo tolka*) were not doctrinally opposed to having designated prayer houses yet found themselves unable to do so because of state restrictions. The religious teachings of the Don Molokans diverged in a number of respects from other strains of the Molokan faith, including a willingness to fulfill certain sacraments (although without priests) and a readiness to recognize state power.[16] In an article of 1870, one Don Molokan expressed the group's belief in the necessity of church buildings.

> From all of this it is clear that the community of believers comprises a living church. However, it is necessary to the community to have a place—a house for prayer and the carrying out of all church demands. Gathering together for this in a residential house or other building is not conducive. The community acted in this way out of extreme need; and for this reason if the benevolent government would be so kind as to permit the Molokans to build a separate house for their prayer services, then the followers of the Don branch of the Molokans will forever thank the government with heartfelt feelings and pray to God about the government's good deeds.[17]

To be sure, such laws did not prevent Molokans from meeting to pray, but they did tend to restrict meetings to private homes where they could more easily hide from government surveillance. Especially in the South Caucasus where the tsarist administration was relatively weak, Molokans found themselves with greater religious freedom than was often the case in the central provinces.[18] From the 1850s on, most tsarist officials in the Caucasus knew that Molokans had some form of designated space for prayer, often residential, and yet took few actions to stop these activities.[19]

Kolesnikov and the Trials of Church Building

Despite traditional Molokan beliefs, three factors appear to have been most important in setting Kolesnikov on his path to constructing a separate religious building. First, the changing context of tsarist laws emboldened Kolesnikov to pursue the construction project. The issue of prayer houses was a pivotal component of the most recent comprehensive law on Christian dissenters: the decree of May 3, 1883. This law, which revised the statutes of 1864, was the culmination of more than twenty years of discussions in various St. Petersburg commissions concerning the place of Old Believers and sectarians in Russian polity and society. The 1883 statute granted "schismatics" seemingly blanket rights to "carry out communal prayer, fulfill spiritual rites, and conduct worship to God according to their rites both in private homes and equally in buildings specially designated for that function."[20] For the sectarians, the new laws dramatically expanded their freedom to practice their faith unmolested and allowed them for the first time to have their own buildings specially designated for religious functions— and Kolesnikov strove to take advantage of this opportunity.[21] However, other articles of the decree placed a series of restrictions on these rights in an effort to ensure that the sectarians did not bathe in too much freedom. Sectarians and Old Believers were required to receive permission from their local governor or the Ministry of the Interior (MVD) (in consultation with the Synod) if they wished to repair or build religious structures—and such permission frequently proved elusive, particularly because the Synod was staunchly opposed to it. Significantly, for the Kolesnikov case, the statute continued not to prohibit prayer meetings in private homes, which legislation had allowed since 1864.

If the 1883 changes in religious policy encouraged Kolesnikov to build his church, personal factors and power struggles among the Baku Molokans also played an important role. By building the prayer house, he hoped to free himself and his followers from communal turmoil and, in the opinion of one observer, to gain "supremacy among the people in the congregation."[22] The discord reflected, in part, a confrontation between the Kolesnikov and Kashcheev families over both business and religious issues. Kolesnikov had arrived in 1862 as a poor orphan along with his two brothers. In the succeeding years, they amassed an enormous fortune through various trade and industrial ventures (including the burgeoning oil business), becoming merchants of the second guild. The Kashcheev family arrived in Baku a year later, and they, too, became millionaires through the oil trade. As one Tiflis Molokan described the ensuing conflict, "[The Kolesnikovs] soon appeared as opponents of Kashcheev and his children, both in terms of Church affairs and issues of trade. . . . Kashcheev strongly came to hate Kolesnikov, and an uninterrupted quarrel continued in the church for twenty-five years."[23] Kolesnikov and one of the Kashcheev brothers vied for prominence in the Baku Molokan community, speaking frequently at services and meetings, acting as elders (*nastavniki*) and presbyters (*presvitery*), and doing what they could to determine the spiritual direction of the community. Much to Kashcheev's frustration, however, it appears that the congregation more readily supported Kolesnikov, who had a wide knowledge of the Scriptures and even spent five years studying ancient Hebrew in order to read texts in the original.[24]

In tandem with these personal conflicts was apparently a series of spiritual and social struggles (unspecified in extant sources) within the Baku Molokan community, and the fallout from these difficulties helped to impel Kolesnikov to construct his building. Tensions grew to such a degree in 1884 that efforts on the part of one unnamed Molokan elder to suspend another from the congregation— at least the second attempt in a few months—"produced a large commotion in the local Molokan community, which even to this moment cannot calm itself, and which is divided into two parties."[25]

It also seems clear that Kolesnikov proposed a new building—and found widespread support for it among the Molokan community—because of increasingly insufficient space for a growing congregation and the desire to unite disparate congregations. Before Kolesnikov's prayer house, the Baku Molokans met in four locations to pray and carry out various religious ceremonies; each one was in the private home of a member of the congregation, and none was large enough to hold the entire congregation of approximately one thousand Molokans. When one of the private homes "fell into disrepair and was threatening danger," the Molokans who had gathered there embraced the idea of moving their services into Kolesnikov's house.[26]

In the context of this legal climate and community troubles, in late 1884 or early 1885 Kolesnikov submitted two requests for permission to build, one to the gubernatorial administration to construct a Molokan prayer house on a plot of land that he owned in Baku's Kubin Square, and another to the Baku town Duma to erect a private residence next door on the same property. He submitted two sets of architectural plans, with a different layout for each building. Despite his aspirations, however, Kolesnikov received permission only for the residential structure. Here, as was frequently the case, Synod officials blocked authorization, arguing that "the construction of a new prayer house in the town of Baku, given the existing ones, could not be permitted as it posed a powerful danger to Orthodoxy."[27]

Kolesnikov was officially informed that permission was denied in 1887, but by then it was a moot point since he had already erected a building on his property a year earlier. He claimed in later testimony that this edifice was the private residence authorized by the city council. However, as is evident from the sketch in figure 9.1, the house was designed with one extremely large central room linked to two smaller rooms, a hallway, and an entranceway—a layout that later testimony indicates followed the architectural designs of the structure originally designated in his petitions as the prayer house.[28] Whatever the building's original intent, for approximately one and a half years Kolesnikov lived in this building before moving to other quarters erected on the lot.

In October 1889, supported by eighty other Molokan signatories, Kolesnikov petitioned the emperor for state authorization to re-designate his new building as a prayer house. Among many arguments, he tried to entice the tsar's support by saying that in "memory of the visitation to the city of Baku of your Imperial Highness," he wanted to convert his "private residential house" into "a prayer house in which the Molokan community . . . can freely conduct prayer services, carrying to God heartfelt prayers about the health of You and Your August Family."[29] All these promises and gilded language were of no avail, however, and the MVD turned down the request.

It is worth reflecting on why the MVD denied Kolesnikov's 1889 petition. Most notable is that the explanation given by the Department of General Affairs

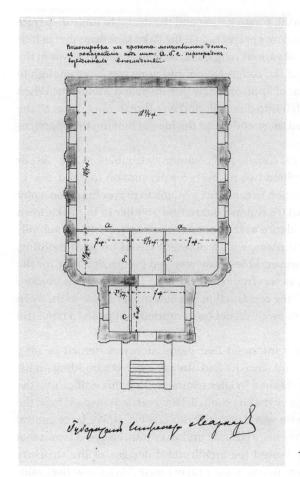

Figure 9.1. Architectural plans for I. F. Kolesnikov's Molokan Church (Prayer House) in Baku. *RGIA, f. 1284, op. 22–1893, d. 81, l. 21.*

(DOD) for its actions diverges from the laws as they existed on the books, and, consciously or unconsciously, the MVD sidestepped the legal code. The MVD–DOD asserted that because the Molokans were recognized as "one of the more pernicious" sects, they were not permitted to build communal chapels. Yet the edict of 1883 not only had granted this right to the Molokans but at the same time had done away with the previous classification system that divided the sectarians into more or less harmful categories, in theory equalizing treatment for them.[30]

In many respects the MVD's misreading—or outright defiance—of the rules reflects the ambiguous and reluctant nature of tsarist steps toward religious rights. It also demonstrates the frequent disjuncture between tsarist laws and administrative practice in late imperial Russia. Kolesnikov's case was by no means unique. When Molokans from the village of Nizhnie Akhty in Erevan Province petitioned numerous times between 1897 and 1905 for permission to open an already constructed prayer house, they, too, were denied for similar reasons: that as "a most pernicious sect" they were not entitled to the benefits of the May 3, 1883, law. A great deal of confusion arose at different levels of officialdom as to how to act in this case. While the MVD denied authorization, the Erevan governor, Count Tizengauzen, argued that the 1883 legislation gave the Nizhnie Akhty villagers full rights to build the church and he personally saw no reason not to permit it. The Chief Administrator of the Caucasus, G. S. Golitsyn, was more confused: he generally agreed with Tizengauzen's interpretation but was unsure how to integrate the 1883 rules with unspecified MVD circulars of 1894 dealing with the Shtundists.[31]

Additionally, the denial of the applicability of the 1883 laws to Molokans regarding religious questions stands in stark contrast to other decisions on the part of the MVD concerning the Molokans' economic prerogatives. When officials in the South Caucasus approached the MVD asking whether the 1883 statutes concerning entitlement to merchant status, and to freer movement for trade purposes, applied to the Molokans, the MVD replied unequivocally that it did and that Molokans were now granted the same rights (and restrictions) in these business matters as the Orthodox population. Given the Molokans' significant economic role in the South Caucasus and elsewhere, it is not surprising, perhaps, that the MVD would be willing to implement the 1883 regulations differently when it suited the ministry.[32]

Despite repeated prohibitions, Kolesnikov allowed the building to be used regularly for Molokan prayer services and meetings without payment from March 1890 on, which quickly became known to the authorities. In response, the provincial administration ordered that Kolesnikov be brought to criminal accountability for allowing sectarian worship in an illegally constructed prayer house. An inquest was opened in the autumn of 1891, but the administrative system was slow and it was not until December 1893 that the Georgian-Imeretian Office of the Synod ordered that Kolesnikov (and many of the Molokans who prayed in the building) be brought to trial.[33]

However, because the Molokans had refused to stop their prayer services despite active police surveillance, Rogge had already ordered Kolesnikov's building forcibly shut down and sealed on January 30, 1892. The report describing the closure of the prayer house indicates that the police found three tenants and their families there, two occupying the smaller rooms and the third living in the larger hall, where stacks of benches lined the walls. Since the police were concerned solely with the room where Molokan services were held, they only sealed the large hall, allowing two of the three tenants to remain in their apartments.[34]

By not waiting for the impending decision of the court trial, the governor opened up the opportunity for Kolesnikov to argue that he had acted arbitrarily in shutting down the church. Rogge countered that he was only following official orders which gave him the right—indeed, required him—to act as he had. He pointed, in particular, to a circular sent out by the chief Caucasian administrator S. A. Sheremetev in 1892 that laid out general guidelines (from the specific case of a Subbotnik temple) for what governors were to do in cases of unauthorized church building on the part of sectarians. Sheremetev asserted that these cases were to be correctly investigated by police and then sent to the court institutions for the appropriate trials. But he also underscored that the provincial administration was not deprived of the right to close such prayer houses on its own authority. Rogge asserted further that, according to general laws, "governors and all official people are required, with all means in their possession, to prevent and suppress any criminal actions," and he believed that this is exactly what he was doing in the Molokan case.[35]

Soon after his building was sealed, Kolesnikov filed a lawsuit against Rogge. He took two approaches in the suit. He argued that he had broken no laws and that the decree of 1883 granted Molokans the right to carry out their faith as they wished. At the same time he asserted that Rogge's order was an illegitimate challenge to Kolesnikov's economic rights, and that he was losing rental money from the building with each passing month and demanded remuneration from Rogge. Two and a half years later, on December 8, 1894, the Senate's Cassation Department dismissed the case, declaring that Kolesnikov's arguments were not convincing.[36]

Earlier, in January 1894, the Baku Justice of the Peace found Kolesnikov guilty of building a Molokan prayer house without state authorization.[37] Throughout the trial one detail was considered most important for both the prosecution and defense: whether the building in question was classified as a private residence or a prayer house. The distinction was crucial to the case, because the 1883 laws permitted Molokans to conduct services of worship according to their faith in their private homes without any prior permission. If the building was considered a residence, then Kolesnikov (and the Molokans who worshiped there) had committed no crime. But if the building was legally defined as a prayer house, they were guilty.

The state and the sectarians went through an elaborate dance of categorizing the building. This definitional process reflects the complexities and difficulties—and the sometimes incongruous results—generated in the gray zones of the partial toleration that characterized the laws of 1864 and 1883. It seems clear that Kolesnikov knew he was building a prayer house and yet had to prove it was not. In contrast, the prosecutors had to demonstrate, without much evidence on their side, that it was without doubt a church. For his part, Kolesnikov maintained that the building was simply the private residence approved by the Baku town council, in which Molokans happened to meet for religious services. According to reports from the trial, Kolesnikov argued that the large hall did not make his building a church:

> He built the large hall in that building for weddings or for the meeting at his house of a large number of guests. By the request of [other Molokans] he permitted them gratis from time to time during large holidays to carry out prayer services in his building according to the Molokan rite, and so they did conduct prayer services there because they did not have a big building.[38]

He bolstered his case by noting that two separate police inspections of the house found in the building "all the things necessary for permanent habitation."[39] Kolesnikov's lawyer at the trial added:

> Judging from the furniture described in the [police report] . . . one can come to the conclusion that the building was intended for habitation. The external signs of the building also cannot serve as criteria from which to judge about whether the building was specifically designed for a chapel.[40]

The prosecution, of course, worked to prove the opposite—"that the room was specially and only designated" for Molokan prayer services.[41] The police officer testified that the building that was actually built matched the architectural plans that Kolesnikov originally submitted for the prayer house and not those of the residence. The prosecution also called in an Orthodox priest, Potashev, as an expert witness to substantiate official reports. Given the stipulations of the law codes, he found himself required to assert that the building resembled a Molokan church, despite the absence of any tradition of church architecture among the Molokans.

> Judging from the external appearance and internal decoration of the building . . . [including] the benches, tables, cupboards, lamps; and the form of the building—an oblong quadrangle—he comes to the full conviction that this building is intended to serve not as living quarters but rather for Molokan prayer. This fact is also indicated by the absence of a throne and images. A similar type of structure is recognized by the Molokans; a chapel according to their religious views should have the form of a regular room. The hall of the building is in all ways not conducive for habitation. That this is a chapel is clear from the fact that this building is entirely fenced off from the remaining outbuildings.[42]

His argument approached the outlandish when, according to newspaper accounts of the trial, Potashev argued that "the attributes of a residential place of habitation" were clear evidence that the structure was in fact a church. The more it resembled a residence, he asserted, the more likely it was a Molokan prayer house. Not unexpectedly, Kolesnikov's lawyer challenged Potashev's claims, noting: "if one followed the conclusions of the expert, then one can conclude that any large room can be designated a prayer house."[43] That said, the lawyer himself was also not averse to making improbable explanations. He tried to argue that the building could not be a Molokan prayer house because of the absence of crosses affixed to the walls. Yet Molokans doctrinally eschewed graven images of any sort in their worship, including crosses.[44] In the end, the justice of the peace found the evidence and argumentation of the prosecution convincing. For this crime, Kolesnikov was sentenced to two months in prison and required either to raze the structure or renovate it into a residential dwelling. In contrast, the Molokans who had worshiped in the building were found not guilty.[45]

Changing Architectures of Prayer and Community

Kolesnikov's attempt to build a prayer house for Molokans in Baku was one of the earliest examples of a larger, empire-wide change in religious practice during the imperial period. Molokans shifted away from a refutation of the need for specially designated spaces in which to worship to an acceptance of purpose-specific sacred space, which was considered essential to the fulfillment of their Christianity and which increasingly took on distinct architectural characteristics. A flurry of church construction efforts is apparent across Russia from the 1890s on, and especially after 1905. Notably Molokan church-building movements appear to have been part of a larger zeitgeist in Christian religious life in Russia, involving, each in its own way and for its own reasons, Orthodox peasants, Old Believers, and Subbotniks.[46]

The change in practice toward more established churches was by no means an abrupt transformation. Molokans had met for decades to worship in the apartments and houses of certain of their members. Although not in specially designated buildings, the rooms used for this sort of prayer meeting generally became institutionalized as the place of worship, at times taking on enhanced meaning for the Molokans. Also, whereas in the early years Molokans would crowd into whatever space they could find in a member's house, later they began to build residences with design elements—such as an oversized room— that deliberately distinguished them as special prayer buildings. In this way, Kolesnikov's multi-use building, with its space for residents and for prayer meetings, was a further step in a longer evolution. At the same time, the very blurring between a residential house and a church in the Kolesnikov case—so disconcerting to tsarist and Orthodox authorities—took on a very different meaning for the Molokans themselves for whom mono-functional sacred space was not necessarily a particularly familiar concept.[47]

Moreover, despite this wave of church building, the transformation to designated religious space was by no means complete or uncontested, and was not necessarily accompanied by simultaneous changes in theology. Indeed, the struggles over the meaning of space—and who defines it—that were at the heart of the standoff between Kolesnikov and state power were also being played out within the Molokan community, albeit in quite different ways. Even after many of these churches were up and running, some Molokans polemicized against their use, asserting that the faithful could meet anywhere and that churches were unnecessary and even contrary to proper Christianity. Notably, when Molokans began to publish their religious doctrines after 1905, these books did not mention the massive Molokan construction projects and uniformly affirmed the traditional views.[48] In addition, there were writers in the Molokan periodical press who raised their voices in direct opposition to the church-building trend. In anguished pleas, they turned to examples from the Scriptures and the lives of the early Christian fathers as clear evidence that true Christians should eschew church buildings. Grievously, in their view, the new Molokan preference for prayer houses was diverting them from the correct path that had long distinguished them from the Orthodox Church and its "idols."[49]

Molokan erection of prayer houses around the empire occurred for reasons not dissimilar to the Kolesnikov case, with the spiritual reasons for church construction hard to discern. Molokan proponents of churches note that they had been unable properly to fulfill their spiritual needs when praying in people's homes, but they do not specify why. They assert that certain architectural and design elements of larger churches would aid them in reaching up to God, and to filling a certain, ill-defined void that they felt. At the same time, Molokans declared their desire to build such prayer houses as a way to bring together their communities (both locally and nationally), and to break down any divisions that might exist among them. Prayer as a single community would permit them more readily to fulfill their spiritual needs. Yet, while earlier Molokan writings substantiated their belief that church buildings were unnecessary through multiple references to the Scriptures, those who advocated new church buildings tended not to take this tack. Occasionally they might argue that Jesus had not specifically excluded the possibility of praying in churches, and had Himself preached in the Jerusalem temple, citing Luke 21: 37–38, for example. However, these biblical justifications appear infrequently. In contrast, those Molokan voices that publicly decried the trend to church construction, like their counterparts from the early nineteenth century, marshaled a vast array of biblical citations as evidence that any prayer house built by human hands went against Christ's intentions.[50]

Examples of Molokan church building from around the empire help to elucidate these broader patterns.[51] Like Kolesnikov in Baku, Molokans in Tiflis also endeavored to construct distinct prayer houses that would serve as the focal point of communal activity and institutions. The first Molokan congregation appeared in Tiflis in 1840, and not long afterward the two primary assemblies—Peski and Kuki, named for the neighborhoods where they met—began to convene each week in one or another apartment to worship.[52] However, in 1888 and 1897, respectively, the Kuki and Peski congregations bought land and built two-story communal prayer houses (the Peski one worth twelve thousand rubles) in order to overcome problems with lack of space, structural disrepair, and fire damage.[53]

Additional church building was taking place in smaller Molokan settlements in rural Transcaucasia. For example, beginning in 1897 and continuing through to 1905, the Molokans of Nizhnie Akhty petitioned the authorities on at least four occasions for permission to open an already completed prayer house in their village.[54] In their various appeals, the villagers underscored how they had previously met in private homes in order to carry out their worship, but that the absence of a specialized architectural space was preventing them from fulfilling their spiritual rites and "religious feelings." The 1900 petition of Fedil Ivanovich Shubin noted the need for a separate church because of the "constant and unceasing flow of tears, tormenting sorrow, and sadness of our children about not having a prescribed house and no other asylum necessary for prayer worship to God of those believing Christians."[55]

Molokans of the Siberian city of Blagoveshchensk also dedicated an impressive-looking church in 1908, "replete with polished marble columns/walls" (figure 9.2). Like the Baku Molokans, their co-religionists on the Amur were successful economically and played a prominent role in urban life. Indeed, Blagoveshchensk was commonly known as "Molokan city." These Siberian Molokans began their efforts to build a prayer house in 1894 when they petitioned the town Duma for a building lot for a church, noting as reasons for this endeavor a lack of space and cramped quarters in private houses and the changes in laws that had once prevented Molokan prayer houses. In contrast to Kolesnikov's troubles, the municipal board (made up of eighteen Orthodox and fourteen Molokan members) immediately approved the request. When a lone dissenting Orthodox voice noted that the Molokans required MVD approval, the land allotment was made conditional on such permission (for which they apparently waited until after 1905). The church was built with an attached school that the Blagoveshchensk Molokans named in honor of Alexander I.[56]

In Baku the church building movement culminated in 1915 when Molokans in that city came together to erect a new prayer house, this one substantially

Figure 9.2. Molokan Church (Prayer House) in Blagoveshchensk,
dedicated 1908, photograph c. 1920. *Photograph courtesy of
Edward Samarin.*

bigger than Kolesnikov's. They still felt that they were suffering from a lack of
space, "cooped up in cramped personal houses, with little air and little light,
where it was not difficult to long for space, light, and air." Through the church,
Baku Molokans hoped to bring about the merger of their five different congregations, and to begin to break down the doctrinal and procedural differences between their communities.[57] They felt that they could not achieve this
unification in Kolesnikov's church (re-opened after 1905), in part because he
had fallen out of favor with the community and was dogged by accusations of
wrong-doing.[58]

The 1915 church reflects the development of certain design elements and
aesthetics that were embryonic in the earlier church building endeavors both in
Baku and Tiflis. In particular, Molokans in the South Caucasus appear to have
settled on a two-storied structure as appropriate for their churches, in which
the lower floor was symbolically linked to the body and the upper floor to the
spirit, a physical arrangement reflecting the "subordination of the flesh to the
soul." The building also demonstrated the Molokans' opposition to decoration
of any sort, with plain interior walls and outside elements. At the same time, as
they moved out of praying in the cramped rooms of private apartments, they
reveled in the "space and light" of the second floor which had tall ceilings and
seventeen long windows on three sides of the prayer house. "One receives

the feeling as if people, weary in a tight darkness, suddenly had escaped into freedom, to the light."[59]

Just how important prayer houses had become for this religious community in fin-de-siècle Russia can be seen in the rising wave of Molokan requests for emigration from the South Caucasus that began in the late nineteenth century and then accelerated after 1900. As part of a larger package of complaints about tsarist treatment, Molokans specifically mentioned government prohibitions on separate prayer houses. Indeed, this very frustration impelled many Molokans to leave Russia at the turn of the century—most traveling halfway around the world to California, where they quickly constructed new church buildings as part of their immigrant community development.[60] Moreover, the significance of designated, communal prayer houses is apparent in the large number of signatures attached to the various petitions for churches sent to the government;[61] in the crowds of Molokan spectators who overflowed out of the courtroom at Kolesnikov's trial waiting with baited breath for the resolution;[62] and in the honors, praise, and rise in stature that Kolesnikov received as a result of his willingness to build the new prayer house for the Molokan community and to suffer tsarist persecution for his faith.[63] The importance of prayer houses can, finally, be witnessed in the celebrations that Molokans put on after 1905 for the opening of new churches. These jubilees could last for many days; were filled with feasting, prayers, and much singing; included invited guests from other Molokan communities; and usually also involved tsarist provincial governors, officials, and dignitaries.[64]

Entering the Public Sphere: Molokans as "Civil Society"

In addition to being a crucial moment of change in Molokan religiosity that increasingly linked religious practice and architectural space, the efforts of Kolesnikov and others to build designated prayer houses represent the first act in a larger drama of Molokan institutionalization, standardization, and community building. This formalization was often embryonic and incomplete, particularly before 1905, and failed to achieve the desired ends even by the end of the old regime.[65] Nonetheless, Molokan institutionalization—an important process in its own right—was also an integral part of the increasing role that Molokans came to play in Russia's fledgling public sphere, especially in the South Caucasus and Siberia. As they took the first steps in institution building through designated prayer houses, Molokans came to take up a physical presence in the public arena. Their place in civil society was partly defined by what they did: political participation, philanthropic work, economic lobbying, publication endeavors, and the development of nongovernmental, voluntary organizations. It was also defined by what they demanded—greater civil rights and more freedom of action in Russian society—and by the tactics with which they went about pushing for these rights. At the origin of both these processes were changing notions of sacred space and the construction of churches.

Church Building as Community Building

Churches were a deliberate first step on the part of the Molokans to standardize not only the tenets and practices of their faith—as the 1915 Baku church underscores—but also the administration of their communities and the intercongregational relations between their different branches and geographic centers. Communal prayer buildings were to act as the hub from which newly organized social organizations, educational institutions, publication ventures, congresses, business ventures, and social activities would radiate.

Molokans considered schools and youth centers to be a crucial part of these new communal structures. Like the Blagoveshchensk Molokans, part of Kolesnikov's original plan was to attach to his church a Molokan school that would then give members of the congregation the opportunity to educate their children outside the state system and provide a standard religious and cultural curriculum for Molokan youth. In fact, schools, educational centers, and other youth organizations were considered of special importance to Molokans as a way to develop new religious leaders and protect their children from the religious advances of Orthodox and particularly Baptist proselytizers.[66]

Following on the shift to building prayer houses, and especially after 1905, Molokans embarked on a series of other forms of institution building as they evolved from a marginal, persecuted religious community into an increasingly established and influential subgroup of Russian society. Many Molokan congregations in the South Caucasus came to register themselves officially with the state, documenting their prayer buildings as their communal anchor. Other Molokan communities also took on increasingly elaborate organizational structures and institutional practices. Like their brethren in Tiflis, Vladikavkaz, and Kars, for instance, the Baku Molokans drew up a charter for an official association with rules and regulations concerning the administration of the community. "The goal of the Society is to unite all spiritual Christians-Molokans living in Baku and the Baku city region in a correctly organized Society for the development and fulfillment of the religious-moral and educational needs of its members and with the goal of mutual material support."[67]

The institutionalization project is vividly seen in two other post-1905 undertakings. The first was a series of congresses, often involving hundreds if not thousands of people, which brought together Molokans in the South Caucasus, and eventually Molokans from around the empire. These meetings generally had five goals: to celebrate their heritage, discuss the finer points of their religious beliefs, plan how best to ensure the growth and longevity of their faith, build national ties among Molokans and between Molokans and other sectarian communities in Russia, and highlight for the authorities all the Molokans' positive contributions to the Russian Empire.[68] Second, after 1905, Molokans rapidly developed their publishing efforts in an endeavor to document their past and provide a forum in which to discuss (and hopefully standardize) their faith. They began to produce a number of Molokan-oriented periodicals, such as *Molokanin, Molokanskii vestnik,* and *Dukhovnyi Khristianin.* At the same time, Molokan contributions to Russian print culture also included an explosion in the publication of prayer books, books on Molokan history, discussions of Christianity from the Molokan perspective, and explorations of Molokan life.[69]

Church Building and Molokan Civil Rights Aspirations

In addition to being an important part of Molokan institutionalization, the question of church building, from the 1880s to 1905, became a central point of Molokan demands for greater civil and religious rights and freedom of opportunity in tsarist society. Here, too, Molokan pressure for their rights moved in lockstep with the gradual shifts toward liberties and equal status taken by the tsarist government from the 1860s on. These political and legal changes made possible the Molokans' increasingly aggressive and conscious struggle for rights within the tsarist political system. For example, post-1905, Molokans asserted that they "more than others ... need freedom of conscience, speech, assembly, and unions, for these freedoms will open before them the doors of all state and societal institutions, and for this reason, naturally, the Manifesto of October 17, 1905, opened for them the hope for the elimination of all the evil that previously had prevented [their] spiritual growth."[70]

Kolesnikov's struggles to build his prayer house highlight the links between churches and Molokan strategies for increasing civil rights. He utilized three approaches to challenge the administrative decision that closed his prayer house, and thereby to protect and expand what he considered his legal rights. First, he hoped to take advantage of the newly developing judicial structures of the post-reform period as a means of challenging the powers of the administration and undo the sealing of his building. The Molokans saw the court system in general as a means to counter administrative orders and to carve out greater rights for themselves, even if (as in Kolesnikov's case) they had only a wobbly legal leg to stand on. In doing so, these dissenters took advantage of the tensions of the Great Reform period, here particularly the frequent butting of heads between an independent judiciary and the policy goals of the administration with its traditions of governing by decree. As Rogge himself noted about the Molokans in the Kolesnikov case:

> They venture to act toward those decrees with sharp disdain and dis-obedience, and when the established organs of power, fulfilling instruc-tions, . . . obstruct the possibility for them further to continue their crimes, then they turn to the court in the form of a civil lawsuit, banking that on the soil of private civil law relations some sort of more propitious solution could be possible for them.[71]

These Molokan legal tactics sent chills through the spines of tsarist admin-istrators in the South Caucasus, who feared for the "prestige of the local author-ities." As Rogge noted:

> The very demands of explanation during the civil legal proceedings cre-ate for the sectarians a form of relations to the local authorities that is undesirable in the highest degree. It is also not without danger because it provides the sectarians the means to believe that the orders of the administrative authorities can be changed by the court authorities, and that which is strictly forbidden by the first, will be met with some sort of encouragement and patronage on the part of the second.[72]

Kolesnikov also attempted to manipulate the ambiguities of the post-1883 religious laws by advancing Molokan legal interpretations in order to open up greater civil space for religious minorities. Indeed, his appeal to build a prayer house reflects the Molokans' increasing legal savvy. In arguing their cases, both Kolesnikov and the Molokans of Nizhnie Akhty demonstrated a clear knowl-edge of the laws affecting their religious lives. They did what they could to take advantage of the blurring boundaries of tsarist religious policy—particularly to point out when state agents were ignoring these laws and to exploit the uncer-tainty of laws that extended toleration while privileging Orthodoxy and that cre-ated crucial distinctions between churches and residences as worship sites.[73]

In protecting and expanding Molokan rights, Kolesnikov was not unwilling to bend the truth of his case. On the one hand, at the trial he rightly underscored that being a practicing Molokan and meeting to worship according to Molokan beliefs were no longer against the law, based on the 1883 rules. In both trials, however, he made the argument that his building was not a prayer house but the personal residence for which he had received permission from the town Duma. While not entirely untrue, Kolesnikov's contention that this was simply a private home was stretching veracity. Clearly from the outset Kolesnikov intended to build a space, preferably separate and use-specific, for Molokan prayer ser-vices and other religious functions. His assertions that the building was simply a residence reflect one (or both) of two possibilities. First, Kolesnikov, like many Molokans, may simply not have made the distinction between private home and church that the laws required him to make, because, traditionally, Molokans had not made such distinctions in their theology. Thus, for Kolesnikov, the building could be both a dwelling and a sacred space simultaneously. Second, and more likely in my view, Kolesnikov's assertions may also have been a conscious ploy to take advantage of the peculiarities of Russian law in order to better his legal claims. It was, of course, a quirk of the laws that the Molokans could hold as many religious services as they wanted in the building as long it was designated private space but were required to close the building if it was labeled a "church," even if no religious services took place there. Whatever the explanation, or some combination of the two, the nature of Russian laws which required a firm distinction between secular and sacred space created a gray zone in which Kolesnikov could press his case for Molokan rights.

In addition, compared to other subjects, Kolesnikov and other Molokans used the very dearth of their rights as an argument. Molokans in the South Caucasus were keenly aware of their second-class status—a situation they believed was barring the attainment of their spiritual enlightenment, economic well-being, philanthropic goals, and their ability to organize or institutionalize their communities.[74] In his 1889 petition to the emperor, Kolesnikov argued that the Molokans were denied many of the religious freedoms granted to other, even non-Russian, subjects and he pushed to be eligible for those rights, too.

> Under your rule, all *inovertsy* . . . have always and everywhere made use of religious freedom and freedom of worship. On the strength of High Mercy, given by You, all confessions can have their Temples and Prayer Houses and freely can carry out the rites according to their religious faith. But we, Spiritual Christians, belonging to the Molokan sect, are deprived of this great happiness and, for carrying out prayer services of worship, gather together in private residential houses.[75]

Whether Molokans knew it or not, their logic should have struck a chord with St. Petersburg administrators. The Special Commission that developed the regulations of 1864 concerning sectarians also noted the disparity—which they considered unwanted—between the religious rights of Christian nonconformists and those of non-Christians who generally held much greater freedoms.[76]

Elsewhere the Molokans used a somewhat different tactic, asserting that they had earned these rights through service to the state. In one petition, Molokans from Nizhnie Akhty argued that they deserved the opportunity to receive the prayer house because they had lived for fifty years in the South Caucasus, had proven themselves to be loyal subjects of the tsar, and would continue to do so.

As contributing subjects, their comparative lack of rights was insulting and unacceptable.[77]

Third, in tandem with his manipulation of Russian religious laws, Kolesnikov shifted the discussion from religious questions to economic rights, which the tsarist government was in less of a position to deny. He founded his lawsuit against Rogge on economic laws and freedom of trade, arguing that the governor had arbitrarily violated "his private interests, involving material losses." In this way, he attempted an end-run around the laws that might restrict Molokan religious practice and hoped to achieve his ends of greater religious freedom without actually having to confront the religious laws themselves. Kolesnikov claimed that he was losing as much as one hundred rubles a month from residential rents that he would otherwise have received. He also asserted that, without ventilation or renovation, the sealed building was beginning to fall apart. Thus he was threatened with the "complete destruction" of a house that cost more than twenty thousand rubles.[78]

The lawsuit, based on the economic losses, was even more of a stretch than Kolesnikov's statement that the house was private and residential. As Rogge was quick to point out, the tenants, with only one exception, had been allowed to remain in the house, and the closing of the large room should not have reduced Kolesnikov's rents substantially. Kolesnikov also declared, in his testimony before the Justice of the Peace, that he had allowed the Molokan community to use the property (for worship and prayer) without charge. In turn, Rogge argued: "The contract by which he calculated his losses and which forms the foundation of the lawsuit is a fiction."[79] Whether Kolesnikov's arguments were true or not is less important than the tactic he employed. Here he combined his use of the courts as a means to challenge administrative power with the strategic use of economic laws. In doing so, he strove to uphold the religious rights that he believed the state had granted to Molokans, to expand those rights even further, and, certainly, to enhance his role in the Molokan community.

Civic Activism and the Public Sphere

As institutionalization progressed in tandem with demands for civil and religious rights, Molokans took on an increasingly active role in the public life of the Russian Empire. As the Kolesnikov case suggests, church building became both a symbol of their growing presence in civic life and a physical cornerstone of public activity: a place to meet, talk, publish, educate, and develop economic and philanthropic activities. As elsewhere, the legal climate affected Molokan civic activism and encouraged them to take on a more public communal persona. In 1870, for example, a Molokan from Tavriia Province underscored how

the rulings of 1864 allowed him to carry out his faith more openly and emboldened him to publish an article in *Otechestvennye zapiski* about his faith and the
Molokan experience.[80]

Baku Molokans had already begun to take on public roles in the economy
through their active involvement in the oil business (and other industries) and
the growth of conspicuous wealth. Kolesnikov's church building was both a
manifestation of, and an outlet for, these growing riches. Moreover, Molokans
also became actively involved in local (and later national) politics. In the Baku
town Duma in 1894, for example, four of the fifty-three members were Molokans
(two representatives each from the Kolesnikov and Kashcheev families). With
this level of representation, Molokans had a disproportionately large presence
in local affairs, with 7.6 percent of the seats held by Molokans when they only
comprised a little less than 1 percent of the town's population. Molokans also
served disproportionately in the Lenkoran town Duma as a result of tsarist
laws that dramatically restricted Muslim political activity, and they were also
a notable presence in municipal governance in Tiflis. Molokans were a dominant force in the Blagoveshchensk town government as well, and, after 1905,
a small number of them were elected to the national Duma, again taking part
in Russia's larger political arena to a degree not justified by their numerical
presence.[81]

Molokans were also becoming more involved in national politics beginning
in the 1870s with public proclamations of support for the tsar and his government. While many of these declarations of endorsement and adulation were
used instrumentally, designed to attain one end or another, others appear to be
relatively heartfelt affirmations of loyalty. Whatever the origin, Molokans in late
imperial Russia were engaging with an approved public discourse concerning
the tsarist administration. In one of hundreds of examples, the newspaper *Kaspii*
noted that, on May 19, 1883, "on the day of the celebration of the holy coronation
of Their Imperial Highnesses, the Lenkoran Molokans assembled in a prayer
house and carried out warmhearted prayers for the health and productivity of
the emperor and empress."[82]

Significantly Molokans chose their prayer houses as the institutionalized
site from which to vocalize many of these announcements. In this way they linked
the development of churches with their increasingly prominent and public role
in Russian life. On the one hand, they underscored their physical, permanent
presence through the prayer buildings. On the other, they asserted a certain
legitimacy for their faith by highlighting the fact that they prayed for the royal
family using Molokan rites. They simultaneously indicated to a traditionally
dubious state that, despite being religious dissenters, they could nonetheless be
loyal and contributing members of tsarist society.[83]

In tandem with this public voicing of their support for the tsar, Molokans in the Caucasus increasingly backed up these proclamations with philanthropic works in the public sphere. In 1881 one group of Baku Molokans proposed to build, through donations from their community, an orphanage and monument in Baku that would honor the recently murdered Alexander II.[84] Molokans in Blagoveshchensk provided medical care to soldiers during the Russo-Japanese War, as well as food and assistance for soldiers returning at the end of the war.[85] Similarly the Baku community opened an infirmary during World War I that was used to tend to the sick and wounded from the southern front, and also made significant donations to the Red Cross and to the Baku town government to carry out similar activities.[86]

Conclusions: From Sacred Space to Public Sphere

Kolesnikov's efforts to build a Molokan prayer house in Baku, and the larger process of Molokan church building in the late nineteenth and early twentieth centuries, indicate that the socioeconomic and political shifts in Russia that accompanied the Great Reforms, industrialization, and urbanization did not leave the Molokans unaffected. In this evolving context, they began to explore new communal structures, spiritual practices, and meanings of religious space. Whereas Molokans had traditionally eschewed the need for physical, use-specific church buildings, their notions of secular versus sacred—and private versus public—space changed in the late imperial period as they began to erect numerous church buildings. Debates and uncertainties surrounded such alterations of long-standing convention, and some Molokans were dismayed at the trend. Nevertheless, for a significant portion of the Molokan community around the empire, a new form of public, sacred space became considered necessary in order more fully to worship God. The apartments and private houses in which Molokans had previously met were certainly sacred spaces, but in ways different from the designated church buildings in which architectural characteristics became components of the religious experience. The new prayer houses also represented a neutral meeting ground for the entire community that could be used to unify Molokans. Indeed, the Kolesnikov prayer house was a transitional moment in a burgeoning process of communal and religious institutionalization.

In addition to their own desires for the greater spiritual fulfillment of their notions of Christianity, the religious evolution that Kolesnikov's church building entails was also the result of external changes in state policies. In shaping and defining the Molokan community, the influence of the state was crucial. Changing state laws toward religious pluralism from the 1860s through 1905 made the building of permanent prayer houses increasingly conceivable, just as earlier laws barring the public performance of their rites had forced them into secretive meetings in private apartments. Contestations between state officials and Molokans (like Kolesnikov) over prayer houses—and the state's legal distinctions between sacred and secular space—required Molokans to conceive, if only partially, in similar terms. The evolving laws—and the very different ways that different strata and subsections of the state interpreted and (mis)applied those laws—presented the sectarians with choices and prospects in addition to restrictions and obstacles. Kolesnikov, like other Molokans, attempted to manipulate tsarist religious laws as leverage to demand further civil rights concessions.

In their endeavors to transform their religious practices and their communal structures, Molokans, both deliberately and unintentionally, were entering into a larger public sphere in Russia and, in the process, helping to define it. Indeed, the story of Molokan church building indicates the importance of religious groups, especially nonconformist religious communities, to the formation of a public sphere, or spheres, in tsarist Russia. As the Molokans transformed their religious practice toward designated church spaces, and from there began to develop institutions and organizations to strengthen their communities, they created the kinds of autonomous social groups, communications networks, and communal infrastructure considered crucial to the formation of a public sphere. Especially after 1905 they produced numerous community publications, developed philanthropic and educational associations, launched numerous publishing ventures, organized regional and national congresses and jubilees, prodded the state for increased religious and civil rights, and became active in tsarist political life by holding office (particularly at the municipal level), involving the local and regional administration in their activities, and engaging in a political discourse of both real and symbolic loyalty to state power.

The Molokan case underscores that the public sphere in tsarist Russia was characterized by a symbiotic relationship between state and society. The burgeoning Molokan civic presence was beholden to the tsarist state as the purveyors of freedoms and opportunities. For all their long-standing anger toward a persecuting Orthodox government, Molokans realized that they could not achieve their goals without the administration's involvement. They could not separate their societal aims from state power, and, as such, they made sure to voice their thanks and loyalty to the tsarist state whenever they could.

As Molokans increased their public presence through church building, they did not actively reach out to other civic, ethnic, or confessional groups but rather strove to link themselves more closely with their co-religionists (or, at the most, with other sectarian communities) across the country. Thus institution building among the Molokans was liable, with the exception of their various wartime philanthropic and medical efforts, to be primarily concerned with pushing their own Molokan religious agenda (and commercial interests). Unlike religious dissenters in central and Western Europe for whom intolerance and legal religious restrictions "served as a stimulus for [them] to sympathize with the claims of oppressed people and radical causes," Molokans tended neither to extrapolate their own demands for religious and civil freedoms into a campaign for broader sociopolitical rights nor to foster a pan-imperial civic-mindedness that went beyond communal interests.[87]

On one level, this sectional (rather than societal) focus, with its fissures between different associational groupings, was a common characteristic of the Russian public sphere in general. Certainly the Molokan story reinforces the understanding of Russian civil society as disparate and disunited but at the same time highlights that the tsarist public sphere was also fractured by religious divisions as well as by the distinctions of social status, profession, and ethnicity (among others) that have tended to receive the focus of scholarly attention.[88] On another level, Molokan linking across a larger societal stage was made more difficult by two other factors. First, that most Molokans lived in borderland regions, such as Kolesnikov in Baku, meant that the ethno-cultural divisions of Russia's diverse periphery raised other obstacles to a more unified civic life. Second, generations of religious persecution and segregation left their communities inward-looking and distrustful of connections to those outside the Molokan sphere. They needed first to institutionalize themselves internally before they could begin to branch out and forge ties with other groupings in Russian society.

Notes

I thank Heather Coleman, Mark Steinberg, the anonymous reader from Indiana University Press, Eugene Clay, and the participants at the "Sacred Stories" conference for their stimulating suggestions on earlier versions of this essay; Andy Conovaloff for his assistance in tracking down photographs; and Kristin Collins for her research assistance. The research and writing of this article were supported by grants from the National Endowment for the Humanities, the National Council for Eurasian and East European Research, the Fulbright-Hays Doctoral Dissertation Research Program, the International Research and Exchanges Board (IREX), the Kennan Institute for Advanced Russian Studies, the Mershon Center, Ohio State University, and the University of Pennsylvania.

1. I use the term "church" in its broadest sense to mean "a building for public and especially Christian worship" (*Merriam-Webster's Collegiate Dictionary,* 10th ed.).

2. This blurring or overlapping of public and private—of state and civil society—is also a common theme in recent reinterpretations of the public sphere and civil society elsewhere in Europe. On Russia, see Joseph Bradley, "Subjects into Citizens: Societies, Civil Society, and

248 *Nicholas B. Breyfogle*

Autocracy in Tsarist Russia," *American Historical Review* 107, no. 4 (October 2002): 1084–1123, Gramsci quotation at 1096; Edith W. Clowes, Samuel D. Kassow, and James L. West, eds., *Between Tsar and People: Educated Society and the Quest for Public Identity in Late Imperial Russia* (Princeton, N.J., 1991); and Cynthia Hyla Whittaker, *Russian Monarchy: Eighteenth-Century Rulers and Writers in Political Dialogue* (DeKalb, Ill., 2003). On other parts of Europe, see Jürgen Habermas, *The Structural Transformation of the Public Sphere: An Inquiry into a Category of Bourgeois Society*, trans. Thomas Burger (Cambridge, Mass., 1989); Craig Calhoun, ed., *Habermas and the Public Sphere* (Cambridge, Mass., 1992); and Frank Trentmann, ed., *Paradoxes of Civil Society: New Perspectives on Modern German and British History* (New York, 2000).

3. For an exception, see the fascinating discussion of the role of Russian Baptists in "push[ing] open the boundaries of the public sphere," in Heather Coleman, "The Most Dangerous Sect: Baptists in Tsarist and Soviet Russia, 1905–1929" (Ph.D. dissertation, University of Illinois, 1998), quote at 418.

4. Peter van der Veer, *Imperial Encounters: Religion and Modernity in India and Britain* (Princeton. N.J., 2001), 27–28.

5. Compare to James E. Bradley and Dale K. Van Kley, eds., *Religion and Politics in Enlightenment Europe* (Notre Dame, Ind., 2001), esp. James Van Horn Melton, "Pietism, Politics, and the Public Sphere in Germany," 294–333; Róisín Healy, "Religion and Civil Society: Catholics, Jesuits, and Protestants in Imperial Germany," in Trentmann, *Paradoxes*, 244–262; and David Zaret, "Religion, Science, and Printing in the Public Spheres in Seventeenth-Century England," in Calhoun, *Habermas*, 212–235.

6. *Sobranie postanovlenii po chasti raskola* (St. Petersburg, 1875) (hereafter, *SPChR* [1875]), 609–617, 672–682; *Polnoe sobranie zakonov Rossiiskoi imperii* (hereafter, *PSZ*) (3) May 3, 1883, no. 1545, 219–221; GMIR, f. 2, op. 26, d. 63, n.d., l. 340b.; V. I. Iasevich-Borodaevskaia, *Bor'ba za veru. Istorichesko-bytovye ocherki i obzor zakonodatel'stva po staroobriadchestvu i sektantstvu v ego posledovatel'nom razvitii* (St. Petersburg, 1912), 1–108, 397–656; N. L. Solov'ev, *Polnyi krug dukhovnykh zakonov* (Moscow, 1907), 18–44, 64–77; K. K. Arsen'ev, *Svoboda sovesti i veroterpimost': Sbornik statei* (St. Petersburg, 1905), 61–201; Paul Werth, *At the Margins of Orthodoxy: Mission, Governance, and Confessional Politics in Russia's Volga-Kama Region, 1827–1905* (Ithaca, N.Y., 2002), 245–254; and Peter Waldron, "Religious Toleration in Late Imperial Russia," in *Civil Rights in Imperial Russia*, ed. Olga Crisp and Linda Edmondson (Oxford, 1989), 103–120. For a pan-European context, see Rainer Liedtke and Stephan Wendehorst, *The Emancipation of Catholics, Jews and Protestants: Minorities and the Nation State in Nineteenth-Century Europe* (Manchester, 1999); and Healy, "Religion and Civil Society."

7. For an introduction to Molokan history and religious beliefs, see Nicholas B. Breyfogle, *Heretics and Colonizers: Forging Russia's Empire in the South Caucasus* (Ithaca, N.Y. 2005); Andy Conovaloff, *The Molokan Homepage*, http://www.molokane.org/molokan/Index. htm (February 6, 2005); and Svetlana Inikova, "Russkie sekty," in V. A. Aleksandrov et al., eds., *Russkie* (Moscow, 1999), 733–740.

8. A. I. Stollov, "Svedenie o molokanakh Tavricheskoi gubernii," *Otechestvennye zapiski* no. 6 (June 1870): 301.

9. Respectively, Eugénie Lineff, "Psalms and Religious Songs of Russian Sectarians in the Caucasus," in *Report of the Fourth Congress of the International Musical Society* (London, 1912), 188; and an unnamed Molokan quoted in Pauline V. Young, *The Pilgrims of Russian-Town: The Community of Spiritual Christian Jumpers in America. The Struggle of a Primitive Religious Society to Maintain Itself in an Urban Environment* (Hacienda Heights, Calif., 1932; Reprint 1932), 30.

10. In addition to the discussion below, on traditional Molokan opposition to temples of any sort, see Rossiiskii gosudarstvennyi istoricheskii arkhiv (hereafter, RGIA), f. 1661, op. 1, d. 445, l. 1490b; Young, *Pilgrims*, 30–31; George W. Mohoff and Jack P. Valov, *A Stroll through Russiantown* (N.p., 1996), 89; and Ivan Ivanovich Sergeev, "Dukhovnye khristiane v Rossii (Istoricheskii ocherk)," *Dukhovnyi Khristianin* (hereafter, *DKh*) 7, no. 8 (August 1912): 91–92.

11. He also pointed to Ephesians 2:21–22, and 1 Corinthians 3:11, 6:19, and 12:12, among other passages, as scriptural support. N. F. Kudinov, *Stoletie Molokanstva v Rossii 1805–1905 gg.* (Baku, 1905), 36–38. Biblical translations are from the Revised Standard Version. See also August von Haxthausen, *Studies on the Interior of Russia,* ed. S. Frederick Starr, trans. Eleanore L. M. Schmidt (Chicago, 1972), 154; Andy Conovaloff, ed., "Dogmas: Principles of the True Spiritual Christian Russian Molokans, since 1803," <http://www.molokane.org/molokan/Dogma/Dogma_US_Jumpers.htm> (February 6, 2005); and Fedor Malitskii, "Khram, kak dom Bozhii i kak dom molitvy (Protiv, tak nazyvaemykh 'dukhovnykh khristian')," *Tambovskie Eparkhial'nye vedomosti,* no. 21 (1888): 1139–1153.

12. Roy R. Robson, *Old Believers in Modern Russia* (DeKalb, Ill., 1995), 54–56.

13. *SPChR* (1875), 189–191; and Gosudarstvennyi muzei istorii religii (hereafter, GMIR) f. 14, op. 3, dd. 1962, 1902, ll. 1–5.

14. RGIA f. 1284, op. 221–1889, d. 92, l. 2; and A. O., "Otkrytie molennogo doma dukh. khrist. v g. Blagoveshchenske na Amure," *DKh* 3, no. 12 (December 1908): 19.

15. RGIA, f. 1284, op. 198–1838, d. 66, ll. 1–10b.

16. Stollov, "Svedenie," 305, 310–311. On the Don branch of the Molokans, see also *Ispovedanie very Molokan donskogo tolka tavricheskoi gubernii* (Simferopol', 1875); and T. I. Butkevich, *Obzor russkikh sekt i ikh tolkov* (Petrograd, 1915), 426–432.

17. Stollov, "Svedenie," 311.

18. RGIA, f. 1284, op. 221–1886, d. 75, l. 3; RGIA, f. 1284, op. 197–1837, d. 143, ll. 1–10b.; Breyfogle, *Heretics,* 62–63.

19. See, for example, *Kaspii* 1, no. 95 (December 9, 1881): 2; *Kaspii* 3, no. 65 (June 10, 1883): 2; *Kaspii* 2, no. 79 (July 30, 1882): 2; and N. Kalashev, "Selenie Ivanovka, Lagichskago uchastka, Geokchaiskago uezda, Bakinskoi gubernii." *Sbornik materialov dlia opisaniia mestnostei i plemen Kavkaza,* vol. 13 (Tiflis, 1892), otd. II, 242.

20. *PSZ* (3) May 3, 1883, no. 1545, article 5, 219–220.

21. In contrast, for Old Believers, 1883 was in many respects a step backward from the freedoms of 1864 (Robson, *Old Believers,* 55).

22. GMIR, f. 2, op. 8, d. 237, 1910, l. 46.

23. GMIR, f. 2, op. 8, d. 237, 1910, ll. 45–46; *Kaspii* 2, no. 59 (May 30, 1882): 2; *Kaspii* 2, no. 76 (July 23, 1882): 1; *Kaspii* 10, no. 137 (June 28, 1890): 2; and RGIA, f. 1287, op. 38, d. 3035, 1895–1907, ll. 50b.–6.

24. GMIR, f. 2, op. 8, d. 237, 1910, ll. 45–46; and Kudinov, *Stoletie,* 73–79, 84–85.

25. *Kaspii* 4, no. 87 (April 21, 1884): 1.

26. RGIA, f. 1354, op. 3, d. 1267, l. 480b., 530b.; RGIA f. 1284, op. 222–1893, d. 81, ll. 4–40b.; GMIR, f. 2, op. 8, d. 237, 1910, ll. 66–71, 82–84; and "Sudebnaia khronika" (January 16, 1894): 3.

27. RGIA, f. 1354, op. 3, d. 1267, ll. 48–480b., 520b.–53. The pattern of Synod officials barring the construction or reopening of Old Believer prayer houses was also commonplace. See Robson, *Old Believers,* 55.

28. RGIA, f. 1284, op. 222–1893, d. 81, ll. 3–4, 160b.–17.

29. RGIA, f. 1284, op. 221–1889, d. 92, l. 2. The petition of Fedil Ivanovich Shubin, a Molokan from the village of Nizhnie Akhty, to the emperor in 1900 was similar in tone, promising "to pray to God and Jesus Christ for the future health and success of the tsar and his family," if the tsar would grant them the right to their communal prayer house (RGIA, f. 1284, op. 222–1899, d. 114, ll. 5–50b.).

30. RGIA, f. 1284, op. 221–1889, d. 92, ll. 8–80b.

31. RGIA, f. 1284, op. 222–1899, d. 114, ll. 1–10b., 2–3, 14–15, 17; Iasevich-Borodaevskaia, *Bor'ba,* 37–108, 559–560; *Vsepoddanneishii otchet ober-prokurora sviateishego sinoda po vedomstvu pravoslavnogo ispovedaniia za 1894 i 1895 gody* (St. Petersburg, 1898), 229–231; and A. Iu. Polunov, *Pod vlast'iu ober-prokurora: Gosudarstvo i tserkov' v epokhu Aleksandra III* (Moscow, 1996), 97–109.

32. RGIA, f. 1284, op. 221–1883, d. 43, ll. 1–40b.; RGIA f. 1284, op. 221–1883, d. 64, ll. 1–60b.; and Breyfogle, *Heretics,* 87–172.

33. RGIA, f. 1284, op. 222–1893, d. 81, ll. 4, 17–170b.; and RGIA, f. 1354, op. 3, d. 1267, ll. 480b.–49.

34. RGIA, f. 1284, op. 222–1893, d. 81, ll. 13–14, 18–180b.

35. RGIA, f. 1284, op. 222–1893, d. 81, ll. 180b.–190b., 22–220b.

36. RGIA, f. 1284, op. 222–1893, d. 81, l. 24.

37. RGIA, f. 1354, op. 3, d. 1267, ll. 490b.–570b.: and "Sudebnaia khronika," *Kaspii*, no. 10 (January 14, 1894): 2; no. 12 (January 16, 1894): 3; and no. 13 (January 18, 1894): 3.

38. RGIA, f. 1354, op. 3, d. 1267, l. 520b.

39. "Sudebnaia khronika" (January 16, 1894): 3.

40. RGIA, f. 1354, op. 3, d. 1267, l. 540b.

41. RGIA, f. 1284, op. 222–1893, d. 81, l. 18.

42. RGIA, f. 1354, op. 3, d. 1267, ll. 530b.–54.

43. "Sudebnaia khronika," (January 16, 1894): 3.

44. Ibid.

45. RGIA, f. 1354, op. 3, d. 1267, ll. 56–560b.

46. Vera Shevzov, "Chapels and the Ecclesial World of Prerevolutionary Russian Peasants," *Slavic Review* 55, no. 3 (fall 1996): 585–613; A. I. Masalkin, "K istorii zakavkazskikh sektantov: II Subbotniki," *Kavkaz*, no. 307 (November 19, 1893): 2; RGIA, f. 1284, op. 222–1893, d. 81, ll. 22–220b.; and Robson, *Old Believers*, 53–74.

47. GMIR, f. 2, op. 8, d. 237, 1910, ll. 66–71, 82–84.

48. See, for example, S. K. Zhabin, *K dukhovnomu svetu. Kratkii kurs Zakona Bozhiia dlia dukhovnykh khristian (postoiannykh molokan)* (Tiflis, 1912), 282–285; *Kratkoe izlozhenie dogmaticheskо-religioznogo ucheniia dukhovnykh khristian* (Tiflis, 1909), 28; N. F. Kudinov, *Dukhovnye khristiane. Molokane. Kratkii istoricheskii ocherk* (Vladikavkaz. 1913), 31; P. A. Suvorov, *Uchebnik dukhovnykh khristian* (Baku, 1915), 94; and P. T. Mazaev, "Ibo vy Khram Boga Zhivogo," *DKh* 3, no. 4 (April 1908): 11–14.

49. T. F. Gavrilov, "O nerukotvorennom khrame," *DKh* 1, no. 9 (August 1906): 15–23; 1, no. 10 (September 1906): 19–24; 1, no. 11 (October 1906): 7–13; and 1, no. 12 (November–December 1906): 31–38.

50. Ibid.

51. In addition to the examples discussed here, Molokan church building took place in numerous other locations across tsarist Russia; see I. N. Minnikov, "Iz g. Shemakhi," *DKh* 3, no. 11 (November 1908): 39; "Iz s. Astrakhanki Shemakh. u Bakin. g., *DKh* 2, no. 12 (December 1907): 47–48; P. M. Druzhinin and V. I. Druzhinin, "Otkrytie molitvennogo doma dukhovnykh khristian v s. Prishibe Astrakhanskoi gubernii," *DKh* 3, no. 12 (December 1908): 22–27; and Gosudarstvennyi arkhiv Rossiiskoi Federatsii (hereafter, GARF), f. 102, 5 d-vo, op. 1901, d. 509, l. 500b.

52. GMIR, f. 2, op. 8, d. 237, 1910, l. 82; and Lineff, "Psalms," 188–193.

53. GMIR, f. 2, op. 8, d. 237, 1910, ll. 66–71, 82–84.

54. RGIA, f. 1284, op. 222–1905, d. 35, l. 11.

55. RGIA, f. 1284, op. 222–1905, d. 35, l. 30b.

56. A. O., "Otkrytie," 18–22; M. T. Gurikov, "Iz g. Blagoveshchensk (Sibir)," *DKh* 1, no. 7–8 (June, 1906): 78–79; *Vsepoddanneishii otchet ober-Prokuratora*, 233–236; "Dukhovnye khristiane molokane na Amure," *Molokanin* 1, no. 1 (April 1910): 35–38; and, for the photograph in figure 9.2, *Spiritual Christian Molokan News*, no. 6 (January–March 1994): 20. On the Molokans of Blagoveshchensk generally, see A. I. Klibanov, *History of Religious Sectarianism in Russia (1860s–1917)*, trans. Ethel Dunn (New York, 1982), 184–196.

57. While many Molokans hoped to use this new prayer house as the physical foundations of greater unity, others realized that the simple fact of bringing the different communities together to pray under one roof would only be a small first step. The differences in religious practice and competition of different leadership also posed fundamental problems to the Molokans (RGIA, f. 821, op. 133, d. 213, 1915, ll. 5–50b.; and GMIR, f. 2, op. 26, d. 63, n.d., l. 340b.).

58. RGIA, f. 821, op. 133, d. 213, 1915, ll. 5, 19.
59. RGIA, f. 821, op. 133, d. 213, 1915, l. 5.
60. Breyfogle, *Heretics*, 299–304; John K. Berokoff, *Molokans in America* (Whittier, Calif., 1969); and Mohoff and Valov, *Stroll*, 89–109.
61. RGIA, f. 1284, op. 222–1899, d. 114.
62. "Sudebnaia khronika" (January 16, 1894): 3.
63. GMIR, f. 2, op. 8, d. 237, 1910, l. 46; RGIA, f. 821, op. 133, d. 213, 1915, l. 19; and Kudinov, *Stoletie*, 84–85.
64. See, of numerous examples, I. T. Fefelov and V. G. Kalmykov, "Soobshchenie iz sela Astrakhanki, Shemakhanskogo uezda, Bakinskoi g.," *Molokanin* 1, no. 8–9 (November–December 1910): 61–64; V. I. Kalmykov, "Pis'mo po sluchaiu obnovleniia molitvennogo doma v Astrakhanke," *Molokanin* 1, no. 8–9 (November–December, 1910): 65–67; A. O., "Otkrytie," 18–22; Druzhinin and Druzhinin, "Otkrytie," 22–27; and Minnikov, "Iz g. Shemakhi," 39.
65. Kudinov, *Stoletie*, 81.
66. RGIA, f. 1284, op. 222–1893, l. 81, l. 3; GMIR, f. 2, op. 8, d. 297, 1907; Kudinov, *Stoletie*, 81; RGIA, f. 821, op. 133, d. 213, 1915, l. 50b.; I. E. Platonov, "O dukhovnykh shkolakh," *DKh* 2, no. 4 (April 1907): 33–37; "Brat'ia vorontsovtsy soobshchaiut," *DKh* 1, no. 4 (March 1906): 31–33; "4-go oktiabria proshlogo 1909," *Molokanin* 1, no. 1 (April 1910): 38–41; "Iz zhizni tiflisskikh Molokan," *Molokanin* 1, no. 1 (April 1910): 42–43; "Sredi sektantov," *Tiflisskii listok*, no. 122 (May 31, 1913): 2; GARF, f. 102, 5 d-vo, op. 1901, d. 509, l. 500b.; GARF, f. 102, oo d-vo, op. 1906, d. 194, ch. 2, ll. 420b.–45; and GARF, f. 102, 4 d-vo, op. 1908, d. 75, ch. 9.
67. RGIA, f. 821, op. 150, d. 445, ll. 440b.–48, 500b.–51, 126–1270b.; *Ustav Bakinskogo Obshchestva dukhovnykh khristian (Molokan) goroda Baku i raiona Bakinskogo gradonachal'stva* (Baku, 1908), quote at 5; "Proekt ustava Bakinskogo obshchestva dukhovnykh khristian," *DKh* 2, no. 7 (July 1907): 21–25; "Iz Tiflisa," *DKh* 2, no. 7 (July 1907): 26–27; GMIR, f. 2, op. 26, d. 63, n.d., l. 340b.; and the articles by N. F. Kudinov, "Khronika," "Proekt ustava 'Soiuz Vladikavkazskikh molokan,'" "Proekt ustava 'Soiuz dukhovnykh khristian (Molokan) gor. Karsa i Karskoi oblasti,'" and "Ustav Obshchetva pod imenovaniem 'Soiuz bakin. Molokan progressistov,'" *Molokanskii vestnik* 1, no. 1 (March 1906): 21–44.
68. On Molokan congresses, see Kudinov, *Stoletie*; *Karsskii oblastnoi s"ezd dukhovnykh khristian 1-go, 2-go i 3-go iiunia 1908 g.* (Kars, 1908); *Otchet o Vserossiiskom s"ezde dukhovnykh khristian (Molokan), sostoiavshemsia 22 iiulia 1905 goda* (Tiflis, 1907); "Vserossiiskii s"ezd Molokan," *Missionerskoe obozrenie* 10, no. 9 (June 1905): 1416; "Glasnye tiflisskoi gorodskoi . . . " *DKh* 2, no. 8 (August 1907): 30; I. S. Grushenkov, "O neobkhodimosti s"ezda vsekh sektantov," *DKh* 2, no. 9 (September 1907): 25–29; I. G. Vodop'ianov, "Vserossiiskii s"ezd dukhov. Khristian v Balkashov," *DKh* 3, no. 4 (April 1908): 20–22; A.V., "S"ezd 'dukhovnykh' v Delizhane," *Tiflisskii listok*, no. 119 (May 27, 1910): 2; Robert Sloan Latimer, *Under Three Tsars: Liberty of Conscience in Russia, 1856–1909* (London, 1909), 41–42; and Berokoff, *Molokans*, opposite 104.
69. Of the numerous titles, see, for example, Zhabin, *K dukhovnomu svetu*; Kudinov, *Dukhovnye*; I. F. Kolesnikov, *Dogmaty i ustav dukhovnykh khristian molokanskogo veroispovedaniia* (Baku, 1910); Suvorov, *Uchebnik*; and *Kratkoe izlozhenie*.
70. GMIR, f. 2, op. 26, d. 63, n.d., l. 340b.
71. RGIA, f. 1284, op. 222–1893, d. 81, l. 70b.
72. RGIA, f. 1284, op. 222–1893, d. 81, ll. 2, 80b.–9.
73. RGIA, f. 1284, op. 222–1893, d. 81, l. 10; RGIA f. 1284, op. 221–1889, d. 92, l. 2; RGIA, f. 1284, op. 222–1899, d. 114, ll. 11–110b., 16; and RGIA, f. 1284, op. 222–1905, d. 35, l. 3.
74. Only with the manifestos of 1905 did they begin to feel that their civil rights and religious rights were properly established. See *Ustav*, 3–4; and GMIR, f. 2, op. 26, d. 63, n.d., l. 340b.
75. RGIA, f. 1284, op. 221–1889, d. 92, l. 2. An almost identical sentiment is found in Stollov, "Svedenie," 305.
76. Iasevich-Borodaevskaia, *Bor'ba*, 13.
77. RGIA, f. 1284, op. 222–1905, d. 35, l. 30b.; and Breyfogle, *Heretics*, chap. 4.

252   *Nicholas B. Breyfogle*

78. RGIA, f. 1284, op. 222–1893, d. 81, ll. 6, 100b.–11.

79. RGIA, f. 1354, op. 3, d. 1267, ll. 47–470b.

80. Stollov, "Svedenie," 312; and Solov'ev, *Polnyi krug,* 18–25. Rogge himself argued similarly, although not unexpectedly attaching a different valence, that the decrease in legal restrictions on the part of the state toward the sectarians had led the latter to act more overtly in society and to show the authorities less submissiveness (RGIA f. 1284, op. 222–1893, d. 81).

81. RGIA, f. 1287, op. 38, d. 3045, 1895–1907, ll. 2–9; GMIR, f. 2, op. 26, d. 63, n.d., l. 340b.; *Vsepodanneishii otchet o proizvedennoi v 1905 godu po Vysochaishchuiu poveleniiu Senatorom Kuzminskim Revizii goroda Baku i Bakinskoi gubernii* (St. Petersburg, 1906), 359; *Vsepoddanneishii otchet ober-Prokuratora,* 235; "Glasnye tiflisskoi," 30; and Latimer, *Under Three Tsars,* 42.

82. *Kaspii* 3, no. 65 (June 10, 1883): 2; *Kaspii* 1, no. 95 (December 9, 1881): 2; RGIA, f. 821, op. 133, d. 213, 1915, l. 2; Kudinov, *Stoletie;* RGIA, f. 1284, op. 221–1885, d. 22, ll. 1–30b.; and "Iz zhizni tifflisskikh Molokan," 42–43.

83. See also RGIA, f. 1284, op. 221–1885, d. 22, ll. 1–30b.; and Breyfogle, *Heretics,* 158–163.

84. *Kaspii* 1, no. 95 (December 9, 1881): 2. For the broader context, see Adele Lindenmeyr, *Poverty Is Not a Vice: Charity, Society, and the State in Imperial Russia* (Princeton, N.J., 1996).

85. "Dukhovnye khristiane molokane," 35–36.

86. *Otchet komiteta po okazaniiu pomoshchi ranenym voinam pri Bakinskoi Obshchin Dukhovnykh Khristian (Molokan)* (Baku, 1915); V. V. Ivanov, "Na pomoshch ranenym voinam," *Baptist* no. 15/16 (1914): 17–18; Klibanov, *History,* 206–208; and RGIA, f. 821, op. 133, d. 213, 1915, ll. 1, 19. Cf. Nicholas B. Breyfogle, "Caught in the Crossfire? Russian Sectarians in the Caucasian Theater of War, 1853–56 and 1877–78," *Kritika: Explorations in Russian and Eurasian History* 2, no. 4 (fall 2001): 713–750.

87. Cf. James E. Bradley, "The Religious Origins of Radical Politics in England, Scotland, and Ireland, 1662–1800," in Bradley and Van Kley, *Religion,* 187–253, quote at 234.

88. Joseph Bradley, "Voluntary Associations, Civic Culture, and *Obshchestvennost'* in Moscow," in Clowes, Kassow, and West, *Between Tsar and People,* 147–148; and Samuel D. Kassow, "Russia's Unrealized Civil Society," in ibid., 367.

10

Divining the Secular in the Yiddish Popular Press

Sarah Abrevaya Stein

————◦⟨∞⟩◦————

S cholars of Russian Jewry are accustomed to dividing modern Yiddish print culture and, arguably, Jewish culture more generally, into two distinct camps: the religious and the secular. According to this formulation, *tekhines* literature (prayers and weekly Torah readings in Yiddish designed, at least in part, for female readers) and vernacular rabbinical commentary are understood as religious texts, whereas Yiddish poetry, prose, potboilers, and the press are secular. Few would argue that Russian Yiddish secular culture of the turn of the twentieth century was not intricately referential of religious sources and experiences, and that this was in a certain sense unavoidable given the personal background of the Jewish intelligentsia, whose members by and large sprung from traditional milieus.[1] There remains, however, an implicit assumption that secular and religious readers were using print culture to delineate themselves from one another in the early twentieth century or, at the very least, that Yiddish texts exploited distinctions that were already discernible among Russian Jews.

The following pages consider the accuracy of these assumptions. An examination of the early history of the Yiddish daily press reveals that, apparently, "religious" and "secular" Jewish readers in Russia were not easily distinguishable from each other at the turn of the century, and, in any case, readers were not necessarily strict in their choice of reading matter. Thus turn-of-the-century Yiddish newspapers that might appear profoundly secular to the contemporary eye could be embraced by observant readers with an almost religious zeal, often not with the blessing of editors and journalists, but despite their evident discomfort. And although editors of self-consciously "modern" Yiddish newspapers actively eschewed religious readers and content that was imagined to appeal to them, the content of Yiddish newspapers inevitably reflected the interests and needs of readers who considered themselves observant.

Indeed, it was not until the interwar period that the producers of Yiddish newspapers sought to target religious readers in their own right. Until this time, these readers were assiduously ignored, as editors and journalists sought to divine a secular Yiddish press that would both signal and catalyze the changing fabric of Russian Jewish culture. Strikingly, observant readers were not put off by these ambitions. Instead, they subverted the intended nature of Yiddish newspapers by the act of reading and by shaping the content of newspapers themselves. Observant Jews were employed to typeset and censor Yiddish periodicals. They penned letters to the editor, submitted advertisements, pressed for the introduction of new material or shifts of focus. Another measure of their visibility may be found in the advertising pages of the Yiddish press. Advertisers were quicker than editors to understand that Yiddish newspapers were destined for observant hands and that these readers would be eager consumers. Thus Jewish merchants throughout the empire interested in attracting a wide clientele posted advertisements in the Yiddish press promoting goods and services designed explicitly for religious readers.

As was true of Russia's emerging worker culture, in early-twentieth-century Russian Yiddish newspapers "secular" was an imagined, if not a fanciful, category. Just as Russian proletarian writing could be suffused with sacred themes and metaphors, Jewish readers could remain "observant" and yet succumb to the lure of worldly texts.[2] At least until the interwar period, which saw the emergence not simply of Jewish newspapers designed for the religious but also political parties designed for this niche, the world of secular Yiddish letters was far from hermetic. The nature of Russian Jewish culture and the fabric of the Yiddish reading public prevented this from being so. The religious and the secular were simply too tightly interwoven, and the meaning of both was yet to be defined.

Messianic Modernism and the Emergence of the Yiddish Daily

The story of one Russian Jewish newspaper reader illustrates these dynamics succinctly. In 1903 Morris Shaten was a teenager living in Kutno, a small town with a sizable Jewish population located just north of Lodz, in the Polish region of the Russian Pale of Settlement.[3] Shaten considered himself to be Hasidic: he grew up in a Hasidic home, prayed in a Hasidic *shtibl,* and was schooled in a Hasidic house of study. Although he dreamed of becoming a bookseller, it was unthinkable that Shaten would leave this world to attend a gymnasium or university. At this time in the early years of the twentieth century, Russian soldiers commonly passed through Kutno, and among them were a number of Jewish soldiers from Russia's interior. These were worldly, educated, radical men, or at least so they seemed to young Shaten. These Jewish soldiers often lingered in Kutno, talking politics with the town's self-made intellectuals, flirting with local women, occasionally falling in love and making the town their home. The soldiers tended to gather for conversation and company in the home of one of Kutno's wealthier Jewish residents; so popular was this meeting place that it soon came to be called a *men'hoyze,* a people's house, and in this house Shaten and his childhood friend, Zundel Tsonber, encountered *Der fraynd,* the only Yiddish daily newspaper either boy had ever seen. *Der fraynd,* Shaten has recalled, "opened our eyes [and showed us] that there was a big and rich world, and that in this world people were fighting for improvements.... [The paper] made a strong impression on me ... It felt like the Messiah had come."[4] Thrilled with their discovery, Shaten and Tsonber wrote to St. Petersburg to order a subscription to the paper, and so they became the first residents of their town to subscribe to a Yiddish newspaper.

Shaten and Zundel read and discussed the paper together, and soon people were eavesdropping on their conversations. Friends began to borrow copies of *Der fraynd:* first a schoolmate, then the schoolmate's brother, then the tailor, and then the sons of the town's *shoykhet* (ritual slaughterer). "People saw us reading, saw us talking. We were speaking about new things. [Thus] we created a circle of *Fraynd* readers ... friendships based on shared knowledge (*a gevisen frayndshaft*)."[5]

The circle's appetite was whet, and soon "reading *Der fraynd* was not enough." In the pages of *Der fraynd* Shaten and his friends discovered advertisements for works of fiction by the day's leading Yiddish authors: Mendele Moykher-Sforim (pseudonym of Sh.Y. Abramovitsh), Sholem Aleichem (pseudonym of Sh. Rabinovitsh), Yitshok Leyb Peretz, Sholem Asch, and Dovid Pinsky. Pooling their rubles, they sent away for these books of fiction, as well as scientific books on physics, chemistry, and astronomy, and new writings by Tolstoy translated into German. Soon they had built an informal library containing between forty and fifty volumes. Fearing their actions would arouse the suspicion of the authorities—according to Shaten it was forbidden to maintain either a public or a private library in Kutno—Shaten's circle stored the books in a factory where a member of the group worked. Readers would cautiously enter one at a time to borrow the books, which were stored in a glass cabinet. As further subterfuge, readers spoke of the collection as "private," although in truth it functioned as a lending library. For Shaten and his circle, *Der fraynd* served as a gateway to a rich world of Yiddish in print. The newspaper—and the library that emerged from its pages—provided them with the secular education they were otherwise unable to acquire. According to Shaten, "it was our *folks-shul,* our primary school."[6]

This story, while colorful, is not unusual. In the first years of the twentieth century Jews of all educational, social, economic, and religious backgrounds, those who lived in towns and those who lived in cities, those in the Russian Pale of Settlement and those in the Russian interior, were beginning to discover, read, and discuss a medium so novel as to be perceived as messianic: the Yiddish popular press. By the late nineteenth century it was not uncommon for Russia's Jews—men, women, and children—to read. Jewish rates of literacy, in Yiddish, Russian, and, to a lesser extent, Hebrew, were high. The Russian census of 1897 indicated that 97 percent of Jews in the empire declared Yiddish their mother tongue, and nearly 65 percent of Jewish men and just over 36 percent of Jewish women older than ten were literate in a non-Russian language, almost always Yiddish. Both these figures, moreover, were significant underestimations.[7] By the end of the nineteenth century, meanwhile, it was no longer unusual for Russian Jews to read fluently in Russian. On average, nearly 50 percent of Russian Jewish men and 21 percent of Russian Jewish women between the ages of ten and fifty were literate in Russian. The number was as high as 51 percent for urban males and 35 percent for urban females.[8] By 1897 nearly fifty thousand Jews residing in the Pale of Settlement alone declared Russian their mother tongue.[9]

Still, the majority of turn-of-the-century Russian Jewish readers had access to an extraordinarily limited variety of published material, which was largely religious in nature. By 1900 secular Yiddish texts—including romances, novellas, and adaptations of European literature—had been in print for more than a century and Yiddish periodicals for some four decades. But this material was published inconsistently and its circulation tended to be small. Information about the day's news was particularly scarce. As the new century began the combined circulation of secular periodicals designed for Russian Jewish readers was less than twenty thousand. In just a decade this number would explode: by the outbreak of the First World War the circulation of Yiddish periodicals in Russia numbered in the hundreds of thousands. By the interwar period, the number of Jewish newspapers in circulation would rise still further. In Warsaw alone, the combined circulation of Yiddish newspapers exceeded 150,000.[10] Arguably the Yiddish press provided many Russian Jews with their first encounter with popular and quotidian print culture, and their first acquaintance with the notion of secular Yiddish culture in print.[11]

Inventing the Secular in the Yiddish Press

The importance of the Yiddish press to Jewish readers is exemplified by the first Yiddish daily newspaper published in Russia, a newspaper that, on its arrival, Morris Shaten heralded as "messianic": *Der fraynd*, published in St. Petersburg from 1903 to 1914. Not only was *Der fraynd* the first Yiddish daily published in the empire but, at least for its first five years of publication, was one of the most influential Yiddish periodicals in print.[12] In only two years *Der fraynd* helped to demonstrate that a Yiddish daily newspaper was a viable intellectual and commercial project, not least by building a circulation of nearly one hundred thousand.[13] This far surpassed the circulation of any Russian Jewish periodical up to that time: indeed, in 1903, the combined circulation of all periodicals designed for Russian Jewish readers was around twenty thousand. In some sense, *Der fraynd*'s impressive circulation exceeded what it justly deserved. Until about 1906, *Der fraynd,* arguably, held a kind of artificial sway over Russian Jewish readers of Yiddish; it had been the first Yiddish daily allowed by the Russian Ministry of the Interior, an office that refused to approve the publication of a Yiddish daily despite dozens of requests over at least two decades by Russian Jewish intellectuals. The Ministry of the Interior, it seemed, feared the idea of Yiddish news in print, a medium the ministry had little ability to control.[14] After the appearance of *Der fraynd,* the ministry would continue to put obstacles in the path of would-be editors of Yiddish dailies, particularly those based in Warsaw, for some three years. This lid on cultural expression aggressively limited *Der fraynd*'s competition, thereby facilitating its success.[15]

In its early years of publication, *Der fraynd* positioned itself around three axes: it assumed a Zionist tone, although a rather moderate one; it defended the use of Yiddish; and it declared itself a secular and modern Jewish newspaper. The paper rarely published outright assaults on observance and only rarely drew attention to its secular posture. Notably secularism was rarely named as a phenomenon, a sign, perhaps, that it was not a category that was or could be rigorously policed. Thus the Yiddish synonyms for secular (*veltlekh, nit geystlekh*) scarcely appeared in the pages of *Der fraynd*. Secularism was, instead, absorbed into the more general category of the modern. Contributors to *Der fraynd* acknowledged that life was fundamentally different for Russian Jews at the turn of the century. "Jewish life has changed dramatically in the last years," the paper's first editorial announced: "Jewish life is no longer tied up in the old order of things. New times have awoken new desires."[16] Readers, the editorial continued, need a daily newspaper that will provide information about "daily life" and answer the questions that daily life raises.[17] Traditionally, of course, it was to rabbinical authorities and courts that Jewish men and women would go with their daily queries. But now, *Der fraynd* implied, the pace of change had become too rapid for rabbinical authorities to accommodate, and the religious establishment was unable to address the sheer quantity of questions that modern Jews faced. In the pages of *Der fraynd,* information was presented as the antidote to religion, and a daily newspaper as its most reliable vehicle.

As this suggests, the pages of *Der fraynd* were not free of references to religious life; on the contrary, the paper often referred to the religious establishment and religious readers as a way to clarify its agenda. Humorous contributions to *Der fraynd* frequently parodied observant Jews and often appeared in a column entitled "Shtet un shtetlakh" (Cities and towns), penned pseudonymically by "Emes" (Truth).[18] One installment described a collection of Jewish men in the shtetl of Zhgersh, who, fearing that the imminent arrival of *Der fraynd* would corrupt their wives, declared the paper *trayf* (not kosher) and issued a *herem* (writ of excommunication) against the journal. "If God helped our wives to improve themselves by creating a newspaper in *taytsh yedn tog* (everyday speech)," the townsmen declare, "we will not read it: and wherever this is heard, so will it be! And further, maintained the wives of Zhgersh, '*Der fraynd* will be *trayf* for everyone.'"[19] Such humorous references to traditional Jewish mores were never balanced by reporting on issues of importance in the Jewish religious world. Indeed, one could easily gain the impression from *Der fraynd* that nothing noteworthy ever happened in the worlds of the Orthodox or Hasidic. The paper's disinterest in addressing observant readers was most evident, in fact, in such absences. This point was made quite clearly by Emes:

> Yiddish newspapers in Russia have always had a penchant for writing more about Paris, Berlin, Madrid, or the furthest cities in Australia and Calcutta, India, than we do of the Jewish shtetls where one million of the five million [Jews] who reside in Russia actually live.... The Jewish cities and towns for which Yiddish newspapers are produced aren't even on the "geographic map" of the Yiddish press.[20]

Thus *Der fraynd*'s supplement offered readers the chance to explore Jewish life in New York, Bucharest, Prague, and Nagasaki before it deigned to speak of Jewish life in the Russian Pale or the Russian interior. And when serious news of local communities did reach the pages of *Der fraynd*, more often than not it was negative. One such article disparaged the education young men received at yeshivas; the author complained that one could graduate from a yeshiva without knowing Russian or, in extreme cases, Hebrew.[21]

Der fraynd was apparently little interested in appealing to observant readers. Indeed, the editorial board may well have actively discouraged them. Shoyl Ginzburg, one of the first editors of the paper, has recounted in his memoirs that, on one occasion, a "grey beard" (which might be understood as an older, Orthodox Jewish man) approached him offering to contribute a weekly article on the *parsha* (a portion of the Torah). Ginzburg's response was terse and scornful: Couldn't the reader see that *Der fraynd* was "not that kind of paper?"[22] This response may more accurately have reflected the era in which Ginzburg penned his memoirs than the early years of *Der fraynd*'s publication. In truth, "that kind of paper," that is, daily newspapers in Yiddish designed for Orthodox readers, would not emerge until the interwar period.[23] Prior to the emergence of these newspapers, Orthodox readers were more likely to turn to the Hebrew *maskilic* (Enlightened) press than to the Yiddish. But nothing prevented them from reading Yiddish periodicals as well.

Der fraynd's secular agenda was further checked by the sobriety of the newspapers' creators. In the paper's early years, its editors were stubbornly unwilling to mimic the kinds of Russian "boulevard" tabloids devoted to daily news and sensationalism. In accordance with this disdain, telegrams announcing the day's news that dominated Russian journals like *Peterburgskii listok* were relegated to the back pages of *Der fraynd*, leaving its front pages for verbose editorials and lead stories expounding on such matters as the nature of the Austrian parliament, the state of Jewish education, or race relations in the United States, and thus reflecting the *maskilic* origins and instincts of *Der fraynd*'s editors.[24] In this sense *Der fraynd* was profoundly conservative and in many ways had not strayed far from the "European" goals of journals like *Hashiloah* (Odessa, 1896–1918) that aimed to educate readers in a didactic manner.[25] Put another way, while *Der fraynd* eschewed religious culture, it retained a conventional sense of the *trayf* (non-kosher) inherited from its more conservative literary predecessors. The editors of *Der fraynd* thus found a fine line for their writers to toe. They disdained the rigidities and complacencies of the old Jewish order, and yet they were unwilling to fully embrace the riot of rapid news and scandal espoused by their Russian-language (and soon to be Yiddish-language) counterparts. *Der fraynd*'s editors therefore showed a preference for a conservative readership over an informed one. This agenda was not so different, after all, than that of the Orthodox order, with an obvious difference: it would be *Der fraynd*—not the rabbinic elite—that educates the people and interprets events for them. This didactic tone would ultimately contribute to the paper's undoing, as a new generation of newspapers began to successfully vie with *Der fraynd* for the attention of readers (especially those in Warsaw).[26]

In any case, it was impossible for a turn-of-the-century Russian Yiddish daily to survive—let alone garner a circulation of one hundred thousand as did *Der fraynd*—without relying on observant readers. This was largely because the observance of some degree of Jewish law was still widespread among Russian Jews in the early years of the twentieth century, and included members of the intelligentsia, just as old and new forms of religion and spirituality held remarkable appeal for Russia's lower and elite classes.[27] It is impossible, however, to quantify the number of "religious" or "secular" Jews who lived in Russia in the early years of the twentieth century, as the terms were used so flexibly that they could not easily be distinguished; perhaps this is why no scholar of Russian Jewry has attempted such an estimation, although the task becomes less difficult when one turns to the interwar period when one can rely on measures such as educational enrollments, party affiliations, and voting practices.[28] More to the point, prior to the emergence of political parties and popular sources designed for the religious, the very meaning of "observant" was difficult to pin down. Where, precisely, did the secular begin and the observant end? What signs and symbols might mark this shift? How was one to define, much less monitor, the boundaries of the religious?

Inevitably there was no shortage of answers to these questions. Members of the rabbinical elite, for example, attempted to restrict Jewish readers' access to secular sources such as the press, while certain newspaper editors feigned indifference to this same pool of readers. As is so often the case, however, reality proved far murkier than either rabbinical law or intellectual ambition anticipated. Religiously minded readers tended to overlap with secularly minded ones, and texts designed with these two readerships in mind frequently crossed the line that was imagined to divide them.

The nature of reading at this time and the constitution of Russian Jewish space further muddied the distinction between religious and secular readers. At the point at which *Der fraynd* emerged, newspaper sales depended on word of mouth, as street sales would not be introduced for more than a decade.[29] This, in turn, meant that readers acquired their newspapers—and their news—in unpredictable places and fashions. In a 1901 essay the theoretician Ahad Ha'am suggested that Russian Jews' favored space for discussing news and politics—and, one assumes, the day's news—was around the synagogue stove sometime between morning and afternoon prayers.[30] Ahad Ha'am was not alone in his assessment: Yiddish common parlance coins this kind of activity *lezhanke politik* (stove-side politics) and the (sometimes limited) knowledge it presupposes *khokmey lezhanke* (stove-side smarts). The marketplace was another favored location to discuss current events and, besides the tavern, may well have served as one of the most important contact zones of Russian (and Russian Jewish) society. In the marketplace, newspapers were sold by traveling vendors, passed from hand to hand, and read aloud to large groups. The founding editor of *Der fraynd*, Shoyl Ginzburg, recorded in his memoirs that one of the most meaningful moments in his career was when he saw a copy of *Der fraynd* being read aloud, by "simple old Jews," in Vilna's marketplace.[31] This ritual has been described by a bystander in the marketplace, Joseph Buloff, who made a practice of listening to the town's educated recluse, "Barve's Son," summarize news of the Russo-Japanese War gleaned from the press.[32] One might imagine that no two places could be more distinct than the synagogue and the marketplace, but actually the two were not as dissimilar as one might think. Religious and secular Jews, after all, had reason to pass through both, and because these were social as well as commercial spaces, both facilitated the proliferation of the Yiddish press.

The library, too, was a space that extended the reach of the Yiddish newspaper, not simply to more readers but to a wider array of readers. While individuals like Morris Shaten were constructing libraries with friends, organizations were beginning to build their own. The 1903 minutes of a painters union (*ferayn*) testifies to just such a practice: "We have now enlarged our library [and] have subscribed to the daily Yiddish paper, *Der fraynd,* which is always to be found in our painters' quarters."[33] Public and private libraries, whether formal and legal or informal and underground, like Shaten's, could be frequented by dozens of readers every day, allowing *Der fraynd* and newspapers like it to extend their reach far beyond their subscribers and undoubtedly beyond the kind of modern, secular reader their creators imagined. One measure of this is the extent to which libraries availed their collections to women, scarcely the target audience of most editors of Yiddish sources at the turn of the century. According to a study conducted in 1907, Jewish women constituted nearly half (42 percent) of the membership of a typical Russian Jewish lending library.[34]

All this is to suggest that Morris Shaten, a self-proclaimed observant Jew, could hardly have been among a minority of *Der fraynd*'s readers. Indeed, other Orthodox readers announced themselves in letters to the editor challenging the paper's secular posture.[35] A number of observant Jews were even on the newspaper's staff. Israel Landau was a Hasid employed by the authorities as the official censor of *Der fraynd.*[36] Despite his religious and political leanings, he was often in the newspaper office as late as two in the morning, chuckling over the latest contribution by Sholem Aleichem. Landau's friendship with Ginzburg, the paper's editor, developed to such an extent that the two arranged for Ginzburg to "censor the paper himself" in order to save Landau "the trouble."[37] And *Der fraynd* could count other observant Jews among its staff. The paper's first typesetters were fifteen Orthodox Jews imported from Vilna to operate the paper's typesetting machines. Shoyl Ginzburg has recalled with chagrin (and, no doubt, hyperbole) that these men were often found absorbed not in work but in prayer, their side-locks and ritual fringes swinging. In spite of Ginzburg's discontent, the presence of observant Jews in a St. Petersburg newspaper office should not, on the surface, have come as a surprise. Since the early nineteenth century Jewish publishing had been dominated by the religious by official decree; for years the state had permitted only two Jewish presses to operate in the empire, both located in Zhitomir and controlled by Hasidim.[38] This arrangement made it difficult for *maskilim,* the supporters of the Jewish Enlightenment, to learn to operate printing presses or to create presses of their own. This had a bearing not only on Yiddish-language publishing but also on the publication of Russian-language sources. In the late nineteenth century it was not unusual for printing presses to be run by immigrants from lands annexed by the Russian Empire, Jews among them. In 1881 Jews from the Pale ran fully 12 percent of the printing firms in St. Petersburg.[39] Hasidic censors and Yiddish typesetters may have been exceptional figures in turn-of-the-century Russia. Nonetheless, they are reminders of the permeable line that divided religious and secular cultural Jewish production in the first decade of the twentieth century. This line was blurred by necessity, the camps it divided far from discrete.

Advertising Observance

If *Der fraynd*'s editors maintained a stubborn disinterest in observant readers, they did not attempt to monitor, or simply could not monitor, all corners of their newspaper to deter such readers. The newspaper's advertising section, in particular, revealed that religious readers were not only among the paper's regular subscribers but were envisioned as active consumers of culture and commodities. Among such advertisements some announced the sale of items to aid in the celebration of Jewish holidays; in the weeks leading up to Passover, *Der fraynd* would consistently publish a flurry of advertisements promoting kosher food and drink appropriate for the occasion. The most prominent purveyor of kosher wine, at least in the pages of *Der fraynd*, was "Carmel," a company whose advertisements normally read: "drink only Carmel wine." Around the time of Passover, advertisers for Carmel wine replaced this terse Yiddish text with an equally terse statement in Hebrew ("drink Carmel wine for all the days of Passover)," as if to draw attention to the purity of the product.[40] Other advertisements promoted items specially koshered for Passover, including tea sold in Moscow; meat, cigars, and sweets sold in Warsaw; kefir sold in Frankfurt; and a special implement for preparing matzo sold in Vilna.[41]

Holidays stimulated emotions as well as the appetite, and advertisements were quick to cater to such needs. One advertisement offered readers "*di shenste ekht yidishe* [the most beautiful and most Jewish]" New Year's cards. Another publicized the reproduction of a painting of Yom Kippur (the Day of Repentance) by M. Yafo, announcing: "[this] large gorgeous picture that has already become famous among artists and academics is now available in fourteen colors. This picture shows in a lifelike way the moving scene of Erev Yom Kippur, when grandfathers and grandmothers pray over their grandchildren before going to synagogue."[42] Elsewhere an advertisement promoted "Jewish historical pictures" that included twenty-seven illustrations of biblical figures and events.[43] The following Yiddish posting promoted an item that arguably was intended to appeal not only to religious readers but to historically minded ones:

> *The letter of Joseph the Righteous.* What he sent his father Jacob through his brothers. He describes everything that happened to him from the time

that they threw him in the ditch until the time he was a duke in Egypt. The letter is 104 pages long and written in the Roman alphabet. It is more than 2000 years old. Price with postage 40 kopecks. Send a postcard of request, Typografia B. Tursch, Warsaw, Nalevki 39.[44]

One could argue that products like these were designed for consumers more nostalgic than pious. To borrow loosely from Gregory Freeze, one might call this "clumsy manipulation of the sacred."[45] But although this may be true, these advertisements, like those designed for explicitly observant readers, nonetheless introduced the theme of religion to an arena where it was otherwise ignored. Advertisements for pious images and Passover foods suggest that, despite the goals of Shoyl Ginzburg and other producers of the paper, *Der fraynd*'s readers were not altogether secular; or perhaps the editors' intention to produce a paper only for secular readers misjudged the extensive and often undetectable overlap between religious and secular readers and between religious and secular reading matter.

To the extent that tension surrounded the wedding of advertisements designed for the religious and a newspaper designed for the secular, it was captured linguistically: advertisements targeting observant readers were often published, at least in part, in Hebrew, a gesture suggesting that these advertisements were separate from the medium in which they appeared. One advertisement for a kosher restaurant in St. Petersburg was even complemented by a handwritten Hebrew note of approval and a *heksher* (seal of kashrut) by local Jewish authorities.[46] Such attempts to draw distinctions between the religious and the secular were not foolproof, however. One did not need to be religiously observant to be able to read an advertisement in Hebrew, recognize a *heksher*, want to locate a kosher restaurant in Berlin, learn where to purchase religious texts or ritual objects in Warsaw, or be interested in the publication of a new book for cantors.[47] The secular and the religious were categories that were blurred by merchants wise enough to understand that a secular Yiddish newspaper was bound to reach the hands of observant readers.

Der fraynd's advertising pages were not only utilized by merchants selling wares or services; readers also submitted their own advertisements or announcements to the newspaper. Women, especially, saw the advertising section as inviting participation. *Der fraynd*, like other Yiddish newspapers of the day, frequently published advertisements penned by women in pursuit of truant husbands. According to Jewish law, abandoned wives are forbidden to remarry without a rabbi's approval, and permission hinges either on proof of death or a husband's consent. Traditionally the search for errant husbands was managed by the religious authorities, but as early as the late nineteenth century, the popular press was usurping some of this authority by serving as a mouthpiece for desperate women.[48] In 1903 one such advertisement featured the capitalized heading "WHO KNOWS?" and the plea of a woman seeking her husband, "a tailor from Vasilevka" named Yankev Viderman," who abandoned her and their five-year-old child. "Is he alive or dead?" the text asks, pleading: "Have pity! Jews with pity who are the children of Jews with pity."[49] A similar advertisement appeared some years later with the heading, in bold type, "Searching for My Husband!" The text read:

> It is already a year since my husband left for London, and since then my friend who lives there wrote me that he has left London with another woman. Here are his details: he is thirty-six years old, his hair already gray, with blond whiskers, a pock-marked face and long nose, he is of middling height, not very confident, his name *Zalmen Hersh Skunk*, a sock maker, who lived in Braynsk. Have pity, Jews, on a young woman with three small children! If you know such a man, inform this address.[50]

Such advertisements testify to the way in which the mass-circulating daily Yiddish press renegotiated traditional media of communication and arbitration among Russian Jewry. While we have no reason to assume that the women who posted these advertisements did not simultaneously seek help from rabbis, that they would turn to the daily press to publicize their husbands' abandonment suggests that a rabbi's abilities were considered to be newly circumscribed in ways the press was not.[51] This posting speaks not only of new symbolic roles but of shifting economic and leadership responsibilities: these young mothers were aware that their abandonment was as much an economic as a religious concern, best suited to a commercial rather than, or as well as, a communal or religious arbitrator.

A short while after "Searching for My Husband!" was published, *Der fraynd* seemed to prove that it could, indeed, help readers who felt that the religious authorities were impotent. In February 1908 a small article appeared on the second page of *Der fraynd* with the title "Yisroel Prayse," and an accompanying photograph of a grim-looking man. "In order to warn Jewish daughters away from abandonment and swindling," the text reads, "we are printing a picture of the well-known Yisroel Prayse who married 30 times in various towns, abandoning the women each time until he was arrested in Minsk."[52] With the awareness that women turned to the paper for defense against fleeing husbands, this article seems to acknowledge the kind of influence *Der fraynd*, and the Yiddish press in general, had seized. Were readers tempted to shun the daily newspaper, this posting seems to suggest, then they would be jeopardizing their very security and even, perhaps, their ability to live according to Jewish law.

This otherwise self-confidently secular medium had inadvertently become an architect of Jewish arbitration.

The story of Yisroel Prayse had another installment. About a week after *Der fraynd* published its warning about Prayse, it ran a cartoon in *Der fraynd baylage* (*Der fraynd*'s weekly literary supplement) that satirized the scandal. The cartoon pictures two infants, one seated on a low stool, the other in a high chair. Each child grips in chubby fists a copy of an adult-sized newspaper with the heading *Hehaver* (The friend), while a doll lies on the ground in front of them, forsaken for this more interesting toy. The caption reads, "A scandal! A children's paper—and not a single reference to Yisroel Prayse and his 80 wives!"[53] Printed at a time when *Der fraynd* was beginning to lose control over its readers, this cartoon reflects the anxiety with which the paper reported on this cause célèbre, appealing to readers' zeal for scandal while at the same time poking fun at it. It indicates that publishing an article about Yisroel Prayse was a way for the paper to respond to the needs that readers had aggressively introduced to the paper's advertising pages, but also that the paper's shapers remained nervous about transgressing the boundary between the pious and the profane. After all, although *Der fraynd*'s creators may have disdained readers' "childish" tastes or impulses, they had no choice but to consider and even cater to them. These impulses compelled the readers to become the paper's creators, and the creators, in turn, to become its readers.

Piety Satirized/Piety Normalized

Cartoons made their appearance in the Yiddish press only in 1905, and they quickly proved to be a medium well suited to negotiating tensions between secular-minded editors and religiously inclined readers.[54] The immediate catalyst advancing this medium was the lifting of censorship, a product of Tsar Nicholas's otherwise halfhearted 1905 October Manifesto, and the general revolutionary spirit that gripped the Russian street in 1905 and 1906. In the wake of October, hundreds of new periodicals blossomed into print, among them myriad satirical papers venting opposition to the old regime in visual form. Between 1905 and 1907 satirical journals featuring political cartoons, caricatures, and radical graphics were published in virtually all the languages of this most multilingual of empires. During these years nearly fifty such papers were also published in Yiddish.[55]

Although for the first few years of its existence, *Der fraynd* had positioned itself as a moderate Zionist organ, by early 1906 the newspaper refashioned itself into a mouthpiece of the Left. This realignment responded to shifts in Russian Jewish politics; by 1905 the Zionist movement was losing its grasp on Jewish popular opinion, and the Bund, then less than ten years old, was emerging as the dominant force of Russian Jewish party politics. This shift had many causes. The Bund gained popularity because the party had successfully organized self-defense groups and had led the general strike movement. The Zionist movement, meanwhile, entered 1905 in disarray. Theodor Herzl, the movement's symbolic leader, had died only a year earlier, leaving in his wake the messy memory of the failed Uganda proposal.[56] Together, these factors ensured that Jewish popular opinion was increasingly cast in favor of social-ism, and that the Zionist movement was thrown on the defensive. In May 1905 the Zionist leadership in Russia issued its support for radical change, and most Russian Zionists, like most Russian Zionist institutions, began to ally themselves with opposition politics, subordinating their call for Jewish national rights to the demand for democratic reform in Russia.[57] Inclined to adaptation rather than isolation, many Zionist institutions saw little choice but to join the fold.

Among them was *Der fraynd*, renamed *Dos lebn* the previous winter as a guard against censorship, not an uncommon maneuver for Russian newspapers of the late imperial period. In part to express its support for the revolution-ary cause, the paper developed a satirical supplement entitled *Der bezim*, and both here and in the main body of *Dos lebn* a series of cartoons announced the paper's new political leanings. Elsewhere I have explored the way in which these cartoons articulated a new relationship with domestic Russian politics; but of interest here is the way that the paper's turn to the Left and its newfound reli-ance on cartoons facilitated a kind of reconciliation with observant readers.[58] This reconciliation is illustrated by *Der bezim*'s mascot, a broom (*bezim*) pictured in the hands of a comical sweeper. We discern from his dress that *Der bezim*'s sweeper is of the working class and is Orthodox: his head is covered, and he wears a caftan and tallis, a beard and *peysis* (side-locks). His pants are tucked into shiny ankle-high workman's boots. Although his broom is raised behind him, his left foot airborne as if he is in motion, the sweeper looks less intent on the task of sweeping than on confronting the reader. The sweeper's gaze is amused but at the same time rather fierce; his mouth is open in a wide grin, teeth exposed, giving him a slightly deranged look.

This image could not have appeared in Russian Jewish periodicals of the late nineteenth century, such as *Voskhod* (St. Petersburg, 1881–1906), *Razsvet* (Odessa, 1860–1861), or *Hashiloah* (Odessa, 1896–1918) nor, for that matter, in the young *Der fraynd*. These journals prided themselves on their appeal to educated, Russified, urban Jewish intellectuals, readers thought to be clean-shaven men who might sport a fashionable mustache, a waistcoat, elegant shoes, men who would go about bare-headed, carrying books, not brooms. *Der bezim*'s mascot displays a very different sense of self, not because the journal's readers necessarily were

Figure 10.1. *Der bezim* masthead, 1906.

imagined to resemble this sweeper (although many of them may well have) but because they were perceived as willing to interpret the image as satire rather than threat, an asset rather than a disability. *Der bezim*'s banner head suggests that, by 1906, the producers of the Yiddish press were gaining confidence that observant Jews could be counted among—indeed visually represent—their readership as a whole, at least in satiric form.

There is radicalism in *Der bezim*'s depicting what was once unthinkable to portray, but also moderation. The sweeper, after all, is the ultimate socialist symbol: a poor, working-class, angry man, all symbols guaranteed to appeal to Russian Jews newly politicized by the Bund. If *Der bezim* was reaching out to its readers, then, it was also struggling to remain relevant at a time when the political stakes were changing for Russian Jewish party politics. Not only was the Bund growing in influence but the institution of the press was itself evolving. Partly because of the politicization of Russian Jewry, by 1906 the Russian Yiddish popular press was expanding at an unprecedented rate. One could argue, then, that the producers of *Der bezim* and *Der fraynd* had reason to fear obsolescence more than observance. Thus it was not only, as Mark Steinberg has demonstrated, that religious sensibilities or tropes infused Russia's emerging worker culture.[59] In the era of revolution, observant readers themselves had acquired a kind of political cachet for the Jewish Left: they were perceived as warriors and custodians of uprising at a moment when it was impolitic *not* to support the revolutionary cause. In this sense, *Der fraynd*'s sudden, though arguably much overdue, embrace of the observant reader did not so much betray its producers' democratic leanings as it concealed a deep-seated conservatism and fear of being left behind.

Perhaps the most entertaining evidence of this trend materialized in the summer of 1913, long after the revolution was forcibly concluded. Six years earlier, *Der fraynd* had relocated to Warsaw in what many saw as a desperate bid to remain competitive. Early in the second decade of the twentieth century, Warsaw was emerging as a preeminent center of Yiddish letters and home to the greatest concentration of East European Yiddish periodicals.[60] The city was also known for the ferocious battles that engaged its literary luminaries, which *Der fraynd* could hardly avoid.[61] Perhaps the most famous butt of humor and promulgator of controversy in the Warsaw Yiddish press was Hillel Tsaytlin, who contributed first to the daily *Haynt* and subsequently to its competitor, *Der moment.*[62] Once a secular intellectual, Tsaytlin had, in an act that invoked the derision of many of his secular peers, recently embraced Orthodoxy. Among his critics was the editor of *Der fraynd*, Shmuel Rosenfeld, who accused Tsaytlin of hypocrisy and, far worse, of posturing: Tsaytlin, Rosenfeld insisted, habitually violated the Sabbath and had been seen consuming pork on Yom Kippur, the year's holiest day dedicated to fasting and repentance.[63] The paper's claims were not widely accepted: few were inclined to view the high-handed *Der fraynd* as a sentinel of Orthodoxy. However, that *Der fraynd* dared to voice such accusations in the first place, strongly suggests the evolving relationship between the secular Yiddish press and religious readers. This episode demonstrates that *Der fraynd* had come to acknowledge the significance not only of Orthodox readers but of religious sensibilities more generally. The Yiddish press and its representatives could no longer ignore these forces, let alone disparage them. By this time personal and institutional reputations had come to rest on the normalization, indeed the veneration, of religiously minded readers, if not the notion of religion itself.

The episode involving Tsaytlin may have bridged two very different historical moments in the world of Yiddish letters. It was preceded by the invention of the Yiddish newspaper reader, a reader interested in worldly affairs far removed from the traditional milieu of the Russian Pale. It would be succeeded by an era in which Yiddish newspapers were understood not only as sources of information but as a medium that could illuminate and deepen the predilections that fissured Jews along religious, class, aesthetic, political, and geographic lines. In the interwar period, religious readers would be viewed not as members of an overall Yiddish reading public but rather as a distinct reading public with needs, interests, and buying powers of its own.[64]

Conclusion

This paper has sought evidence in the pages of the early Russian Yiddish daily press of a profound overlap between religious and secular Jews, on the one hand, and religious and secular texts, on the other, that might be understood as a central feature of early-twentieth-century Russian Jewish culture. *Der fraynd* proves a useful case study not because it was a typical newspaper, nor because it represented the views of its many readers. It is provocative, instead, because it was one of very few Yiddish newspapers to emerge at a critical moment of transition in Russian Jewish culture. It appeared before Jewish party politics had become rigid and polarized, before the genre of the Yiddish daily had become a permanent feature of the East European landscape, and before the will of Yiddish readers came to dominate the industry of Yiddish publishing. Partly as a result of all this, its pages were sites of experimentation: spaces where readers and producers of the Yiddish press could test the possibilities inherent in this novel genre and, in the process, learn a great deal about themselves.

This essay suggests that the emergence of a popular literature and press in the Russian Jewish vernacular did not, as many scholars have assumed, irrevocably sharpen the divide between religious and secular Jewish readers, on the one hand, and sacred and profane texts, on the other. Although the rabbinical elite and the pioneers of avowedly secular Jewish culture both attempted to control the substance and form of reading matter for Jews, neither could succeed. Partially this was because the proliferation of affordable and accessible texts allowed readers of Yiddish the freedom to read independently, quite possibly for the first time. But it was also because Jewish readers appear not to have been dissuaded by the binaries (religious or secular, sacred or profane) that elites imposed upon Jewish readers. Like their non-Jewish peers, Russian Jews' experience of the sacred was not controlled by traditional mores but was profoundly influenced by emerging technologies, evolving socioeconomic realities, and a fluid sense of self.

Notes

1. That the vast majority of Eastern European *maskilim* came from traditional backgrounds is an unavoidable reality of turn-of-the-century Russian Jewish History. This is conveyed in a number of biographies of the period that retrace family lineages of prominent Jewish intellectuals. To list a few among many: Sophie Dubnov-Erlich, *The Life and Works of S. M. Dubnov: Diaspora Nationalism and Jewish History* (Bloomington, Ind., 1991); Amia Lieblich, *Conversations with Dvora: An Experimental Biography of the First Modern Hebrew Woman Writer,* trans. Naomi Seidman (Berkeley, Calif., 1997); Michael Stanislawski, *For Whom Do I Toil? Judah Leib Gordon and the Crisis of Russian Jewry* (New York, 1988); Steven Zipperstein, *Elusive*

Prophet: Ahad Ha'am and the Origins of Zionism (Berkeley, Calif., 1993); and Ruth Wisse, *I. L. Peretz and the Making of Modern Jewish Culture* (Seattle, Wash., 1991).

2. Mark D. Steinberg, *Proletarian Imagination: Self, Modernity, and the Sacred in Russia, 1910–1925* (New York, 2002), esp, chaps. 6, 7.

3. Information about Morris Shaten has been culled from an interview conducted by his son, Dr. Haim Shaten, in 1965. It is held in the archives of the Jewish Institute for Scientific Research (YIVO) as part of its collection of oral histories of American Jewish labor activists.

4. Morris Shaten (1965), "Interview with Morris Shaten by his son, Dr. Haim F. Shaten," YIVO Institute for Jewish Research, 4.

5. Ibid., 5.

6. Ibid., 5–6.

7. In judging literacy levels, the census defined Jews by language, not nationality. Thus nearly two hundred thousand Jews who identified their mother tongue as Russian (including some who wished to disassociate themselves from Yiddish for political reasons) were not counted as literate Jews. Results of the Russian census of 1897 may be found in a variety of sources. See, for example: "Gramotnost' evreev v Rossii," in *Evreiskaia entsiklopediia* (St. Petersburg, 1908–1913). This information is also summarized in English by I. M. Rubinow, *Economic Conditions of the Jews in Russia*, vol. 15 (New York, 1907). At roughly the same time as the Russian census was collected, the Jewish Colonization Association undertook its own study of Russian Jewry. These findings are reported in *Sbornik materialov ob ekonomicheskom polozhenii Evreev v Rossii* (St. Petersburg, 1904). Unfortunately this study does not include a more detailed accounting of Jewish literacy rates.

8. "Gramotnost' evreev v Rossii"; Rubinow, *Economic Conditions of the Jews in Russia*.

9. Arcadius Kahan, *Essays in Jewish Social and Economic History*, ed. Roger Weiss (Chicago, 1986), 4 n. 3. As Kahan points out, most of these Jews were concentrated in Warsaw, Lodz, Odessa, and Kiev.

10. Michael C. Steinlauf, "The Polish-Jewish Daily Press," *Polin* 2 (1987): 219–245. See also Keith Ian Weiser, "The Politics of Yiddish: Noyekh Prilutski and the Folkspartey in Poland, 1900–1926" (Ph.D. dissertation, Columbia University, 2001).

11. I explore the emergence and impact of the popular Yiddish press in more detail in Sarah Abrevaya Stein, *Making Jews Modern: The Yiddish and Ladino Press of the Russian and Ottoman Empires* (Bloomington, Ind., 2003).

12. For a more thorough description of the creation of *Der fraynd* and the state of Jewish publishing in the empire at the turn of the century, see ibid. See also D. A. Eliashevich, *Evrei v Rossii: Istoriia i kultura: Sbornik nauchnykh trudov*, Vol. 5, *Trudy po iudaike. Istoriia i etnografiia* (St. Petersburg, 1998); Dovid Druk, *Tsu der geshikhte fun der yidisher prese in rusland un poylen* (Warsaw, 1920); Tsitron, *Di geshikhte fun der yidisher prese fun yorn 1863–1889* (New York, 1923); Shabsay Rapoport, "Der anheyb fun 'fraynd'," *Yubileum-baylage fraynd, tsenter yorgang*, no. 12 (1913): 2–5; *Dokumenty Sobrannye Evreiskoi Istoriko-arkheograficheskoi Komissiei Vseukrainskoi akademii nauk*, ed. Viktoriia Khiterer, "Sovremennye issledovaniia" series (Kiev and Jerusalem, 1999); David E. Fishman, "The Politics of Yiddish in Tsarist Russia," in *From Ancient Israel to Modern Judaism, Intellect in Quest of Understanding*, ed. Ernest Frerichs et al. (Atlanta, 1989), 155–173; and Shoyl Ginzburg, *Amolike peterburg*, 2 vols., Vol. 1, *Historishe verk* (New York, 1944).

13. In contrast to most Russian-language dailies, which tended to circulate within particular cities, *Der fraynd*'s readership was spread throughout the empire's Western Provinces, and many of its contributors and readers lived not in St. Petersburg but in Warsaw, which provoked considerable friction between its editors and journalists. There is some debate about the scope of the paper's circulation. Zalman Reyzen attributes the lowest circulation to *Der fraynd* at fifty thousand (*Leksikon fun der yidisher literatur, prese, un filologye* [Vilna, 1926]). The editor Shoyl Ginzburg estimates it to have been ninety thousand (*Amolike peterburg*). Dovid Druk, a historian of the Yiddish press, who offers the most thorough accounting of the history

of Yiddish publishing, cites a higher figure of one hundred thousand (*Tsu der geshikhte fun der yidisher prese in rusland un poylen*).

14. These fears were well founded to some extent; the Jewish socialist underground press, printed abroad and smuggled to Russian Jewish readers was—like the Bundist movement as a whole—swiftly gaining popularity at this time. Further, ministry officials indeed lacked the means to effectively censor and control Yiddish in print. Available censors tended to be converts or Hasidic opponents of secular Jewish culture, both of whom the ministry had reasons to distrust. Recent explorations of Russian archives have considerably deepened our understandings of the nature of Russian censorship of Yiddish sources. For example, see D. A. Eliashevich, *Pravitel'stvennaia politika i evreiskaia pechat'*; and Khiterer, *Dokumenty Sobrannye Evreiskoi Istoriko-arkheograficheskoi Komissiei*. See also Rapoport, "Der onheyb fun 'fraynd'; Druk, *Tsu der geshikhte fun der yidisher prese;* Tsitron, *Di geshikhte fun der yidisher prese;* Ginzburg, *Amolike peterburg;* Fishman, "The Politics of Yiddish in Tsarist Russia"; Stephen D. Corrsin, *Warsaw before the First World War: Poles and Jews in the Third City of the Russian Empire 1880–1914* (Boulder, Colo., 1989); idem, "Language Use in Cultural and Political Change in Pre-1914 Warsaw: Poles, Jews, and Russification," *Slavonic and East European Review* 68, no. 1 (1990): 69–90; Alexander Orbach, *New Voices of Russian Jewry* (Leiden, 1980); Dan Miron, *A Traveler Disguised: A Study in the Rise of Modern Yiddish Fiction in the Nineteenth Century* (New York, 1973); and Emanuel Goldsmith, *Modern Yiddish Culture: the Story of the Modern Yiddish Language Movement* (New York, 1987).

15. One consequence of the Ministry of Interior's policies was the enforced dependence of Yiddish readers in Congress Poland on periodicals published in Odessa (in the last decades of the nineteenth century) and St. Petersburg (in the first years of the twentieth). This proved inconvenient, as readers in Poland received their papers after a delay of several days, and, moreover, these sources tended to be oblivious to local news. This geographic divide also highlighted the political schisms that divided Jewish intellectuals in these erstwhile and up-and-coming literary centers. While the founders of *Der fraynd* gained the approval of the Ministry of Interior because of the paper's Russophilism, readers and writers of Yiddish in Warsaw voiced criticism of the paper's disinterest in affairs in "the provinces" in general, and in Warsaw in particular, a city that would soon outpace Odessa and St. Petersburg as the Yiddish literary center of Eastern Europe. In turn, *Der fraynd*'s editors disdained the more radical literary and political sensibilities of Warsaw's emerging literary elite. Nonetheless, as Warsaw rose in preeminence, the paper's editorial board saw no option but to succumb to the new norms in Yiddish publishing. Thus, in 1909, the paper relocated to Warsaw, a move that was viewed by critics as a superficial reckoning with a deeply rooted problem. I describe this dynamic in more detail in *Making Jews Modern*. See also Corrsin, *Warsaw before the First World War;* and Chone Shmeruk, "Aspects of the History of Warsaw as a Yiddish Literary Center," in *The Jews in Warsaw: A History*, ed. Wladyslaw T. Bartoszewski and Antony Polonsky (Oxford, 1991), 232–246.

16. *Der fraynd,* no. 1, 5 (18) January 1903.

17. Ibid.

18. This column bears the same title as one penned by I. L. Peretz in the weekly *Der yud,* and may well have been penned by Peretz using the pseudonym "Emes." References to the series in an article by Bal Makhshoves, however, attribute it to S. An-sky. See Bal Makhshoves (Isador Eliashev), "Notizn fun a kritik," *Kunst un lebn,* no. 1 (June 1908): 49–54; Ruth Wisse, "Not the 'Pintele Yid' but the Full-Fledged Jew," *Prooftexts* 15, no. January (1995): 33–61.

19. "Shtet un shtetlakh," *Der fraynd,* no. 21, 29 January (11 February) 1903.

20. "Shtet un shtetlakh," *Der fraynd,* no. 60, 17 (30) March 1903.

21. "Di rusishe shprakhe in yeshivas," *Der fraynd,* no. 36, 3 (16) March 1903.

22. Ginzburg, *Amolike peterburg,* 231.

23. Newspapers designed for observant readers did emerge earlier: among the first was *Halevanon,* published in the 1870s in Hebrew. Its founder, Rabbi Ya'acov Lifshits, sensed the

opportunity to use the newspaper medium to combat the influence of the Haskalah and of Zionism. According to Lifshits, *Halevanon* was read by almost every rabbi in Poland, Lithuania, and the Ukraine. It took some thirty years, however, for the genre of the "religious newspaper" to catch on. For Lifshits's reflections on the history of *Halevanon,* see Ya'akov Lifshits, *Zikhron Ya'akov,* 3 vols. (Frankfurt and Kovno, 1924–1930), 2:99. For a brief discussion of the history of *Halevanon,* see Ehud Luz, *Parallels Meet: Religion and Nationalism in the Early Zionist Movement (1882–1904)* (Philadelphia, Pa., 1988), 15–16. A more general discussion of the rise of Orthodox politics and cultural production in the interwar period is the subject of Gershon Bacon's *Politics of Tradition: Agudat Yisrael in Poland, 1916–1939* (Jerusalem, 1996).

24.   Notably *Der fraynd's* coverage of cultural affairs in the United States had a profound impact on young émigrés. In an autobiographical essay, Elbert Aidline Trommer has recalled how strongly *Der fraynd's* coverage of American Jewish writers affected him in the years before he left Russia for New York. See Elbert Aidline Trommer (Khaym eliezer ben mordkhe-dov). "Far vos ikh bin avek fun der alter heym un vos ikh hob dergreykht in amerike" (YIVO Institute, American Autobiography, Folder 182), 35.

25.   Zipperstein, *Elusive Prophet,* 118–119.

26.   These dailies were devoted to providing readers with sensational stories about crime and romance (filled, in one writer's words, with "blood and love"), and, of course, the day's news, which focused on local as well as international events, a practice long avoided by *Der fraynd.* This new generation of newspapers, periodicals like *Haynt* (Warsaw, 1910–1939) and *Der moment* (Warsaw, 1910–1939), were inexpensive, fiercely competitive, and known to woo readers aggressively. For the first time they relied on street sales rather than subscriptions, and they were in great demand. Both *Haynt* and *Der moment* gained a circulation of more than thirty-five thousand. These readerships are striking because they were concentrated in a single city and competed with dozens of new Polish, Yiddish, and Hebrew papers.

27.   See, for example Gregory Freeze, "Counter-Reformation in Russian Orthodoxy: Popular Response to Religious Innovation, 1922–1925," *Slavic Review* 54, no. 2 (summer 1995): 305–339; Jeffrey Burds, *Peasant Dreams and Market Politics* (Pittsburgh, Pa., 1998); Laura Engelstein, *Castration and the Heavenly Kingdom* (Ithaca, N.Y., 1999); Heather J. Coleman, "Becoming a Russian Baptist: Conversion Narratives and Social Experience," *Russian Review* 61, no. 1 (January 2002): 94–112, Vera Shevzov, *Russian Orthodoxy on the Eve of Revolution* (Oxford, 2004).

28.   See, for example, Bacon, *The Politics of Tradition;* Ezra Mendelsohn, "Interwar Poland: Good for the Jews or Bad for the Jews," in *The Jews in Poland,* ed. Chimen Abramsky, Maciej Jachimczyk, and Antony Polonsky (Oxford, 1986), 130–139; Shimon Frost, *Schooling as a Socio-Political Expression: Jewish Education in Interwar Poland* (Jerusalem, 1998); Ezra Mendelsohn, "Jewish Politics in Interwar Poland: An Overview," in *The Jews of Poland between Two World Wars,* ed. Yisrael Gutman et al. (Hanover, N.H., 1989), 9–19; and Edward D. Wynot, "Jews in the Society and Politics of Inter-war Warsaw," in Bartoszewski and Polonsky, *The Jews in Warsaw,* 291–311.

29.   By 1905 *Der fraynd* was available for purchase in cities throughout the Pale of Settlement and Congress Poland, as well as in the imperial capital, and relied on distribution agents in St. Petersburg (through the *Der fraynd* office), Vilna (through the "Shtesel House"), Warsaw (through H. D. Perlman), Odessa (through bookseller S. Hornshteyn), Kiev (through "Pedagogue" booksellers), Lodz (through *Wygoda* publishing house), Kovel (through Heinrich Geller), and Riga (through the bookseller Y. L. Ashkenazi). In 1908 *Der fraynd* took to publishing its list of distributing "agents" in its advertising pages. Three years later the paper could be bought in dozens of cities in Russia and numerous cities abroad: in England from the book-seller L. Friedman (in Oxford) and in Berlin, from the bookseller P. Gontser. See, for example, *Der fraynd,* no. 18, 22 January (4 February) 1908. For a reference to sellers abroad, see *Der fraynd,* no. 195, 27 August (9 September) 1908.

30.   Zipperstein, *Elusive Prophet,* 151. This account is echoed in "Mendl Turk," a short story by S. An-sky, author, ethnographer, and occasional contributor to *Der fraynd.* The narrator of

An-sky's tale, a secular Jewish tutor, is shocked to discover that the local synagogue is home not to the spiritual ambiance of "amity and love" that he remembers from his youth but to a vociferous debate over the ongoing Russo-Turkish War (S. An-sky, "Mendl Turk," in *The Dybbuk and Other Writings,* ed. David Roskies [New York, 1992], 93–117).

31. Ginzburg, *Amolike peterburg,* 218, 217.

32. Joseph Buloff, *In the Old Marketplace* (Cambridge, 1991), 13. For more on the practice of public reading, see Natalie Zemon Davis, "Printing and the People," in *Society and Culture in Early Modern France* (Stanford, Calif., 1975), 189–227.

33. Cited in Ezra Mendelsohn, *Class Struggle in the Pale: The Formative Years of the Jewish Workers' Movement in Tsarist Russia* (Oxford, 1970), 147.

34. Shlomo Goldenberg. "Hayesh korim 'evrim?" *Hashiloah* 17 (1907): 417–422. Notably this point was often challenged in the pages of *Der fraynd.* While articles in the paper often pointed to the intimacy women felt for Yiddish, contributors seemed unwilling to imagine women as constituting a significant portion of their readers. One "letter from a woman," which was, in fact, penned by a male member of the newspaper's staff, extolled the relationship between women and the Yiddish language while simultaneously degrading women's interest in reading the Yiddish press. "Jewish women read few books and newspapers in Yiddish," the article begins; [t]he average woman doesn't have enough time, while upper-class women have no interest in reading in Yiddish. Very few of us women, mind you, will open a Yiddish book or newspaper, and, when we do, we understand very little of what is written there." See Dina Tsaytlin, "Fun a fremde velt, (a briv fun a froy)," *Der fraynd,* no. 6, 12 (25) January 1903. That Tsaytlin was but a pseudonym is documented in H. D. Horovits, "Unzer ershte teglikhe tsaytung (tsu der tsen-yoriger geshikhte fun'm Fraynd)," in *Der pinkes, yorbukh fun der geshikhte fun der yidisher literatur un shprakh, far folklor, kritik un bibliografie,* ed. Shmuel Niger (Vilna, 1912), 244–265. For more on the practice of male journalists using women's names, see Naomi Seidman, *A Marriage Made in Heaven: The Sexual Politics of Hebrew and Yiddish* (Berkeley, Calif., 1997).

35. The article "Di rusishe shprakhe in yeshivas," for example, responded to a letter published in the preceding issue of *Der fraynd.* This letter, penned by a (self-proclaimed) religious reader, criticized the assumption that yeshiva students ought to be fluent in Russian (*Der fraynd,* no. 36, 3 [17] March 1903).

36. The practice of hiring Hasidic censors was not an uncommon one for the state; the Hasidim, who were, at least theoretically, hostile to secular Jewish culture, were thought to be reliable checks on the spread of radicalism. In addition, they, like converts, were among the few Yiddish speakers on whom the Ministry of Interior felt they could rely. See Shoyl Ginzburg, "Tsu der geshikhte fun yidishn drukvezn," in *Historishe verk, fun yidishen leben un shafen in tsarishen rusland.* 3 vols. (New York, 1937), 1:48–62; Druk, *Tsu der geshikhte fun der yidisher prese;* Shmuel Leyb Tsitron, *Di geshikhte fun der yidisher prese fun yorn 1863–1889* (New York, 1923).

37. Ginzburg's lengthy description of Landau can be found in his memoirs, *Amolike peterburg,* 224–227.

38. Ginzburg, "Tsu der geshikhte fun yidishn drukvezn."

39. Mark D. Steinberg, *Moral Communities: The Culture of Class Relations in the Russian Printing Industry, 1867–1907* (Berkeley, Calif., 1992), 13.

40. See, for example, *Der fraynd,* no. 59, 11 (24) March 1904.

41. *Der fraynd,* no. 45, 1 (14) March 1905; the advertisements for meat are in *Der fraynd,* no. 59, 11 (24) March 1904, and for tea in *Der fraynd,* no. 42, 11 (23) March 1903. A. Aronovitch's advertisement for a matzo-making accouterment is in *Der fraynd,* no. 27, 1 (14) February 1908.

42. *Der fraynd,* no. 173, 9 (22) August 1905. M. Yafo's painting would be promoted in the pages of *Der fraynd* around the time of Yom Kippur for years to come.

43. *Der fraynd,* no. 235, 25 October (10 November) 1903.

44. *Der fraynd,* no. 54, 23 (11) March 1903.

45. Gregory L. Freeze, "Subversive Piety: Religion and the Political Crisis in Late Imperial Russia," *Journal of Modern History* 68 (June 1996): 312.

46. *Der fraynd*, no. 228, 10 (23) December 1908.

47. Advertisements for the Hotel Orient's kosher restaurant appeared in *Der fraynd* for countless years. Ritual objects could be bought from Y. Shekman, among other sellers. See *Der fraynd*, no. 195, 27 August (9 September) 1908. The guide for cantors was promoted in *Der fraynd*, no. 173, 1 (14) August 1908.

48. Beginning in the 1860s abandoned Jewish women turned to the daily press for assistance in seeking truant spouses. At this time, the editor Eliezer Lipman Zilberman devoted the last page of his Hebrew periodical *Hamagid* to advertisements searching for truant husbands. See Mark Baker, "The Voice of the Deserted Jewish Women, 1867–1870," *Jewish Social Studies* 2, no. 1 (1995): 98–124. Arguably the need for such postings was exacerbated by the fact that Jewish widows were considerably more prevalent than Jewish widowers in late-nineteenth- and early-twentieth-century Russia. See Arcadius Kahan, *Essays in Jewish Social and Economic History*, ed. Roger Weiss (Chicago, 1986).

49. *Der fraynd*, no. 245, 8 (21) November 1903.

50. *Der fraynd*, no. 25, 31 January (13 February) 1907.

51. For more on the evolving nature of Jewish marriage and divorce in late imperial Russia, see ChaeRan Y. Freeze, *Jewish Marriage and Divorce in Imperial Russia* (Waltham, Mass., 2002).

52. *Der fraynd*, no. 44, 21 February (5 March) 1908.

53. *Der fraynd baylage*, no. 9, 2 March 1908.

54. As Edward Portnoy has demonstrated, by the interwar period Yiddish cartoons satirizing religious motifs were a common feature of the press ("Exploiting Tradition: Religious Iconography in Cartoons of the Polish Yiddish Press," *Polin*, November 2003).

55. The history of cartoons of the 1905 era are explored in Vladimir Botsiavnovskii and E. F. Gollerbakh, eds., *Russkaia satira pervoi revoliutsii 1905–1906* (Leningrad, 1925); E. P. (Evgeniia Petrovna) Demchenko, *Politicheskaia grafika Kieva, perioda revoliutsii, 1905–1907* (Kiev, 1976); idem, *Politicheskaia grafika v pechati Ukrainy, 1905–1907* (Kiev, 1984); David King and Cathy Porter, *Images of Revolution: Graphic Art from 1905 Russia* (New York, 1983); E. L. Nemirovskii, ed., *Russkaia satiricheskaia periodika, 1905–1907 gg.* (St. Petersburg, 1980); and V. V. (Vladimir Vasil'evich) Shleev, ed., *Revoliutsiia 1905–1907 goda i izobrazitel'noe iskusstvo*, vol. 3 (Moscow, 1977).

56. For the most thorough exploration of the Bund's rise to power, see Jonathan Frankel, *Prophecy and Politics: Socialism, Nationalism, and the Russian Jews, 1862–1917* (Cambridge, 1981). See also Henry J. Tobias, *The Jewish Bund in Russia from Its Origins to 1905* (Stanford, Calif., 1972). In 1903, in the wake of the Kishinev pogrom, Theodor Herzl proposed that the Zionist movement accept Uganda as a destination for the mass settlement of Jews. The proposal caused a schism in the movement between those territorialists who would settle for nothing less than the settlement of the Jews in Palestine and those who sought an immediate solution to the Russian Jewish "problem." The failure of Herzl's proposal caused widespread disillusionment with the movement, which was failing to realize its territorial ambitions. See, for example, Jehuda Reinharz and Anita Shapira, eds., *Essential Papers on Zionism* (New York, 1996); and David Vital, *Zionism: The Formative Years* (Oxford, 1982).

57. For a description of the evolutions in Russian Jewish politics in this period, see, in addition to the sources listed in the preceding notes, Eliyahu Feldman, *Yehude Rusyah biyeme hamahpekhah harishonah vehapogromim*. (Jerusalem, 1999); Christoph Gassenschmidt, *Jewish Liberal Politics in Tsarist Russia, 1900–1914: The Modernization of Russian Jewry* (Oxford, 1995); and Yitzhak Maor, *Hatenuah hatsiyonit berusyah* (Jerusalem, 1986).

58. Sarah Abrevaya Stein, "Faces of Protest: Yiddish Cartoons of the 1905 Revolution," *Slavic Review* 61, no. 4 (winter 2002).

59. Steinberg, *Proletarian Imagination*, see, esp., chaps. 6, 7.

60.   The paper's relocation gained *Der fraynd* enemies among Yiddish journalists and publishers in Warsaw. Dovid Druk, a journalist for *Haynt,* although willing to credit *Der fraynd* as being the first Yiddish daily to gain a wide-reaching circulation (*Der fraynd,* he once wrote, "shaped readers of Yiddish: improved them") described the move with anger, commenting that "anyone with a sense for newspapers knew that *Der fraynd* would not succeed in Warsaw." Hidden behind Druk's ire seems to be the accusation that *Der fraynd*'s move was opportunistic, duplicitous. And it is true that the claims of *Der fraynd*'s new editorial staff were incongruous with the paper's history, a history that many of the fiction writers, journalists, and readers of Warsaw knew firsthand. See Druk, *Tsu der geshikhte,* 92, quote at 9. See also Bal Makhshoves, "Notizn fun a kritik."

61.   Stephen D. Corrsin, *Warsaw before the First World War: Poles and Jews in the Third City of the Russian Empire, 1880–1914* (Boulder, Colo., 1989); Chone Shmeruk, "Aspects of the History of Warsaw as a Yiddish Literary Center," in Bartoszewski and Polonsky, *The Jews in Warsaw,* 232–246; and Stephen D. Corrsin, "Language Use in Cultural and Political Change in Pre-1914 Warsaw: Poles, Jews, and Russification," *Slavonic and East European Review* 68, no. 1 (1990): 69–90.

62.   For more on these newspapers, see the contributions to *Di yidishe prese vos iz geven,* ed. Mordechai Tsanin, Dovid Flinker, and Sholem Rosenfeld (Tel Aviv, 1975); *Haynt yoyvl bukh* (Warsaw, 1938); Corrsin, *Warsaw before the First World War;* Druk, *Tsu der geshikhte fun der yidisher prese;* Yakov Shatzky, "Geshikhte fun der yidisher prese," in *Algemeyne entsiklopedye* (New York, 1942), 199–285; and Weiser, "The Politics of Yiddish."

63.   Rosenfeld aired these grievances in a series of articles signed "R." See, for example, R, "Arop di maske!" *Der fraynd,* no. 188, 28 August 1913. My thanks to Edward Portnoy for drawing this episode to my attention.

64.   On the evolving climate of interwar Jewish culture, see David Flinker and Moshe Ron. "Di yidishe presse in poyln tsvishn beyde velt-milkhomes," in *Yorbukh,* ed. Arye Tartakower, 266–325 (New York, 1967); Nahman Mayzel, *Geven a mol a lebn, dos yidishe kultur-lebn in poyln tsvishen beyde velt-milkhomes,* vol. 71, *Bikher seria, dos poylishe yudentum* (Buenos Aires, 1951); Michael C. Steinlauf, "The Polish-Jewish Daily Press," *Polin* 2 (1987): 219–245; Shmuel Werses, "The Hebrew Press and Its Readership in Interwar Poland," in *The Jews of Poland between Two World Wars,* ed. Yisrael Gutman et al. (Hanover, N.H., 1989), 312–333.

11

Revolutionary Rabbis: Hasidic Legend and the Hero of Words

Gabriella Safran

———————— ·•◦∞◦•· ————————

And now if worship even of a star had some meaning in it, how much more might that of a hero! Worship of a Hero is transcendent admiration of a Great Man. I say great men are still admirable; I say there is, at bottom, nothing else admirable! No nobler feeling than this of admiration for one higher than himself dwells in the breast of man. It is to this hour, and at all hours, the vivifying influence in man's life.
Religions I find stand on it.
Thomas Carlyle, *On Heroes, Hero-Worship, and the Heroic in History* (1841)

When young Jewish men and women from the Pale of Settlement joined the Russian radical movements at the beginning of the twentieth century, they tended to imagine themselves as rejecting the conservatism, deep piety, and inwardly focused worldview associated with traditional Judaism and especially with the popular mystical movement of Hasidism. But when the Russian Jewish ethnographer and writer, and prominent Socialist Revolutionary (SR) activist, S. An-sky (Shloyme-Zanvl Rappoport, 1863–1920) tried to define heroism in a way that was relevant to the modernizing Jews of his era, he turned for his heroes to Hasidic legends, along with other Jewish folkloric material. One legend, in particular, of a Hasidic *rebbe* who puts God on trial and determines that He is in the wrong, seemed to appeal to An-sky tremendously. He included it in his 1908 essay in Russian, "Jewish Folk Art" ("Evreiskoe narodnoe tvorchestvo") and rewrote it three more times, once more in Russian in poetic form, and twice in Yiddish, once as a poem and once in prose.

Although he is best known today as the author of the play *The Dybbuk*, An-sky published many other significant works. He lived and wrote on the border between the radical Russian intelligentsia and the traditional Jews of the Pale of Settlement, and he crossed that border many times, writing in Russian, then Yiddish, then both at once, producing novellas, stylized folktales, ethnographic

276

and political articles, poetry, war reportage, and the famous drama, *The Dybbuk*, which is often seen as the embodiment of traditional Eastern European Jewish life and beliefs. Although he is best remembered by Jewish historians and scholars of Yiddish literature, he played a visible role among the Russian radicals. In the 1880s he worked among and read to peasants and miners in the Don region; in 1892 he moved in Populist circles in St. Petersburg and wrote articles for the Populist "thick" journal *Russkoe bogatstvo* (Russian wealth); at the turn of the century he lived in Europe among radical Russian émigrés, worked for the Populist theorist Petr Lavrov until the latter's death in 1900, supported Viktor Chernov's efforts to create a unified SR party, and coauthored, with Father Georgii Gapon, a pamphlet on the 1905 pogroms. Like many émigré radicals, An-sky returned to the Russian Empire after the 1905 Revolution.

For a number of groups within the Russian intelligentsia, the first decades of the twentieth century and particularly the years after the 1905 Revolution were a time for questioning the materialistic, mechanistic, and atheistic positivism of the radical tradition, a time for affirming or challenging religious ideas and "fighting with God" (*bogoborchestvo*).[1] Russian writers of poetry, prose, and propaganda used religious imagery in this period for diverse purposes, whether to articulate ideals of revolutionary messianism and the dream of redemption through martyrdom, to argue for an individual-centered view of history, or to express their own emotions, hopes, and fears.[2] So when An-sky turned to Hasidic legend in 1908, he was responding to larger trends in his Russian as well as his Jewish milieu.

In this essay I examine some of An-sky's work during his first years back in Russia, comparing his various versions of the legend of God on trial to the Hasidic original in order to understand why this narrative appealed to him so much and what he accomplished in his many returns to it. The existence of so many contemporaneous versions of a single story by a single author in two languages provides an opportunity to consider questions of language, genre, and audience, and to speculate about the different messages that one plot could carry. I situate the various versions within a number of conversations in which Russian and Jewish thinkers were engaged at the time: the consideration by Russified Jews of the "value" of Jewish culture for themselves; the Russian discourse on Jews, which often portrayed them as posing some kind of threat to the well-being of non-Jews; and the broader European discussion of the relevance of mysticism for the modern artist and intellectual. As a bilingual and bicultural intellectual, An-sky participated in more conversations than most. His revisions of the legend of God on trial contributed to each of these discussions, I will argue, by designing a new kind of Jewish hero who might allow readers to tell—and perhaps to live out—new kinds of stories.

A Hero for the Folklorist

In his essay, "Jewish Folk Art," An-sky related dozens of Jewish folktales, all of which, he argued, show that the Jewish folk imagination celebrates not people who have mastered "physical" or "material" power but rather those who possess "spiritual" (*dukhovnaia*) strength and conquer by means of "the word or the spirit" (*slovom ili dukhom*).[3] He drew on many sources of Jewish folklore, ancient and modern, written and oral. In the section of his essay devoted to the characterization of Jewish folkloric heroes, he asserted that all bodies of folklore provide powerful idealized images of heroes whom the people can admire. Although he conceded that Jewish monotheism in principle makes it impossible to imagine heroes as gods who walk among humans, Jewish folklore manages to achieve the desired effect by creating "man in the image and likeness of God, having constructed a bridge between them in the form of the Torah."[4] After retelling a well-known Talmudic episode about a group of rabbis who insist that they, rather than God, have the right to define justice on earth (Baba Metsia 59B), An-sky moved to more recent narratives about Hasidic rabbis: "Like the Talmudic sages, the heroes of modern legends do not feel obligated to obey the heavenly voice, and they deal with God simply, as an equal."[5] He found the following legend "most typical":

> The king of Romania issued some kind of cruel decree against the Jews. One righteous Jew, a certain Rabbi Faivel, who spent days and nights in the synagogue studying the Torah, learned of the new law and became very angry. Although it was midnight, he ran immediately to the local rabbi, a great sage (*pravednik*), Rabbi Elimelekh.
>
> "Rabbi!" he cried. "I come to you with a complaint. In the holy Torah the Jews are called 'God's slaves.' The slaves of one owner are not obligated to suffer from the commands of another owner. On what basis should the Jews suffer from the decree of the king of Romania? Make a judgment, Rabbi!"
>
> "You are right, my son," Rabbi Elimelekh answered. "Come back tomorrow and I will resolve this matter. At night one does not pass judgment."
>
> The next day three great *tsaddiks*, including the rabbi of Opatov, came to Rabbi Elimelekh. Rabbi Elimelekh sent for Rabbi Faivel and ordered him to present his complaint.
>
> "I don't have that same passion that I did last night," Rabbi Faivel answered.
>
> "I give you the power of the word (*Daiu tebe silu slova*)!" Rabbi Elimelekh said.
>
> Then Rabbi Faivel again presented the complaints of the night before.
>
> "We have the following custom," said the rabbi from Opatov. "After the two sides complete their discussions, they must leave. Thus you, Rabbi

Faivel, must go away. And you, too, Creator, should also go away. But since your glory fills the world, we permit you to stay, but know that we will not be at all partial. We will make our decision based on the law."

For a long time all four righteous men (*pravednika*) discussed whether the king of Romania had the right to issue his cruel decree against the Jews, and finally they decided that he did not have that right. Having proven their decision with appropriate texts from holy books, they wrote their verdict and signed it. In three days the cruel decree was canceled.[6]

This story provided a compelling example of rabbis deciding that human justice, as defined in discussion, takes precedence over divine will. In fact, in An-sky's retelling, the tale lends itself to that conclusion far more readily than does the original legend. The theme of controversy and even legal controversy with God appears in various Hasidic legends.[7]

An-sky's best-known story of a rabbi who puts God on trial is associated with Rabbi Levi Yitzkhak of Berdichev, an early Hasidic leader (1740–1810) known for his compassion for the sufferings of the Jewish people. He is believed to have composed a poem called "The Kaddish of Rebbe Levi Yitzkhak" (the kaddish is a central Jewish prayer praising God; the poem introduces the liturgical kaddish) or "A din-toyre mit got" (God on trial), in which he rebukes God for permitting an excess of Jewish suffering.[8] Levi Yitzkhak summons God to a trial because He has demanded too much of the Jews. God does not, apparently, respond, but Levi Yitzkhak's song nonetheless concludes with a line from the prayers affirming his faith: "*Yisgadal v'yiskadash shmei raboh*" (Magnified and sanctified is thy great name).[9]

An-sky may have known of the kaddish of Levi Yitzkhak of Berdichev already in 1908; he certainly knew it later.[10] Nonetheless, he based his tale of God on trial instead on a less well-known legend, one focusing on Rebbe Elimelekh of Lyzhansk (1717–1787), one of the founders of Hasidism in Galicia. This legend was published in Hebrew by Shlomo Gabriel Rozental in Warsaw in 1901 and again in 1905.[11] The basic plot of that legend is the same as An-sky's: a king issues an evil decree; a poor man comes to Rebbe Elimelekh and argues that the situation is not fair; Rebbe Elimelekh encourages the man to voice his complaint and then decides to put God on trial; during the trial, Elimelekh and other rabbis determine that God is in the wrong; and after they make their decision, the decree is lifted. Against the background of these similarities, the differences between this original plot and the legend An-sky recounts in "Jewish Folk Art" reveal the polemical function of his storytelling.

By careful editing, An-sky turned a pious tale of the wonder-working abilities of a Hasidic rebbe into a subversive parable. The first lines of An-sky's legend make his change of focus evident, but whereas An-sky set the legend in

Romania, Rozental's legend is set in Austria (actually in Lyzhansk or, in modern Polish spelling, Leżajsk, which is in southeast Poland, in the Galician part of the Austro-Hungarian Empire). The reason for the Romanian setting is that readers of the Russian-Jewish press were used to seeing articles that used anti-Semitism or anti-Jewish legislation in Romania as opportunities to voice potentially controversial opinions about those very problems in the Russian Empire; so, by moving the location of the legend to Romania, An-sky signaled to his readers that the story could be read through Aesopian lenses as a veiled commentary on the situation in Russia.[12] In Rozental's legend the evil decree requires Jews to pay four hundred gold coins to the royal treasury before any marriage, thereby preventing them from obeying the first divine command given to them, "Be fruitful and multiply" (Gen. 2:28). But by not mentioning the decree specifically, An-sky both generalized the legend, suggesting it might serve as an example in any situation of governmental oppression, and distanced himself from the Russian discourse surrounding Jewish sexuality, which manifested itself in an obsessive fascination among certain writers about the results of the command to be fruitful and multiply.[13]

Rozental, as one might expect of an editor who seemed to have had pious Hasidic readers in mind, focused the narrative on the Hasidic rebbe, whereas An-sky, by shifting the emphasis to Faivel, depicted a non-rabbinical hero who could serve his readers as a model. In Rozental's legend, the person who brings the complaint to Elimelekh was introduced as "one honest man who feared the Lord."[14] An-sky gave this character a name and has him, rather than Elimelekh, locate the crucial precedent in the Jewish textual tradition demonstrating that God is in the wrong. At the same time he simplified the legal discussion; for although his Faivel simply points out that the Bible refers to Hebrews as "God's slaves," Rozental's Elimelekh quotes the Talmudic tractate Gittin 41 to the effect that when a person's enslavement makes it impossible for him to marry, he must be liberated.[15] An-sky also diminished Rozental's focus on Elimelekh himself and the rebbe's wonder-working abilities. In Rozental, after hearing the arguments, the rebbe spends a few moments in *dvekut*, that is, ecstatic silent communion with the divine, and finally emerges with "his face like a torch of burning fire" and with the solution to the problem. Once he articulates his decision, he has only to raise his eyes and his hands to heaven, and the evil decree is immediately rescinded.[16] An-sky, in contrast, has the rebbe (now joined by several other rebbes) reach his conclusion after lengthy and heated debates, and the verdict must be spoken and then written down before it can take effect. With this new ending, An-sky depicted the source of real power as not the Hasidic rebbe himself and his privileged relationship with God but rather the words he and others speak and write. The rebbe commands this power of the word, but it can also be used by another. Thus when Elimelekh in An-sky's version tells Faivel, "I give you the power of the word" (a line entirely missing from Elimelekh's encouragement of the man in Rozental), the rebbe gives the hero access to the source of his strength.

With his adaptation of Rozental's story, An-sky created a compelling image of a hero who can change the world through his deliberate use of language, his ability to cite relevant sources and weave persuasive arguments. The abilities of Rabbi Faivel might be meant to inspire the readers of the article to change the world as well. First of all, the reader might use language in taking up An-sky's challenge to develop Jewish folkloristics in order to revive Jewish culture. In the first lines of his essay, An-sky condemned the ineffective use of language:

> One can boldly say that there is no people that has talked about itself as much and knows itself as little as the Jews. In the Jewish press for many years now there have been endless debates and passionate fights about the essence of Jewishness, about folk culture [*narodnost'*], about national-ism, about the great spiritual heritage, about the national-cultural values and so on, but still, in fact one encounters among Jews neither serious interest in Jewish culture nor concern about its preservation and further development.[17]

Here An-sky defined the problems of the Jewish people as based in incompe-tent speaking and writing. Jews talk so much and print endless debates, but they do not manage to accomplish the task at hand.

This task, as An-sky defined it, was to establish Jewish culture itself on a firmer foundation. "We have no significant cultural institutions, and our litera-ture in all three languages (Yiddish, Hebrew, and Russian) has no underlying material base [*ne imeet pod soboi nikakoi material'noi pochvy*]." And the situation was only getting worse. "With every year, with every day, the most precious pearls of folklore are dying, disappearing." The urgency of the matter should itself be sufficient to unify the "best forces of our people."[18] Modern Jews must collect and study Jewish folklore, he said, because in that way they can become familiar with the roots of Jewish culture, which he describes as "*suffused* with the idea of monotheism, which in its basis is opposed to any warfare [*bor'ba*], does not permit any personality cult, and admires spiritual perfection above mate-rial and, especially, physical perfection."[19] All the tales he collected, he asserted, support his claim that although the folklore of the Jews may share many narra-tive elements with other European folklores, it transfers these elements "from material to spiritual ground."[20] Once Jews read and retell their own folktales, it seems, they will find confirmation of the potential force of their own verbal activities. Unified by their orientation toward "the spiritual" over "the material," these readers, like the heroes they read about, will be able to accomplish miracles with their words alone.

Given the functions he wanted Jewish folklore to perform, An-sky's revision of the story of God on trial makes perfect sense. His commitment to the notion that folklore can give Jews useful heroic models explains his emphasis on the force of the rabbis' words. Rather than being satisfied with stories that conclude with a nod toward the awesome power of God or the tsaddik, he emphasized the power of human speech, creating the kind of heroes and heroism that Russian Jews seemed to need, heroes who could achieve the work of cultural renovation. Although An-sky paid lip service to the centrality of monotheism in Jewish culture, he represented that culture as more atheistic or even polytheistic than monotheistic, since the heroes he described usurp a portion of the power and respect that God enjoys in traditional Judaism.

A Hero in an Empire

Having defined—or invented—his hero of words, An-sky did not appear satisfied to confine him within a single scholarly text. In that same year of 1908, he wrote a poem in Russian, ten pages long, titled "Sud. Skazanie" (The trial. A legend).[21] Since the poem is so much longer than the story of God's trial in "Jewish Folk Art," An-sky probably wrote the poem after he wrote the article; having transformed the story once, he was inspired to do so again, yet more radically. Whereas in "Jewish Folk Art" he had argued for reestablishing Jewish identity on the foundation of carefully selected folktales, in "The Trial" he attempted to put this doctrine into practice using a single tale. As he rewrote his Hasidic legend as a poem in standard literary Russian, he simultaneously worked to present the Jewish people as a standard, rather than a dangerously deviant, element of the empire's multiethnic population. With this work, he suggested that the Jews should be imagined as commensurate with other nationalities in the empire, each with a folk culture of its own, and not seen as posing any particular threat to non-Jews.[22]

One of An-sky's first readers of the poem, Vera Zhitlovskaia (the estranged wife of his good friend, Haim Zhitlowsky), pointed out that the form, trochaic tetrameter, reminded her of "Konek-gorbunok" (The hunchbacked horse), a stylized 1834 folktale in verse by Petr Pavlovich Ershov. She wrote discouragingly, "I read your 'Trial.' It's a good idea, but unfortunately you used the meter of 'Konek-gorbunok,' and when one reads your 'Trial,' one keeps seeing a racing horse in the distance. Basically, you should stop writing poems in Russian."[23] Zhitlovskaia was correct that trochaic tetrameter was associated in Russian with stylized folklore, but she slightly misidentified the meter of "Trial." It is not rhyming trochaic tetrameter (like "Konek-gorbunok") but a rarer form, unrhymed trochaic tetrameter. This unusual meter, I will argue, hints at a similarity between Jewish culture and one of the best-known bodies of folklore of a non-Russian nationality in the empire, that of the Finns.

For the Russian-educated public, the connections between Finnish oral poetry and the Russian *bylina* tradition (also preserved in the far North) exemplified an aesthetically compelling, authentic folk tradition.[24] Admiration for Finnish folklore and sympathy for the Finnish nationalist movement went hand in hand for Russian intellectuals.[25] The most famous product of Finnish oral poetry was the *Kalevala*, a book-length poem woven together in the 1830s and 1840s from a collection of folk poems by Elias Lönnrot, a Finnish doctor and folklore enthusiast. At the beginning of the twentieth century, when Finns felt that their culture was threatened by Russification, the *Kalevala* gained significance as a focal point for national identity and resistance to St. Petersburg.[26] First translated into Russian in 1881, the *Kalevala* was retranslated in 1888 and republished a number of times.[27] Although the 1881 translation was in prose, the 1888 version (subsequently reprinted), like the *Kalevala*, used unrhymed trochaic tetrameter, a logical meter for Finnish folk poetry, since it preserves the rhythm of Finnish speech, in which stress always falls on the first syllable of a word, but less logical for Russian with its shifting stress.[28] The meter of the *Kalevala* has been imitated by writers of faux folk epics, most effectively by Henry Wadsworth Longfellow in *Hiawatha*, which was translated into Russian by Ivan Bunin in 1896 and became popular.[29] Thus, by retelling the legend of Elimelekh of Lyzhansk as a narrative poem in unrhymed trochaic tetrameter, An-sky evoked the political connotations clinging to the *Kalevala*: the struggle of a minority nationality, proud of its ancient folk traditions, against the might of the empire. By using this meter, otherwise uncommon in Russian, An-sky suggested that his poem should be placed in the same category as the *Kalevala* (and *Hiawatha*), as an ancient national epic, as a foundational myth of a people.[30]

The poem's vocabulary reinforces the suggestion that it is a founding epic. A preface announces the legend's venerability and significance:

In Jassy, in the old synagogue,
Just at midnight on the night of Yom Kippur,
In the sad flickering
Of the gloomy candles
The old synagogue servant
Told those present a true story [*byl'*]
A true story that he had heard
From the sinless, righteous lips of the holy Elimelekh,

Whose greatness and glory
Resounded in all Romania.[31]

Every line here speaks of age. The synagogue and the servant are both "old,"
the term *byl'*, used twice, implies a true story from the past (the word literally
means "that which was"). Throughout the poem the vocabulary reinforces the
notion of age: "old Rabbi Faivel" (4) speaks with "old Rabbi Elimelekh" (5);
the trial begins with the words of "the oldest / of the judges, the rabbi from
Apta" (6); Rabbi Faivel cites "the ancient holy books" (7), "the ancient forgotten
books" (11); and all the rabbis act as befits the elderly: they speak "seriously,
slowly, calmly" (10), and they quietly stroke their beards (10). All these images
create the impression of a significant event that provides a link to the past of
the Jewish people. The substance of the tale therefore speaks to the function
that the epic genre can perform in constructing a national identity by linking a
group of people to an imagined past.

Even as "The Trial" presents a past specific to the Jews, it simultaneously
makes that past—and, by extension, Jewish culture—transparent to non-Jews.
A few occasions of switching languages, when An-sky introduces Hebrew and
Yiddish terms into the Russian text, display Jewish culture instructively. The
rabbis wear tallises and *tfilin* (phylacteries) (6), and explanatory footnotes briefly
define these objects for the reader. Whereas the version of the tale in "Jewish Folk
Art" gives no indication when during the year the events described occurred,
the second line of "The Trial," as we saw, is "just at midnight on the eve of Yom
Kippur," and a footnote defines the holiday as the "Day of Forgiveness, a great
fast" (2). Along with its footnote, the addition of that date, seemingly borrowed
from the kaddish of Levi-Yitzkhak of Berdichev and indicating that An-sky knew
of that better-known "God on Trial,") suggests that the author intended the piece
not only to inspire pride in Jewish culture but also to provide ethnographic
information about Jewish traditions to readers who were ignorant of them.

The decision probably had a different impact on readers with a traditional
Jewish background who became Russified as adolescents or adults. For persons
familiar with Jewish traditions, the date highlights the radicalism of An-sky's
poem. During the Yom Kippur prayer service, Jews affirm God's omnipotence
and human frailty; they plead for mercy during the coming year but do not
demand it, accepting that only God can understand the logic dictating that some
people will prosper, others suffer. By locating his Russian poem on the eve of
Yom Kippur, An-sky signaled to such readers that his vision of Judaism offered
an alternative to passivity in the face of an omnipotent deity.

For readers either familiar with or unaware of the traditions, the text's
bilingualism creates a bridge between Russian culture, especially the Russian

radical culture that An-sky had embraced as an adult, and the Jewish way of life he knew from his own traditional childhood. Simply by writing of Jewish sages in Russian, using terms associated with Russian Orthodoxy and the narrative traditions surrounding it (for example, using the word *pravednik*, or "righteous man," for the rabbis), An-sky argued for the universality of his vision of Jewishness. He also used Hebrew words to suggest that Jewish values were commensurate with those of the radicals. When Faivel comes to Elimelekh with his complaint against God, the latter responds with strong language:

> "My son!" softly answered
> The old Rabbi Elimelekh,
> "Publicly accusing God
> Of diverging from the law,
> Summoning Him to a rabbi
> For judgment and reprisal [*rasprava*]
> Is, I think, a foolish step,
> A sinful and a dangerous one! . . .
> But it's not hard to understand you:
> In a dark hour of great sorrow
> You are prepared to plead
> For the Jewish community
> You are prepared for "*msiras nefesh.*"
> Know, my son, for the community
> I, too, am prepared for a heroic deed [*podvig*]!"(5)

In a footnote, An-sky defined *msiras nefesh* as *samopozhertvovanie* (self-sacrifice). The term is traditionally used for self-endangerment or self-sacrifice on behalf of the Jewish community, although it was used broadly among the Ashkenazic Jews of Eastern Europe to mean any kind of self-sacrifice. The Russian equivalent An-sky chose for it, like the terms *rasprava* (reprisal) and *podvig* (heroic deed), creates a symbolic link between the actions of the Romanian rabbis and those of radicals such as Gregory Gershuni, An-sky's friend and an SR terrorist mastermind. The terrorist acts that Gershuni oversaw were often described by those within SR circles using this language, the revolutionaries figuring as heroes (ascetic ones) who were willing to expose themselves to terrible dangers in order to mete out just punishment (*rasprava*).[32] The term *podvig* strongly evokes the worldview of Russian Orthodoxy and refers to an act of self-denial meant to bring the worshiper close to God.[33] Thus, when Rabbi Elimelekh equated *msiras nefesh* with *podvig,* An-sky was translating the arguments of his rabbis not simply into standard literary Russian but into the semi-secular, semi-religious language of the SRs, adapting a narrative and terminology from Ashkenazi culture to bring it closer to the narratives and language of the radicals.

The narrator points out the radicalism of Rabbi Faivel's defiance of God: the other Jews "cried bitterly, prayed" (3), which was "useless" (*naprasno*), but Faivel's angry response to the situation stands out (4). The rabbinical council that judges the case is equally defiant. When the Rabbi of Apta tells God that even though the rabbis understand that He cannot leave the room during their deliberations, they will not be prejudiced in His favor, he paraphrases Deuteronomy 30:12, "Remember: the Torah is not in heaven / You gave it to the Jews / And we will make judgments based on it!" (11). An-sky's hero of words defies any autocrat, whether the king of Romania or God himself, who, Faivel insists, "like any mortal / Himself is obligated to obey / All the Torah's holy laws!" (9). An-sky's poem gestured toward the situation facing Gershuni and the Russian radical intelligentsia in 1908: both the cruel king of Romania and the God whom Faivel accuses undoubtedly recalled Nicholas II, an autocrat in the process of reneging on his 1905 promise to place the law above himself, and the folktales keep alive the fantasy that the clever use of words might ultimately bring about the tsar's defeat. Also, for An-sky's Russian audience, "The Trial" demonstrated that the Jewish folk tradition was an epic tradition comparable to the traditions of other nations, one that could furnish contemporary readers with the positive heroic examples needed to inspire action.

By translating the legend of God's trial into Russian, An-sky invited his Russian readers to recognize similarities between Jewish culture and those of other nationalities in the empire, including Russian culture, whether Orthodox or radical. At the same time he pointed to the disjunction between common Russian stereotypes about Jews and the folkloric world he put on display. In his colorful illustration of the debating rabbis, An-sky evoked one of the most enduring Russian stereotypes of the Jew as talking at greater length and in a less controlled way than the Russian. The length of the rabbis' debate—three days!—suggests the kind of ability to go on talking that alarmed Russian writers. While the rabbis insist on the adherence of their argumentation to strict rules, pointing out to God that they will not be partial even though He is unable to absent himself from the courtroom, they also trespass the bounds of conventional civility. The Russian poem indicates that the rabbis "cursed and scolded and reproached one another" (*i rugalis', i branilis'/i drug druga ukoriali*);[34] the three verbs suggest a kind of verbal excess. These descriptions recall the images of Jews in Russian Realist fiction whose speech, both in everyday usage and in a religious context, is depicted as disorderly, offensive, even possibly dangerous.

Fedor Dostoevsky, in portraying the Jew Isai Fomich at prayer in his 1860–1862 prison memoir, *Notes from the House of the Dead*, stressed the disorder of Isai

Fomich's verbal expressions: he shouts, gesticulates wildly, and draws attention to himself through his absurd gestures and sounds.[35] The narrator suspects that, despite Isai Fomich's protests, all his sounds and motions are prescribed by law, are actually a calculated performance, although the actor's goal remains unclear. The connections between Isai Fomich's religion and his absurd speech indicate that, for Dostoevsky, this unappealing verbal expression, with its apparent disorder that may conceal a hidden motivation, was central to the character's identity as a Jew. Although Dostoevsky represented a Judeophobic extreme in many of his views of the "Jewish Question," Isai Fomich's speech and prayers resemble the speech of other Russian writers' Jewish characters. Felix Dreizin notes the persistence of Russian stereotypes of the Jew who "is noisy, fussy, and gesticulates excessively."[36] For example, the speech of the Jewish innkeeper in Chekhov's 1888 novella, *The Steppe,* is confused, confusing, and unattractive. He greets his guests while "twisting, gesticulating, cringing and uttering ecstatic cries, believing all these antics essential to the display of supreme courtesy and affability."[37] In some cases, nineteenth-century Russian writers depicted Jews as using their noisy, fussy speech neither to create a spectacle (as Isai Fomich does) nor to curry favor (as Moses does) but to commit a crime. In Mikhail Saltykov-Shchedrin's *Diary of a Provincial in Petersburg,* written in the early 1870s, the Jew Gershka Zaltsfish first starts one rumor to raise stock prices and then another to make them fall. Saltykov-Shchedrin depicted the Jew's speech as wild, outrageous, an apparently out-of-control (but secretly controlled) performance.[38] The Jewish speech he described was not only unattractive but also dangerous, since it helped the Jews take advantage of peasants or other innocent non-Jews whom, it seemed, the Jews were always trying to cheat.

The prevalent image of Jewish speech as dangerous and in need of control in late-nineteenth-century fiction recurred in the anti-Jewish Russian discourse of the first years of the twentieth century. The *Protocols of the Elders of Zion,* an anti-Jewish tract written by Sergei Nilus and circulated by the tsarist secret police in 1905,[39] imagined the Jews as relishing the "triumph of free babbling" in the modern press and in legislatures, encouraging and contributing to the unrestrained speech that could eventually lead to the downfall of legitimate governments, and their replacement by a Jewish regime.[40] The *Protocols* themselves reified the fantasy of a threatening Jewish voice, since the document was presented as the written minutes of meetings of a secret organization of Jews who aim to take over the world and hope to accomplish their goal by means of the speeches they give at their gatherings.[41] The vision of Jews who gather and speak together as part of their campaign to subjugate other nations harkened back to the master-text of modern Russian Judeophobia, Yakov Brafman's *Kniga Kagala* (Book of the Kahal), and the central image of a threatening gathering of talking Jews remained powerful throughout An-sky's lifetime.[42] In the words of Vasily Shul'gin, a self-professed anti-Semite, Jewish speech and Jewish writing could be held responsible for all the violence of the revolutionary years: "Everywhere and in every place—at meetings, unions, organizations, demonstrations, congresses, which were then becoming popular (for example, the lawyers' congress in Kiev), and especially in print—those in charge, whether openly or behind the scenes, were Jews."[43] Shul'gin and Nilus associated the threatening speech of Jews with lawyers, the law, and legislatures, as well as with revolutionary meetings such as the SR Congress that An-sky described, where many of the participants, including Gershuni, were indeed Jews. The stereotype of Jews as excessively concerned with law relates closely to their stereotype as loving to argue. Both, of course, might have been reinforced by differences between Jewish and Russian speech habits, as well as by the perception (and the fact) that the legal profession in the Russian Empire contained a disproportionate number of Jews.[44]

At the same time Judeophobes such as Shul'gin and Nilus evoked a powerful dualism in Christian thought. The Gospel of John begins with this dichotomy: "For the law was given by Moses, but grace and truth came by Jesus Christ" (John 1:17). In the Gospels, Jesus and his followers flout a number of laws, including Jewish regulations about diet and hand washing and Roman strictures against attacking tax collectors. They spent the longest time, however, discussing the law requiring Jewish men to be circumcised, and Paul ultimately concluded that this law is meaningless and that a person who obeys it should not imagine that he has thereby done anything to gain God's favor: "Behold, I, Paul, say unto you, that if ye be circumcised, Christ shall profit you nothing. . . . Christ is become of no effect unto you, whosoever of you are justified by the law; ye are fallen from grace. . . . For in Jesus Christ neither circumcision availeth anything nor uncircumcision, but faith which worketh by love" (Galatians 5:2, 4, 6). With verses such as these, the Greek Bible indicated that the material proof of obedience to the law represented by circumcision carries no meaning for the new religion. With their attention toward the rejection of circumcision, Christians such as Paul distinguished their practices from those of the Jews around them and defined their new religion against Judaism. They thereby initiated a tradition identifying Judaism itself with an obsolescent legal system, one already made irrelevant by the new possibility of Christian grace. This tradition would live on in Russia;[45] indeed, it has been a familiar theme in Russian literary culture from medieval times.[46]

An-sky's contentious rabbis have something in common with the talkative, legalistically minded Jews depicted by Dostoevsky, Chekhov, Saltykov-Shchedrin, and other Russian writers, and in those rabbis' three-day meeting behind closed doors they even recall the imagined "Elders of Zion." However, the depiction of the rabbis' speech in "The Trial" exemplifies An-sky's reclamation and valorization of those specific attributes of Jewish culture that seemed most off-putting to Russians. By choosing to retell the Talmudic and folkloric legends of rabbis who insist that the law they study takes precedence over the words and the actions of God, An-sky based his depiction of Jewishness on precisely the concern with law at the center of hostile Christian images of Judaism; however, his texts break down the dualism that identifies Jews with the law, the material world, the static, and all that is not truly Christian. Like his choice of meter, his imagery of venerability, and his insistence on the heroism of his defiant rabbis, An-sky's reclamation of the image of excessive Jewish talking and uncompromising Jewish legalism contributes to his deliberate creation of an epic poem around which a modern citizen of the Russian Empire could base a new, positive identification with Judaism. In this poem, he challenged head-on the widespread belief that Jewish culture, especially Jewish speech, made Jews dangerous to non-Jews. He suggested, instead, that Jews were no more inherently threatening than Finns, and they possessed as attractive a folk culture as that of the Finns. The Jews' seemingly excessive speech, rather than posing a danger, might actually offer the empire's subjects a useful model for achieving justice.

An Authentic Yiddish Hero

Evidently feeling that his two Russian versions of the story of God's trial were not enough, An-sky also rewrote the story twice in Yiddish: first, dated 1908 in his Yiddish collected works, as a poem called *"A din-toyre mit Got"* (God on trial), which was again in unrhymed trochaic tetrameter, and then a prose version titled *"A din-toyre"* (A trial) published early in 1909 in Russia and America, in the St. Petersburg Yiddish newspaper *Der fraynd,* and in *Dos naye lebn* (The new life), a Yiddish newspaper edited in New York by his childhood friend, Haim Zhitlowsky.[47] In a passage offering a glimpse into his work as a bilingual writer, An-sky wrote to Zhitlowsky about his work in the fall and winter of 1908.

> Recently, having settled in Terioki [in the Finnish territory near St. Petersburg], I wrote a whole series of articles . . . The most significant work was the translation of "Ashmedai" [a stylized epic poem that An-sky had written in Yiddish in 1904, also in unrhymed trochaic tetrameter] into Russian. In fact, I translated only chapters one and two from Yiddish, and I wrote completely new versions of the remaining five chapters. I think I succeeded with the meter no worse than I did in Yiddish, and, as

for the content, I gave it a completely different character: a serious, naïve, religious poema [a modern Russian poetic genre, a long poem that tells a story].... I gave a public reading of the first part in Petersburg at a literary soirée and there was unending applause, and the press praised it.... In short, this is a period of animated creativity.

By the way, I've written a few folk legends and tales in verse. One of them, "The Trial," came out in the first issue of *Jewish World* [*Evreiskii mir*]. I wrote the same legend in Yiddish and I'm sending it to you. Please put it in the February issue of your journal, no later than that, because I also want to give it to [I. L.] Peretz for his *Jewish Weekly* [*Yudishe vokhenshrift*], but with the assumption that it will appear there a week later than it does in your publication, since in America they get the *Weekly* three weeks late.... If you take this little thing [*veshchitsu*] and you can send me the payment due, let me know.... If you don't like it, also tell me. I can give you a lot of little things like this. I think it's something you like [*kazhetskia eto v tvoem vkuse*].[48]

With "Ashmedai," An-sky saw the translation of his own poem from one language into another as an occasion to produce an essentially new text. Rather than feeling any kind of obligation to produce a Russian version that accurately reproduced the content of the Yiddish original, he happily reported that he had turned the original poem, a satirical portrayal of a divorce between the devil and his wife, with covert attacks on traditional Jews, reformers, and others, into "a serious, naïve religious poema."[49]

With his simultaneous Yiddish and Russian versions of "The Trial," An-sky experimented again with the possibilities each language offered him. The Yiddish poem shares with the Russian text the meter associated with the *Kalevala* and the imagery of venerability, and, like the Russian, it can be seen as an attempt to create an epic text, endowed with powerful epic heroes, on which modern Jews might base a renewed national identity. A host of small differences show, however, that even in this "little thing" that he claims to have tossed off quickly, the writer tailored each text for its audience, offering slightly different messages to his Russian-speaking and Yiddish-speaking readers.

The Yiddish poem displays the effective power of the rabbis' word of rebellion even more vividly than the Russian. When the rabbis quote the Torah or other texts, they do so in Hebrew, which is standard in such Yiddish speech. For example, when they agree that God cannot leave the courtroom because the Torah acknowledges that "*k'vode mole olom*," "his glory fills the world,"[50] they cite a text that Jews recite every day in the kedushah prayer. For a Yiddish speaker with a traditional religious background, such citations could have had opposing effects. On the one hand, they testify to the legitimacy of the legendary rabbis: they are not simply the invention of the Russified An-sky but seem to be native speakers of the rabbinic language, making this version of the legend appear more authentic, less startling. On the other hand, the disjunction between the familiar language of the prayer and the rabbis' defiance of God could have added to the humor of the poem and heightened its departure from tradition. (The Yiddish poem, unlike the other versions, draws on this same disjunction to pull readers into the text, concluding the description of the revocation of the evil decree with "amen!")[51]

When describing the central argument between the rabbis, the Russian text offers little legalistic discourse. In the Russian, the rabbis cite only the best-known rabbinic texts.

> Citations poured in a torrent
> From the Bible, the Talmud,
> Old forgotten books,
> There were even hints
> About the legends of the "hidden Torah."

> *Gradom sypalis' tsitaty*
> *Iz Pisan'ia, iz Talmuda,*
> *Iz starinnykh knig zabytykh,*
> *Byli dazhe i nameki*
> *Na predan'ia "skrytoi Tory."*[52]

By calling the rabbinic works "forgotten" and "hidden" in Russian rather than listing their specific titles, An-sky appealed to the fin-de-siècle fascination with the ancient and the exotic.[53] Of course, he knew perfectly well that the traditional study of these books in yeshivas continued, albeit somewhat abated, in the Russian Empire and elsewhere; thus the books the rabbis could have cited were by no means forgotten. But he seems to have calculated that for his Jewish or non-Jewish Russian readers, the image of rabbinical disputes as vibrant, legalistic, and often rude would be less attractive than the vision of rabbis as the solemn masters of ancient, barely accessible, mysterious sources.

The Yiddish version, unlike the Russian, contains more details about the argument and the culture of argumentation surrounding it: as the rabbis argue, one says to another, "Well said!" and another strokes his beard confidently while speaking.[54] The rabbis get excited, applauding one another for an effective argument but responding to an ineffective one with curses such as *sheygets* (smart aleck; literally, non-Jew), *shnek* (worm), and *am-ha-arets* (ignoramus).[55] The differing characterization of the rabbis' reference works speaks eloquently to the writer's sensitivity about his multiple audiences. Whereas the Russian mentions only the Torah, the Talmud, and the unnamed "forgotten books," in the Yiddish the rabbis display the range of logical devices making up their legal discourse:

> *A fortiori* arguments, arguments on the basis of biblical or rabbinic
>   analogy,
> Points of halakhah, precedent cases,
> Interpretations of abbreviations, mystic hints
> From the Kabbalah and the Zohar,
> From the precious few words of the Ba'al Shem Tov
> And from the deep mysteries of the Torah.
>
> *Kal ve-khoymers, gzeyre shaves,*
> *un halokhes, un inyonim,*
> *un notrikons un remozim,*
> *fun kabole un fun zo(y)er,*
> *fun balshems getseylte verter*
> *un fun tife sisre-toyre.*[56]

In his Yiddish text, An-sky created a compelling image of rabbinic argumentation, emphasizing the seriousness of the endeavor, the remarkable number of sources used, the variety of legal arguments available, and the importance accorded to a persuasive argument, which can inspire one rabbi to praise another or to insult him. He depicted the tradition of rabbinic dispute attractively as dynamic, rich, and intellectually intense.

In both versions, he illustrated the Jewish tradition of argumentation and the Jewish voice, but in the Yiddish he accentuated even more strongly the material that Russian readers might find unattractive. This difference may be understood in various ways. Perhaps a conscious or subconscious self-censorship prevented An-sky from going too far in his description in Russian of talkative Jews; he did not want to shock his Russian readers or to confirm anyone's negative stereotypes. At the same time the possibilities offered by the languages themselves may have inspired the differences. Once he was working with Yiddish, he may have found it easy and fun to imagine the specific insults that the rabbis yelled, whereas rendering those same terms in Russian would have felt artificial or difficult. In any event, while the differences between the texts signal his awareness of his varied audiences and their potential reactions, An-sky reclaimed and valorized Jewish talkativeness in both languages.

With his final transformation of the legend into Yiddish prose, An-sky brought it full circle, since one can assume that before Rozental published it in Hebrew, it had been told by Hasidim in Yiddish. From the perspective of language and form, the version he published in *Dos naye lebn* and *Der fraynd* mimics that original, while the subtitle, "A Hasidic Folktale," suggests that An-sky simply transcribed it as he heard it from an actual member of the folk, presumably a pious Hasid. The changes he made in the prose version all appear calculated to reinforce the impression of authenticity. The Yiddish prose version retains much of the trochaic tetrameter, giving it an unusual rhythm for a prose piece and suggesting that the author simply took his Yiddish poem, removed the line breaks, and adapted it slightly before sending it in. At a few points he made the sentence structure, which had been distorted to conform to the meter, a bit closer to the rhythm of Yiddish, rather than Finnish, speech; for example, he changed the first line from *"Un gesheyen iz di mayse / Nor nit lang, in yene tsaytn"* to *"Gesheyen iz di mayse gor nit lang, in yene tsaytn."* Both lines mean, "The story happened not long ago, in those times," but only the first one is in trochaic tetrameter.

An-sky altered content as well as form in the prose version. His depictions of the debating rabbis in the prose version include impressive Hasidic genealogies: the narrator introduces Rabbi Elimelekh as a "student of the Ba'al Shem Tov," the eighteenth-century founder of Hasidism, and the Rabbi of Apta is likewise "the Ba'al Shem's beloved student."[57] However, these descriptions are not historically accurate: the Hasidic rabbi and kabbalist Meir Apta was born in 1760, the year when the Ba'al Shem Tov died, and so could not have been his student, and Elimelech of Lyzhansk was a disciple not of the Ba'al Shem Tov himself but rather of the Ba'al Shem's student, Dov Baer of Mezhirech. But by associating the heroes of his story with the Ba'al Shem, An-sky worked to legitimate them, and therefore his text, as a pure product of the Hasidic imagination, told by a narrator who is suitably concerned with Hasidic genealogy. A change of a single word reinforces the specificity (not to say insularity) of that narrative voice: in the Russian and Yiddish poetic versions, Rabbi Faivel insists that a God who follows the law is prohibited from destroying "the whole world" (in Russian) or "humanity" (in Yiddish).[58] In the Yiddish prose version, Rabbi Faivel evokes instead the specter of a God willing to destroy "all the Jews."[59] Finally, in the Yiddish prose version, the rabbis elaborate on their decision that God was wrong in permitting the king to pass the evil decree: whereas in the other versions he made a "mistake," in the prose tale "he had poorly interpreted a verse and unclearly understood the literal meaning of a deep word in the Zohar (*er hot shlekht getaytsht dem posek un nit klor dem pshat farshtanen fun a tifn vort in zo(y)er).*"[60] The additional explanation emphasizes the narrator's unwillingness to criticize God.

With these changes, An-sky disguised a story that he had for the most part invented as a faithfully transcribed legend, concealing the defiant tone of his additions to the tale under the reverent notes of a Hasidic storyteller.

In selecting and then retelling the legend of God's trial originally in "Jewish Folk Art," An-sky had offered it as evidence to support a scientific theory; in writing poetic versions of the tale in Russian and Yiddish, he presented it as an appropriate subject for a heroic epic that might compare with the epic traditions of other nations. The forms of all three of these versions—the Russian language and the trochaic tetrameter—draw attention to the conscious labor of the ethnographer-writer who, like Lönnrot, transformed the raw material of the folktale into a more "sophisticated" text that might be appreciated by a non-folk audience. In this final prose version, in contrast, An-sky drew attention away from his own artifice and represented the story as a found object that could speak authoritatively of its own origins.

A Hasidic Hero for the Fin de Siècle

In writing Hasidic tales in a modern language and arguing for their significance, An-sky was not alone. Two other well-known Jewish writers published retellings of Hasidic stories in 1908: Martin Buber, whose *Die Legende des Baal Schem,* a German reworking of the stories of the Ba'al Shem Tov, came out in Frankfurt am Main, and I. L. Peretz, whose *Khsidish,* a collection of his Yiddish stories on themes from the lives and tales of Hasidic rabbis, was republished in Vilna that same year. (The stories it contained had originally been published in the 1890s and early 1900s. His first collection titled *Khsidish* came out in 1901.) The three writers' projects contain similarities and telling differences. The connections between An-sky and Peretz are most obvious; whereas An-sky may or may not have read Buber, he definitely knew I. L. Peretz and his work well, and acknowledged that it influenced him.[61] Indeed, as he wrote to Zhitlowsky, he thought of Peretz's short-lived journal as a good venue for the publication of his Yiddish poem. An-sky seems to have sympathized especially with Peretz's vision of a new Yiddish-oriented high culture as the potential center of a revitalized Jewish national identity.[62] Peretz wanted to re-create Jewish folklore as "a source of modern national pride and a means of preserving tradition, the folk's defining character, in a new secular key."[63] He hoped that this folklore would be appreciated by a generation of Jewish intellectuals who had grown apart from traditional spirituality and a belief in God but who felt the pull of a spiritual nationalism, centered on the romanticized notion of the Jewish people and on the mystical figure of the creative artist who speaks for them.

Even while An-sky shared some of Peretz's views of art and Jewish community, the two writers' depictions of the Jewish intellectual tradition differed significantly. For instance, Peretz's "Between Two Mountains," reprinted in

Khsidish, could be read as condemning a hierarchy that values rabbinic learning above all. That tale counterpoises two rabbis, the *mitnaged* (anti-Hasidic) Brisker Rov, a learned scholar, and the Hasidic Bialer Rebbe, his former student. Having condemned his teacher's scholarly edifice as a palace made of ice that barred him from contact with the Jewish people, the Bialer Rebbe presents an alternative vision of Judaism as a chorus of voices, in which the melodies of the worshipers blend with the song of "the soul of the world."[64] At least on first reading, the story appears to come out against the Jewish legal tradition as cold, empty, and inhumane, when contrasted with the aesthetic appeal of Hasidic spirituality.

Martin Buber, in his own 1908 revisions of Hasidic legends, attempted, like Peretz, to fashion a Judaism and Jewish culture that would appeal to modern European audiences, and he hoped to persuade his early-twentieth-century German readers that the Jews could boast a mystical patrimony. "Behind the strange exterior of Hasidism, Buber disclosed a remarkable spiritual universe of mystical profundity. He rendered Hasidism respectable, as it were, by integrating this most distinctive manifestation of East European Jewish spirituality into the general discourse and idiom of the New Romanticism (and, later, of Expressionism)."[65] As Peretz did in "Between Two Mountains," Buber drew attention away from the verbal tradition of rabbinic debate and toward the inarticulate feelings that may be drowned out by such debate. In the introduction to his 1908 volume, Buber wrote of a young boy taken to a Yom Kippur service. Although it is forbidden to play an instrument on this day, the boy asks his father repeatedly if he can express his emotional response to the prayers by blowing on his whistle. Finally, the boy "could no longer suppress his ecstasy; he tore the whistle from his pocket and let its voice powerfully resound. All stood startled and bewildered. But the Baal-Shem raised himself above them and spoke: 'The judgment is suspended, and wrath is dispelled from the face of the earth.'" Buber explained that the boy's expression of his feelings could move God to suspend the judgment because of the quality of the boy's soul: "every service which proceeds from a simple or unified soul is complete."[66] Such service is superior to the words of the articulate worshiper. "No prayer is stronger in grace and penetrates in more direct flight through all the worlds of heaven than that of the simple man who does not know anything to say and only knows to offer God the unbroken promptings of his heart. God receives them as a king receives the singing of a nightingale in his gardens at twilight, a singing that sounds sweeter to him than the homage of the princes in his throne-room."[67] With these words Buber exalted passion over words, and inarticulateness over articulateness. The "princes in his throne-room" may symbolize the traditional heroes of the Jewish tradition, the rabbis who have mastered the textual tradition and use the words of the texts to praise (or to question) God. Their spiritual example, according to Buber, may be less valuable for a modern Jew than that of the ignorant man, the *"am ha-arets"* whom the rabbis, such as those in An-sky's poem, tend to scorn.[68]

It would appear from this analysis that, like Peretz, Buber's retellings of Hasidic legends presented Judaism in general and Hasidism in particular as attractively exotic, ancient, and mysterious; both deemphasized or even criticized the tradition of rabbinic argumentation, with its unpleasant links to stereotypes about Jews and the Jewish voice. Whereas An-sky, in the Russian and even more in the Yiddish, wove his reclamation of Jewish mysticism into an appealing depiction of legal disputes, Buber and Peretz turned their backs on that tradition of debate.

Nonetheless, I do not want to insist too strongly on the differences between An-sky and the other re-tellers of Hasidic legends without pointing out the similarities in their motifs. For instance, for both Buber and An-sky the word *hitlahavut,* or in Yiddish *hislayves,* played a key role in a redefined Judaism and in the art that makes it possible. When the Hasidim themselves define the ecstatic state of the worshiper during prayer, they use *hitlahavut* (from the Hebrew *lahav,* meaning flame), or "burning enthusiasm," to denote their ideal: in the words of one scholar, "to be completely absorbed in prayer, to lose the self and 'strip off one's corporeal nature' . . . to burn in longing for the divine."[69] For Buber, *hitlahavut* was the most important attribute of Jewish spirituality. He defined it as "'the burning,' the ardor of ecstasy," it "unlocks the meaning of life. . . . He who is in it is in holiness. . . . it is an ascent to the infinite from rung to rung."[70] According to Buber, this yearning for the divine motivates the thought of the Hasidim; it stands at a central point in his retellings of their stories.

An-sky used that same word to talk about a writer's inspiration. In October 1908 he told Haim Zhitlowsky that he feared not having enough energy to produce creative work. "I really want to work with you [on *Dos naye lebn*], but I don't know if I'll have the mood, the inspiration, the *hislayves,* and whatever else is needed."[71] Two months later, when he produced "The Trial" and other poems in a burst of productivity, he used this same word in his Yiddish texts. In the version of "The Trial" that he had retold in "Jewish Folk Art," when Rabbi Faivel goes back to Rabbi Elimelekh the morning after his midnight complaints, he has lost the courage to voice his complaint against God, but Rabbi Elimelekh says, "I give you the power of the word [*silu slova*]." In the Russian poem, Rabbi Faivel says that he does not have "yesterday's passion" (*vcherashnego poryva*), and one of Rabbi Elimelekh's visitors responds:

> Faivel! I, the Rabbi of Apta,
> I order you

Again to find spiritual peace,
Clarity of thoughts, the power of the word!
Speak, disclose to the court
What your complaint is
Against God. Be certain:
We will judge according to the law!⁷²

In the Yiddish versions Faivel tells the assembled rabbis that he no longer has "*di nekhtige hislayves*" (yesterday's *hitlahavut*), and the Apter Rabbi answers in the poem, "I give you strength, / Knowledge, insight, and *hitlahavut*" (*koyakh, / Deye, bine un hislayves*).⁷³ Thus, what An-sky saw as the basis of the Jewish folk imagination and the source of his own energy as a writer, the power of the word, may have had something in common with that unquenchable yearning for the divine that Buber placed at the center of his own ecstatic re-envisioning of Jewish spirituality. In both cases, modern writers strove to identify and harness not just passion itself but a passion that might provide the centripetal force necessary to re-create a national and a religious community. They located that passion, however, in different places: the *hitlahavut* of the pipe player in Buber's story could be best expressed without words, whereas the *hislayves* that Rabbi Faivel gains allows him to speak clearly and strongly.

Conclusions

When Buber revisited his own 1908 tales of the Ba-al Shem Tov, he admitted, a bit ruefully, that he had transformed his Hasidic stories fundamentally, but An-sky never published any expression of doubt or regret about his 1908 and 1909 revisions of the legend of God on trial.⁷⁴ Literary historians who have examined An-sky's legacy for Jewish folkloristics, however, have noted his cavalier attitude toward his sources. The Israeli scholar Haya Bar-Yitzhak observes that, of all his ethnographic writings, it is far from clear which texts he is analyzing and whether he has a firm basis for the sweeping generalizations in his articles.⁷⁵ As shown in his competing versions of the legend of God's trial, An-sky did not simply document his sources inadequately but dramatically altered his folk material. In the case of the Yiddish prose version in particular, he presented the product of his own imagination as an accurately transcribed bit of oral lore.

Modern folklore studies offer some terminology to describe the effect of An-sky's folkloric revisions. Richard Bauman and Charles L. Briggs note that products of verbal art are uniquely "susceptible to treatment as self-contained, bounded objects separable from their social and cultural contexts of production and reception."[76] In other words, a person or people—anthropologists or members of a traditional culture—can "de-center" or detach a stretch of discourse from its original location in speech or in a written text. Bauman and Briggs call this process "entextualization," meaning "the process of rendering discourse extractable, of making a stretch of linguistic production into a unit—a *text*—that can be lifted out of its interactional setting."[77] Once one has defined such a unit, one can say of it, "This is a text (a story, a poem) and it has a certain meaning." By selecting the legend of God on trial from Rozental's collection, translating it into Russian, and using it as proof for his theory in "Jewish Folk Art," An-sky could be seen as de-centering the legend, entextualizing it, and re-centering it. Each of his literary adaptations of the legend, in different languages and genres, would then be another instance of re-centering, and thus a further distortion of the original folk discourse.

In response to the ideas of Bauman and Briggs, and other scholars, Dan Ben-Amos questions the dichotomy between authentic, ideally oral folklore and the implicitly spurious re-centering of folk texts outside the traditional contexts. He notes that in adaptations of folklore "such events, productions, and performances have their own contexts which are authentic unto themselves."[78] Ben-Amos's hesitation about the binary division separating authentic and inauthentic folklore is particularly appropriate for the discussion of Jewish folklore, which, as he observes, has always been characterized by the interaction of oral and written genres, and the potential transfer of a text in a literary source from one social and historical setting to another.[79] Indeed, as pointed out by the French theorist of oral poetry Paul Zumthor, it may be unproductive to imagine a stark contrast between the authentic oral folk text and the less genuine written one; the model of a truly and purely oral tradition, in which texts are preserved with no resort to writing, has long been a fantasy for most of the world.[80]

Keeping in mind the useful corrections of Ben-Amos and Zumthor to the paradigm that draws a strict distinction between genuine oral texts and ersatz written ones, I would like to return to An-sky's four transformations of the legend of God's trial. As we saw, An-sky did not only translate this legend that he found in Rozental's Hebrew into Russian and Yiddish but added details with each adaptation. Following Bar-Yitzhak, with her hesitation about An-sky's lack of footnotes, one might simply dismiss the results as no longer pertaining to his work as an ethnographer. These literary texts, one might say, may be inspired by a legend, but they differ from it fundamentally. While Rozental's Hebrew edition of Hasidic tales may still possess some genuine connection to an oral tradition, An-sky's adaptations of these stories, to follow this logic, simply go too far. But rather than adopting this perspective, I prefer to characterize An-sky's adaptations as contributing to the lifespan of this folk text, accepting that a legend is a dynamic phenomenon that passes from one language to another, one literary form to another, one medium to another, undergoing transformations in plot and imagery the whole time.[81] It follows that the Hasidic legend that Rozental heard, Rozental's Hebrew translation of it, and An-sky's four revisions of the legend might be seen as equally legitimate utterances, each participating in conversations that are as much oral as written. These conversations might be about the holiness of a specific *rebbe*, the value of Jewish culture for Russified intellectuals, the place of Jews in a multiethnic empire, or the reclamation of mysticism by the modern artist.

The urgency with which An-sky told and retold this particular legend may stem not only from his evident need to take part in all these conversations but also from the ways in which "God on Trial" thematizes the power of the word written and spoken. When An-sky encountered this legend, in which the words that one person says to another have the force to change the world, he may have recognized the object of his own enduring fascination. This fascination explains his use of the terminology of Hasidic prayer. Whereas in Rozental's version of the legend, as we saw, Rabbi Elimelekh experiences *dvekut*, a meditative closeness to God, An-sky's Faivel is granted *hitlahavut, hislayves,* an ecstatic condition of a burning longing for the divine, and An-sky equated *sila slova*, the power of the word, precisely with that ecstatic state. The *hislayves* of his Faivel, it seems to me, is simultaneously a burning longing for the divine and a passionate striving for an effective, powerful language. And I suspect that An-sky himself also wanted to attain that ecstasy along with that power of the word.

The central irony of An-sky's encounter with the legend of God's trial emerges from the evident appeal of *hitlahavut* for him. By putting God on trial and declaring that He is in the wrong, An-sky's revolutionary rabbis measure their distance from traditional piety and their closeness to the Russian radicals. At the same time, by yearning to have a burning longing for the divine and thereby master the power of the word, they strive for the ecstatic ideal of the pious. Although An-sky's growing interest in Jewish folklore in this period could be seen simply as a return to Jewish culture and a turning away from Russian culture—and indeed he himself presented it that way at times[82]—a close reading of the folktale revisions shows that he continued to look back over his shoulder at Russian culture, talking all the while. Each version of the tale responds to one or several subsets of potential readers, Russian and Jewish, as well as, undoubtedly, internal interlocutors corresponding to these readers. The paradox of An-sky's seemingly mutually exclusive attitudes toward Hasidism is emblematic of his position as a bilingual and bicultural intellectual who, like his heroes, did not necessarily need to reconcile the divergent statements he made to different audiences.

Notes

I am grateful to many people who have helped me research and think through this topic: Zachary Baker, Dan Ben-Amos, David Roskies, Heather Coleman, Mark Steinberg, and the participants in the Sacred Stories conference (Urbana, 2002) and the Borderlines conference (Syracuse, 2002). The epigraph opening this chapter is from Thomas Carlyle, *On Heroes, Hero-Worship, and the Heroic in History*, ed. George Wherry (Cambridge, 1911), 11.

1. See Christopher Read, *Religion, Revolution and the Russian Intelligentsia, 1900–1912: The Vekhi Debate and Its Intellectual Background* (London, 1979).

2. See Mark D. Steinberg, "Workers on the Cross: Religious Imagination in the Writings of Russian Workers, 1910–1924," *Russian Review* 53, no. 2 (April 1994): 213–239; Jay Bergman, "The Image of Jesus in the Russian Revolutionary Movement: The Case of Russian Marxism," *International Review of Social History* 35, no. 2 (1990): 220–248.

3. S. An-sky, "Evreiskoe narodnoe tvorchestvo," *Perezhitoe* (1908), 298.

4. Ibid.

5. Ibid., 300.

6. Ibid., 301.

7. See the ten examples collected in Louis I. Newman, ed., *The Hasidic Anthology: Tales and Teachings of the Hasidim* (New York, 1934), 56–59.

8. See the articles "Kaddish" and "Levi Isaac ben Meir of Berdichev" in the *Encyclopedia Judaica*, 16 vols. (Jerusalem, 1971), 10: 660–663, 11: 102–104.

9. *Listserve Mendele: Yiddish Literature and Language*, vol. 07.136, January 20, 1998. For the text of the song in Yiddish and English, see Samuel H. Dresner, *The World of a Hasidic Master: Levi Yitzkhak of Berdichev* (Northvale, N.J., 1994), 86–87.

10. During the ethnographic expeditions that he led in Ukraine in 1912, An-sky recorded his colleague, Zinovy Kisel'hof, singing a version of the song. See "Dem berdichever rovs kaddish," on *Treasury of Jewish Culture in Ukraine* (Kiev, 1997). The song was performed by Paul Robeson at a 1958 concert at Carnegie Hall and appears on the CD of that performance, "Chasidic Chant," on *Paul Robeson, Live at Carnegie Hall* (1985).

11. Shelomoh Gavriel ben Mordekhai Zeev, *Sefer Hitgalut ha-tsadikim: ve-sipurim moraim, u-mafli pelaim* (Warsaw, 1901; republished 1905). I cite the text from an Israeli scholarly edition: Shlomo Gabriel Rozental, *Hithgaluth Ha-Zaddikim. Tifereth Ha-Zaddikim*, ed. Gedalyah Nigal (Jerusalem, 1996), 81–83. There is evidence that this story circulated orally; a version of it was collected in Kiev in 1925, published in 1934, and republished in 1999 in *Evreiskie narodnye skazki: predaniia, bylichki, rasskazy, anekdoty*, originally collected by E.S. Raize and reedited with an introduction and commentary by Valerii Dymshits (St. Petersburg, 1999). Then again, An-sky himself may have popularized the story, causing it to reach Raize—in a version that resembled his own more than Rozental's—seventeen years after he retold it.

12. For examples of such Aesopian references to the Jewish question in Romania, see the journal *Russkii evrei* (1879–1884).

13. On Vasily Rozanov's obsession with Jewish sexuality, see Laura Engelstein, *The Keys to Happiness: Sex and the Search for Modernity in fin-de-siècle Russia* (Ithaca, N.Y., 1992), chap. 8.

14. Rozental, *Hithgaluth Ha-Zaddikim*, 81.

15. Ibid., 83.

16. Ibid.

17. An-Sky, "Jewish Folk Art," 276.

18. Ibid., 276, 277, 278.

19. Ibid., 279.

20. Ibid., 314.

21. S. An-skii, "Sud. (Skazanie)," *Evreiskii mir,* January 1909. There it is dated "December 1908. Terioki." I cite S. An-sky, *Sobranie sochinenii* (St. Petersburg, 1911), vol. 1.

22. My thinking on An-sky's attitude toward the Jews' position in the empire has been greatly influenced by Seth Wolitz, and I am grateful to him.

23. Undated letter, Vera Zhitlovskaia to S. Rappoport, Rappoport papers, the Judaica section of the manuscript division of the Vernadsky National Library of Ukraine in Kiev, f. 339, no. 810.

24. See the article on the *Kalevala* in *Entsiklopedicheskii slovar'.*

25. On the political situation in Finland during the first years of the twentieth century, see *Russification in the Baltic Provinces and Finland, 1855–1914,* ed. Edward Thaden (Princeton, N.J., 1981), esp. pt. 5, "Finland," by C. Leonard Lundin. On the Russian liberal attitude toward the Finnish nationalist movement, see Alexis E. Pogorelskin, "Vestnik Evropy and the Finnish Question, 1885–1904," *Journal of Baltic Studies* 11, no. 2 (1980): 127–141; on the attitude of Petr Lavrov, Haim Zhitlowsky, and other radicals in An-sky's circles, see E. K. Zhigunov, "P. L. Lavrov i russkaia emigratsiia o finliandskom voprose," *Skandinavskii sbornik* (1972): 17.

26. See William Albert Wilson, *Folklore and Nationalism in Modern Finland* (Bloomington, Ind., 1976), esp. 57–59.

27. *Kalevala. Finskii narodnyi epos,* trans. E. Granstrom (St. Petersburg, 1881); *Kalevala. Finskaia narodnaia epopeia,* trans. L. P. Belskii (St. Petersburg, 1888).

28. E. J. Moyne, *Hiawatha and Kalevala: A Study of the Relationship between Longfellow's "Indian Edda" and the Finnish Epic.* Folklore Fellows Communication, no. 192 (Helsinki, 1963).

29. Genri Longfellow, "Pesn' o Gaiavate," trans. I. Bunin, *Orlovskii vestnik* (1896), nos. 114–252. Hiawatha was translated into Yiddish by Yehoash (New York, 1910).

30. An-sky had also used unrhymed trochaic tetrameter earlier, in 1904, in another folkloric stylization. See S. An-sky, "Ashmedai," in *The Dybbuk and the Yiddish Imagination,* ed. and trans. Joachim Neugroschel (Syracuse, N.Y., 2000), 306.

31. An-sky, "Sud," 3.

32. On the discourse of SR terror, see Manfred Hildermeier, *The Russian Socialist Revolutionary Party before the First World War* (New York, 2000), 54–55.

33. On *podvig,* see G. N. Skliarevskaia, *Slovar' pravoslavnoi tserkovnoi kul'tury* (St. Petersburg, 2000), 183; and *Polnyi pravoslavnyi bogoslovskii entsiklopedicheskii slovar'* (St. Petersburg, 1913; reprint London, 1971), 1820–1821.

34. "Sud," 11.

35. F. M. Dostoevskii, *Polnoe sobranie sochinenii,* 30 vols. (Leningrad, 1972), 4: 95–96.

36. Felix Dreizin, *The Russian Soul and the Jew* (Lanham, Md., 1990), 3.

37. A. P. Chekhov, *Polnoe sobranie sochinenii i pisem,* 30 vols. (Moscow, 1977), 7: 32; translation from Anton Chekhov, "The Steppe: The Story of a Journey," in *The Oxford Chekhov,* trans. Ronald Hingley, 9 vols. (New York, 1980), 4: 31.

38. M. E. Saltykov-Shchedrin, "Dnevnik provintsiala," *Sobranie sochinenii* 20 vols. (Moscow, 1970), 10: 508–509.

39. See Norman Cohn, *Warrant for Genocide: The Myth of the Jewish World-Conspiracy and the Protocols of the Elders of Zion* (New York, 1966).

40. See *The Protocols and World Revolution* (Boston, 1920), 18–19.

41. Ibid., 8.

42. See Heinz-Dietrich Löwe, *The Tsars and the Jews: Reform, Reaction, and Anti-Semitism in Imperial Russia, 1772–1917* (Chur, Switzerland, 1993), 155ff.; and A. I. Solzhenitsyn, *Dvesti let vmeste (1795–1995),* 2 vols. (Moscow, 2001), 1: 106–156.

43. V. V. Shul'gin, "Chto NAM v NIKH ne nravitsia . . . ". *Ob antisemitizme v Rossii* (St. Petersburg, 1992), 44. This book was first published in 1929 in Paris.

44. For statistics on the numbers of Jewish lawyers, and debates around their dominance of the profession, see Benjamin Ira Nathans, *Beyond the Pale: The Jewish Encounter with Late Imperial Russia* (Berkeley, Calif., 2002), 314ff.

45. "Sermon on Law and Grace" (between 1037 and 1050) defines Russia precisely within the context of the binary opposition between law and grace.

46. Dostoevsky's fascination with law, grace, Jews, and Russians is discussed in David Goldstein, *Dostoyevsky and the Jews* (Austin, Tex., 1980); see Peter J. S. Duncan, *Russian Messianism: Third Rome, Revolution, Communism and After* (New York, 2000), 34–41; and Marina Kostalevsky, *Dostoevsky and Soloviev: The Art of Integral Vision* (New Haven, Conn., 1997), 136, on Dostoevsky's *Diary of a Writer*.

47. Sh. An-sky, "A din-toyre mit Got," *Gezamelte shriftn*, 15 vols. (New York, 1927), 1: 147–158; idem, "A din toyre," *Dos naye lebn*, February 1909, 142–146; idem "A din-toyre. (A khsidishe folks-mayse)," *Der fraynd*, no. 62, 16 (29) March 1909. For a translation, see Tony Kushner and Joachim Neugroschel, *A Dybbuk and Other Tales of the Supernatural* (New York, 1998), 160.

48. Letter from S. Rappoport to H. Zhitlowsky, 7(20) January 1909, YIVO, Zhitlowsky papers, no. 834. Rappoport also touched on this poem in two undated letters from YIVO, which begin "Neskol'ko dnei t. n. poluchil tvoe serdechnoe pis'mo" and "Ochen' obradoval menia tvoe serdechnoe pis'mo. Davno ne poluchal ot tebia takogo." There he writes, "Thank you for printing 'Din toyre.' It came out better in Russian." The poem never came out in *Yudishe vokhenshrift*, which ceased publication with issue no. 4 on 18 February (3 March) 1909.

49. For a translation of "Ashmedai," see *The Dybbuk and the Yiddish Imagination: A Haunted Reader*, ed. and trans. Joachim Neugroschel (Syracuse, 2000). Neugroschel notes that the *Kalevala* meter developed a humorous function in Yiddish literature (306).

50. An-sky, "A din-toyre mit got," 156.

51. Ibid., 158.

52. An-sky, "Sud," 11.

53. See the Jewish mysticism in Andrei Belyi's 1908 novel *Serebrianyi golub'* (The silver dove).

54. An-sky, "A din-toyre mit got," 154, 156.

55. Ibid., 158.

56. Ibid., 157.

57. An-sky, "A din-toyre, 142–143.

58. An-sky, "Sud," 9; "A din-toyre mit got," 155.

59. "A din-toyre," 145.

60. Ibid., 146.

61. David Roskies discusses the influence of Peretz on An-sky in his excellent "S. Ansky and the Paradigm of Return," in *The Uses of Tradition: Jewish Continuity in the Modern Era*, ed. Jack Wertheimer (New York, 1992). See An-sky's reminiscences of Peretz in his *Gezamelte shriftn*, vol. 10.

62. On An-sky's ideology, see Michael C. Steinlauf, "Dybbuks on and off the Polish Stage," *The Jews in Poland* (Krakow, 1999), vol. 2.

63. Mark W. Kiel, "Vox Populi, Vox Dei: The Centrality of Peretz in Jewish Folkloristics," *Polin* 7 (1992): 93.

64. I. L. Peretz, "Between Two Mountains," in *The I. L. Peretz Reader*, ed. Ruth R. Wisse (New York, 1990), 195.

65. Paul Mendes-Flohr, "*Fin-de-Siècle* Orientalism, the *Ostjuden* and the Aesthetics of Jewish Self-Affirmation," in *Studies in Contemporary Jewry*, ed. Jonathan Frankel, vol. 1 (Bloomington, Ind., 1984), 105.

66. Martin Buber, *The Legend of the Baal-Shem*, trans. Maurice Friedman (New York, 1969), 31.

67. Ibid., 30.

68. In 1916 An-sky wrote his own version of the story of the boy with the whistle. Whereas Buber concentrated on the boy's pure soul, An-sky returned to the theme of conflict with God, drawing attention to the effectiveness of the whistle in breaking through the doors of Heaven (An-sky, *Gezamelte shriftn*, 1:144–146; for an English translation, see idem, *A Dybbuk*, 181–182).

69. Louis Jacobs, *Hasidic Prayer* (New York, 1973), 93ff.

70. Buber, *The Legend of the Baal-Shem,* 17, 18, 19.

71. Letter from Rappoport to Zhitlowsky, 17 (30) October 1908, YIVO, Zhitlowsky papers, no. 826.

72. An-sky, "Sud," 7.

73. An-sky, "A din-toyre mit got," 152.

74. "Where I retold the legendary tradition, I still did so just as the Western author that I was" (Martin Buber, *Hasidism and Modern Man,* ed. and trans. M. Friedman [New York, 1958], 22; cited in Mendes-Flohr, "*Fin-de-Siècle* Orientalism," 112).

75. Haya Bar-Yitzhak, "Hearot le-masah 'Ha-etnopoetika ha-yehudit' leshin An-ski," *Khuliot* (winter 1999): 367. Cf. Dov Noy, "Mekomo shel Shin An-ski be-folkloristikah ha-yehudit," *Mekhkare yerushalaim befolklor yehudi,* bet.

76. Richard Bauman and Charles L. Briggs, "Poetics and Performance as Critical Perspectives on Language and Social Life," *Annual Review of Anthropology* 19 (1990): 72.

77. Ibid., 73.

78. Dan Ben-Amos, "Context in Context," *Western Folklore* 53 (April 1993): 220.

79. Dan Ben-Amos, "Jewish Folk Literature," *Oral Tradition* 14, no. 1 (March 1999): 140ff.

80. Paul Zumthor, *Oral Poetry: An Introduction* (Minneapolis, Minn., 1990), 17, 25.

81. On legends as dynamic phenomena, see Linda Degh, *Legend and Belief: Dialectics of a Folklore Genre* (Bloomington, Ind., 2001).

82. As An-sky said in 1910, "Bearing within me an eternal yearning toward Jewry, I nevertheless turned in all directions and went to labor on behalf of another people." See Moyshe Shalit, *Fun noentn over,* vol. 1 (Warsaw, 1937–1938), 231. Cf. Roskies, "S. Ansky and the Paradigm of Return," 246.

12

"A Path of Thorns": The Spiritual Wounds and Wandering of Worker-Poets

Mark D. Steinberg

⸺⸻❈⸻⸺

Two paradoxical stories connect in this essay: manual workers who wrote poetry and a religious language that was not necessarily the language of religion. Both are stories about suffering and searching, and their interpretation in a sacred key, marked by emotional pathos and a sense of transcendent meaning, by faith but also by doubt. These are stories about language—its irrepressibility and power. And these are stories about boundaries, about the porosity and ambiguity of hermeneutic divides in people's experiences of the world, in their experience of the transcendent, and in our own categories and definitions, especially of the elusive boundaries of secular and sacred.

In the early years of the twentieth century, hundreds of working-class Russians, with little formal schooling, found themselves inexplicably "driven," by their own accounts, to express themselves in verse and, although less often, in fictional prose, criticism, and reminiscence.[1] The language with which they wrote was rich in religious images, tropes, and narratives. They wrote of their own lives, and of the world and its meanings, as a "way of the cross" and "path of thorns," as "crucifixion" and "martyrdom." They spoke of awakening to "sacred truth" and of the promises of redemption and salvation. Few of these writers, in their use of this language, meant literally to interpret life according to Christian theological belief; their biographies tell us that most of them were avowedly secular Marxists. But neither was this mere metaphor, pointing entirely to something beyond itself, emptied of all referential sense of the original. "It is absolutely impossible," it has been suggested, "to empty out words filled to bursting,"[2] especially when words are full of the long human effort to give meaning and sense to life, and even imbue it with awe and hope.

I find the same resistance to "emptying out" in the pervasive use of religious vocabulary and images by worker-poets. Sacred symbols and metaphors, it has long been argued, have a distinctive power to express deeper, mysterious, and sacramental structures of meaning in the world, and to voice, with all necessary multiplicity and paradox, the otherwise inexpressible.[3] In the poetry of Russian workers, the symbolic language of the sacred, however much the intended narrative concerned this world (*saecularis*, in the Christian Latin, means to be of, or pertaining to, this world and this time), served in just such a way to read the disjointed fragments of everyday experience as part of a meaningful and purposeful narrative, a coherent conception of existence and time. Where secular and sacred begin and end in this language is characteristically ambiguous. Most important, this discourse, although formally atheological, drew deeply on the sensibilities and emotions of religious language, especially the pathos of Christ's Passion, in order to articulate a sense of awe before the world, to voice the imagination, and to dream of salvation. At the same time, and for many inescapably, however much they sought to flee it, this was an emotional pathos expressing a deep sense of melancholy and dread, but not one that can simply be reduced to secular skepticism.

This language, in the hands of workers, cannot be fully understood apart from the peculiar story of these workers' lives. Worker-poets well understood that workers writing poetry was transgressive. They often painfully felt the contradictoriness of their position at the boundaries of physical labor and mental creativity, of class and cultural difference. Indeed, their position as proletarian authors was full of the unease and power we have come to associate with liminal and hybrid identities. The hyphen that helps to name these identities, Jacques Derrida has suggested, is often a bridge that does not bridge, a "silence" that cannot pacify "a single torment" or ease "wounds."[4] It is also a linguistic sign of transgressive reach. Worker-poets, we find in their writings, felt both this torment and this daring. This awkwardness and transgressiveness is an essential part of the story of the worker-poet's language. These worker-poets may also be seen as archetypal "strangers," much as the linguist and psychoanalyst Julia Kristeva has described in writing about the hyphenated experiences of immigrants but also about the essential, psychological, strangeness stirred by other, more inward paths of cultural and social leaving "home" and wandering. Kristeva characterizes strangers as marked by feelings of "solitude, even in the midst of a crowd," by an "interior distance," by the occasional pleasures of solitude and melancholy, by nostalgia (the "melancholy love of a vanished [or, I would add, yet to be] space . . . and time"), and by the ultimate drive to "make oneself for oneself" rather than for others.[5] This applies well to the experiences of many Russian worker-poets, although also of many contemporaries who felt no less strange (perhaps painfully lost, perhaps exhilarated, perhaps both) amid the characteristically modern displacements of Russian life at the fin de siècle of the tsarist imperial order in Russia. And this strangeness is inseparable from what drew them to the language of the sacred.

Kristeva's suggestion that "a secret wound ... drives the stranger to wandering"[6] is a useful metaphor. Of course, it is not only a metaphor. We know that Russian workers were in fact physically harmed by their working-class lives and that many literally took to the road to find work, to improve their life, to see what lay beyond home. But these workers also made it clear that they felt "wounded" and thus "wandered" in much more subtle ways. Preoccupied with the self (the individual, the inward person, *lichnost'*) and with the soul (*dusha, dukhovnost'*), workers wrote constantly about the natural dignity of each human being and the suffering of the self, especially the worker's self, from the "insults" and "humiliations" society daily heaped upon it.[7] In search of explanation and answer and hope, they set out on a path of "wandering" which they themselves often viewed as essentially "spiritual" (*dukhovnyi*). The biographies of worker-poets are filled with obsessive reading, preoccupation with self-improvement and self-perfection, intense exploration of inner feelings, and a search for universal "truth." Writing itself was a form of wandering—across the boundaries of identity and across terrains of meaning. These "wounds," and the "wandering" to which they led, can be seen as analogous to one of the central narratives and functions of religion: the promise and the journey of suffering and healing, but also the search to know God. This essay, at its heart, concerns such a story but one that is never freed of ambiguity in defining the boundaries of secular and sacred languages, nor the uncertainty, especially when formal religious faith is absent, of the ultimate promise of healing, nor the sense of ultimate inaccessibility of the full knowledge of truth.

Spiritual Upheaval

The plebeian religious voice I explore in this essay was an inseparable part of the revival of religion, spirituality, mysticism, and myth in Russia during the last decades of the old regime.[8] Writing about another age (our own) marked by the "return of the religious," Derrida has pointed to the upheaval of the sacred, especially of sacred language, as a "volcano," or a fiery "abyss," that refuses to be "dominated, tamed, instrumentalized, secularized."[9] In 1908 the Russian poet Alexander Blok spoke of just such an upheaval of the "elemental," of emotion, fear, and fury, breaking through the "crusted lava" of civilization.[10] For many Russians of the fin de siècle, like Blok, the spiritual ferment of the age seemed so immense that an explosion, much like that of a volcano, was certainly approaching.[11] And the spiritual ferment among the Russian lower classes was one of its most potent, and potentially most explosive, signs.

Contemporaries and historians have often written of the loss of faith and decline in religious practice, as well as a rise of anti-clericalism, among urban workers in Russia by the turn of the century and after.[12] Memoirs by workers, including worker-writers, typically profess atheism. The Orthodox Church itself acknowledged the growing influence of secular mentalities among the urban classes, against which, in the latter years of the nineteenth century and the early years of the twentieth, it organized a sustained public campaign of religious talks, sermons, and mission work.[13] But the secularization of urban workers should not be oversimplified. Alienation from the established Church—common, although far from universal—and even crises of faith led often not toward secularism and atheism but toward alternative forms of religious faith and enthusiasm. In the 1870s, for example, as Reginald Zelnik has shown, the "seductive power" that student radicals often had among workers who participated in their circles resulted partly from a syncretic joining of social and political dissent to religious fervor and sacred moral purpose.[14] The same seductive effect was visible in the mass influence among workers, on the eve of 1905, of the movement led by Father Georgii Gapon, who similarly voiced social protest in a religious idiom and fostered a charismatic atmosphere of moral fervor and sacred mission.[15] After 1905, as among the educated—and reflecting the same dissatisfaction with an established Church that poorly satisfied spiritual, psychological, or moral needs—we see a continued revival of spiritual and religious searching among the urban lower classes. Unorthodox religious movements—although many of their followers rejected accusations of sectarianism and saw themselves as seeking only to renew and restore the true Orthodox faith—proliferated in urban areas, especially in working-class neighborhoods. These included followers of deviant Orthodox movements such as the moralistic and charismatic "Brethren" (*brattsy*) or the "Ioannites" (who venerated Father Ioann of Kronstadt), widespread sympathy for Tolstoy's religion of ethics and spiritual feeling but shorn of Church dogma and ritual, followers of individual mystics and healers, adherents of newly established sects such as the "free Christians" or the "sons of the apocalypse," older Russian groups like the *skoptsy* (castrates) and *khlysty* (flagellants), and growing evangelical and Baptist congregations.[16] These movements represented more complex, and perhaps more troubling, challenges to religious orthodoxy than secularization.

In many of these movements, religious *feeling* alongside fervent morality was a defining feature, and central to their appeal. The *brattsy* were typical. Founded in St. Petersburg in the mid-1890s, when the former fish and bread trader Ivan Churikov began converting the urban poor to a life of sober self-mastery, it spread, especially in the post-1905 years, to Moscow and other cities, as large numbers of artisans, workers in shops and factories, domestic servants, petty tradesmen, salesclerks, laborers, and the unemployed flocked to their meetings. The ethical teachings of the *brattsy* were much the same as that of other dissident religious movements of the day as well as of the missionaries and temperance advocates of the official Church: stop drinking, live moral lives, keep your families together, and stop the violence between spouses and against children, in order to honor God and live with a dignity befitting human beings, who carry within themselves the flame of the Holy Spirit. Their appeal reflected in large measure the way the message was expressed—its linguistic, ritual, and performative presentation. The Brethren spoke, it was said, in simple and direct language, with real sympathy and understanding for the sufferings of the poor, and with deep spiritual passion. The worker-writer Mikhail Loginov underscored this difference: "In the churches they instruct the common people with Orthodox teachings, which are absorbed, like any teaching, by the mind, but leave people's feelings untouched. 'Brother' Ivan knew how to set fire to the emotions: he created not a new teaching [*verouchenie*], but a faith, which, in the words of Christ, can move mountains."[17] Their meetings, like those of other popular urban "sects," had the atmosphere of a revival rather than of an Orthodox service—the congregation was exultant and active, continually interrupting the preaching with shouts of agreement, repetition of the preacher's phrases, and song, and meetings often featured moving testimonials by "sisters" and "brothers" who were saved from lives of drink, sin, and despair.[18] A "feeling for faith"[19] as much as theological belief itself was central to the Brethren's message and appeal. Among the growing number of lower-class adherents to Protestant and "sectarian" communities, and among followers of Father Ioann of Kronstadt, who had sought to restore fervency and the presence of the miraculous in liturgical celebration, stories of conversion and faith speak similarly of the centrality of emotion. Russian socialists and even many Marxists shared in the turn toward the spiritual, toward complexly intertwining supposedly secular and sacred languages. Most essential in this religious turn was the perception of the power of sacred emotion. The Bolshevik "God-builders," in particular, argued for the importance in any collective movement of appealing to the subconscious and the emotional, of harnessing the inspiring force of sacred "myth."[20]

Worker-writers shared the perception that ideas must touch the emotions to be of consequence. They filled their texts with hyperboles, metaphors, and symbols partly because these spoke the language of emotion most powerfully. And they found the symbolic language of the sacred especially resonant. According to Fedor Kalinin, who had been a worker-student of the God-builders, worker-writers were inspired by a distinctively proletarian epistemology that recognized, out of everyday experience, that the world cannot be understood with rational reason alone but required emotional intuition and knowledge.[21]

Religious idioms and images were appealing partly because they were so familiar, a part of the workers' world, especially their emotional world, since childhood. In autobiographies, including those written after 1917, worker-writers
often testified to the strong influence in their youths (and the warmth of feeling
for these memories), of religious stories, especially the lives of the saints and
martyrs and the Gospels, religious festivals, and the music, scents, and ritual of
the liturgy. Some sang in church choirs or read the Psalter at funerals. Some went
on pilgrimages—among these to sites where the boundaries between secular
and sacred were vague, to Tolstoy at Iasnaia Poliana, for example—or even spent
time in monasteries.[22]

Most worker-writers, however, considered themselves to have become
modern and secular. Certainly, for some, religious language expressed actual
religious knowledge and faith (of course, the extent and forms of personal belief
among workers remain necessarily obscure to us). Many certainly felt that the
story of Christ's Passion, and the promise inherent in Christianity that suffering was a meaningful sign of coming salvation, was (or, at least, was hoped to
be) literally true. But most worker-writers had at least superficially rejected the
faith of their parents and youths, and insisted that true knowledge was secular and materialistic and that the beliefs and rituals of the Church were mere
"superstition." Yet they often held onto religious imagery and language, even
a religious sensibility. Only partly did this involve translating religious images
into a secular (typically socialist) setting: dreaming of an earthly paradise, for
example, or insisting on Christ's socially subversive message. More often the
boundaries of secular and sacred were less neatly preserved. Religious motifs
and language were complexly compelling as an emotionally meaningful way to
interpret the world and envision change, even in the absence of formal "belief."
As the worker-poet Sergei Obradovich would later put it, symbolic language
best reflected truths that were most clearly understood through the emotions.[23]
Religious language remained a potent symbolic language precisely because
it so powerfully revealed, in Mircea Eliade's description, "a structure of the
world that is not evident on the level of immediate experience," raising stories
of the everyday to a more elevated, numinous sphere, and reaching toward the
universal.[24]

The Wounded Self

A vivid vocabulary of spiritual affliction pervaded the writing of worker-
poets. They wrote constantly of *grust'* and *pechal'* (sadness), *skorb'* (sorrow), *gore*
(misery, grief), *muka* and *muchenie* (torment, martyrdom), *stradanie* (suffering),
and *toska* (melancholy, anguish, longing). As a naming of the "wound" that

"drives the stranger to wandering," and of the wandering in which boundaries of secular and sacred were continually crossed and blurred, *toska* was
particularly telling and pervasive. *Toska* is difficult to translate, its meaning a
multilayered pastiche of longing (for something lost or not yet found), nostalgia
(the yearning, as Svetlana Boym has defined it, not only for a lost or nonexistent
place but for a different time), and melancholy (which Kristeva has defined as
"exquisite depression").[25] *Toska* was an essential, even defining component of
the pervasive strangeness these writers expressed—feelings (as Kristeva has
described in defining the stranger) of "interior distance," a "passion for solitude" (and for its pain), a "baroque" love of words and speech. The *toska* of the
stranger also entailed insistent "dreaming" about "a beyond," about "another
land, always a promised one."[26]

More tangibly, like Albert Camus' archetypal stranger, Meursault, worker-
poets were "never at one with men, nor with things."[27] This was especially true
of their industrial environment and the working-class men among whom they
lived. The landscape of cities and factories was the proletarian's "home," which,
Marxist intellectuals argued, shaped workers' spirits and won their unique
class "love." Yet very often this modern landscape felt cold and alien to workers, leading them to dream of some "beyond." This was not simply a matter of
poverty and long hours of labor. Worker-poets pointed to a more subtle spiritual alienation. Mikhail Gerasimov, a metalworker, miner, and railroad worker
(and probably the best-known and most accomplished Bolshevik worker-poet
of the time), was attracted by the city's "flash of bright colors / and noise of
street pleasures," but also felt that here he had become "a stranger to his own
inward self" (*dushe svoei chuzhei*).[28] Others wrote similarly of the industrial city
as a "prison" for the self, with its "high, cold, and gloomy" walls, its "stone
corridors," blocking out the warmth and light of the sun.[29] Factories and their
machinery, the most immediate physical environment for workers, seemed
especially cold and empty spiritually. The semi-autobiographical hero of the
metalworker Aleksei Bibik's novel of industrial life, for example, saw "in the
soulless din of the factory . . . inward indifference and even insolent unbelief. It
seemed to him that there was something here that was strange [*strannym*] and
needless. And he waited for it to die."[30]

The human beings with whom these workers shared the modern city stirred
an even deeper sense of estrangement and desire for a "beyond." In the "huge
and alien" city, it was said, even "streets crowded with people" felt empty and
"cursed," peopled by the "gloomy and soulless crowd," by strangers filled with
"hatred" and "enmity" for one another.[31] Vladimir Kirillov, who had come to city
work from a village in Smolensk Province, saw that the people of the modern
city looked at one another with "uncomprehending gazes" and "all wear masks

on their souls."[32] A trade unionist, commenting in 1910 on an "epidemic" of suicides among workers, blamed not poverty or unemployment (objective conditions were relatively good) but workers' feelings that modern life was a "big, dark, empty, and cold barn."[33] The spiritual condition of the human life of the city was made still worse by pervasive "vulgarity" (*poshlost'*), "dissoluteness" (*raspushennost'*), and "debauchery" (*razvrata*).[34]

The degraded world of workers was an especially painful, and preoccupying, danger; the spiritual ills of urban life was not limited to the decadence of the bourgeoisie. The overwhelming experience of the "thinking worker" amid his class "comrades," wrote the Marxist printing worker Ivan Dement'ev ("Kubikov"), was the "feeling of being alone . . . amid the gray and backward mass." Seeing "in what filth the soul of man is stewing," the awakened worker feels like "an alien creature among these people."[35] This spiritual "filth" was the subject of a great deal of writing by workers, who endlessly expressed their dismay, even disgust, at the pervasive drunkenness, swearing, and cruelty they saw all around them. They were nauseated by the smells of lower-class life—the village, the factory, the tavern, the street. And they expressed a deep sense of alienation and loathing before the "savage manners" and crass tastes of ordinary workers: widespread "drunkenness, violence, and depravity," "indifference" to "self-betterment," wasteful and harmful time spent in taverns, and a "darkness and chaos" that pervaded the life of common people.[36] The very vocabulary with which "thinking workers" judged everyday working-class life expressed their moral disgust and alienation: they wrote of widespread *poshlost'* (self-satisfied vulgarity), *razvrat* (debauchery), *raznuzdannost'* (licentiousness), *nechesnost'* (dishonesty, dishonor), *skandal* (scandalous behavior), *deboshirstvo* (rowdy disorder), *pakosti* (trash, depravities, obscenities), and *nravstvennaia khalatnost'* (moral apathy).[37] Every day, "thinking workers" had to struggle in such an environment to "defend their inner world from being spit upon."[38] As a result, they had become "cultural loners" (*kul'turnye odinochki*).[39] Many even sensed that their inner self had become a stranger to their own social self: as the miner and poet Aleksei Chizhikov wrote, the "workers' soul," no different in essence from the soul of even a tsar, was "imprisoned in a rough worker's hide."[40] The depth of estrangement in this writing bordered on a sort of cultural and moral nausea.

This spiritual "wound" led to spiritual "wandering." Worker-poets, in the face of this world, became, by their accounts, seekers and wanderers in search of higher meaning in life. The bakery worker Mikhail Savin wrote, in 1909, that he felt so out of place amid "the prose of everyday life" that he preferred "living in dreams, drunk with poetry, and the thirst for light."[41] The glassworker Egor Nechaev similarly felt that the world around him was a "prison" in which the only comfort was an inner fire, his "best friend," calling him to an unknown future.[42] Aleksei Mashirov, a Petersburg-born metalworker and a Bolshevik, described a worker sitting alone in his cramped room after work, trying to ignore the "laughter and tears of carefree fellows" on "the other side of the wall," reading by the "pale light of a lamp."[43] They wandered in search of meaning through books and inward thoughts but also did so literally. Their memoirs are filled with stories of traveling around the empire in search of work; a few even worked in Western Europe or sailed the seas as merchant marines. Very often these were described as spiritual journeys in search of "the meaning of human life."[44] For some, this was the explicit purpose of the journey. Ivan Nazarov, for example, recalled that he was so disgusted with the crass everyday world of workers and bosses in his native Suzdal that he fled to a monastery and became a monk; not finding the answers there that he was seeking, however, he went back into the world and began "wandering" (*peredvizhenie*).[45] Aleksei Solov'ev, a construction worker, wrote of "fleeing" the "petty and monotonous" life of the urban working class to "tramp around old Rus'" (*brodiazhit' po Rusi*), although he soon discovered that he preferred the phantoms of literature to the real people he met on the road, and therefore turned to a more inward journey.[46] Such spiritual wandering, as these workers certainly knew, was part of a familiar tradition in Russian culture, much of it on the ambiguous boundary of secular and sacred, of wandering artists (*peredvizhniki*), literary wanderers like Gorky and Tolstoy, roaming religious mystics (*stranniki*), lay preachers, pilgrims, and the vast genre of popular literary and folk tales of questing vagabonds, heroes, and saints.

For worker-poets, especially those who embraced socialist ideologies, the journey for meaning was a search to explain suffering—a theodicy. This suffering was often quite tangible. Workers' poetry was filled with images of suffering easily constructed out of the raw materials of lower-class life: childhoods ruined and lost, brutal conditions at work, filthy housing, poor food, hunger; even escape into sleep and dreams was "tortured by exhaustion."[47] Death, mainly premature, figured prominently in writing as in life. We see factory workers crushed to death by machines, workers dying of hunger, of disease associated with poverty, dying young and innocent. And when they died, one poet suggested, black blood flowed from their mouths, a sign of lifelong suffering.[48]

Suffering, of course, is interpretation. Physical injury, hunger, disease, and death are primarily material facts. Suffering is a category through which such facts are perceived, valued, and represented. In this sense, the poetics of suffering was an act of witnessing. As in much Russian literature, the discourse of suffering was hyperbolic, an expression of pathos. But it was also symbolic, an expression of meaning. Symbolic language, we know, universalizes the particular and points to deeper structures of meaning in the world, to less visible truths. Existential facts, transubstantiated into meaningful images by being inscribed into poetry, become, in this sense, sacramental—physical signs of a more meaningful reality. Workers' heightened sense of the value of the self, and the estrangement of self from both matter (the physical world of modern industrial life) and man (especially the working-class man), which we see in much worker writing, was such a story of revealed meaning, offered with great pathos. These feelings and meanings, however, remain elusive and even ambiguous.

Moral Stories

Images of suffering in workers' poetry echoed, in part, the Christian interpretation, underscored repeatedly in the liturgy, of suffering as the necessary lot of sinful man. Thus workers repeatedly portrayed their lives as "a harsh way of the cross filled with suffering" (*tiazhelyi krestnyi put' stradanii*), a "path of thorns," along which one must "bear one's heavy cross" and drink to the depths from the "overflowing chalice of suffering."[49] However, most worker-poets, especially those influenced by radical ideologies, tended instead to read suffering as moral wrong, as evil, but also as bearing within itself, as repeated allusions to Jesus' own suffering implied, the promise of redemption and deliverance. Contrary to those who have argued for the overwhelming weight of a deeply seated Russian cultural inclination toward self-abnegation and passive acceptance of suffering—the alleged "long-suffering" essence of the Russian soul[50]—Russian culture has also long nurtured a quite different narrative of suffering as possessing the power to transcend itself and redeem the sufferer. As narrative and argument, suffering was often understood not simply in connection to the fate of a sinful earthly world but also, in kenotic emulation of Christ's Passion,[51] as an elevating, empowering, and, above all, critical moral practice, and as a path to transcendence and salvation. It was not necessary to retain Christian canonical belief to find the structure and pathos of this Christian narrative compelling, although this hybrid language of suffering complicated rather than simplified the relation between secular and sacred, and the boundaries of each, in images and stories of suffering.

Representing suffering was often a critical moral practice: a condemnation of the harm to human beings caused by modern conditions of life. For some, this moral interpretation was cast explicitly within religious teachings and spiritual values. Admiration for Lev Tolstoy as a voice of spiritual and moral criticism of the status quo was one expression of this critical Christian moral vision. Although Tolstoy had been excommunicated from the Russian Orthodox Church in 1901, he remained widely admired for his popular moral writings, his simplified theology, and his own sufferings. His death in 1910, during his own journey of pilgrimage, wandering, and escape from everyday life, evoked an outpouring of praise for his role as a moral prophet. "Your books became for us a Gospel," wrote one poet in the trade-union paper of the St. Petersburg metalworkers' union to the recently deceased writer, "thank you for every sacred word."[52] Numerous worker-poets described Tolstoy as a "sun that has set," a "prophet of labor and love," a "titan," a "genius," and a "demigod," who spoke "sacred words that will remain eternal," and at whose unmarked grave pilgrims gathered and even the trees bowed low in honor.[53] Radical intellectuals, including Lenin,[54] nervously advised workers to embrace Tolstoy's ideals cautiously. The editors of the newspaper of the Petersburg metalworkers' union, for example, recommended that Tolstoy be appreciated "not as a Christian teacher, but as a great artist and tireless seeker of truth and justice [*pravda*], as defender of the oppressed, opponent of inequality, and fighter for free thought."[55] Many workers made it clear, however, that they were attracted precisely to Tolstoy's search for deeper spiritual truth (*istina*) and his teachings of spiritual love.

Mikhail Loginov—who became a writer and journalist after many years of tramping and odd jobs, and appears to have been one of those workers who turned away from the established Church but not from Christian belief—devoted the last years before his death from tuberculosis at the age of forty-one to promoting among the urban poor a socially critical morality, imbued with Christian imagery. The truth (*istina*) that Christ taught, Loginov insisted, has been "lost amid human contrivances and rites," hidden from people just as the "Gospels are hidden from people behind heavy silver and golden covers and clasps." The message taught by Christ—although also by Buddha and Mohammed, Loginov added—is "love of humankind, which alone can save the world from its senseless and cruel life." Loginov called on workers and the poor to awaken from their dark lives of "coarse swearing, fights, and drunken carouses" to "godly light and truth." Addressing the rich, he accused them of "sacrificing to Mammon," and quoted the scriptural threat, "he who does not work shall not eat." Like Tolstoy, Loginov repeatedly insisted that the spirit of God is within each person: if you recognize this inner spirit it will "make you free, as you were created to be."[56]

Other lower-class writers, also possibly still believers, often agreed openly with those who criticized the Church for the preponderance of religious form over feeling and thought, and especially for its neglect of true Christian ethics. This, of course, was also the message of the religious "sectarians" whose influence among urban workers grew dramatically after 1905. Many worker-poets shared this critical view of proper religiosity. "My God is not dressed in gold / Nor ornamented with diamonds / On the walls of churches and towers," wrote the textile worker Sergei Gan'shin, "My God is love and light."[57] Candles should be lit, Mikhail Loginov argued, not to "illuminate the cold and dark walls of a cathedral" but on "the altar of justice" in the name of people.[58] Were Christ to return now to the world and see the current state of Christian faith and practice, it was often said, "he would be ashamed for people" and saddened. His wounds would bleed at the sight of rich cathedrals standing complacently beside prisons where men "suffering for the truth" were bound in chains.[59] If one had to insist on the boundaries between secular and sacred thinking, it can be said that secular notions of social justice were affecting sacred vocabularies. But it is more useful to speak of a dialogue in which each infused the other with meaning, even for "believers."

While moral anger at the ethical passivity and hypocrisy of the Church led some to sectarian and Protestant movements, many strayed onto more distinctive, even individual, paths. The newspaper of the union of sales-clerical workers of Ekaterinodar, for example, offered the story of a young worker who had elaborated his own religious philosophy and practice. Interpreting the Gospels "in his own way," he transformed his workplace (a shoe store, a strik-ingly profane image even if it were not the actual site of this transformation) in his imagination into "a monastery" where he would practice a godly life of humility, honest labor, and just relations to others.[60] But many were led away from religion altogether, precisely in the name of the religious principles that made Church practice hypocritical: "I cannot pray to one / Who cannot hear the howl of the poor / . . . Who cannot hear the cry of the oppressed / Who is alien to misery and tears. / I can pray no more / To one who is friend to the rich. / I no longer believe! I will not!"[61]

Many worker-writers fashioned a critical ethics out of religious teachings, whether or not they continued to "believe." The biblical narrative of creation, fall, searching, incarnation, and salvation became a metaphor for interpreting the world, as it did for many Russian intellectuals. And the story of the Passion— the exemplary union of materiality and divinity, of profane and sacred, in which the boundaries were especially ambiguous but the promise of redemption unwavering—was particularly compelling. Egor Nechaev emphasized Christ's life of poverty and labor, his simple and honest speech, his willingness to speak truth to power, his sacrificial death in defense of love.[62] The Moscow weaver and poet Filipp Shkulev imagined himself at Christ's resurrection, sharing in the joy and renewal, hearing the "song of great love" but also feeling his own heart "burn from pain / Seeing how everywhere the common people are suffocating, / In evil, struggle, and blood."[63] Pondering their own hardships, worker-writers often drew on sacred moral teachings. The printer Sergei Obradovich, as a sol-dier in the trenches during the First World War, wrote verses and fragmented thoughts, between battles, in a diary made of pieces of folded paper, cursing war as an evil that "makes people insolent and sour, [and] makes people forget the commandments of love and charity."[64] Above all, worker-poets spoke of seeking and standing for "truth" (*pravda*) as a moral universal: for "Eternal sacred / Truth: martyr and brother."[65] And next to truth, as in the new "temple" (*khram*) that Sergei Gan'shin imagined, stood "peace, love, and beauty."[66]

Salvation

Even before the revolution inspired an imaginative leap toward millenarianism, secular conceptions of freedom and transformation of the world were intermixed with mythic, even mystic dreams of salvation. Although some placed their hope literally only in the "kingdom of heaven after death,"[67] more common were expectations of earthly deliverance from suffering. But very often these secular dreams were constructed of transcendent and sacred materials. Worker-poets often imagined themselves and their fellow sufferers as on a journey from suffering to deliverance, described with language steeped in the images and sensibility of the Passion. And although this language was "secularized" in its application to the world, it was characteristically too full to be "emptied out" of its spirit of sacred passion and perception. The Bolshevik metalworker Aleksei Mashirov ("Samobytnik") was inclined to view the hell of the factory as a place of "prayer" in which he was clad in *verigi* (the heavy chains worn by religious ascetics for penance and to chasten the flesh).[68] Workers often wrote of the suffering common people, and especially of themselves, as living through "martyred days" upon their own hard "way of the cross."[69] And death, the most liminal and potentially sacred moment in human life, was easily viewed in transcendent terms. At the end of a life of suffering, death, too, could be linked to Christ's passion. In a poem by the Bolshevik worker Mikhail Gerasimov, this symbolic association was made literal in the portrayal of a worker killed in an accident in a foundry:

> A sudden cry. A figure lay
> Crucified on the golden sheet,
> Embraced by serpentine flames,
> Burning on a fiery cross.
>
> He died amid the noise of machines;
> The pig iron boiled, the steel glistened.
> But shackled to his smoky throne,
> A bloodied angel thrust forward into the distance.[70]

The Passion, itself an elaboration of the biblical messianic narrative, embodied, especially as it appeared in workers' writings, the promise of deliverance from evil and suffering. Certainly some workers still grounded such belief in theistic faith: "no doubts are in one's soul / and with a heart at peace one believes in God."[71] But most often these were stories about secular hopes that were "filled to bursting" with the pathos and transcendent feeling of the sacred. Most generally, worker-poets wrote of their optimism in the future, their "faith" in change, their certainty that all obstacles would be overcome.[72] This faith was often cast in religious language and imagery, even by self-identified Marxist proletarians. For example, a church bell heard in the distance could be understood as the sound of "a bright divine muse," a "symbol of tears and misery," that awakened the spirit to be ready for new battles for a new future.[73] This spirit was conveyed repeatedly with symbolic images of the coming physical transformation of the world, driven by cosmic forces: approaching dawn, the rising sun, the force of wind, streams cutting though granite, spring rains and rebirth.[74]

Hints of apocalyptic redemption were common but nothing like what would be heard in the years following the 1917 Revolution. Worker-writers imagined, using familiar and potent symbols, an apocalyptic time of tempests, thunder, and catastrophes, followed by a new heaven and a new earth. Many wrote of a coming "golden time," of faith in an approaching age when the "miracle of goodness" will triumph, of a time when crowds will emerge from "the depths of melancholy longing and barrenness" (*iz nedr toski i proziaban'ia*) to meet "the sacred truth" of the coming new world free of suffering and oppression.[75] An exiled trade unionist offered this catechism of faith from the far North: "I believe in the coming eternal happiness / I believe in the poetry of life, in goodness and love / I believe that after the storms and thunder / The burning sun will appear again."[76] As in much millenarian thinking, the coming of the new age was expected to reunite the dead with the living. Aleksei Gastev, writing while in exile in Siberia in a poem published by the Petersburg metalworkers' union, characteristically envisioned the dead rising to join the struggle and even lead the revolution: "We are coming! We cannot but come; the dark specters of fighters struck down not long ago now arise; the living traditions of the past, fathers felled by wounds, stand up. We follow."[77]

Many wrote of saviors. Believing workers were likely to look to the promised second coming of Christ, although often with a radically apocalyptic spirit and a secular presence and physicality. Filipp Shkulev, for example, described Christ returning to earth with a message of revolutionary deliverance from suffering: finding the people in agony—"harsh ranks of gloomy faces," and chains rattling in "gloomy prisons," framed by the golden cupolas on "rich cathedrals"— Christ, with blood seeping from his wounds, comforts a man bowed in lament and prayer, "Do not cry / A time will come, when the haughty butchers / As in an ocean seething with waves / Will be repaid in blood."[78] More "secularized" workers were likely to seek new saviors. Thus the glassworker Egor Nechaev "prayed" to "freedom" that, "in the dark of night" when his "eyes are break-ing with tears" and his heart "can no longer endure the sorrow," she would come as a "savior" to "touch the sores" on his body with her "healing hand."[79] (Freedom is linguistically feminine in Russian, but the gendering of this image may also have drawn on the familiar cultural association of salvation with both the abstract "divine feminine" and the Mother of God.)

Very often worker-poets saw *themselves* as possessing mysterious salvific powers. Ideas about the special mission and power of the writer were wide-spread in Russian culture. And poets from the common people, creating lit-erature with little formal education, had additional reason to see themselves as having been given a sacred "gift."[80] Many writers from among the workers and peasants claimed that a "mysterious force" (*nevedomaia sila*) had com-pelled them to write.[81] Egor Nechaev, for example, spoke of the appearance of a "delightful fire" that burned in his mind calling him to a "distant unknown."

> In hours of labor and in brief sleep,
> Through the noise of machines and the talk of people,
> It always, God knows from where,
> Appears to me like a best friend:
> Here in the tender whisper of a wave,
> There in the rebirth of spring.[82]

Ideas about the sacred value of writing and the mysterious power that inspired it were often bound up with notions of worker-poets coming to the people as saviors. Some saw themselves as gentle redeemers, able to comfort the "sorrowing people" through "simple prayers" of catharsis and "quiet joy."[83] Others, especially the more politicized like Vasilii Aleksandrovskii, imagined themselves coming to the people, like the Christ of the gospels, not with peace but with a sword:

> I will be there, where backs are bent,
> Where labor is profaned and defiled,
> Where cries of grief are heard
> Amid the noise and roar of machines.
> I will be there, where children perish
> In the grasp of rough labor,
> Where unbearable need
> Casts its nets.
> I will instill in them indignation,
> Protest and bitter vengeance against their enemies,
> I will give them new thoughts
> And instinctual distant desires.

Each are within me, and I am in everyone.
If you are bold enough, then together
We will penetrate the Mysteries of the World [*Tainy Mira*],
And from there take everything.[84]

The entwining of the secular and sacred, of the worldly and transcendent, is captured not only in the narrative of the savior who is in and of all people, inspiring the suffering with "instinctual distant desires," but in the promised knowledge of the "Mysteries [*Tainy*] of the World," which echo the physical embodiment of the sacred in the sacraments (*tainstva*), mysteries simultaneously seen and unseen, present and transcendent, knowable and ineffable.

Wings often grew on the bodies of human saviors. Aleksei Gastev, in a prose poem that appeared in 1913 in the newspaper of the Petersburg metalworkers' union, of which he was then a leader, envisioned, if only metaphorically, the winged transfiguration of revolutionary workers as the struggle advances:

Higher still, yet higher! In the smoke of victory, we dash from the highest rocks, from the most treacherous cliffs to the most distant heights!
We have no wings?
We will! They will be born in an explosion of burning wish.[85]

Repeatedly worker-writers envisioned themselves symbolically in flight returning to earth as saviors. Egor Nechaev wished that he were an eagle or the sun, bringing happiness and freedom to the world.[86] Sergei Gan'shin described himself as "an eagle from the skies . . . from which my mighty voice / like a tocsin" rings out for victory "in the great and sacred struggle."[87] And Aleksei Mashirov portrayed awakened workers like himself coming to the people in inspiring flight: as birds in a black sky, as flashes of summer lightning, or as a "meteor falling into the deep abyss"—a redeeming sacrifice illumining the way for others.[88]

However metaphoric, winged human flight inescapably gave the ideas represented—escape, freedom, struggle—a mythic quality. Flight, of course, is a potent symbol, a dream of transcendent power and freedom, of a mystical break with the universe of everyday experience. Its roots lay equally in Christian tradition and older mythic cultures, and also, it has been argued, in the human subconscious. "Magical flight," as Eliade termed it, may be one of the most universal religious tropes, in which the boundaries of the everyday and the material world, and even of time and space, could be penetrated and transformed. Appearing in the myths and sacred lore of many cultures, and especially in shamanistic practices, magical flight can denote freedom from monstrous and evil forces, a link between the profane and the sacred, a mysterious understanding and power, and transcendence above the physical bonds of the human condition.[89] In a more secular vein, Nietzsche's Superman, widely influential in

Russian culture, was "an enemy of the spirit of gravity," who would "one day teach men to fly."[90] And Maxim Gorky, whose works were well known among writers from the lower classes and who was himself influenced by Nietzsche, also mythologized flight as transcendent and emancipatory.[91] In other words, flight was a metaphor that was not easily emptied out of the qualities of the sacred that filled it "to bursting." With images of flight, these writers typically blurred the line separating secular notions of civic and social emancipation from transcendent and mystical visions of transcendence, redemption, and salvation. This was not a stylistic inconsistency but a reflection of perceptions and attitudes that themselves may have been unstable and ambiguous but could not avoid reaching for images, and answers, that lay beyond the everyday and the profane.

No Exit

The reach for transcendent meaning and the promise of deliverance, however, sometimes came up empty-handed. Certain knowledge of the world, especially in the absence of canonical faith, often remained elusive. Suffering remained a narrative unmoored from the telos of certain salvation. Instead, a number of worker-poets articulated a tragic view of life's meaning and course. At best, this was a philosophical sense of the tragic, a view of suffering as inescapable and inevitable, but also as elevating the human spirit and deepening the soul. This was the philosophical tradition that looked back to Schopenhauer and Nietzsche, both influential in fin-de-siècle Russia, but also to Russian writers like Dostoevsky. Nietzsche, for example, argued that tragedy enables people to see "something sublime and significant" in their "struggles, strivings, and failures," in order ultimately to know, especially in the face of the modern knowledge that we are all ultimately destined to extinction, that "the individual must be consecrated to something higher than himself."[92] This tragic sense, implicit in much of the writing about suffering by worker-poets, would be even more starkly voiced, by Marxist workers as well, after the path of thorns that came with war, revolution, and civil war. The metalworker Nikolai Liashko, for example, writing in 1921, described modern existence as an essentially tragic but vital experience. The explosive furies of change in modern life, he maintained, have thrown humanity into an "abyss":

> For some it is heaven in the abyss, for others hell. . . . Wonders grow into horrors and horrors into wonders. To enumerate the changes would fill thousands of pages, and to describe them would fill millions of pages. Unexpected pains and joys, emptiness and profound meaning, versatile coping, spiritual breakdown, tragedies of immense weight appearing at every step. People sicken, go mad from exhaustion—but really live![93]

Andrei Platonov, the most accomplished and renowned Russian working-class author, would offer much the same philosophical argument: "Despair, torment, and death—these are the true reasons for heroic human action and the most powerful motors of history."[94]

This philosophical sense of the tragic was too optimistic for some, however, especially before the heroic romanticism of the years of revolution and civil war. If, as one worker-poet suggested, by virtue of their position in the social world, workers "drank to the very bottom the bitter cup of truth,"[95] that truth was often a nagging philosophical and historical skepticism. This was a more common sense of the tragic, or even what might be called an existentialist sense that there was no exit, no redemption—only "man" alone in the present world. Many worker-poets voiced their anxiety that there was no exit from the iron cage of human life as it was. They described shattered hopes for a "bright life," growing feelings of anguished melancholy and depression (*toska*), knowledge that it was pointless to "ask for happiness," and a deepening sense of the meaninglessness of life.[96] Even socialist workers, notwithstanding the promises of redemption that ideology offered, often could not sustain faith. The young socialist metal-worker Vasilii Aleksandrovskii wrote of troubled thoughts while sitting beside a dying friend: death appeared here not as a moral symbol of an unjust social order nor as a promise of deliverance, not even into rest and oblivion, but as only the final marker of life's grim course, of "dark, faceless dread / concealed somewhere, beyond the gloom."[97] Mikhail Gerasimov, a Bolshevik, admitted (in an unpublished poem) feeling that he was beyond meaningful suffering: "My soul . . . can now love no more, nor suffer / It is dead and empty."[98]

These reflections often expanded into more explicitly existential despair over life's meaning. The awakening of nature in springtime, for example, could be viewed not as a sign of hope but only as a reminder of the "melancholy, pain, and bitterness" in one's "weary soul," or of the truth that life's hardships "have no reason."[99] And these writers would sometimes admit to doubts that any savior would ever come. Egor Nechaev, especially in poems collected in his volume of 1913, *Vechernie pesni* (Evening songs), spoke of people, perhaps himself, whose "prayers go without answer / Hopes perish without trace," for whom "rays of hope and the flame of faith in God / long since burned out."[100] Like so many of these proletarian poets, Sergei Obradovich, a socialist worker whose verses appeared in many labor journals, and who wrote, on many occasions, of heroic struggle and faith in the future, succumbed to dark thoughts about existence:

I thought to myself: in this world of vanities
I am a hollow and superfluous thing,
Nothing and unnoticed

> Beneath the weight of suffering and misfortune . . .
> Loving all that the soulless world despised,
> I called upon death as if it were joy,
> And, in that indifferent darkness, in anguished doubt,
> I sought an answer to my question:
> Is there a place where life shimmers,
> Or are we fated to suffer forever?
> There was no answer.[101]

Even in the midst of the revolution, worker-writers found themselves subject to such existential doubt. The Marxist literary critic Aleksandr Voronskii, surveying workers' writings of the first years after October, noted the startling abundance of "melancholy [*toska*], sorrow, and solitariness, a tendency to dreaminess, to phantasms, to reveries and daydreams, to contemplativeness."[102] Indeed, *toska*, both by name and in spirit, continued to pervade workers' poetry, as they wrote, amid the heroic struggles and sufferings of 1917 to 1921, of loneliness, exhausted searching, autumnal sadness, and hearts weighed down with melancholy.[103] Like Sergei Obradovich, many "called upon death" in the face of the silence that met their questions about meaning. Thus a worker-poet and pianist active in local club work in provincial Kostroma (he claimed to love music as a way to express the "sorrows" of his "soul") wrote of his fascination with "the darkness of eternity" that lay beyond the end of life.[104]

A Feeling for the Sacred

The vocabulary, imagery, and pathos we see in much worker writing may be viewed as epiphanic, as writing in which the sacred is made manifest although without necessarily insisting on the literal truth of the images or stories evoked. What is the meaning of the sacred so translated and displaced? The suggestive metaphor "spilt religion," applied originally to Romantic art, also simply envisions religion as a vessel, or as contained in one, that can be spilled, and the secular world as a similarly bounded material that can absorb that "other" substance.[105] Nor is it adequate to interpret workers' use of religious vocabularies and images, even their narrative representation of human existence, as a mythic journey through suffering toward deliverance from affliction and evil, as merely a functionalist device, a way to communicate with the still religious common people (a tactic long employed by Russian socialists). Nor, I think, is it sufficient to speak of this language as simply the residue of faith, or empty linguistic habit, vacated of original referents and meanings. This is less spillage of religion into "other" spheres than interpenetration, dialogue, and plenitude (in Bakhtin's terms), even "presence" (in liturgical and sacramental terms). Of course, we cannot entirely know what workers believed or what they felt. We must be cautious of the hazardous allure of imagining transparency and lucidity—which, arguably, is precisely the foundation of the canonical faith we know to be so in doubt among many worker-poets. Workers' religious language was likely many things at once (or at different moments), including device and residue. But it is abundantly clear that many sacred words, images, and narratives are so imbued with accrued meanings and feelings that they are impossible to empty out.

Feeling was at the heart of workers' poetic language. Worker-poets created a discourse rich in emotion and sentiment, overflowing with much the same pathos that filled the religious language on which they so often drew. When the Marxist Vasilii Aleksandrovskii declared himself feeling "close to the new-born God" as Christmas approached, this was a matter not of Christian faith but of an admittedly mysterious spiritual pleasure—"a sharp knocking within my soul / from where I do not know"—at feelings evoked by glistening silver snows, winter stars, and "trembling nature."[106] In Sergei Gan'shin's imagined temple of truth and love, the altar was illumined "with the fire of feeling," in this case with the feelings of insult and injury felt by the people.[107] It would not be an overstatement to speak of a cult of feeling in workers' writings. Fascinated with the feelings inspired by their own suffering and dreaming—reading (and literally writing) these as holding transcendent meaning—strong feeling acted as a source both of pain and pleasure, as the ultimate measure of truth. As the "worker-philosopher" Fedor Kalinin maintained in an essay published in 1912, "the intellectual can still *think* for the young [working] class, but he cannot *feel* for it." And feelings most mattered in seeking the true. Non-proletarian intellectuals could analyze the "external facts and phenomena" of "political economy," Kalinin acknowledged, but true knowledge of the world (the ability, in Vasilii Aleksandrovskii's phrase, to "penetrate the Mysteries of the World") demands an emotional understanding that derives from experience[108]—from the fact, as it were, that workers "drank to the very bottom the bitter cup of truth." In many ways, this was a sacramental cup.

Feeling is central to the constitution of the sacred. Religion, it has often been argued, fundamentally involves the use of stories and symbols to evoke moods linked to transcendental interpretations of life—to see meaning in the chaos of existence, to name the good and predict its triumph, and to give form to potent feelings of mystery, awe, and the sublime. This emotional spirit is essential: there is no sacred, and hence no religion, without the play of sensibilities, passions, nostalgias, and imagination.[109] When Russian worker-poets wrote in a religious idiom, theirs, too, was a complex way of speaking in universalizing terms about sacred moral right, of articulating things sublime and mysterious, of voicing faith in deliverance—of "seeing," "flying," witnessing, and perhaps saving. It was a type of witnessing, of reaching beyond rational and material expressions of meaning to view the world much as literal religion does—as marked by the presence of mysterious structures of meaning. This may have seemed the only adequate language to voice the otherwise inexpressible and inexplicable. Indeed, with the fading power of formal theological belief, the force of sentiment and emotion, of the feeling for faith, may have become all the stronger. When a worker viewed the cruel and often senseless reality of his life, even if only metaphorically, as a religious journey, it may have become, if not kind or rational, at least emotionally understandable and bearable. Suffering was ennobled and valued as a sign of moral goodness; one's tormentors were damned; and affliction was made to contain the promise of salvation.

But not always. Religion is also about uncertainty and unknowability. Sergei Bulgakov, Vladimir Lossky, and others have similarly emphasized that religion, especially Orthodoxy, tends toward apophasis, the mystical theology that insists on the ultimate unknowability of "God," the impossibility of rationally comprehending the simultaneous transcendence and immanence of the divine.[110] Worker-poets, with all the pathos of religious feeling, also often hesitated before the certain knowledge and faith in the future that was so central to socialist ideology and struggle. And, at least at times, many felt that their searching remained without end, without exit—that they heard "no answer" to their questions about life's meaning and direction. Crucifixion, or apocalyptic images of storms, blood, and death, did not necessarily bring certainty of resurrection and salvation. At best, sometimes, suffering could become precious and powerful as a mark of sanctifying and dignifying experience—the pleasurable pain of the wandering "stranger," the melancholy (*tosklivyi*) love of an always anticipated sacred place and time.[111]

Notes

1. An earlier discussion of worker-writers and of their language of the sacred, here rethought and revised, can be found in Mark Steinberg, *Proletarian Imagination: Self, Modernity, and the Sacred in Russia, 1910–1925* (Ithaca, N.Y., 2002).

2. Letter of Gershom Sholem to Franz Rozenzweig (26 December 1926) quoted and discussed in Jacques Derrida, *Acts of Religion* (New York, 2002), 191–227. In the quote Sholem refers to the attempt to secularize the sacred language of Hebrew.

3. Mircea Eliade, "Methodological Remarks on the Study of Religious Symbolism," in *The History of Religions: Essays in Methodology,* ed. Mircea Eliade and Joseph Kitagawa (Chicago, 1959), 98–102; Clifford Geertz, "Ethos, World View, and the Analysis of Sacred Symbols," in idem, *The Interpretation of Cultures* (New York, 1973), 126–141.

4. Jacques Derrida, *Monolingualism of the Other; or, The Prosthesis of Origin* (Stanford, Calif., 1996), 10–11, cited and discussed in Gil Anidjar's introduction to Derrida, *Acts of Religion,* 9.

5. Julia Kristeva, *Strangers to Ourselves* (New York, 1991), esp. chap. 1.

6. Ibid., 5.

7. See Steinberg, *Proletarian Imagination,* chap. 2.

8. See the introduction to this volume.

9. Derrida, "The Eyes of Language," in idem, *Acts of Religion,* 191–227; quote at 198.

10. Aleksandr Blok, "Stikhiia i kul'tura" (December 1908), in *Aleksandr Blok, Andrei Belyi: Dialog poetov o Rossii i revoliutsii,* ed. M. F. Pianykh (Moscow, 1990), 396–405.

11. Ibid., 400–404.

12. For example, L. M. Kleinbort, "Ocherki rabochei demokratii," pt. 2, *Sovremennyi mir* (May 1913): 169–170; and M. M. Persits, *Ateizm russkogo rabochego, 1870–1905* gg. (Moscow, 1965).

13. See, for example, Gregory Freeze, "Counter-reformation in Russian Orthodoxy: Popular Response to Religious Innovation, 1922–1925," *Slavic Review* 54, no. 2 (Summer 1995): 305–339; idem, "Subversive Piety: Religion and the Political Crisis in Late Imperial Russia," *Journal of Modern History* 68 (June 1996): 308–350.

14. Reginald E. Zelnik, "'To the Unaccustomed Eye': Religion and Irreligion in the Experience of St. Petersburg Workers in the 1870s," *Russian History* 16, no. 2–4 (1989): 313–326; quote at 315.

15. S. I. Somov, "Iz istorii sotsialdemokraticheskogo dvizheniia v Peterburge v 1905 g.," *Byloe,* 1907, no. 4: 33–34; Gerald Surh, "Petersburg's First Mass Labor Organization: The Assembly of Russian Workers and Father Gapon," *Russian Review* 40, no. 4 (October 1981): 436–440.

16. See the introduction to this volume.

17. *Dumy narodnye,* no. 6 (6 March 1910): 1.

18. Pankratov, *Ishchushchie boga,* 52–53; A. M., "U trezvennikov," *Malen'kaia gazeta,* 1 (14) October 1914; *Dumy narodnye,* no. 3 (13 February 1910): 4.

19. The phrase is Mikhail Bakhtin's. See discussions in Susan Felch and Paul Contino, eds., *Bakhtin and Religion: A Feeling for Faith* (Evanston, Ill., 2001).

20. A. V. Lunacharskii, "Ateizm," *Ocherki po filosofii marksizma: filosofskii sbornik* (St. Petersburg, 1908), esp. 115–116, 148–157; idem, *Religiia i sotsializm,* 2 vols. (St. Petersburg, 1908 and 1911).

21. See, for example, F. Kalinin, "Tip rabochego v literature," *Novyi zhurnal dlia vsekh,* 1912, no. 9 (September): 96–97, 106.

22. For example, P. Ia. Zavolokin, ed., *Sovremennye raboche-krest'ianskie poety* (Ivanovo-Voznesensk, 1925), 41–42, 62, 168. See other sources cited in Steinberg, *Proletarian Imagination,* 231.

23. S. Obradovich, "Obraznoe myshlenie," *Kuznitsa,* no. 2 (June 1920): 24–25.

24. Eliade, "Methodological Remarks on the Study of Religious Symbolism," 98–103.

25. Svetlana Boym, *The Future of Nostalgia* (New York, 2001), xv; Kristeva, *Strangers to Ourselves,* 10.

26. Kristeva, *Strangers to Ourselves,* 5, 10, 12, 13, 21, 27.

27. Albert Camus, *L'Etranger* (1942), quoted ibid., 27.

28. M. Gerasimov, "V gorode," in *Pervyi sbornik proletarskikh pisatelei* (St. Petersburg, 1914), 51.

29. P. Zaitsev, "Sapozhnik ia," *Kolotushka,* no. 4 (Easter 1911): 2; Sergei Gan'shin, "Ia syn stepei," *Zhivoe slovo,* no. 18 (May 1913): 6; M. T-ts [M. A. Loginov], "Gorodskiia kvartiry," *Zvezda iasnaia* [*Zvezda utrenniaia*], no. 6 (29 February 1912): 2.

Mark D. Steinberg

30. A. Bibik, *K shirokoi doroge (Ignat iz Novoselovki)* (St. Petersburg, 1914), 30. See also I. Sm. "Zhizn' cheloveka v raznykh vremenakh," *Rabochii po metallu,* no. 24 (14 November 1907): 3–4; A. Zorin [Gastev], "Rabochii mir: s parizhskogo zavoda," *Zhizn' dlia vsekh,* no. 7 (July 1910): 144.

31. M. Artamonov, "Taet," *Metallist,* 1914, no. 4/41 (1 April): 5–6; S. Gan'shin, "Ia syn stepei," *Zhivoe slovo,* no. 18 (May 1913): 6; P. Zaitsev, "Sapozhnik ia," *Kolotushka,* no. 4 (Easter 1911); A. Dikii, "Bezrabotnye," *Edinstvo,* no. 6 (15 June 1909): 3.

32. V. Kirillov, "Gorod," *Stikhotvoreniia 1914–1918* (Petersburg [*sic*], 1918), 26.

33. Syryi, "Pomnite o samoubiitsakh," *Golos portnogo,* no. 3 (10 July 1910): 3–4, 8.

34. For example, Kvadrat [I. Kubikov], "Kul'tura i prosveshcheniia," *Pechatnoe delo,* no. 8 (27 June 1909): 5; M. Tikhoplesets [M. Loginov], "Epikuritsy," *Zvezda iasnaia [Zvezda utreniaia],* no. 6 (29 February 1912): 5–6; M. Volkov, "Obzor pechati," *Narodnaia sem'ia,* no. 4 (19 February 1912): 12–14; S. Gan'shin, "Krest'ianka," *Zhivoe slovo,* no. 20 (May 1913); M. Gerasimov, "U vitriny," *Prosveshchenie,* 1914, no. 1 (January): 6.

35. Kvadrat [Dement'ev-Kubikov], in *Novaia rabochaia gazeta,* no. 5 (13 August 1913): 2.

36. For example, the writings by M. Savin and M. Chernysheva in *Balalaika* (1910–1911); Blizhnyi, "Prosvetimsia liudi," *Rodnye vesti,* 1912, no. 4 [Easter]: 3; *Dumy narodnye,* 1910, no. 2 [February]: 1; *Zvezda iasnaia [Zvezda utreniaia],* no. 6 (29 February 1912): 2–4; *Zvezda utreniaia,* no. 17 (23 May 1912): 2; M. T-ts [M. Loginov], *Dumy narodnye,* 1910, no. 1 [February]: 2.

37. See sources cited in Steinberg, *Proletarian Imagination,* 85–89.

38. Kvadrat in *Novaia rabochaia gazeta,* no. 5 (13 August 1913): 2.

39. G. Deev-Khomiakovskii, "Kul'turnye ugolki i kul'turnye odinochki," *Drug naroda,* 1915, no. 2 (31 January): 10–11.

40. Aleksei Chizhikov, letter accompanying verses submitted to *Pravda* by the miner, March 4, 1914. RGASPI (former Central Party Archive), f. 364, op. 1, d. 315, ll. 1–3; quote at 4.

41. A. A. Tiulenev, ed., *Gallereia sovremennykh poetov* (Moscow, 1909), 11.

42. Nechaev, "Moia pesnia," *Vechernie pesni: stikhotvoreniia* (Moscow, 1914), 79–80.

43. Mashirov, "Posle raboty," *Pravda,* 8 November 1912; and *Pervyi sbornik proletarskikh pisatelei,* 160.

44. Mikhail Kiriushkin, autobiography, in RGALI, f. 1068, op. 1, d. 72, l. 1.

45. RGALI, f. 1068, op. 1, d. 106, ll. 23–24.

46. Zavolokin, *Sovremennye raboche-krest'ianskie poety,* 214.

47. On destroyed childhoods, for example, see Egor Nechaev, "Moia pesnia" [1906], *Vecherniia pesni: stikhotvoreniia* (Moscow, 1914): 79; M. Chernysheva, "Ne prigliadite kartiny . . . ," *Balalaika,* 1910, no. 18: 2. On tortured sleep, see, for example, F. Gavrilov, "Son," in *Proletarskie poety,* 3 vols. (Leningrad, 1935–1939), 1: 197–201; S. Obradovich, "Bezsonnoiu noch'iu," *Severnoe utro* (Archangel'sk), no. 52 (6 March 1913): 2; M. Gerasimov, "Zavodskii gudok," *Pervyi sbornik proletarskikh pisatelei* (St. Petersburg, 1914), 91–92.

48. [Chechenets], "Nevol'niki truda," *Nash put',* 1911, no. 17 (23 May): 8–9; S. Bruskov, "Smert' byvshago cheloveka," *Rodnye vesti,* 1912, no. 3: 2–3; M. Chernysheva, "Zaveshchanie," *Dumy narodnye,* no. 7 ([13 March] 1910): 5; F. Shkulev, "Pil'shchik," *Narodnaia mysl',* no. 2 (February 1911): 107; N. Dodaev, "Trud," *Zhizn' pekarei,* 1914, no. 1/4 (10 March): 2.

49. G. Deev-Khomiakovskii in *Drug naroda,* 1915, no. 5–7: 2–3; S. Drozhzhin, ibid., 13; A-ch, "Ternistyi put'," *Samopomoshch' 2,* no. 1 (18 December 1911): 6; S. Aleksandrov, "K dnei rabochego pechati," poem sent to *Pravda,* 10 June 1914, RGASPI, f. 364 (Pravda), op. 1, d. 337, l. 1.

50. Anna Feldman Leibovich, *The Russian Concept of Work: Suffering, Drama, and Tradition in Pre- and Post-Revolutionary Russia* (Westport, Conn., 1995); Daniel Rancour-Laferriere, *The Slave Soul of Russia: Moral Masochism and the Cult of Suffering* (New York, 1995).

51. The classic accounts of Russian "kenotic Christianity" are Nadejda Gorodetzky, *The Humiliated Christ in Modern Russian Thought* (New York, 1938); and G. P. Fedotov, *The Russian Religious Mind* (Cambridge, 1946), chap. 4.

52. *Nash put'*, no. 19 (3 December 1910): 3.

53. *Balalaika*, 1910, no. 21: 2; I. Kornev, "Velikaia mogila," *Chelovek*, no. 2 (6 March 1911): 5–6.

54. V. I. Lenin, "L. N. Tolstoi" (16 November 1910) and "L. N. Tolstoi i sovremennoe rabochee dvizhenie" (28 November 1910), in *Polnoe sobranie sochinenii*, 55 vols. (Moscow, 1958–1965), 20: 19–24, 38–41.

55. *Nash put'*, no. 10 (3 December 1910): 1–2.

56. *Dumy narodnye*, no. 1 (1910): 1–2; no. 3 (13 February 1910): 1; no. 5 (27 February 1910): 2; *Zvezda utrenniaia*, no. 16 (16 May 1912): 2. Loginov alludes to John 8:32: "And you shall know the truth [*istina*] and the truth shall make you free."

57. S. Gan'shin-Gremiacheskii, "Moi Bog . . . ," *Dumy narodnye*, no. 1 (1910): 5. See also the editorial on page 1.

58. *Zvezda utrennaia*, no. 9 (25 March 1912): 2.

59. F. Shkulev, "Khristos," *Narodnaia mysl'*, no. 1 (January 1911): 14; *Dumy narodnye*, no. 5 (27 February 1910): 1. See also E. Nechaev, "Patriot," *Ostriak*, 1910, no. 70, in *U istokov russkoi proletar'skoi poezii* (Moscow and Leningrad, 1965), 113–114.

60. A-ch, "Ternistyi put'," *Samopomoshch' 2*, no. 1 (18 December 1911): 6–7.

61. S. Gan'shin, "Ne mogu," RGASPI, f. 433 (*Zvezda*), op. 1, d. 91, l. 3.

62. E. Nechaev, "Khristos," *Vechernie pesni*, 124–125.

63. F. Shkulev, "V den'Voskreseniia," *Zvezda utrenniaia*, no. 9 (25 March 1912): 3–4.

64. RGALI, f. 1874, op. 1, d. 185, l. 26 (entry of 23 November 1916).

65. M. Savin, "Pravda," *Bulochnik*, no. 3 (12 March 1906).

66. S. Gan'shin, "Postroim Khram," *Vpered!*, no. 157 (14 September 1917): 3. See also *Drug naroda*, no. 2 (31 January 1915): 16.

67. A-ch, "Ternistyi put'," *Samopomoshch' 2*, no. 1 (18 December 1911): 7. See also D. Bogdanov, "Na cherdak," *Narodnaia mysl'*, no. 2 (February 1911): 130.

68. Samobytnik [Mashirov], "Vesennye grezy," *Voprosy strakhovaniia*, 30 July 1916, reprinted in *Proletarskie poety*, 3: 26; idem, "Posle raboty," *Pravda*, 8 November 1912, reprinted in *Proletarskie poety*, 2: 88.

69. E. Nechaev, "K rodine" (1907), in *U istokov*, 98; D. Bogdanov, "Na cherdak," *Narodnaia mysl'*, no. 2 (February 1911): 130; G. Deev-Khomiakovskii in *Drug naroda*, no. 5–7 (1915): 1–2; I. Golikov, "Bog v pomoshch'," RGALI, f. 1068, op. 1, d. 41, l. 15.

70. M. Gerasimov, "Krest," in *Sbornik proletarskikh pisatelei*, ed. M. Gorkii, A. Serebrov, and A. Chapygin (Petrograd, [1917]), 3.

71. M. Zakharov, "Nastroenie," *Rodnye vesti*, 1911, no. 3(4): 7.

72. Many examples can be found in Soviet anthologies of proletarian poetry, such as the three volumes of *Proletarskie poety* (Leningrad, 1935–1939); and *Poeziia v bol'shevistskikh izdaniiakh, 1901–1917* (Leningrad, 1967).

73. M. Tsarev, "V lesu" (1915), *Proletarskie poety*, 3: 36–37; S. Gan'shin, "Slyshite-l'?" *Vpered!* no. 115 (25 July 1917): 5.

74. See, for example, poems by Aleksei Mashirov (Samobytnik), such as "Ruch'i," "Na rassvete vesennyi zori," "Grebtsy," "Vesennyi dozhd'," most of them first printed in *Pravda* in 1912 and 1913, reprinted in *Poeziia v bol'shevistskikh izdaniiakh*, 218–219, 227, 304; or Aleksandrovskii in *Novaia rabochaia gazeta*, no. 31 (13 September 1913): 2.

75. I. Volodinskii, "Dumy naborshchika," *Nashe pechatnoe delo*, no. 18 (21 February 1915): 5; I. Golikov, "Blagoslovi," RGALI, f. 1068, op. 1, d. 41, l. 130b. See also E. Nechaev, "Starik," *Vechernie pesni*, 96–97.

76. O. R-n, "Iz ssylki," *Edinstvo*, no. 4 (23 April 1909): 3.

77. I. Dozorov [Gastev], "My idem!" *Metallist*, 1914, no. 1/38 (13 January): 3–4.

78. F. Shkulev, "Khristos," *Narodnaia mysl'*, no. 1 (January 1911): 14. See a similar poem by S. Gan'shin in *Narodnaia sem'ia*, no. 3 (16 January 1912): 1.

79. E. Nechaev, "O svobode" (1907), *Vechernie pesni*, 94–95.

80. *Narodniki*, no. 1 (1912): 2.

81. M. Gorkii, "O pisateliakh-samouchkakh" (1911), in *Sobranie sochinenii*, 30 vols. (Moscow, 1949–1956), 24: 105–108.

82. E. Nechaev, "Moia pesnia," *Vecherniia pesni*, 79–80; and *U istokov*, 92.

83. Korolev, *Vsem skorbiashchim*, 5–6.

84. V. Aleksandrovskii, "Novye pesni," *Nashi pesni*, 2 vols. (Moscow, 1913–1914), 1: 11.

85. Dozorov [Gastev], "My Idem!" 3–4.

86. E. Nechaev, "Pesnia nevol'nika," *Vechernie pesni*, 151; and *U istokov*, 98–99.

87. S. Gan'shin "Orel," a manuscript poem sent to Maxim Gorky, in 1914, in Arkhiv A. M. Gor'kogo, RAV-PG, 37–13–1; "Orlam," *Vpered!* no. 121 (1/14 August 1917): 2.

88. A. Mashirov (Samobytnik), "Zarnitsy," *Proletarskaia pravda*, 18 September 1913; and "Moim sobrat'iam," *Prosnuvshaiasia zhizn* [rukopisnyi zhurnal] (1913), both reprinted in *Proletarskie poety*, 2: 89–90.

89. Mircea Eliade, *Myths, Dreams, and Mysteries* (New York, 1960), 75–84, 99–110.

90. Friedrich Nietzsche, *Thus Spoke Zarathustra*, trans. Walter Kaufmann (New York, 1966), 192. *Tak govoril Zaratustra* was first published in Russia in 1898.

91. See, especially, his "Pesnia o sokole" (1895) and "Pesnia o burevestnike" (1901).

92. Friedrich Nietzsche, *Richard Wagner in Bayreuth* (1876), quoted in Laurence Lampert, *Nietzsche and Modern Times* (New Haven, Conn., 1993), 295–297, 417.

93. N. Liashko, "O byte i literature perekhodnogo vremeni," *Kuznitsa*, no. 8 (April–September 1921): 29–30, 34.

94. A. Platonov, "Zhizn' do kontsa," *Voronozhskaia kommuna*, 25 August 1921.

95. A. Smirnov, "Dumy proletarii," *V bure i plameni* (Iaroslavl', 1918), 57.

96. For example, the many poems by V. Vegenov that were the featured literary works in *Novoe pechatnoe delo* in 1911 and 1912; S. Obradovich, "Zhizn'," *Sever Rossii* (Arkhangel'sk), no. 1 (23 August 1913): 3; S. Gan'shin, "Tiazhelo na dushe," manuscript poem sent to Maxim Gorky in 1914, in Arkhiv A. M. Gor'kogo, RAV-PG, 37–13–1; Vladimir Korolev, *Vsem skorbiashchim* (Iaroslavl', 1915), 5–6, 46.

97. V. Aleksandrovskii, "Pered razsvetom (M.E.K.)," *Novaia rabochaia gazeta*, no. 9 (18 August 1913): 2.

98. M. Gerasimov, "V dushe rany zazhili davno," RGALI, f. 1374, op. 1, d. 6, l. 10 (unpublished poem).

99. S. Popov, "Vesna," *Chelovek*, no. 4 (24 April 1911): 32.

100. E. Nechaev, "V bezsonnitsu," "Starik," "V Tiurme," *Vechernie pesni*, 96–98, 110 (reprinted in *U istokov*, 93, 94, 97).

101. Obradovich, "Bezsonnoiu noch'iu," *Severnoe utro* (Archangel'sk), no. 52 (6 March 1913): 2.

102. Voronskii, "O gruppe pisatelei 'Kuznitsa,'" 126.

103. A. Platonov, "Toska," *Zheleznyi put'*, 1919, no. 9 (April): 13; and "Nad golubymi ozerami . . .," *Krasnaia derevnia*, 5 May 1920 (quotation); V. Aleksandrovskii, "U zhertvennika," *Tvori*, no. 2 (1921): 4; and many of the writings in the journal *Kuznitsa*.

104. V. Zafran, "U roialia" and "Boi," *Sbornik Kostromskogo proletkul'ta*, no. 1 (1919): 41–42.

105. See T. E. Hulme, "Romanticism and Classicism," in *Speculations: Essays on Humanism and the Philosophy of Art*, ed. Herbert Read (London, 1936), 41. I am grateful to Laura Engelstein for this suggestion.

106. V. Aleksandrovskii, "V noch' pod Rozhdestvo," *Zhivoe slovo*, 1913, no. 51–52 (December): 6.

107. S. Gan'shin, "Postroim Khram," *Vpered!* no. 157 (14 September 1917): 3.

108. F. Kalinin, "Tip rabochego v literature," *Novyi zhurnal dlia vsekh*, 1912, no. 9 (September): 96–97, 106.

109. See, especially, Clifford Geertz, "Religion As a Cultural System," in idem, *The Interpretation of Cultures* (New York, 1973), esp. 89–103; Mircea Eliade, *The Sacred and the Profane: The Nature of Religion* (New York, 1959); and idem, *Myths, Dreams, and Mysteries,* esp. 74, 107.

110. Vladimir Lossky, *The Mystical Theology of the Eastern Church* (first published in French in 1944) (London, 1957). See the discussion, in relation to Bakhtin's "feeling for faith," in Randall Poole, "The Apophatic Bakhtin," in Felch and Contino, *Bakhtin and Religion,* 151–175.

111. Kristeva has written of "those who transcend: living neither before nor now but beyond, they are bent with a passion that, although tenacious, will remain forever unsatisfied. It is a passion for another land, always a promised one" (*Strangers to Ourselves,* 10).

13

A New Spirituality: The Confluence of Nietzsche and Orthodoxy in Russian Religious Thought

Bernice Glatzer Rosenthal

———••⟨∞⟩••———

Friedrich Nietzsche's writings, of enormous influence in late-nineteenth- and early-twentieth-century Russian thought and culture,[1] seemed to speak directly to the crisis of values induced by modernization, especially for intellectuals dissatisfied with the prevailing ideologies and seeking new ideals and values by which to live. Nietzsche's challenge to rationalism, positivism, and Christianity nourished Russian religious thought and was eventually absorbed into new interpretations of Orthodoxy. Facilitating the absorption were surprising affinities between Nietzsche and Orthodoxy. The most significant text in this interaction was *The Birth of Tragedy from the Spirit of Music* (1872), in which Nietzsche counterposed forces he saw as symbolized by Apollo, the Greek god of clarity and form, and Dionysus, the Greek god of orgiastic ecstasy. "Apollo [is] the transfiguring genius of the *principium individuationis* through which alone the redemption in illusion is truly to be obtained; while by the mystical triumphant cry of Dionysus the spell of individuation is broken, and the way lies open to the Mothers of Being, to the innermost heart of things."[2] The union of Apollo and Dionysus gives birth to new forms of art.

Nietzsche believed that myth is essential to the health of a culture. By "myth" he meant a ruling idea or ideal, that which gives a society its coherence and from which are derived personal and national identity, morality, art, science, and government. "Myth" springs from the Dionysian substratum of suffering and wisdom that underlies all existence and is given form in Apollonian images. For Nietzsche, "myth" is not the antonym of "truth"; as the universe is in constant flux there is no ultimate "truth." Moreover, life has no intrinsic meaning; human beings endow it with meaning in the form of myth. There is nothing in *The Birth of Tragedy* about the Superman, the will to power, the death of God, or the individualism often associated with Nietzsche. In this book Nietzsche exalted "the oneness of everything existent, the conception of individuation as the primal cause of evil and of art as the joyous hope that the spell of individuation would be broken in augury of a restored oneness."[3]

Among Nietzsche's most ardent Russian admirers were the symbolists—poets and writers who viewed phenomenal reality as a symbol of a higher or occult reality. Primarily interested in the "inner man" (the soul or the psyche), they perceived Nietzsche as a mystic, a prophet, and a liberator of passions repressed by Christianity and bourgeois civilization. Intent on a Nietzschean "revaluation of all values," they wanted to create a new man and a new culture. They came to believe (contra Nietzsche) that ultimate truth does exist, beyond the Dionysian flux, and the poet could reach it. In the first years of the twentieth century, the symbolists became interested in religion. They and their allies were dubbed God-seekers (*bogoiskateli*), even though some were already believers, because they sought new religious truths, or new understandings of old truths, to guide humankind in the twentieth century.

This essay delineates the surprising affinities between Nietzsche and Orthodoxy and then turns to the combinations of Nietzsche and Orthodoxy by Dmitry Merezhkovsky (1865–1941), popularizer of symbolism and of Nietzsche and founder of the St. Petersburg Religious-Philosophical Society; Viacheslav Ivanov (1866–1949), symbolist poet and one of the movement's most influential theorists; and the polymath priest and Orthodox theologian Pavel Florensky (1882–1937), a God-seeker before he became a priest. All three considered conventional Orthodoxy too remote from the problems of life on earth. Nietzsche helped shape their critiques of conventional Orthodoxy and their attempts to revitalize it.

Affinities between Nietzsche and Orthodoxy

When Nietzsche's first admirers found his philosophy inadequate, for reasons explained below, they tried to combine it with Christianity. When that venture foundered, they absorbed aspects of his thought in new interpretations of Orthodoxy. The affinities examined here help to explain Nietzsche's initial appeal as well as the subsequent modifications and embellishments of his thought.

Anti-rationalism

Orthodox theology is mystical. Orthodox Christians associated rationalism with the "Latin West" (the Roman Catholic West), and then with the "pagan"

Enlightenment and its nineteenth century derivatives—positivism, liberalism, and socialism. Nietzsche attacked Socratic rationalism and faulted the rationalism of his own time for "actually holding out the prospect of the lawfulness of an entire solar system,"[4] by which he meant Newton's laws, the epistemological basis of the Enlightenment. Orthodoxy presumes a universe of dynamic becoming that is closer to Nietzsche's Dionysian universe than to Newton's vision of the world as a mechanism. Moreover, Orthodoxy distinguishes between Divine Essence (*Ousia*) and Divine Energies (*Energeia*). The Divine Essence remains unapproachable, but Divine energies come down to us, imbuing all creation, including man. If Divine Essence is removed, and teleology along with it, we have Nietzsche's Dionysian universe, a world without the Logos. Such was Merezhkovsky's view until, terrified by the specter of a meaningless universe, he turned to Christ.[5] The philosopher Nikolai Berdiaev, part of Merezhkovsky's circle for a time, came to advocate a "Christian Dionysianism," a Dionysianism illuminated by the Logos.

Beauty

Russia's conversion to Orthodox Christianity, so the *Primary Chronicle* tells us, was inspired by beauty: "The Greeks led us to the edifices where they worship their God, and we knew not whether we were in heaven or on earth. For on earth there is no such splendor or such beauty, and we are at a loss how to describe it. We only know that God dwells there among men."[6] Orthodox ontology presumes organic wholeness and conflates that wholeness with beauty. The Russian word for ugliness, *bezobraznyi*, literally means formlessness, that is, chaos as opposed to cosmos. Radiant beauty is associated with holiness and salvation. Dostoevsky predicted that "beauty will save the world," and Soloviev insisted that "beauty *is* saving the world." Both were major influences on symbolism and God-seeking. Nietzsche did not promise salvation, of course, but he exalted art as the "highest task and the truly metaphysical activity in this life." Indeed, "it is only as an *aesthetic phenomenon* that existence and the world are eternally *justified*."[7] Merezhkovsky made early Russian symbolism into a religion of art; worship of beauty was the first commandment.

Organic Wholeness

The Orthodox ontology of wholeness underlies the Slavophile conceptions of *sobornost'* (a union of believers in love and freedom) and *tsel'noe znanie* (integral knowledge). Although German romanticism was the original impetus for Slavophilism, its proponents soon realized that the elements that appealed to them, such as organic unity, intuitive knowledge, and beauty, were anticipated by the Greek Fathers. "What began as a historical quest for a distinctive

Russian culture resulted in a rediscovery and recognition of Eastern Orthodoxy and the question of Russia and Europe became a transcription of the question of Orthodoxy and Western Christianity and vice versa."[8] A similar process occurred in the late nineteenth and early twentieth centuries, except that the neo-Slavophilism of those years included Nietzschean elements. The ontology of wholeness also underlies Soloviev's philosophy, especially his ideals of a free theocracy (a variant of *sobornost'*), and total unity (*vseedinstvo*), an all-enveloping synthesis of art, philosophy, religion, and science (a variant of "integral knowledge"). For Nietzsche, myth is the integrating force. The symbolists tried to create new myths that would unite art and life, reintegrate Russian society, and transfigure the world.

Transfiguration

The Orthodox conception of transfiguration pertains to the body as well as the soul, and to matter as well as spirit, and is associated with radiant beauty, the radiance of the uncreated light of Mount Tabor (Matthew 17:1–4, Mark 9:2–14, Luke 9:28–36). The presence of the divine light in the transfigured world is celebrated in the liturgy of the feast of the Transfiguration, in which the Church anticipated the light of Christ's Second Coming. Nietzsche talked about the "Apollonian power of transfiguration" and the need for a "new transfiguring illusion."[9] Transfiguration was a source of the symbolists' conception of art as a theurgical activity, which they later expanded to "life creation" (*zhiznetvorchestvo*), a new world created by artists—poets and writers as well as painters. Implicitly the artist has divine powers or is a conduit for divine energies or both.

Deification

Transfiguration is closely linked with another Orthodox concept, deification, which stems from the idea that God made man in his own image (in Greek, *ikon*) and likeness (Genesis 1:26–27). In Timothy Ware's words: The Greek Fathers "dared to speak of 'deification' (in Greek *theosis*). If man is to share in God's glory, they argued, if he is to be 'perfectly one' with God, this means in effect that man must be 'deified'; he is called to become by grace what God is by nature. Saint Athanasius summed up the purpose of the Incarnation by saying 'God became man that we might be made God.'"[10] The words "image" (*obraz*) and "likeness" (*podobie*) reflected the inherent presence in the icon of a vision of paradise that a true believer could regain, a view of a transformed and transfigured world where man could contemplate his likeness to God lost in the Fall.[11]

Far from being an esoteric theological construct, the concept that "man may be made God" formed the cornerstone of Orthodox mysticism, sacramental theology, soteriology (the doctrine of salvation through Jesus Christ), and

Incarnation theology. Orthodoxy emphasizes the authority inherent in the body of the faithful (the *oikoumene*) by virtue of their participation in and identification with God, as distinct from the Catholic belief in an infallible Pope or the Protestant emphasis on Scripture as the word of God. The vesting of authority in the *oikoumene* is another manifestation of the ontology of wholeness.

The concept of deification helps to explain, at least in part, Soloviev's surprisingly positive response to Nietzsche's Superman. Soloviev recognized the elitist and amoral aspects of Nietzsche's idea, but he chose to concentrate on the "good sides." Man "naturally" wants to be better, higher, greater than he is in reality, Soloviev said, and this inclination draws him "naturally" to the "idea of the Superman."[12] Emphasizing human agency, "self-activity" (*samodeiatel'nost'*), and free choice, Soloviev interpreted Nietzsche's idea not in a biological or Darwinian sense, that is, man as a "wild half-animal," but as spiritual and psychological growth and the ability to defeat death. Taking Jesus as his model, Soloviev declared that the authentic Superman is "one who has vanquished death," the "first born from the dead" (Colossians 1:18), the "first begotten of the dead" (Revelation 1:5). He follows "a superhuman path" on which mortal and suffering man is transformed into an immortal and blessed superman."[13] In his last work, "A Tale of Antichrist," which was part of his book, *War, Progress, and the End of History: Three Conversations* (1900), Soloviev depicted the Antichrist as a Nietzschean figure; "many called him a Superman." Seemingly a benefactor of humanity, his real goal is power and he loves only himself. His attempt to replace the "preliminary Christ" for the "final one" (himself) leads to the Apocalypse and the Second Coming.[14]

Symbolists who became God-seekers exalted Jesus, the God-man, over the demonic man-god Dostoevsky predicted. They rejected the will to power and advocated "individuality" (self-expression or self-affirmation in a communal framework) rather than "individualism" (self-affirmation apart from or against the community). Nevertheless, theirs was a Nietzsche-influenced Christianity that sanctioned liberation of the passions and transgression of established boundaries and norms. Some symbolists linked Dionysus and Christ; others conflated Jesus and the Superman. Berdiaev went so far as to proclaim that "man has not only the right but the duty to become a Superman, because the Superman is the path from man to God."[15]

Hesychasm

Transfiguration and deification were interwoven in Hesychasm, a strain of Orthodox mysticism that became established at Mount Athos (the spiritual center of Orthodox monasticism) in the fourteenth century and spread to

Russia in the fifteenth century. Hesychast monks claimed to have experienced a transfiguration comparable to that of Christ, in other words, deification. Just as Christ had been only temporarily transfigured at Mount Tabor (His permanent transfiguration taking place after His resurrection), so, too, did the Hesychasts experience a temporary transfiguration, which would become permanent after the Last Judgment, when the entire universe, people and matter, would be transfigured into something radiantly beautiful.

Hesychasts claimed, by virtue of their union with God, to possess suprarational knowledge superseding even that of the most learned theologians, and which would not be revealed to the undeified until after the Resurrection. The possibility of achieving a temporary transfigured state—and the superiority of such individuals over the undeified majority—became a fundamental doctrine within Orthodox monasticism. Hesychast spirituality was characterized by the submission of the self to a spiritual master, for example, an Elder, some form of apophatic exercise related to "spiritual silence," contemplation of the psychosomatic nexus (the heart), continuous prayer with bodily movement and controlled breathing (the Jesus prayer), and the vision of the uncreated light. The Elder (in Greek, *Geron;* in Russian, *Starets*), is a person of spiritual discernment and wisdom whom other monks and lay people adopt as their guide. He receives no special ordination or appointment to this role but is guided to it by the direct inspiration of the Spirit and advises people through his special gift or charisma.

Hesychasm was perpetuated in Russia by Nils Sorsky (ca. 1453–1508), leader of the Volga Hermits, or "non-possessors," who had lived at Mount Athos. Nils emphasized solitude (*Heschia*), interior prayer, and manual labor but not beauty for fear that it would become an idol. The "non-possessors" believed that monks must be detached from the world and that only those vowed to complete poverty can achieve true detachment. Stressing prayer, contemplation, and an inner spiritual light, together with a striving for moral perfection, they opposed ecclesiastical formalism and ritualism and insisted that church and state be independent of each other. Moreover, the state belonged to a lower order of reality, so it had no right to interfere in religious matters. Their opponents, the "possessors" or Josephites (after Joseph of Volokalamsk, 1439–1515), argued that to do its work in the world, for example, care for the sick and the needy, shelter travelers, and teach, the Church needed wealth. These monks espoused a rigid, legalistic obedience to the letter of the law, upheld Church services, rituals, practices, and teachings as sacrosanct, and stressed the beauty of the Orthodox liturgy. They advocated a close union of church and state, regarded the tsar as the final arbiter in doctrinal disputes, and urged complete suppression of all dissent, by violence if necessary. The Church Council of 1503 supported the

Josephites and repressed the "non-possessors." Both Nils and Joseph were canonized, however, and Hesychast teachings were kept alive by writers, painters, and mystics, including the Elders of Optina Pustyn, a monastery that became a center of pilgrimage in the mid-nineteenth century. Among the pilgrims were the Slavophiles Aleksei Khomiakov and Ivan Kireevsky, and the writers Konstantin Leontiev (who was called the "Russian Nietzsche" because of his aestheticism and elitism), Lev Tolstoy, and Fedor Dostoevsky.[16]

Through their writings, aspects of Hesychasm filtered into lay culture. Dostoevsky modeled Elder Zossima (in *The Brothers Karamazov*) on an Optina Elder. Hesychasm informed the Slavophiles' conception of *sobornost'*, Dostoevsky's and Soloviev's apotheoses of beauty, Leontiev's aestheticism, and Soloviev's concept of "Godmanhood" (*Bogochelovechestvo*, sometimes translated Divine Humanity), by which he meant the salvation, transfiguration, and deification of all humankind, not just righteous individuals—a corollary of the ontology of wholeness. Soloviev criticized the Hesychasts for their interiority, however. He wanted an activist Christianity, one that would truly change the world.

Without Church discipline the doctrine of deification could nourish visions of an amoral Superman, a free spirit above the law, as it did in fin-de-siècle Russia, with the help of Nietzsche. And beauty did become an idol, as Nils Sorsky feared. Nietzsche also facilitated an appreciation, on the part of some intellectuals, of the aesthetic and mythopoeic aspects, or potential, of Orthodoxy. Nietzsche mentioned Hesychasm in *On the Genealogy of Morals*. "Nor is there any ground for considering this program of starving the body [he meant vegetarianism] and the desires as necessarily a symptom of lunacy . . . it is certainly capable of opening the way to all kinds of spiritual disturbances, to 'an inner light' for instance, as with the Hesychasts of Mount Athos."[17] For God-seekers, the "inner light" was not a "spiritual disturbance" but an inspiration, a source of new religious truths.

The Kenotic Christ

"Kenosis" means emptying in Greek, "the 'self-emptying abasement of the Son of God,' the renunciation of His own will in order to accomplish the will of the Father, by his obedience to Him unto death and the Cross."[18] The image of the humiliated and suffering Christ pervades Russian spirituality, culture, and literature.[19] We see it in the canonization of the young Kievan princes Boris and Gleb, because they submitted meekly to their murderers, even refusing an opportunity to escape, and in St. Seraphim of Sarov, who was beaten by robbers but offered no resistance and refused to testify at their trial. The image of the kenotic Christ underlies Dostoevsky's ideal of redemption through suffering.

To Dostoevsky, suffering was not just something to be endured if necessary; it had a positive value as part of a Christian morality of humility and love. Nietzsche's first Russian admirers rejected the kenotic values of humility, asceticism, and altruism, only to rehabilitate at least one of them later on.

Anti-legalism

Jesus said: "Think not that I am come to destroy the law, or the prophets: I am come not to destroy, but to fulfill" (Matthew 5:17). And "I say unto you, till heaven and earth pass, one jot or one tittle shall in no wise pass from the law, till all be fulfilled" (Matthew 5:18). Until then, presumably, the Mosaic law stands. But Jesus made other statements that have anti-legal implications. He told his followers to forgive injuries rather than seek redress, and to "judge not, that ye be not judged" (Matthew 7:1). Paul abrogated aspects of the Mosaic law (e.g., circumcision, *kashruth*), saying that "the epistle of Christ . . . is written not with ink, but with the Spirit of the living God, not in tables of stone, but in fleshy tables of the heart." "The new testament [is] not of the letter, but of the spirit: for the letter killeth, but the spirit giveth life" (II Corinthians 3:3, 3:6). For centuries Christians have proclaimed that theirs is a religion of love and hence superior to Judaism, which is a religion of law, and that grace is superior to law. Hillarion, the first Russian Metropolitan of Kievan Rus' said exactly that in his "Sermon on Law and Grace."

In Western Christendom, the subordination of law to grace nourished an antinomian heresy, the cult of the Free Spirit, that emerged around 1200 and persisted as a recognizable tradition for some five centuries. (Antinomianism is the belief that Christians are freed from the moral law by the dispensation of grace set forth in the Gospel.) Essentially Gnostics, adepts of the Free Spirit believed that they had attained a perfection so absolute that they were incapable of sin. The political corollary of their views, says the historian Norman Cohn, was "a quasi-mystical anarchism—an affirmation of freedom so reckless and unqualified that it amounted to a total denial of every kind of restraint and limitation." Their "total amoralism" frequently included "promiscuity on principle." Cohn considers the adepts remote precursors of the Russian anarchist Bakunin and Nietzsche in their "wildest moments."[20] Nietzsche considered himself and Wagner (in his pro-Wagner period) free spirits.

A striking feature of Orthodox Christianity is its lack of features that depend on a conception of religion as a legal relationship with God (as in Judaic, Roman Catholic, and Protestant conceptions of the covenant). "Sin" in Eastern Christianity is ontological, a turning away or separation from God, rather than juridical or legalistic. This is not to say there is no law in Orthodoxy. There are a great many laws and regulations, often of great strictness and rigor. But the main emphasis is on tradition, "a sense of *living continuity* with the Church of ancient times," which includes "the Bible, the Creed, the Service Books, the Holy Icons, in fact the whole system of doctrine, Church government, worship and art which Orthodoxy has articulated over the ages."[21]

In Russia, partly in response to Roman Catholic missionaries and theologians from the West, especially from Poland, alegalism turned into anti-legalism. Roman Catholicism incorporated Roman law, which included the idea of natural law, and which John Locke reformulated as natural rights (life, liberty, and property) guaranteed by a social contract. The Slavophiles opposed Western "legalism" and "juridical rationalism," which they considered peculiar to the West, and the very idea of a social contract. But they accepted the moral law, Orthodox canon law, the dogmas of the seven ecumenical councils, and customary law and usage.[22]

Nietzsche enjoined creators to "smash the old tables of values," to write "new values on new tablets,"[23] and to go beyond slavish conceptions of good and evil. He praised authentic Christianity for being nonjudgmental.

> In the entire psychology of the "Gospel" the concept guilt and punishment is lacking: likewise the concept reward. "Sin," every kind of distancing relation between God and man, is abolished—*precisely this is the "glad tidings."* Blessedness is not promised, it is not tied to any conditions: it is the *only* reality—the rest is signs for speaking of it ...
>
> The consequence of such a condition projects itself into a new practice, the true evangelic practice. It is not a "belief" which distinguishes the Christian: the Christian acts, he is distinguished by a different mode of acting. Neither by words nor in his heart does he resist the man who does him evil ... He neither appears in courts of law nor claims their protection.[24]

In fin-de-siècle Russia, Nietzsche helped to inspire a Christian amoralism (or antinomianism) in which all is permitted because all is forgiven; there is no punishment. Almost all of Nietzsche's admirers ended up rejecting Kant's moral imperatives. Florensky called Kant "the great deceiver," because he reduced religion to ethics. In Florensky's words: "The Church in the highest sense sees ethical morality as alien ... If one is to speak in a Christian way about behavior, one must speak out only ontologically and never moralistically and, above all, never legalistically."[25]

Apocalypticism

The Revelation of St. John predicts terrible wars, earthquakes, plagues, and other calamities as a prelude to the Second Coming of Christ and the New

Heaven and New Earth. Apocalypticism can turn into an ideology of protest against the existing order. The Medieval Roman Catholic Church discouraged apocalyptic speculation for that reason, but it remained an underground current that surfaced in difficult times. In Russia apocalypticism became part of the religion of the Old Believers (or Old Ritualists), who refused to accept Patriarch Nikon's reforms and called him the Antichrist. Peter the Great and Napoleon were also called the Antichrist, and not only by Old Believers. Dostoevsky warned that the Antichrist is approaching. Soloviev also seemed to think so. Apocalypticism was often linked with messianism, the belief that Moscow is the Third Rome or that Russians are the God-bearing people (Dostoevsky's view) or both. Berdiaev considered messianic eschatology one of the primary components of "the Russian idea."[26]

Nietzsche called himself the Antichrist and his writings abound with allusions to the Last Days and the Final Conflict. For example:

> For when truth enters into a fight with the lies of millennia, we shall have upheavals, a convulsion of earthquakes, a moving of mountains and valleys, the like of which has never been dreamed of. The concept of politics will have merged entirely with a war of spirits: all power structures of the old society will have been exploded—all of them are based on lies: there will be wars the like of which have never yet been seen on earth.[27]

The symbolists mingled biblical visions of the Last Days with subsequent visions, including those of Soloviev, Nietzsche, and Wagner. They perceived the Revolution of 1905 as the beginning of an apocalypse that would usher in a new world of freedom, beauty, and love.

Language

The Christian Bible says: "In the beginning was the Word and the Word was with God and the Word was God" (John 1:1). "All things were made by him" (John 1:3). Orthodoxy adds another element: the Word has divine energies that pervade and transfigure the cosmos. Orthodoxy also assumes, following Plato's Cratylus, that names have a cosmic meaning and incarnate the essence of things. Implicitly the power to name is the power to create new things.

Nietzsche used biblical language, albeit to subvert the Bible. Trained as a classical philologist, and psychologically oriented, he was very aware of the power of words. In *The Birth of Tragedy*, he connected word and myth: a new word leads to a new myth, and vice versa. Every myth has its own language; when a myth fades, its language becomes hackneyed and stale. In subsequent works, he emphasized the thought-structuring power of language and the ability of new words to (eventually) create new things. The symbolists combined Nietzsche's ideas on language with the Orthodox concept of the generative word. They sought a salvific "new word" that would actually create a new world.

Merezhkovsky, Ivanov, and Florensky's Combinations of Nietzsche and Orthodoxy

Merezhkovsky, the first Russian to combine Nietzsche and Orthodoxy, sought a balance of Apollo and Dionysus and accentuated the Superman. Ivanov's Nietzschean Christianity was almost entirely Dionysian until 1908–1909, when it took on Apollonian elements. Florensky's Orthodox theology incorporated symbolist and Nietzschean themes. Each one reworked the aspects of Nietzsche's thought that appealed to him and defined his interpretation of Orthodoxy against the aspects to which he objected. All three were aware of Nietzsche's belief that myth is the "prerequisite of religion."[28] Merezhkovsky and Ivanov mythologized Orthodoxy. Florensky believed that myth is already a secularization, so he emphasized unmediated religious experience.

Merezhkovsky

Merezhkovsky founded the Religious-Philosophical Society of St. Petersburg a decade or so after he began to popularize symbolism and Nietzsche in the early 1890s. The Society, which sponsored debates between clergymen and lay intellectuals on burning issues of the day, became a focal point of attempts to reinterpret Orthodoxy. Among the issues debated were freedom of speech, Christian attitudes to sex, Tolstoy's excommunication (by the Holy Synod in 1901), whether new Christian dogma is needed (Merezhkovsky said it was) and, if so, who has the power to create it. Merezhkovsky's views changed drastically over time, but Nietzsche was an important component throughout.[29] His thought provided Merezhkovsky with verbal ammunition in his campaign against populism and positivism, and helped him make Russian symbolism into a militant religion of art. When that religion failed him, he tried to reconcile paganism, "the truth of the earth" (from Zarathustra's injunction "Be true to the earth"), with Christianity, "the truth of heaven" (eternal life), in a yet unknown higher truth. Pushkin, Merezhkovsky declared, reconciled these truths unconsciously, and he resolved to find the poet's "secret." In his eyes, Pushkin was a superman, a perfect combination of Apollo and Dionysus.[30]

In 1899 Merezhkovsky announced his "turn to Christ" and embarked on a "revaluation of all [Christian] values" in the light of Nietzsche's critique. Soon after, Merezhkovsky proclaimed that "historical Christianity" (Christianity as taught in the churches) is obsolete, because the Second Coming is imminent.

Jesus Christ Himself would grant humankind a Third Revelation, or Third Testament, that would reconcile all dualisms. Christians would then enjoy personal immortality, love, and the pleasures of this world, including sex. Jesus would be the sole ruler and His only law would be love. From then on, Merezhkovsky cast all problems and issues—paganism versus Christianity, Russia versus Europe, spirit versus flesh, and so on—in terms of an eschatological dualism that only the Apocalypse could resolve.

He now discerned a polarity *within* Christianity between the flesh and the spirit, which, in his view, was symbolized, respectively, by Tolstoy and Dostoevsky. Maintaining that "historical Christianity" emphasized the spirit at the expense of the flesh, he advocated "holy flesh," the sanctification of sex, not realizing he was advocating transfiguration. In his study of Tolstoy and Dostoevsky, he treated Dostoevsky and Nietzsche as kindred souls, pointing out the many parallels in their thought, while considering Tolstoy to be Nietzsche's antipode. Outraged by Tolstoy's condemnation of modern art and his preachments of celibacy, even in marriage, Merezhkovsky claimed that Tolstoy's ethics and epistemology were Buddhist, not Christian. Nevertheless, he was outraged at Tolstoy's excommunication, for he realized that his own "religious quest" required free speech. Indeed, the government shut down the Religious-Philosophical Society in April 1903 as a forum for heresy (it reopened after the 1905 Revolution). These developments led Merezhkovsky to challenge the subordination of the Orthodox Church to the state and, eventually, to demand a new church.

Merezhkovsky was convinced that the fate of all humanity, not just Russians, hinged on whether his generation opted for a Superman/man-god or the God-man Jesus Christ. He believed that Christ had two faces, the "dark face" of "historical Christianity" and a second face, that of the apparent Antichrist but in truth that of the real Christ, which would be revealed in the near future. Authentic Christianity is not a slave morality, as Nietzsche charged, but a religious supramoral phenomenon that transgresses all limits and barriers of moral law; it is a phenomenon of the greatest freedom beyond good and evil. Jesus's teaching does not imply leveling, as Nietzsche alleged, but the creation of new and deeper valleys, new and higher mountains.[31] Christianity is not self-denying; the Christian doctrine of personal immortality is the greatest self-affirmation of all. The man-god and God-man are united in Jesus Christ.

Shortly before the Revolution of 1905 Merezhkovsky declared that autocracy is from the Antichrist. During that uprising he advocated a religious revolution, one that went beyond political change, and proclaimed that "Jesus was a revolutionary." The savior brought humankind "not peace but a sword" and came to turn the old world upside down. Merezhkovsky's revolutionary Jesus was a frontal challenge to "slavish" historical Christianity and to Tolstoy's pacifism, which was inspired by Jesus's injunction "resist not evil" (Matthew 5:39). Merezhkovsky's Jesus is also reminiscent of Nietzsche's depiction of Him in revolt against the "Jewish church," a "holy anarchist who roused up the lowly, the outcastes, and 'sinners,' the Chandala within Judaism to oppose the ruling order—in language which, if the Gospels can be trusted, would even today lead to Siberia," a "political criminal" uttering a "no towards everything that was priest and theologian."[32] Merezhkovsky did not quote such statements, possibly because the censor would never have passed them and also because by then he wanted to found an entirely new church, a Church of the Holy Spirit, after the third person in the Trinity. Merezhkovsky's Nietzschean Christianity was not purely Dionysian but required definite forms and structures, that is, Apollonian elements.

Merezhkovsky's Christian revolutionism featured attacks on *meshchanstvo*, a perennial target of his, as the most dangerous face of the Beast of the Apocalypse. *Meshchanstvo* originally denoted the lower middle classes, but it came to mean philistinism. According to Merezhkovsky, the Revolution of 1905 slayed autocracy, mortally wounded Orthodoxy, but rendered *meshchanstvo* stronger than ever; it empowered liberals and socialists who value material well-being more than eternal life. An aristocrat by birth, as well as by temperament, Merezhkovsky considered prosperity a bourgeois ideal. His fulminations against *meshchanstvo* echo Nietzsche's contempt for the "last man" (*der letzte Mensch*, sometimes translated "the ultimate man"), who seeks security, contentment, and comfort.

In the 1890s Merezhkovsky had wanted Russian culture to become an equal part of European culture, that is, to give as well as to take. During the 1905 Revolution, which lasted until mid-1907, he championed a revolutionary neo-Slavophilism and claimed that *meshchanstvo*, rather than Christianity, was the true religion of Europe. He also claimed that Russia and Europe formed an eschatological dualism.

> Russia is to Europe as the left hand is to the right. . . . Speaking in Kantian language, your province is the phenomenal, ours is the transcendental. Speaking in Nietzschean language, in you is Apollo, in us Dionysus; your genius is moderation, ours is extremism . . . you love the middle, we love the ends; you are sober, we are drunk; you are rational, we are frenzied; you are just, we are lawless . . . for you politics is knowledge, for us it is religion."[33]

"Run," he told European intellectuals in the same essay, "we will burn you." Russia and Europe must both go through the purifying fire.

In contemporaneous pieces Merezhkovsky said that a "religious revolution" would reconcile the "truth of anarchism" (freedom) and the "truth of socialism" (community), and claimed, too, that Nietzsche was an anarchist. Merezhkovsky himself was closer to anarchism than to socialism. Propounding a "religious anarchism," he believed that if Christ's law, love, were engraved on every human heart, then law would be unnecessary and the state would collapse. "No violence, no law: no law, no state." Freedom meant voluntary acceptance of God's law (love); love was "absolute power" and "absolute freedom," and human reason had to be subordinated to "divine reason" (the Logos).[34]

After the 1905 Revolution Merezhkovsky repudiated Nietzsche, or claimed to, called Nietzscheanism a "childhood sickness" dangerous to adults, and attributed the nihilism and amoralism of postrevolutionary Russian society to Nietzsche's influence. In retrospect, Merezhkovsky viewed his own Nietzscheanism of the 1890s as a "religious trial" and said that to realize the truth about Jesus Christ he had to pursue falsehood to the end. He had been "dangerously close" to the Antichrist, but he now realized that both truths (heaven and earth, spirit and flesh) are contained in the person of Jesus Christ. Nietzsche's error was in discovering America after Columbus. The Superman had already appeared; He was the God-man Jesus Christ. To associate Christ and the Antichrist (as he had done) was dangerous blasphemy.[35] From then on, Merezhkovsky used Nietzsche's name pejoratively even while making other aspects of Nietzsche's thought his own. He accused other people of egotism, amoralism, pride, and lust for power—traits commonly associated with Nietzsche—and discussed Nietzsche's thought under other rubrics, such as "Lermontov" for Nietzschean individualism and "Tiutchev" for Dionysian chaos.

Merezhkovsky fled Bolshevik Russia, "the realm of the Antichrist," in December 1919. In books he wrote after emigrating, there are numerous references to Apollo and Dionysus. For example, Napoleon was an incarnation of the sun god (Apollo), the last hero of the West, the setting sun, but he was also "Napoleon-Dionysus." The world cannot live without the Son (Jesus), so it lives by His shadow. The shadow of the Son is "Napoleon-Dionysus." Dionysus was the last of a series of "suffering" and "baptized" gods that began in the ancient Near East. Tammuz, Osiris, Dionysus, and others were all precursors of Christ. (This is an expansion of Ivanov's idea, discussed below). Contra both Nietzsche and Dostoevsky, Merezhkovsky considered Napoleon a Christian; his advent was a Christian mystery.[36]

Merezhkovsky wrote several books about the ancient Near East—not just Greece but also Crete, Egypt, Babylon, and Atlantis. Dionysus appears in *Taina trekh: Egipet i Vavilon* (The mystery of the three: Egypt and Babylon; 1925) as Father Dionysus, along with Mother Demeter and son Laikh as the Holy Family of the Eleusinian mysteries. "Eternal Egypt" sanctified sex and defeated death, while Babylon emphasized reason and knowledge, producing insatiable, unhappy Faustian types. (He considered Goethe's Faust a precursor of Nietzsche's Superman). In *The Secret of the West: Atlantis Europe* (1930), Merezhkovsky lambasted the would-be Supermen of Atlantis for their rapacity and overweening pride, and warned that unless Europeans choose Christ over the Antichrist they will destroy themselves or be destroyed, just as the Atlantenes were.[37] One of his favorite themes throughout was the need for ecstasy (one of Ivanov's favorite words) including sexual ecstasy. Merezhkovsky counterposed "Christian ecstasy" to the "demonic ecstasy" of war and predicted that the lack of "Christian ecstasy" would lead to a second Great War. In studies of medieval Western mystics and church reformers, he alluded to "divine ecstasy," a special mystical ecstasy, that connected people to God and inspired individuals and entire nations to uplift themselves.

Nietzsche's abiding influence on Merezhkovsky can be seen in the latter's lifelong emphasis on passion, his mythopoeic approach to religion and politics, his vision of Jesus as the Superman, and his search for a new myth that would reconcile all dualisms, including Apollo and Dionysus.

Ivanov

Ivanov developed the Dionysian aspects of Nietzsche's thought almost to the exclusion of the Apollonian. He claimed that the suffering Dionysus was a precursor of the crucified Christ, and, unlike Nietzsche, he treated the Cult of Dionysus as primarily a religious phenomenon.[38] Focused on the inner life, on self-expression and self-definition, Ivanov considered politics superficial and sought to transcend it in a new mythic vision.

In "The Hellenic Religion of the Suffering God" (1904–1905) Ivanov asserted that the "passion of Dionysus was the distinctive feature of the cult, the nerve of its religion, to the same degree that the passion of the Christian God is the soul of Christianity."[39] Aristotle called man a "political animal"; Ivanov said that man is a "religious animal" and, since ecstasy is the "alpha and omega" of the religious state, an "ecstatic animal."[40] He pointed out that a distinguishing feature of the religion of Dionysus was a cult of sex, placed more emphasis than Nietzsche did on the frenzy and cruelty of the cultic rituals, and restored the "ecstatic women," the ferocious maenads, whom Nietzsche mentioned only in passing.

Ivanov knew that the original Dionysian rites were not just sexual orgies but were also sacrificial rituals and, as such, were violent, bloody, and cruel. The sacrificial object was literally torn to pieces, which were then distributed to the celebrants to be eaten. Cannibalism was later replaced by animal sacrifice, but, to the first celebrants, the god himself was the victim. When they ate god, they became god, or so they believed. Ivanov considered animal sacrifice a falsification of religious authenticity; indeed, religious cannibalism was the purest form because it destroyed the *principium individuationis.*

In Ivanov's eyes, the frenzied rituals were a "merry bacchanal" with "two primordial features, religious ecstasy (in which he included sexual ecstasy) and blood sacrifice.[41] The cult itself was an "orgiastic commune" (*obshchina;* note his use of the Slavophile term) united for sacrifice.[42] The Religion of Dionysus contained mystical truth, "the truth of the duality of god as sacrificial offering and executioner, as theomachist [*bogoborets*] and tragic conqueror, as the murdered one and the murderer."[43] Ivanov's concept of theomachy was drawn in part from Dostoevsky's Ivan Karamazov, who refused to accept the world God created, and in part from Prometheus, who defied the Olympian gods.

The sacrificial object, Ivanov emphasized, was not a wrongdoer. The religion of Dionysus was undogmatic, polymorphic, and amoral. A striving to moralize the gods was a later development and a symptom of religious decline. The tie between morality and religion remained weak and external, however, and the system of mystical purification continued. The mystery of catharsis was a means to restore the inner world and to purify the soul from the pollution of sin. The Greeks were religious in the highest sense, but morality was not part of the essence of their religion.[44] Religion is like music; it cannot be confined to a narrow space but must soar to heaven.

> Dionysian rapture [*vostorg*] was the only force that released [people] from pessimistic despair. It was a legitimate first reaction of the [human] spirit, gazing at the grief and torment of existence, at the undeniable reality of the collapse of high hopes and the triumph of evil forces, at the eternal horror of all-extinguishing death. Dionysus teaches us to breathe deeply, with a full chest, to breathe the whole—with it and in it—as much as it is possible to do so.[45]

The religion of Dionysus was "like virgin soil waiting to be fertilized by Christianity; it needed it as its final issue, the last word that it had not uttered."[46]

On the eve of the Revolution of 1905 Ivanov urged his fellow symbolists to become myth-creators, to forge the myths around which Russian society could unite, thereby ending social and political conflict. During that revolution he supported a doctrine called "Mystical Anarchism," a politicized Dionysianism that aimed at replacing government, law, and morality with internal and invisible bonds—specifically myth, eros, and sacrifice. The myth would be created in a Dionysian theater-temple devoted to "myth-creation" (*mifotvorchestvo*) and "collective creativity" in which there would be no separation between actors and spectators. Together the people (*narod*), functioning as a Dionysian chorus, and the symbolist poet, articulator of the "new word," would create the myth, or reformulate an eternal myth, that would become the embryo of a new cult, a new culture, and a "new organic society," in that order.

Specifically rejecting the "will to power," Ivanov proposed a new ideal—powerlessness—a society in which no person rules another, and dominance and subordination have ceased to exist. His social ideal was a cultic version of *sobornost'* in which eros replaces agape; a "new religious synthesis" (myth) replaces the state religion; a Dionysian theater-temple replaces the state church; and direct religious experience, including orgiastic experience, replaces dogma. The "new religious synthesis" would be Christian, but not exclusively Christian, and it would include orgiastic rituals. "Orgies of action" and "orgies of purification," to be conducted in the theater-temple, would induce self-forgetting in "mystical ecstasy," thereby breaking the spell of individuation and restoring the lost oneness. Ivanov's public statements on myth-creation lacked an Apollonian image. He did not specify who or what would be sacrificed nor who or what would be worshiped.

In 1908, however, for much the same reasons that Merezhkovsky repudiated Nietzscheanism, and also having been chastened by the untimely death of his wife, Ivanov declared that "Dionysus in Russia is dangerous." He stopped invoking eros, ecstasy, and orgiasm (*orgiazm*), and condemned "Luciferan self-affirmation," the wish to be as gods. Noting that Zarathustra was a lawgiver as well as a lawbreaker, Ivanov began to theorize about Apollo (the ethical deity) and Apollonianism. But he still believed that self-sacrifice (the kenotic ideal) was morally preferable to self-preservation, "the law of Moses and of our culture."[47] Christianity transcends (or negates) natural law.

As Ivanov became more emphatically Christian, his vocabulary and imagery changed. The symbol became the Word, with its explicitly Christian connotations. Christianity, rather than an eclectic "new religious synthesis," became the new all-unifying myth (he treated Christianity rather unconventionally as a myth), and Jesus's face replaced the amorphous Christ/Dionysus archetype. To Ivanov, Jesus's face symbolized His personhood and distinguished Christianity from diffuse mysticism, from the faceless All of Buddhism, and from "impersonal" (soulless) secular ideologies. The cultic community became a transcendental church or nation (depending on the context), and the passions became the "Russian soul." In 1908–1909 Ivanov coined a new word, *sovlechenie*, to denote, depending on the context, passion, energy, will, rejection of egoism, casting off material possessions, laying oneself bare in order to merge spiritually with others, and unmasking hypocrisy and lies. He considered *sovlechenie* the entelechy of the "Russian idea" and the moving force of Russian life.[48]

In the "Russian Idea" (1909), a term coined by Dostoevsky and popularized by Soloviev, Ivanov propounded a new myth. This one did have an Apollonian image, the visage of Jesus. Every nation has its own idea, Ivanov insisted; it stems from the unconscious depths of the folk soul. The "Russian Idea" is a Christian idea. He contrasted "organic" Christian culture to the "critical culture" of the modern era, marked by differentiation, egoism, and self-will, and redefined Apollonianism as the principle of unity and Dionysianism as the principle of multiplicity or fragmentation. He attributed to the "passion of *sovlechenie*" the intelligentsia's "will to descent and service (to the *narod*)" and the *narod*'s "will to ascend (to God)," and predicted that the intelligentsia and the *narod* would meet in the "still invisible light of Christ."

Ivanov believed that only Christian regeneration could save Russia and that new religious truths must be "hidden in mystery," in the form of myth. As an example, he gave the religious innovations of Pisistratus, founder of the orphic mystery religion, which were so in tune with the subliminal yearnings of the people that their novelty was forgotten. Pisistratus is remembered as a tyrant but not as a renegade from the popular faith. By contrast, Socrates, progenitor of critical rationalism, was perceived as a heretic and a danger to the state. He did not understand the people, and they did not understand him.

The horrors of World War I reinforced Ivanov's apocalyptic expectations and deepened his conviction that only Christian regeneration could save Russia. After the February Revolution, he insisted that a mere change in the political order was insufficient; a truly creative revolution required the religious awakening of the Russian people. The Bolshevik Revolution and the civil war he interpreted as a religious trial and as part of an eschatological transition that was primarily internal and would culminate in a new consciousness, the recognition that all are one, for which Ivanov coined a new term, "monantropism"—etymologically a movement toward "one-man-ness" or a feeling of "one-man-ness."[49]

Florensky

One of the foremost Orthodox theologians of the twentieth century, as well as a scientist, mathematician, art critic, and student of archaeology and anthropology, Pavel Florensky reworked ideas derived from Nietzsche, God-seeking, and symbolism along specifically Orthodox lines, sometimes connecting the wisdom of the Greek Fathers and Hesychast concepts to the latest scientific discoveries and contemporary issues.

Occasionally he alluded to Nietzsche to make a point. For example, in a discussion of inner experience, he quoted an aphorism from *The Gay Science* (book 4, no. 298).

I caught this insight on the way and quickly seized the rather poor words that were closest to hand to pin it down lest it fly away again. And now it has died of these arid words and shakes and flaps in them—and I hardly know anymore when I look at it how I could ever have felt so happy when I caught this bird.[50]

"What is clear today can be muddy tomorrow," Florensky continued, so it is essential to "register [*oformit'*] inner experience, to attach living flesh to the bones of concepts and charts. This is where reason rightly comes in." He then distinguished between dogmatics (the right use of reason) and dogmatism (abstract formulas), describing dogmatics as "a system of basic charts of the most ineffable experience, as an abridged guide to eternal life," and as a turn to "conciliar reason, to a supra-individual collective consciousness, to the super-personal organization of the church," that expresses spiritual life in all its fullness. But in Florensky's time dogmatics had become dogmatism, "lifeless formulas," "theories and systems floating in the air." That is why "contemporary Christians are cold to the beauty of dogmatics."[51] Florensky may have had Ivanov's anti-dogmatism in mind. He knew Ivanov's thought and quoted his verse.[52]

Nietzsche held that rationalistic systems falsify reality. Florensky maintained that rationalism is necessarily self-contradictory because truth is an antinomy. There is "one Truth," but only in heaven. "Here on earth, we have a multitude of truths, fragments of the Truth, noncongruent to another."[53] Rationalists cannot reconcile them. In a different discussion of antinomies, Florensky wrote: "The world is tragically beautiful in its fragmentedness. Its harmony is in its dishar-mony; its unity is in its discord. Such is the paradoxical teaching of Heraclitus, later paradoxically developed by Friedrich Nietzsche in the theory of 'tragic optimism.'"[54] "Tragic optimism," the expression of humankind without grace, is the "forced smile of a slave" who does not want to show his master that he is afraid of him, and who is "afraid of his own fear. The forms are beautiful [an allusion to Nietzsche's aestheticism], but is it a secret for ancient man that 'beneath them Chaos moves?'"[55] Florensky considered rationalism unnatural, destructive, and, implicitly, an expression of the will to power: "The rational-ist intellectual . . . 'loves' in words the whole world and considers everything 'natural.' But in practice he hates the whole world in its concrete life and would like to destroy it, in order to replace it with the concepts of his rational mind, i.e. with in essence, his self-assertive I."[56]

The one way to understand Orthodoxy, Florensky insisted, is through direct Orthodox experience (rather than diffuse mystical experience). Catholicism and Protestantism are based on concepts, but "to become Orthodox it is necessary to immerse oneself all at once in Orthodoxy, to begin living in an Orthodox way."[57] For him, this entailed becoming part of a church community. Ecclesiality (*tserkovnost'*) was a prominent feature of Florensky's theology. As he used the term, ecclesiality had several layers of meaning, all related to the Holy Spirit, the invisible Church, and the unity of all believers in the mystic body of Christ (the original meaning of *sobornost'*). Ecclesiality, in Florensky's view, is the spiritual beauty that manifests itself when one is united with all creation by way of love for its creator. The emphasis on love was not from Nietzsche, of course, but a good part of the aestheticism was, both directly and by way of the symbolists. On another level, ecclesiality was Florensky's answer to Ivanov's vision of a cultic community. Loving union is possible only in a church, Florensky maintained. Moreover, there are different kinds of love. Eros is "a passion that erupts."[58] Rather than the orgiastic passions that "erupt" in the Dionysian rites, Florensky emphasized the passion of jealousy, quoting the Bible, the ancient Greeks, and Nietzsche to support his view. He connected jealousy with ardent love and pointed out that "jealousy" (*revnost'*) and "zeal" (*rvenie*) are etymologically related.[59]

Florensky's theology combined Apollonian and Dionysian elements. Among the former are insistence on concreteness, on definite forms and structures. Also Apollonian is his emphasis on "free choice" in love, the personal element rather than impersonal instinct (the Dionysian element) or blind will. He considered each loving relationship unique, for while love is unbounded, it must also be bounded (Apollo draws boundaries).

> Together with a uniting force that takes one outside individual existence, there must be an isolating force, which sets a limit to diffuseness and impersonality. This force is jealousy; and its function is to isolate, separate, delimit, differentiate. If this force did not exist, there would be no concrete church life with its specific order. Instead we would have protestant, anarchistic, Tolstoyan, etc. mixing of all with all. We would have total formlessness and chaos.[60]

Florensky's desire for "definiteness of connections and constancy of unions"[61] was related to his desire to overcome Dionysianism. When he read about Dionysus, he once told a friend (Elchaninov), he had gotten as excited as if he himself had participated in the orgies. In *Pillar*, Florensky maintained that God is present in every loving relationship. Moreover, "without love (and to have love it is first necessary to have God's love), a person disintegrates into fragments of psychological elements and aspects. God's love is what unifies a person." Without God's love, "the soul loses its substantial unity, the consciousness of its creative nature. It is lost in a chaotic vortex of its own states, ceasing to be their substance. The I drowns in the 'mental deluge' of passions."[62]

> Even individual parts of the body announce their "autonomy" and independence. The whole organism, both corporeal and psychic is transformed

from an integral and harmonious instrument from an organ of the person, into an accidental colony, a motley assembly of mutually incompatible self-acting mechanisms.[63]

Compare Nietzsche:

What is the sign of every literary decadence? That life no longer dwells in the whole. The word becomes sovereign and leaps out of the sentence, the sentence reaches out and obscures the meaning of the page, the page gains life at the expense of the whole—the whole is no longer a whole. But this is the simile of every style of decadence; every time, the anarchy of atoms, disaggregation of the will.[64]

Florensky counterposed "Apollonian" and "Titanic," as Nietzsche did in *The Birth of Tragedy*.[65] The Titans were creatures of the earth, Florensky explained, representatives of an impersonal force, of pure power. The person is an Apollonian principle, Christianity's answer to the impersonal "Titanic principle" and the unbridled passions of Dionysianism. "Titanism" is not a sin, however, but a good, the power of life, existence itself, even though "Titanism" can lead to sin—the sin of self-affirmation.[66] Florensky idealized the humble Elder Isidore.[67]

Florensky did not speak out on political issues after 1906, but he could not ignore an event of the magnitude of the Bolshevik Revolution, especially since the new rulers were militant atheists. Between 1917 and about 1923 "cult" replaced "ecclesiality" as the central concept of Florensky's theology. He even called Christianity a cult and said, "to a cult [presumably Bolshevism] one can oppose only a cult."[68] Claiming that cults have metaphysical importance, he interpreted Church art and Church rituals in cultic terms, and attempted to revalue all aspects of culture, including mathematics and science, from a specifically Orthodox perspective. He was intent on an Orthodox "revaluation of all values."

Although the cult of Dionysus was Florensky's model, he also drew on archaeological and anthropological studies of cults. In his view, a cult is a living organism, centered on a real person, and united by powerful emotional bonds. Every cult has *its own* way of organizing the world, *its own* conception of space and time, and *its own* rituals. Rituals sanctify reality; they are the core of religion. Man is a liturgical animal.[69] In the ancient world, Florensky maintained, the cult was the center of life. He wanted Christianity to return to its cultic origin, to the worship of Jesus as a living person, to His real body, His real blood, a real cross. The Dionysian rites centered on the real body and real blood of Dionysus. "Only wine" did not exist for ancient man or for Christians either. The Greeks drunk the real blood of Dionysus.[70] Florensky's mystique of blood included a "modern" element, racist anti-Semitism, which he combined with the medieval "blood libel," the allegation that Jews kill Christian children and use their blood in religious rituals.[71]

Florensky was a member of the Commission on the Preservation of Historical Monuments, which was under the jurisdiction of the Commissariat of Enlightenment, headed by Anatoly Lunacharsky, a Nietzschean Marxist, a Wagnerophile, and a proponent of a politicized version of Ivanov's idea of a Dionysian theater. Florensky's report, "Church Ritual as a Synthesis of the Arts," was an attempt to dissuade cultured Bolsheviks (such as Lunacharsky) from turning the nationalized Sergeev-Trinity Monastery into a "dead" museum.[72] Using concepts derived from Nietzsche, Wagner, and symbolism that might appeal to the new rulers, Florensky argued that the synthesis of the arts, for which "contemporary aestheticians" yearn, was achieved long ago in Church rituals that addressed all the senses in a unique theatricality. In Church rituals, everything is subordinated to a single goal, to the supreme effect of this musical drama's catharsis, and so everything is coordinated to everything else; it does not exist if taken separately, or at least it exists falsely. A work of art is a living entity that requires special conditions in which to live. Icons cannot be isolated from the organism of Church ritual, the only artistic environment in which they have true artistic meaning. The union of art and life (a goal of symbolists, futurists, and Bolsheviks) could be achieved by "bringing the museum out into life and bringing life into the museum, thereby creating a living museum for the people that would educate the masses on a daily basis . . . (rather than collecting rarities for art gourmets); a thorough assimilation of human creativity into life."[73] Florensky concluded his report on a Nietzschean note: "It is not to the arts but to Art that our age aspires, to the very depths of Art's core as a primordial unifying activity."[74]

He frequently contrasted the "rich organic wholeness of Church culture" with "eclectic and contradictory" Renaissance culture. He hated the Renaissance as the time when people fell away from God. His ideal was a society in which religion permeated every aspect of life. The separate will, in its individual uniqueness, had to coincide with God's will. Christian culture was the "sanctification of nature, of all areas of life. Art, philosophy, science, politics, economics, et al., cannot be seen as self-contained entities separate and apart from Christ." Christianity could not be passive with regard to this world.[75] For Florensky, as for Lenin, there were no neutral zones.

In "Iconostasis" (which started out as part of his report), Florensky related "Dionysian" and "Apollonian" to mystical experience.

> The soul is raised up from the visible realm to where visibility itself vanishes and the field of the invisible opens: this is the Dionysian dissolution

[*rastorzhenie*] of the bonds of the visible. And having reached the heights, the invisible, the soul descends again into the visible—and then, before its very eyes, arise the symbolic forms of the invisible world—the faces of things, ideas. This is the Apollonian vision [*videnie*] of the spiritual world.[76]

As for icons (windows into the spiritual world), in the fourteenth and fifteenth centuries Russian icon painting "reached a height of perfection without parallel in the whole history of world art—a pinnacle shared, perhaps, only by classical Greek sculpture (which also incarnated a spiritual vision), and (again like Greek sculpture), whose brilliance was corrupted by rationalism and empiricism."[77] Note the resemblance to Nietzsche's description of the death of Greek tragedy at the hands of Euripedes and Socrates. Florensky described icon painting as a collective process (a version of Ivanov's "collective creativity"), saying that even if the painter works alone, "the collectivity of work is necessarily implicit in the icon, for the primary goal is always the clarity of a collectively carried and transmitted truth. Hence, if by chance some purely subjective view of things spontaneously creeps into one moment of the icon painting process, it will be balanced in the final icon by other masters mutually correcting one another."[78]

Also discussed in "Iconostasis" are masks, a favorite theme of Nietzsche's and of the symbolists. Nietzsche regarded the heroes of Greek tragedy as masks of Dionysus. Ivanov broadened Nietzsche's idea to include Shakespeare's tragic heroes and Don Quixote. Symbolist theater employed tragic and comic masks extensively as a device to visualize an alter ego or a psychological state. Florensky noted that, in classical cultures, masks were more like icons but, "when the ancient religions became corrupted and spiritually drained, and the cultic icons became correspondingly profaned, then from this blasphemy there arose the modern meanings of the mask: deceptive illusion, spiritual fraudulence, and even the triviality of some kind of horror."[79] But the mask has a "spiritual essence that does not die in the decomposition of the old image; that essence separates itself from the corpse, creating an artistic body. This is the icon."[80] He traced the icon to the Egyptian death mask, which revealed the deified spirit of the deceased resting in eternity. This was not an illusion but the real essence of the deceased person.

In other pieces Florensky developed his own interpretation of perspectivism, a signature device of the avant garde, Russian and European, that was informed by Nietzsche, Bergson, and contemporary scientific studies of perception, spatial orientation, and optics. In *The Gay Science,* a key Nietzsche text for Florensky, Nietzsche said, "the human intellect cannot avoid seeing itself in its own perspectives and *only* in these. We cannot look around our own corner. . . . But I should think that today we are at least far from the ridiculous immodesty that would be involved in decreeing from our corner that perspectives are permitted only from this corner."[81] In *Ecce Homo,* Nietzsche asserted: "Now I know how, have the know-how, to *reverse perspective:* the first reason why the 'revaluation of values' is perhaps possible for me alone."[82] Florensky's essay "Reverse Perspective" (1922) was part of his Orthodox revaluation of all values.[83] Rejecting the linear perspective that dominated European painting since the Renaissance, he argued that icons do have perspectival unity, a special system of depicting reality centered on the Gospels, hence theocentric not naturalistic. Icons express a "*special* point of view, with its *special* center of perspective, and sometimes with its own special horizon," and a complex reworking of perspective in every detail.[84] This special perspective was not a mistake, or a product of naïveté, but a daring breaking of rules that had positive force. The icon painters rejected the Euclidean-Kantian conception of space, which placed the self in the center and subordinated reality to its laws. In "pure art" (in which Florensky included Egyptian and Babylonian art), liberation from perspective or a primordial nonrecognition of its power is the expression of "an objective and supra-personal metaphysic" as opposed to the individual judgment of a separate person with his particular point of view.[85] Linear perspective was the pictorial expression of the self-centered subjectivism of Descartes and Kant.

Linear perspective arose in the applied arts, Florensky continued, especially in the theater, which subordinated painting to its own tasks. "Theatrical decoration wants, as much as possible, to *replace* reality ... decoration is a deception, even if it is pretty ... It is a screen that blocks the light of existence [in Nietzschean terms, 'an illusion']."[86] Rationalists do not demand the truth of life but an external likeness that is pragmatically useful. "Pure art" has higher demands; it is a wide-open window on reality. Ancient and medieval man affirmed authentic reality within himself (the soul) and outside himself, therefore objectively. The Middle Ages developed an authentic culture with "its *own* science, its *own* art, its *own* state system."[87] Modern man wants to escape reality so he makes his own laws. His subjectivism is a form of illusionism.

Rationalistic humanism emerged in the Renaissance, Florensky pointed out, and with it a new attitude to perspective that put man at the center of the universe and made him the measure of all things. As a result, purely religious action degenerated into semi-theatrical mystery, and "the icon of so-called religious painting ... became more and more only a pretext for the depiction of the body and the landscape."[88] In *Pillar,* Florensky held that Leonardo da Vinci's paintings epitomized the new worldview—an arrogant assertion of the human "I know." The smiles of Leonardo's subjects expressed spiritual waywardness and confusion; Mona Lisa's smile betokened lecherousness and corruption.[89] In "Reverse Perspective," Florensky treated Leonardo's "Last Supper" as a replication of Euclid's abstract geometrical space and as a prelude to the abstract laws of Newtonian mechanics and Kantian space. In *The Imaginary in Geometry: Extension of the Field of Two-Dimensional Geometry* (1922), Florensky argued that, from the perspective of relativity theory, the Ptolemaic system is just as valid as the Copernican system.

Florensky made no overt political statements in the 1920s, but he did expect some sort of apocalypse, which he described in scientific terms as a black hole that swallows everything up. In 1933, however, he penned an essay on the hypothetical state structure of the future, in which he envisioned a "true autocrat" (as distinct from current pretenders such as "Mussolini, Hitler, and others," presumably Stalin), a kind of Christian "artist-tyrant" who would create the structure of a new society and a new culture.[90] Evert van der Zweerde traces Florensky's hypothetical vision to the theocratic-hierarchic order that Florensky envisioned in an early essay, "On the Goal and Meaning of Progress" (1905), in which he criticized "Protestant" and "socialist" theories of progress and rejected the very goal of a "normal society."[91]

Conclusion

We have seen how Merezhkovsky, Ivanov, and Florensky picked up the aspects of Nietzsche's thought that appealed to them, modified and embellished these aspects in the light of their own concerns, and eventually absorbed them into their reinterpretations of Orthodoxy. Merezhkovsky used Nietzsche to make symbolism into a militant religion of art, then to preach an apocalyptic Christianity, and finally to champion a "religious revolution" and claim that Jesus was a revolutionary. He regarded Jesus as the Superman Nietzsche sought in vain. Ivanov believed that Dionysus was a precursor of Christ and that the cult of Dionysus was primarily a religious phenomenon. During the 1905 Revolution he advocated reviving the Theater of Dionysus and dedicating it to creating the new myths, or revitalizing the old ones, that would reunify Russia. A few years later he proposed a specifically Christian unifying myth, the "Russian Idea." Florensky constructed a specifically Orthodox theology centering on ecclesiality, aestheticism, and direct religious experience. After the Bolshevik Revolution he tried to make Christianity into a cult, used concepts derived from Nietzsche and symbolism to analyze Church rituals and icons, and advocated the revaluation of all values from a specifically Orthodox perspective. Ironically the herald of the death of God inspired and helped shape Russian religious thought, thanks, in part, to the surprising affinities between Florensky's thought and Orthodoxy.

Notes

1. For the extent of Nietzsche's influence, see Bernice Glatzer Rosenthal, ed., *Nietzsche in Russia* (Princeton, N.J., 1986); idem, ed., *Nietzsche and Soviet Culture: Ally and Adversary* (Cambridge, 1994), introduction, pt. 1; idem, *New Myth, New World: From Nietzsche to Stalinism,* esp. secs. 1, 2 (University Park, Pa., 2002). See also Edith W. Clowes, *The Revolution of Moral Consciousness: Nietzsche in Russian Literature, 1890–1914* (DeKalb, Ill., 1988); Inna Boiskaia, *Fridrikh Nitsche i russkaia religioznaia filosofiia* (Minsk, 1993), N.V. Motroshilova and Iulia Sineokaia, ed., *F. Nitsshe i filosofiia v Rossii* (St. Petersburg, 1999); and Iulia Sineokaia, ed., *Nietzsche Pro et Contra* (St. Petersburg, 2001).

2. Friedrich Nietzsche, *The Birth of Tragedy from The Spirit of Music,* trans. Walter Kaufmann (New York, 1967), 99–100.

3. Ibid., 74.

4. Ibid., 96.

5. Merezhkovsky spelled this out in an essay about Tiutchev, *Dve tainy russkoi poezii, Nekrasov i Tiutchev* (Petrograd, 1916) which was really about himself. Details in B. G. Rosenthal, *D. S. Merezhkovsky and the Silver Age* (The Hague, 1975), 95–97.

6. In Basil Dmytryshyn, ed., *Medieval Russia, A Source Book* (Fort Worth, 1991), 32.

7. Nietzsche, *The Birth of Tragedy,* 31–32, 52.

8. Boris Jakim and Robert Bird, "General Introduction," in *On Spiritual Unity: A Slavophile Reader* (Hudson, N.Y., 1998), 11.

9. Nietzsche, *The Birth of Tragedy,* 143.

10. Timothy Ware, *The Orthodox Church* (Baltimore, Md., 1963), 29.

11. Stephen Baehr, *The Paradise Myth in Eighteenth-Century Russia* (Stanford, Calif., 1991), 20.

12. Soloviev, "Ideia sverkhcheloveka" (1899), in *Vladimir Sergeevich Soloviev: Sochinenii,* 2 vols. (Moscow, 1990): 2:628–29.

13. Ibid., 2:632–34.

14. Soloviev, "Kratkaia povest' ob antikhriste," in *Sochinenii,* 2:740–41.

15. Nikolai Berdiaev "Eticheskaia problema v svete filosofskogo idealizma," in *Problema idealizma* (Moscow, 1902), 124.

16. Vasily Rozanov, a luminary of the St. Petersburg Religious-Philosophical Society, was also called the "Russian Nietzsche" because of his diatribes against the Christian exaltation of celibacy, virginity, and death. Nevertheless, he found supreme beauty in Orthodox rituals and in the visage of Jesus.

17. Friedrich Nietzsche, *On the Genealogy of Morals,* trans. Walter Kaufmann (New York, 1969), 132.

18. Vladimir Lossky, *The Mystical Theology of the Eastern Church* (Crestwood, N.Y., 1976), 144.

19. Natalia Gorodetsky, *The Humiliated Christ in Russian Thought* (New York, 1938).

20. Norman Cohn, *The Pursuit of the Millennium* (New York, 1972), 148–50, 176–80.

21. Ware, *Orthodox Church,* 203–204.

22. The first four councils—the Councils of Nicea (325), Constantinople (381), Ephesus (431), and Chalcedon (451)—hold a special place in the structure of dogmatic authority, comparable to that of the four Gospels. See Jaroslav Pelikan, *The Spirit of Eastern Christendom* (600–1700) (Chicago, 1974), 25–30.

23. Friedrich Nietzsche, *Thus Spoke Zarathustra,* trans. R. J. Hollingdale (New York, 1961), 51–52.

24. Friedrich Nietzsche, *The Antichrist*, trans. R. J. Hollingdale (Baltimore, Md., 1968), 145.

25. "Ikonostas," in *Sviachshennik Pavel Florenskii. Sochineniia*, 4 vols. (Moscow, 1994–1999), 2:520.

26. Nikolai Berdyaev, *The Russian Idea* (Lindisfarne, N.Y., 1992 [1946]), passim.

27. Friedrich Nietzsche, *Ecce Homo*, in same volume as *Genealogy of Morals*, trans. Walter Kaufmann, 327.

28. Nietzsche, *The Birth of Tragedy*, 111.

29. Details in B. G. Rosenthal, "Stages of Nietzscheanism: Merezhkovsky's Intellectual Evolution," in *Nietzsche in Russia*, 69–94.

30. "Pushkin" in D. S. Merezhkovskii, *Pol'noe sobranie sochinenii* (hereafter, *PSS*), 24 vols. (Moscow, 1914), 18: 89–171.

31. Merezhkovskii, *PSS*, 11:186; 12:24, 201.

32. Nietzsche, *The Antichrist*, 140.

33. Merezhkovskii, *PSS*, 13:162–63. First published as the introduction to *Le tsar et la revolution* (Paris, 1907).

34. Merezhkovskii, *PSS*, 13:36–42, 147; *PSS*, 14:21–22, 119–20, 171–72.

35. Ibid., 1:vi–vii; 13:69–71, 81–84.

36. D. S. Merezhkovskii, *Napoleon*, 2 vols. (Belgrade, 1929). The English translation is in two volumes, *Napoleon the Man* (New York, 1929) and *The Life of Napoleon* (New York, 1929), both translated by Catherine Zveginstov.

37. D. S. Merezhkovsky, *Taina zapada: Atlantida-Evropa* (Belgrade, 1930).

38. See, especially, "Ellenskaia religiia stradaiushchego boga" (The Hellenic religion of the suffering God), published in Merezhkovsky's revue, *Novyi put'* (hereafter, *NP*) (1904), nos. 1–3, 5, 8, and 9, and continued as "Religiia dionis" (The religion of Dionysus), *Voprosy zhizni* (hereafter, *VZ*) (1905), nos. 6, 7. I thank Robert Bird for providing me with photocopies.

39. *NP*, 1:115.

40. *VZ*, 7:137, 144.

41. *NP*, 2:48.

42. *NP*, 9:59.

43. *NP*, 8:23.

44. *VZ*, 7:145–46.

45. *VZ*, 7:148.

46. *VZ*, 7:142.

47. Ivanov, "O zakone i sviazi" (1908), in *Viacheslav Ivanov: Sobranie sochinenii*, ed. D. V. Ivanov and I. O. Deschartes, 4 vols. (Brussels, 1979), 3:126.

48. Details in Rosenthal, "Vyacheslav Ivanov's Conceptions of *Sobornost'*," *California Slavic Studies* 14 (1992): 154–57.

49. Rosenthal, "Ivanov's Conceptions," 161–62.

50. "Dogmatizm i dogmatika" (1905), *Sviashchennik Pavel Florenskii. Sochineniia*, 1:556.

51. Ibid., 1:556–62.

52. See, for example, ibid., 551, 552.

53. Pavel Florensky, *The Pillar and the Ground of the Truth*, trans. Boris Jakim (Princeton, N.J., 1997), 117.

54. Ibid., 115.

55. Ibid., 202. The line is Tiutchev's; Merezhkovsky quoted it, too.

56. Ibid., 215.

57. Ibid., 9.

58. Ibid., 288.

59. Ibid., 335.

60. Ibid., 330.

61. Ibid., 330.

62. Ibid., 129.

63. Ibid., 130.

64. Nietzsche, *The Case of Wagner,* in same volume as *The Birth of Tragedy,* trans. Walter Kaufmann, 170.

65. Nietzsche, *The Birth of Tragedy,* 46.

66. *Sviashchennik Pavel Florenskii. Iz Bogoslovskogo naslediia, Bogoslovskie trudy* 17 (1977); henceforth, cited as *Iz naslediia.*

67. See Florensky, *Salt of the Earth. An Encounter with a Holy Russian Elder: Isidore of Gethsemane Hermitage,* trans. Richard Betts (Piatina, Calif., 1987).

68. *Iz naslediia,* 123.

69. Ibid., 107.

70. Ibid., 131, 221.

71. Details in Michael Hagemeister, "Wiederverzauberung der Welt: Pavel Florenskij's Neues Mittelalter" in *Pavel Florenskij,* 33–41 (the section titled "Vom Antijudaismus zum Antisemitismus").

72. Florenskii, "Khramovoe deistvo kak sintes iskusstv," *Sochineniia,* 2:370–82.

73. Ibid., 2:374.

74. Ibid., 2:382.

75. *Iz naslediia,* 54.

76. *Ikonostas,* 429.

77. Ibid., 460.

78. Ibid., 502.

79. Ibid., 435.

80. Ibid., 522.

81. Friedrich Nietzsche, *The Gay Science,* trans. Walter Kaufmann (New York, 1974), 336.

82. Nietzsche, *Ecce Homo,* 223.

83. Florenskii, "Obratnaia perspektiva," *Sochineniia* 3(1), 46–103.

84. Ibid., 48.

85. Ibid., 49.

86. Ibid., 53.

87. Ibid., 59–60.

88. Ibid., 64–65.

89. Florensky, The *Pillar and the Ground of the Truth,* 129–30.

90. Details in B. G. Rosenthal, "Florenskii's Russifications of Nietzsche," in *Pavel Florenskij—Tradition und Moderne,* ed. Norbert Franz, Michael Hagemeister, Frank Haney (Frankfurt am Main, 2001), 256–58.

91. Evert van der Zweerde, "'*Sobornost'* als Gesellschaftsideal bei Vladimir Solov'ev und Pavel Florenskij," in *Pavel Florenskij,* 233–42.

14

Malevich's Mystic Signs: From Iconoclasm to New Theology

Alexei Kurbanovsky

————•┅⟨∞⟩┅•————

Kazimir Severinovich Malevich (1878–1935) was an innovator as well as a prophet, as profound in his theoretical insights as he was radical in reforming conventional painterly language. His work, as artist and cultural theorist, was deeply engaged with the crisis and searching in spiritual life of his time. In a brochure printed to coincide with "0.10: The Last Futurist Painting Exhibition," held in Petrograd in December 1915, Malevich wrote: "All former and contemporary painting before suprematism, and sculpture, the word, and music were enslaved by the form of nature, and they await their liberation in order to speak in their own tongue and not depend upon the intellect, sense, logic, philosophy, psychology, the various laws of causality and technical changes in life."[1] One could observe that, at the turn of the nineteenth and twentieth centuries, notions of uncertainty and doubt invaded theoretical thought and artistic creative discourse. There appeared an open abyss between experimental sciences, which were grounded in testing and observation of natural facts, and those fields of knowledge where interpretation predominated. And this abyss grew even deeper as a result of vulgar, nonreflective positivism that penetrated into philosophy from natural sciences. That system of analytical thought, in spite of its operational possibilities, had no basis in the process of reason's self-reflection. Philosophy appeared an easy prey for critical skepticism—before thinking could arrive at certain conclusions by way of reflection upon the process that gave birth to these very conclusions.

Some important thinkers, as well as artists, both in Russia and Europe, analyzed this situation and predicted it would change slowly. Alexander Benois, the influential Russian art critic and artist, wrote:

> Along with individualism, and depending on it, the long-derided idealism acquired new life in the [18]80s.... Materialism, which provided

an amazingly simplistic explanation of life, could satisfy no longer. . . . All social teachings have lost their charm, and the mystical spirit of poetry, the eternal striving to abandon the chains of mundane prose, have come back to life with a new force.[2]

Another important young painter, Igor Grabar, observed that "people feel the necessity for something to replace the broken religion, and, getting nothing, they find nothing better than to turn back to it. Positivism is trembling, and metaphysics clears itself a road in the sphere of modern philosophy."[3] Both artists were referring to various activities that were taking place in the Russian religious-philosophical sphere. The way out of the positivist dead end was at that time associated with renewed quests of spirituality, religion, and aesthetics. Art was considered an important field into which relevant methods of theoretical thought were projected. Conversely, if we compare actual artistic tendencies of that time to contemporary spiritual and intellectual projects, we find each illuminating the other, revealing essential characteristics of the spiritual moment.

It is generally accepted that at the turn the century European and Russian art passed through a series of stylistic phases that ruined traditional representational practices. The subject of artistic perception, whose right to an autonomous bodily experience was positively asserted in impressionism and dramatically challenged by post-impressionism and symbolism, was deeply compromised by cubism's rejection of the single perspective viewpoint and by its integration of the spectator's gaze into a picture. And then the subject was completely eliminated by technical progress—by "the new iron and the machine life, the roar of automobiles, the glitter of electric lights, the whirring of propellers," as Malevich put it[4]—a fact noisily celebrated by international futurism. To maintain its importance, painting was forced constantly to demonstrate innovation. This was the logical conclusion of the ideology of scientific and industrial progress, which penetrated all spheres of thought. Still, the unyielding, accelerated tempo of formal inventiveness was unusual. In contrast to classical art history, which was based on stylistic factors, the early-twentieth-century avant-garde, proceeding from its own notions of "means" and "ends" in art, introduced *strategic* difference as the most essential.[5] This meant that henceforth every artist must draw his own conclusions from every successive stage of imminent painterly evolution.

The aim of this essay is to sketch the evolution of Malevich's creative thinking. I intend to show that the artist was well aware of some important theoretical issues discussed in contemporary philosophy and aesthetics. His own development followed from the overthrow of old forms of authority—social, artistic, and other (what could be termed "iconoclasm")—to the formulation of strong ideological dogmas which merit description as a "new theology." Malevich's choice seems logical and symptomatic for Russian culture of the early twentieth century.

Kazimir Malevich's intellectual and artistic maturation proceeded unevenly, both for subjective reasons (his Polish Catholic origins and provincial background, lack of systematic education and limited access to relevant knowledge) and for objective ones (Russia was still lagging artistically behind the West in the late nineteenth century). Only when twenty-nine-year-old Malevich came to Moscow in 1908, finding himself in the midst of various exhibitions and aesthetic manifestations, did he begin rapidly to assimilate theoretical and artistic influences.[6] His painting of the first decade of the twentieth century reflects the initial stages of the future Russian avant-garde, which would both be influenced by and help to shape the Europe-wide problematic of modernism. Malevich began with symbolism, having absorbed the influence of Paul Gauguin and the Pont-Aven School (from pictures available in the Ivan Morozov and Sergei Shchukin collections in Moscow). But equally strong was the impact of Russian icons, which were for the first time appreciated by educated Russians not only "ethnographically" but also as examples of profound spirituality, valid in themselves as artistic expressions however different their aesthetic program.

Connected with these was the next important source that played a crucial part in Malevich's early development: the nonprofessional, "primitive" art of Russian peasants to which Mikhail Larionov introduced him. Ancient Russian icons, as well as peasant art, were interpreted as authentic artistic forms and, in their distinctly Slavic/Eastern character, as an alternative to the Western classical, rationalist tradition in art—the arguments of such Russian futurists, or *budetlyane,* as Benedikt Livshits, Alexei Kruchenykh, and Velemir Khlebnikov. Malevich developed a deep and sustained interest in Orthodox spirituality, manifested throughout his career. Stylistically his paintings of the early 1910s show that he also readily accepted cubist stylization, as well as some "simultaneist" techniques of the futurists.

Russian artists were familiar with cubism both as an artistic practice, via works by Pablo Picasso and Georges Braque in the Morozov and Shchukin collections, and as an aesthetic doctrine. Albert Gleizes and Jean Metzinger's book, *Du cubisme,* was published in 1913 in two different Russian translations: Malevich's friend, Mikhail Matiushin, edited one of these. Its significance was far-reaching. It is important to note that cubist formal innovation for Malevich went hand in hand with his interest in the poetic, linguistic innovations of the Russian literary Futurists. In such paintings as *Portrait of I. V. Kliun (Improved)* (1913) and *Aviator* (1914) (both in the State Russian Museum, St. Petersburg) and *An Englishman in Moscow* (1914; Stedelijk Museum, Amsterdam) there are puns with Russian words as well as the motif of a saw (which can be connected to a metaphor in one of Kruchenykh's manifestoes).[7] Russian artists built a steady connection between word-creation, the new language of art, and renovation of life. This is precisely why their cubist works can be compared to the theory of language as a sign, much like the structural linguistics elaborated at this very time in Switzerland by Ferdinand de Saussure (his highly influential *Cours de linguistique generale* was published posthumously in 1916).[8]

It is important to realize, first, that a picture, like language, is a synchronistic, relative system, coherent and whole as a unit at every moment of its existence. Thus cubist paintings (for example, Malevich's *Aviator* or *Composition with Mona Lisa*—both painted in 1914 and housed in the State Russian Museum) are structured by pairs of binary oppositions: details drawn/painted and cut out/glued in the collage technique, colored and white surfaces, straight and curved lines. Malevich himself remarked on this binarity:

> The main axis of Cubist construction was the straight and the curved line. The first category called forth other lines, forming angles, and the second axis called forth curves of reverse shape. On these axes were grouped different types of painterly texture: lacquered, prickly, and matt. Collages were introduced for textural and graphic variety. Plaster was introduced.[9]

These details possess not absolute but relative value: they are not elements of narrative but acquire meaning exactly from being juxtaposed to each other, inside the picture. It means that the artist proceeded from the Saussurian definition of the relative and independent quality of the signifier: "In language there are only differences without positive terms. Whether we take the signified or the signifier, language has neither ideas nor sounds that existed before the linguistic system, but only conceptual and phonic differences that have issued from the system. The idea or phonic substance that a sign contains is of less importance than the other signs that surround it."[10] This does not presuppose Malevich's knowledge of the work of Saussure. The parallel realization (in painting and in language theory) of the arbitrary and differential nature of the sign created the very possibility of the modernist critique of representation.

This highlights a more important perspective, relevant in the case of Malevich. If a painting as a succession of signifiers is understood as a kind of text, this reminds us of the analogous approach that existed in Russian religious culture toward icons. Icon painting was considered not a form of representation but a special mediation between man and God, as a type of sacred *text*. The image should somehow diminish and efface itself before the letter of the Holy Scripture; the eye's transition to the sacred meaning must be made smooth and obstacle free. This understanding is evident in the harsh critique by a prominent Russian religious figure, Archpriest Avvakum (1620–1682), who wrote the following, sometime between 1669 and 1675:

> They paint the image of Our Savior Emmanuel with a puffy face, scarlet mouth, curly hair, his arms and muscles fat, fingers thick; and, in the same manner, legs with fat thighs, and the entire figure is made with a swelled belly, and fat like a German. . . . Painting like that is produced after a carnal design, for the Heretics themselves love obese corporeality and have cast down all that is Celestial, while Christ Our Lord had all His limbs delicate, as the Holy Fathers teach us.[11]

Judging the art of icon painting on theological grounds, Avvakum lamented the deterioration of this noble craft (as a result of a corrupting Western influence); and as he referred to the Holy Fathers' authority, it meant that the Archpriest implicitly read icons as a form of divine Scripture. A similar attitude was adopted in the early twentieth century by the Orthodox priest and influential theorist Pavel Florensky (1882–1937), who maintained, in his *Iconostasis* (1919), that the true authors of the icons were not the artists who painted them but the Holy Church Fathers on whose written revelations the icons were based.[12] We shall see how Malevich problematized the notion of authorship in his suprematist *Black Square* of 1915.

Signs in language, as in visual art (in cubism but also in Orthodox icons) appear as the products of some differential system. Thus a cubist formal analysis is based on the undermining of positive elements of likeness and stresses the inner difference as the prevailing instance—as in language, which is constituted by differences. But in icon painting it is precisely the moment of difference that specifies its nature, as icons must not come too close to the material world, being images of Transcendence. Both an icon master and Malevich the cubist start with the relative value of plastic signs and their arbitrary, rather than substantial, character. The condition of signifying is precisely the *difference* of the pictorial sign from the material nature of its referent (as is true also of the Orthodox icon); an *f*-shaped curve in Malevich's *Composition with Mona Lisa* is as valid a structural signifier of a violin as, say, a single tree in a Russian icon is for "forest," "wilderness," or any place of "external natural scenery."

Composition with Mona Lisa was also important as an example of Malevich's portentous aesthetic iconoclasm. In this picture of 1914, the artist glued to the canvas a reproduction of Leonardo da Vinci's famous painting and violently crossed it out, in red, on the face and the neck—as he was to comment later, "people ought to examine what is painterly, and not the samovar, cathedral, pumpkin or Mona Lisa."[13] As is well known, Leonardo's *Mona Lisa* was stolen

from the Louvre on August 25, 1911; the police investigations led to the inter-
rogation and temporary arrest of the ardent modernists Pablo Picasso and
Guillaume Apollinaire. The painting was subsequently found, but in the eyes of
all the young artist innovators of Europe it became associated with institutionalized art, protected by the police, the judicial system, and the whole repressive
apparatus of the bourgeois state. So it was extremely tempting to show contempt for this famous artifact: lack of respect signified both aesthetic revolution
and political radicalism. Notably Malevich discredited the *Mona Lisa* five years
earlier than did Marcel Duchamp, whose infamous *L.H.O.O.Q.* [*Mona Lisa with
Moustache*] of 1919 was acclaimed by the Dadaists as *the* gesture of nihilistic-
ritualistic dismissal of the past. But for Kazimir Malevich it must have meant
also a ritualistic refutation of all Western mimetic, illusionist representation,
in the name of a supreme aesthetic tradition (what he, in the above quotation,
called "painterly") that could be associated with the Eastern-Orthodox religious
symbolism of the icon.

Mystical cosmogony as well as defiance of the traditional forms of production and consumption of art can also be seen in the staging in December 1913
of the Russian futurist opera *Victory over the Sun*. Mikhail Matiushin composed
the music, Kruchenykh and Khlebnikov wrote the text, and Malevich did the
designs and costumes. Cubist geometry of scenography and dynamics of light
complemented the radicalism of the word-creation and the innovative treatment of plot in the opera. The very motif of "victory over the sun" meant a victory over the linear conception of time, to be replaced by everlasting eternity.[14]
The chief importance of this opera should be seen in the fact that the Russian
futurists believed in their *priestly power* to transform reality, which must capitu-
late before a futuristic "trans-rational" (*zaumnyi*) text. At approximately this
same time, Velemir Khlebnikov predicted the "fall of the state" in 1917. These
artists presumed a quasi-religious position ("In the beginning was the Word")
as well as a truly shamanistic attitude to the creative word.

***

Discussion of the origins of Malevich's formal painterly evolution must be
supplemented by the analogous analysis of his theoretical sources. Malevich
considered his articles, manifestoes, and brochures an essential part of his
artistic stance. Indeed, we must keep in mind his special attitude to sacred text.
In the symbolist rhetoric, metaphors, and figures of speech that he used one
cannot fail to discover the strong influence—and sometimes indirect, intertex-
tual references—to the works of contemporary Russian philosophers and religious thinkers such as Vladimir Soloviev, Pavel Florensky, Mikhail Gershenzon,
as well as of the major European "founders of discursivity" such as Arthur

Schopenhauer, Friedrich Nietzsche, and Henri Bergson. Allusions are also made to Russian translations of texts constitutive of Western modernism, especially manifestoes of the Italian futurists, and the Gleizes and Metzinger treatise *Du Cubisme*. Compare some of the following examples:

"If we **take** any of the things that man has defined and try to **investigate** them, we see that, under pressure from our tool of investigation, it immediately **disintegrates** into a large number of **component parts** which are fully independent."—Malevich, "God Is Not Cast Down" (1922)[15]

"Whatever we **take**, we inevitably **fragment** the object we are considering, **split it** into **incompatible aspects.** When we look at one and the same thing from different points of view ... we can arrive at antinomies."—Pavel Florensky, *The Pillar and Ground of the Truth* (1914)[16]

"The [**black**] **square** is a **living, royal infant.** ... In the art of Suprematism forms will **live,** like all **living** forms of nature."—Malevich, "From Cubism and Futurism to Suprematism: The New Realism in Painting" (1916)[17]

"It is not the case that **black Death** attacks **luminous Life** from outside; rather, life itself conceals in its depths the pitilessly **growing embryo** of Death."—Florensky, *The Pillar and Ground of the Truth*[18]

"I have destroyed the ring of the **horizon** and escaped from the circle of things, from the horizon-ring ... This accursed ring which opens up newer and newer prospects, leads the artist away from the **target of destruction.**"—Malevich, "From Cubism and Futurism to Suprematism" (1916)[19]

"I love all those who are like heavy drops falling singly from the **dark cloud** that hangs **over** mankind: they prophesy the coming of the lightning and as prophets they **perish.**"—Friedrich Nietzsche, *Thus Spoke Zarathustra* ("Zarathustra's Prologue") (1884)[20]

"Before ours, all forms of art are **old blouses,** which are changed just like your **silk dresses.** And throwing them away, you acquire new ones. Why do you not put on the **costumes of your grandmothers,** when you go into ecstasies before the pictures of their powdered images?"—Malevich, "From Cubism and Futurism to Suprematism" (1916)[21]

"All ages and all peoples gaze motley out of your **veils** ... He who tore away from you your **veils and wraps and paint** and gestures would have just enough left over to frighten the birds."—Nietzsche, *Thus Spoke Zarathustra* ("Of the Land of Culture")[22]

"I have conquered the **lining** of the heavenly, have torn it down and, **making a bag,** put in colors and tied it with **a knot.** Sail forth! The white, free chasm, infinity is before us."
—Malevich, "Non-Objective Creation and Suprematism" (1919)[23]

"Once in possession of the form of space, mind uses it like **a net** with **meshes** that can be **made and unmade** at will, which, thrown over matter, divides it as the needs of our action demand."—Henri Bergson, *Creative Evolution* (1907)[24]

"**Intuition** is the kernel of **infinity.** Everything that is visible on our globe disperses itself in it. Forms originated from the **intuitive energy** that conquers the **infinite.**"— Malevich, "On New Systems in Art" (1919)[25]

"But it is to the very inwardness of life that *intuition* leads us—by **intuition** I mean instinct that has become disinterested, self-conscious, capable of reflecting upon its object and enlarging it **indefinitely.**"—Henri Bergson, *Creative Evolution* (1907)[26]

The number of these examples could easily be multiplied. While they do not necessarily demonstrate any conscious, deliberate use of quotations, they clearly show parallels in the *production* of a signifying thought. This allows one to conclude that we here confront the case of *intertextuality* as the "overlapping and intersection of semiotic practices," such as Julia Kristeva described.[27] This testifies to a kinship of Malevich's thinking with synchronous Russian and European discursive projects that share similar or analogous creative genealogies, for both the formal-plastic language of art and the language of conceptual thinking possess their own inner logic—and this cannot but lead to quite comparable results.

In the contemporary art-historical literature the question of Malevich's philosophical competence is given some attention: he is claimed to have fair knowledge of works by Plato, Kant, and Hegel, and to have developed parallels with Max Scheler and Martin Heidegger.[28] But the principal comparison one ought to make is between Malevich and the contemporary project of phenomenology, as exemplified by Edmund Husserl (1859–1938). His basic work, *Ideas toward a Pure Phenomenology, Book One,* was published in 1913. Husserl proceeded from the idea of a deep crisis of discursive practices of knowledge (although his important *Philosophy and the Crisis of European Humanity* was published only in 1935), just as Malevich proceeded from the crisis of representative practices in painting. The German philosopher saw his main task as clarifying how reason takes possession of experience by connecting a thought with its object in an act of structured perception, which would lead to breaking out of the vicious circle of subjective consciousness. The philosophical enterprise of phenomenology was to mark those structures of experience and judgment that could not be subjected to doubt, or questioned, even by the most skeptical forms of reason. This brings to mind a similar task formulated in Malevich's painterly suprematism: "The system is constructed in time and space, independently of all aesthetic beauties, experiences and moods: it is more a philosophical color system for realizing the latest achievements of my ideas, more as knowledge."[29] His principles were purely structural and ultimately transcendental, aimed at the "preservation of the sign." Whatever comparison we make, however, such analogies to contemporary Western philosophy consistently show that Malevich's discourse was developing not by a chain of logical conclusions but by flashes of mystical associations, even revelations.

In the avant-garde strategy a painting is considered noteworthy only when it breaks away from all former criteria of quality. At the same time artistic innovation acquires the status of a new quality only when it is projected back onto the very qualitative hierarchy that it rewrites. This is demonstrated with particular clarity by interpretations of Malevich's famous *Black Square* (1915; Tretyakov Gallery, Moscow). The painting was first shown at "0.10: The Last Futurist Painting Exhibition." It was given primacy of place in the installation—suspended

Figure 14.1. Kazimir Malevich, *Black Square*, 1915.

across a corner of the room, as Russian icons were usually placed. Its creation presupposed some kind of aesthetic-religious act: to substitute an object of representation with another reality—supposedly supreme and transcendental—which thus proved its incompatibility with representation.[30] *Black Square,* being a handmade, painterly work, demonstrated the artist's negative but also pious attitude: aware of his failure to compete with the Absolute, he demonstrated "zero" craftsmanship—exactly as ancient Russian icon painters did when they felt inadequate to the task of representing God. Similarly, what Malevich produced was a "black letter," a mystic sign—a signifier that simultaneously stood for the pain of the impossibility of reaching the Absolute and the ecstasy of ascending to its existence. Thus *Black Square* signified absolute contemplation, the negative (apophatic) quality of thinking,[31] and its color could mean the Supreme Emanation of God unbearable for human sight—according to Pseudo-Dionysius the Areopagite. It questioned the technical quality of the artifact (production) in the name of the quality of theoretical/theological thinking (revelation).

After *Black Square* Malevich produced *Black Cross* (1915; Beaubourg Foundation, Paris) and *Black Circle* (1920 [repeats an earlier version that was lost]; State Russian Museum). The mystic significance of this series is undeniable: the square, the traditional symbol of the Earth in medieval iconography,

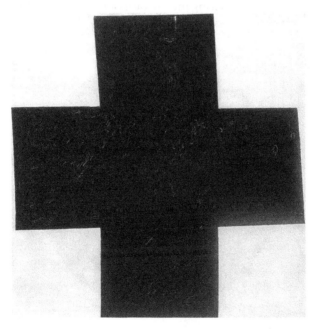

Figure 14.2. Kazimir Malevich, *Black Cross,* 1915.

may be said to designate all things earthly, the circle to represent the skies or God or both, and the cross to signify the Church as the union of the earth and the heavens. Notably Malevich painted a Greek cross to emphasize the Orthodox tradition.

This series of black signs also problematized the notion of authorship, since Malevich could not claim to have invented either the forms or the color. Like an ancient Russian icon painter, he could only claim to be a mediator through whom these transcendental concepts came into existence. But Malevich was also driven by the modernist ideology of innovation; hence his constant anxiety to maintain his priority in this important painterly discovery. As the one responsible for these first black signs of a new aesthetic (soon followed by red and white ones), he wanted to be universally recognized as a kind of high priest of the "Suprematist religion" and to maintain his exclusive right to its exegesis.

Traditional painting for Malevich was linked to the loss of the "proper" understanding of the essence of the world, which he thought indecipherable and which pictures resembled only superficially and in quite an "improper" manner. Corresponding with the notion of pictorial representations were more or less appropriate artifacts that served as symbolic messages such as *Venus de Milo, Mona Lisa,* or Paul Cezanne's still lifes. But neither the idea of representation nor the symbolic language of the artifacts were equivalent to each other, nor were they adequate for rendering the divine essence of the world. The language

Figure 14.3. Kazimir Malevich, *Plane in Rotation,* called *Black Circle,* 1915.

of contemporary art for Malevich was among the most impoverished, because it failed to account for the arrival of powerful new technologies and knowledge, remaining helplessly chained to what he often described, degradingly, as the "old green world, the world of flesh and bone." His own art, as he repeatedly stressed, was born of the spiritual need to transcend all earthly reality.

In analyzing codes of visual representation in all art of the past Malevich was especially critical of the linear, or Italian, perspective. As he wrote in 1919, "thus was created the perspective, whose beams converged in one point making a cuneiform path: this was art's path; this was how the entire world was viewed. . . . In our comprehension and view of the world our body always moved along lines of perspective . . . Had they remained as unshakable as they did for art our body would have grown into a cuneiform shape just as art did."[32] This critique resembles the phenomenological approach, such as that developed later by Maurice Merleau-Ponty, who considered the Italian Renaissance perspective not a natural way of seeing but a cultural artifact.[33] Merleau-Ponty demonstrated how this scientific, mathematical perspective presumed a watching, static subject at the point of the conventional visual cone, and thus really produced that subject. The prerevolutionary Russian art critic Genrikh Tasteven wrote that the futurists, on the contrary, wanted the spectator (the subject) to be engulfed by their dynamic pictures.[34] Malevich intended to break up the "cuneiform catacombs" and thus to put an end to representation. The Russian painter Lazar (El) Lissitzky, who underwent a full course of suprematist instruction, wrote, significantly, that "suprematism projected the top of the finite visual pyramid of perspective into infinity."[35] This presumed that the surface of a suprematist painting must not produce the illusion of transparency but must be unyielding and flat. It also suggested the sort of *reverse perspective* championed at the same time by Pavel Florensky, which had the receding point in the mind of the spectator.

Malevich considered his suprematism to be the final stage not only of Russian and European painting but of the artistic craft itself. Life and art became for him interchangeable: "Our contemporaries must understand that life will not be the content of art, but rather art must become the content of life, since only thus can life be beautiful."[36] So *White Square* [*White on White*] (1918; Museum of Modern Art, New York) must be considered his most radical painting. This painting marked a moment of the closure of visuality (in which literally nothing remained to see). Visuality was transcended by the artist's quest for immaterial transcendence, after which all painting, Malevich believed, became equivalent to a variety of empty formal tricks that could be taught. As a professor at the State Institute of Artistic Culture (GINKhUK), he showed his students exactly how various artistic styles were "made"—and easily produced pictures in his own early manners, from cubism to impressionism.[37] To be accepted as a professor at a Soviet state institution, Malevich consented that his *Red Square: Painterly Realism of a Peasant Woman in Two Dimensions* (1915; State Russian Museum) was interpreted not just as an "aesthetic theory" but also as *the* symbol of the victorious proletarian revolution, which effectively changed the history of humanity.

***

When Kazimir Malevich painted his black, red, and white signs in succession, he sought to put an end not only to his own painterly development but to the idea of representation as such (apart from as art pedagogy).[38] Thus, on December 15, 1920, he declared: "I myself have entered a remote and for me new realm of thought; as best as I can, I shall give an account of what I see in the infinite space of the human skull."[39] All his paintings executed henceforth should be understood as a part of his theory: pedagogical exercises for his students, or illustrations/icons of his "new theology."

Among all the important theoretical treatises that Malevich wrote, one particularly stands out: *God Is Not Cast Down: Art, Factory, and Church,* published in Vitebsk in 1922. This work has been understood by many as a sustained attack upon the materialist worldview held by the Marxist public, including artists and critics. Malevich even had to defend himself against critic Sergei Isakov's accusations that he was a "religious obscurantist."[40] Indeed, this short brochure reads like a theological treatise.

Without attempting a prolonged analysis of this rather multifaceted and complex work, it is nevertheless important to indicate that it contains a proof of God's existence, deduced from the perfection of God's creation. Malevich approached this problem as an artist, when he wrote: "Man, finding himself in the nucleus of universal stimulus, feels himself to be before the secret of perfection and fearing the darkness of mystery, hastens to find it out . . . Thus everything that is clear in nature tells him by the power of its perfection that the universe, as perfection, is God. The comprehension of God or of the universe, as perfection, became his prime objective."[41] This was not a sensual discovery but an intellectual one, for it presumed a preexisting idea of perfection in the mind of the subject; the idea, of course, must also be a divine revelation. Compare a passage in St. Augustine's *Confessions*: "And I replied unto all the things which encompass the door of my flesh: 'Ye have told me of my God, that ye are not He; tell me something of Him.' And they cried out with a loud voice, 'He made us.' My questioning them, was my thoughts on them: and their form of beauty gave the answer."[42] This reasoning in Roman Catholic theology was later called the "ontological argument": a being conceived perfect must of necessity exist, because existence is the essential feature of perfection.[43] We should presume that St. Augustine's *Confessions* were easily available to Malevich in many Russian translations; but this similarity testifies probably not so much to his knowledge of the book as to the painter's semiconscious affiliation with the Western Roman Catholic tradition, possibly linked to his Polish origins.

Still further into *God Is Not Cast Down* Malevich developed ideas that seemed much closer to Orthodox, Eastern mysticism. He wrote of the complete incomprehensibility of God to human reason, which he called "sense": "God cannot be sense, for sense always begs the question 'of what?'; accordingly God cannot be human sense either, for attaining it as the final sense man will not attain God. . . . Hence God is not sense, but senselessness. His senselessness should be seen in the absolute final limit as non-objective."[44] That approach followed from his reductionist artistic practice which already demonstrated this apophatic quality of his thought. Here, this postulate is formulated with the rigor of his "new Suprematist theology."

The logic of his argument led Malevich to describe the ultimate separation of the human person from the world—even the universe—as the creation of some totally alien Supreme Power: "The universe, like a crazy brain, moves in a whirling vortex, irresponsible as to its destination and purpose. Thus the universe is the senselessness of God liberated and concealing himself in rest."[45] Malevich's *Black Square* can be said to embody this negative attitude to the universe (which is also an expression of perfection). The next stage, the "rest," corresponds to *White on White* resembling a form of divine light.[46] The inaccessibility and incomprehensibility of God also refers to the central concept of the Orthodox mystic teaching—hesychasm, which prescribed strict forms of spiritual discipline, asceticism, and "inner silence" (*hesychia*) for the mental contemplation of God's supernatural light such as the apostles witnessed on Mount Tabor at the time of Christ's Transfiguration.

Malevich increasingly devoted his thought to the role of the state. In his later theoretical writings, he envisioned the state as penetrating everything and as all-powerful. Malevich saw his own ideology as the only logically possible one, such that one can see the totalitarian qualities of the Soviet state as matching, in his view, the suprematist absolute. Not only physical reality but humanity, too, must become the material for utopian construction. In his *Introduction to the Theory of the Additional Element in Painting*, written sometime in 1926 but not published during his lifetime, Malevich wrote: "Any state is such an apparatus by means of which the nervous system of its inhabitants is regulated; in it there are people who are called state conscious, and who comprise in a given system the idea of the state, people in whom all subjective individual consciousness is already killed."[47] As the higher nervous activity also involved thinking, this meant a total control over every person's spiritual life in the thoroughly ideological state that quite resembled theocracy. Included in his pictorial theory, these reflections show that Malevich was mentally projecting himself onto the leading role in the official Soviet "Communist theology."

Among Malevich's later writings, a central place is occupied by his treatise *The World as Non-Objectivity* (1924–1925; not published during his lifetime). It exists in several manuscript versions, extended or abridged. Ideas of a theocratic state are developed here as well. Malevich paid particular attention to the symbolism of state power and to Leninism as the new religion of the Soviet state (he drew deliberate parallels between the cult of Lenin and Christianity). Still contemplating the possibility of becoming an official ideologist, Malevich imagined this symbolism in the suprematist fashion. Thus, he wrote, "the point of view that Lenin's death is not death, that he is alive and eternal, is symbolized in the new object which has the aspect of a cube. The cube is no longer a geometrical body. In this new object we attempt to depict eternity, to create such a circumstance by which the eternal life of Lenin will be affirmed, the eternal life that has overcome death"[48] Producing the first icon of modern art in his *Black Square*, Malevich foresaw suprematist/Leninist icons in every Russian home, when he wrote that "every Leninist workman must have a cube in his house as a reminder of the eternal, constant doctrine of Leninism, which becomes symbolic, dividing the patterns of material life into a cult."[49] The archaic mystical power of this new icon, competing with the Egyptian pyramids, expressed the ultimate "victory over the sun"—the idea of a reversed progress, or a transhistorical, "post-apocalyptic" state reached after the Communist revolution.

Here Malevich could be said to have run ahead of the official Soviet culture with its new proletarian rituals and quasi-religious symbols, although he essentially predicted the coming orthodoxy. One can observe that the new Soviet "theocratic state" eventually considered its "communist religion" to be so strong that it aimed at utilizing not suprematist squares or cubes but the classical formal repertoire, narratives, and even names of the geniuses of the past for its own propaganda. Thus the motto "Rembrandt, Rubens, and Repin in the Service of the Working People" was formulated and put into practice.[50] Soviet artists actually utilized Renaissance and Baroque compositional devices for pictures showing the glory of the leaders, scenes of labor, and sport. Looking now at Malevich's late paintings of the 1930s, we find that he also adapted academic forms of Russian nineteenth-century naturalism and even Italian quattrocento for his solemn portraits (*Self-Portrait*, 1933; State Russian Museum).[51] The artist shared the predominant utopian, even postmodern, attitude that made all artistic forms redundant and qualified them for appropriation. In other words, after the craft of painting experienced its transcendental death in *Black Square*, it was only the post-apocalyptic Soviet reality that could give it a new life. A Soviet artist could reestablish his connections with reality as an act of conscious choice. Refutation of tradition could not be the signifier of artistic liberty, because it immediately was built into the same tradition as its negative term. Absolute freedom was to be found in the creative rewriting of reality itself; this was assumed to be the most important task of Soviet culture in the Stalin era. Malevich's parallel painterly and theoretical development proved that he truly belonged to the spiritual atmosphere of his times.

When Russian avant-garde artists eventually confronted official culture, it appeared that both shared utopian, life-building intentions. Soviet Communism as a "totalitarian artifact," however, could have only one author: Stalin the Leader, identified with the "collective reason" of the Bolshevik Party. Some of the original innovators such as Larionov, Kandinsky, Chagall, and Gabo emigrated in the 1920s; others, including Malevich, were ostracized, gradually squeezed into the periphery of Soviet Russia's artistic life, deprived of the possibility to teach, show their new work, and propagate aesthetic theories. Those who were deemed guilty of "counterrevolutionary propaganda" or "distortion of Soviet socialist reality" were arrested (Malevich had to spend several days in custody in 1930). One can observe that aesthetic-political rigor demonstrated by the majority of the avant-garde artists when they were able to exercise a degree of power was the very quality that helped to prepare and effect their own destruction.

Thus the formal evolution of Malevich's art demonstrates the route of reduction and abandonment of mimetic representation that became the principal feature of all twentieth-century art. As one contemporary critic observed, the entire program of modernism was exhausted during the short time span that separated Seurat from Malevich.[52] But this Russian artist's personal theoretical and spiritual evolution from daring painterly iconoclasm to profound mysticism and religious awareness of his later painted signs is an altogether unique, and yet characteristic, "sacred story," demonstrating clearly the intensity of the Russian religious-philosophical quest in the early revolutionary decades of the last century.

Notes

1. Kazimir Malevich, "From Cubism to Suprematism in Art, to the New Realism of Painting, to Absolute Creation" (1915); cf. Charlotte Douglas, *Swans of Other Worlds: Kazimir Malevich and the Origins of Abstraction in Russia* (Ann Arbor, Mich., 1980), 107.

2. Alexander Benois, *Istoria russkoi zhivopisi v XIX veke* (History of Russian painting in the 19th century) (Moscow, 1998 [1902]), 343–344.

3. Igor Grabar, "Upadok ili vozrozhdenie? Ocherk sovremennykh techenii v iskusstve" (Decline or revival? An outline of contemporary trends in art), *Niva: Ezhemesiachnye literaturnye prilozheniia*, 1897, no. 1:67.

4. K. S. Malevich, *Essays on Art: Unpublished Writings*, ed. Troels Andersen, vols. 1–3 (Copenhagen, 1968–1976), vol. 1 (1915–1928): 29.

5. This point is held by many contemporary scholars; cf. "To speak of the history of painting in terms of the avant-garde is thus to recognize that modern painting, not only in its margins or in its sociological context but also in its very heart—the "painterliness" of painting—is strategic" (Thierry de Duve, *Pictorial Nominalism: On Marcel Duchamp's Passage from Painting to the Readymade*, trans. Dana Polan [Minneapolis, 1991], 27).

6. "Malevich never made any attempt to disguise the sources of his stylistic experiments," writes a modern scholar. "The strongest intellectual influences seem to have come through the ideas of Kulbin, Kandinsky, Matiushin, Kruchenykh and Bergson, from Worringer, Helmholtz, Denis, Fechner, Wundt and Lipps; in other words, from Expressionism. Malevich's ready use of P. D. Uspensky's formal vocabulary derives from this orientation" (Douglas, *Swans of Other Worlds*, 3).

7. In his manifesto, *Slovo kak takovoe* (The Word as such; 1913), illustrated by Malevich, Kruchenykh wrote: "We . . . think that language must be foremost language, and if it would resemble something, let it resemble a saw or a poisonous arrow of a savage"; cf. *Russkii Futurizm: Teoriia, praktika, kritika, vospominaniia* (Russian futurism: Theory, practice, criticism, reminiscences) (Moscow, 2000), 47.

8. Contemporary international scholars including Leo Steinberg, Yve-Alain Bois, Rosalind Krauss, and Christine Poggi developed a parallel comparative analysis of Saussurian linguistics and the French cubism of Picasso and Braque. See Christine Poggi, *In Defiance of Painting: Cubism, Futurism, and the Invention of Collage* (New Haven, Conn., 1992), 48–49; see also the bibliography on page 263.

9. Malevich, *Essays on Art*, 1:98.

10. Ferdinande de Saussure, *Course in General Linguistics*, ed. C. Bally and A. Sechehaye, in collaboration with A. Riedlinger, trans. W. Baskin (New York, 1966), 120.

11. *Zhitie Avvakuma i drugie ego sochineniia* (The life of Avvakum, together with his other writings) (Moscow, 1991), 253. For the purpose of this essay it is not important that Avvakum later acted as the principal figure of the Russian schism, was unfrocked, arrested, and, after torture, burned alive at the stake.

12. "This direct proclamation is not setting forth some supposedly anti-artistic dogma against—or any doctrinal censorship of—icon-painting creativity; rather, it reveals precisely the ones whom the church has always known to be true icon-painters: the Holy Fathers. They create the art because they are the ones who contemplate the persons and events that the icon must depict" (Pavel Florensky, *Iconostasis*, trans. Donald Sheehan and Olga Andrejev [Crestwood, N.Y., 1996], 67).

13. Malevich, *Essays on Art*, 1:109.

14. John Milner connected this opera with the vision of the "fourth dimension" according to P. D. Uspensky. See John Milner, *Kazimir Malevich and the Art of Geometry* (New Haven, Conn., 1996), 90. Katerina Clark, accentuating the role of the "futurist strongmen," placed it into the "Nietzschean/Wagnerian" context; see her *Petersburg, Crucible of Cultural Revolution* (Cambridge, Mass., 1995), 39–41.

15. Malevich, *Essays on Art*, 1:194.

16. Pavel Florensky, *The Pillar and Ground of the Truth*, trans. B. Jakim. (Princeton, N.J., 1997), 118.

17. Malevich, *Essays on Art*, 1:38.

18. Florensky, *The Pillar and Ground of the Truth*, 375.

19. Malevich, *Essays on Art*, 1:19.

20. Friedrich Nietzsche, *Thus Spoke Zarathustra: A Book for Everyone and No One*, trans. R. J. Hollingdale (London, 1969), 45. The similarity is even more striking in the Russian translation by Yury Antonovsky, published in 1911 and widely available, because in both Malevich and Nietzsche the Russian word *pogibel'* (destruction, death) is used.

21. Malevich, *Essays on Art*, 1:27.

22. Nietzsche, *Thus Spoke Zarathustra*, 142.

23. Malevich, *Essays on Art*, 1:122.

24. Henri Bergson, *Creative Evolution*, trans. A. Mitchell (New York, 1931), 202. This book was translated into Russian in 1914 by V. A. Flerova and avidly discussed in various artistic circles.

25. Malevich, *Essays on Art*, 1:104.

26. Bergson, *Creative Evolution*, 176.

27. "The *text* is defined as a trans-linguistic apparatus that redistributes the order of language by relating speech, which aims to inform directly, to different kinds of anterior or synchronic utterances. The text is therefore a *productivity*, and this means: first, that its relationship to language in which it is situated is redistributive (destructive-constructive) [...] and second, that it is a permutation of texts, an intertextuality: in the space of a given text, several utterances, taken from other texts, intersect and neutralize one another" (Julia Kristeva, *Desire in Language: A Semiotic Approach to Literature and Art*, trans. T. Gora, A. Jardine, and L. S. Roudinez (New York, 1980), 36.

28. Troels Andersen drew a detailed comparison of Malevich's main philosophical treatise, *The World as Non-Objectivity*, with Arthur Schopenhauer's *The World as Will and Representation* in his preface to K. S. Malevich, *The World as Non-Objectivity. Unpublished Writings 1922–25*, trans. X. Glowacki-Prus/ E.T. Little, vol. 3 (Copenhagen, 1976), 7–9. Boris Groys placed Malevich in philosophical perspective alongside Martin Heidegger in his essay "Malevich i Khaidegger," *Wiener Slawistischer Almanach*, no. 9 (1982): 355–366.

29. Malevich, *Essays on Art*, 1:120.

30. Apart from parallels with icon painting, important for my study, this idea could have a Bergsonian genealogy. Cf. "To represent the object A non-existent can only consist, therefore, in *adding* something to the idea of this object: we add to it, in fact, the idea of an *exclusion* of this particular object by actual reality in general" (Bergson, *Creative Evolution*, 285).

31. "Malevich thought that *Black Square* had given him access to a vision of the pure materiality coinciding (in the best Aristotelian tradition) with the nothingness that arose after the disintegration of the Divine Logos—the world of Divine Forms, which (interpreted in the best Thomist traditions) were superimposed by God the Artist upon material chaos" (Boris Groys, *The Total Art of Stalinism: Avant-Garde, Aesthetic Dictatorship, and Beyond*, trans. C. Rougle [Princeton, N.J., 1992], 72). I am indebted to Groys's *Total Art of Stalinism* for the concept of Stalinist art as a "post-Apocalyptic" phenomenon.

32. Malevich, *Essays on Art*, 1:113–114.

33. See Maurice Merleau-Ponty, *Le Visible et l'Invisible* [*suivi de notes de travail*] (Paris, 1964), 264–265. In English: *The Visible and the Invisible, followed by Working Notes*, trans. A. Lingis (Evanston, Ill., 1968), 212–213.

34. See Genrikh Tasteven. *Futurizm: na puti k novomu simvolizmu* (Futurism: Toward a new symbolism) (Moscow, 1914), 39–40.

35. El Lissitzky, *K. und Pangeometrie* (1925), in *Maler, Architekt, Typograf, Fotograf: Erinnerungen, Briefe, Schriften*, collected by Sophie Lissitzky-Kuppers (Dresden, 1976), 355.

36. Malevich, *Essays on Art*, 2:17.

37. This created considerable misunderstanding with the dating of certain of Malevich's paintings; recent examinations involving X rays made it possible to establish much later dates for many pictures traditionally thought to have been painted in the 1900s. See Elena Basner, *Zhivopis' Malevicha pozdnego perioda: fenomen rekonstruktsii khudozhnikom svoego tvorcheskogo*

puti (Malevich's later painting: A phenomenon of the artist's reconstruction of his own creative path) Avtoreferat dissertatsii na soiskanie uchenoi stepeni kandidata iskusstvoznaniia (St. Petersburg, 1999).

38. Later, in 1921, Alexander Rodchenko also "did away" with the art of painting as such; in that same year the prominent Russian critic Nikolai Tarabukin delivered a public lecture entitled "The Last Picture Has Been Painted."

39. Malevich, *Essays on Art*, 1:128.

40. The brochure was probably an extended version of the lecture "Art, Factory, and Church" presented by Malevich in June 1922 at the Petrograd Museum of Artistic Culture. The artist's response to criticism, a short article called *Van'ka-Vstan'ka* (The Tumbler) was published in May 1923. See Malevich, *Essays on Art*, 2:168.

41. Malevich, *Essays on Art*, 1:196.

42. St. Augustine, *The Confessions of Saint Augustine*, trans. E. B. Pusey, D.D. (New York, 1949), 201.

43. The "ontological argument" was developed by St. Anselm, Archbishop of Canterbury (1033–1109), in his *Monologium;* cf. "There is, then, some one being which alone exists in the greatest and in the highest degree of all. But that which is greatest of all, and through which exists whatever is good or great, and, in short, whatever has any existence—that must be supremely good, and supremely great, and the highest of all existing beings" (St. Anselm, *Proslogium; Monologium; An Appendix in behalf of the Fool by Gaunilon; and Cur Deus homo*, trans. Sidney Norton Deane, B.A. [Chicago, 1903], 42–43).

44. Malevich, *Essays on Art*, 1:204.

45. Ibid., 1:214.

46. Cf. again, in St. Anselm, "So the supreme Being, and *to be* in the highest degree, and *being* in the highest degree, bear much the same relations, one to another, as *the light* and *to light* and *lucent*" (*Monologium*, 49).

47. Malevich, *Essays on Art*, 3:154.

48. Ibid., 3:344.

49. Ibid., 3:326.

50. Coined, in the 1930s, by the Soviet critic and artistic administrator Ivan Gronsky. For details, see the exhibition catalogue *Agitatsiia za schastie* (Agitation for happiness), State Russian Museum; and Documenta Archiv, Kassel (St. Petersburg and Bremen, 1994), 52.

51. In his thorough and detailed study cited above, *Kazimir Malevich and the Art of Geometry*, John Milner showed possible connections of Malevich's geometric suprematism with European Renaissance theories of harmony and proportion (the Golden Section, the Fibonacci numbers, Vitruvius, Alberti, Leonardo, Durer). This indicates that Malevich's late "Renaissance" paintings of the 1930s were well researched and prepared. But compare Groys: "the source of both the [avant-garde] project and the will to destroy the world as we know it to pave the way for the new was in the mystical, transcendental, 'sacred' sphere, and in this sense completely 'irrational'" (Groys, *The Total Art of Stalinism*, 64). In this essay I am in full agreement with Groys's approach here of trying to explore Malevich's nonrational—religious, mystical—side; it seems by far more important for an adequate appreciation of Malevich's achievement.

52. Thierry de Duve, *Kant after Duchamp* (Cambridge, 1998), 174.

15

The Theology of Culture in Late Imperial Russia

Paul Valliere

The emergence of a highly original tradition of religious philosophy operating along the boundary between philosophy and theology, and to some
extent contesting that boundary, was one of the most distinctive developments
in Russian culture in the late imperial period. Suppressed at home by the Soviets
and eclipsed in the postrevolutionary Russian diaspora by the neotraditionalist
turn in Orthodox theology beginning in the 1930s, Russian religious philosophy
began to be rediscovered by dissident intellectuals in the later Soviet period and,
with glasnost, to be published again. By now, a large if by no means complete corpus of Russian religious philosophy is available in good contemporary editions.
Systematic interpretation of this material has not kept pace with production,
however, and interpreters do not agree on how the story of Russian religious
philosophy should be told. Some even question whether there *is* a unified story.
Suspicion of grand narratives runs deep in humanist and philosophical circles
today, making it difficult to win appreciation for macro-historical theses of any
kind. Forty years ago Nicolas Zernov was able to construe a great variety of theological, philosophical, and literary products of the Silver Age (1900–1917) and of
the postrevolutionary Russian diaspora as evidence for "the Russian religious
renaissance of the twentieth century," which he construed as the story of the
return of the prodigal sons and daughters of Russia to the Orthodox faith.[1] It is
difficult to imagine such a presentation winning wide acceptance at the present
time, at least among specialists on the history and culture of imperial Russia.

Yet historical scepticism, unless we absolutize it, is not a reason for suspend-
ing inquiry into commonalities that might be shown to connect small stories
to larger ones. The theme of "sacred stories" invites this sort of inquiry. What
makes an ordinary story into a sacred story if not a perceived or projected link
between the little story and an overarching one? Russian religious philosophers

certainly viewed themselves as part of a larger story, and their storymaking needs to be taken seriously as a historical phenomenon.

What comprised the unity of Russian religious philosophy? The answer is not to be found in the specific theological positions foregrounded by the practitioners, for here we find not only a great variety but also profound and often irreconcilable differences. A more promising avenue is the investigation of the shared idealist background of Russian religious philosophy. Differences between Russian religious thinkers may be connected to divergent currents within idealism, while their unity, such as it is, may be explained by the thought-forms underlying all types of modern idealism. So, for example, whereas some of the differences between the religious philosophers Nikolai Berdiaev (1874–1948) and Sergei Bulgakov (1871–1944) may be interpreted as deriving from Kantian and Schellingian idealism, respectively, the features that distinguish Kantian, Schellingian, and other types of idealism from positivism, pragmatism, materialism, scepticism, and so on, would form the common ground occupied by Berdiaev and Bulgakov. Sergei Khoruzhii construes the unity of Russian religious philosophy similarly but in terms of Neoplatonism rather than modern idealism.[2]

More recently interest has gravitated to the institutional vehicles of Russian religious philosophy, such as publishing houses, philosophical societies, and political associations. The motivation of this scholarship is to situate the religious philosophers in the Russian ideological debates of the period, in effect to recontextualize and perhaps demystify religious philosophy.[3]

Still another approach, the one I develop in this essay, is to locate the common ground of Russian religious philosophy in an intellectual *project*, namely, that of overcoming the disjunction between religious tradition and modern secular civilization by means of a theology of culture. When Pavel Florensky (1882–1937), against the wishes of his family, abandoned a university career in mathematics and entered the service of the Church, he explained his intentions in a letter to his mother:

> To bring about a synthesis of the Church's values [*tserkovnost'*] and secular culture, to unite myself completely with the Church, but without any sort of compromises, honorably, to grasp the whole positive doctrine of the Church and [also] the scientific-philosophical worldview along with art, etc.—this is how I view one of the most immediate aims of practical activity.[4]

It is significant that the compromises Florensky mentions in this passage are not just religious but secular; that is, he worries not only about measuring up to the demands of the Church but also about falling short of the challenges of modern civilization. To be sure, the cited passage bears the distinctive Florenskian signature of a strong ecclesiastical commitment. But this is only one way of going about the theology of culture, a variation distinct from the theme. Theology of culture is the theme.

A considerable variety of approaches to the theology of culture can be documented in the history of Russian religious philosophy. Most of the forms described in H. Richard Niebuhr's comprehensive typology in *Christ and Culture* can be found there.[5] Lev Tolstoy represented the position of "Christ against culture." The Kierkegaardian position of "Christ and culture in paradox" was articulated by Lev Shestov and, to some extent, by Berdiaev. Soloviev and Bulgakov clearly thought in terms of "Christ the transformer of culture." In Florensky one sees a tension between Solovievian transformationism and a neo-medievalist view of "Christ beyond culture." Slavophilism showed affinities for the "Christ of culture." Yet the application of a pluralistic typology such as Niebuhr's sidesteps the question of the unity of Russian religious philosophy and the related issue of why the theology of culture so preoccupied Russian thinkers and indeed modern religious thinkers everywhere, including Niebuhr. These more basic questions are better illuminated by another important modern contribution to the theology of culture, Paul Tillich's theory of theonomy.

Theonomy, as Tillich defined it, concerns the sacred *nomos* or divine *logos* which is disclosed in all branches of human creative activity—science, politics, arts and letters, and so on.[6] Theonomy clarifies the religious substance *of* culture without necessarily justifying traditional religious or ecclesiastical interventions *in* culture. The basic assumption is that all human creativity responds to the divine ground of being, however diverse the manifestations of creative eros may be. In other words, sacred stories witness to a sacred ground without which there would be no sacred stories. The concept of theonomy is particularly relevant to the modern religious situation in that it offers a way of grounding civilization in the sacred without the tutelage of specifically religious institutions. The concept is designed to accommodate secularization without surrendering a theological perspective.

The concept of theonomy is best clarified by distinguishing it from the related concepts of autonomy and heteronomy. A Russian example will illustrate these distinctions. In 1923 Pavel Florensky composed a "Note on Christianity and Culture" to gloss a manifesto composed in 1918 by his friend and mentor, the distinguished philosopher and psychologist Lev Lopatin (1855–1920). Lopatin's manifesto, entitled "Theses of a Worldwide Union for the Rebirth of Christianity," was published along with Florensky's "Note" in English translation in the Anglican journal *The Pilgrim: A Review of Christian Politics and Religion* in 1924. The editor of the journal was William Temple, then bishop of

Manchester, who went on to write one of the great works of cosmic theology in the Anglican tradition, *Nature, Man, and God* (1934), and ended his career as Archbishop of Canterbury (1942–1944). Temple was also one of the pioneers of the modern ecumenical movement, which explains his interest in Lopatin's essay. In his "Theses" Lopatin argues that Christians of all confessions should learn to distinguish between the essentials of the Christian faith—matters on which most historic Christian confessions agree (according to Lopatin)—and the multitude of nonessential beliefs and practices that divide them. Lopatin's ecumenism clearly derives from that of his friend and forerunner, Vladimir Soloviev; it is interesting to find Florensky lending support to the project, as he is not often associated with ecumenism. Florensky's approach to the theology of culture in this essay is characterized by Bernice Glatzer Rosenthal:

> Florenskii frequently contrasted the "rich organic wholeness of Church culture" with "eclectic and contradictory" Renaissance culture. His ideal was a society in which religion permeated every aspect of life. The separate will, in its individual uniqueness, must coincide with God's will. Christian culture is the "sanctification of nature, of all areas of life. Art, philosophy, science, politics, economics, et al., cannot be seen as self-contained entities separate and apart from Christ." Christianity must not be passive with regard to this world. For Florenskii, as for Bogdanov and Lenin, there are no neutral zones.[7]

Rosenthal is quite right to relate Florensky's ideal to his lifelong polemic against the culture of the Renaissance in the name of "organic wholeness," something Florensky viewed as characteristic of medieval culture, whence his call for a "new Middle Ages."[8] Of course, Florensky was not a medieval thinker but a modern one, and one must be careful not to take his picture of the Middle Ages at face value. Florensky's organicism was a legacy from Russian Slavophilism and, by the same token, a modern response to a modern problem, namely, the problem of religion and culture under discussion here.

One will not succeed in capturing the essence of this problem, however, by limiting oneself to the two alternatives offered in Rosenthal's analysis, namely, a religiously neutral or secular culture, on the one hand, and a culture dominated by religious hegemons, on the other, the latter alternative presumably justifying Rosenthal's comparison of Florensky with the Marxist revolutionaries Bogdanov and Lenin. In the modern theology of culture these are the alternatives of autonomy and heteronomy, respectively. Autonomy is a view of human cultural activities as containing their own *nomos* or *logos*, a view of the world as sufficient unto itself, "*samodovleiushchii*," as Florensky puts it. Of course, Florensky rejects this view as inconsistent with belief in God. But this does not mean that he opts for heteronomy, that is, for the subordination of culture to religious hegemony, the external and forced domination of culture by religious authorities. In the text discussed by Rosenthal, Florensky explicitly rejects this approach:

> Western Christianity of the Baroque period committed an essential error when it tried to assimilate pieces of anti-Christian culture as raw material and, without spiritualizing them from within, covered them over with a lacquer of piety or touched them up with an ecclesiastical coloring. The scientific and cultural activity of the Jesuits deserves deep respect as far as its basic idea is concerned, namely, to supply Christianity with a Christian culture. But it was profoundly mistaken in that [its constructions] are not real buildings but show-pavilions and plaster models; such a culture is something one builds to impress unthoughtful novices but not for one's own consumption.[9]

Regardless of the justice of Florensky's historical characterizations, this passage makes it clear that, at least in intention, Florensky did not seek the domination of culture by religion, an arrangement relying on force rather than freedom. On the contrary, Florensky sought a *nomos* expressing the immediate relation of cultural activity ("spiritualized from within") to the sacred ground of being. This is not a relationship constituted by religious authorities but one that exists already in the depths of cultural activity, in the *theo-nomos* of culture. The antagonism between autonomy and heteronomy is transcended by theonomy, the disclosure of the sacred ground and intentionality of holiness in every serious cultural pursuit. The clarification of this connection as it figures in the various spheres of culture is the business of the theologian of culture.

The search for the sacred ground of cultural activity motivated modern Russian religious philosophy from the beginning. Aleksandr Bukharev (Archimandrite Feodor, 1824–1871) wrote in his theological manifesto, *On Orthodoxy in Relation to the Modern World* (1860):

> Our truly innate, spiritual ideas of truth and goodness, of beauty and being, and the supreme laws of our reason are fundamentally and essentially luminous and shining indications of "the Light that enlightens every human being who comes into the world" (John 1:9), namely, Christ the Divine Word, the foundation of all things; [they are] indications of our spiritual nature even in its present state of disorder and alienation from God.[10]

This was not pious rhetoric. Bukharev backed up his idea by taking an active interest in the Russian cultural life of his day. He was the first ecclesiastical writer to discuss Gogol's works. He wrote a probing essay on the artist A. A. Ivanov, whose painting, *The Appearance of Christ to the People*, he regarded as one of the great theological statements of modern times. He wrote substantial pieces on Turgenev's *Fathers and Sons,* Chernyshevsky's *What Is to Be Done?* and Dostoevsky's *Crime and Punishment,* as well as on a wide range of social and cultural issues.[11]

Fifty years later Florensky looked back to Bukharev as "the little-known but creative first source of those ideas which we are accustomed to view as the characteristic features of our particular Russian philosophical thought and which excite our own time under the pretentious and profoundly unfounded name of 'the new religious consciousness.'" Florensky argued that Bukharev's ideas, and those of the New Religious Consciousness of the Silver Age, revolved around the problem of "the relation of God and the world," which Florensky also called "the Christological problem," "the Christocosmic problem," "the Christo-Sophianic problem," and "the problem of anthropodicy, [namely,] the problem of the justification of the world before God, and to this end the sanctification and transformation of the flesh of the World."[12] Florensky's neologisms, pushing at the limits of traditional dogmatic-theological language, are all ways of getting at what Mark Steinberg and Heather Coleman identify as the central theme of the sacred stories recounted in this volume: the dialogue of religion with the modern world.[13] Modern Russian theology of culture, seeking to justify human creative activity by relating it to "the light that enlightens every human being who comes into the world" (John 1:9), was one of the chief agencies of this dialogue in the sphere of Russian intellectual culture.

The verse from the Fourth Gospel (John 1:9) was a favorite scriptural topos of Russian theologians of culture from Bukharev through Bulgakov. In an address, "The Dogmatic Foundation of Culture," delivered at a meeting of the League of Orthodox Culture in 1930, Bulgakov glosses the verse with yet another unconventional term: "cosmiurge." "Christ is the light 'which enlightens every human being who comes into the world.' In these words 'world' means 'cosmos,' in which the human being is the cosmiurge. Jesus Christ carries out and affirms that participation of human beings in the creation of the world which was given to them from the beginning."[14] The idea of the human being as "cosmiurge," that is, as world builder and co-creator with God, is a Christianization of the Platonic concept of the "demiurge," the artisan who fashions the material world. The specifically Christian contribution here is by no means superficial, however, for Plato's demiurge was a god, not a human being. It is faith in the incarnation of the Word that opens the way for the elevation of human beings to a status they did not enjoy in the Platonic cosmos.

Concepts like Sophia, cosmiurge, demiurge, theurgy, and so on, have often tempted scholarly interpreters of Russian religious philosophy to undertake ambitious programs of theological speculation in which the task of the theology of culture gets lost in a maze of gnostic and theosophical scholasticism. Against this tendency it is important to underscore the connection of the theology of culture with the concrete problem of how religious forces and secular civilization should relate to each other in modern times. In late imperial Russia this problem had reached an acute stage. While the established Orthodox Church was by no means as cut off from the world around it as was once believed, it would be wrong to run to the opposite extreme and suppose that the imperial church was comfortable with the secular society emerging around it. The tensions and blockages were real, and Russian theologians of culture acknowledged them candidly. Florensky has a nice metaphor for the situation. Although he introduces it with reference to Orthodox dogmatic theology rather than the entire patrimony of Orthodoxy, his thought is applicable to the wider context as well:

> The body and the soul of the religious worldview have parted company. We [churchmen] worry only about ourselves, unwilling even for a moment to descend from our vantage point, and so we have forgotten how we got there to begin with. It is no wonder that people cannot find the way into this grand, Gothic cathedral, so beautiful in its ensemble and its parts, but lacking a parvis and steps by which to enter. The innumerable windows are gloomy, enmeshed in spiderwebs, and the passer-by, fearfully casting a sidelong glance, keeps on walking and heads for his own domestic chapel. Meanwhile, the faithful, not knowing how to exit the cathedral, walk pale and lifeless amid the grand columns, peep out of the arched windows, and, instead of prayers, mutter impotent anathemas against the people in the street who (as happens quite often) might actually wish to come in and pray in the church. [15]

These lines come from a presentation Florensky made at the inaugural meeting of a philosophy club at the Moscow Theological Academy in January 1906 (draft dated September 26, 1905). One did not have to be a social activist or revolutionary to recognize that Russia was in the grip of a profound crisis at the time. Florensky's picture of a church which the public cannot find its way into, nor believers a way out, is a poignant emblem for the problem addressed by the modern theology of culture.

The most systematic outline of a theology of culture in late imperial Russia can be found in the work of the philosopher and lay theologian Vladimir Soloviev (1853–1900). An example is afforded by the masterpiece of his early career, *The Critique of Abstract Principles* (1880). Here Soloviev criticizes all the hegemonic ideologies of the nineteenth century for "abstraction," by which he means the substitution of an intellectually constructed world for the buzzing, blooming, spiritually alive world we actually live in. Against abstraction, Soloviev argues for a "positive" philosophy of life that takes living experience seriously, including

religious experience. To elaborate his idea, Soloviev follows the Kantian precedent of a threefold critique: an epistemological critique of pure reason, an
ethical critique of practical reason, and a critique of aesthetics in the broadest
sense, an investigation of "the principles of creativity."[16] This threefold program,
when submerged in the regenerative waters of Soloviev's "positive" transvaluation of values, generates the famous trio of theo-notions which thereafter define
his agenda. The transvaluation of pure reason generates "free theosophy"; of
practical reason, "free theocracy"; of aesthetics, "free theurgy."

Rich and complex, the three theo-notions comprise the substance of
Soloviev's philosophy, which I will not elaborate here. Relevant to the present
discussion, however, is how clearly Soloviev's concepts instantiate the idea of
theonomy. What is the goal of the projects of free theosophy, theocracy and
theurgy if not the clarification of the *theo-nomos* of the basic enterprises of
culture, namely, science, morality (including politics), and art? And what is
the function of the modifier "free" if not to distinguish the three theo-projects
from their heteronomous cousins in unfree church-states and state-churches?
Soloviev's theo-projects are experiments in theonomy.

The three theo-projects—and let it be noted that in Soloviev they are projects, not systems—illustrate the practical task of theonomy, the search for ways
to bridge the gap between secular and religious culture. Soloviev's free theosophy builds a bridge between science and religion; free theocracy, between
society and church; free theurgy, between art and piety. The process of secularization in late imperial Russia was pulling these things apart, polarizing public opinion between conservative defenders of the traditional theocracy and
advocates of militant secularism. Soloviev, by contrast, advanced his religious
philosophy as a mediating force. Whether it played such a role during his lifetime is debatable, given the controversy he stirred, especially during the 1880s,
the most activist decade of his career. But the mediating character of Soloviev's
thought was clearly appreciated in the next generation. In his 1903 essay, "What
the Philosophy of Vladimir Soloviev Offers the Modern Mind," Bulgakov's
answer was "wholeness":

> Soloviev's ideal—wholeness in knowledge, wholeness in life, wholeness
> in creativity [*ideal tsel'nogo znaniia, tsel'noi zhizni, tsel'nogo tvorchestva*]—is
> inherent in every cultivated mind. Nevertheless, despite a great wealth
> of information and the progress of science, modern thought presents a
> picture of inner disintegration and weakness. Elements which ought to be
> in harmony are now at war with each other and exist in a state of mutual
> alienation: positive science suspects metaphysics of violating its rights,
> metaphysics along with science is suspicious of religion, while practical life
> runs its course without depending on either metaphysics or religion.[17]

The idea of theonomy with its goal of mediation can be seen in some of the most abstract and difficult ideas in the Solovievian corpus, beginning with the concept of *bogochelovechestvo*. The term is traditionally translated as "God-manhood," more recently as "divine humanity" or "humanity of God." The word is an abstract noun derived from *Bogochelovek*, God-man, an appellation of Christ the Word of God Incarnate. *Bogochelovechestvo* thus means something like "divine incarnatedness." But consider Soloviev's use of the term in the first of his celebrated *Lectures on Divine Humanity* (1878–1881):

> The old, traditional form of religion proceeds from faith in God but does not follow it to the end. Modern extra-religious civilization proceeds from faith in human beings but it, too, is inconsistent; it does not follow its faith to the end. Both these faiths, faith in God and faith in human beings, when pursued consistently and finally realized, come together in the one full and all-inclusive truth of Divine Humanity.[18]

Before running to gnostic, theosophical, or even patristic Christian sources to gloss *bogochelovechestvo*, one should note how clearly the modern Russian theology of culture is instantiated in this concept. Soloviev introduces *bogochelovechestvo* as a formula for mediating between heteronomous religious tradition and autonomous modern civilization—in other words, as a strategy for theonomy.

Some of the best-known attempts at cultural mediation in the closing decades of imperial Russia, such as the early-twentieth-century Religious-Philosophical Meetings and the essay collection *Vekhi* (Landmarks, 1909), were projects of Solovievian inspiration, not to mention avowedly Solovievian essays in the theology of culture such as Bulgakov's *Philosophy of Economy* (1912). Bulgakov's outline of a "sophic economy" (*Evtuhov*) is a particularly good example of the ideal of theonomy: concrete yet spiritual, worldly yet pious, neither deterministic nor anarchic—in a word, divine-human (*bogochelovecheskii*).[19]

The theonomous ideal is also discernible in some of the cultural and religious stereotyping one finds in the annals of Russian religious philosophy, especially the three-way contrast between Protestantism, Roman Catholicism, and Orthodoxy, where Protestantism stands for autonomy (individualism, secularism), Catholicism for heteronomy (authoritarianism, clericalism), and Orthodoxy for the sanctification of the world through a mediating religious principle, or theonomy.[20] The scheme is a self-serving apologia for Orthodoxy when taken literally but a fairly accurate formulation of the ideal of theonomy when linked to the project of theology of culture.

The self-promotion of Orthodoxy by means of the negative stereotyping of other traditions raises the question of whether the theology of culture in late imperial Russia was a device for confessional and national egoism. In a postmodern context, virtually all projects of mediation have become suspect. The postmodern category of alterity, with its radical scepticism about the possibility of knowing the Other, can readily be applied to depict Solovievian "wholeness" as a formula for oppressive closure and exclusivity. But this critique overlooks an important feature of the theology of culture in Russian religious philosophy, namely, its connection with the campaign for religious liberty in the Russian Empire and, in general, for a more humanistic, less hegemonic approach to the relations between the Russian nation and other peoples inside and outside the empire. The connection was forged by Soloviev during the 1880s when he followed up his abstract sketch of a theology of culture in *The Critique of Abstract Ideals* with two series of essays under the title *The National Question in Russia* (1883–1891) in which he distanced himself from the Slavophilism of his day. His celebrated essay, "The Jews and the Christian Question" (1884), in which he excoriated his fellow Christians for failing to manifest love of neighbor in their relations with Jews, also dates from this period, as does his impassioned call for religious liberty in Russia in *La Russie et L'Eglise universelle* (1889).[21] The political implications Soloviev drew from his theology of culture were by no means arbitrary but issued from the inner logic of the theory. The difference between the modern concept of theonomy and traditional approaches to the relationship between religion and culture lies in the contrast between direct and indirect means of establishing the relationship. In traditional theocracies a historic religious tradition, such as Russian Orthodoxy, enjoys hegemony or at least privileged establishment in state and society. The connection between religion and culture is direct, confessionally explicit, and guaranteed by state power. Theonomous theologies of culture, by contrast, arise when the direct links between religion and culture become problematized or begin to break down. The whole point of such theologies is to formulate the connection between culture and the sacred ground of being in a fresh way, without recourse to traditional heteronomy. Theology of culture is thus a sign of what Soloviev called "national adulthood" and "spiritual maturity" in contrast to the paternalism of defending religion by means of "criminal laws and ecclesiastical censorship."[22]

The link between theology of culture and a modern enlightened approach to religious and national diversity was inherited by the Silver Age philosophers inspired by Soloviev. In these thinkers, however, one notes a certain displacement of Solovievian universalism by a growing nationalism. P. B. Struve's call for the intelligentsia to adopt a "national face" ("Russian-national" [*russkii*] as distinct from "Russian-imperial" [*rossiiskii*]) was especially significant given Struve's role as the political mentor of many Silver Age idealist philosophers.[23] The causes of this shift should probably be sought in the significantly changed historical circumstances faced by the new generation. With a real, if still limited, religious liberty operative in the Russian Empire after 1905, the debate about the desirability of liberty gave way to the debate about how to define and nurture both Russian and Orthodox identities in the changed constitutional order. Domestic concerns overshadowed Soloviev's pan-Europeanism and ecumenism. Nationalist and neo-Slavophile tendencies in Russian religious philosophy became even more prominent with the outbreak of World War I, as one might have expected. Growing anxieties about the integrity of the Russian state itself, whether based on political prescience or on the fashionable apocalypticism of the Silver Age, also destabilized the Solovievian vision. A distinction made by Soloviev himself in the preface to *The National Question in Russia* may be relevant here. Soloviev observed that for many peoples in the world, for example, stateless peoples, the "national question" is a question concerning their very existence as a people, whereas, for Russia, "a unified, independent and great power," the national question "is not a question about existence but *about worthy existence*," that is, the moral question of how Russia should treat her neighbors and domestic minorities.[24] Clearly the political and international upheavals of 1905–1906 and 1914–1917 altered Russia's status in this regard. The existence of the Russian imperial state was an issue for Silver Age thinkers in a way that it had not been for Soloviev.

One of the thorniest issues concerning theonomy is why the culture builders to whom the concept applies—artists, scientists, moralists, activists, and others—are not more aware of the connection with the sacred ground of being posited by the notion of theonomy. The modern cultural scene yields countless examples of individuals who view their creative activities in purely secular, autonomous terms. To explain this, proponents of theonomy have devised the theory of unconscious faith or anonymous Christianity, that is, the theory that creative activity involves an act of faith regardless of the practitioners' religious or confessional views. It is hardly surprising that the best-known theorist of unconscious faith in modern theology, Paul Tillich, was also the leading expositor of the concept of theonomy.[25] On Russian soil it was Sergei Bulgakov who introduced the notion. Bulgakov and Tillich arrived at their theory of faith independently, of course, but their affinity was not accidental. The common source was the thought of the German idealist philosopher F. W. J. Schelling (1775–1854), on whom Tillich wrote two dissertations.[26] In Bulgakov's case, the Schellingian legacy was mediated by Soloviev, the greatest European Schellingian after Schelling himself.

The idea of unconscious or implicit faith figures in several of Bulgakov's earliest articles. The most theoretical of these is "Fundamental Problems of the Theory of Progress," the lead essay in *Problems of Idealism,* the opening fusillade of Russian neo-idealism published in 1902.[27] There Bulgakov argues that the notion of historical progress underlying most modern social ideologies (liberal, positivist, Marxist) is not at all a scientific or rational idea, as its proponents would have us believe, but an expression of faith, that is, a religious or quasi-religious idea.[28] Bulgakov also explored the issue of faith in articles on Russian cultural figures. His procedure is relevant to a discussion of sacred stories, because it illustrates the process of story making in the philosophical arena. Bulgakov's essays on Dostoevsky, Soloviev, Herzen, and Chekhov, all published before 1905, are an example of myth making in Russian religious philosophy, an effort to demonstrate the pertinence of the latter by enveloping it in a sacred story embracing even luminaries of modern Russian civilization who did not present themselves as religious, such as the radical social critic Aleksandr Herzen (1812–1870) and the prose writer and dramatist Anton Chekhov (1860–1904).

Herzen is the easier of the two cases for Bulgakov to handle because Herzen was a natural-born believer, a man who experienced all the dynamics of faith from passionate belief to loss of faith to despair and recovery of faith, albeit faith in the traditional Russian peasant commune, an object of faith which Bulgakov, as a professional economist, could not fail to regard as dubious. But it is precisely the spell of such unpromising objects of faith that demonstrates human beings' deep need of faith. "The spiritual drama of Herzen," as Bulgakov called it, lay in the mismatch between Herzen's believing personality and an impoverished (materialist, positivist) worldview that could not possibly satisfy it.[29]

Chekhov, by contrast, had the temperament of a sceptic. Yet Bulgakov is convinced that the dynamics of faith can be observed in Chekhov, too, albeit in the privative mode. Chekhov's characters, as construed by Bulgakov, are studies in moral weakness, portraits of "the powerlessness of the good in the soul of the average man," depictions of "spiritual *meshchanstvo* [philistinism]."[30] But instead of living their unexalted lives with an easy conscience, Chekhov's "gloomy folk" (*khmurye liudi*) suffer from their condition: they think poorly of themselves, denigrate themselves in public, torture one another morally, *know* they are weak specimens of humanity—symptoms implying the presence of an ideal, albeit darkly veiled. Chekhov's "universal sadness presupposes this passive idealism (so to speak) as its self-evident premise or necessary basis, the confession of an ideal at least in the form of a *norm* for the evaluation of reality." Bulgakov compares Chekhov's characters to deep-sea plants whose existence depends on the sun even though the sun is not visible from the depths they inhabit. Without the ideal, Chekhov would present a case of "Buddhist quietism," an unmitigated metaphysical pessimism providing no basis for the intimations of the power of goodness and beauty that one finds in his works, or for the "mystical chords" which are occasionally struck, such as at the end of *Uncle Vanya* and *Three Sisters*.[31]

As one might expect, Bulgakov greatly admired Chekhov's "A Boring Story" ("Skuchnaia istoriia," 1889), the tale of an eminent professor of medicine who, old and sick, admits to himself that, "in my passion for science, in my desire to live, in my attendance on others and my striving to know myself, in all the thoughts, feelings, and concepts I have had about things, there is no common thread tying everything together into a single whole." This "spiritual drama" or "story of the religious bankruptcy of a living and noble human soul" is read by Bulgakov as an invitation to conversion from scepticism to religious idealism.[32]

Bulgakov also finds a Christian and democratic moral outlook in Chekhov. "This exclusive attention which Chekhov gives to the poor in spirit, the spiritual cripples, the blind from birth, the paralytics and enfeebled, those who have failed and been defeated in the struggle of life, makes him in thought and feeling a profoundly democratic writer in the ethical meaning of this word. Chekhov stood close to the idea which is the cornerstone of Christian morality, and which is the true ethical basis of all democratism: that every living soul, every human life, is something absolutely valuable in its own right, irreplaceable, something which cannot and should not be regarded as a means only but as something which has a right to the alms of human attention." Bulgakov is keen to distinguish this Christian and democratic faith from the promethean humanism of a Nietzsche. "What ennobles a human being, what makes him a human being in the true sense, is not this strange deification of the natural, zoological Superman, Nietzsche's 'blond beast,' but faith in the really super-human and all-powerful force of the Good which is capable of regenerating the injured and supporting the weak human being. Only by believing in this can we believe in ourselves and in our fellows, in humanity."[33] Chekhov, in other words, was not just an idealist but a Christian and democratic idealist.

At this point, to be sure, Bulgakov's Chekhov begins to look suspiciously like Bulgakov himself. If one were to search for the "real" Chekhov, one would surely have to consider levels of irony that Bulgakov does not plumb in his essay, such as whether the title of "A Boring Story" might apply to *everything* in the story, including the old professor's belated confession of the absence of wholeness in his life. But the search for the real Chekhov is (mercifully) not the task here. At issue is how a religious philosopher assimilated Chekhov's oeuvre into a sacred story designed to put flesh on the theology of culture. Many examples of this procedure—the harnessing of Pushkin, Herzen, Dostoevsky, and others to the theology of culture—can be found in the annals of Russian religious philosophy. Most religious philosophers were convinced that modern Russian cultural history itself was a sacred story.

The religious use of cultural figures and cultural products was a matter of some debate in Russian religious philosophy. Berdiaev's sparkling culturo-theological essay on the poet and literary critic Viacheslav Ivanov (1866–1949), "The Enchantment of Reflected Cultures" (1916), is a good example. Nominally a review of Ivanov's *Borozdy i mezhi* (Furrows and boundaries), the essay is, in fact, an assessment of Ivanov's status in the Russian religious renaissance, a story in which Berdiaev numbers Gogol, Dostoevsky, Tolstoy, Scriabin, and others among philosophers and theologians. Berdiaev's verdict is that "Ivanov's place in Russian culture and art is obvious and considerable, but in the Russian religious movement he cannot claim a place of his own."[34] Why not? The answer is implied by the title of Berdiaev's essay: Ivanov's world, while religiously animated, is illuminated by "reflected" light, by cultural products received from a distance rather than by immediate religious experience. Ivanov, adopting the approach of "pan-philologism" or "super-philologism," found religious value and mystical enchantment in the poetry of ancient Greece and other sources from the past but not in the messy, fleshly, crisis-ridden present. Ivanov's spirituality was accordingly beautiful, serene, refined, measured, but disconnected from actual being and in that sense secondary. "In V. Ivanov's consciousness the severe problem of culture and being, of culture and life, is not present, he does not feel the tragedy of culture, he is satisfied with culture, enraptured by its riches."[35] Berdiaev sees this as the characteristic theological mistake of philologists and practitioners of the humanities generally:

> With Ivanov the line between primary being and reflected being is always being erased. The word does not become flesh, rather the flesh becomes word, being passes over into word. In its essence the word is ontological. But in Ivanov's view of the world this solidity disappears. Nowhere and never does one sense the solidity of primary being. In everything there is a strange mobility [*zybkost'*], the mobility of reflected, philological being.[36]

Postmodernists would doubtless side with Ivanov in this quarrel between poetry and philosophy, rejecting Berdiaev's criticism as an instance of logocentrism. Yet more than logocentrism is at stake here, as Berdiaev shows when he shifts to the language of theology proper. Berdiaev's essay is a good example of how the modern theology of culture from time to time approaches the precincts of dogmatic theology. In Christian dogmatic proclamation the Word does not become story, even though a story of the incarnation of the Word certainly exists. The Word becomes flesh, incarnate in a particular human being (Jesus), situated in a particular history (Israel), existing in an actual world ("the whole creation [that] groaneth and travaileth in pain together until now,"

Rom. 8:22). The theology of culture in Russia was deeply invested in this sort of incarnationalism.

The emergence of dogmatic categories in the theology of culture points the way to some of the most creative experiments undertaken by Russian thinkers at the end of the imperial period and thereafter, namely, experiments in the reconstruction of Orthodox dogmatic theology itself. At first glance, dogmatics and theology of culture appear to be antagonists. Traditionally dogma resists enculturation in so far as it is regarded as the revelation of unchanging divine truth. Dogma is conventionally regarded as a trans-cultural verity, "a brief guidebook to eternal life," as Florensky put it.[37] For this reason, among others, the modern theology of culture never begins with dogmatics. This makes it all the more interesting to discover that theology of culture often *ends* with dogmatics, as in the work of Bulgakov and Florensky in Russia and of Paul Tillich in the West, all thinkers who devoted much of their later career to dogmatic or systematic theology.

The convergence of theology of culture upon dogmatics has to do with the bridge building between religion and modern civilization which is the business of theology of culture in the first place. Dogma is the last bastion of the Church's isolation from the world, the final sealed cathedral, to use Florensky's metaphor. To further their mission of mediating between Church and world, theologians of culture must bring Church dogma into the conversation in the long run. But the active role does not lie exclusively with theologians of culture. Dogmatic theologians, roused from their slumbers by the challenges of modern civilization, discover that they, too, have resources to bring to the task of mediation. What is the dogma of the incarnation of the Word, after all, if not a bridge to the world? Thus, what begins as a *Streit der Fakultäten* between dogmatics and theology of culture sometimes ends in the mutually enriching project of "church-and-world dogmatics," as I have called it; or in Bulgakov's Solovievian language, *bogochelovecheskaia dogmatika*, "divine-human dogmatics"; or in Florensky's language, *opytnaia dogmatika*, "experiential dogmatics."[38]

Florensky's call for an experiential dogmatics arose from his perception that the Orthodox Church of his day, while trying to defend dogma, was, in fact, purveying "dogmatism," that is, belief in belief itself as opposed to personal encounter with the substance of dogma. Dogmatism occurs when the authority of dogma is abstracted from the living meaning of dogma. "Not without reason," writes Florensky, "has L. Tolstoy observed that many people believe not in dogmas but in the fact that they ought to believe in dogmas; the moribund empty form does not communicate inner truth and so becomes an idol."[39] The antidote to this pathology is experiential dogmatics. "We have a system of Orthodox dogmas; what we need to do is present Orthodox dogmatics as an actually living

religious worldview; in other words, the system of dogmas needs a propaedeutic."[40] What a "propaedeutic" means is difficult to ascertain on the basis of this
essay alone but becomes clear when we turn to Florensky's best-known work, *The
Pillar and Ground of the Truth* (1914), the first sentence of which reads: "Living
religious experience as the sole legitimate way to gain knowledge of the
dogmas—that is how I would like to express the general theme of my book or,
rather, my jottings, which have been written at different times and in different
moods."[41] In other words, *The Pillar and Ground of the Truth* is the propaedeutic
Florensky envisioned in 1905: not a dogmatics but a preparation *for* dogmatics,
an effort to re-experientialize the terms and concepts necessary for dogmatics,
such as faith, doubt, tri-unity, sin, Gehenna, creation, sophia, and many others.

But if *The Pillar and Ground of the Truth* is the propaedeutic, where is the
dogmatics itself? Did Florensky ever get to it? He did, although like Bulgakov
only after the close of the imperial period. The cycle of lectures and essays on
"cult" which Florensky launched in 1918 and continued in 1921–1922 are in
effect a body of dogmatic theology, or at the very least a detailed sketchbook for
a dogmatic theology.[42] What makes these lectures a dogmatic theology is that
they are concerned not with background conceptions ("propaedeutic") but with
the positive data of Orthodox worship and piety. To be sure, Florensky presents
Orthodox dogma in an unconventional, experientializing, and contextualizing
manner quite different from that of traditional dogmatics. The procedure is
analogous to Bulgakov's experientializing of dogmatic concepts by means of
Solovievian idealism and other catalysts. Bulgakov's late works are a dogmatics
of *orthodoxia* in the sense of "right doctrine"; Florensky's, a dogmatics of *orthodoxia* in the sense of "right worship" ("cult"). The two projects are analogous
and complementary. The point to be noted in both cases is the renovation of
dogmatic theology in such a way as to incorporate rather than reject the dialogue of Orthodoxy with the modern world.[43]

In short, thanks to the theology of culture, even Orthodox dogmatics was
becoming "a dialogic cultural practice" in late imperial Russia, just like the other
sectors of religion canvassed in this volume.[44] Certainly dogmatic theology in
most historical circumstances deserves its reputation for formalism and rigid-
ity. But the early twentieth century was not "most circumstances" for Russian
Orthodoxy, and Bulgakov and Florensky both knew it. The often hostile attitude
toward their dogmatic theological experiments by the traditionalist Orthodox
is not evidence of the failure of their project but rather of their success at
bringing a new kind of discussion into the very heart of the Orthodox dogmatic-
theological establishment, a discussion of the dogmatic tradition *in relation to*
human experience and human creativity. Indeed, it may well be in the ongoing annals of Orthodox dogmatics that the theology of culture of late imperial
Russia will find its most enduring afterlife.

Notes

1. Nicolas Zernov, *The Russian Religious Renaissance of the Twentieth Century* (New York and Evanston, Ill., 1963).

2. He writes: "The philosophical process in Russia in the beginning of the 20th century was characterized by great intensity and accelerated development. This fact brings forth the problem of structuring this process into different currents, trends and schools. It is a large historicophilosophical problem studied only superficially so far and having no generally accepted solution. It is indisputable, however, that the core of the process is provided by the famous Russian religious-philosophical renaissance and the philosophy of the latter has the metaphysics of All-Unity founded by Vladimir Solov'ev as its main part. We maintain that at the last stage of the metaphysics of All-Unity, just in the years preceding its violent end in Russia, a new philosophical current has been formed which we propose to call the 'Moscow School of Christian Neoplatonism.'" ("The Idea of Energy in the 'Moscow School of Christian Neoplatonism,'" in *Pavel Florenskij: Tradition und Moderne*, Beiträge zum Internationale Symposium an der Universität Potsdam, 5. bis 9. April 2000, ed. Norbert Franz, Michael Hagemeister, and Frank Haney [Frankfurt am Main, 2001], 69). See also "Neopatristicheskii sintez i russkaia filosofiia," in Sergei Khoruzhii, *O starom i novom* (St. Petersburg, 2000), 35–61.

3. See the review article by Robert Bird, "Russian Philosophy as Ideology," *Slavic and East European Journal* 43 (fall 2001): 531–37. The works in question, among others, are Modest Kolerov, *Ne mir, no mech: Russkaia religiozno-filosofskaia pechat' ot "Problem idealizma" do "Vekh"* 1902–1909 (St. Petersburg, 1996); Kolerov, *Industriia idei: Russkie obshchestvenno-politicheskie i religiozno-filosofskie sborniki, 1887–1947* (Moscow, 2000); and Evgenii Gollerbakh, *K nezrimomu gradu: Religiozno-filosofskaia gruppa "Put'" (1910–1919) v poiskakh novoi russkoi identichnosti* (St. Petersburg, 2000). See also Kristiane Burchardi, *Die Moskauer "Religiös-Philosophische Vladimir-Solov'ev-Gesellschaft" (1905–1918)*, Forschungen zur osteuropäischen Geschichte 53 (Wiesbaden, 1998).

4. Sviash. Pavel Florenskii, *Sochineniia*, ed. Igumen Andronik (A. S. Trubachev) et al., 4 vols. (Moscow, 1994–1999), 1:8–9. The letter is dated March 3, 1904.

5. H. Richard Niebuhr, *Christ and Culture* (New York, 1951).

6. On the concept before Tillich, see Friedrich Wilhelm Graf, *Theonomie: Fallstudien zum Integrationsanspruch neuzeitlicher Theologie* (Gütersloh, 1987). A huge bibliography is provided for Tillich's theology of culture. For orientation, see *Theonomy and Autonomy: Studies in Paul Tillich's Engagement with Modern Culture*, ed. John J. Carey (Macon, Ga., 1984); Victor Nuovo, *Visionary Science: A Translation of Tillich's "On the Idea of a Theology of Culture" with an Interpretive Essay* (Detroit, Mich., 1987); and Peter Haigis, *Im Horizont der Zeit: Paul Tillichs Projekt einer Theologie der Kultur*, Marburger Theologische Studien 47 (Marburg, 1998).

7. Bernice Glatzer Rosenthal, "Florenskii's Russifications of Nietzsche," in Franz, Hagemeister, and Haney, *Pavel Florenskij: Tradition und Moderne*, 254. The quotations are from P. A. Florenskii, "Khristianstvo i kul'tura," *Zhurnal Moskovskoi patriarkhii*, 1983, no. 4:54. For the corresponding passage in the latest edition of Florensky's works, see Florenskii, *Sochineniia*, 2:550. The title of Florensky's essay in the latter source is "Zapiska o khristianstve i kul'ture."

8. Florensky's medievalism is analyzed by Michael Hagemeister, "Wiederverzauberung der Welt: Pavel Florenskijs Neues Mittelalter," in Franz, Hagemeister, and Haney, *Pavel Florenskij: Tradition und Moderne*, 21–41.

9. Florenskii, "Zapiska o khristianstve i kul'ture," in *Sochineniia*, 2:550–51.

10. "O Bozhestvennom zakonodatel'stve chrez sv. proroka i Bogovidtsa Moiseia," in *O pravoslavii v otnoshenii k sovremennosti* (St. Petersburg, 1860), 143–44.

11. For a discussion of Bukharev's theology of culture, see Paul Valliere, *Modern Russian Theology: Bukharev, Soloviev, Bulgakov* (Grand Rapids, Mich., 2000), 19–106.

12. Sviash. Pavel Florenskii, "Arkhimandrit Feodor (A.M. Bukharev)," in *Arkhimandrit Feodor (A.M. Bukharev): pro et contra. Lichnost' i tvorchestvo arkhimandrita Feodora (Bukhareva) v otsenke russkikh myslitelei i issledovatelei: Antologiia*, ed. B. F. Egorov et al. (St. Petersburg, 1997), 586–87.

13. See the introduction to this volume.

14. S. N. Bulgakov, "Dogmaticheskoe obosnovanie kul'tury," in idem, *Sochineniia*, ed. S. Khoruzhii, 2 vols. (Moscow, 1993), 2:640.

15. Florenskii, "Dogmatizm i dogmatika," in *Sochineniia*, 1:561.

16. V. S. Solov'ev, "Predislovie," *Kritika otvlechennykh nachal*, in idem, *Polnoe sobranie sochinenii i pisem*, 20 vols. (Moscow, 2000–), 3:12.

17. Sergei Bulgakov, "Chto daet sovremennomu soznaniiu filosofiia Vladimira Solov'eva?" in idem, *Ot marksizma k idealizmu: sbornik statei, 1896–1903*(St. Petersburg, 1903), 196.

18. V. S. Solov'ev, *Chteniia o bogochelovechestve*, in *Sobranie sochinenii Vladimira Sergeevicha Solov'eva*, ed. S. M. Solov'ev and E. L. Radlov, 10 vols., 2nd ed. (St. Petersburg, 1911–1914), 3:26.

19. See Sergei Bulgakov, *Philosophy of Economy: The World as Household*, trans. Catherine Evtuhov (New Haven, Conn., and London, 2000); Catherine Evtuhov, *The Cross and the Sickle: Sergei Bulgakov and the Fate of Russian Religious Philosophy* (Ithaca, N.Y., and London, 1997); and Valliere, *Modern Russian Theology*, 253–78.

20. For a good example, see Bulgakov, "Dogmaticheskoe obosnovanie kul'tury," 641–42.

21. In the introduction Soloviev expressed the hope that he would live to "see the day when my country will possess the good which it needs first of all—religious liberty" (*La Russie et l'Eglise universelle*, 4th ed. [Paris, 1922], lxi). For an orientation to Soloviev's thinking on the so-called Jewish question, see Judith Deutsch Kornblatt and Gary Rosenshield, "Vladimir Solovyov: Confronting Dostoevsky on the Jewish and Christian Questions," *Journal of the American Academy of Religion* 68 (March, 2000): 69–98.

22. V. S. Solov'ev, *National'nyi vopros v Rossii*, in Solov'ev and Radlov, *Sobranie sochinenii*, 5:5, 80–81.

23. For two debates on nationalism in which Struve played a central role, see *Natsionalizm: Polemika 1990–1917*, ed. M. A. Kolerov (Moscow, 2000). The first debate, in 1909, concerned Russian nationalism and anti-Semitism, with Struve recommending "asemitism" as an alternative to anti-Semitism and philo-Semitism, "benign neglect" in American parlance. The second debate, in 1916–1917, concerned Russian nationalism and the war effort, with Struve defending the value of "national eros" for strengthening the Russian state, Evgenii Trubetskoi opposing him in the tradition of Solovievian Christian universalism, and Berdiaev (as ever) claiming to occupy an independent position above the fray.

24. Solov'ev, *Natsional'nyi vopros v Rossii*, in Solov'ev and Radlov, *Sobranie sochineii*, 5:3.

25. See Paul Tillich, *Dynamics of Faith* (New York, 1957).

26. See Jerome Arthur Stone, "Tillich and Schelling's Later Philosophy," *Kairos and Logos: Studies in the Roots and Implications of Tillich's Theology*, ed. John J. Carey (Macon, Ga., 1984), 3–35.

27. For an English translation, see *Problems of Idealism: Essays in Russian Social Philosophy*, trans. and ed. Randall A. Poole (New Haven, Conn., and London, 2003).

28. For a full discussion, see Valliere, *Modern Russian Theology*, 227–44.

29. "Dushevnaia drama Gertsena," in Bulgakov, *Ot marksizma k idealizmu*, 161–94.

30. "Chekhov kak myslitel'," in Bulgakov, *Sochineniia*, 2:139–41.

31. Ibid., 2:149–51.

32. Ibid., 2:137–38.

33. Ibid., 2:147–48.

34. "Ocharovanie otrazhennykh kul'tur," in Nikolai Berdiaev, *Tipy religioznoi mysli v Rossii*, in *Sobranie sochinenii* (Paris, 1989), 3:528.

35. Ibid., 3:519.
36. Ibid., 3:520.
37. Florenskii, "Dogmatizm i dogmatika," 1:557.
38. On Bulgakov's "church-and-world dogmatics," see Valliere, *Modern Russian Theology,* 291–371. For *opytnaia dogmatika* see Florenskii, "Dogmatizm i dogmatika," 1:570. In a footnote on the same page Florensky adds, as clarification: "Experiential dogmatics would be in full accord with the whole of contemporary science, which also seeks to build upon an experiential, immediately given foundation." This thought conforms exactly with Florensky's rejection of religiously inspired but scientifically harmful "compromises" in the letter to his mother cited above, in note 4.
39. Florenskii, "Dogmatizm i dogmatika," 1:560–61.
40. Ibid., 1:559.
41. *The Pillar and Ground of the Truth: An Essay in Orthodox Theodicy in Twelve Letters,* trans. Boris Jakim (Princeton, N.J., 1997), 5.
42. The lectures are collected in Sviash. Pavel Florenskii, "Iz bogoslovskogo naslediia," *Bogoslovskie trudy* 17 (Moscow, 1977), 85–248. Florensky's "Ikonostas," *Bogoslovskie trudy* 7 (Moscow, 1972), belongs to the same cycle of works.
43. There are other ways of interpreting Florensky's lectures on cult. Bernice Rosenthal has suggested that "after the Bolshevik Revolution, 'cult' replaced 'ecclesiality' [*tserkovnost'*] as the central concept of Florensky's theology" ("Florenskii's Russifications of Nietzsche," 252). In effect, this interpretation drives a wedge between the late lectures and the ecclesiastical values which my interpretation assumes to have been primary throughout Florensky's career. Hence, whereas I compare Florensky to Bulgakov, who was unquestionably an ecclesial theologian in his later years, Rosenthal compares him to the Nietzschean Marxist and revolutionary Aleksandr Bogdanov.
44. See the introduction to this volume.

Further Reading

---··◆··---

Religion in Russia

Batalden, Stephen K. *Seeking God: The Recovery of Religious Identity in Orthodox Russia, Ukraine, and Georgia.* DeKalb, Ill., 1993.

Bergman, Jay. "The Image of Jesus in the Russian Revolutionary Movement: The Case of Russian Marxism." *International Review of Social History* 35 (1990): 220–248.

Breyfogle, Nicholas B. *Heretics and Colonizers: Forging Russia's Empire in the South Caucasus.* Ithaca, N.Y., 2005.

Burchardi, Kristiane. *Die Moskauer "Religiös-Philosophische Vladimir-Solov'ev-Gesellschaft" (1905–1918). Forschungen zur osteuropäischen Geschichte* 53. Wiesbaden, 1998.

Burds, Jeffrey. "A Culture of Denunciation: Peasant Labor Migration and Religious Anathematization in Rural Russia, 1860–1905." In *Accusatory Practices: Denunciation in Modern European History, 1789–1989,* ed. Sheila Fitzpatrick and Robert Gellately, 40–72. Chicago, 1997.

Carlson, Maria. *"No Religion Higher Than Truth": A History of the Theosophical Movement in Russia, 1875–1922.* Princeton, 1993.

Coleman, Heather J. *Russian Baptists and Spiritual Revolution, 1905–1929.* Bloomington, Ind., 2005.

Chulos, Chris J. *Converging Worlds: Religion and Community in Peasant Russia, 1861–1917.* DeKalb, Ill., 2003.

Cunningham, James W. *A Vanquished Hope: The Movement for Church Renewal in Russia, 1905–1906.* Crestwood, N.Y., 1981.

Curtiss, John Sheldon. *Church and State in Russia: The Last Years of the Empire 1900–1917.* New York, 1940.

Engelstein, Laura. *Castration and the Heavenly Kingdom: A Russian Folktale.* Ithaca, N.Y., 1999.

———. "The Dream of Civil Society in Tsarist Russia: Law, State, and Religion." In *Civil Society before Democracy: Lessons from Nineteenth-Century Europe.* Lanham, Md., 2000.

———. "Holy Russia in Modern Times: An Essay on Orthodoxy and Cultural Change." *Past and Present* no. 173 (November 2001): 129–156.

Etkind, Aleksandr. *Khlyst: sekty, literatura i revoliutsiia.* Moscow, 1998.

Evtuhov, Catherine. *The Cross and the Sickle: Sergei Bulgakov and the Fate of Russian Religious Philosophy, 1890–1920.* Ithaca, N.Y., 1997.

Freeze, Gregory L. "A Case of Stunted Anticlericalism: Clergy and Society in Imperial Russia." *European Studies Review* 13 (1983): 177–200.

———. "Handmaiden of the State? The Church in Imperial Russia Reconsidered." *Journal of Ecclesiastical History* 36, no. 1 (January 1985): 78–103.

———. *The Parish Clergy in Nineteenth-Century Russia: Crisis, Reform, Counter-Reform.* Princeton, N.J., 1983.

———. "Subversive Piety: Religion and the Political Crisis in Late Imperial Russia." *Journal of Modern History* 68 (June 1996): 308–350.

Geraci, Robert P., and Michael Khodarkovsky. *Of Religion and Empire: Missions, Conversion, and Tolerance in Tsarist Russia.* Ithaca, N.Y., 2001.

Heier, Edmund. *Religious Schism in the Russian Aristocracy 1860–1900. Radstockism and Pashkovism.* The Hague, 1970.

Himka, John-Paul, and Andriy Zayarnyuk, eds. *Letters from Heaven: Popular Religion in Russia and Ukraine.* Toronto, 2006.

Hosking, Geoffrey, ed. *Church, Nation, and State in Russia and Ukraine.* New York, 1991.

Hughes, Robert P., and Irina Paperno, eds. *Russian Culture in Modern Times.* Vol. 2 of *Christianity and the Eastern Slavs.* California Slavic Studies 17. Berkeley, Calif., 1994.

Ivanits, Linda J. *Russian Folk Belief.* Armonk, N.Y., 1989.

Kivelson, Valerie A., and Robert H. Greene, eds. *Orthodox Russia: Belief and Practice under the Tsars.* University Park, Pa., 2003.

Kizenko, Nadieszda. *A Prodigal Saint: Father John of Kronstadt and the Russian People.* University Park, Pa., 2000.

Klibanov, A. I. *Istoriia religioznogo sektantstva v Rossii (60-e gody XIX v.–1917g.).* Moscow, 1965.

Kline, George L. *Religious and Antireligious Thought in Russia.* Chicago, 1968.

Lossky, Nicholas O. *History of Russian Philosophy.* New York, 1951.

Löwe, Heinz-Dietrich. *The Tsars and the Jews: Reform, Reaction, and Anti-Semitism in Imperial Russia, 1772–1917.* Chur, Switzerland, 1993.

Nathans, Benjamin Ira. *Beyond the Pale: The Jewish Encounter with Late Imperial Russia.* Berkeley, Calif., 2002.

Nichols, Robert L., and Theofanis George Stavrou. *Russian Orthodoxy under the Old Regime.* Minneapolis, Minn., 1978.

Pascal, Pierre. *The Religion of the Russian People.* Trans. Rowan Williams. London, 1976.

Polunov, A. Iu. *Pod vlast'iu ober-prokurora. Gosudarstvo i tserkov' v epokhu Aleksandra III.* Moscow, 1996.

Read, Christopher. *Religion, Revolution and the Russian Intelligentsia 1900–1912: The Vekhi Debate and Its Intellectual Background.* London, 1979.

Robson, Roy R. *Old Believers in Modern Russia.* DeKalb, Ill., 1995.

———. *Solovki: The Story of Russia Told Through Its Most Remarkable Islands.* New Haven, Conn., 2004.

Rosenthal, Bernice Glatzer, ed. *The Occult in Russian and Soviet Culture.* Ithaca, N.Y., 1997.

Rosenthal, Bernice Glatzer, and Martha Bohachevsky-Chomiak, eds. *A Revolution of the Spirit: Crisis of Value in Russia, 1890–1924.* New York, 1990.

Safran, Gabriella. *Rewriting the Jew: Assimilation Narratives in the Russian Empire.* Stanford, Calif., 2000.

Scherrer, Jutta. "Ein gelber und ein blauer Teufel: zure Entstehung der Begriffe 'bogostroitel'stvo' und 'bogoiskatel'stvo.'" *Forschungen zur osteuropäischen Geschichte* 25 (1978): 319–329.

———. "L'intelligentsia russe: sa quête de la 'vérité religieuse du socialisme.'" *Le temps de la réflexion*, no. 2 (1981): 134–151.

———. *Die Petersburger Religiös-Philosophischen Veriningungen. Forschungen zur osteuropäischen Geschichte* 19 (1973).

Shevzov, Vera. "Poeticizing Piety: The Icon of Mary in Russian Akathistoi Hymns." *St. Vladimir's Theological Quarterly* 44, nos. 3–4 (2000): 343–373.

———. *Russian Orthodoxy on the Eve of Revolution.* New York, 2004.

Smolich, I. K. *Istoriia russkoi tserkvi 1700–1917,* chaps. 1, 2. Moscow, 1996. Published previously in German.

Stein, Sarah Abrevaya. *Making Jews Modern: Yiddish and Ladino Press of the Russian and Ottoman Empires.* Bloomington, Ind., 2003.

Steinberg, Mark D. *Proletarian Imagination: Self, Modernity, and the Sacred in Russia, 1910–1925.* Ithaca, N.Y., 2002.

Timberlake, Charles E., ed. *Religious and Secular Forces in Late Tsarist Russia. Essays in Honor of Donald W. Treadgold.* Seattle, Wash., 1992.

Tuchtenhagen, Ralph. *Religion als minderer Status: die Reform der Gesetzgebung gegenüber religiösen Minderheiten in der verfaßten Gesellschaft des russischen Reiches 1905–1917.* Frankfurt am Main, 1995.

Valliere, Paul. *Modern Russian Theology: Bukharev, Soloviev, Bulgakov.* Grand Rapids, Mich., 2000.

Wagner, William G. "Paradoxes of Piety: The Nizhegorod Convent of the Exaltation of the Cross, 1807–1928." In *Orthodox Russia: Studies in Belief and Practice, 1492–1936,* ed. V. A. Kivelson and R. H. Greene, 211–238. University Park, Pa., 2003.

Waldron, Peter. "Religious Reform after 1905: Old Believers and the Orthodox Church." *Oxford Slavonic Papers* (new series) 20 (1987): 110–139.

———. "Religious Toleration in Late Imperial Russia." In *Civil Rights in Imperial Russia,* ed. Olga Crisp and Linda Edmondson. 103–120. Oxford, 1989.

Werth, Paul W. *At the Margins of Orthodoxy: Mission, Governance, and Confessional Politics in Russia's Volga-Kama region, 1827–1905.* Ithaca, N.Y., 2002.

———. "From 'Pagan' Muslims to 'Baptized' Communists: Religious Conversion and Ethnic Particularity in Russia's Eastern Provinces." *Comparative Studies in Society and History* 42, no. 3 (2000): 497–523.

———. "The Limits of Religious Ascription: Baptized Tatars and the Revision of 'Apostasy,' 1840s–1905." *Russian Review* 59, no. 4 (2000): 493–451.

Worobec, Christine D. *Possessed: Women, Witches, and Demons in Imperial Russia.* DeKalb, Ill., 2001.

Zernov, Nicolas. *The Russian Religious Renaissance of the Twentieth Century.* New York, 1963.

Zipperstein, Steven J. *The Jews of Odessa: A Cultural History, 1794–1881.* Stanford, Calif., 1985.

Comparative and Theoretical Works

Badone, Ellen, ed. *Religious Orthodoxy and Popular Faith in Europe.* Princeton, N.J., 1990.

Berger, Peter L. *The Sacred Canopy: Elements of a Sociological Theory of Religion.* New York, 1967.

Blackbourn, David. *Marpingen: Apparitions of the Virgin Mary in Nineteenth-Century Germany.* Oxford, 1993.

Comaroff, John, with J. Comaroff. *Of Revelation and Revolution. The Dialectics of Modernity on a South African Frontier.* Chicago, 1997.

Davis, Natalie Zemon. "From 'Popular Religion' to Religious Cultures." In *Reformation Europe: A Guide to Research,* ed. Steven Ozment, 321–341. St. Louis, Mo., 1982.

———. *Society and Culture in Early Modern France.* Stanford, Calif., 1975.

Degh, Linda. *Legend and Belief: Dialectics of a Folklore Genre.* Bloomington, Ind., 2001.

Derrida, Jacques. *Acts of Religion.* Ed. and intro. Gil Anidjar. New York, 2002.

Desan, Suzanne. *Reclaiming the Sacred: Lay Religion and Popular Politics in Revolutionary France.* Ithaca, N.Y., 1990.

Dubisch, Jill. *In a Different Place: Pilgrimage, Gender, and Politics at a Greek Island Shrine.* Princeton, N.J., 1995.

Durkheim, Emile. *The Elementary Forms of the Religious Life.* Trans. Joseph Ward Swain. New York, 1965.

Eade, John, and Michael J. Sallnow, eds. *Contesting the Sacred: The Anthropology of Christian Pilgrimage.* New York, 1991; 2nd ed., Urbana, Ill., 2000.

Eliade, Mircea. *Myths, Dreams, and Mysteries.* New York, 1960.

———. *The Sacred and the Profane: The Nature of Religion.* New York, 1959.

Eliade, Mircea, and Joseph Kitagawa, eds. *The History of Religions: Essays in Methodology.* Chicago, 1959.

Ford, Caroline. "Religion and Popular Culture in Modern Europe." *Journal of Modern History* 65, no. 1 (March 1993): 152–175.

Geertz, Clifford. *The Interpretation of Cultures.* New York, 1973.

Ginzburg, Carlo. *The Cheese and the Worms.* Baltimore, Md., 1980.

Hall, David D. *Lived Religion in America: Toward a History of Practice.* Princeton, N.J., 1997.

Hammond, Phillip E., ed. *The Sacred in a Secular Age: Toward Revision in the Scientific Study of Religion.* Berkeley, Calif., 1985.

Kselman, Thomas A., ed. *Belief in History: Innovative Approaches to European and American Religion.* Notre Dame, Ind., 1991.

———. *Death and the Afterlife in Modern France.* Princeton, N.J., 1993.

———. *Miracles and Prophesies in Nineteenth Century France.* New Brunswick, N.J., 1983.

McLeod, Hugh, ed. *European Religion in the Age of Great Cities 1830–1930.* London, 1995.

———. *Religion and the People of Western Europe 1789–1989.* New ed. Oxford, 1997.

———. *Secularization in Western Europe, 1848–1914.* New York, 2000.

Morris, Marcia A. *Saints and Revolutionaries: The Ascetic Hero in Russian Literature.* Albany, N.Y., 1993.

Nolan, Mary Lee, and Sidney Nolan. *Christian Pilgrimage in Modern Western Europe.* Chapel Hill, N.C., 1989.

Pals, Daniel L. *Eight Theories of Religion.* New York, 2006.

Sabean, David W. *Power in the Blood: Popular Culture and Village Discourse in Early Modern Germany.* Cambridge, 1984.

Turner, Victor, and Edith L. B. Turner. *Image and Pilgrimage in Christian Culture: Anthropological Perspectives.* New York, 1978.

Van der Veer, Peter. *Imperial Encounters: Religion and Modernity in India and Britain.* Princeton, N.J., 2001.

Van der Veer, Peter, and Hartmut Lehmann, eds. *Nation and Religion: Perspectives on Europe and Asia.* Princeton, N.J., 1999.

Viswanathan, Gauri. *Outside the Fold: Conversion, Modernity, and Belief.* Princeton, N.J., 1998.

Contributors

⸺⟨∞⟩⸺

Nicholas B. Breyfogle is Associate Professor of History at The Ohio State University. He is the author of *Heretics and Colonizers: Forging Russia's Empire in the South Caucasus* and articles on the history of Russian religion, pacifism, colonialism, and the civilian experience of war.

Heather J. Coleman is Canada Research Chair in Imperial Russian History and Associate Professor in the Department of History and Classics at the University of Alberta. She is the author of *Russian Baptists and Spiritual Revolution.*

Gregory L. Freeze is the Victor and Gwendolyn Beinfield Professor of History at Brandeis University. He is the author of *The Parish Clergy in Nineteenth-Century Russia* and the editor of *Russia: A History.*

Nadieszda Kizenko is Associate Professor of History at the State University of New York, Albany. She is the author of *A Prodigal Saint: Father John of Kronstadt and the Russian People* and is currently working on a study of confession in modern Russia.

Alexei Kurbanovsky is Senior Research Scholar at the State Russian Museum in St. Petersburg. A specialist in Russian art of the nineteenth and twentieth centuries in its international context, he is the author of *Art History as a Kind of Writing* (in Russian) as well as more than 130 articles and catalogue essays on Russian classical and post-Soviet art.

Roy R. Robson is Associate Professor of History at University of the Sciences in Philadelphia. He is the author of *Old Believers in Modern Russia* and *Solovki: The Story of Russia Told Through Its Most Remarkable Islands.*

Bernice Glatzer Rosenthal is Professor of History at Fordham University. She has published widely on early-twentieth-century Russian thought and culture. Her most recent publications are *New Myth, New World: From Nietzsche to Stalinism* and *The Occult in Russian and Soviet Culture.*

Gabriella Safran is Associate Professor of Slavic Languages and Literatures at Stanford University. She is the author of *Rewriting the Jew: Assimilation Narratives in the Russian Empire* and the co-author of a volume of essays and source materials on S. An-sky. She is currently working on a critical biography of S. An-sky.

Vera Shevzov is Associate Professor of Religion at Smith College and the author of *Russian Orthodoxy on the Eve of Revolution.* She is currently working on a book on Mary in modern Russia.

Sarah Abrevaya Stein is Associate Professor in the Department of History and in the Henry M. Jackson School of International Studies at the University of Washington, Seattle. She is the author of *Making Jews Modern: The Yiddish and Ladino Press in the Russian and Ottoman Empires.*

Mark D. Steinberg is Professor of History at the University of Illinois, Urbana-Champaign and editor of *Slavic Review.* His most recent books include *Voices of Revolution, 1917; Proletarian Imagination: Self, Modernity, and the Sacred in Russia, 1910–1925;* and, with Nicholas Riasanovsky, the seventh edition of *A History of Russia.*

Paul Valliere is McGregor Professor in the Humanities at Butler University in Indianapolis. His publications include *Modern Russian Theology: Bukharev, Soloviev, Bulgakov* and essays on Orthodox Christianity and law in *The Teachings of Modern Christianity on Law, Politics, and Human Nature,* edited by John Witte Jr. and Frank S. Alexander.

William G. Wagner is Dean of the Faculty and Brown Professor of History at Williams College. The author of *Marriage, Property, and Law in Late Imperial Russia,* he currently is engaged in a study of female Orthodox monasticism in imperial and early Soviet Russia.

Paul W. Werth is Associate Professor of History at the University of Nevada, Las Vegas. He is the author of *At the Margins of Orthodoxy: Mission, Governance, and Confessional Politics in Russia's Volga-Kama Region, 1827–1905* and is currently researching problems of religious toleration and confessional diversity in the Russian Empire.

Christine D. Worobec is Presidential Research Professor in the Department of History at Northern Illinois University and the author of *Peasant Russia: Family and Community in the Post-Emancipation Period* and *Possessed: Women, Witches, and Demons in Imperial Russia.*

Index

Printed and bound by CPI Group (UK) Ltd, Croydon, CR0 4YY

09/06/2025

14685946-0001